CRIC

M000074573

FOREWORD

A year ago, just before the book went to press, I had to rewrite portions of the Foreword as it became clear that the COVID-19 pandemic was going to have a dramatic impact on events during the season ahead. Sadly, with the official UK death toll passing 125,000 today, its effects were seen far beyond the cricket fields of our nation and continue to be felt by all of us. This time, we approach the summer with greater hope, as the success of the vaccination roll-out suggests we might return to something closer to normality as the season progresses.

But we're not fully there as yet. The County Championship, with LV= returning as sponsors, is a hybrid of group games, play-offs and a final to decide who will get to lift the Bob Willis Trophy. For the first time, the Royal London One-Day Cup is to be run alongside the ECB's new tournament, The Hundred, leaving the counties deprived of more than a hundred of their top players. I wrote at length about The Hundred in my Foreword two years ago, and don't propose to go over old ground again now, but these aren't propitious times to launch a new format.

However, this is no time to be fighting old battles. After losing so much action – at professional and amateur levels – last summer, the biggest challenge cricket has is to get people to re-engage. There will be nervousness felt by some fans when it comes to going to matches, so grounds have a duty to prepare well for letting the crowds back in and to explain clearly what they have done to make things safe for everyone. Players should also do what they can to interact positively with the supporters; their livelihoods depend on an enthused fanbase, and winning people back has never been more vital. When the opportunity arises, I urge all readers to make an extra effort this summer to watch a game in person, whether at Test level or supporting your local club side. We all lost the rhythm of playing and watching in 2020, and we need to get back into those good habits in 2021.

This year is a huge one for the England team. After their chastening experience in India, the men's team will face up to New Zealand and India in Test series this summer. The two touring sides are currently ranked the best in the world and will also meet in the final of the ICC World Championship – the idea has not yet fully captured the imagination, but it seems a useful step towards ensuring that Test cricket is always meaningful. In a TikTok world, a game that can last for five days has its work cut out to prove its relevance. After the season is over, England then travel to India for the T20 World Cup followed by the Ashes, so it will be a challenging, exciting winter.

We hope that our cover star, Zak Crawley, will further flourish in the Test arena, building on the enormous promise shown by his innings of 267 against Pakistan last summer. Like so many, despite the echoing emptiness of the grounds, he showed true professionalism and skill when it might have been easy to let performance levels dip. Fortunately, he is surrounded by three Test-cap centurions in James Anderson, Stuart Broad and Joe Root who consistently show the attributes required to build a long and successful career. At various times in recent months, each of them has stepped up to deliver remarkable performances, and all three are on the cusp of new landmarks: Anderson needs six wickets to move ahead of Anil Kumble into third place in the leading Test wicket-takers, Broad needs just three to move into third place among fast bowlers, and Root requires one more victory to become the England captain with most wins. I look forward to seeing all those landmarks passed this summer. But most importantly of all, I can't wait for the crowds to return and for the cricket nets and grounds to be the hives of activity they should be throughout the summer.

Ian Marshall
Eastbourne, 11 March 2021

GUIDE TO USING PLAYFAIR

The basic layout of *Playfair* has remained the same for this edition. The Annual is divided into five sections, as follows: Test match cricket, county cricket, international limited-overs cricket (including IT20), other cricket (IPL, Big Bash, The Hundred, Rachael Heyhoe Flint Trophy, Ireland and women's international cricket), and fixtures for the coming season. Sadly, the National Counties fixtures were not available in time for inclusion in the Annual. Each section, where applicable, begins with a preview of forthcoming events, followed by events during the previous year, then come the player records, and finally the records sections.

Within the players' register, there has been some debate with the county scorers over those who are defined as 'Released/Retired', pointing out that some players are drafted in for a game or two, and may re-appear in the current season, despite not having a contract as the book goes to press. What I try to do is to ensure that everyone who appeared in last season's games is included somewhere – this way, at least, if they do play in 2021 their details are available to readers. Players' Second XI Championship debuts and their England Under-19 Test appearances are given for those under the age of 25.

In the county limited-overs records in the Register, those records denoted by '50ov' cover any limited-overs game of 50 or more overs – in the early days, each team could have as many as 65 overs per innings. The '40ov' section refers to games of 40 or 45 overs per innings.

For both men's and women's IT20 records sections, I have taken the decision to limit the records listed to those games that feature at least one side that has appeared in an official LOI. While I welcome the ICC's efforts to broaden the game's profile, when Uganda's women can beat Mali's by 304 runs (after scoring 314 for two – including a run out), you wonder who really benefits here. Or when Turkey's men set the three lowest scores on record on successive days, do they deserve to be shamed three times over?

ACKNOWLEDGEMENTS AND THANKS

As always, this book could not have been compiled without the assistance of many people giving so generously of their time and expertise, often in more challenging circumstances thanks to lockdown, so I must thank the following for all they have done to help ensure this edition of *Playfair Cricket Annual* could be written:

At the counties, I would like to thank the following for their help over the last year: Derbyshire – Stephen Martin and John Brown; Durham – Sam Blacklock and William Dobson; Essex – George Haberman and Tony Choat; Glamorgan – Andrew Hignell; Gloucestershire – Lizzie Allen and Adrian Bull; Hampshire – Tim Tremlett and Kevin Baker; Kent – Freddie Young and Lorne Hart; Lancashire – Diana Lloyd and Chris Rimmer; Leicestershire – Dan Nice and Paul Rogers; Middlesex – Steven Fletcher and Don Shelley; Northamptonshire – Tony Kingston; Nottinghamshire – Helen Palmer and Roger Marshall; Somerset – Spencer Bishop and Polly Rhodes; Surrey – Steve Howes and Phil Makepeace; Sussex – Colin Bowley and Graham Irwin; Warwickshire – Keith Cook and Mel Smith; Worcestershire – Carrie Lloyd and Sue Drinkwater; Yorkshire – Cecilia Allen and John Potter.

Thanks to Alan Fordham for the Principal and Second XI Fixtures and Chris Kelly for the first-class umpires. I am hugely grateful as always to Philip Bailey for providing the first-class and List A career records, and for supplying – at incredibly short notice – a new feature: T20 career records.

At Headline, my thanks go to Jonathan Taylor for his help throughout the year; Louise Rothwell ensures the Annual is printed at great speed; Ellie Morley kindly looked after the *Playfair* website last summer so it provided all the latest information on newcomers. John Skermer has been diligently checking the proofs since 2008. At Letterpart, the *Playfair* typesetter since 1994, Chris Leggett and Caroline Leggett play a vital part in the process, delivering the page proofs in record time to ensure we can remain as up-to-date as possible.

Finally, I should thank the government for re-opening schools a week before the final deadline, which meant that my daughters, Kiri and Sophia, were out of the house at the busiest time. My wife, Sugra, was as supportive, patient and helpful as ever. Thank you all.

ENGLAND v NEW ZEALAND

SERIES RECORDS
1928 to 2019-20

HIGHEST INNINGS TOTALS

England	in England	567-8d	Nottingham	1994
	in New Zealand	593-6d	Auckland	1974-75
New Zealand	in England	551-9d	Lord's	1973
	in New Zealand	615-9d	Mt Maunganui	2019-20

LOWEST INNINGS TOTALS

England	in England	126	Birmingham	1999
	in New Zealand	58	Auckand	2017-18
New Zealand	in England	47	Lord's	1958
	in New Zealand	26	Auckland	1954-55
HIGHEST MATCH AGGREGATE		1610 for 40 wickets	Lord's	2015
LOWEST MATCH AGGREGATE		390 for 30 wickets	Lord's	1958

HIGHEST INDIVIDUAL INNINGS

England	in England	310*	J.H.Edrich	Leeds	1965
	in New Zealand	336*	W.R.Hammond	Auckland	1932-33
New Zealand	in England	206	M.P.Donnelly	Lord's	1949
	in New Zealand	222	N.J.Astle	Christchurch	2001-02

HIGHEST AGGREGATE OF RUNS IN A SERIES

England	in England	469	(av 78.16)	L.Hutton	1949
	in New Zealand	563	(av 563.00)	W.R.Hammond	1932-33
New Zealand	in England	462	(av 77.00)	M.P.Donnelly	1949
	in New Zealand	347	(av 69..40)	P.G.Fulton	2012-13

RECORD WICKET PARTNERSHIPS – ENGLAND

1st	231	A.N.Cook (116)/N.R.D.Compton (117)	Dunedin	2012-13
2nd	369	J.H.Edrich (310*)/K.F.Barrington (163)	Leeds	1965
3rd	245	J.Hardstaff jr (114)/W.R.Hammond (140)	Lord's	1937
4th	266	M.H.Denness (181)/K.W.R.Fletcher (216)	Auckland	1974-75
5th	242	W.R.Hammond (227)/L.E.G.Ames (103)	Christchurch	1932-33
6th	281	G.P.Thorpe (200*)/A.Flintoff (137)	Christchurch	2001-02
7th	149	A.P.E.Knott (104)/P.Lever (64)	Auckland	1970-71
8th	246	L.E.G.Ames (137)/G.O.B.Allen (122)	Lord's	1931
9th	163*	M.C.Cowdrey (128*)/A.C.Smith (69*)	Wellington	1962-63
10th	59	A.P.E.Knott (49)/N.Gifford (25*)	Nottingham	1973

RECORD WICKET PARTNERSHIPS – NEW ZEALAND

1st	276	C.S.Dempster (136)/J.E.Mills (117)	Wellington	1929-30
2nd	241	J.G.Wright (116)/A.H.Jones (143)	Wellington	1991-92
3rd	213*	K.S.Williamson (104*)/L.R.P.L.Taylor (105*)	Hamilton	2019-20
4th	155	M.D.Crowe (143)/M.J.Greatbatch (68)	Wellington	1987-88
5th	180	M.D.Crowe (142)/S.A.Thomson (69)	Lord's	1994
6th	142	B.J.Watling (85)/C.de Grandhomme (72)	Christchurch	2017-18
7th	260	B.J.Watling (205)/M.J.Santner (126)	Mt Maunganui	2019-20
8th	104	D.A.R.Moloney (64)/A.W.Roberts (66*)	Lord's	1937
9th	118	J.V.Coney (174*)/B.L.Cairns (64)	Wellington	1983-84
10th	118	N.J.Astle (222)/C.L.Cairns (23*)	Christchurch	2001-02

BEST INNINGS BOWLING ANALYSIS

England	in England	7- 32	D.L.Underwood	Lord's	1969
	in New Zealand	7- 47	P.C.R.Tufnell	Christchurch	1991-92
		7- 47	R.J.Sidebottom	Napier	2007-08
New Zealand	in England	7- 74	B.L.Cairns	Leeds	1983
	in New Zealand	7-143	B.L.Cairns	Wellington	1983-84

BEST MATCH BOWLING ANALYSIS

England	in England	12-101	D.L.Underwood	The Oval	1969
	in New Zealand	12- 97	D.L.Underwood	Christchurch	1970-71
New Zealand	in England	11-169	D.J.Nash	Lord's	1994
	in New Zealand	10-100	R.J.Hadlee	Wellington	1977-78

HIGHEST AGGREGATE OF WICKETS IN A SERIES

England	in England	34	(av 7.47)	G.A.R.Lock	1958
	in New Zealand	24	(av 17.08)	R.J.Sidebottom	2007-08
New Zealand	in England	21	(av 26.61)	R.J.Hadlee	1983
	in New Zealand	15	(av 19.53)	R.O.Collinge	1977-78
		15	(av 24.73)	R.J.Hadlee	1977-78
		15	(av 18.33)	T.A.Boult	2017-18

RESULTS SUMMARY: ENGLAND v NEW ZEALAND – IN ENGLAND

	Tests	Series E	NZ	D	Lord's E	NZ	D	The Oval E	NZ	D	Manchester E	NZ	D	Leeds E	NZ	D	Birmingham E	NZ	D	Nottingham E	NZ	D
1931	3	1	–	2			1	1					1									
1937	3	1	–	2			1			1	1											
1949	4	–	–	4			1			1			1			1						
1958	5	4	–	1	1					1	1			1			1					
1965	3	3	–	–	1									1			1					
1969	3	2	–	1	1			1														1
1973	3	2	–	1			1							1						1		
1978	3	3	–	–	1			1												1		
1983	4	3	1	–	1			1							1					1		
1986	3	–	1	2			1			1											1	
1990	3	1	–	2			1										1					1
1994	3	1	–	2			1						1							1		
1999	4	1	2	1		1			1				1				1					
2004	3	3	–	–	1									1						1		
2008	3	2	–	1			1				1									1		
2013	2	2	–	–	1									1								
2015	2	1	1	–	1										1							
	54	30	5	19	8	1	8	4	1	4	3	–	4	5	2	1	4	–	–	6	1	2

ENGLAND v NEW ZEALAND – IN NEW ZEALAND

	Tests	Series E	NZ	D	Christchurch E	NZ	D	Wellington E	NZ	D	Auckland E	NZ	D	Dunedin E	NZ	D	Hamilton E	NZ	D	Napier E	NZ	D	Mt Maunganui E	NZ	D
1929-30	4	1	–	3	1					1			2												
1932-33	2	–	–	2			1						1												
1946-47	1	–	–	1			1																		
1950-51	2	1	–	1			1	1																	
1954-55	2	2	–	–							1			1											
1958-59	2	1	–	1	1								1												
1962-63	3	3	–	–	1			1			1														
1965-66	3	–	–	3			1						1			1									
1970-71	2	1	–	1	1								1												
1974-75	2	1	–	1			1				1														
1977-78	3	1	1	1	1				1				1												
1983-84	3	–	1	2		1				1			1												
1987-88	3	–	–	3			1			1			1												
1991-92	3	2	–	1	1					1	1														
1996-97	3	2	–	1	1			1					1												
2001-02	3	1	1	1	1					1		1													
2007-08	3	2	1	–				1										1		1					
2012-13	3	–	–	3						1			1			1									
2017-18	2	–	1	1			1					1													
2019-20	2	–	1	1															1					1	
	51	18	6	27	8	1	7	4	1	6	4	2	11	1	–	2	–	1	1	1	–	–	–	1	–
Totals	105	48	11	46																					

ENGLAND v INDIA
SERIES RECORDS

1932 to 2020-21

HIGHEST INNINGS TOTALS

England	in England	710-7d	Birmingham	2011
	in India	652-7d	Madras	1984-85
India	in England	664	The Oval	2007
	in India	759-7d	Chennai	2016-17

LOWEST INNINGS TOTALS

England	in England	101	The Oval	1971
	in India	81	Ahmedabad	2020-21
India	in England	42	Lord's	1974
	in India	83	Madras	1976-77
HIGHEST MATCH AGGREGATE	1614 for 30 wickets		Manchester	1990
LOWEST MATCH AGGREGATE	387 for 30 wickets		Ahmedabad	2020-21

HIGHEST INDIVIDUAL INNINGS

England	in England	333	G.A.Gooch	Lord's	1990
	in India	218	J.E.Root	Chennai	2020-21
India	in England	221	S.M.Gavaskar	The Oval	1979
	in India	303*	K.K.Nair	Chennai	2016-17

HIGHEST AGGREGATE OF RUNS IN A SERIES

England	in England	752	(av 125.33)	G.A.Gooch	1990
	in India	594	(av 99.00)	K.F.Barrington	1961-62
India	in England	602	(av 100.33)	R.S.Dravid	2002
	in India	655	(av 109.16)	V.Kohli	2016-17

RECORD WICKET PARTNERSHIPS – ENGLAND

1st	225	G.A.Gooch (116)/M.A.Atherton (131)	Manchester	1990
2nd	241	G.Fowler (201)/M.W.Gatting (207)	Madras	1984-85
3rd	350	I.R.Bell (235)/K.P.Pietersen (175)	The Oval	2011
4th	266	W.R.Hammond (217)/T.S.Worthington (128)	The Oval	1936
5th	254	K.W.R.Fletcher (113)/A.W.Greig (148)	Bombay	1972-73
6th	189	J.M.Bairstow (93)/C.R.Woakes (137*)	Lord's	2018
7th	162*	M.J.Prior (103*)/S.C.J.Broad (74*)	Lord's	2011
8th	168	R.Illingworth (107)/P.Lever (88*)	Manchester	1971
9th	103	C.White (94*)/M.J.Hoggard (32)	Nottingham	2002
10th	198	J.E.Root (154*)/J.M.Anderson (81)	Nottingham	2014

RECORD WICKET PARTNERSHIPS – INDIA

1st	213	S.M.Gavaskar (221)/C.P.S.Chauhan (80)	The Oval	1979
2nd	314	G.Gambhir (179)/R.S.Dravid (136)	Chandigarh	2008-09
3rd	316	G.R.Viswanath (222)/Yashpal Sharma (140)	Madras	1981-82
4th	249	S.R.Tendulkar (193)/S.C.Ganguly (128)	Leeds	2002
5th	214	M.Azharuddin (110)/R.J.Shastri (111)	Calcutta	1984-85
6th	204	K.L.Rahul (149)/R.R.Pant (114)	The Oval	2018
7th	235	R.J.Shastri (142)/S.M.H.Kirmani (102)	Bombay	1984-85
8th	241	V.Kohli (235)/J.Yadav (104)	Mumbai	2016-17
9th	104	R.J.Shastri (93)/Madan Lal (44)	Delhi	1981-82
10th	111	B.Kumar (58)/Mohammed Shami (51*)	Nottingham	2014

BEST INNINGS BOWLING ANALYSIS

England	in England	8-31	F.S.Trueman	Manchester	1952
	in India	7-46	J.K.Lever	Delhi	1976-77
India	in England	7-74	I.Sharma	Lord's	2014
	in India	8-55	M.H.Mankad	Madras	1951-52

BEST MATCH BOWLING ANALYSIS

England	in England	11- 93	A.V.Bedser	Manchester	1946
	in India	13-106	I.T.Botham	Bombay	1979-80
India	in England	10-188	C.Sharma	Birmingham	1986
	in India	12-108	M.H.Mankad	Madras	1951-52

HIGHEST AGGREGATE OF WICKETS IN A SERIES

England	in England	29	(av 13.31)	F.S.Trueman	1952
	in India	29	(av 17.55)	D.L.Underwood	1976-77
India	in England	19	(av 26.63)	B.Kumar	2014
	in India	35	(av 18.91)	B.S.Chandrasekhar	1972-73

1500 RUNS

	Tests	I	NO	HS	Runs	Avge	100	50
S.R.Tendulkar (I)	32	53	4	193	2535	51.73	7	13
S.M.Gavaskar (I)	38	67	2	221	2483	38.20	4	16
A.N.Cook (E)	30	54	3	294	2431	47.66	7	9
R.S.Dravid (I)	21	37	5	217	1950	60.03	7	8
G.R.Viswanath (I)	30	54	4	222	1880	37.60	4	12
J.E.Root (E)	20	36	3	218	1789	54.21	5	9
V.Kohli (I)	23	41	3	235	1742	45.84	5	6
G.A.Gooch (E)	19	33	2	333	1725	55.64	5	8
D.B.Vengsarkar (I)	26	43	6	157	1589	42.94	5	6
K.P.Pietersen (E)	16	28	1	202*	1581	58.55	6	6

70 WICKETS

	Tests	Balls	Runs	Wkts	Avge	Best	5wI	10wM
J.M.Anderson (E)	30	6432	2985	118	25.29	5- 20	4	–
B.S.Chandrasekhar (I)	23	6199	2591	95	27.27	8- 79	8	–
A.Kumble (I)	19	6434	2815	92	30.59	7-115	4	1
R.Ashwin (I)	19	5444	2516	88	28.59	6- 55	6	1
B.S.Bedi (I)	22	7173	2539	85	29.87	6- 71	4	–
Kapil Dev (I)	27	6343	3174	85	37.34	6- 91	4	–
S.C.J.Broad (E)	22	4020	1875	70	26.78	6- 25	2	–

RESULTS SUMMARY – ENGLAND v INDIA – IN ENGLAND

	Tests	Series			Lord's			Manchester			The Oval			Leeds			Nottingham			Birmingham			Southampton		
		E	I	D	E	I	D	E	I	D	E	I	D	E	I	D	E	I	D	E	I	D	E	I	D
1932	1	1	–	–	1	–	–																		
1936	3	2	–	1	1	–	–	–	–	1	1	–	–												
1946	3	1	–	2	1	–	–	–	–	1	–	–	1												
1952	4	3	–	1	1	–	–	1	–	–	–	–	1	1	–	–									
1959	5	5	–	–	1	–	–	1	–	–	1	–	–	1	–	–	1	–	–						
1967	3	3	–	–	1	–	–							1	–	–				1	–	–			
1971	3	–	1	2	–	–	1	–	–	1	–	1	–												
1974	3	3	–	–	1	–	–	1	–	–										1	–	–			
1979	4	1	–	3	–	–	1				–	–	1	–	–	1				1	–	–			
1982	3	1	–	2	1	–	–	–	–	1	–	–	1												
1986	3	–	2	1	–	1	–							–	1	–				–	–	1			
1990	3	1	–	2	1	–	–	–	–	1	–	–	1												
1996	3	1	–	2	–	–	1										–	–	1	1	–	–			
2002	4	1	1	2	1	–	–				–	–	1	–	1	–	–	–	1						
2007	3	–	1	2	–	–	1				–	–	1				–	1	–						
2011	4	4	–	–	1	–	–				1	–	–				1	–	–	1	–	–			
2014	5	3	1	1	–	1	–	1	–	–	1	–	–				–	–	1				1	–	–
2018	5	4	1	–	1	–	–				1	–	–				–	1	–	1	–	–	1	–	–
	62	34	7	21	12	2	4	4	–	5	5	1	7	3	2	1	2	2	3	6	–	1	2	–	–

ENGLAND v INDIA – IN INDIA

	Tests	Series			Mumbai			Kolkata			Chennai			Delhi			Kanpur			Bangalore		
		E	I	D	E	I	D	E	I	D	E	I	D	E	I	D	E	I	D	E	I	D
1933-34	3	2	–	1	1	–	–	–	–	1	1	–	–									
1951-52	5	1	1	3	–	–	1	–	–	1	–	1	–	–	–	1	1	–	–			
1961-62	5	–	2	3	–	–	1	–	1	–	–	1	–	–	–	1	–	–	1			
1963-64	5	–	–	5	–	–	1	–	–	1	–	–	1	–	–	1	–	–	1			
1972-73	5	1	2	2	–	–	1	–	1	–	–	1	–	1	–	–	–	–	1			
1976-77	5	3	1	1	–	–	1	1	–	–	1	–	–	1	–	–				–	1	–
1979-80	1	–	1	–	–	1	–															
1981-82	6	–	1	5	–	1	–	–	–	1	–	–	1	–	–	1	–	–	1	–	–	1
1984-85	5	2	1	2	–	1	–	–	–	1	1	–	–	1	–	–	–	–	1			
1992-93	3	–	3	–	–	1	–	–	1	–	–	1	–									
2001-02	3	–	1	2																–	–	1
2005-06	3	1	1	1	1	–	–															
2008-09	2	–	1	1							–	1	–									
2011-12	4	2	1	1	1	–	–	1	–	–												
2016-17	5	–	4	1	–	1	–				–	1	–									
2020-21	4	1	3	–							1	1	–									
	64	14	22	28	4	4	5	2	3	5	4	7	2	3	–	4	1	–	5	–	1	2

	Tests	Chandigarh			Ahmedabad			Nagpur			Rajkot			Visakhapatnam		
		E	I	D	E	I	D	E	I	D	E	I	D	E	I	D
2001-02		–	1	–	–	–	1									
2005-06		–	1	–				–	–	1						
2008-09		–	–	1												
2011-12					–	1	–	–	–	1						
2016-17		–	1	–							–	–	1	–	1	–
2020-21					–	2	–									
		–	3	1	–	3	1	–	–	2	–	–	1	–	1	–

	Tests	E	I	D
Totals	126	48	29	49

TOURING TEAMS REGISTER 2021

Neither New Zealand nor India had selected their 2021 touring teams at the time of going to press. The following players, who had represented those teams in Test matches since 1 December 2019, were still available for selection:

NEW ZEALAND

Full Names	Birthdate	Birthplace	Team	Type	F-C Debut
ASTLE, Todd Duncan	24.09.86	Palmerston N	Canterbury	RHB/LB	2005-06
BLUNDELL, Thomas Ackland	01.09.90	Wellington	Wellington	RHB/WK	2012-13
BOULT, Trent Alexander	22.07.89	Rotorua	Northern D	RHB/LFM	2008-09
DE GRANDHOMME, Colin	22.07.86	Harare, Zim	Northern D	RHB/RMF	2005-06
FERGUSON, Lachlan Hammond	13.06.91	Auckland	Auckland	RHB/RF	2012-13
HENRY, Matthew James	14.12.91	Christchurch	Canterbury	RHB/RFM	2010-11
JAMIESON, Kyle Alex	30.12.94	Auckland	Auckland	RHB/RFM	2014-15
LATHAM, Thomas William Maxwell	02.04.92	Christchurch	Canterbury	LHB/WK	2010-11
MITCHELL, Daryl Joseph	20.05.91	Hamilton	Canterbury	RHB/RM	2011-12
NICHOLLS, Henry Michael	15.11.91	Christchurch	Canterbury	LHB/OB	2011-12
PATEL, Ajaz Yunus	21.10.88	Bombay, India	Central D	LHB/SLA	2012-13
PHILLIPS, Glenn Dominic	06.12.96	East London, SA	Auckland	RHB/OB	2016-17
RAVAL, Jeet Ashok	22.09.88	Gujarat, India	Northern D	LHB/LB	2008-09
SANTNER, Mitchell Josef	05.02.92	Hamilton	Northern D	LHB/SLA	2011-12
SOMERVILLE, William Edgar Richard	09.08.84	Wadestown	Auckland	RHB/OB	2004-05
SOUTHEE, Timothy Grant	11.12.88	Whangarei	Northern D	RHB/RMF	2006-07
TAYLOR, Luteru Ross Poutoa Lote	08.03.84	Lower Hutt	Central D	RHB/OB	2002-03
WAGNER, Neil	13.03.86	Pretoria, SA	Northern D	LHB/LMF	2005-06
WATLING, Bradley-John	09.07.85	Durban, SA	Northern D	RHB/WK	2004-05
WILLIAMSON, Kane Stuart	08.08.90	Tauranga	Northern D	RHB/OB	2007-08
YOUNG, William Alexander	22.11.92	New Plymouth	Central D	RHB/OB	2011-12

INDIA

Full Names	Birthdate	Birthplace	Team	Type	F-C Debut
AGARWAL, Mayank Anurag	16.02.91	Bangalore	Karnataka	RHB/OB	2013-14
ASHWIN, Ravichandran	17.09.86	Madras	Tamil Nadu	RHB/OB	2006-07
BUMRAH, Jasprit Jasbirsingh	06.12.93	Ahmedabad	Gujarat	RHB/RFM	2013-14
GILL, Shubman	08.09.99	Firozpur	Punjab	RHB/OB	2017-18
JADEJA, Ravindrasinh Anirudsinh	06.12.88	Navagam-Khed	Saurashtra	LHB/SLA	2006-07
KOHLI, Virat	05.11.88	Delhi	Delhi	RHB/RM	2006-07
MOHAMMED SHAMI	03.09.90	Jonagar	Bengal	RHB/RFM	2010-11
NADEEM, Shahbaz	12.08.89	Bokaro	Jharkhand	RHB/SLA	2004-05
NATARAJAN, Thangarasu	27.05.91	Salem	Tamil Nadu	LHB/LFM	2014-15
PANDYA, Hardik Himanshu	11.10.93	Choryasi	Baroda	RHB/RMF	2013-14
PANT, Rishabh Rajendra	04.10.97	Haridwar	Delhi	LHB/WK	2015-16
PATEL, Axar Rajeshbhai	20.01.94	Anand	Gujarat	LHB/SLA	2012-13
PUJARA, Cheteshwar Arvindbhai	25.01.88	Rajkot	Saurashtra	RHB/LB	2005-06
RAHANE, Ajinkya Madhukar	06.06.88	Ashwi Khurd	Mumbai	RHB/RM	2007-08
SAHA, Wriddhaman Prasanta	24.10.84	Siliguri	Bengal	RHB/WK	2007-08
SAINI, Navdeep Amarjeet	23.11.92	Karnal	Delhi	RHB/RM	2013-14
SHARMA, Ishant	02.09.88	Delhi	Delhi	RHB/RMF	2006-07
SHARMA, Rohit Gurunath	30.04.87	Bansod	Mumbai	RHB/OB	2006-07
SHAW, Prithvi Pankaj	09.11.99	Thane	Mumbai	RHB/OB	2016-17
SIRAJ, Mohammed	13.03.94	Hyderabad	Hyderabad	RHB/RFM	2015-16
THAKUR, Shardul Narendra	16.10.91	Palghar	Mumbai	RHB/RFM	2012-13
VIHARI, Gade Hanuma	13.10.93	Kakinada	Andhra	RHB/OB	2010-11
WASHINGTON SUNDAR, M.S.	05.10.99	Chennai	Tamil Nadu	LHB/OB	2016-17
YADAV, Kuldeep	14.12.94	Kanpur	Uttar Pradesh	LHB/SLC	2014-15
YADAV, Umesh Tilak	25.10.87	Nagpur	Vidarbha	RHB/RFM	2008-09

STATISTICAL HIGHLIGHTS IN 2020 TESTS

Including Tests from No. 2376 (Australia v New Zealand, 3rd Test) and No. 2378 (South Africa v England, 2nd Test) to No. 2396 (Australia v India, 2nd Test), No. 2399 (New Zealand v Pakistan, 1st Test) and No. 2401 (South Africa v Sri Lanka, 1st Test).

† = National record

TEAM HIGHLIGHTS
HIGHEST INNINGS TOTALS

621	South Africa v Sri Lanka	Centurion
583-8d	England v Pakistan (*3rd Test*)	Southampton
560-6d	Bangladesh v Zimbabwe	Dhaka

LOWEST INNINGS TOTALS

36†	India v Australia	Adelaide

HIGHEST MATCH AGGREGATE

1197-28	Sri Lanka (396 & 180) v South Africa (621)	Centurion

LARGE MARGINS OF VICTORY

Inns & 134 runs	New Zealand (519-7d) beat West Indies (138 & 247)	Hamilton
Inns & 106 runs	Bangladesh (560-6d) beat Zimbabwe (265 & 189)	Dhaka
279 runs	Australia (454 & 217-2d) beat New Zealand (256 & 136)	Sydney
269 runs	England (369 & 226-2d) beat West Indies (197 & 129)	Manchester

MOST EXTRAS IN AN INNINGS

	B	LB	W	NB		
47	11	23	1	12	New Zealand (519-7d) v West Indies	Hamilton

BATTING HIGHLIGHTS
DOUBLE HUNDREDS

Z.Crawley	267	England v Pakistan (*3rd Test*)	Southampton
M.Labuschagne	215	Australia v New Zealand	Sydney
A.D.Mathews	200*	Sri Lanka v Zimbabwe (*1st Test*)	Harare
Mushfiqur Rahim	203*	Bangladesh v Zimbabwe	Mirpur
K.S.Williamson	251	New Zealand v West Indies	Hamilton

HUNDREDS IN THREE CONSECUTIVE INNINGS

Shan Masood	135	Pakistan v Sri Lanka	Karachi
	100	Pakistan v Bangladesh	Rawalpindi
	156	Pakistan v England	Manchester

MOST RUNS IN BOUNDARIES IN AN INNINGS

Runs	6s	4s			
148	2	34	K.S.Williamson	New Zealand v West Indies	Hamilton

LONG INNINGS (Qualification: 600 mins and/or 400 balls)

Mins	Balls			
600	468	A.D.Mathews (200*)	Sri Lanka v Zimbabwe (*1st Test*)	Harare
624	412	K.S.Williamson (251)	New Zealand v West Indies	Hamilton

NOTABLE PARTNERSHIPS

Qualifications: 1st-6th wkts: 200 runs; 7th-8th: 150; 9th-10th: 100.

Fourth Wicket

260	D.P.Sibley/B.A.Stokes	England v West Indies (*2nd Test*)	Manchester
222	Mominul Haque/Mushfiqur Rahim	Bangladesh v Zimbabwe	Dhaka

Fifth Wicket

359†	Z.Crawley/J.C.Buttler	England v Pakistan (*3rd Test*)	Southampton
203	B.A.Stokes/O.J.D.Pope	England v South Africa	Port Elizabeth

Seventh Wicket

155	J.Blackwood/A.S.Joseph	West Indies v New Zealand	Hamilton

BOWLING HIGHLIGHTS

SEVEN WICKETS IN AN INNINGS

Sikandar Raza	7-113	Zimbabwe v Sri Lanka (*2nd Test*)	Harare

TEN WICKETS IN A MATCH

S.C.J.Broad	10- 67	England v West Indies (*3rd Test*)	Manchester
N.M.Lyon	10-118	Australia v New Zealand	Sydney

FIVE WICKETS IN AN INNINGS ON DEBUT

B.E.Hendricks	5-64	South Africa v England	Johannesburg

HAT-TRICK

Naseem Shah		Pakistan v Bangladesh	Rawalpindi

At 16 years 359 days, Naseem Shah became the youngest bowler ever to take a Test hat-trick, beating Abdul Razzaq, who was 20.

MOST OVERS IN AN INNINGS

K.A.Maharaj	58-15-180-5	South Africa v England	Port Elizabeth

MOST RUNS CONCEDED IN AN INNINGS

L.Ambuldeniya	42.3-8-182-4	Sri Lanka v Zimbabwe (*2nd Test*)	Harare

WICKET-KEEPING HIGHLIGHTS

FIVE WICKET-KEEPING DISMISSALS IN AN INNINGS

Q.de Kock	5ct	South Africa v England	Cape Town
R.W.Chakabva	5ct	Zimbabwe v Bangladesh	Dhaka
T.D.Paine	5ct	Australia v India	Adelaide

EIGHT WICKET-KEEPING DISMISSALS IN A MATCH

Q.de Kock	8ct	South Africa v England	Cape Town
B.J.Watling	8ct	New Zealand v Pakistan	Mt Maunganui

FIELDING HIGHLIGHTS

FOUR OR MORE CATCHES IN AN INNINGS IN THE FIELD

B.A.Stokes	5ct	England v South Africa	Cape Town

SIX CATCHES IN A MATCH IN THE FIELD

O.J.D.Pope	6ct	England v South Africa	Port Elizabeth
B.A.Stokes	6ct	England v South Africa	Cape Town

LEADING TEST AGGREGATES IN 2020

600 RUNS IN 2020

	M	I	NO	HS	Runs	Avge	100	50
B.A.Stokes (E)	7	12	1	176	**641**	58.27	2	2
D.P.Sibley (E)	9	14	1	133*	**615**	37.89	2	2

RECORD CALENDAR YEAR RUNS AGGREGATE

	M	I	NO	HS	Runs	Avge	100	50
M.Yousuf (P) (2006)	11	19	1	202	**1788**	99.33	9	3

RECORD CALENDAR YEAR RUNS AVERAGE

	M	I	NO	HS	Runs	Avge	100	50
G.St A.Sobers (WI) (1958)	7	12	3	365*	**1193**	132.55	5	3

1000 RUNS IN DEBUT CALENDAR YEAR

	M	I	NO	HS	Runs	Avge	100	50
M.A.Taylor (A) (1989)	11	20	1	219	**1219**	64.15	4	5
A.C.Voges (A) (2015)	12	18	6	269*	**1028**	85.66	4	3
A.N.Cook (E) (2006)	13	24	2	127	**1013**	46.04	4	3

30 WICKETS IN 2020

	M	O	R	W	Avge	Best	5wI	10wM
S.C.J.Broad (E)	8	242.5	561	38	**14.76**	6-31	1	1
T.G.Southee (NZ)	5	187.5	511	30	**17.03**	5-32	2	–

RECORD CALENDAR YEAR WICKETS AGGREGATE

	M	O	R	W	Avge	Best	5wI	10wM
M.Muralitharan (SL) (2006)	11	588.4	1521	90	**16.90**	8-70	9	5
S.K.Warne (A) (2005)	14	691.4	2043	90	**22.70**	6-46	6	2

25 WICKET-KEEPING DISMISSALS IN 2020

	M	Dis	Ct	St
J.C.Buttler (E)	9	30	30	–
B.J.Watling (NZ)	5	25	25	–

RECORD CALENDAR YEAR DISMISSALS AGGREGATE

	M	Dis	Ct	St
J.M.Bairstow (E) (2016)	17	70	66	4

12 CATCHES BY FIELDERS IN 2020

	M	Ct
J.E.Root (E)	8	14
B.A.Stokes (E)	8	14

RECORD CALENDAR YEAR FIELDER'S AGGREGATE

	M	Ct
G.C.Smith (SA) (2008)	15	30

TEST MATCH SCORES
ENGLAND v WEST INDIES (1st Test)

At The Rose Bowl, Southampton, on 8, 9, 10, 11, 12 July 2020.
Toss: England. Result: **WEST INDIES** won by four wickets.
Debuts: None.

ENGLAND

R.J.Burns	lbw b Gabriel	30	c Campbell b Chase	42
D.P.Sibley	b Gabriel	0	c Dowrich b Gabriel	50
J.L.Denly	b Gabriel	18	c Holder b Chase	29
Z.Crawley	lbw b Holder	10	c and b Joseph	76
*B.A.Stokes	c Dowrich b Holder	43	c Hope b Holder	46
O.J.D.Pope	c Dowrich b Holder	12	b Gabriel	12
†J.C.Buttler	c Dowrich b Holder	35	b Joseph	9
D.M.Bess	not out	31	b Gabriel	3
J.C.Archer	lbw b Holder	0	c Dowrich b Gabriel	23
M.A.Wood	c Hope b Holder	5	c Dowrich b Gabriel	2
J.M.Anderson	b Gabriel	10	not out	4
Extras	(LB 6, NB 2, W 2)		(B 4, LB 10, NB 3)	17
Total	**(67.3 overs)**	**204**	**(111.2 overs)**	**313**

WEST INDIES

K.C.Brathwaite	lbw b Stokes	65	b Archer	4
J.D.Campbell	lbw b Anderson	28	not out	8
S.D.Hope	c Stokes b Bess	16	b Wood	9
S.S.J.Brooks	c Buttler b Anderson	39	lbw b Archer	0
R.L.Chase	lbw b Anderson	47	c Buttler b Archer	37
J.Blackwood	c Anderson b Bess	12	c Anderson b Stokes	95
†S.O.Dowrich	c Buttler b Stokes	61	c Buttler b Stokes	20
*J.O.Holder	c Archer b Stokes	5	not out	14
A.S.Joseph	b Stokes	18		
K.A.J.Roach	not out	1		
S.T.Gabriel	b Wood	4		
Extras	(LB 21, NB 1)	22	(LB 7, NB 1, W 5)	13
Total	**(102 overs)**	**318**	**(6 wkts; 64.2 overs)**	**200**

WEST INDIES	O	M	R	W		O	M	R	W
Roach	19	6	41	0		22	8	50	0
Gabriel	15.3	3	62	4		21.2	4	75	5
Joseph	13	4	53	0	(5)	18	2	45	2
Holder	20	6	42	6	(3)	22	8	49	1
Chase					(4)	25	6	71	2
Brathwaite						3	0	9	0

ENGLAND	O	M	R	W		O	M	R	W
Anderson	25	11	62	3		15	3	42	0
Archer	22	3	61	0		17	3	45	3
Wood	22	2	74	1		12	0	36	1
Stokes	14	5	49	4	(5)	10.2	1	39	2
Bess	19	5	51	2	(4)	10	2	31	0

FALL OF WICKETS

	E	WI	E	WI
Wkt	1st	1st	2nd	2nd
1st	0	43	72	7
2nd	48	102	113	7
3rd	51	140	151	27
4th	71	173	249	100
5th	87	186	253	168
6th	154	267	265	189
7th	157	281	278	–
8th	157	306	279	–
9th	174	313	303	–
10th	204	318	313	–

Umpires: R.K.Illingworth (*England*) (48) and R.A.Kettleborough (*England*) (65).
Referee: B.C.Broad (*England*) (101). **Test No. 2387/158 (E1023/WI546)**
J.D.Campbell retired hurt at 6-0 (2nd innings) and resumed at 189-6.

ENGLAND v WEST INDIES (2nd Test)

At Old Trafford, Manchester, on 16, 17, 18 (*no play*), 19, 20 July 2020.
Toss: West Indies. Result: **ENGLAND** won by 113 runs.
Debuts: None.

ENGLAND

R.J.Burns	lbw b Chase	15		b Roach	11
D.P.Sibley	c Roach b Chase	120			
Z.Crawley	c Holder b Chase	0		b Roach	11
*J.E.Root	c Holder b Joseph	23		run out	22
B.A.Stokes	c Dowrich b Roach	176	(1)	not out	78
O.J.D.Pope	lbw b Chase	7	(5)	not out	12
†J.C.Buttler	c Joseph b Holder	40	(2)	b Roach	0
C.R.Woakes	c Hope b Roach	0			
S.M.Curran	c Brathwaite b Chase	17			
D.M.Bess	not out	31			
S.C.J.Broad	not out	11			
Extras	(B 4, LB 7, NB 8, W 10)	29		(B 1, LB 1, NB 1, W 3)	6
Total	**(9 wkts dec; 162 overs)**	**469**		**(3 wkts dec; 19 overs)**	**129**

WEST INDIES

K.C.Brathwaite	c and b Stokes	75		lbw b Woakes	12
J.D.Campbell	lbw b Curran	12		c Buttler b Broad	4
A.S.Joseph	c Pope b Bess	32	(10)	c Bess b Stokes	9
S.D.Hope	c Buttler b Curran	25	(3)	b Broad	7
S.S.J.Brooks	lbw b Broad	68	(4)	lbw b Curran	62
R.L.Chase	lbw b Woakes	51	(5)	lbw b Broad	6
J.Blackwood	b Broad	0	(6)	c Buttler b Stokes	55
†S.O.Dowrich	lbw b Broad	0	(7)	lbw b Woakes	0
*J.O.Holder	c Root b Woakes	2	(8)	b Bess	35
K.A.J.Roach	not out	5	(9)	c Pope b Bess	5
S.T.Gabriel	b Woakes	0		not out	0
Extras	(B 1, LB 12, NB 2, W 2)	17		(LB 3)	3
Total	**(99 overs)**	**287**		**(70.1 overs)**	**198**

WEST INDIES	O	M	R	W		O	M	R	W
Roach	33	9	58	2		6	0	37	2
Gabriel	26	2	79	0		7	0	43	0
Joseph	23.1	5	70	1	(4)	2	0	14	0
Holder	32	10	70	1	(3)	4	0	33	0
Chase	44	3	172	5					
Brathwaite	3.5	0	9	0					

ENGLAND	O	M	R	W		O	M	R	W
Broad	23	7	66	3		15	5	42	3
Woakes	21	10	42	3		16	3	34	2
Curran	20	4	70	2		8	3	30	1
Bess	21	3	67	1		15.1	3	59	2
Root	1	1	0	0	(6)	1.2	1	0	0
Stokes	13	3	29	1	(5)	14.4	4	30	2

FALL OF WICKETS

	E	WI	E	WI
Wkt	1st	1st	2nd	2nd
1st	29	16	1	7
2nd	29	70	17	19
3rd	81	123	90	23
4th	341	199	—	37
5th	352	242	—	137
6th	395	248	—	138
7th	395	252	—	161
8th	426	260	—	183
9th	427	287	—	192
10th	—	287	—	198

Umpires: M.A.Gough (*England*) (15) and R.K.Illingworth (*England*) (49).
Referee: B.C.Broad (*England*) (102). **Test No. 2388/159 (E1024/WI547)**

ENGLAND v WEST INDIES (3rd Test)

At Old Trafford, Manchester, on 24, 25, 26, 27 (*no play*), 28 July 2020.
Toss: West Indies. Result: **ENGLAND** won by 269 runs.
Debuts: None.

ENGLAND

R.J.Burns	c Cornwall b Chase	57	c sub (J.Da Silva) b Chase	90
D.P.Sibley	lbw b Roach	0	lbw b Holder	56
*J.E.Root	run out	17	not out	68
B.A.Stokes	b Roach	20		
O.J.D.Pope	b Gabriel	91		
†J.C.Buttler	c Holder b Gabriel	67		
C.R.Woakes	b Roach	1		
D.M.Bess	not out	18		
J.C.Archer	c Holder b Roach	3		
S.C.J.Broad	c Blackwood b Chase	62		
J.M.Anderson	c Cornwall b Holder	11		
Extras	(B 12, LB 4, NB 6)	22	(B 6, LB 3, NB 3)	12
Total	**(111.5 overs)**	**369**	**(2 wkts dec; 58 overs)**	**226**

WEST INDIES

K.C.Brathwaite	c Root b Broad	1	lbw b Broad	19
J.D.Campbell	c Burns b Archer	32	c Root b Broad	0
S.D.Hope	c Buttler b Anderson	17	(4) c Broad b Woakes	31
S.S.J.Brooks	c Buttler b Anderson	4	(5) c Buttler b Woakes	22
R.L.Chase	lbw b Broad	9	(6) run out	7
J.Blackwood	b Woakes	26	(7) c Buttler b Broad	23
*J.O.Holder	lbw b Broad	46	(8) lbw b Woakes	12
†S.O.Dowrich	c Woakes b Broad	10	(9) lbw b Woakes	8
R.R.S.Cornwall	lbw b Broad	10	(10) lbw b Woakes	2
K.A.J.Roach	c Root b Broad	0	(3) c Buttler b Broad	4
S.T.Gabriel	not out	0	not out	0
Extras	(B 4, LB 5, NB 1, W 5)	15	(LB 1)	1
Total	**(65 overs)**	**197**	**(37.1 overs)**	**129**

WEST INDIES	O	M	R	W		O	M	R	W
Roach	25.4	4	72	4		11	4	34	0
Gabriel	23.2	5	77	2		5	0	19	0
Holder	24.5	5	83	1		9	2	24	1
Cornwall	27	5	85	0	(5)	19	2	79	0
Chase	11	3	36	2	(4)	14	2	61	1
ENGLAND									
Anderson	16	5	28	2		8	4	18	0
Broad	14	4	31	6		8.1	1	36	4
Archer	17	1	72	1	(4)	10	1	24	0
Woakes	18	2	57	1	(3)	11	0	50	5

FALL OF WICKETS

	E	WI	E	WI
Wkt	*1st*	*1st*	*2nd*	*2nd*
1st	1	1	114	0
2nd	47	44	226	6
3rd	92	58	–	45
4th	122	59	–	71
5th	262	75	–	79
6th	267	110	–	87
7th	272	178	–	99
8th	280	188	–	117
9th	356	188	–	119
10th	369	197	–	129

Umpires: M.A.Gough (*England*) (16) and R.A.Kettleborough (*England*) (66).
Referee: B.C.Broad (*England*) (103). **Test No. 2389/160 (E1025/WI548)**

ENGLAND v WEST INDIES
SERIES AVERAGES 2020

ENGLAND – BATTING AND FIELDING

	M	I	NO	HS	Runs	Avge	100	50	Ct/St
B.A.Stokes	3	5	1	176	363	90.75	1	1	2
D.M.Bess	3	4	3	31*	83	83.00	–	–	1
S.C.J.Broad	2	2	1	62	73	73.00	–	1	1
R.J.Burns	3	5	–	90	234	46.80	–	2	1
D.P.Sibley	3	5	–	120	226	45.20	1	2	–
J.E.Root	2	4	1	68*	130	43.33	–	1	4
O.J.D.Pope	3	5	1	91	134	33.50	–	1	2
J.C.Buttler	3	5	–	67	151	30.20	–	1	12
Z.Crawley	2	4	–	76	97	24.25	–	1	–
J.M.Anderson	2	3	1	11	25	12.50	–	–	2
J.C.Archer	2	3	–	23	26	8.66	–	–	1
C.R.Woakes	2	2	–	1	1	0.50	–	–	1

Also batted (one Test): S.M.Curran 17; J.L.Denly 18, 29; M.A.Wood 5, 2.

BOWLING

	O	M	R	W	Avge	Best	5wI	10wM
S.C.J.Broad	60.1	17	175	16	10.93	6-31	1	1
B.A.Stokes	52	13	147	9	16.33	4-49	–	–
C.R.Woakes	66	15	183	11	16.63	5-50	1	–
J.M.Anderson	64	23	150	5	30.00	3-62	–	–
D.M.Bess	65.1	13	208	5	41.60	2-51	–	–
J.C.Archer	66	8	202	4	50.50	3-45	–	–

Also bowled: S.M.Curran 28-7-100-3; J.E.Root 2.2-2-0-0; M.A.Wood 34-2-110-2.

WEST INDIES – BATTING AND FIELDING

	M	I	NO	HS	Runs	Avge	100	50	Ct/St
J.Blackwood	3	6	–	95	211	35.16	–	2	1
S.S.J.Brooks	3	6	–	68	195	32.50	–	2	–
K.C.Brathwaite	3	6	–	75	176	29.33	–	2	1
R.L.Chase	3	6	–	51	157	26.16	–	1	–
J.O.Holder	3	6	1	46	114	22.80	–	–	5
S.O.Dowrich	3	6	–	61	126	21.00	–	1	7
A.S.Joseph	2	3	–	32	59	19.66	–	–	2
S.D.Hope	3	6	–	31	105	17.50	–	–	3
J.D.Campbell	3	6	1	32	84	16.80	–	–	1
K.A.J.Roach	3	5	2	5*	15	5.00	–	–	1
S.T.Gabriel	3	5	3	4	4	2.00	–	–	–

Also batted (one Test): R.R.S.Cornwall 10, 2 (2 ct).

BOWLING

	O	M	R	W	Avge	Best	5wI	10wM
J.O.Holder	111.5	31	301	10	30.10	6- 42	1	–
S.T.Gabriel	98.1	14	355	11	32.27	5- 75	1	–
R.L.Chase	94	14	340	10	34.00	5-172	1	–
K.A.J.Roach	116.4	31	292	8	36.50	4- 72	–	–
A.S.Joseph	56.1	11	182	3	60.66	2- 45	–	–

Also bowled: K.C.Brathwaite 6.5-0-18-0; R.R.S.Cornwall 46-7-164-0.

ENGLAND v PAKISTAN (1st Test)

At Old Trafford, Manchester, on 5, 6, 7, 8 August 2020.
Toss: Pakistan. Result: **ENGLAND** won by three wickets.
Debuts: None.

PAKISTAN

Shan Masood	lbw b Broad	156	c Buttler b Broad		0
Abid Ali	b Archer	16	c Woakes b Bess		20
*Azhar Ali	lbw b Woakes	0	lbw b Woakes		18
Babar Azam	c Root b Anderson	69	c Stokes b Woakes		5
Asad Shafiq	c Stokes b Broad	7	run out		29
†Mohammad Rizwan	c Buttler b Woakes	9	lbw b Stokes		27
Shadab Khan	c Root b Bess	45	lbw b Broad		15
Yasir Shah	c Buttler b Broad	5	c Buttler b Broad		33
Mohammad Abbas	c Root b Archer	0	(10) not out		3
Shaheen Shah Afridi	not out	9	(9) c Burns b Stokes		2
Naseem Shah	c Buttler b Broad	4	b Archer		4
Extras	(B 1, LB 7, NB 2)	10	(B 4, LB 5, NB 4)		13
Total	**(109.3 overs)**	**326**	**(46.4 overs)**		**169**

ENGLAND

R.J.Burns	lbw b Afridi	4	lbw b Abbas		10
D.P.Sibley	lbw b Abbas	8	c Shafiq b Yasir		36
*J.E.Root	c Rizwan b Yasir	14	c Azam b Naseem		42
B.A.Stokes	b Abbas	0	c Rizwan b Yasir		9
O.J.D.Pope	c Khan b Naseem	62	c Khan b Afridi		7
†J.C.Buttler	b Yasir	38	lbw b Yasir		75
C.R.Woakes	b Yasir	19	not out		84
D.M.Bess	c Shafiq b Yasir	1	(9) not out		0
J.C.Archer	c Rizwan b Khan	16			
S.C.J.Broad	not out	29	(8) lbw b Yasir		7
J.M.Anderson	lbw b Khan	7			
Extras	(B 8, LB 4, NB 8, W 1)	21	(LB 2, NB 5)		7
Total	**(70.3 overs)**	**219**	**(7 wkts; 82.1 overs)**		**277**

ENGLAND	O	M	R	W		O	M	R	W
Anderson	19	6	63	1		9	2	34	0
Broad	22.3	9	54	3		10	3	37	3
Woakes	20	6	43	2	(5)	5	1	11	2
Archer	22	4	59	3	(3)	6.4	0	27	1
Bess	20	4	74	1	(4)	12	2	40	1
Root	6	0	25	0					
Stokes					(6)	4	1	11	2
PAKISTAN									
Shaheen Shah Afridi	18	4	51	1		15.1	1	61	1
Mohammad Abbas	15	6	33	2		16	4	36	1
Naseem Shah	16	4	44	1		13	4	45	1
Yasir Shah	18	2	66	4		30	2	99	4
Shadab Khan	3.3	0	13	2		8	0	34	0

FALL OF WICKETS

Wkt	P	E	P	E
	1st	1st	2nd	2nd
1st	36	4	6	26
2nd	43	12	33	86
3rd	139	12	48	96
4th	150	62	63	106
5th	176	127	101	117
6th	281	159	120	256
7th	291	161	122	273
8th	291	170	158	—
9th	317	197	158	—
10th	326	219	169	—

Umpires: R.K.Illingworth (*England*) (50) and R.A.Kettleborough (*England*) (67).
Referee: B.C.Broad (*England*) (104).   Test No. 2390/84 (E1026/P429)

ENGLAND v PAKISTAN (2nd Test)

At The Rose Bowl, Southampton, on 13, 14, 15 (*no play*), 16, 17 August 2020.
Toss: Pakistan. Result: **MATCH DRAWN**.
Debuts: None.

PAKISTAN

Shan Masood	lbw b Anderson	1
Abid Ali	c Burns b Curran	60
*Azhar Ali	c Burns b Anderson	20
Babar Azam	c Buttler b Broad	47
Asad Shafiq	c Sibley b Broad	5
Fawad Alam	lbw b Woakes	0
†Mohammad Rizwan	c Crawley b Broad	72
Yasir Shah	c Buttler b Anderson	5
Shaheen Shah Afridi	run out	0
Mohammad Abbas	lbw b Broad	2
Naseem Shah	not out	1
Extras	(B 9, LB 12, NB 1, W 1)	23
Total	**(91.2 overs)**	**236**

ENGLAND

R.J.Burns	c Shafiq b Afridi	0
D.P.Sibley	c Rizwan b Abbas	32
Z.Crawley	lbw b Abbas	53
*J.E.Root	not out	9
O.J.D.Pope	lbw b Yasir	9
†J.C.Buttler	not out	0
C.R.Woakes		
S.M.Curran		
D.M.Bess		
S.C.J.Broad		
J.M.Anderson		
Extras	(LB 3, NB 3, W 1)	7
Total	**(4 wkts; 43.1 overs)**	**110**

ENGLAND	O	M	R	W	O	M	R	W	FALL OF WICKETS		
										P	E
Anderson	27	5	60	3					*Wkt*	*1st*	*1st*
Broad	27.2	9	56	4					1st	6	0
Curran	18	3	44	1					2nd	78	91
Woakes	19	3	55	1					3rd	102	92
									4th	117	105
PAKISTAN									5th	120	–
Shaheen Shah Afridi	10	3	25	1					6th	158	–
Mohammad Abbas	14	5	28	2					7th	171	–
Naseem Shah	5	0	10	0					8th	176	–
Yasir Shah	11	2	30	1					9th	215	–
Shan Masood	3	0	14	0					10th	236	–
Azhar Ali	0.1	0	0	0							

Umpires: M.A.Gough (*England*) (17) and R.A.Kettleborough (*England*) (68).
Referee: B.C.Broad (*England*) (105). **Test No. 2391/85 (E1027/P430)**

ENGLAND v PAKISTAN (3rd Test)

At The Rose Bowl, Southampton, on 21, 22, 23, 24, 25 August 2020.
Toss: England. Result: **MATCH DRAWN**.
Debuts: None.

ENGLAND

R.J.Burns	c Masood b Afridi	6
D.P.Sibley	lbw b Yasir	22
Z.Crawley	st Rizwan b Shafiq	267
*J.E.Root	c Rizwan b Naseem	29
O.J.D.Pope	b Yasir	3
†J.C.Buttler	c and b Alam	152
C.R.Woakes	c Yasir b Alam	40
D.M.Bess	not out	27
S.C.J.Broad	b Afridi	15
J.C.Archer		
J.M.Anderson		
Extras	(B 4, LB 13, NB 4, W 1)	22
Total	**(8 wkts dec; 154.4 overs)**	**583**

PAKISTAN

Shan Masood	lbw b Anderson	4	lbw b Broad		18
Abid Ali	c Sibley b Anderson	1	lbw b Anderson		42
*Azhar Ali	not out	141	c Root b Anderson		31
Babar Azam	lbw b Anderson	11	not out		63
Asad Shafiq	c Root b Anderson	5	c sub (J.R.Bracey) b Root		21
Fawad Alam	c Buttler b Bess	21	not out		0
†Mohammad Rizwan	c Buttler b Woakes	53			
Yasir Shah	c Root b Broad	20			
Shaheen Shah Afridi	c Buttler b Broad	3			
Mohammad Abbas	run out	1			
Naseem Shah	c Sibley b Anderson	0			
Extras	(B 2, LB 7, NB 2, W 2)	13	(LB 9, NB 3)		12
Total	**(93 overs)**	**273**	**(4 wkts; 83.1 overs)**		**187**

PAKISTAN	O	M	R	W		O	M	R	W
Shaheen Shah Afridi	33.4	5	121	2					
Mohammad Abbas	33	8	82	0					
Yasir Shah	39	3	173	2					
Naseem Shah	27	6	109	1					
Fawad Alam	12	0	46	2					
Shan Masood	3	1	11	0					
Asad Shafiq	7	0	24	1					

ENGLAND	O	M	R	W		O	M	R	W
Anderson	23	3	56	5		19	3	45	2
Broad	20	5	40	2		14.1	5	27	1
Archer	17	3	58	0	(4)	14	8	14	0
Woakes	15	2	42	1	(3)	8	2	14	0
Bess	18	2	68	1		21	4	54	0
Root						6	0	17	1
Sibley						1	0	7	0

FALL OF WICKETS			
	E	P	P
Wkt	1st	1st	2nd
1st	12	6	49
2nd	73	11	88
3rd	114	24	109
4th	127	30	172
5th	486	75	–
6th	530	213	–
7th	547	241	–
8th	583	247	–
9th	–	261	–
10th	–	273	–

Umpires: M.A.Gough (*England*) (18) and R.K.Illingworth (*England*) (51).
Referee: B.C.Broad (*England*) (106).   Test No. 2392/86 (E1028/P431)

ENGLAND v PAKISTAN
SERIES AVERAGES 2020

ENGLAND – BATTING AND FIELDING

	M	I	NO	HS	Runs	Avge	100	50	Ct/St
Z.Crawley	2	2	–	267	320	160.00	1	1	1
J.C.Buttler	3	4	1	152	265	88.33	1	1	9
C.R.Woakes	3	3	–	84*	143	71.50	–	1	1
J.E.Root	3	4	1	42	94	31.33	–	–	6
D.M.Bess	3	3	2	27*	28	28.00	–	–	–
S.C.J.Broad	3	3	1	29*	51	25.50	–	–	–
D.P.Sibley	3	4	–	36	98	24.50	–	–	3
O.J.D.Pope	3	4	–	62	81	20.25	–	1	–
J.C.Archer	2	1	–	16	16	16.00	–	–	–
J.M.Anderson	3	1	–	7	7	7.00	–	–	–
R.J.Burns	3	4	–	10	20	5.00	–	–	3

Also played (one Test): S.M.Curran did not bat; B.A.Stokes 0, 9 (2 ct).

BOWLING

	O	M	R	W	Avge	Best	5wI	10wM
S.C.J.Broad	94	31	214	13	16.46	4-56	–	–
J.M.Anderson	97	19	258	11	23.45	5-56	1	–
C.R.Woakes	67	14	165	6	27.50	2-11	–	–
J.C.Archer	59.4	15	158	4	39.50	3-59	–	–
D.M.Bess	71	12	236	3	78.66	1-40	–	–

Also bowled: S.M.Curran 18-3-44-1; J.E.Root 12-0-42-1; D.P.Sibley 1-0-7-0; B.A.Stokes 4-1-11-2.

PAKISTAN – BATTING AND FIELDING

	M	I	NO	HS	Runs	Avge	100	50	Ct/St
Azhar Ali	3	5	1	141*	210	52.50	1	–	–
Babar Azam	3	5	1	69	195	48.75	–	2	1
Mohammad Rizwan	3	4	–	72	161	40.25	–	2	5/1
Shan Masood	3	5	–	156	179	35.80	1	–	1
Abid Ali	3	5	–	60	139	27.80	–	1	–
Yasir Shah	3	4	–	33	63	15.75	–	–	1
Asad Shafiq	3	5	–	29	67	13.40	–	–	3
Fawad Alam	2	3	–	21	21	10.50	–	–	1
Shaheen Shah Afridi	3	4	1	9*	14	4.66	–	–	–
Mohammad Abbas	3	4	1	3*	6	2.00	–	–	–
Naseem Shah	3	4	1	4	5	1.66	–	–	–

Also batted (one Test): Shadab Khan 45, 15 (2 ct).

BOWLING

	O	M	R	W	Avge	Best	5wI	10wM
Yasir Shah	98	9	368	11	33.45	4- 66	–	–
Mohammad Abbas	78	23	179	5	35.80	2- 28	–	–
Shaheen Shah Afridi	76.5	13	258	5	51.60	2-121	–	–
Naseem Shah	61	14	208	3	69.33	1- 44	–	–

Also bowled: Asad Shafiq 7-0-24-1; Azhar Ali 0.1-0-0-0; Fawad Alam 12-0-46-2; Shadab Khan 11.3-0-47-2 Shan Masood 6-1-25-0.

NEW ZEALAND v WEST INDIES (1st Test)

At Seddon Park, Hamilton, on 3, 4, 5, 6 December 2020.
Toss: West Indies. Result: **NEW ZEALAND** won by an innings and 134 runs.
Debut: New Zealand – W.A.Young.

NEW ZEALAND

T.W.M.Latham	b Roach	86
W.A.Young	lbw b Gabriel	5
*K.S.Williamson	c Chase b Joseph	251
L.R.P.L.Taylor	c Brooks b Gabriel	38
H.M.Nicholls	c Holder b Roach	7
†T.A.Blundell	lbw b Gabriel	14
D.J.Mitchell	c Holder b Roach	9
K.A.Jamieson	not out	51
T.G.Southee	not out	11
N.Wagner		
T.A.Boult		
Extras	(B 11, LB 23, NB 12, W 1)	47
Total	**(7 wkts dec; 145 overs; 658 mins)**	**519**

WEST INDIES

K.C.Brathwaite	c Blundell b Boult	21		c Blundell b Southee	10
J.D.Campbell	c Williamson b Southee	26		c Latham b Boult	2
S.S.J.Brooks	c Taylor b Southee	1	(4)	c sub (D.P.Conway) b Wagner	2
D.M.Bravo	b Jamieson	9	(3)	c Southee b Wagner	12
R.L.Chase	lbw b Wagner	11		lbw b Jamieson	6
J.Blackwood	c Latham b Southee	23		c Southee b Wagner	104
*J.O.Holder	not out	25		lbw b Mitchell	8
A.S.Joseph	c Mitchell b Southee	0		c sub (M.J.Santner) b Jamieson	86
K.A.J.Roach	b Jamieson	2		not out	0
S.T.Gabriel	lbw b Wagner	1		b Wagner	0
†S.O.Dowrich	absent hurt			absent hurt	
Extras	(B 8, LB 7, NB 3, W 1)	19		(LB 7, NB 2, W 8)	17
Total	**(64 overs; 295 mins)**	**138**		**(58.5 overs; 283 mins)**	**247**

WEST INDIES	O	M	R	W		O	M	R	W
Roach	30	7	114	3					
Gabriel	25	6	89	3					
Holder	31	12	60	0					
Joseph	31	8	99	1					
Chase	25	0	109	0					
Brathwaite	3	0	14	0					

NEW ZEALAND	O	M	R	W		O	M	R	W
Southee	19	7	35	4		15	2	62	1
Boult	17	5	30	1		15	1	61	1
Jamieson	13	3	25	2	(4)	12	2	42	2
Wagner	15	3	33	2	(3)	13.5	2	66	4
Mitchell						3	0	71	1

FALL OF WICKETS

	NZ	WI	WI
Wkt	1st	1st	2nd
1st	14	53	4
2nd	168	55	25
3rd	251	55	27
4th	281	79	27
5th	353	79	53
6th	409	119	89
7th	503	119	244
8th	–	135	247
9th	–	138	247
10th	–	–	–

Umpires: C.B.Gaffaney (*New Zealand*) (34) and W.R.Knights (*New Zealand*) (1).
Referee: J.J.Crowe (*New Zealand*) (100). **Test No. 2393/48 (NZ443/WI549)**

NEW ZEALAND v WEST INDIES (2nd Test)

At Basin Reserve, Wellington, on 11, 12, 13, 14 December 2020.
Toss: West Indies. Result: **NEW ZEALAND** won by an innings and 12 runs.
Debuts: West Indies – J.Da Silva, C.K.Holder.

NEW ZEALAND

*T.W.M.Latham	c Da Silva b C.K.Holder	27
T.A.Blundell	b Gabriel	14
W.A.Young	c J.O.Holder b Gabriel	43
L.R.P.L.Taylor	c Da Silva b Gabriel	9
H.M.Nicholls	c Brathwaite b Chase	174
†B.J.Watling	b Joseph	30
D.J.Mitchell	lbw b C.K.Holder	42
K.A.Jamieson	c J.O.Holder b Joseph	20
T.G.Southee	b Joseph	11
N.Wagner	not out	66
T.A.Boult	c Brooks b Chase	6
Extras	(B 2, LB 7, W 9)	18
Total	**(114 overs; 535 mins)**	**460**

WEST INDIES

K.C.Brathwaite	c Taylor b Southee	0	c Young b Boult	24
J.D.Campbell	c Latham b Jamieson	14	b Jamieson	68
D.M.Bravo	c and b Southee	7	c Nicholls b Boult	4
S.S.J.Brooks	b Jamieson	14	c Watling b Wagner	36
R.L.Chase	b Jamieson	0	c Latham b Jamieson	0
J.Blackwood	c Latham b Southee	69	b Boult	20
*J.O.Holder	c Boult b Jamieson	9	b Southee	61
†J.Da Silva	c Watling b Southee	3	lbw b Wagner	57
A.S.Joseph	c Watling b Jamieson	0	c Watling b Southee	24
C.K.Holder	not out	8	not out	13
S.T.Gabriel	b Southee	2	b Wagner	0
Extras	(LB 3, NB 1, W 1)	5	(B 1, LB 7, NB 1, W 1)	10
Total	**(56.4 overs; 265 mins)**	**131**	**(79.1 overs; 366 mins)**	**317**

WEST INDIES	O	M	R	W	O	M	R	W
Gabriel	26	7	93	3				
J.O.Holder	27	6	85	0				
Joseph	22	2	109	3				
C.K.Holder	26	1	110	2				
Chase	13	1	54	2				

NEW ZEALAND	O	M	R	W	O	M	R	W
Southee	17.4	6	32	5	22	4	96	2
Boult	14	5	34	0	21	3	96	3
Wagner	12	5	28	0	(4) 17.1	4	54	3
Jamieson	13	4	34	5	(3) 15	4	43	2
Mitchell					4	0	20	0

	FALL OF WICKETS		
	NZ	WI	WI
Wkt	1st	1st	2nd
1st	31	0	37
2nd	63	22	41
3rd	78	29	130
4th	148	29	131
5th	203	97	134
6th	286	111	170
7th	336	117	252
8th	359	117	282
9th	454	127	307
10th	460	131	317

Umpires: C.M.Brown (*New Zealand*) (1) and C.B.Gaffaney (*New Zealand*) (35).
Referee: J.J.Crowe (*New Zealand*) (101).   **Test No. 2394/49 (NZ444/WI550)**

AUSTRALIA v INDIA (1st Test)

At Adelaide Oval, on 17, 18, 19 December 2020 (day/night).
Toss: India. Result: **AUSTRALIA** won by eight wickets.
Debut: Australia – C.D.Green.

INDIA

P.P.Shaw	b Starc	0		b Cummins	4
M.A.Agarwal	b Cummins	17		c Paine b Hazlewood	9
C.A.Pujara	c Labuschagne b Lyon	43	(4)	c Paine b Cummins	0
*V.Kohli	run out	74	(5)	c Green b Cummins	4
A.M.Rahane	lbw b Starc	42	(6)	c Paine b Hazlewood	0
G.H.Vihari	lbw b Hazlewood	16	(7)	c Paine b Hazlewood	8
†W.P.Saha	c Paine b Starc	9	(8)	c Labuschagne b Hazlewood	4
R.Ashwin	c Paine b Cummins	15	(9)	c Paine b Hazlewood	0
U.T.Yadav	c Wade b Starc	6	(10)	not out	4
J.J.Bumrah	not out	4	(3)	c and b Cummins	2
Mohammed Shami	c Head b Cummins	0		retired hurt	1
Extras	(B 2, LB 8, NB 7, W 1)	18			–
Total	**(93.1 overs; 414 mins)**	**244**		**(21.2 overs; 118 mins)**	**36**

AUSTRALIA

M.S.Wade	lbw b Bumrah	8		run out	33
J.A.Burns	lbw b Bumrah	8		not out	51
M.Labuschagne	lbw b Yadav	47		c Agarwal b Ashwin	6
S.P.D.Smith	c Rahane b Ashwin	1		not out	1
T.M.Head	c and b Ashwin	7			
C.D.Green	c Kohli b Ashwin	11			
†*T.D.Paine	not out	73			
P.J.Cummins	c Rahane b Yadav	0			
M.A.Starc	run out	15			
N.M.Lyon	c Kohli b Ashwin	10			
J.R.Hazlewood	c Pujara b Yadav	8			
Extras	(LB 3)	3		(LB 1, NB 1)	2
Total	**(72.1 overs; 318 mins)**	**191**		**(2 wkts; 21 overs; 93 mins)**	**93**

AUSTRALIA	O	M	R	W		O	M	R	W
Starc	21	5	53	4		6	3	7	0
Hazlewood	20	6	47	1	(3)	5	3	8	5
Cummins	21.1	7	48	3	(2)	10.2	4	21	4
Green	9	2	15	0					
Lyon	21	4	68	1					
Labuschagne	1	0	3	0					
INDIA									
Yadav	16.1	5	40	3		8	1	49	0
Bumrah	21	7	52	2		7	1	27	0
Mohammed Shami	17	4	41	0					
Ashwin	18	3	55	4	(3)	6	1	16	1

FALL OF WICKETS				
	I	A	I	A
Wkt	1st	1st	2nd	2nd
1st	0	16	7	70
2nd	32	29	15	82
3rd	100	45	15	–
4th	188	65	15	–
5th	196	79	15	–
6th	206	111	19	–
7th	233	111	26	–
8th	235	139	26	–
9th	240	167	31	–
10th	244	191	–	–

Umpires: B.N.J.Oxenford (*Australia*) (60) and P.R.Reiffel (*Australia*) (49).
Referee: D.C.Boon (*Australia*) (58).   **Test No. 2395/99 (A831/I543)**

AUSTRALIA v INDIA (2nd Test)

At Melbourne Cricket Ground, on 26, 27, 28, 29 December 2020.
Toss: Australia. Result: **INDIA** won by eight wickets.
Debuts: India – S.Gill, M.Siraj.

AUSTRALIA

J.A.Burns	c Pant b Bumrah	0	(2) c Pant b Yadav		4
M.S.Wade	c Jadeja b Ashwin	30	(1) lbw b Jadeja		40
M.Labuschagne	c Gill b Siraj	48	c Rahane b Ashwin		28
S.P.D.Smith	c Pujara b Ashwin	0	b Bumrah		8
T.M.Head	c Rahane b Bumrah	38	c Agarwal b Siraj		17
C.D.Green	lbw b Bumrah	12	c Jadeja b Bumrah		45
†T.D.Paine	c Vihari b Ashwin	13	c Pant b Jadeja		1
P.J.Cummins	c Siraj b Jadeja	9	c Agarwal b Bumrah		22
M.A.Starc	c Siraj b Bumrah	7	not out		14
N.M.Lyon	lbw b Bumrah	20	c Pant b Siraj		3
J.R.Hazlewood	not out	4	b Ashwin		10
Extras	(B 10, NB 3, W 1)	14	(LB 5, NB 3)		8
Total	**(72.3 overs; 326 mins)**	**195**	**(103.1 overs; 423 mins)**		**200**

INDIA

M.A.Agarwal	lbw b Starc	0	c Paine b Starc		5
S.Gill	c Paine b Cummins	45	not out		35
C.A.Pujara	c Paine b Cummins	17	c Green b Cummins		3
*A.M.Rahane	run out	112	not out		27
G.H.Vihari	c Smith b Lyon	21			
†R.R.Pant	c Paine b Starc	29			
R.A.Jadeja	c Cummins b Starc	57			
R.Ashwin	c Lyon b Hazlewood	14			
U.T.Yadav	c Smith b Lyon	9			
J.J.Bumrah	c Head b Lyon	0			
M.Siraj	not out	0			
Extras	(B 12, LB 6, NB 2, W 2)	22			–
Total	**(115.1 overs; 540 mins)**	**326**	**(2 wkts; 15.5 overs; 68 mins)**		**70**

INDIA	O	M	R	W	O	M	R	W		FALL OF WICKETS			
Bumrah	16	4	56	4	27	6	54	2			A	I	A	I
Yadav	12	3	39	0	3.3	0	5	1		*Wkt*	*1st*	*1st*	*2nd*	*2nd*
Ashwin	24	7	35	3	(4) 37.1	6	71	2		1st	10	0	4	16
Jadeja	5.3	1	15	1	(5) 14	5	28	2		2nd	35	61	42	19
Siraj	15	4	40	2	(3) 21.3	4	37	3		3rd	38	64	71	–
										4th	124	116	98	
AUSTRALIA										5th	134	173	98	
Starc	26	5	78	3	4	0	20	1		6th	155	294	99	
Cummins	27	9	80	2	5	0	22	1		7th	155	306	156	
Hazlewood	23	6	47	1	3	1	14	0		8th	164	325	177	
Lyon	27.1	4	72	3	2.5	0	5	0		9th	191	325	185	
Green	12	1	31	0						10th	195	326	200	
Labuschagne					(5) 1	0	9	0						

Umpires: B.N.J.Oxenford (*Australia*) (61) and P.R.Reiffel (*Australia*) (50).
Referee: D.C.Boon (*Australia*) (59). **Test No. 2396/100 (A832/1544)**

AUSTRALIA v INDIA (3rd Test)

At Sydney Cricket Ground, on 7, 8, 9, 10, 11 January 2021.
Toss: Australia. Result: **MATCH DRAWN**.
Debuts: Australia – W.J.Pucovski; India – N.Saini.

AUSTRALIA

W.J.Pucovski	lbw b Saini	62	(2) c sub (W.P.Saha) b Siraj		10
D.A.Warner	c Pujara b Siraj	5	(1) lbw b Ashwin		13
M.Labuschagne	c Rahane b Jadeja	91	c sub (W.P.Saha) b Saini		73
S.P.D.Smith	run out	131	lbw b Ashwin		81
M.S.Wade	c Bumrah b Jadeja	13	c sub (W.P.Saha) b Saini		4
C.D.Green	lbw b Bumrah	0	c sub (W.P.Saha) b Bumrah		84
†*T.D.Paine	b Bumrah	1	not out		39
P.J.Cummins	b Jadeja	0			
M.A.Starc	c Gill b Saini	24			
N.M.Lyon	lbw b Jadeja	0			
J.R.Hazlewood	not out	1			
Extras	(B 4, NB 5, W 1)	10	(LB 5, NB 3)		8
Total	**(105.4 overs)**	**338**	**(6 wkts dec; 87 overs)**		**312**

INDIA

R.G.Sharma	c and b Hazlewood	26	c Starc b Cummins		52
S.Gill	c Green b Cummins	50	c Paine b Hazlewood		31
C.A.Pujara	c Paine b Cummins	50	b Hazlewood		77
*A.M.Rahane	b Cummins	22	c Wade b Lyon		4
G.H.Vihari	run out	4	(6) not out		23
†R.R.Pant	c Warner b Hazlewood	36	(5) c Cummins b Lyon		97
R.A.Jadeja	not out	28			
R.Ashwin	run out	10	(7) not out		39
N.Saini	c Wade b Starc	3			
J.J.Bumrah	run out	0			
M.Siraj	c Paine b Cummins	6			
Extras	(LB 2, NB 2, W 5)	9	(LB 3, NB 6, W 2)		11
Total	**(100.4 overs)**	**244**	**(5 wkts; 131 overs)**		**334**

INDIA	O	M	R	W		O	M	R	W
Bumrah	25.4	7	66	2		21	4	68	1
Siraj	25	4	67	1		25	5	90	1
Ashwin	24	1	74	0	(4)	25	1	95	2
Saini	13	0	65	2	(3)	16	2	54	2
Jadeja	18	3	62	4					

AUSTRALIA	O	M	R	W		O	M	R	W
Starc	19	7	61	1		22	6	66	0
Hazlewood	21	10	43	2		26	12	39	2
Cummins	21.4	10	29	4		26	6	72	1
Lyon	31	8	87	0		46	17	114	2
Labuschagne	3	0	11	0	(6)	4	2	9	0
Green	5	2	11	0	(5)	7	0	31	0

FALL OF WICKETS

	A	I	A	I
Wkt	1st	1st	2nd	2nd
1st	6	70	16	71
2nd	106	85	35	92
3rd	206	117	138	102
4th	232	142	148	250
5th	249	195	208	272
6th	255	195	312	–
7th	278	206	–	–
8th	310	210	–	–
9th	315	216	–	–
10th	338	244	–	–

Umpires: P.R.Reiffel (*Australia*) (51) and P.Wilson (*Australia*) (3).
Referee: D.C.Boon (*Australia*) (60).
Test No. 2397/101 (A833/1545)

AUSTRALIA v INDIA (4th Test)

At Woolloongabba, Brisbane, on 15, 16, 17, 18, 19 January 2021.
Toss: Australia. Result: **INDIA** won by three wickets.
Debuts: India – T.Natarajan, M.S.Washington Sundar.

AUSTRALIA

D.A.Warner	c Sharma b Siraj	1	(2)	lbw b Washington Sundar	48
M.S.Harris	c Washington Sundar b Thakur	5	(1)	c Pant b Thakur	38
M.Labuschagne	c Pant b Natarajan	108		c Sharma b Siraj	25
S.P.D.Smith	c Sharma b Washington Sundar	36		c Rahane b Siraj	55
M.S.Wade	c Thakur b Natarajan	45		c Pant b Siraj	0
C.D.Green	b Washington Sundar	47		c Sharma b Thakur	37
†*T.D.Paine	c Sharma b Thakur	50		c Pant b Thakur	27
P.J.Cummins	lbw b Thakur	2		not out	28
M.A.Starc	not out	20		c Saini b Siraj	1
N.M.Lyon	b Washington Sundar	24		c Agarwal b Thakur	13
J.R.Hazlewood	b Natarajan	11		c Thakur b Siraj	9
Extras	(B 4, LB 5, NB 6, W 5)	20		(B 5, LB 2, NB 4, W 2)	13
Total	**(115.2 overs; 517 mins)**	**369**		**(75.5 overs; 335 mins)**	**294**

INDIA

R.G.Sharma	c Starc b Lyon	44		c Paine b Cummins	7
S.Gill	c Smith b Cummins	7		c Smith b Lyon	91
C.A.Pujara	c Paine b Hazlewood	25		lbw b Cummins	56
*A.M.Rahane	c Wade b Starc	37		c Paine b Cummins	24
M.A.Agarwal	c Smith b Hazlewood	38	(6)	c Wade b Cummins	9
†R.R.Pant	c Green b Hazlewood	23	(5)	not out	89
M.S.Washington Sundar	c Green b Starc	62		b Lyon	22
S.N.Thakur	b Cummins	67		c Lyon b Hazlewood	2
N.Saini	c Smith b Hazlewood	5		not out	0
M.Siraj	b Hazlewood	13			
T.Natarajan	not out	1			
Extras	(B 5, LB 7, NB 2)	14		(B 18, LB 8, NB 3)	29
Total	**(111.4 overs; 504 mins)**	**336**		**(7 wkts; 97 overs; 435 mins)**	**329**

INDIA	O	M	R	W	O	M	R	W		FALL OF WICKETS			
										A	I	A	I
Siraj	28	10	77	1	19.5	5	73	5	Wkt	1st	1st	2nd	2nd
Natarajan	24.2	3	78	3	14	4	41	0	1st	4	11	89	18
Thakur	24	6	94	3	(4) 19	2	61	4	2nd	17	60	91	132
Saini	7.5	2	21	0	(5) 5	1	32	0	3rd	87	105	123	167
Washington Sundar	31	6	89	3	(3) 18	1	80	1	4th	200	144	123	228
Sharma	0.1	0	1	0					5th	213	161	196	265
									6th	311	186	227	318
AUSTRALIA									7th	313	309	242	325
Starc	23	3	88	2	16	0	75	0	8th	315	320	247	–
Hazlewood	24.4	6	57	5	22	5	74	1	9th	354	328	274	–
Cummins	27	5	94	2	24	10	55	4	10th	369	336	294	–
Green	8	1	20	0	3	1	10	0					
Lyon	28	9	65	1	31	7	85	2					
Labuschagne	1	1	0	0	1	0	4	0					

Umpires: B.N.J.Oxenford (*Australia*) (62) and P.Wilson (*Australia*) (4).
Referee: D.C.Boon (*Australia*) (61).   Test No. 2398/102 (A834/I546)

NEW ZEALAND v PAKISTAN (1st Test)

At Bay Oval, Mount Maunganui, on 26, 27, 28, 29, 30 December 2020.
Toss: Pakistan. Result: **NEW ZEALAND** won by 101 runs.
Debuts: None.

NEW ZEALAND

T.W.M.Latham	c Azhar b Afridi	4	c Abid b Naseem	53
T.A.Blundell	c Yasir b Afridi	5	b Abbas	64
*K.S.Williamson	c Sohail b Yasir	129	c Rizwan b Naseem	21
L.R.P.L.Taylor	c Rizwan b Afridi	70	not out	12
H.M.Nicholls	c Masood b Naseem	56	c Abbas b Naseem	11
†B.J.Watling	c Yasir b Afridi	73	run out	5
M.J.Santner	c Rizwan b Ashraf	19	not out	6
K.A.Jamieson	c Rizwan b Abbas	32		
T.G.Southee	b Yasir	0		
N.Wagner	c Masood b Yasir	19		
T.A.Boult	not out	8		
Extras	(LB 5, NB 6, W 5)	16	(LB 2, NB 5, W 1)	8
Total	**(155 overs; 688 mins)**	**431**	**(5 wkts dec; 45.3 overs; 224 mins)**	**180**

PAKISTAN

Shan Masood	c Watling b Jamieson	10	c Taylor b Southee	0
Abid Ali	b Jamieson	25	c Watling b Boult	0
Mohammad Abbas	c Taylor b Boult	5	(9) lbw b Santner	1
Azhar Ali	c Watling b Southee	5	(3) c Watling b Boult	38
Haris Sohail	c Nicholls b Southee	3	(4) c Santner b Southee	9
Fawad Alam	c Watling b Wagner	9	(5) c Watling b Wagner	102
†*Mohammad Rizwan	run out	71	(6) lbw b Jamieson	60
Faheem Ashraf	c Watling b Jamieson	91	(7) c Watling b Wagner	19
Yasir Shah	b Boult	4	(8) c Southee b Jamieson	0
Shaheen Shah Afridi	c Latham b Wagner	6	not out	8
Naseem Shah	not out	0	c and b Santner	1
Extras	(B 3, LB 4, NB 1, W 2)	10	(B 16, LB 7, NB 8, W 2)	33
Total	**(102.2 overs; 458 mins)**	**239**	**(123.3 overs; 566 mins)**	**271**

PAKISTAN	O	M	R	W		O	M	R	W
Shaheen Shah Afridi	36	7	109	4		11	0	47	0
Mohammad Abbas	31	14	49	1		11	2	33	1
Faheem Ashraf	19	8	40	1	(4)	4	1	18	0
Naseem Shah	25	3	96	1	(3)	12.3	1	55	3
Yasir Shah	37	4	113	3		6	0	21	0
Shan Masood	2	1	2	0		1	0	4	0
Haris Sohail	5	0	17	0					

NEW ZEALAND	O	M	R	W		O	M	R	W
Southee	26	7	69	2		23	8	33	2
Boult	26	4	71	2		25	9	72	2
Jamieson	23.2	13	35	3		26	13	35	2
Wagner	21	5	50	2		28	9	55	2
Santner	6	2	7	0		19.3	3	52	2
Williamson						2	1	1	0

FALL OF WICKETS

	NZ	P	NZ	P
Wkt	1st	1st	2nd	2nd
1st	4	28	111	0
2nd	13	39	139	0
3rd	133	43	147	37
4th	266	51	165	75
5th	281	52	170	240
6th	317	80	–	242
7th	383	187	–	251
8th	388	196	–	259
9th	421	235	–	261
10th	431	239	–	271

Umpires: C.B.Gaffaney (*New Zealand*) (36) and W.R.Knights (*New Zealand*) (2).
Referee: J.J.Crowe (*New Zealand*) (102).   Test No. 2399/59 (NZ445/P432)

NEW ZEALAND v PAKISTAN (2nd Test)

At Hagley Oval, Christchurch, on 3, 4, 5, 6 January 2021.
Toss: New Zealand. Result: **NEW ZEALAND** won by an innings and 176 runs.
Debut: Pakistan – Zafar Gohar.

PAKISTAN

Shan Masood	lbw b Southee	0		c Southee b Jamieson	0
Abid Ali	c Southee b Jamieson	25		c sub (W.A.Young) b Jamieson	26
Azhar Ali	c Taylor b Henry	93	(4)	c Watling b Jamieson	37
Haris Sohail	c Nicholls b Jamieson	1	(5)	c Watling b Jamieson	15
Fawad Alam	c Watling b Jamieson	2	(6)	c Taylor b Boult	16
†*Mohammad Rizwan	c Watling b Jamieson	61	(7)	b Jamieson	10
Faheem Ashraf	c Taylor b Jamieson	48	(8)	c Watling b Jamieson	28
Zafar Gohar	c Jamieson b Southee	34	(9)	c Henry b Boult	37
Shaheen Shah Afridi	c Nicholls b Boult	4	(10)	c Taylor b Williamson	7
Mohammad Abbas	not out	0	(3)	c Watling b Boult	3
Naseem Shah	c Latham b Boult	12		not out	0
Extras	(B 2, LB 9, W 6)	17		(B 1, NB 2, W 4)	7
Total	**(83.5 overs; 385 mins)**	**297**		**(81.4 overs; 356 mins)**	**186**

NEW ZEALAND

T.W.M.Latham	c Sohail b Afridi	33
T.A.Blundell	lbw b Ashraf	16
*K.S.Williamson	c Masood b Ashraf	238
L.R.P.L.Taylor	c Masood b Abbas	12
H.M.Nicholls	c Naseem b Abbas	157
†B.J.Watling	c Sohail b Afridi	7
D.J.Mitchell	not out	102
K.A.Jamieson	not out	30
M.J.Henry		
T.G.Southee		
T.A.Boult		
Extras	(B 27, LB 8, NB 12, W 17)	64
Total	**(6 wkts dec; 158.5 overs; 703 mins)**	**659**

NEW ZEALAND	O	M	R	W	O	M	R	W		FALL OF WICKETS			
Southee	23	7	61	2	20	8	45	0			P	NZ	P
Boult	20.5	3	82	2	18.4	6	43	3		*Wkt*	*1st*	*1st*	*2nd*
Jamieson	21	8	69	5	20	6	48	6		1st	4	52	3
Henry	17	2	68	1	15	5	25	0		2nd	66	52	17
Mitchell	2	1	6	0	5	1	8	0		3rd	70	71	46
Williamson					3	0	16	1		4th	83	440	79
										5th	171	452	88
PAKISTAN										6th	227	585	98
Shaheen Shah Afridi	35.5	8	101	2						7th	260	–	126
Mohammad Abbas	34	11	98	2						8th	282	–	145
Naseem Shah	26	2	141	0						9th	285	–	171
Faheem Ashraf	28	4	106	2						10th	297	–	186
Shan Masood	2	0	17	0									
Zafar Gohar	32	0	159	0									
Haris Sohail	1	0	2	0									

Umpires: C.M.Brown (*New Zealand*) (2) and C.B.Gaffaney (*New Zealand*) (37).
Referee: J.J.Crowe (*New Zealand*) (103).   **Test No. 2400/60 (NZ446/P433)**

SOUTH AFRICA v SRI LANKA (1st Test)

At SuperSport Park, Centurion, on 26, 27, 28, 29 December 2020.
Toss: Sri Lanka. Result: **SOUTH AFRICA** won by an innings and 45 runs.
Debuts: South Africa – L.L.Sipamla; Sri Lanka – P.W.H.de Silva.   ‡ (H.D.R.L.Thirimanne)

SRI LANKA

*F.D.M.Karunaratne	b Ngidi	22		b Ngidi	6
M.D.K.J.Perera	c de Kock b Mulder	16		c de Kock b Nortje	64
B.K.G.Mendis	c Ngidi b Nortje	12		c van der Dussen b Ngidi	0
L.D.Chandimal	c du Plessis b Mulder	85		b Mulder	25
D.M.de Silva	retired hurt	79		absent hurt	
†D.P.D.N.Dickwella	lbw b Mulder	49	(5)	c de Kock b Mulder	10
M.D.Shanaka	not out	66	(6)	c de Kock b Sipamla	6
P.W.H.de Silva	b Sipamla	18	(7)	c Bavuma b Sipamla	59
C.A.K.Rajitha	c Elgar b Sipamla	12		c Maharaj b Nortje	0
M.V.T.Fernanado	b Sipamla	0	(8)	run out	0
C.B.R.L.S.Kumara	c van der Dussen b Sipamla	0	(10)	not out	0
Extras	(B 16, LB 9, NB 6, W 6)	37		(B 4, LB 2, NB 4)	10
Total	**(96 overs)**	**396**		**(46.1 overs)**	**180**

SOUTH AFRICA

D.Elgar	c and b Shanaka	95
A.K.Markram	c Shanaka b Fernando	68
H.E.van der Dussen	c Dickwella b Kumara	15
F.du Plessis	c Karunaratne b P.W.H.de Silva	199
†*Q.de Kock	c sub‡ b P.W.H.de Silva	18
T.Bavuma	c Dickwella b Shanaka	71
P.W.A.Mulder	c Dickwella b P.W.H.de Silva	36
K.A.Maharaj	c P.W.H.de Silva b Fernando	73
A.A.Nortje	c Dickwella b Fernando	0
L.L.Sipamla	lbw b P.W.H.de Silva	0
L.T.Ngidi	not out	2
Extras	(B 9, LB 18, NB 7, W 10)	44
Total	**(142.1 overs)**	**621**

SOUTH AFRICA	O	M	R	W		O	M	R	W
Ngidi	19	3	64	1		10	2	38	2
Sipamla	16	1	76	4	(4)	5	0	24	2
Nortje	22	3	88	1	(2)	10.1	1	47	2
Mulder	20	4	69	3	(3)	12	1	39	2
Maharaj	19	3	74	0		6	3	20	0
Markram						3	2	6	0

SRI LANKA	O	M	R	W
Fernando	31.1	3	129	3
Rajitha	2.1	0	16	0
Shanaka	28.5	2	98	2
P.W.H.de Silva	45	5	171	4
Kumara	21.1	0	103	1
Karunaratne	6.5	0	36	0
Mendis	7	0	41	0

FALL OF WICKETS			
	SL	SA	SL
Wkt	1st	1st	2nd
1st	28	141	10
2nd	54	200	22
3rd	54	200	85
4th	284	220	99
5th	296	399	114
6th	320	476	142
7th	387	609	148
8th	387	610	179
9th	396	611	180
10th	–	621	–

Umpires: M.Erasmus (*South Africa*) (63) and A.T.Holdstock (*South Africa*) (1).
Referee: A.Pycroft (*Zimbabwe*) (77).   **Test No. 2401/30 (SA440/SL290)**
D.M.de Silva retired hurt at 185-3.

SOUTH AFRICA v SRI LANKA (2nd Test)

At New Wanderers Stadium, Johannesburg, on 3, 4, 5 January 2021.
Toss: Sri Lanka. Result: **SOUTH AFRICA** won by ten wickets.
Debuts: Sri Lanka – A.M.Fernando, M.B.Ranasinghe.

SRI LANKA

*F.D.M.Karunaratne	c de Kock b Nortje	2	c Mulder b Nortje		103
M.D.K.J.Perera	c Markram b Mulder	60	b Ngidi		1
H.D.R.L.Thirimanne	c du Plessis b Mulder	17	c de Kock b Ngidi		31
B.K.G.Mendis	c van der Dussen b Mulder	0	c de Kock b Ngidi		0
M.B.Ranasinghe	c van der Dussen b Nortje	5	c Maharaj b Nortje		1
†D.P.D.N.Dickwella	c de Kock b Nortje	7	c Bavuma b Ngidi		36
M.D.Shanaka	c de Kock b Nortje	4	c Sipamla b Mulder		8
P.W.H.de Silva	c de Kock b Sipamla	29	b Sipamla		16
P.V.D.Chameera	c de Kock b Nortje	22	c de Kock b Sipamla		0
M.V.T.Fernando	not out	2	not out		1
A.M.Fernando	b Nortje	4	b Sipamla		0
Extras	(LB 5)	5	(B 9, LB 2, NB 2, W 1)		14
Total	**(40.3 overs)**	**157**	**(56.5 overs)**		**211**

SOUTH AFRICA

D.Elgar	c Thirimanne b Chameera	127	(2) not out	31
A.K.Markram	c Mendis b A.M.Fernando	5	(1) not out	36
H.E.van der Dussen	c Dickwella b Shanaka	67		
F.du Plessis	c Dickwella b Shanaka	8		
†*Q.de Kock	c Mendis b M.V.T.Fernando	10		
T.Bavuma	lbw b M.V.T.Fernando	19		
P.W.A.Mulder	lbw b M.V.T.Fernando	7		
K.A.Maharaj	c Dickwella b A.M.Fernando	2		
A.A.Nortje	c Mendis b M.V.T.Fernando	13		
L.L.Sipamla	c Shanaka b M.V.T.Fernando	5		
L.T.Ngidi	not out	14		
Extras	(B 8, LB 14, W 3)	25		
Total	**(75.4 overs)**	**302**	**(0 wkts; 13.2 overs; 47 mins)**	**67**

SOUTH AFRICA	O	M	R	W		O	M	R	W
Ngidi	10	3	44	0		15	5	44	4
Nortje	14.3	1	56	6		19	2	64	2
Sipamla	9	3	27	1	(4)	9.5	1	40	3
Mulder	7	3	25	3	(3)	13	3	52	1

SRI LANKA	O	M	R	W		O	M	R	W
M.V.T.Fernando	23.4	0	101	5		4	0	23	0
A.M.Fernando	19	6	61	2		1	1	20	0
Chameera	14	1	53	1					
Shanaka	15	3	42	2		3	1	8	0
De Silva	4	0	23	0	(3)	2.2	0	16	0

FALL OF WICKETS

	SL	SA	SL	SA
Wkt	1st	1st	2nd	2nd
1st	19	34	1	–
2nd	71	218	86	–
3rd	71	218	92	–
4th	80	235	109	–
5th	84	241	176	–
6th	93	257	181	–
7th	110	262	190	–
8th	128	276	209	–
9th	151	283	210	–
10th	157	302	211	–

Umpires: M.Erasmus (*South Africa*) (64) and A.T.Holdstock (*South Africa*) (2).
Referee: A.Pycroft (*Zimbabwe*) (78). Test No. 2402/31 (SA441/SL291)

SRI LANKA v ENGLAND (1st Test)

At Galle International Stadium, on 14, 15, 16, 17, 18 January 2021.
Toss: Sri Lanka. Result: **ENGLAND** won by seven wickets.
Debut: England – D.W.Lawrence.

SRI LANKA

H.D.R.L.Thirimanne	c Bairstow b Broad	4	(2) c Buttler b Curran		111
M.D.K.J.Perera	c Root b Bess	20	(1) c Leach b Curran		62
B.K.G.Mendis	c Sibley b Broad	0	c Buttler b Leach		15
A.D.Mathews	c Root b Broad	27	(5) c Root b Leach		71
*L.D.Chandimal	c Curran b Leach	28	(6) c Root b Bess		20
†D.P.D.N.Dickwella	c Sibley b Bess	12	(7) c Buttler b Bess		29
M.D.Shanaka	c Buttler b Bess	23	(8) b Leach		4
P.W.H.de Silva	c Root b Bess	19	(9) c Root b Leach		12
M.D.K.Perera	b Bess	0	(10) st Buttler b Leach		24
L.Ambuldeniya	run out	0	(4) c Sibley b Bess		0
A.M.Fernando	not out	0	not out		0
Extras	(LB 1, NB 1)	2	(B 7, LB 1, NB 3)		11
Total	**(46.1 overs)**	**135**	**(136.5 overs)**		**359**

ENGLAND

Z.Crawley	c de Silva b Ambuldeniya	9	c Mendis b Ambuldeniya	8
D.P.Sibley	c Thirimanne b Ambuldeniya	4	b Ambuldeniya	2
J.M.Bairstow	c Mendis b Ambuldeniya	47	not out	35
*J.E.Root	c Ambuldeniya b M.D.K.Perera	228	run out	1
D.W.Lawrence	c Mendis b M.D.K.Perera	73	not out	21
†J.C.Buttler	c Dickwella b Fernando	30		
S.M.Curran	b Fernando	0		
D.M.Bess	run out	0		
M.J.Leach	lbw b M.D.K.Perera	4		
M.A.Wood	c Dickwella b M.D.K.Perera	2		
S.C.J.Broad	not out	11		
Extras	(B 7, NB 6)	13	(B 4, LB 5)	9
Total	**(117.1 overs)**	**421**	**(3 wkts: 24.2 overs; 91 mins)**	**76**

ENGLAND	O	M	R	W	O	M	R	W
Broad	9	3	20	3	17	11	14	0
Curran	4	2	8	0	11	1	37	2
Wood	6	1	21	0	(4) 21	5	49	0
Bess	10.1	3	30	5	(3) 33	4	100	3
Leach	17	2	55	1	41.5	6	122	5
Root					11	1	19	0
Lawrence					2	0	10	0

SRI LANKA	O	M	R	W	O	M	R	W
Ambuldeniya	45	4	176	3	12	3	29	2
Fernando	14	1	44	2				
De Silva	15	1	63	0	1	0	4	0
M.D.K.Perera	36.1	2	109	4	(2) 11.2	2	34	0
Shanaka	7	1	22	0				

	FALL OF WICKETS			
	SL	E	SL	E
Wkt	1st	1st	2nd	2nd
1st	16	10	101	3
2nd	16	17	155	12
3rd	25	131	158	14
4th	81	304	210	
5th	81	372	243	
6th	105	372	291	
7th	126	382	296	
8th	126	398	314	
9th	130	406	352	
10th	135	421	359	

Umpires: H.D.P.K.Dharmasena (*Sri Lanka*) (66) and R.S.A.Palliyaguruge (*Sri Lanka*) (4).
Referee: R.S.Madugalle (*Sri Lanka*) (194).   Test No. 2403/35 (SL292/E1029)

SRI LANKA v ENGLAND (2nd Test)

At Galle International Stadium, on 22, 23, 24, 25 January 2021.
Toss: Sri Lanka. Result: **ENGLAND** won by six wickets.
Debut: Sri Lanka – R.T.M.Wanigamuni.

SRI LANKA

H.D.R.L.Thirimanne	c Buttler b Anderson	43	(2) c Crawley b Leach	13
M.D.K.J.Perera	c Root b Anderson	6	(1) lbw b Leach	14
B.O.P.Fernando	b Anderson	0	c Crawley b Bess	3
A.D.Mathews	c Buttler b Anderson	110	b Bess	5
*L.D.Chandimal	lbw b Wood	52	c Anderson b Leach	9
†D.P.D.N.Dickwella	c Leach b Anderson	92	c Lawrence b Bess	7
R.T.M.Wanigamuni	c Buttler b Wood	0	c Buttler b Leach	16
M.D.K.Perera	c Leach b Curran	67	c Crawley b Bess	4
R.A.S.Lakmal	c Crawley b Anderson	0	not out	11
L.Ambuldeniya	c Root b Wood	7	c Bairstow b Root	40
A.M.Fernando	not out	0	b Root	0
Extras	(LB 2, NB 1, W 1)	4	(B 3, NB 1)	4
Total	**(139.3 overs)**	**381**	**(35.5 overs)**	**126**

ENGLAND

Z.Crawley	c Thirimanne b Ambuldeniya	5	c B.O.P.Fernando b Ambuldeniya	13
D.P.Sibley	lbw b Ambuldeniya	0	not out	56
J.M.Bairstow	c B.O.P.Fernando b Ambuldeniya	28	lbw b Ambuldeniya	29
*J.E.Root	run out	186	b Wanigamuni	11
D.W.Lawrence	c Thirimanne b Ambuldeniya	3	c Dickwella b Ambuldeniya	2
†J.C.Buttler	c B.O.P.Fernando b Wanigamuni	55	not out	46
S.M.Curran	c Thirimanne b Ambuldeniya	13		
D.M.Bess	c Thirimanne b Ambuldeniya	32		
M.A.Wood	c Thirimanne b Ambuldeniya	1		
M.J.Leach	lbw b M.D.K.Perera	1		
J.M.Anderson	not out	4		
Extras	(B 8, LB 3, NB 5)	16	(LB 4, NB 3)	7
Total	**(116.1 overs)**	**344**	**(4 wkts; 43.3 overs; 181 mins)**	**164**

ENGLAND	O	M	R	W	O	M	R	W		FALL OF WICKETS			
Anderson	29	13	40	6	2	0	6	0			SL	SL	E	E
Curran	18.3	3	60	1	2	0	9	0		*Wkt*	*1st*	*1st*	*2nd*	*2nd*
Leach	38	5	119	0	(4) 14	1	59	4		1st	7	4	19	17
Wood	28	4	83	3						2nd	7	5	29	62
Bess	26	2	76	0	(3) 16	1	49	4		3rd	76	116	37	84
Root					(5) 1.5	1	0	2		4th	193	132	37	89
										5th	232	229	47	–
SRI LANKA										6th	243	252	66	–
Lakmal	16	7	31	0						7th	332	333	70	–
Ambuldeniya	42	6	137	7	(1) 20	3	73	3		8th	332	337	78	–
A.M.Fernando	10	2	31	0						9th	364	339	126	–
M.D.K.Perera	32.1	4	86	1	(2) 13.3	1	39	0		10th	381	344	126	–
Wanigamuni	16	1	48	1	(3) 10	0	48	1						

Umpires: H.D.P.K.Dharmasena (*Sri Lanka*) (67) and R.S.A.Palliyaguruge (*Sri Lanka*) (5).
Referee: R.S.Madugalle (*Sri Lanka*) (195).   Test No. 2404/36 (SL293/E1030)

PAKISTAN v SOUTH AFRICA (1st Test)

At National Stadium, Karachi, on 26, 27, 28, 29 January 2021.
Toss: South Africa. Result: **PAKISTAN** won by seven wickets.
Debuts: Pakistan – Imran Butt, Nauman Ali.

SOUTH AFRICA

Batsman	Dismissal 1	R		Dismissal 2	R
D.Elgar	c Azam b Nauman	58	(2)	c Rizwan b Shah	29
A.K.Markram	c Butt b Afridi	13	(1)	c Abid b Nauman	74
H.E.van der Dussen	run out	17		c Abid b Shah	64
F.du Plessis	c Rizwan b Shah	23		lbw b Shah	10
†*Q.de Kock	c Butt b Nauman	15	(6)	c Abid b Shah	2
T.Bavuma	run out	17	(7)	lbw b Nauman	40
G.F.Linde	c sub (Mohammad Nawaz) b Hasan	35	(8)	c Butt b Nauman	11
K.A.Maharaj	b Shah	0	(5)	b Hasan	2
K.Rabada	not out	21		b Nauman	1
A.A.Nortje	b Shah	0		c Alam b Nauman	3
L.T.Ngidi	lbw b Afridi	8		not out	3
Extras	(B 5, LB 1, NB 7)	13		(LB 1, NB 7, W 1)	9
Total	**(69.2 overs)**	**220**		**(100.3 overs)**	**245**

PAKISTAN

Batsman	Dismissal 1	R		Dismissal 2	R
Imran Butt	c sub (K.D.Petersen) b Rabada	9		c de Kock b Nortje	12
Abid Ali	b Rabada	4		b Nortje	10
Azhar Ali	c de Kock b Maharaj	51		not out	31
*Babar Azam	lbw b Maharaj	7		lbw b Maharaj	30
Shaheen Shah Afridi	b Nortje	0			
Fawad Alam	c Bavuma b Ngidi	109	(5)	not out	4
†Mohammad Rizwan	c du Plessis b Ngidi	33			
Faheem Ashraf	b Nortje	64			
Hasan Ali	b Rabada	21			
Nauman Ali	lbw b Maharaj	24			
Yasir Shah	not out	38			
Extras	(B 1, LB 7, NB 10)	18		(B 1, LB 2)	3
Total	**(119.2 overs)**	**378**		**(3 wkts; 22.5 overs)**	**90**

PAKISTAN	O	M	R	W		O	M	R	W
Shaheen Shah Afridi	11.2	0	49	2		17	1	61	0
Hasan Ali	14	5	61	1		16	1	61	0
Faheem Ashraf	5	0	12	0	(5)	9	6	8	0
Nauman Ali	17	4	38	2	(3)	25.3	6	35	5
Yasir Shah	22	6	54	3	(4)	33	7	79	4

SOUTH AFRICA	O	M	R	W		O	M	R	W
Rabada	27	7	70	3		8	2	21	0
Nortje	27	4	105	2		7	1	24	2
Ngidi	17	1	57	2	(4)	3	0	17	0
Maharaj	32.2	4	90	3	(3)	1.5	0	12	1
Linde	13	4	38	0		3	0	13	0
Markram	3	0	10	0					

FALL OF WICKETS

	SA	P	SA	P
Wkt	1st	1st	2nd	2nd
1st	30	5	48	22
2nd	63	15	175	23
3rd	108	26	185	86
4th	133	27	185	–
5th	136	121	187	–
6th	179	176	192	–
7th	179	278	234	–
8th	194	295	238	–
9th	195	323	240	–
10th	220	378	245	–

Umpires: Ahsan Raza (*Pakistan*) (1) and Alim Dar (*Pakistan*) (133).
Referee: Mohammad Javed (*Pakistan*) (1).

Test No. 2405/27 (P434/SA442)

PAKISTAN v SOUTH AFRICA (2nd Test)

At Rawalpindi Cricket Stadium, on 4, 5, 6, 7, 8 February 2021.
Toss: Pakistan. Result: **PAKISTAN** won by 95 runs.
Debuts: None.

PAKISTAN

Batsman	1st innings		2nd innings	
Imran Butt	c de Kock b Maharaj	15	lbw b Rabada	0
Abid Ali	c Markram b Nortje	6	c de Kock b Maharaj	13
Azhar Ali	lbw b Maharaj	0	lbw b Linde	33
*Babar Azam	c du Plessis b Nortje	77	lbw b Maharaj	8
Fawad Alam	run out	45	c Markram b Linde	12
†Mohammad Rizwan	c Rabada b Nortje	18	not out	115
Faheem Ashraf	not out	78	c Nortje b Linde	29
Hasan Ali	c Elgar b Maharaj	8	lbw b Maharaj	5
Yasir Shah	c and b Mulder	8	c de Kock b Linde	23
Nauman Ali	c Markram b Nortje	8	c Elgar b Rabada	45
Shaheen Shah Afridi	c Elgar b Nortje	0	b Linde	4
Extras	(B 2, LB 2, NB 5)	9	(B 9, NB 2)	11
Total	**(114.3 overs)**	**272**	**(102 overs)**	**298**

SOUTH AFRICA

Batsman	1st innings		2nd innings	
D.Elgar	c Rizwan b Hasan	15	(2) c Rizwan b Afridi	17
A.K.Markram	c Afridi b Nauman	32	(1) c Butt b Hasan	108
H.E.van der Dussen	b Hasan	0	b Hasan	48
F.du Plessis	c Rizwan b Ashraf	17	lbw b Hasan	5
T.Bavuma	not out	44	c Rizwan b Afridi	61
†*Q.de Kock	b Afridi	29	c Butt b Hasan	0
P.W.A.Mulder	run out	33	b Shah	20
G.F.Linde	b Hasan	21	c Ashraf b Hasan	4
K.A.Maharaj	b Hasan	1	c Butt b Afridi	0
K.Rabada	run out	0	b Afridi	0
A.A.Nortje	b Hasan	0	not out	2
Extras	(NB 9)	9	(LB 2, NB 7)	9
Total	**(65.4 overs)**	**201**	**(91.4 overs)**	**274**

SOUTH AFRICA	O	M	R	W		O	M	R	W
Rabada	21	2	72	0		14	3	34	2
Nortje	24.3	8	56	5		17	7	57	0
Maharaj	45	11	90	3		38	4	118	3
Linde	5.5	2	4	0	(5)	26	9	64	5
Elgar	1.1	0	6	0					
Mulder	17	7	40	1	(4)	7	1	16	0

PAKISTAN	O	M	R	W		O	M	R	W
Shaheen Shah Afridi	13	2	37	1		21	6	51	4
Hasan Ali	15.4	2	54	5		16	2	60	5
Faheem Ashraf	8	2	20	1	(5)	10	2	37	0
Nauman Ali	17	8	36	1	(3)	20	6	63	0
Yasir Shah	12	2	54	0		23.4	5	56	1
Fawad Alam						1	0	5	0

FALL OF WICKETS

Wkt	1st P	1st SA	2nd P	2nd SA
1st	21	26	0	33
2nd	21	26	28	127
3rd	22	55	45	135
4th	145	81	63	241
5th	149	114	76	241
6th	190	164	128	253
7th	221	186	143	258
8th	251	192	196	268
9th	272	201	293	268
10th	272	201	298	274

Umpires: Ahsan Raza (*Pakistan*) (2) and Alim Dar (*Pakistan*) (134).
Referee: Mohammad Javed (*Pakistan*) (2). **Test No. 2406/28 (P435/SA443)**

BANGLADESH v WEST INDIES (1st Test)

At Zahur Ahmed Chowdhury Stadium, Chittagong, on 3, 4, 5, 6, 7 February 2021.
Toss: Bangladesh. Result: **WEST INDIES** won by three wickets.
Debuts: West Indies – N.E.Bonner, K.R.Mayers, S.A.R.Moseley.

BANGLADESH

Shadman Islam	lbw b Warrican	59		c Da Silva b Gabriel	5
Tamim Iqbal	b Roach	9		lbw b Cornwall	0
Nazmul Hossain	run out	25		c Blackwood b Cornwall	0
*Mominul Haque	c Campbell b Warrican	26		c Roach b Gabriel	115
Mushfiqur Rahim	c Cornwall b Warrican	38		lbw b Cornwall	18
Shakib Al Hasan	c Brathwaite b Cornwall	68			
†Liton Das	b Warrican	38	(6)	c Mayers b Warrican	69
Mehedi Hasan	c sub (K.A.R.Hodge) b Cornwall	103	(7)	b Warrican	7
Taijul Islam	c Da Silva b Gabriel	18	(8)	b Warrican	3
Nayeem Hasan	b Bonner	24	(9)	not out	1
Mustafizur Rahman	not out	3			
Extras	(B 2, LB 7, NB 5, W 5)	19		(NB 4, W 1)	5
Total	**(150.2 overs; 598 mins)**	**430**		**(8 wkts dec; 67.5 overs; 300 mins)**	**223**

WEST INDIES

*K.C.Brathwaite	b Nayeem	76		c sub (Yasir Ali) b Mehedi	20
J.D.Campbell	lbw b Mustafizur	3		lbw b Mehedi	23
S.A.R.Moseley	lbw b Mustafizur	2		lbw b Mehedi	12
N.E.Bonner	c Nazmul b Taijul	17		lbw b Taijul	86
K.R.Mayers	lbw b Mehedi	40		not out	210
J.Blackwood	c Liton b Mehedi	68		b Nayeem	9
†J.Da Silva	c Liton b Nayeem	42		b Taijul	20
R.R.S.Cornwall	b Mehedi	2	(9)	not out	0
K.A.J.Roach	c sub (Mithun Ali) b Mehedi	0	(8)	c sub (Saif Hasan) b Mehedi	0
J.A.Warrican	b Taijul	4			
S.T.Gabriel	not out	0			
Extras	(LB 1, NB 4)	5		(B 11, LB 4)	15
Total	**(96.1 overs; 375 mins)**	**259**		**(7 wkts; 127.3 overs; 514 mins)**	**395**

WEST INDIES	O	M	R	W		O	M	R	W
Roach	20	5	60	1		7	1	17	0
Gabriel	26	4	69	1	(3)	12	0	37	2
Cornwall	42.2	5	114	2	(2)	27	2	81	3
Mayers	7	2	16	0	(7)	11	0	11	0
Warrican	48	8	133	4	(4)	17.5	0	57	3
Brathwaite	4	0	13	0		1	0	7	0
Bonner	3	0	16	1	(5)	2	0	11	0

BANGLADESH	O	M	R	W		O	M	R	W
Mustafizur Rahman	15	4	46	2		13	1	71	0
Shakib Al Hasan	6	1	16	0					
Mehedi Hasan	26	9	58	4		35	3	113	4
Taijul Islam	33.1	11	84	2	(2)	45	18	91	2
Nayeem Hasan	16	1	54	2	(4)	34.3	4	105	1

FALL OF WICKETS

	B	WI	B	WI
Wkt	1st	1st	2nd	2nd
1st	23	11	1	39
2nd	66	24	1	48
3rd	119	75	33	59
4th	134	130	73	275
5th	193	154	206	292
6th	248	253	214	392
7th	315	253	222	394
8th	359	253	223	–
9th	416	259	–	–
10th	430	259	–	–

Umpires: R.K.Illingworth (*England*) (52) and Sharfuddoula (*Bangladesh*) (1).
Referee: Neeyamur Rashid (*Bangladesh*) (1).   **Test No. 2407/17 (B120/WI551)**

BANGLADESH v WEST INDIES (2nd Test)

At Shere Bangla National Stadium, Mirpur, Dhaka, on 11, 12, 13, 14 February 2021.
Toss: West Indies. Result: **WEST INDIES** won by 17 runs.
Debuts: None.

WEST INDIES

Batsman	1st innings		2nd innings	
*K.C.Brathwaite	c Nazmul b Soumya	47	c Liton b Nayeem	6
J.D.Campbell	lbw b Taijul	36	b Taijul	18
S.A.R.Moseley	b Abu	7	c Mithun b Mehedi	7
N.E.Bonner	c Mithun b Mehedi	90	b Nayeem	38
K.R.Mayers	c Soumya b Abu	5	(6) lbw b Abu	6
J.Blackwood	c and b Taijul	28	(7) st Liton b Taijul	9
†J.Da Silva	b Taijul	92	(8) c Soumya b Taijul	20
A.S.Joseph	c Liton b Abu	82	(9) c Nazmul b Nayeem	9
R.R.S.Cornwall	not out	4	(10) c Mushfiqur b Nayeem	1
J.A.Warrican	c Liton b Abu	2	(5) lbw b Abu	1
S.T.Gabriel	c Mushfiqur b Taijul	8	not out	1
Extras	(B 4, LB 2, NB 2)	8		–
Total	**(142.2 overs; 590 mins)**	**409**	**(52.5 overs; 237 mins)**	**117**

BANGLADESH

Batsman	1st innings		2nd innings	
Tamim Iqbal	c Moseley b Joseph	44	c Moseley b Brathwaite	50
Soumya Sarkar	c Mayers b Gabriel	0	c Cornwall b Brathwaite	13
Nazmul Hossain	c Bonner b Gabriel	4	c Moseley b Cornwall	11
*Mominul Haque	c Da Silva b Cornwall	21	c Cornwall b Warrican	26
Mushfiqur Rahim	c Mayers b Cornwall	54	c Da Silva b Warrican	14
Mithun Ali	c Brathwaite b Cornwall	15	c Bonner b Cornwall	10
†Liton Das	c Blackwood b Cornwall	71	c Da Silva b Cornwall	22
Mehedi Hasan	c Brathwaite b Gabriel	57	c Cornwall b Warrican	31
Nayeem Hasan	c Blackwood b Cornwall	0	(10) lbw b Brathwaite	14
Taijul Islam	not out	13	(9) lbw b Cornwall	8
Abu Jayed	c Bonner b Joseph	1	not out	0
Extras	(B 5, LB 10, W 1)	16	(B 8, LB 4, NB 2)	14
Total	**(96.5 overs; 466 mins)**	**296**	**(61.3 overs; 240 mins)**	**213**

BANGLADESH	O	M	R	W		O	M	R	W
Abu Jayed	28	6	98	4	(4)	10	4	32	2
Mehedi Hasan	33	9	75	1	(3)	6	1	15	1
Nayeem Hasan	24	3	74	0	(2)	15.5	5	34	3
Taijul Islam	46.2	8	108	4	(1)	21	4	36	4
Soumya Sarkar	11	1	48	1					

WEST INDIES	O	M	R	W		O	M	R	W
Gabriel	21	3	70	3	(3)	2	0	5	0
Cornwall	32	8	74	5	(1)	30	5	105	4
Joseph	17.5	3	60	2	(2)	2	0	16	0
Mayers	8	2	15	0					
Warrican	13	2	48	0		16.3	4	47	3
Bonner	3	0	17	0					
Brathwaite	3	2	9	0	(5)	2	0	9	0

FALL OF WICKETS

	WI	B	WI	B
Wkt	1st	1st	2nd	2nd
1st	66	1	11	59
2nd	87	11	20	70
3rd	104	69	39	78
4th	116	71	50	101
5th	178	142	62	115
6th	266	155	73	147
7th	384	281	104	153
8th	396	281	114	188
9th	398	283	116	188
10th	409	296	117	213

Umpires: R.K.Illingworth (*England*) (53) and Sharfuddoula (*Bangladesh*) (2).
Referee: Neeyamur Rashid (*Bangladesh*) (2). **Test No. 2408/18 (B121/WI552)**

INDIA v ENGLAND (1st Test)

At M.A.Chidambaram Stadium, Chennai, on 5, 6, 7, 8, 9 February 2021.
Toss: England. Result: **ENGLAND** won by 227 runs.
Debuts: None.

ENGLAND

Batsman	1st innings		2nd innings	
R.J.Burns	c Pant b Ashwin	33	c Rahane b Ashwin	0
D.P.Sibley	lbw b Bumrah	87	c Pujara b Ashwin	16
D.W.Lawrence	lbw b Bumrah	0	lbw b I.Sharma	18
*J.E.Root	lbw b Nadeem	218	lbw b Bumrah	40
B.A.Stokes	c Pujara b Nadeem	82	c Pant b Ashwin	7
O.J.D.Pope	lbw b Ashwin	34	c R.G.Sharma b Nadeem	28
†J.C.Buttler	b I.Sharma	30	st Pant b Nadeem	24
D.M.Bess	lbw b Ashwin	34	lbw b Ashwin	25
J.C.Archer	b I.Sharma	0	b Ashwin	5
M.J.Leach	not out	14	not out	8
J.M.Anderson	b Ashwin	1	c and b Ashwin	0
Extras	(B 7, LB 17, NB 20, W 1)	45	(NB 7)	7
Total	**(190.1 overs)**	**578**	**(46.3 overs)**	**178**

INDIA

Batsman	1st innings		2nd innings	
R.G.Sharma	c Buttler b Archer	6	b Leach	12
S.Gill	c Anderson b Archer	29	b Anderson	50
C.A.Pujara	c Burns b Bess	73	c Stokes b Leach	15
*V.Kohli	c Pope b Bess	11	b Stokes	72
A.M.Rahane	c Root b Bess	1	b Anderson	0
†R.R.Pant	c Leach b Bess	91	c Root b Anderson	11
M.S.Washington Sundar	not out	85	c Buttler b Bess	0
R.Ashwin	c Buttler b Leach	31	c Buttler b Leach	9
S.Nadeem	c Stokes b Leach	0	c Burns b Leach	0
I.Sharma	c Pope b Anderson	4	not out	5
J.J.Bumrah	c Stokes b Anderson	0	c Buttler b Archer	4
Extras	(B 4, LB 1, NB 1)	6	(B 8, LB 5, NB 1)	14
Total	**(95.5 overs)**	**337**	**(58.1 overs)**	**192**

INDIA	O	M	R	W		O	M	R	W
I.Sharma	27	7	52	2	(3)	7	1	24	1
Bumrah	36	7	84	3	(4)	6	0	26	1
Ashwin	55.1	5	146	3	(1)	17.3	2	61	6
Nadeem	44	4	167	2	(2)	15	2	66	2
Washington Sundar	26	2	98	0		1	0	1	0
R.G.Sharma	2	0	7	0					

ENGLAND	O	M	R	W		O	M	R	W
Anderson	16.5	5	46	2	(3)	11	4	17	3
Archer	21	3	75	2	(1)	9.1	4	23	1
Stokes	6	1	16	0	(5)	4	1	13	1
Leach	24	5	105	2	(2)	26	4	76	4
Bess	26	5	76	4		8	0	50	1
Root	2	0	14	0					

FALL OF WICKETS

	E	I	E	I
Wkt	1st	1st	2nd	2nd
1st	63	19	0	25
2nd	63	44	32	58
3rd	263	71	58	92
4th	387	73	71	92
5th	473	192	101	110
6th	477	225	130	117
7th	525	305	165	171
8th	525	312	167	179
9th	567	323	178	179
10th	578	337	178	192

Umpires: A.K.Chaudhary (*India*) (1) and N.N.Menon (*India*) (4).
Referee: J.Srinath (*India*) (54).

Test No. 2409/123 (1547/E1031)

INDIA v ENGLAND (2nd Test)

At M.A.Chidambaram Stadium, Chennai, on 13, 14, 15, 16 February 2021.
Toss: India. Result: **INDIA** won by 317 runs.
Debut: India – A.R.Patel.

INDIA

Batsman	1st innings		2nd innings	
R.G.Sharma	c Ali b Leach	161	st Foakes b Leach	26
S.Gill	lbw b Stone	0	lbw b Leach	14
C.A.Pujara	c Stokes b Leach	21	run out	7
*V.Kohli	b Ali	0	lbw b Ali	62
A.M.Rahane	b Ali	67	(6) c Pope b Ali	10
†R.R.Pant	not out	58	(5) st Foakes b Leach	8
R.Ashwin	c Pope b Root	13	(8) b Stone	106
A.R.Patel	st Foakes b Ali	5	(7) lbw b Ali	7
I.Sharma	c Burns b Ali	0	(10) c Stone b Leach	7
Kuldeep Yadav	c Foakes b Stone	0	(9) lbw b Ali	3
M.Siraj	c Foakes b Stone	4	not out	16
Extras		–	(B 5, LB 15)	20
Total	**(95.5 overs)**	**329**	**(85.5 overs)**	**286**

ENGLAND

Batsman	1st innings		2nd innings	
R.J.Burns	lbw b I.Sharma	0	c Kohli b Ashwin	25
D.P.Sibley	c Kohli b Ashwin	16	lbw b Patel	3
D.W.Lawrence	c Gill b Ashwin	9	st Pant b Ashwin	26
*J.E.Root	c Ashwin b Patel	6	(5) c Rahane b Patel	33
B.A.Stokes	b Ashwin	18	c Kohli b Ashwin	8
O.J.D.Pope	c Pant b Siraj	22	(7) c I.Sharma b Patel	12
†B.T.Foakes	not out	42	(8) c Patel b Yadav	2
M.M.Ali	c Rahane b Patel	6	(9) st Pant b Yadav	43
O.P.Stone	c R.G.Sharma b Ashwin	1	(10) lbw b Patel	0
M.J.Leach	c Pant b I.Sharma	5	(4) c R.G.Sharma b Patel	0
S.C.J.Broad	b Ashwin	0	not out	5
Extras	(B 4, LB 4, NB 1)	9	(B 6, LB 1)	7
Total	**(59.5 overs)**	**134**	**(54.2 overs)**	**164**

ENGLAND	O	M	R	W		O	M	R	W
Broad	11	2	37	0	(5)	9	3	25	0
Stone	15.5	5	47	3	(1)	6.5	1	21	1
Leach	27	3	78	2	(2)	33	6	100	4
Stokes	2	0	16	0					
Ali	29	3	128	4	(3)	32	7	98	4
Root	11	3	23	1	(4)	4	0	15	0
Lawrence					(6)	1	0	7	0

INDIA	O	M	R	W		O	M	R	W
I.Sharma	5	1	22	2		6	3	13	0
Ashwin	23.5	4	43	5	(3)	18	5	53	3
Patel	20	3	40	2	(2)	21	5	60	5
Kuldeep Yadav	6	1	16	0	(5)	6.2	1	25	2
Siraj	5	4	5	1	(4)	3	1	6	0

FALL OF WICKETS

	I	E	I	E
Wkt	1st	1st	2nd	2nd
1st	0	0	42	17
2nd	85	16	55	49
3rd	86	23	55	50
4th	248	39	65	66
5th	249	52	86	90
6th	284	87	106	110
7th	301	105	202	116
8th	301	106	210	116
9th	325	131	237	126
10th	329	134	286	164

Umpires: N.N.Menon (*India*) (5) and V.K.Sharma (*India*) (1).
Referee: J.Srinath (*India*) (55).

Test No. 2410/124 (I548/E1032)

INDIA v ENGLAND (3rd Test)

At Narendra Modi Stadium, Ahmedabad, on 24, 25 February 2021 (day/night).
Toss: England. Result: **INDIA** won by ten wickets.
Debuts: None.

ENGLAND

Z.Crawley	lbw b Patel	53	b Patel	0
D.P.Sibley	c R.G.Sharma b I.Sharma	0	c Pant b Patel	7
J.M.Bairstow	lbw b Patel	0	b Patel	0
*J.E.Root	lbw b Ashwin	17	lbw b Patel	19
B.A.Stokes	lbw b Patel	6	lbw b Ashwin	25
O.J.D.Pope	b Ashwin	1	lbw b Ashwin	12
†B.T.Foakes	b Patel	12	lbw b Patel	8
J.C.Archer	b Patel	11	lbw b Ashwin	0
M.J.Leach	c Pujara b Ashwin	3	c Rahane b Ashwin	9
S.C.J.Broad	c Bumrah b Patel	3	not out	1
J.M.Anderson	not out	0	c Pant b Washington Sundar	0
Extras	(B 1, LB 2, NB 3)	6		–
Total	**(48.4 overs; 204 mins)**	**112**	**(30.4 overs; 126 mins)**	**81**

INDIA

R.G.Sharma	lbw b Leach	66	not out	25
S.Gill	c Crawley b Archer	11	not out	15
C.A.Pujara	lbw b Leach	0		
*V.Kohli	b Leach	27		
A.M.Rahane	lbw b Leach	7		
†R.R.Pant	c Foakes b Root	1		
R.Ashwin	c Crawley b Root	17		
M.S.Washington Sundar	b Root	0		
A.R.Patel	c Sibley b Root	0		
I.Sharma	not out	10		
J.J.Bumrah	lbw b Root	1		
Extras	(B 2, LB 2, W 1)	5	(B 8, LB 1)	9
Total	**(53.2 overs; 273 mins)**	**145**	**(0 wkts; 7.4 overs; 26 mins)**	**49**

INDIA	O	M	R	W		O	M	R	W
I.Sharma	5	1	26	1					
Bumrah	6	3	19	0					
Patel	21.4	6	38	6	(1)	15	0	32	5
Ashwin	16	6	26	3	(2)	15	3	48	4
Washington Sundar					(3)	0.4	0	1	1

ENGLAND	O	M	R	W		O	M	R	W
Anderson	13	8	20	0					
Broad	6	1	16	0					
Archer	5	2	24	1					
Leach	20	2	54	4	(1)	4	1	15	0
Stokes	3	0	19	0					
Root	6.2	3	8	5	(2)	3.4	0	25	0

FALL OF WICKETS

	E	I	E	I
Wkt	1st	1st	2nd	2nd
1st	2	33	0	–
2nd	27	34	0	–
3rd	74	98	19	–
4th	80	114	50	–
5th	81	115	56	–
6th	81	117	66	–
7th	93	125	68	–
8th	98	125	80	–
9th	105	134	80	–
10th	112	145	81	–

Umpires: A.K.Chaudhary (*India*) (2) and N.N.Menon (*India*) (6).
Referee: J.Srinath (*India*) (56).   **Test No. 2411/125 (1549/E1033)**

INDIA v ENGLAND (4th Test)

At Narendra Modi Stadium, Ahmedabad, on 4, 5, 6 March 2021.
Toss: England. Result: **INDIA** won by an innings and 25 runs.
Debuts: None.

ENGLAND

Z.Crawley	c Siraj b Patel	9	c Rahane b Ashwin		5
D.P.Sibley	b Patel	2	c Pant b Patel		3
J.M.Bairstow	lbw b Siraj	28	c R.G.Sharma b Ashwin		0
*J.E.Root	lbw b Siraj	5	lbw b Ashwin		30
B.A.Stokes	lbw b Washington Sundar	55	c Kohli b Patel		2
O.J.D.Pope	c Gill b Ashwin	29	st Pant b Patel		15
D.W.Lawrence	st Pant b Patel	46	b Ashwin		50
†B.T.Foakes	c Rahane b Ashwin	1	c Rahane b Patel		13
D.M.Bess	lbw b Patel	3	c Pant b Patel		2
M.J.Leach	lbw b Ashwin	7	c Rahane b Ashwin		2
J.M.Anderson	not out	10	not out		1
Extras	(B 3, LB 5, NB 1, W 1)	10	(B 4, LB 8)		12
Total	**(75.5 overs; 320 mins)**	**205**	**(54.5 overs; 210 mins)**		**135**

INDIA

S.Gill	lbw b Anderson	0
R.G.Sharma	lbw b Stokes	49
C.A.Pujara	lbw b Leach	17
*V.Kohli	c Foakes b Stokes	0
A.M.Rahane	c Stokes b Anderson	27
†R.R.Pant	c Root b Anderson	101
R.Ashwin	c Pope b Leach	13
M.S.Washington Sundar	not out	96
A.R.Patel	run out	43
I.Sharma	lbw b Stokes	0
M.Siraj	b Stokes	0
Extras	(B 10, LB 6, NB 3)	19
Total	**(114.4 overs; 546 mins)**	**365**

INDIA	O	M	R	W		O	M	R	W
I.Sharma	9	2	23	0					
Siraj	14	2	45	2	(1)	4	0	12	0
Patel	26	7	68	4	(2)	24	6	48	5
Ashwin	19.5	4	47	3	(3)	22.5	4	47	5
Washington Sundar	7	1	14	1	(4)	4	0	16	0

ENGLAND	O	M	R	W
Anderson	25	14	44	3
Stokes	27.4	6	89	4
Leach	27	5	89	2
Bess	17	1	71	0
Root	18	1	56	0

FALL OF WICKETS			
	E	I	E
Wkt	1st	1st	2nd
1st	10	0	10
2nd	15	40	10
3rd	30	41	20
4th	78	80	30
5th	121	121	65
6th	166	146	65
7th	170	259	109
8th	188	365	111
9th	189	365	134
10th	205	365	135

Umpires: N.N.Menon (*India*) (7) and V.K.Sharma (*India*) (2).
Referee: J.Srinath (*India*) (57).   **Test No. 2412/126 (I550/E1034)**

ENGLAND v INDIA SERIES AVERAGES 2020-21

ENGLAND – BATTING AND FIELDING

	M	I	NO	HS	Runs	Avge	100	50	Ct/St
J.E.Root	4	8	–	218	368	46.00	1	–	3
B.A.Stokes	4	8	–	82	203	25.37	–	2	5
D.W.Lawrence	3	6	–	50	149	24.83	–	1	–
O.J.D.Pope	4	8	–	34	153	19.12	–	–	5
D.P.Sibley	4	8	–	87	134	16.75	–	1	1
Z.Crawley	2	4	–	53	67	16.75	–	1	2
D.M.Bess	2	4	–	34	64	16.00	–	–	–
B.T.Foakes	3	6	1	42*	78	15.60	–	–	4/3
R.J.Burns	2	4	–	33	58	14.50	–	–	3
M.J.Leach	4	8	2	14*	48	8.00	–	–	1
J.M.Bairstow	2	4	–	28	28	7.00	–	–	–
S.C.J.Broad	2	4	2	5*	9	4.50	–	–	–
J.C.Archer	2	4	–	11	16	4.00	–	–	–
J.M.Anderson	3	6	3	10*	12	4.00	–	–	1

Also batted (one Test): M.M.Ali 6, 43 (1 ct); J.C.Buttler 30, 24 (5 ct); O.P.Stone 1, 0 (1 ct).

BOWLING

	O	M	R	W	Avge	Best	5wI	10wM
J.M.Anderson	65.5	31	127	8	15.87	3-17	–	–
O.P.Stone	22.4	6	68	4	17.00	3-47	–	–
J.E.Root	45	7	141	6	23.50	5- 8	1	–
M.M.Ali	61	10	226	8	28.25	4-98	–	–
M.J.Leach	161	26	517	18	28.72	4-54	–	–
J.C.Archer	35.1	9	122	4	30.50	2-75	–	–
B.A.Stokes	42.4	8	153	5	30.60	4-89	–	–
D.M.Bess	51	6	197	5	39.40	4-76	–	–

Also bowled: S.C.J.Broad 26-6-78-0; D.W.J.awrence 1-0-7-0.

INDIA – BATTING AND FIELDING

	M	I	NO	HS	Runs	Avge	100	50	Ct/St
M.S.Washington Sundar	3	4	2	96*	181	90.50	–	2	–
R.G.Sharma	4	7	1	161	345	57.50	1	1	5
R.R.Pant	4	6	1	101	270	54.00	1	2	8/5
R.Ashwin	4	6	–	106	189	31.50	1	–	2
V.Kohli	4	6	–	72	172	28.66	–	2	4
C.A.Pujara	4	6	–	73	133	22.16	–	1	3
S.Gill	4	7	1	50	119	19.83	–	1	2
A.M.Rahane	4	6	–	67	112	18.66	–	1	8
A.R.Patel	3	4	–	43	55	13.75	–	–	1
M.Siraj	2	3	1	16*	20	10.00	–	–	1
I.Sharma	4	6	2	10*	26	6.50	–	–	1
J.J.Bumrah	2	3	–	4	5	1.50	–	–	1

Also batted (one Test): S.Nadeem 0, 0; K.Yadav 0, 3.

BOWLING

	O	M	R	W	Avge	Best	5wI	10wM
A.R.Patel	127.4	27	286	27	10.59	6-38	4	1
R.Ashwin	188.1	33	471	32	14.71	6-61	3	–
I.Sharma	59	15	160	6	26.66	2-22	–	–
J.J.Bumrah	48	10	129	4	32.25	3-84	–	–
S.Nadeem	59	6	233	4	58.25	2-66	–	–

Also bowled: R.G.Sharma 2-0-7-0; M.Siraj 26-7-68-3; M.S.Washington Sundar 38.4-3-130-2; K.Yadav 12.2-2-41-2.

INTERNATIONAL UMPIRES AND REFEREES 2021

ELITE PANEL OF UMPIRES 2021

The Elite Panel of ICC Umpires and Referees was introduced in April 2002 to raise standards and guarantee impartial adjudication. Two umpires from this panel stand in Test matches while one officiates with a home umpire from the Supplementary International Panel in limited-overs internationals.

Full Names	Birthdate	Birthplace	Tests	Debut	LOI	Debut
ALIM Sarwar DAR	06.06.68	Jhang, Pakistan	135	2003-04	211	1999-00
DHARMASENA, H.D.P.Kumar	24.04.71	Colombo, Sri Lanka	67	2010-11	105	2008-09
ERASMUS, Marais	27.02.64	George, South Africa	64	2009-10	92	2007-08
GAFFANEY, Christopher Blair	30.11.75	Dunedin, New Zealand	37	2014	68	2010
GOUGH, Michael Andrew	18.12.79	Hartlepool, England	18	2016	63	2013
ILLINGWORTH, Richard Keith	23.08.63	Bradford, England	53	2012-13	69	2010
KETTLEBOROUGH, Richard Allan	15.03.73	Sheffield, England	68	2010-11	90	2009
MENON, Nitin Narendra	02.11.83	Indore, India	7	2019-20	24	2016-17
OXENFORD, Bruce Nicholas James	05.03.60	Southport, Australia	62	2010-11	97	2007-08
REIFFEL, Paul Ronald	19.04.66	Box Hill, Australia	51	2012	71	2008-09
TUCKER, Rodney James	28.08.64	Sydney, Australia	71	2009-10	85	2008-09
WILSON, Joel Sheldon	30.12.66	Trinidad, West Indies	19	2015	66	2011

ELITE PANEL OF REFEREES 2021

Full Names	Birthdate	Birthplace	Tests	Debut	LOI	Debut
BOON, David Clarence	29.12.60	Launceston, Australia	61	2011	146	2011
BROAD, Brian Christopher	29.09.57	Bristol, England	106	2003-04	326	2003-04
CROWE, Jeffrey John	14.09.58	Auckland, New Zealand	103	2004-05	298	2003-04
MADUGALLE, Ranjan Senerath	22.04.59	Kandy, Sri Lanka	196	1993-94	363	1993-94
PYCROFT, Andrew John	06.06.56	Harare, Zimbabwe	78	2009	178	2009
RICHARDSON, Sir Richard Benjamin	12.01.62	Five Islands, Antigua	29	2016	54	2016
SRINATH, Javagal	31.08.69	Mysore, India	57	2006	223	2006-07

INTERNATIONAL UMPIRES PANEL 2021

Nominated by their respective cricket boards, members from this panel officiate in home LOIs and supplement the Elite panel for Test matches. The number of Test matches/LOI in which they have stood is shown in brackets.

Afghanistan	Ahmed Shah Pakteen (1/15)	Ahmed Shah Durrani (-/6)	Bismallah Jan Shinwari (-/8)
			Izafullah Safi (-/3)
Australia	S.A.J.Craig (-/-)	P.Wilson (4/32)	S.J.Nogajski (-/6)
			G.A.Abood (-/2)
Bangladesh	Tanvir Ahmed (-/1)	Sharfuddoula (2/45)	Masudur Rahman (-/9)
			Gazi Sohel (-/1)
England	A.G.Wharf (-/6)	D.J.Millns (-/3)	M.Burns (-/1)
			M.J.Saggers (-/2)
India	C.Shamshuddin (-/43)	A.K.Chaudhary (2/20)	V.K.Sharma (2/2)
			K.N.Ananthapadmanabhan (-/-)
Ireland	M.Hawthorne (-/30)	R.E.Black (-/13)	A.J.Neill (-/8)
			P.A.Reynolds (-/3)
New Zealand	W.R.Knights (2/15)	C.M.Brown (2/17)	S.B.Haig (-/6)
Pakistan	Shozab Raza (-/24)	Ahsan Raza (2/37)	Asif Yaqoob (-/2)
			Rashid Riaz (-/2)
South Africa	A.T.Holdstock (2/23)	S.George (-/54)	B.P.Jele (-/11)
			A.Paleker (-/2)
Sri Lanka	R.M.P.J.Rambukwella (-/-)	R.S.A.Palliyaguruge (5/79)	R.R.Wimalasiri (-/14)
			L.E.Hannibal (-/7)
West Indies	G.O.Brathwaite (-/44)	L.S.Reifer (-/4)	P.A.Gustard (-/-)
			N.Duguid (-/7)
Zimbabwe	L.Rusere (-/14)	I.Chabi (-/1)	C.Phiri (-/-)
			F.Mutizwa (-/-)

Test Match and LOI statistics to 9 March 2021.

TEST MATCH CAREER RECORDS

These records, complete to 9 March 2021, contain all players registered for county cricket or The Hundred in 2021 at the time of going to press, plus those who have played Test cricket since 1 October 2019 (Test No. 2362). Some players who may return to Test action have also been listed, even if their most recent game was earlier than this date.

ENGLAND – BATTING AND FIELDING

	M	I	NO	HS	Runs	Avge	100	50	Ct/St
M.M.Ali	61	106	8	155*	2831	28.88	5	14	33
J.M.Anderson	160	223	94	81	1223	9.55	–	1	97
J.C.Archer	13	20	–	30	155	7.75	–	–	2
J.M.Bairstow	74	131	7	167*	4197	34.12	6	21	186/13
J.T.Ball	4	8	–	31	67	8.37	–	–	1
G.S.Ballance	23	42	2	156	1498	37.45	4	7	22
G.J.Batty	9	12	2	38	149	14.90	–	–	3
D.M.Bess	14	19	5	57	319	22.78	–	1	3
R.S.Bopara	13	19	1	143	575	31.94	3	–	6
S.G.Borthwick	1	2	–	4	5	2.50	–	–	2
T.T.Bresnan	23	26	4	91	575	26.13	–	3	8
S.C.J.Broad	146	213	36	169	3355	18.95	1	13	47
R.J.Burns	23	42	–	133	1291	30.73	2	8	19
J.C.Buttler	50	87	8	152	2728	34.53	2	18	123/1
R.Clarke	2	3	–	55	96	32.00	–	–	1
A.N.Cook	161	291	16	294	12472	45.35	33	57	175
M.S.Crane	1	2	–	4	6	3.00	–	–	–
Z.Crawley	12	20	–	267	683	34.15	1	4	10
S.M.Curran	21	33	4	78	741	25.55	–	3	4
T.K.Curran	2	3	1	39	66	33.00	–	–	–
L.A.Dawson	3	6	2	66*	84	21.00	–	1	2
J.L.Denly	15	28	–	94	827	29.53	–	6	7
B.M.Duckett	4	7	–	56	110	15.71	–	1	1
S.T.Finn	36	47	22	56	279	11.16	–	1	8
B.T.Foakes	8	16	3	107	410	31.53	1	1	14/5
A.D.Hales	11	21	–	94	573	27.28	–	5	8
H.Hameed	3	6	–	82	219	43.80	–	2	4
K.K.Jennings	17	32	1	146*	781	25.19	2	1	17
C.J.Jordan	8	11	–	35	180	18.00	–	–	14
D.W.Lawrence	5	10	1	73	248	27.55	–	2	1
M.J.Leach	16	28	8	92	273	13.65	–	1	9
A.Lyth	7	13	–	107	265	20.38	1	–	8
D.J.Malan	15	26	–	140	724	27.84	1	6	11
E.J.G.Morgan	16	24	1	130	700	30.43	2	3	11
C.Overton	4	8	2	41*	124	20.66	–	–	1
S.R.Patel	6	9	–	42	151	16.77	–	–	3
L.E.Plunkett	13	20	5	55*	238	15.86	–	1	3
O.J.D.Pope	17	28	3	135*	798	31.92	1	5	19
A.U.Rashid	19	33	5	61	540	19.28	–	2	4
S.D.Robson	7	11	–	127	336	30.54	1	1	5
T.S.Roland-Jones	4	6	2	25	82	20.50	–	–	–
J.E.Root	103	189	14	254	8617	49.24	20	49	134
J.J.Roy	5	10	–	72	187	18.70	–	1	1
D.P.Sibley	18	31	–	133*	882	30.41	2	4	10
B.A.Stokes	71	130	5	258	4631	37.04	10	24	81
O.P.Stone	2	4	–	19	20	5.00	–	–	–
M.D.Stoneman	11	20	1	60	526	27.68	–	5	1
J.M.Vince	13	22	–	83	548	24.90	–	3	8
T.Westley	5	9	1	59	193	24.12	–	1	1
C.R.Woakes	38	60	12	137*	1321	27.52	1	5	17
M.A.Wood	18	30	6	52	402	16.75	–	1	7

ENGLAND – BOWLING

	O	M	R	W	Avge	Best	5wI	10wM
M.M.Ali	1889.4	275	6850	189	36.24	6- 53	5	1
J.M.Anderson	5721	1474	16251	614	26.46	7- 42	30	3
J.C.Archer	434.5	95	1304	42	31.04	6- 45	3	–
J.T.Ball	102	23	343	3	114.33	1- 47	–	–
G.S.Ballance	2	1	5	0			–	–
G.J.Batty	285.4	38	914	15	60.93	3- 55	–	–
D.M.Bess	417	82	1223	36	33.97	5- 30	2	–
R.S.Bopara	72.2	10	290	1	290.00	1- 39	–	–
S.G.Borthwick	13	0	82	4	20.50	3- 33	–	–
T.T.Bresnan	779	185	2357	72	32.73	5- 48	1	–
S.C.J.Broad	4886	1164	14328	517	27.71	8- 15	18	3
R.Clarke	29	11	60	4	15.00	2- 7	–	–
A.N.Cook	3	0	7	1	7.00	1- 6	–	–
M.S.Crane	48	3	193	1	193.00	1-193	–	–
S.M.Curran	441.1	86	1431	44	32.52	4- 58	–	–
T.K.Curran	66	14	200	2	100.00	1- 65	–	–
L.A.Dawson	87.4	12	298	7	42.57	4-101	–	–
J.L.Denly	65	11	219	2	109.50	2- 42	–	–
S.T.Finn	1068.4	190	3800	125	30.40	6- 79	5	–
A.D.Hales	3	1	2	0			–	–
K.K.Jennings	12.1	1	55	0			–	–
C.J.Jordan	255	74	752	21	35.80	4- 18	–	–
D.W.Lawrence	3	0	17	0			–	–
M.J.Leach	617.1	101	1859	62	29.98	5- 83	2	–
A.Lyth	1	1	0	0			–	–
D.J.Malan	26	4	70	0			–	–
C.Overton	117.5	15	403	9	44.77	3-105	–	–
S.R.Patel	143	23	421	7	60.14	2- 27	–	–
L.E.Plunkett	443.1	71	1536	41	37.46	5- 64	1	–
A.U.Rashid	636	50	2390	60	39.83	5- 49	2	–
T.S.Roland-Jones	89.2	23	334	17	19.64	5- 57	1	–
J.E.Root	513.1	103	1604	37	43.35	5- 8	1	–
D.P.Sibley	1	0	7	0			–	–
B.A.Stokes	1545.5	286	5115	163	31.38	6- 22	4	–
O.P.Stone	34.4	9	97	7	13.85	3- 29	–	–
J.M.Vince	4	1	13	0			–	–
T.Westley	4	0	12	0			–	–
C.R.Woakes	1085.2	240	3282	112	29.30	6- 17	4	1
M.A.Wood	548.5	122	1772	53	33.43	5- 41	2	–

TESTS **AUSTRALIA – BATTING AND FIELDING**

	M	I	NO	HS	Runs	Avge	100	50	Ct/St
C.T.Bancroft	10	18	1	82*	446	26.23	–	3	16
J.A.Burns	23	40	1	180	1442	36.97	4	7	23
P.J.Cummins	34	50	7	63	708	16.46	–	2	16
A.J.Finch	5	10	–	62	278	27.80	–	2	7
C.Green	4	7	–	84	236	33.71	–	1	5
P.S.P.Handscomb	16	29	5	110	934	38.91	2	4	28
M.S.Harris	10	19	1	79	428	23.77	–	2	7
J.R.Hazlewood	55	68	31	39	445	12.02	–	–	19
T.M.Head	19	31	2	161	1153	39.75	2	7	12
U.T.Khawaja	44	77	6	174	2887	40.66	8	14	35
M.Labuschagne	18	31	–	215	1885	60.80	5	10	15
N.M.Lyon	100	129	39	47	1101	12.23	–	–	50
M.R.Marsh	32	55	5	181	1260	25.20	2	3	16
G.J.Maxwell	7	14	1	104	339	26.07	1	–	5
T.D.Paine	35	57	10	92	1534	32.63	–	9	150/7
J.L.Pattinson	21	25	9	47*	417	26.06	–	–	6
W.J.Pucovski	1	2	–	62	72	36.00	–	–	–
J.A.Richardson	2	1	–	1	1	1.00	–	–	–
P.M.Siddle	67	94	15	51	1164	14.73	–	2	19
S.P.D.Smith	77	139	17	239	7540	61.80	27	31	123
M.A.Starc	61	91	19	99	1596	22.16	–	10	31
M.S.Wade	36	63	9	117	1613	29.87	4	5	74/11
D.A.Warner	86	159	7	335*	7311	48.09	24	30	69

AUSTRALIA – BOWLING

	O	M	R	W	Avge	Best	5wI	10wM
P.J.Cummins	1289	318	3542	164	21.59	6- 23	5	1
A.J.Finch	2	0	8	0	–	–	–	–
C.Green	44	7	118	0	–	–	–	–
J.R.Hazlewood	1981.1	515	5438	212	25.65	6- 67	9	–
T.M.Head	21	4	76	0	–	–	–	–
U.T.Khawaja	2	0	5	0	–	–	–	–
M.Labuschagne	137	14	500	12	41.66	3- 45	–	–
N.M.Lyon	4281.4	815	12816	399	32.12	8- 50	18	3
M.R.Marsh	475.3	83	1623	42	38.64	5- 46	1	–
G.J.Maxwell	77	4	341	8	42.62	4-127	–	–
J.L.Pattinson	660.3	142	2133	81	26.33	5- 27	4	–
J.A.Richardson	51	15	123	6	20.50	3- 26	–	–
P.M.Siddle	2317.5	615	6777	221	30.66	6- 54	8	–
S.P.D.Smith	230.1	25	960	17	56.47	3- 18	–	–
M.A.Starc	2095.5	415	7031	255	27.57	6- 50	13	2
M.S.Wade	5	1	28	0	–	–	–	–
D.A.Warner	57	1	269	4	67.25	2- 45	–	–

TESTS SOUTH AFRICA – BATTING AND FIELDING

	M	I	NO	HS	Runs	Avge	100	50	Ct/St
K.J.Abbott	11	14	–	17	95	6.78	–	–	4
H.M.Amla	124	215	16	311*	9282	46.64	28	41	108
T.Bavuma	44	73	8	102*	2097	32.26	1	15	20
T.B.de Bruyn	12	23	1	101	428	19.45	1	–	11
Q.de Kock	51	86	5	129*	3008	37.13	5	21	208/11
M.de Lange	2	2	–	9	9	4.50	–	–	1
F.du Plessis	69	118	14	199	4163	40.02	10	21	63
D.Elgar	67	117	10	199	4260	39.81	13	16	71
M.Z.Hamza	5	10	–	62	181	18.10	–	1	5
S.R.Harmer	5	6	1	13	58	11.60	–	–	1
B.E.Hendricks	1	2	1	5*	9	9.00	–	–	–
H.Klaasen	1	2	–	6	11	5.50	–	–	3/1
H.G.Kuhn	4	8	–	34	113	14.12	–	–	1
G.F.Linde	3	6	–	37	135	22.50	–	–	–
K.A.Maharaj	34	54	6	73	721	15.02	–	3	10
P.J.Malan	3	6	–	84	156	26.00	–	1	3
A.K.Markram	24	44	1	152	1760	40.93	5	8	19
P.W.A.Mulder	4	6	–	36	110	18.33	–	–	2
S.Muthusamy	2	4	2	49*	98	49.00	–	–	2
L.T.Ngidi	8	13	7	14*	42	7.00	–	–	4
A.A.Nortje	10	18	4	40	104	7.42	–	–	2
D.Olivier	10	12	5	10*	26	3.71	–	–	2
W.D.Parnell	6	4	–	23	67	16.75	–	–	3
D.Paterson	2	4	3	39*	43	43.00	–	–	1
V.D.Philander	64	94	20	74	1779	24.04	–	8	17
D.L.Piedt	9	12	1	56	131	11.90	–	1	5
D.Pretorius	3	6	–	37	83	13.83	–	–	2
K.Rabada	45	68	12	34	628	11.21	–	–	23
L.L.Sipamla	2	2	–	5	5	2.50	–	–	1
H.E.van der Dussen	8	14	–	98	485	34.64	–	5	121
S.van Zyl	12	17	2	101*	395	26.33	1	–	6
D.J.Vilas	6	9	–	26	94	10.44	–	–	13

SOUTH AFRICA – BOWLING

	O	M	R	W	Avge	Best	5wI	10wM
K.J.Abbott	346.5	95	886	39	22.71	7- 29	3	–
H.M.Amla	9	0	37	0	–	–	–	–
T.Bavuma	16	1	61	1	61.00	1- 29	–	–
T.B.de Bruyn	17	1	74	0	–	–	–	–
M.de Lange	74.4	10	277	9	30.77	7- 81	1	–
F.du Plessis	13	0	69	0	–	–	–	–
D.Elgar	171.4	12	665	15	44.33	4- 22	–	–
S.R.Harmer	191.2	34	588	20	29.40	4- 61	–	–
B.E.Hendricks	38.3	5	175	6	29.16	5- 64	1	–
G.F.Linde	78.5	17	252	9	28.00	5- 64	1	–
K.A.Maharaj	1255.1	229	4055	120	33.79	9-129	6	1
P.J.Malan	2	0	5	0	–	–	–	–
A.K.Markram	33.2	5	103	0	–	–	–	–
P.W.A.Mulder	83	22	253	11	23.00	3- 25	–	–
S.Muthusamy	37.3	2	180	2	90.00	1- 63	–	–
L.T.Ngidi	197.1	47	640	24	26.66	6- 39	1	–
A.A.Nortje	315.4	53	1164	39	29.84	6- 56	3	–
D.Olivier	240	43	924	48	19.25	6- 37	3	1
W.D.Parnell	92.4	11	414	15	27.60	4- 51	–	–
D.Paterson	57.5	11	166	4	41.50	2- 86	–	–
V.D.Philander	1898.3	507	5000	224	22.32	6- 21	13	2
D.L.Piedt	304	46	1175	26	45.19	5-153	1	–
D.Pretorius	80	22	252	7	36.00	2- 26	–	–
K.Rabada	1405.1	284	4720	202	23.36	7-112	9	4
L.L.Sipamla	39.5	5	167	10	16.70	4- 76	–	–
S.van Zyl	67.1	15	148	6	24.66	3- 20	–	–

TESTS **WEST INDIES – BATTING AND FIELDING**

	M	I	NO	HS	Runs	Avge	100	50	Ct/St
J.Blackwood	35	63	4	112*	1903	32.25	2	14	28
N.E.Bonner	2	4	–	90	231	57.75	–	2	3
C.R.Brathwaite	3	5	1	69	181	45.25	–	3	–
K.C.Brathwaite	66	126	7	212	3876	32.57	8	20	31
D.M.Bravo	56	102	5	218	3538	36.47	8	17	51
S.S.J.Brooks	8	15	–	111	422	28.13	1	3	8
J.D.Campbell	13	26	3	68	572	24.86	–	2	6
R.L.Chase	37	68	4	137*	1869	29.20	5	8	15
R.R.S.Cornwall	5	9	2	14	39	5.57	–	–	11
M.L.Cummins	14	22	7	24*	114	7.60	–	–	2
J.Da Silva	3	6	–	92	234	39.00	–	2	7
S.O.Dowrich	35	62	8	125*	1570	29.07	3	9	85/5
S.T.Gabriel	52	78	29	20*	216	4.40	–	–	16
S.O.Hetmyer	16	30	–	93	838	27.93	–	5	7
C.K.Holder	1	2	2	13*	21	–	–	–	–
J.O.Holder	45	79	13	202*	2115	32.04	3	9	42
S.D.Hope	34	64	3	147	1603	26.27	2	5	47/1
A.S.Joseph	14	24	–	86	344	14.33	–	2	8
K.R.Mayers	2	4	1	210*	261	87.00	1	–	3
S.A.R.Moseley	2	4	–	12	28	7.00	–	–	3
S.P.Narine	6	7	2	22*	40	8.00	–	–	2
K.A.J.Roach	61	99	20	41	907	11.48	–	–	15
A.D.Russell	1	1	–	2	2	2.00	–	–	1
J.A.Warrican	10	17	9	41	150	18.75	–	–	3

WEST INDIES – BOWLING

	O	M	R	W	Avge	Best	5wI	10wM
J.Blackwood	54	9	194	2	97.00	2- 14	–	–
N.E.Bonner	8	0	46	1	46.00	1- 16	–	–
C.R.Brathwaite	68	9	242	1	242.00	1- 30	–	–
K.C.Brathwaite	344.2	27	1109	21	52.80	6- 29	1	–
D.M.Bravo	1	0	2	0	–	–	–	–
J.D.Campbell	10.1	0	30	0	–	–	–	–
R.L.Chase	858.2	96	3003	71	42.29	8- 60	3	–
R.R.S.Cornwall	284.5	52	832	27	30.81	7- 75	2	1
M.L.Cummins	329.2	60	1084	27	40.14	6- 48	1	–
S.T.Gabriel	1415.5	250	4796	156	30.74	8- 62	6	1
C.K.Holder	26	1	110	2	55.00	2-110	–	–
J.O.Holder	1260	343	3242	116	27.94	6- 59	7	1
A.S.Joseph	383.1	84	1287	34	37.85	3- 53	–	–
K.R.Mayers	16	4	42	0	–	–	–	–
S.P.Narine	275	60	851	21	40.52	6- 91	2	–
K.A.J.Roach	1843.4	414	5721	205	27.90	6- 48	9	1
A.D.Russell	23	2	104	1	104.00	1- 73	–	–
J.A.Warrican	353	46	1157	32	36.15	4- 62	–	–

TESTS   **NEW ZEALAND – BATTING AND FIELDING**

	M	I	NO	HS	Runs	Avge	100	50	Ct/St
T.D.Astle	5	6	1	35	98	19.60	–	–	3
T.A.Blundell	10	16	2	121	538	38.42	2	2	7
T.A.Boult	71	84	40	52*	668	15.18	–	1	39
C.de Grandhomme	24	36	4	105	1185	37.03	1	8	15
L.H.Ferguson	1	2	2	1*	1	–	–	–	–
M.J.Henry	13	16	4	66	224	18.66	–	1	6
K.A.Jamieson	6	6	2	51*	226	56.50	–	1	2
T.W.M.Latham	56	97	4	264*	3929	42.24	11	20	59
D.J.Mitchell	4	4	1	102*	226	75.33	1	1	1
H.M.Nicholls	37	55	6	174	2152	43.91	7	10	25
A.Y.Patel	8	10	3	14	53	7.57	–	–	5
G.D.Phillips	1	2	–	52	52	26.00	–	1	1
J.A.Raval	24	39	1	132	1143	30.07	1	7	21
M.J.Santner	23	31	1	126	766	25.53	1	2	16
W.E.R.Somerville	4	6	2	40*	72	18.00	–	–	–
T.G.Southee	77	109	11	77*	1690	17.24	–	5	58
L.R.P.L.Taylor	105	183	22	290	7379	45.83	19	34	155
N.Wagner	51	65	18	66*	660	14.04	–	1	12
B.J.Watling	73	114	15	205	3773	38.11	8	19	259/8
K.S.Williamson	83	144	13	251	7115	54.31	24	32	72
W.A.Young	2	2	–	43	48	24.00	–	–	1

NEW ZEALAND – BOWLING

	O	M	R	W	Avge	Best	5wI	10wM
T.D.Astle	111.1	16	368	7	52.57	3-39	–	–
T.A.Blundell	3	0	13	0	–	–	–	–
T.A.Boult	2636.3	597	7875	281	28.02	6-30	8	1
C.de Grandhomme	613.5	140	1487	47	31.63	6-41	1	–
L.H.Ferguson	11	1	47	0	–	–	–	–
M.J.Henry	492.1	86	1598	31	51.54	4-93	–	–
K.A.Jamieson	200.2	70	478	36	13.27	6-48	4	1
D.J.Mitchell	36	7	110	1	110.00	1- 7	–	–
A.Y.Patel	270.5	56	733	22	33.31	5-59	2	–
J.A.Raval	14	1	34	1	34.00	1-33	–	–
M.J.Santner	649.5	133	1803	41	43.97	3-53	–	–
W.E.R.Somerville	175.2	30	487	15	32.46	4-75	–	–
T.G.Southee	2897.5	667	8670	302	28.70	7-64	11	1
L.R.P.L.Taylor	16	3	48	2	24.00	2- 4	–	–
N.Wagner	1897.3	400	5766	219	26.32	7-39	9	–
K.S.Williamson	355.3	48	1195	30	39.83	4-44	–	–

TESTS INDIA – BATTING AND FIELDING

	M	I	NO	HS	Runs	Avge	100	50	Ct/St
M.A.Agarwal	14	23	–	243	1052	45.73	3	4	11
R.Ashwin	78	109	14	124	2656	27.95	5	11	27
J.J.Bumrah	19	28	11	10*	43	2.52	–	–	5
S.Gill	7	13	2	91	378	34.36	–	3	4
R.A.Jadeja	51	73	19	100*	1954	36.18	1	15	38
V.Kohli	91	153	10	254*	7490	52.37	27	25	88
Kuldeep Yadav	7	8	–	26	54	6.75	–	–	3
Mohammed Shami	50	66	21	51*	498	11.06	–	1	11
S.Nadeem	2	3	1	1*	1	0.50	–	–	1
T.Natarajan	1	1	1	1*	1	–	–	–	–
R.R.Pant .	20	33	3	159*	1358	45.26	3	6	75/7
A.R.Patel	3	4	–	43	55	13.75	–	–	1
C.A.Pujara	85	142	8	206*	6244	46.59	18	29	57
A.M.Rahane	73	123	12	188	4583	41.28	12	23	95
K.L.Rahul	36	60	2	199	2006	34.58	5	11	46
W.P.Saha	38	52	9	117	1251	29.09	3	5	92/12
N.Saini	2	3	1	5	8	4.00	–	–	1
I.Sharma	101	135	45	57	746	8.28	–	1	22
R.G.Sharma	38	64	8	212	2615	46.69	7	12	41
P.P.Shaw	5	9	1	134	339	42.37	1	2	2
M.Siraj	5	6	2	16*	39	9.75	–	–	3
S.N.Thakur	2	3	1	67	73	36.50	–	1	2
G.H.Vihari	12	21	2	111	624	32.84	1	4	3
M.S.Washington Sundar	4	6	2	96*	265	66.25	–	3	1
U.T.Yadav	48	55	23	31	359	11.21	–	–	17

INDIA – BOWLING

	O	M	R	W	Avge	Best	5wI	10wM
R.Ashwin	3586.4	724	10099	409	24.69	7-59	30	7
J.J.Bumrah	679.1	161	1835	83	22.10	6-27	5	–
R.A.Jadeja	2189.3	553	5351	220	24.32	7-48	9	1
V.Kohli	29.1	2	84	0	–	–	–	–
Kuldeep Yadav	177.1	24	620	26	23.84	5-57	2	–
Mohammed Shami	1499.5	275	4966	180	27.58	6-56	5	–
S.Nadeem	76.2	11	273	8	34.12	2-18	–	–
T.Natarajan	38.2	7	119	3	39.66	3-78	–	–
A.R.Patel	127.4	27	286	27	10.59	6-38	4	1
C.A.Pujara	1	0	2	0	–	–	–	–
N.Saini	41.5	5	172	4	43.00	2-54	–	–
I.Sharma	3084	616	9780	303	32.27	7-74	11	1
R.G.Sharma	63.5	5	224	2	112.00	1-26	–	–
M.Siraj	160.2	39	452	16	28.25	5-73	1	–
S.N.Thakur	44.4	8	164	7	23.42	4-61	–	–
G.H.Vihari	57.3	10	180	5	36.00	3-37	–	–
M.S.Washington Sundar	87.4	10	299	6	49.83	3-89	–	–
U.T.Yadav	1270.1	213	4521	148	30.54	6-88	3	1

TESTS

PAKISTAN – BATTING AND FIELDING

	M	I	NO	HS	Runs	Avge	100	50	Ct/St
Abid Ali	10	17	1	174	569	35.56	2	1	4
Asad Shafiq	77	128	6	137	4660	38.19	12	27	77
Azhar Ali	85	160	10	302*	6417	42.78	17	33	62
Babar Azam	31	57	8	143	2167	44.22	5	16	21
Faheem Ashraf	8	13	1	91	495	41.25	–	4	1
Fawad Alam	9	17	2	168	570	38.00	3	–	5
Haris Sohail	16	27	1	147	847	32.57	2	3	14
Hasan Ali	11	18	5	29	189	14.53	–	–	4
Iftikhar Ahmed	3	5	–	27	48	9.60	–	–	1
Imam-ul-Haq	11	21	2	76	485	25.52	–	3	7
Imran Butt	2	4	–	15	36	9.00	–	–	6
Imran Khan	10	10	3	6	16	2.28	–	–	–
Mohammad Abbas	23	33	14	29	109	5.73	–	–	6
Mohammad Amir	36	67	11	48	751	13.41	–	–	5
Mohammad Rizwan	13	20	3	115*	754	44.35	1	6	32/1
Musa Khan	1	2	2	12*	16	–	–	–	–
Naseem Shah	9	12	5	12	28	4.00	–	–	1
Nauman Ali	2	3	–	45	77	25.66	–	–	–
Shadab Khan	6	11	2	56	300	33.33	–	3	3
Shaheen Shah Afridi	15	23	4	14	85	4.47	–	–	1
Shan Masood	25	47	–	156	1378	29.31	4	6	16
Usman Shinwari	1	–	–	–	–	–	–	–	–
Yasir Shah	45	67	7	113	843	14.05	1	–	23
Zafar Gohar	1	2	–	37	71	35.50	–	–	–

PAKISTAN – BOWLING

	O	M	R	W	Avge	Best	5wI	10wM
Asad Shafiq	56.4	1	196	3	65.33	1- 7	–	–
Azhar Ali	142.3	8	611	8	76.37	2-35	–	–
Faheem Ashraf	173	41	528	15	35.20	3-42	–	–
Fawad Alam	13	0	51	2	25.50	2-46	–	–
Haris Sohail	105	12	294	13	22.61	3- 1	–	–
Hasan Ali	351.1	82	1132	43	26.32	5-45	3	1
Iftikhar Ahmed	31.2	1	141	1	141.00	1- 1	–	–
Imran Khan	272.4	50	917	29	31.62	5-58	1	–
Mohammad Abbas	789.4	238	1916	84	22.80	5-33	4	1
Mohammad Amir	1269.5	292	3627	119	30.47	6-44	4	–
Musa Khan	20	1	114	0	–	–	–	–
Naseem Shah	224.4	33	849	20	42.45	5-31	1	–
Nauman Ali	79.3	26	172	8	21.50	5-35	1	–
Shadab Khan	159	19	513	14	36.64	3-31	–	–
Shaheen Shah Afridi	489.5	89	1552	48	32.33	5-77	1	–
Shan Masood	24	6	92	2	46.00	1- 6	–	–
Usman Shinwari	15	4	54	1	54.00	1-54	–	–
Yasir Shah	2266.5	348	7247	235	30.83	8-41	16	3
Zafar Gohar	32	0	159	0	–	–	–	–

TESTS

SRI LANKA – BATTING AND FIELDING

	M	I	NO	HS	Runs	Avge	100	50	Ct/St
L.Ambuldeniya	9	13	–	40	103	7.92	–	–	2
P.V.D.Chameera	9	17	2	22	91	6.06	–	–	4
L.D.Chandimal	60	109	8	164	4096	40.55	11	20	77/10
D.M.de Silva	32	58	5	173	1942	36.64	6	7	34
P.W.H.de Silva	3	6	–	59	153	25.50	–	1	2
D.P.D.N.Dickwella	41	74	4	92	2163	30.90	–	16	97/23
A.M.Fernando	3	6	3	4	4	1.33	–	–	–
B.O.P.Fernando	7	13	2	102	396	36.00	1	1	7
M.V.T.Fernando	10	16	8	38	57	7.12	–	–	2
F.D.M.Karunaratne	68	132	5	196	4657	36.66	10	24	53
C.B.R.L.S.Kumara	22	30	15	10	52	3.46	–	–	4
R.A.S.Lakmal	62	97	24	42	847	11.60	–	–	18
A.D.Mathews	88	158	22	200*	6194	45.54	11	36	68
B.K.G.Mendis	47	91	4	196	3022	34.73	7	11	71
M.D.K.Perera	43	77	8	95	1303	18.88	–	7	19
M.D.K.J.Perera	22	41	3	153*	1177	30.97	2	7	19/8
M.K.P.A.D.Perera	6	10	2	43*	135	16.87	–	–	4
C.A.K.Rajitha	9	12	2	12	35	3.50	–	–	4
M.B.Ranasinghe	1	2	–	5	6	3.00	–	–	–
M.D.Shanaka	6	12	2	66*	140	14.00	–	1	4
H.D.R.L.Thirimanne	38	74	6	155*	1623	23.86	2	6	27
R.T.M.Wanigamuni	1	2	–	16	16	8.00	–	–	–

SRI LANKA – BOWLING

	O	M	R	W	Avge	Best	5wI	10wM
L.Ambuldeniya	457.3	64	1609	45	35.75	7-137	3	1
P.V.D.Chameera	245.5	20	1037	25	41.48	5- 47	1	–
D.M.de Silva	326.1	39	1091	21	51.95	3- 25	–	–
P.W.H.de Silva	67.2	6	277	4	69.25	4-171	–	–
A.M.Fernando	47	9	156	4	39.00	2- 44	–	–
B.O.P.Fernando	3	0	19	0	–	–	–	–
M.V.T.Fernando	274.2	28	1025	31	33.06	5-101	1	–
F.D.M.Karunaratne	46.2	4	185	2	92.50	1- 12	–	–
C.B.R.L.S.Kumara	672	93	2554	68	37.55	6-122	1	–
R.A.S.Lakmal	1865.5	378	5682	151	37.62	5- 54	3	–
A.D.Mathews	646	158	1745	33	52.87	4- 44	–	–
B.K.G.Mendis	21	1	110	1	110.00	1- 10	–	–
M.D.K.Perera	1800.5	239	5780	161	35.90	6- 32	8	2
M.K.P.A.D.Perera	230.5	33	819	33	24.81	6-115	4	–
C.A.K.Rajitha	235.4	44	779	25	31.16	3- 20	–	–
M.D.Shanaka	127	19	431	13	33.15	3- 46	–	–
H.D.R.L.Thirimanne	14	1	51	0	–	–	–	–
R.T.M.Wanigamuni	26	1	96	2	48.00	1- 48	–	–

M.K.P.A.D.Perera is also known as A.Dananjaya; M.B.Ranasinghe is also known as M.Bhanuka; R.T.M.Wanigamuni is also known as W.R.T.Mendis.

TESTS **ZIMBABWE – BATTING AND FIELDING**

	M	I	NO	HS	Runs	Avge	100	50	Ct/St
R.P.Burl	2	3	–	16	24	8.00	–	–	1
R.W.Chakabva	18	35	2	101	850	25.75	1	4	39/4
C.R.Ervine	18	36	2	160	1208	35.52	3	4	16
K.M.Jarvis	13	24	10	25*	128	9.14	–	–	3
K.T.Kasuza	4	6	1	63	124	24.80	–	1	1
W.N.Madhevere	1	1	–	0	0	0.00	–	–	1
T.Maruma	3	5	–	41	68	13.60	–	–	1
P.S.Masvaure	6	12	1	64	255	23.18	–	2	1
B.S.Mudzinganyama	1	1	–	16	16	16.00	–	–	–
C.T.Mumba	3	5	2	11*	25	8.33	–	–	2
T.K.Musakanda	2	3	–	7	13	4.33	–	–	1
C.T.Mutombodzi	1	2	–	33	41	20.50	–	–	1
B.Muzarabani	2	3	2	12*	26	26.00	–	–	–
A.Ndlovu	2	4	–	5	9	2.25	–	–	2
V.M.Nyauchi	4	6	3	11	30	10.00	–	–	1
Sikandar Raza	16	31	–	127	1080	34.83	1	7	4
B.R.M.Taylor	31	62	4	171	2055	35.43	6	10	28
D.T.Tiripano	11	21	5	49*	303	18.93	–	–	3
C.K.Tshuma	1	2	–	3	3	1.50	–	–	–
S.C.Williams	13	25	1	119	875	36.45	3	3	12

ZIMBABWE – BOWLING

	O	M	R	W	Avge	Best	5wI	10wM
R.P.Burl	14	1	22	1	22.00	1- 13	–	–
K.M.Jarvis	418.3	79	1354	46	29.43	5- 54	3	–
W.N.Madhevere	4	1	6	0	–	–	–	–
P.S.Masvaure	14	0	61	0	–	–	–	–
C.T.Mumba	99.5	17	354	10	35.40	4- 50	–	–
C.T.Mutombodzi	19	3	67	0	–	–	–	–
B.Muzarabani	33	9	110	6	18.33	4- 48	–	–
A.Ndlovu	70	7	277	2	138.50	2-170	–	–
V.M.Nyauchi	111.5	22	309	12	25.75	3- 30	–	–
Sikandar Raza	411.5	52	1362	33	41.27	7-113	2	–
B.R.M.Taylor	7	0	38	0	–	–	–	–
D.T.Tiripano	332.1	78	884	20	44.20	3- 23	–	–
C.K.Tshuma	25	2	85	1	85.00	1- 85	–	–
S.C.Williams	304.3	35	957	21	45.57	3- 20	–	–

TESTS   **BANGLADESH – BATTING AND FIELDING**

	M	I	NO	HS	Runs	Avge	100	50	Ct/St
Abu Jayed	10	18	7	7*	28	2.54	–	–	1
Al-Amin Hossain	7	11	7	32*	90	22.50	–	–	–
Ebadat Hossain	6	10	4	2	4	0.66	–	–	1
Imrul Kayes	39	76	2	150	1797	24.28	3	4	35
Liton Das	22	38	1	94	1059	28.62	–	7	37/3
Mahmudullah	49	93	6	146	2764	31.77	4	16	38/1
Mehedi Hasan	24	46	6	103	836	20.90	1	3	19
Mithun Ali	10	18	–	67	333	18.50	–	2	6
Mominul Haque	42	78	4	181	3048	41.18	10	13	29
Mushfiqur Rahim	72	134	10	219*	4537	36.58	7	22	106/15
Mustafizur Rahman	14	20	7	16	59	4.53	–	–	1
Nayeem Hasan	7	10	3	26	109	15.57	–	–	4
Nazmul Hossain	6	11	–	71	241	21.90	–	1	6
Rubel Hossain	27	47	19	45*	265	9.46	–	–	11
Saif Hasan	2	3	–	16	24	8.00	–	–	–
Shadman Islam	7	13	–	76	339	26.07	–	2	3
Shakib Al Hasan	57	106	7	217	3930	39.69	5	25	24
Soumya Sarkar	16	30	–	149	831	27.70	1	4	23
Taijul Islam	31	52	8	39*	454	10.31	–	–	17
Tamim Iqbal	62	119	1	206	4508	38.20	9	28	17

BANGLADESH – BOWLING

	O	M	R	W	Avge	Best	5wI	10wM
Abu Jayed	270.2	58	909	30	30.30	4- 71	–	–
Al-Amin Hossain	169.2	35	545	9	60.55	3- 80	–	–
Ebadat Hossain	142	29	536	6	89.33	3- 91	–	–
Imrul Kayes	4	0	12	0	–	–	–	–
Mahmudullah	566.3	56	1949	43	45.32	5- 51	1	–
Mehedi Hasan	984.2	129	3242	100	32.42	7- 58	7	2
Mominul Haque	100.1	8	376	4	94.00	3- 27	–	–
Mustafizur Rahman	335.3	68	1102	30	36.73	4- 37	–	–
Nayeem Hasan	220.2	35	656	25	26.24	5- 61	2	–
Nazmul Hossain	0.4	0	13	0	–	–	–	–
Rubel Hossain	703.5	73	2764	36	76.77	5-166	1	–
Shakib Al Hasan	2176	394	6553	210	31.20	7- 36	18	2
Soumya Sarkar	84.4	3	336	4	84.00	2- 68	–	–
Taijul Islam	1320.1	214	4101	126	32.54	8- 39	7	1
Tamim Iqbal	5	0	20	0	–	–	–	–

TESTS   **IRELAND – BATTING AND FIELDING**

	M	I	NO	HS	Runs	Avge	100	50	Ct/St
M.R.Adair	1	2	–	8	11	5.50	–	–	1
A.Balbirnie	3	6	–	82	146	24.33	–	2	3
J.Cameron-Dow	1	2	1	32*	41	41.00	–	–	2
G.H.Dockrell	1	2	–	39	64	32.00	–	–	–
A.R.McBrine	2	4	–	11	18	4.50	–	–	–
J.A.McCollum	2	4	–	39	73	18.25	–	–	2
T.J.Murtagh	3	6	2	54*	109	27.25	–	1	–
K.J.O'Brien	3	6	1	118	258	51.60	1	1	–
W.T.S.Porterfield	3	6	–	32	58	9.66	–	–	2
S.W.Poynter	1	2	–	1	1	0.50	–	–	2/1
W.B.Rankin †	3	6	1	17	43	8.60	–	–	–
P.R.Stirling	3	6	–	36	104	17.33	–	–	4
S.R.Thompson	3	6	–	53	64	10.66	–	1	–
G.C.Wilson	2	4	1	33*	45	15.00	–	–	6

IRELAND – BOWLING

	O	M	R	W	Avge	Best	5wI	10wM
M.R.Adair	27.4	8	98	6	16.33	3-32	–	–
A.Balbirnie	1	0	8	0	–	–	–	–
J.Cameron-Dow	23.5	0	118	3	39.33	2-94	–	–
G.H.Dockrell	40	11	121	2	60.50	2-63	–	–
A.R.McBrine	50	10	159	3	53.00	2-77	–	–
T.J.Murtagh	95	25	213	13	16.38	5-13	1	–
K.J.O'Brien	10	2	31	0	–	–	–	–
W.B.Rankin	73.5	6	304	8	38.00	2- 5	–	–
P.R.Stirling	2	0	11	0	–	–	–	–
S.R.Thompson	68.2	14	204	10	20.40	3-28	–	–

† W.B.Rankin made one Test appearance for England, v A in Jan 2014, scoring 13 and 0, with bowling figures of 0-34 and 1-47.

AFGHANISTAN – BATTING AND FIELDING

	M	I	NO	HS	Runs	Avge	100	50	Ct/St
Abdul Malik	1	2	–	0	0	0.00	–	–	2
Abdul Wasi	1	2	–	9	12	6.00	–	–	–
Afsar Zazai	4	8	1	48*	172	24.57	–	–	5/1
Asghar Stanikzai	5	9	–	92	276	30.66	–	3	2
Hamza Hotak	2	4	2	34	72	36.00	–	–	–
Hashmatullah Shahidi	4	8	2	61	147	24.50	–	1	2
Ibrahim Zadran	3	6	–	87	255	42.50	–	2	5
Ihsanullah Janat	3	6	1	65*	110	22.00	–	1	4
Javed Ahmadi	2	4	–	62	105	26.25	–	1	–
Mohammad Nabi	3	6	–	24	33	5.50	–	–	2
Mujeeb Zadran	1	2	–	15	18	9.00	–	–	–
Munir Ahmad	1	2	–	12	13	6.50	–	–	–
Nasir Ahmadzai	1	2	–	15	17	8.50	–	–	–
Qais Ahmad	1	2	–	14	23	11.50	–	–	–
Rahmat Shah	5	10	–	102	304	30.40	1	2	2
Rashid Khan	4	7	–	51	106	15.14	–	1	–
Yamin Ahmadzai	5	9	–	18	32	3.55	–	–	–
Zahir Khan	3	6	3	0*	0	0.00	–	–	–

AFGHANISTAN – BOWLING

	O	M	R	W	Avge	Best	5wI	10wM
Abdul Wasi	8.5	0	25	0	–	–	–	–
Asghar Stanikzai	2	0	16	0	–	–	–	–
Hamza Hotak	57.5	8	165	12	13.75	6-75	2	–
Ibrahim Zadran	2	0	13	1	13.00	1-13	–	–
Javed Ahmadi	1	0	9	0	–	–	–	–
Mohammad Nabi	91	17	254	8	31.75	3-36	–	–
Mujeeb Zadran	15	1	75	1	75.00	1-75	–	–
Qais Ahmad	9	2	28	1	28.00	1-22	–	–
Rashid Khan	156.2	28	485	23	21.08	6-49	3	1
Yamin Ahmadzai	88.3	18	264	11	24.00	3-41	–	–
Zahir Khan	56	3	239	7	34.14	3-59	–	–

INTERNATIONAL TEST MATCH RESULTS

Complete to 9 March 2021

	Opponents	Tests	E	A	SA	WI	NZ	I	P	SL	Z	B	Ire	Afg	Tied	Drawn
								Won by								
England	Australia	351	110	146	–	–	–	–	–	–	–	–	–	–	–	95
	South Africa	153	64	–	34	–	–	–	–	–	–	–	–	–	–	55
	West Indies	160	51	–	–	58	–	–	–	–	–	–	–	–	–	51
	New Zealand	105	48	–	–	–	11	–	–	–	–	–	–	–	–	46
	India	126	48	–	–	–	–	29	–	–	–	–	–	–	–	49
	Pakistan	86	26	–	–	–	–	–	21	–	–	–	–	–	–	39
	Sri Lanka	36	17	–	–	–	–	–	–	8	–	–	–	–	–	11
	Zimbabwe	6	3	–	–	–	–	–	–	–	0	–	–	–	–	3
	Bangladesh	10	9	–	–	–	–	–	–	–	–	1	–	–	–	0
	Ireland	1	1	–	–	–	–	–	–	–	–	–	0	–	–	0
Australia	South Africa	98	–	52	26	–	–	–	–	–	–	–	–	–	–	20
	West Indies	116	–	58	–	32	–	–	–	–	–	–	–	–	1	25
	New Zealand	60	–	34	–	–	8	–	–	–	–	–	–	–	–	18
	India	102	–	43	–	–	–	30	–	–	–	–	–	–	1	28
	Pakistan	66	–	33	–	–	–	–	15	–	–	–	–	–	–	18
	Sri Lanka	31	–	19	–	–	–	–	–	4	–	–	–	–	–	8
	Zimbabwe	3	–	3	–	–	–	–	–	–	0	–	–	–	–	0
	Bangladesh	6	–	5	–	–	–	–	–	–	–	1	–	–	–	0
S Africa	West Indies	28	–	–	18	3	–	–	–	–	–	–	–	–	–	7
	New Zealand	45	–	–	25	–	4	–	–	–	–	–	–	–	–	16
	India	39	–	–	15	–	–	14	–	–	–	–	–	–	–	10
	Pakistan	28	–	–	15	–	–	–	6	–	–	–	–	–	–	7
	Sri Lanka	31	–	–	16	–	–	–	–	9	–	–	–	–	–	6
	Zimbabwe	9	–	–	8	–	–	–	–	–	0	–	–	–	–	1
	Bangladesh	12	–	–	10	–	–	–	–	–	–	0	–	–	–	2
W Indies	New Zealand	49	–	–	–	13	17	–	–	–	–	–	–	–	–	19
	India	98	–	–	–	30	–	22	–	–	–	–	–	–	–	46
	Pakistan	52	–	–	–	17	–	–	20	–	–	–	–	–	–	15
	Sri Lanka	20	–	–	–	4	–	–	–	9	–	–	–	–	–	7
	Zimbabwe	10	–	–	–	7	–	–	–	–	0	–	–	–	–	3
	Bangladesh	18	–	–	–	12	–	–	–	–	–	4	–	–	–	2
	Afghanistan	1	–	–	–	1	–	–	–	–	–	–	–	0	–	0
N Zealand	India	59	–	–	–	–	12	21	–	–	–	–	–	–	–	26
	Pakistan	60	–	–	–	–	14	–	25	–	–	–	–	–	–	21
	Sri Lanka	36	–	–	–	–	16	–	–	9	–	–	–	–	–	11
	Zimbabwe	17	–	–	–	–	11	–	–	–	0	–	–	–	–	6
	Bangladesh	15	–	–	–	–	12	–	–	–	–	0	–	–	–	3
India	Pakistan	59	–	–	–	–	–	9	12	–	–	–	–	–	–	38
	Sri Lanka	44	–	–	–	–	–	20	–	7	–	–	–	–	–	17
	Zimbabwe	11	–	–	–	–	–	7	–	–	2	–	–	–	–	2
	Bangladesh	11	–	–	–	–	–	9	–	–	–	0	–	–	–	2
	Afghanistan	1	–	–	–	–	–	1	–	–	–	–	–	0	–	0
Pakistan	Sri Lanka	55	–	–	–	–	–	–	20	16	–	–	–	–	–	19
	Zimbabwe	17	–	–	–	–	–	–	10	–	3	–	–	–	–	4
	Bangladesh	11	–	–	–	–	–	–	10	–	–	0	–	–	–	1
	Ireland	1	–	–	–	–	–	–	1	–	–	–	0	–	–	0
Sri Lanka	Zimbabwe	20	–	–	–	–	–	–	–	14	0	–	–	–	–	6
	Bangladesh	20	–	–	–	–	–	–	–	16	–	1	–	–	–	3
Zimbabwe	Bangladesh	17	–	–	–	–	–	–	–	–	7	7	–	–	–	3
	Afghanistan	1	–	–	–	–	–	–	–	–	1	–	–	0	–	0
Bangladesh	Afghanistan	1	–	–	–	–	–	–	–	–	–	0	–	1	–	0
Ireland	Afghanistan	1	–	–	–	–	–	–	–	–	–	–	0	1	–	0
		2413	377	393	167	177	105	162	140	92	13	14	0	2	2	769

56

	Tests	Won	Lost	Drawn	Tied	Toss Won
England	1034	377	308	349	–	505
Australia	834†	394†	226	212	2	418†
South Africa	443	167	152	124	–	210
West Indies	552	177	199	175	1	290
New Zealand	446	105	175	166	–	222
India	550	162	169	218	1	274
Pakistan	435	140	133	162	–	207
Sri Lanka	293	92	113	88	–	159
Zimbabwe	111	13	70	28	–	63
Bangladesh	121	14	91	16	–	62
Ireland	3	–	3	–	–	2
Afghanistan	5	2	3	–	–	2

† total includes Australia's victory against the ICC World XI.

INTERNATIONAL TEST CRICKET RECORDS

(To 9 March 2021)

TEAM RECORDS

HIGHEST INNINGS TOTALS

952-6d	Sri Lanka v India	Colombo (RPS)	1997-98
903-7d	England v Australia	The Oval	1938
849	England v West Indies	Kingston	1929-30
790-3d	West Indies v Pakistan	Kingston	1957-58
765-6d	Pakistan v Sri Lanka	Karachi	2008-09
760-7d	Sri Lanka v India	Ahmedabad	2009-10
759-7d	India v England	Chennai	2016-17
758-8d	Australia v West Indies	Kingston	1954-55
756-5d	Sri Lanka v South Africa	Colombo (SSC)	2006
751-5d	West Indies v England	St John's	2003-04
749-9d	West Indies v England	Bridgetown	2008-09
747	West Indies v South Africa	St John's	2004-05
735-6d	Australia v Zimbabwe	Perth	2003-04
730-6d	Sri Lanka v Bangladesh	Dhaka	2013-14
729-6d	Australia v England	Lord's	1930
726-9d	India v Sri Lanka	Mumbai	2009-10
715-6d	New Zealand v Bangladesh	Hamilton	2018-19
713-3d	Sri Lanka v Zimbabwe	Bulawayo	2003-04
713-9d	Sri Lanka v Bangladesh	Chittagong	2017-18
710-7d	England v India	Birmingham	2011
708	Pakistan v England	The Oval	1987
707	India v Sri Lanka	Colombo (SSC)	2010
705-7d	India v Australia	Sydney	2003-04
701	Australia v England	The Oval	1934
699-5	Pakistan v India	Lahore	1989-90
695	Australia v England	The Oval	1930
692-8d	West Indies v England	The Oval	1995
690	New Zealand v Pakistan	Sharjah	2014-15
687-8d	West Indies v England	The Oval	1976
687-6d	India v Bangladesh	Hyderabad	2016-17
682-6d	South Africa v England	Lord's	2003

681-8d	West Indies v England	Port-of-Spain	1953-54
680-8d	New Zealand v India	Wellington	2013-14
679-7d	Pakistan v India	Lahore	2005-06
676-7	India v Sri Lanka	Kanpur	1986-87
675-5d	India v Pakistan	Multan	2003-04
674	Australia v India	Adelaide	1947-48
674-6	Pakistan v India	Faisalabad	1984-85
674-6d	Australia v England	Cardiff	2009
671-4	New Zealand v Sri Lanka	Wellington	1990-91
668	Australia v West Indies	Bridgetown	1954-55
664	India v England	The Oval	2007
662-9d	Australia v England	Perth	2017-18
660-5d	West Indies v New Zealand	Wellington	1994-95
659-8d	Australia v England	Sydney	1946-47
659-4d	Australia v India	Sydney	2011-12
659-6d	New Zealand v Pakistan	Christchurch	2020-21
658-8d	England v Australia	Nottingham	1938
658-9d	South Africa v West Indies	Durban	2003-04
657-8d	Pakistan v West Indies	Bridgetown	1957-58
657-7d	India v Australia	Calcutta	2000-01
656-8d	Australia v England	Manchester	1964
654-5	England v South Africa	Durban	1938-39
653-4d	England v India	Lord's	1990
653-4d	Australia v England	Leeds	1993
652-8d	West Indies v England	Lord's	1973
652	Pakistan v India	Faisalabad	1982-83
652-7d	England v India	Madras	1984-85
652-7d	Australia v South Africa	Johannesburg	2001-02
651	South Africa v Australia	Cape Town	2008-09
650-6d	Australia v West Indies	Bridgetown	1964-65

The highest for Zimbabwe is 563-9d (v WI, Harare, 2001), and for Bangladesh 638 (v SL, Galle, 2012-13).

LOWEST INNINGS TOTALS

† One batsman absent

26	New Zealand v England	Auckland	1954-55
30	South Africa v England	Port Elizabeth	1895-96
30	South Africa v England	Birmingham	1924
35	South Africa v England	Cape Town	1898-99
36	Australia v England	Birmingham	1902
36	South Africa v Australia	Melbourne	1931-32
36	India v Australia	Adelaide	2020-21
38	Ireland v England	Lord's	2019
42	Australia v England	Sydney	1887-88
42	New Zealand v Australia	Wellington	1945-46
42†	India v England	Lord's	1974
43	South Africa v England	Cape Town	1888-89
43	Bangladesh v West Indies	North Sound	2018
44	Australia v England	The Oval	1896
45	England v Australia	Sydney	1886-87
45	South Africa v Australia	Melbourne	1931-32
45	New Zealand v South Africa	Cape Town	2012-13
46	England v West Indies	Port-of-Spain	1993-94
47	South Africa v England	Cape Town	1888-89
47	New Zealand v England	Lord's	1958

47	West Indies v England			Kingston			2003-04		
47	Australia v South Africa			Cape Town			2011-12		
49	Pakistan v South Africa			Johannesburg			2012-13		

The lowest for Sri Lanka is 71 (v P, Kandy, 1994-95) and for Zimbabwe 51 (v NZ, Napier, 2011-12).

BATTING RECORDS
5000 RUNS IN TESTS

Runs			M	I	NO	HS	Avge	100	50
15921	S.R.Tendulkar	I	200	329	33	248*	53.78	51	68
13378	R.T.Ponting	A	168	287	29	257	51.85	41	62
13289	J.H.Kallis	SA/ICC	166	280	40	224	55.37	45	58
13288	R.S.Dravid	I/ICC	164	286	32	270	52.31	36	63
12472	A.N.Cook	E	161	291	16	294	45.35	33	57
12400	K.C.Sangakkara	SL	134	233	17	319	57.40	38	52
11953	B.C.Lara	WI/ICC	131	232	6	400*	52.88	34	48
11867	S.Chanderpaul	WI	164	280	49	203*	51.37	30	66
11814	D.P.M.D.Jayawardena	SL	149	252	15	374	49.84	34	50
11174	A.R.Border	A	156	265	44	205	50.56	27	63
10927	S.R.Waugh	A	168	260	46	200	51.06	32	50
10122	S.M.Gavaskar	I	125	214	16	236*	51.12	34	45
10099	Younus Khan	P	118	213	19	313	52.05	34	33
9282	H.M.Amla	SA	124	215	16	311*	46.64	28	41
9265	G.C.Smith	SA/ICC	117	205	13	277	48.25	27	38
8900	G.A.Gooch	E	118	215	6	333	42.58	20	46
8832	Javed Miandad	P	124	189	21	280*	52.57	23	43
8830	Inzamam-ul-Haq	P/ICC	120	200	22	329	49.60	25	46
8781	V.V.S.Laxman	I	134	225	34	281	45.97	17	56
8765	A.B.de Villiers	SA	114	191	18	278*	50.66	22	46
8643	M.J.Clarke	A	115	198	22	329*	49.10	28	27
8625	M.L.Hayden	A	103	184	14	380	50.73	30	29
8617	J.E.Root	E	103	189	14	254	49.24	20	49
8586	V.Sehwag	I/ICC	104	180	6	319	49.34	23	32
8540	I.V.A.Richards	WI	121	182	12	291	50.23	24	45
8463	A.J.Stewart	E	133	235	21	190	39.54	15	45
8231	D.I.Gower	E	117	204	18	215	44.25	18	39
8181	K.P.Pietersen	E	104	181	8	227	47.28	23	35
8114	G.Boycott	E	108	193	23	246*	47.72	22	42
8032	G.St A.Sobers	WI	93	160	21	365*	57.78	26	30
8029	M.E.Waugh	A	128	209	17	153*	41.81	20	47
7728	M.A.Atherton	E	115	212	7	185*	37.70	16	46
7727	I.R.Bell	E	118	205	24	235	42.69	22	46
7696	J.L.Langer	A	105	182	12	250	45.27	23	30
7624	M.C.Cowdrey	E	114	188	15	182	44.06	22	38
7558	C.G.Greenidge	WI	108	185	16	226	44.72	19	34
7540	S.P.D.Smith	A	77	139	17	239	61.80	27	31
7530	Mohammad Yousuf	P	90	156	12	223	52.29	24	33
7525	M.A.Taylor	A	104	186	13	334*	43.49	19	40
7515	C.H.Lloyd	WI	110	175	14	242*	46.67	19	39
7490	V.Kohli	I	91	153	10	254*	52.37	27	25
7487	D.L.Haynes	WI	116	202	25	184	42.29	18	39
7422	D.C.Boon	A	107	190	20	200	43.65	21	32
7379	L.R.P.L.Taylor	NZ	105	183	22	290	45.83	19	34
7311	D.A.Warner	A	86	159	7	335*	48.09	24	30
7289	G.Kirsten	SA	101	176	15	275	45.27	21	34

Runs			M	I	NO	HS	Avge	100	50
7249	W.R.Hammond	E	85	140	16	336*	58.45	22	24
7214	C.H.Gayle	WI	103	182	11	333	42.18	15	37
7212	S.C.Ganguly	I	113	188	17	239	42.17	16	35
7172	S.P.Fleming	NZ	111	189	10	274*	40.06	9	46
7115	K.S.Williamson	NZ	83	144	13	251	54.31	24	32
7110	G.S.Chappell	A	87	151	19	247*	53.86	24	31
7037	A.J.Strauss	E	100	178	6	177	40.91	21	27
6996	D.G.Bradman	A	52	80	10	334	99.94	29	13
6973	S.T.Jayasuriya	SL	110	188	14	340	40.07	14	31
6971	L.Hutton	E	79	138	15	364	56.67	19	33
6868	D.B.Vengsarkar	I	116	185	22	166	42.13	17	35
6806	K.F.Barrington	E	82	131	15	256	58.67	20	35
6744	G.P.Thorpe	E	100	179	28	200*	44.66	16	39
6453	B.B.McCullum	NZ	101	176	9	302	38.64	12	31
6417	Azhar Ali	P	85	160	10	302*	42.78	17	33
6361	P.A.de Silva	SL	93	159	11	267	42.97	20	22
6244	C.A.Pujara	I	85	142	8	206*	46.59	18	29
6235	M.E.K.Hussey	A	79	137	16	195	51.52	19	29
6227	R.B.Kanhai	WI	79	137	6	256	47.53	15	28
6215	M.Azharuddin	I	99	147	9	199	45.03	22	21
6194	A.D.Mathews	SL	88	158	22	200*	45.54	11	36
6167	H.H.Gibbs	SA	90	154	7	228	41.95	14	26
6149	R.N.Harvey	A	79	137	10	205	48.41	21	24
6080	G.R.Viswanath	I	91	155	10	222	41.93	14	35
5949	R.B.Richardson	WI	86	146	12	194	44.39	16	27
5842	R.R.Sarwan	WI	87	154	8	291	40.01	15	31
5825	M.E.Trescothick	E	76	143	10	219	43.79	14	29
5807	D.C.S.Compton	E	78	131	15	278	50.06	17	28
5768	Salim Malik	P	103	154	22	237	43.69	15	29
5764	N.Hussain	E	96	171	16	207	37.19	14	33
5762	C.L.Hooper	WI	102	173	15	233	36.46	13	27
5719	M.P.Vaughan	E	82	147	9	197	41.44	18	18
5570	A.C.Gilchrist	A	96	137	20	204*	47.60	17	26
5515	M.V.Boucher	SA/ICC	147	206	24	125	30.30	5	35
5502	M.S.Atapattu	SL	90	156	15	249	39.02	16	17
5492	T.M.Dilshan	SL	87	145	11	193	40.98	16	23
5462	T.T.Samaraweera	SL	81	132	20	231	48.76	14	30
5444	M.D.Crowe	NZ	77	131	11	299	45.36	17	18
5410	J.B.Hobbs	E	61	102	7	211	56.94	15	28
5357	K.D.Walters	A	74	125	14	250	48.26	15	33
5345	I.M.Chappell	A	75	136	10	196	42.42	14	26
5334	J.G.Wright	NZ	82	148	7	185	37.82	12	23
5312	M.J.Slater	A	74	131	7	219	42.84	14	21
5248	Kapil Dev	I	131	184	15	163	31.05	8	27
5234	W.M.Lawry	A	67	123	12	210	47.15	13	27
5222	Misbah-ul-Haq	P	75	132	20	161*	46.62	10	39
5200	I.T.Botham	E	102	161	6	208	33.54	14	22
5138	J.H.Edrich	E	77	127	9	310*	43.54	12	24
5105	A.Ranatunga	SL	93	155	12	135*	35.69	4	38
5062	Zaheer Abbas	P	78	124	11	274	44.79	12	20

The most for Zimbabwe is 4794 by A.Flower (112 innings), and for Bangladesh 4537 by Mushfiqur Rahim (134 innings).

750 RUNS IN A SERIES

Runs			Series	M	I	NO	HS	Avge	100	50
974	D.G.Bradman	A v E	1930	5	7	–	334	139.14	4	–
905	W.R.Hammond	E v A	1928-29	5	9	1	251	113.12	4	–
839	M.A.Taylor	A v E	1989	6	11	1	219	83.90	2	5
834	R.N.Harvey	A v SA	1952-53	5	9	–	205	92.66	4	3
829	I.V.A.Richards	WI v E	1976	4	7	–	291	118.42	3	2
827	C.L.Walcott	WI v A	1954-55	5	10	–	155	82.70	5	2
824	G.St A.Sobers	WI v P	1957-58	5	8	2	365*	137.33	3	3
810	D.G.Bradman	A v E	1936-37	5	9	–	270	90.00	3	1
806	D.G.Bradman	A v SA	1931-32	5	5	1	299*	201.50	4	–
798	B.C.Lara	WI v E	1993-94	5	8	–	375	99.75	2	2
779	E.de C.Weekes	WI v I	1948-49	5	7	–	194	111.28	4	2
774	S.M.Gavaskar	I v WI	1970-71	4	8	3	220	154.80	4	3
774	S.P.D.Smith	A v E	2019	4	7	–	211	110.57	3	3
769	S.P.D.Smith	A v I	2014-15	4	8	2	192	128.16	4	2
766	A.N.Cook	E v A	2010-11	5	7	1	235*	127.66	3	2
765	B.C.Lara	WI v E	1995	6	10	1	179	85.00	3	3
761	Mudassar Nazar	P v I	1982-83	6	8	2	231	126.83	4	1
758	D.G.Bradman	A v E	1934	5	8	–	304	94.75	2	1
753	D.C.S.Compton	E v SA	1947	5	8	–	208	94.12	4	2
752	G.A.Gooch	E v I	1990	3	6	–	333	125.33	3	2

HIGHEST INDIVIDUAL INNINGS

400*	B.C.Lara	WI v E	St John's	2003-04
380	M.L.Hayden	A v Z	Perth	2003-04
375	B.C.Lara	WI v E	St John's	1993-94
374	D.P.M.D.Jayawardena	SL v SA	Colombo (SSC)	2006
365*	G.St A.Sobers	WI v P	Kingston	1957-58
364	L.Hutton	E v A	The Oval	1938
340	S.T.Jayasuriya	SL v I	Colombo (RPS)	1997-98
337	Hanif Mohammed	P v WI	Bridgetown	1957-58
336*	W.R.Hammond	E v NZ	Auckland	1932-33
335*	D.A.Warner	A v P	Adelaide	2019-20
334*	M.A.Taylor	A v P	Peshawar	1998-99
334	D.G.Bradman	A v E	Leeds	1930
333	G.A.Gooch	E v I	Lord's	1990
333	C.H.Gayle	WI v SL	Galle	2010-11
329*	M.J.Clarke	A v I	Sydney	2011-12
329	Inzamam-ul-Haq	P v NZ	Lahore	2001-02
325	A.Sandham	E v WI	Kingston	1929-30
319	V.Sehwag	I v SA	Chennai	2007-08
319	K.C.Sangakkara	SL v B	Chittagong	2013-14
317	C.H.Gayle	WI v SA	St John's	2004-05
313	Younus Khan	P v SL	Karachi	2008-09
311*	H.M.Amla	SA v E	The Oval	2012
311	R.B.Simpson	A v E	Manchester	1964
310*	J.H.Edrich	E v NZ	Leeds	1965
309	V.Sehwag	I v P	Multan	2003-04
307	R.M.Cowper	A v E	Melbourne	1965-66
304	D.G.Bradman	A v E	Leeds	1934
303*	K.K.Nair	I v E	Chennai	2016-17
302*	Azhar Ali	P v WI	Dubai (DSC)	2016-17
302	L.G.Rowe	WI v E	Bridgetown	1973-74
302	B.B.McCullum	NZ v I	Wellington	2013-14
299*	D.G.Bradman	A v SA	Adelaide	1931-32

299	M.D.Crowe	NZ v SL	Wellington	1990-91
294	A.N.Cook	E v I	Birmingham	2011
293	V.Sehwag	I v SL	Mumbai	2009-10
291	I.V.A.Richards	WI v E	The Oval	1976
291	R.R.Sarwan	WI v E	Bridgetown	2008-09
290	L.R.P.L.Taylor	NZ v A	Perth	2015-16
287	R.E.Foster	E v A	Sydney	1903-04
287	K.C.Sangakkara	SL v SA	Colombo (SSC)	2006
285*	P.B.H.May	E v WI	Birmingham	1957
281	V.V.S.Laxman	I v A	Calcutta	2000-01
280*	Javed Miandad	P v I	Hyderabad	1982-83
278*	A.B.de Villiers	SA v P	Abu Dhabi	2010-11
278	D.C.S.Compton	E v P	Nottingham	1954
277	B.C.Lara	WI v A	Sydney	1992-93
277	G.C.Smith	SA v E	Birmingham	2003
275*	D.J.Cullinan	SA v NZ	Auckland	1998-99
275	G.Kirsten	SA v E	Durban	1999-00
275	D.P.M.D.Jayawardena	SL v I	Ahmedabad	2009-10
274*	S.P.Fleming	NZ v SL	Colombo (SSC)	2002-03
274	R.G.Pollock	SA v A	Durban	1969-70
274	Zaheer Abbas	P v E	Birmingham	1971
271	Javed Miandad	P v NZ	Auckland	1988-89
270*	G.A.Headley	WI v E	Kingston	1934-35
270	D.G.Bradman	A v E	Melbourne	1936-37
270	R.S.Dravid	I v P	Rawalpindi	2003-04
270	K.C.Sangakkara	SL v Z	Bulawayo	2004
269*	A.C.Voges	A v WI	Hobart	2015-16
268	G.N.Yallop	A v P	Melbourne	1983-84
267*	B.A.Young	NZ v SL	Dunedin	1996-97
267	P.A.de Silva	SL v NZ	Wellington	1990-91
267	Younus Khan	P v I	Bangalore	2004-05
267	Z.Crawley	E v P	Southampton	2020
266	W.H.Ponsford	A v E	The Oval	1934
266	D.L.Houghton	Z v SL	Bulawayo	1994-95
264*	T.W.M.Latham	NZ v SL	Wellington	2018-19
263	A.N.Cook	E v P	Abu Dhabi	2015-16
262*	D.L.Amiss	E v WI	Kingston	1973-74
262	S.P.Fleming	NZ v SA	Cape Town	2005-06
261*	R.R.Sarwan	WI v B	Kingston	2004
261	F.M.M.Worrell	WI v E	Nottingham	1950
260	C.C.Hunte	WI v P	Kingston	1957-58
260	Javed Miandad	P v E	The Oval	1987
260	M.N.Samuels	WI v B	Khulna	2012-13
259*	M.J.Clarke	A v SA	Brisbane	2012-13
259	G.M.Turner	NZ v WI	Georgetown	1971-72
259	G.C.Smith	SA v E	Lord's	2003
258	T.W.Graveney	E v WI	Nottingham	1957
258	S.M.Nurse	WI v NZ	Christchurch	1968-69
258	B.A.Stokes	E v SA	Cape Town	2015-16
257*	Wasim Akram	P v Z	Sheikhupura	1996-97
257	R.T.Ponting	A v I	Melbourne	2003-04
256	R.B.Kanhai	WI v I	Calcutta	1958-59
256	K.F.Barrington	E v A	Manchester	1964
255*	D.J.McGlew	SA v NZ	Wellington	1952-53
254*	V.Kohli	I v SA	Pune	2019-20
254	D.G.Bradman	A v E	Lord's	1930
254	V.Sehwag	I v P	Lahore	2005-06

254	J.E.Root	E v P	Manchester		2016
253*	H.M.Amla	SA v I	Nagpur		2009-10
253	S.T.Jayasuriya	SL v P	Faisalabad		2004-05
253	D.A.Warner	A v NZ	Perth		2015-16
251	W.R.Hammond	E v A	Sydney		1928-29
251	K.S.Williamson	NZ v WI	Hamilton		2020-21
250	K.D.Walters	A v NZ	Christchurch		1976-77
250	S.F.A.F.Bacchus	WI v I	Kanpur		1978-79
250	J.L.Langer	A v E	Melbourne		2002-03

The highest for Bangladesh is 219* by Mushfiqur Rahim (v Z, Dhaka, 2018-19).

20 HUNDREDS

			200	Inn	E	A	SA	WI	NZ	I	P	SL	Z	B
51	S.R.Tendulkar	I	6	329	7	11	7	3	4	–	2	9	3	5
45	J.H.Kallis	SA	2	280	8	5	–	8	6	7	6	1	3	1
41	R.T.Ponting	A	6	287	8	–	8	7	2	8	5	1	1	1
38	K.C.Sangakkara	SL	11	233	3	1	3	3	4	5	10	–	2	7
36	R.S.Dravid	I	5	286	7	2	2	5	6	–	5	3	3	3
34	Younus Khan	P	6	213	4	4	4	3	2	5	–	8	1	3
34	S.M.Gavaskar	I	4	214	4	8	–	13	2	–	5	2	–	–
34	B.C.Lara	WI	9	232	7	9	4	–	1	2	4	5	1	1
34	D.P.M.D.Jayawardena	SL	7	252	8	2	6	1	3	6	2	–	1	5
33	A.N.Cook	E	5	291	–	5	2	6	3	7	5	3	–	2
32	S.R.Waugh	A	1	260	10	–	2	7	2	2	3	3	1	2
30	M.L.Hayden †	A	2	184	5	–	6	5	1	6	1	3	2	–
30	S.Chanderpaul	WI	2	280	5	5	5	–	2	7	1	–	1	4
28	D.G.Bradman	A	12	80	19	–	4	2	–	4	–	–	–	–
28	M.J.Clarke	A	4	198	7	–	5	1	4	7	1	3	–	–
28	H.M.Amla	SA	4	215	6	5	–	1	4	5	2	2	–	3
27	S.P.D.Smith	A	3	139	11	–	1	2	2	8	2	1	–	–
27	V.Kohli	I	7	153	5	7	3	2	3	–	–	5	–	2
27	G.C.Smith	SA	5	205	7	3	–	7	2	–	4	–	1	3
27	A.R.Border	A	2	265	8	–	–	3	5	4	6	1	–	–
26	G.St A.Sobers	WI	2	160	10	4	–	–	1	8	3	–	–	–
25	Inzamam-ul-Haq	P	2	200	5	1	–	4	3	3	–	5	2	2
24	K.S.Williamson	NZ	4	144	3	2	3	3	–	2	4	3	1	3
24	G.S.Chappell	A	4	151	9	–	–	5	3	1	6	–	–	–
24	Mohammad Yousuf	P	4	156	6	1	–	7	1	4	–	1	2	2
24	D.A.Warner	A	2	159	3	–	4	1	3	4	5	–	–	2
24	I.V.A.Richards	WI	3	182	8	5	–	–	1	8	2	–	–	–
23	V.Sehwag	I	6	180	2	3	5	2	2	–	4	5	–	–
23	K.P.Pietersen	E	3	181	–	4	3	3	2	6	2	–	1	2
23	J.L.Langer	A	3	182	5	–	2	3	4	7	3	–	–	–
23	Javed Miandad	P	6	189	2	6	–	2	7	5	–	1	–	–
22	W.R.Hammond	E	7	140	–	9	6	1	4	2	–	–	–	–
22	M.Azharuddin	I	–	147	6	2	–	4	–	2	–	3	5	–
22	M.C.Cowdrey	E	–	188	–	5	3	6	2	3	3	–	–	–
22	A.B.de Villiers	SA	2	191	2	6	–	1	2	3	4	2	–	2
22	G.Boycott	E	1	193	–	7	1	5	2	4	3	–	–	–
21	I.R.Bell	E	1	205	–	4	2	2	1	4	4	2	–	3
21	R.N.Harvey	A	2	137	6	–	8	3	–	4	–	–	–	–
21	G.Kirsten	SA	3	176	5	2	–	2	3	2	2	1	1	2
21	A.J.Strauss	E	–	178	–	4	3	6	3	3	2	–	–	–
21	D.C.Boon	A	1	190	3	–	3	3	6	1	1	–	–	–
20	K.F.Barrington	E	1	131	–	5	2	3	3	3	4	–	–	–

			200	Inn	E	A	SA	WI	NZ	I	P	SL	Z	B
20	P.A.de Silva	SL	2	159	2	1	–	–	2	5	8	–	1	1
20	J.E.Root	E	5	189	–	3	2	3	2	5	1	4	–	–
20	M.E.Waugh	A	–	209	6	–	4	4	1	1	3	1	–	–
20	G.A.Gooch	E	2	215	–	4	–	5	4	5	1	1	–	–

† Includes century scored for Australia v ICC in 2005-06.

The most for Zimbabwe 12 by A.Flower (112), and for Bangladesh 10 by Mominul Haque (78).

The most double hundreds by batsmen not included above are 6 by M.S.Atapattu (16 hundreds for Sri Lanka), 4 by L.Hutton (19 for England), 4 by C.G.Greenidge (19 for West Indies), 4 by Zaheer Abbas (12 for Pakistan), and 4 by B.B.McCullum (12 for New Zealand).

HIGHEST PARTNERSHIP FOR EACH WICKET

1st	415	N.D.McKenzie/G.C.Smith	SA v B	Chittagong	2007-08
2nd	576	S.T.Jayasuriya/R.S.Mahanama	SL v I	Colombo (RPS)	1997-98
3rd	624	K.C.Sangakkara/D.P.M.D.Jayawardena	SL v SA	Colombo (SSC)	2006
4th	449	A.C.Voges/S.E.Marsh	A v WI	Hobart	2015-16
5th	405	S.G.Barnes/D.G.Bradman	A v E	Sydney	1946-47
6th	399	B.A.Stokes/J.M.Bairstow	E v SA	Cape Town	2015-16
7th	347	D.St E.Atkinson/C.C.Depeiza	WI v A	Bridgetown	1954-55
8th	332	I.J.L.Trott/S.C.J.Broad	E v P	Lord's	2010
9th	195	M.V.Boucher/P.L.Symcox	SA v P	Johannesburg	1997-98
10th	198	J.E.Root/J.M.Anderson	E v I	Nottingham	2014

BOWLING RECORDS

200 WICKETS IN TESTS

Wkts			M	Balls	Runs	Avge	5 wI	10 wM
800	M.Muralitharan	SL/ICC	133	44039	18180	22.72	67	22
708	S.K.Warne	A	145	40705	17995	25.41	37	10
619	A.Kumble	I	132	40850	18355	29.65	35	8
614	J.M.Anderson	E	160	34326	16251	26.46	30	3
563	G.D.McGrath	A	124	29248	12186	21.64	29	3
519	C.A.Walsh	WI	132	30019	12688	24.44	22	3
517	S.C.J.Broad	E	146	29316	14328	27.71	18	3
439	D.W.Steyn	SA	93	18608	10077	22.95	26	5
434	Kapil Dev	I	131	27740	12867	29.64	23	2
433	H.M.R.K.B.Herath	SL	93	25993	12157	28.07	34	9
431	R.J.Hadlee	NZ	86	21918	9612	22.30	36	9
421	S.M.Pollock	SA	108	24453	9733	23.11	16	1
417	Harbhajan Singh	I	103	28580	13537	32.46	25	5
414	Wasim Akram	P	104	22627	9779	23.62	25	5
409	R.Ashwin	I	78	21520	10099	24.69	30	7
405	C.E.L.Ambrose	WI	98	22104	8500	20.98	22	3
399	N.M.Lyon	A	100	25690	12816	32.12	18	3
390	M.Ntini	SA	101	20834	11242	28.82	18	4
383	I.T.Botham	E	102	21815	10878	28.40	27	4
376	M.D.Marshall	WI	81	17584	7876	20.94	22	4
373	Waqar Younis	P	87	16224	8788	23.56	22	5
362	Imran Khan	P	88	19458	8258	22.81	23	6
362	D.L.Vettori	NZ/ICC	113	28814	12441	34.36	20	3
355	D.K.Lillee	A	70	18467	8493	23.92	23	7
355	W.P.J.U.C.Vaas	SL	111	23438	10501	29.58	12	2
330	A.A.Donald	SA	72	15519	7344	22.25	20	3
325	R.G.D.Willis	E	90	17357	8190	25.20	16	–
313	M.G.Johnson	A	73	16001	8891	28.40	12	3
311	Z.Khan	I	92	18785	10247	32.94	11	1

Wkts			M	Balls	Runs	Avge	5 wI	10 wM
310	B.Lee	A	76	16531	9554	30.81	10	–
309	M.Morkel	SA	86	16498	8550	27.66	8	–
309	L.R.Gibbs	WI	79	27115	8989	29.09	18	2
307	F.S.Trueman	E	67	15178	6625	21.57	17	3
303	I.Sharma	I	101	18504	9780	32.27	11	1
302	T.G.Southee	NZ	77	17387	8670	28.70	11	1
297	D.L.Underwood	E	86	21862	7674	25.83	17	6
292	J.H.Kallis	SA/ICC	166	20232	9535	32.65	5	–
291	C.J.McDermott	A	71	16586	8332	28.63	14	2
281	T.A.Boult	NZ	71	15819	7875	28.02	8	1
266	B.S.Bedi	I	67	21364	7637	28.71	14	1
261	Danish Kaneria	P	61	17697	9082	34.79	15	2
259	J.Garner	WI	58	13169	5433	20.97	7	–
259	J.N.Gillespie	A	71	14234	6770	26.13	8	–
255	M.A.Starc	A	61	12575	7031	27.57	13	2
255	G.P.Swann	E	60	15349	7642	29.96	17	3
252	J.B.Statham	E	70	16056	6261	24.84	9	1
249	M.A.Holding	WI	60	12680	5898	23.68	13	2
248	R.Benaud	A	63	19108	6704	27.03	16	1
248	M.J.Hoggard	E	67	13909	7564	30.50	7	1
246	G.D.McKenzie	A	60	17681	7328	29.78	16	3
242	B.S.Chandrasekhar	I	58	15963	7199	29.74	16	2
236	A.V.Bedser	E	51	15918	5876	24.89	15	5
236	J.Srinath	I	67	15104	7196	30.49	10	1
236	Abdul Qadir	P	67	17126	7742	32.80	15	5
235	Yasir Shah	P	45	13601	7247	30.83	16	3
235	G.St A.Sobers	WI	93	21599	7999	34.03	6	–
234	A.R.Caddick	E	62	13558	6999	29.91	13	1
233	C.S.Martin	NZ	71	14026	7878	33.81	10	1
229	D.Gough	E	58	11821	6503	28.39	9	–
228	R.R.Lindwall	A	61	13650	5251	23.03	12	–
226	S.J.Harmison	E/ICC	63	13375	7192	31.82	8	1
226	A.Flintoff	E/ICC	79	14951	7410	32.78	3	–
224	V.D.Philander	SA	64	11391	5000	22.32	13	2
221	P.M.Siddle	A	67	13907	6777	30.66	8	–
220	R.A.Jadeja	I	51	13137	5351	24.32	9	1
219	N.Wagner	NZ	51	11385	5766	26.32	9	–
218	C.L.Cairns	NZ	62	11698	6410	29.40	13	1
216	C.V.Grimmett	A	37	14513	5231	24.21	21	7
216	H.H.Streak	Z	65	13559	6079	28.14	7	–
212	M.G.Hughes	A	53	12285	6017	28.38	7	1
210	Shakib Al Hasan	B	57	13056	6553	31.20	18	2
208	S.C.G.MacGill	A	44	11237	6038	29.02	12	2
208	Saqlain Mushtaq	P	49	14070	6206	29.83	13	3
205	K.A.J.Roach	WI	61	11062	5721	27.90	9	1
202	K.Rabada	SA	45	8431	4720	23.36	9	4
202	A.M.E.Roberts	WI	47	11136	5174	25.61	11	2
202	J.A.Snow	E	49	12021	5387	26.66	8	1
200	J.R.Thomson	A	51	10535	5601	28.00	8	1

35 OR MORE WICKETS IN A SERIES

Wkts			Series	M	Balls	Runs	Avge	5 wI	10 wM
49	S.F.Barnes	E v SA	1913-14	4	1356	536	10.93	7	3
46	J.C.Laker	E v A	1956	5	1703	442	9.60	4	2
44	C.V.Grimmett	A v SA	1935-36	5	2077	642	14.59	5	3
42	T.M.Alderman	A v E	1981	6	1950	893	21.26	4	–
41	R.M.Hogg	A v E	1978-79	6	1740	527	12.85	5	2
41	T.M.Alderman	A v E	1989	6	1616	712	17.36	6	1
40	Imran Khan	P v I	1982-83	6	1339	558	13.95	4	2

Wkts		Series	M	Balls	Runs	Avge	5 wI	10 wM
40	S.K.Warne	A v E	2005	5	1517	797	19.92	3	2
39	A.V.Bedser	E v A	1953	5	1591	682	17.48	5	1
39	D.K.Lillee	A v E	1981	6	1870	870	22.30	2	1
38	M.W.Tate	E v A	1924-25	5	2528	881	23.18	5	1
37	W.J.Whitty	A v SA	1910-11	5	1395	632	17.08	2	
37	H.J.Tayfield	SA v E	1956-57	5	2280	636	17.18	4	1
37	M.G.Johnson	A v E	2013-14	5	1132	517	13.97	3	
36	A.E.E.Vogler	SA v E	1909-10	5	1349	783	21.75	4	1
36	A.A.Mailey	A v E	1920-21	5	1465	946	26.27	4	2
36	G.D.McGrath	A v E	1997	6	1499	701	19.47	2	
35	G.A.Lohmann	E v SA	1895-96	3	520	203	5.80	4	2
35	B.S.Chandrasekhar	I v E	1972-73	5	1747	662	18.91	4	
35	M.D.Marshall	WI v E	1988	5	1219	443	12.65	3	1

The most for New Zealand is 33 by R.J.Hadlee (3 Tests v A, 1985-86), for Sri Lanka 30 by M.Muralitharan (3 Tests v Z, 2001-02), for Zimbabwe 22 by H.H.Streak (3 Tests v P, 1994-95), and for Bangladesh 19 by Mehedi Hasan (2 Tests v E, 2016-17).

15 OR MORE WICKETS IN A TEST († On debut)

19- 90	J.C.Laker	E v A	Manchester	1956
17-159	S.F.Barnes	E v SA	Johannesburg	1913-14
16-136†	N.D.Hirwani	I v WI	Madras	1987-88
16-137†	R.A.L.Massie	A v E	Lord's	1972
16-220	M.Muralitharan	SL v E	The Oval	1998
15- 28	J.Briggs	E v SA	Cape Town	1888-89
15- 45	G.A.Lohmann	E v SA	Port Elizabeth	1895-96
15- 99	C.Blythe	E v SA	Leeds	1907
15-104	H.Verity	E v A	Lord's	1934
15-123	R.J.Hadlee	NZ v A	Brisbane	1985-86
15-124	W.Rhodes	E v A	Melbourne	1903-04
15-217	Harbhajan Singh	I v A	Madras	2000-01

The best analysis for South Africa is 13-132 by M.Ntini (v WI, Port-of-Spain, 2004-05), for West Indies 14-149 by M.A.Holding (v E, The Oval, 1976), for Pakistan 14-116 by Imran Khan (v SL, Lahore, 1981-82), for Zimbabwe 11-257 by A.G.Huckle (v NZ, Bulawayo, 1997-98), and for Bangladesh 12-117 by Mehedi Hasan (v WI, Dhaka, 2018-19).

NINE OR MORE WICKETS IN AN INNINGS

10- 53	J.C.Laker	E v A	Manchester	1956
10- 74	A.Kumble	I v P	Delhi	1998-99
9- 28	G.A.Lohmann	E v SA	Johannesburg	1895-96
9- 37	J.C.Laker	E v A	Manchester	1956
9- 51	M.Muralitharan	SL v Z	Kandy	2001-02
9- 52	R.J.Hadlee	NZ v A	Brisbane	1985-86
9- 56	Abdul Qadir	P v E	Lahore	1987-88
9- 57	D.E.Malcolm	E v SA	The Oval	1994
9- 65	M.Muralitharan	SL v E	The Oval	1998
9- 69	J.M.Patel	I v A	Kanpur	1959-60
9- 83	Kapil Dev	I v WI	Ahmedabad	1983-84
9- 86	Sarfraz Nawaz	P v A	Melbourne	1978-79
9- 95	J.M.Noreiga	WI v I	Port-of-Spain	1970-71
9-102	S.P.Gupte	I v WI	Kanpur	1958-59
9-103	S.F.Barnes	E v SA	Johannesburg	1913-14
9-113	H.J.Tayfield	SA v E	Johannesburg	1956-57

9-121	A.A.Mailey	A v E	Melbourne	1920-21
9-127	H.M.R.K.B.Herath	SL v P	Colombo (SSC)	2014
9-129	K.A.Maharaj	SA v SL	Colombo (SSC)	2018

The best analysis for Zimbabwe is 8-109 by P.A.Strang (v NZ, Bulawayo, 2000-01), and for Bangladesh 8-39 by Taijul Islam (v Z, Dhaka, 2014-15).

HAT-TRICKS

F.R.Spofforth	Australia v England	Melbourne	1878-79
W.Bates	England v Australia	Melbourne	1882-83
J.Briggs[7]	England v Australia	Sydney	1891-92
G.A.Lohmann	England v South Africa	Port Elizabeth	1895-96
J.T.Hearne	England v Australia	Leeds	1899
H.Trumble	Australia v England	Melbourne	1901-02
H.Trumble	Australia v England	Melbourne	1903-04
T.J.Matthews (2)[2]	Australia v South Africa	Manchester	1912
M.J.C.Allom[1]	England v New Zealand	Christchurch	1929-30
T.W.J.Goddard	England v South Africa	Johannesburg	1938-39
P.J.Loader	England v West Indies	Leeds	1957
L.F.Kline	Australia v South Africa	Cape Town	1957-58
W.W.Hall	West Indies v Pakistan	Lahore	1958-59
G.M.Griffin[7]	South Africa v England	Lord's	1960
L.R.Gibbs	West Indies v Australia	Adelaide	1960-61
P.J.Petherick[1/7]	New Zealand v Pakistan	Lahore	1976-77
C.A.Walsh[3]	West Indies v Australia	Brisbane	1988-89
M.G.Hughes[3/7]	Australia v West Indies	Perth	1988-89
D.W.Fleming[1]	Australia v Pakistan	Rawalpindi	1994-95
S.K.Warne	Australia v England	Melbourne	1994-95
D.G.Cork	England v West Indies	Manchester	1995
D.Gough[7]	England v Australia	Sydney	1998-99
Wasim Akram[4]	Pakistan v Sri Lanka	Lahore	1998-99
Wasim Akram[4]	Pakistan v Sri Lanka	Dhaka	1998-99
D.N.T.Zoysa[5]	Sri Lanka v Zimbabwe	Harare	1999-00
Abdul Razzaq	Pakistan v Sri Lanka	Galle	2000-01
G.D.McGrath	Australia v West Indies	Perth	2000-01
Harbhajan Singh	India v Australia	Calcutta	2000-01
Mohammad Sami[7]	Pakistan v Sri Lanka	Lahore	2001-02
J.J.C.Lawson[7]	West Indies v Australia	Bridgetown	2002-03
Alok Kapali	Bangladesh v Pakistan	Peshawar	2003
A.M.Blignaut	Zimbabwe v Bangladesh	Harare	2003-04
M.J.Hoggard	England v West Indies	Bridgetown	2003-04
J.E.C.Franklin	New Zealand v Bangladesh	Dhaka	2004-05
I.K.Pathan[6/7]	India v Pakistan	Karachi	2005-06
R.J.Sidebottom[7]	England v New Zealand	Hamilton	2007-08
P.M.Siddle	Australia v England	Brisbane	2010-11
S.C.J.Broad	England v India	Nottingham	2011
Sohag Gazi	Bangladesh v New Zealand	Chittagong	2013-14
S.C.J.Broad[7]	England v Sri Lanka	Leeds	2014
H.M.R.K.B.Herath	Sri Lanka v Australia	Galle	2016
M.M.Ali	England v South Africa	The Oval	2017
J.J.Bumrah	India v West Indies	Kingston	2019
Naseem Shah	Pakistan v Bangladesh	Rawalpindi	2019-20

[1] On debut. [2] Hat-trick in each innings. [3] Involving both innings. [4] In successive Tests. [5] His first 3 balls (second over of the match). [6] The fourth, fifth and sixth balls of the match. [7] On losing side.

WICKET-KEEPING RECORDS
150 DISMISSALS IN TESTS†

Total			Tests	Ct	St
555	M.V.Boucher	South Africa/ICC	147	532	23
416	A.C.Gilchrist	Australia	96	379	37
395	I.A.Healy	Australia	119	366	29
355	R.W.Marsh	Australia	96	343	12
294	M.S.Dhoni	India	90	256	38
270	B.J.Haddin	Australia	66	262	8
270†	P.J.L.Dujon	West Indies	81	265	5
269	A.P.E.Knott	England	95	250	19
257	B.J.Watling	New Zealand	73	249	8
256	M.J.Prior	England	79	243	13
241†	A.J.Stewart	England	133	227	14
228	Wasim Bari	Pakistan	81	201	27
219	Q.de Kock	South Africa	51	208	11
219	R.D.Jacobs	West Indies	65	207	12
219	T.G.Evans	England	91	173	46
217	D.Ramdin	West Indies	74	205	12
206	Kamran Akmal	Pakistan	53	184	22
201†	A.C.Parore	New Zealand	78	194	7
198	S.M.H.Kirmani	India	88	160	38
189	D.L.Murray	West Indies	62	181	8
187	A.T.W.Grout	Australia	51	163	24
186†	J.M.Bairstow	England	74	173	13
179†	B.B.McCullum	New Zealand	101	168	11
176	I.D.S.Smith	New Zealand	63	168	8
174	R.W.Taylor	England	57	167	7
167	Sarfraz Ahmed	Pakistan	49	146	21
165	R.C.Russell	England	54	153	12
157	T.D.Paine	Australia	35	150	7
156	H.A.P.W.Jayawardena	Sri Lanka	58	124	32
152	D.J.Richardson	South Africa	42	150	2
151†	K.C.Sangakkara	Sri Lanka	134	131	20
151†	A.Flower	Zimbabwe	63	142	9

The most for Bangladesh is 113 (98 ct, 15 st) by Mushfiqur Rahim in 72 Tests.
† Excluding catches taken in the field

25 OR MORE DISMISSALS IN A SERIES

29	B.J.Haddin	Australia v England	2013
28	R.W.Marsh	Australia v England	1982-83
27 (inc 2st)	R.C.Russell	England v South Africa	1995-96
27 (inc 2st)	I.A.Healy	Australia v England (6 Tests)	1997
26 (inc 3st)	J.H.B.Waite	South Africa v New Zealand	1961-62
26	R.W.Marsh	Australia v West Indies (6 Tests)	1975-76
26 (inc 5st)	I.A.Healy	Australia v England (6 Tests)	1993
26 (inc 1st)	M.V.Boucher	South Africa v England	1998
26 (inc 2st)	A.C.Gilchrist	Australia v England	2001
26 (inc 2st)	A.C.Gilchrist	Australia v England	2006-07
26 (inc 1st)	T.D.Paine	Australia v England	2017-18
25 (inc 2st)	I.A.Healy	Australia v England	1994-95
25 (inc 2st)	A.C.Gilchrist	Australia v England	2002-03
25	A.C.Gilchrist	Australia v India	2007-08

TEN OR MORE DISMISSALS IN A TEST

11	R.C.Russell	England v South Africa	Johannesburg	1995-96
11	A.B.de Villiers	South Africa v Pakistan	Johannesburg	2012-13
11	R.R.Pant	India v Australia	Adelaide	2018-19
10	R.W.Taylor	England v India	Bombay	1979-80
10	A.C.Gilchrist	Australia v New Zealand	Hamilton	1999-00
10	W.P.Saha	India v South Africa	Cape Town	2017-18
10	Sarfraz Ahmed	Pakistan v South Africa	Johannesburg	2018-19

SEVEN DISMISSALS IN AN INNINGS

7	Wasim Bari	Pakistan v New Zealand	Auckland	1978-79
7	R.W.Taylor	England v India	Bombay	1979-80
7	I.D.S.Smith	New Zealand v Sri Lanka	Hamilton	1990-91
7	R.D.Jacobs	West Indies v Australia	Melbourne	2000-01

FIVE STUMPINGS IN AN INNINGS

5	K.S.More	India v West Indies	Madras	1987-88

FIELDING RECORDS
100 CATCHES IN TESTS

Total			Tests	Total			Tests
210	R.S.Dravid	India/ICC	164	122	G.S.Chappell	Australia	87
205	D.P.M.D.Jayawardena	Sri Lanka	149	122	I.V.A.Richards	West Indies	121
200	J.H.Kallis	South Africa/ICC	166	121†	A.B.de Villiers	South Africa	114
196	R.T.Ponting	Australia	168	121	A.J.Strauss	England	100
181	M.E.Waugh	Australia	128	120	I.T.Botham	England	102
175	A.N.Cook	England	161	120	M.C.Cowdrey	England	114
171	S.P.Fleming	New Zealand	111	115	C.L.Hooper	West Indies	102
169	G.C.Smith	South Africa/ICC	117	115	S.R.Tendulkar	India	200
164	B.C.Lara	West Indies/ICC	131	112	S.R.Waugh	Australia	168
157	M.A.Taylor	Australia	104	110	R.B.Simpson	Australia	62
156	A.R.Border	Australia	156	110	W.R.Hammond	England	85
155	L.R.P.L.Taylor	New Zealand	105	109	G.St A.Sobers	West Indies	93
139	Younus Khan	Pakistan	118	108	H.M.Amla	South Africa	124
135	V.V.S.Laxman	India	134	108	S.M.Gavaskar	India	125
134	J.E.Root	England	103	105	I.M.Chappell	Australia	75
134	M.J.Clarke	Australia	115	105	M.Azharuddin	India	99
128	M.L.Hayden	Australia	103	105	G.P.Thorpe	England	100
125	S.K.Warne	Australia	145	103	G.A.Gooch	England	118
123	S.P.D.Smith	Australia	77	100	I.R.Bell	England	118

The most for Zimbabwe is 60 by A.D.R.Campbell (60) and for Bangladesh 38 by Mahmudullah (49).

† *Excluding catches taken when wicket-keeping.*

15 CATCHES IN A SERIES

15	J.M.Gregory	Australia v England		1920-21

SEVEN OR MORE CATCHES IN A TEST

8	A.M.Rahane	India v Sri Lanka	Galle	2015
7	G.S.Chappell	Australia v England	Perth	1974-75
7	Yajurvindra Singh	India v England	Bangalore	1976-77
7	H.P.Tillekeratne	Sri Lanka v New Zealand	Colombo (SSC)	1992-93
7	S.P.Fleming	New Zealand v Zimbabwe	Harare	1997-98
7	M.L.Hayden	Australia v Sri Lanka	Galle	2003-04
7	K.L.Rahul	India v England	Nottingham	2018

FIVE CATCHES IN AN INNINGS

5	V.Y.Richardson	Australia v South Africa	Durban	1935-36
5	Yajurvindra Singh	India v England	Bangalore	1976-77
5	M.Azharuddin	India v Pakistan	Karachi	1989-90
5	K.Srikkanth	India v Australia	Perth	1991-92
5	S.P.Fleming	New Zealand v Zimbabwe	Harare	1997-98
5	G.C.Smith	South Africa v Australia	Perth	2012-13
5	D.J.G.Sammy	West Indies v India	Mumbai	2013-14
5	D.M.Bravo	West Indies v Bangladesh	Kingstown	2014
5	A.M.Rahane	India v Sri Lanka	Galle	2015
5	J.Blackwood	West Indies v Sri Lanka	Colombo (PSS)	2015-16
5	S.P.D.Smith	Australia v South Africa	Cape Town	2017-18
5	B.A.Stokes	England v South Africa	Cape Town	2019-20
5	H.D.R.L.Thirimanne	Sri Lanka v England	Galle	2020-21

APPEARANCE RECORDS

100 TEST MATCH APPEARANCES

Opponents

			E	A	SA	WI	NZ	I	P	SL	Z	B
200	S.R.Tendulkar	India	32	39	25	21	24	–	18	25	9	7
168†	R.T.Ponting	Australia	35	–	26	24	17	29	15	14	3	4
168	S.R.Waugh	Australia	46	–	16	32	23	18	20	8	3	2
166†	J.H.Kallis	South Africa/ICC	31	28	–	24	18	18	19	15	6	6
164	S.Chanderpaul	West Indies	35	20	24	–	21	25	14	7	8	10
164†	R.S.Dravid	India/ICC	21	32	21	23	15	–	15	20	9	7
161	A.N.Cook	England	–	35	19	20	15	30	20	16	–	6
160	J.M.Anderson	England	–	32	26	22	14	30	18	14	2	2
156	A.R.Border	Australia	47	–	6	31	23	20	22	7	–	–
149	D.P.M.D.Jayawardena	Sri Lanka	23	16	18	11	13	18	29	–	8	13
147†	M.V.Boucher	South Africa/ICC	25	20	–	24	17	14	15	17	6	8
146*	S.C.J.Broad	England	–	32	22	19	16	22	19	12	–	3
145†	S.K.Warne	Australia	36	–	24	19	20	14	15	13	1	2
134	V.V.S.Laxman	India	17	29	19	22	10	–	15	13	6	3
134	K.C.Sangakkara	Sri Lanka	22	11	17	12	12	17	23	–	5	15
133†	M.Muralitharan	Sri Lanka/ICC	16	12	15	12	14	22	16	–	14	11
133	A.J.Stewart	England	–	33	23	24	16	9	13	9	6	–
132	A.Kumble	India	19	20	21	17	11	–	15	18	7	4
132	C.A.Walsh	West Indies	36	38	10	–	10	15	18	3	2	–
131	Kapil Dev	India	27	20	4	25	10	–	29	14	2	–
131†	B.C.Lara	West Indies/ICC	30	30	18	–	11	17	12	8	2	3
128	M.E.Waugh	Australia	29	–	18	28	14	14	15	9	1	–
125	S.M.Gavaskar	India	38	20	–	27	9	–	24	7	–	–
124	H.M.Amla	South Africa	21	21	–	9	14	21	14	14	2	8
124	Javed Miandad	Pakistan	22	24	–	17	18	28	–	12	3	–
124†	G.D.McGrath	Australia	30	–	17	23	14	11	17	8	1	2
121	I.V.A.Richards	West Indies	36	34	–	–	7	28	16	–	–	–
120†	Inzamam-ul-Haq	Pakistan/ICC	19	13	13	15	12	10	–	20	11	6
119	I.A.Healy	Australia	33	–	12	28	11	9	14	11	1	–
118	I.R.Bell	England	–	33	11	12	13	20	13	10	–	6
118	G.A.Gooch	England	–	42	3	26	15	19	10	3	–	–
118	Younus Khan	Pakistan	17	11	14	15	11	9	–	29	5	7
117	D.I.Gower	England	–	42	–	19	13	24	17	2	–	–
117†	G.C.Smith	South Africa/ICC	21	21	–	14	13	15	16	7	2	8
116	D.L.Haynes	West Indies	36	33	1	–	10	19	16	1	–	–
114	D.B.Vengsarkar	India	26	24	–	25	11	–	22	8	–	–
115	M.A.Atherton	England	–	33	13	28	17	11	7	11	4	4
115†	M.J.Clarke	Australia	35	–	14	12	11	22	10	8	–	2

Opponents

			E	A	SA	WI	NZ	I	P	SL	Z	B
114	M.C.Cowdrey	England	–	43	14	21	18	8	10	–	–	
114	A.B.de Villiers	South Africa	20	24	–	13	10	20	12	7	4	4
113	S.C.Ganguly	India	12	24	17	12	8	–	12	14	9	5
113†	D.L.Vettori	New Zealand/ICC	17	18	14	10	–	15	9	11	9	5
111	S.P.Fleming	New Zealand	19	14	15	11	–	13	9	13	11	6
111	W.P.J.U.C.Vaas	Sri Lanka	15	12	11	9	10	14	18	–	15	7
110	S.T.Jayasuriya	Sri Lanka	14	13	15	10	13	10	17	–	13	5
110	C.H.Lloyd	West Indies	34	29	–	–	8	28	11	–	–	–
108	G.Boycott	England	–	38	7	29	13	13	6	–	–	–
108	C.G.Greenidge	West Indies	29	32	–	–	10	23	14	–	–	–
108	S.M.Pollock	South Africa	23	13	–	16	11	12	12	13	5	3
107	D.C.Boon	Australia	31	–	6	22	17	11	11	9	–	–
105†	J.L.Langer	Australia	21	–	11	18	14	14	11	3	–	2
105	L.R.P.L.Taylor	New Zealand	17	12	8	14	–	14	15	12	4	9
104	K.P.Pietersen	England	–	27	10	14	8	16	14	11	–	4
104†	V.Sehwag	India/ICC	17	23	15	10	12	–	9	11	3	4
104	M.A.Taylor	Australia	33	–	11	20	11	9	12	8	–	–
104	Wasim Akram	Pakistan	18	13	4	17	9	12	–	19	10	2
103	C.H.Gayle	West Indies	20	8	16	–	12	14	8	10	8	7
103	Harbhajan Singh	India	14	18	11	11	13	–	9	16	7	4
103†	M.L.Hayden	Australia	20	–	19	15	11	18	6	7	2	4
103	Salim Malik	Pakistan	19	15	1	7	18	22	–	15	6	–
103*	J.E.Root	England	–	24	12	11	11	20	12	10	–	2
102	I.T.Botham	England	–	36	–	20	15	14	14	3	–	–
102	C.L.Hooper	West Indies	24	25	10	–	2	19	14	6	2	–
101	G.Kirsten	South Africa	22	18	–	13	13	10	11	9	3	2
101	B.B.McCullum	New Zealand	16	16	13	13	–	10	8	12	4	9
101	M.Ntini	South Africa	18	15	–	15	11	10	9	12	3	8
101‡	I.Sharma	India	21	25	15	12	7	–	1	12	–	7
100	A.J.Strauss	England	–	20	16	18	9	12	13	8	–	4
100	G.P.Thorpe	England	–	16	16	27	13	5	8	9	2	4
100	N.M.Lyon	Australia	23	–	15	8	10	22	9	11	–	2

† Includes appearance in the Australia v ICC 'Test' in 2005-06; * includes appearance v Ireland in 2019; ‡ includes appearance v Afghanistan in 2018. The most for Zimbabwe is 67 by G.W.Flower, and for Bangladesh 70 by Mushfiqur Rahim.

100 CONSECUTIVE TEST APPEARANCES

159	A.N.Cook	England	May 2006 to September 2018
153	A.R.Border	Australia	March 1979 to March 1994
107	M.E.Waugh	Australia	June 1993 to October 2002
106	S.M.Gavaskar	India	January 1975 to February 1987
101	B.B.McCullum	New Zealand	March 2004 to February 2016

50 TESTS AS CAPTAIN

			Won	Lost	Drawn	Tied
109	G.C.Smith	South Africa	53	29	27	–
93	A.R.Border	Australia	32	22	38	1
80	S.P.Fleming	New Zealand	28	27	25	–
77	R.T.Ponting	Australia	48	16	13	–
74	C.H.Lloyd	West Indies	36	12	26	–
60	M.S.Dhoni	India	27	18	15	–
60	V.Kohli	India	36	14	10	–
59	A.N.Cook	England	24	22	13	–
57	S.R.Waugh	Australia	41	9	7	–

			Won	Lost	Drawn	Tied
56	Misbah-ul-Haq	Pakistan	26	19	11	–
56	A.Ranatunga	Sri Lanka	12	19	25	–
54	M.A.Atherton	England	13	21	20	–
53	W.J.Cronje	South Africa	27	11	15	–
51	M.P.Vaughan	England	26	11	14	–
50	I.V.A.Richards	West Indies	27	8	15	–
50	M.A.Taylor	Australia	26	13	11	–
50	A.J.Strauss	England	24	11	15	–
50	J.E.Root	England	26	18	6	–

The most for Zimbabwe is 21 by A.D.R.Campbell and H.H.Streak, and for Bangladesh 34 by Mushfiqur Rahim.

65 TEST UMPIRING APPEARANCES

135	Alim Dar	(Pakistan)	21.10.2003 to 03.03.2021
128	S.A.Bucknor	(West Indies)	28.04.1989 to 22.03.2009
108	R.E.Koertzen	(South Africa)	26.12.1992 to 24.07.2010
95	D.J.Harper	(Australia)	28.11.1998 to 23.06.2011
92	D.R.Shepherd	(England)	01.08.1985 to 07.06.2005
84	B.F.Bowden	(New Zealand)	11.03.2000 to 03.05.2015
78	D.B.Hair	(Australia)	25.01.1992 to 08.06.2008
74	I.J.Gould	(England)	19.11.2008 to 23.02.2019
74	S.J.A.Taufel	(Australia)	26.12.2000 to 20.08.2012
73	S.Venkataraghavan	(India)	29.01.1993 to 20.01.2004
71	R.J.Tucker	(Australia)	15.02.2010 to 27.01.2020

THE FIRST-CLASS COUNTIES
REGISTER, RECORDS AND 2020 AVERAGES

All statistics are to 9 March 2021.

ABBREVIATIONS – General

*	not out/unbroken partnership	IT20	International Twenty20
b	born	l-o	limited-overs
BB	Best innings bowling analysis	LOI	Limited-Overs Internationals
Cap	Awarded 1st XI County Cap	Tests	International Test Matches
f-c	first-class	F-c Tours	Overseas tours involving first-class
HS	Highest Score		appearances

Awards

PCA 2020	Professional Cricketers' Association Player of 2020
Wisden 2019	One of Wisden Cricketers' Almanack's Five Cricketers of 2019
YC 2020	Cricket Writers' Club Young Cricketer of 2020

ECB Competitions

CB40	Clydesdale Bank 40 (2010-12)
CC	County Championship
CGT	Cheltenham & Gloucester Trophy (2001-06)
FPT	Friends Provident Trophy (2007-09)
NL	National League (1999-2005)
P40	NatWest PRO 40 League (2006-09)
RLC	Royal London One-Day Cup (2014-19)
T20	Twenty20 Competition
Y40	Yorkshire Bank 40 (2013)

Education

Ac	Academy
BHS	Boys' High School
C	College
CS	Comprehensive School
GS	Grammar School
HS	High School
I	Institute
S	School
SFC	Sixth Form College
SS	Secondary School
TC	Technical College
U	University

Playing Categories

LBG	Bowls right-arm leg-breaks and googlies
LF	Bowls left-arm fast
LFM	Bowls left-arm fast-medium
LHB	Bats left-handed
LM	Bowls left-arm medium pace
LMF	Bowls left-arm medium fast
OB	Bowls right-arm off-breaks
RF	Bowls right-arm fast
RFM	Bowls right-arm fast-medium
RHB	Bats right-handed
RM	Bowls right-arm medium pace
RMF	Bowls right-arm medium-fast
SLA	Bowls left-arm leg-breaks
SLC	Bowls left-arm 'Chinamen'
WK	Wicket-keeper

Teams (see also p 209)

AS	Adelaide Strikers
BH	Brisbane Heat
BMT	Bulawayo Metropolitan Tuskers
CC&C	Combined Campuses & Colleges
CD	Central Districts
CSK	Chennai Super Kings

DC	Deccan Chargers
DCa	Delhi Capitals
DD	Delhi Daredevils
EL	England Lions
EP	Eastern Province
GW	Griqualand West
HB	Habib Bank Limited
HME	Harare Metropolitan Eagles
HH	Hobart Hurricanes
KKR	Kolkata Knight Riders
KRL	Khan Research Laboratories
KXIP	Kings XI Punjab
KZN	KwaZulu-Natal Inland
ME	Mashonaland Eagles
MI	Mumbai Indians
MR	Melbourne Renegades
MS	Melbourne Stars
MSC	Mohammedan Sporting Club
MT	Matabeleland Tuskers
MWR	Mid West Rhinos
ND	Northern Districts
NSW	New South Wales
NT-	Northern Transvaal
NW	North West
(O)FS	(Orange) Free State
PDSC	Prime Doleshwar Sporting Club
PS	Perth Scorchers
PW	Pune Warriors
Q	Queensland
RCB	Royal Challengers Bangalore
RPS	Rising Pune Supergiant
RR	Rajasthan Royals
RS	Rising Stars
SA	South Australia
SH	Sunrisers Hyderabad
SJD	Sheikh Jamal Dhanmondi
SNGPL	Sui Northern Gas Pipelines Limited
SR	Southern Rocks
SS	Sydney Sixers
SSGC	Sui Southern Gas Corporation
ST	Sydney Thunder
Tas	Tasmania
T&T	Trinidad & Tobago
TU	Tamil Union
UB	United Bank Limited
Vic	Victoria
WA	Western Australia
WP	Western Province
ZT	Zarai Taraqiati Bank Limited

DERBYSHIRE

Formation of Present Club: 4 November 1870
Inaugural First-Class Match: 1871
Colours: Chocolate, Amber and Pale Blue
Badge: Rose and Crown
County Champions: (1) 1936
NatWest Trophy Winners: (1) 1981
Benson and Hedges Cup Winners: (1) 1993
Sunday League Winners: (1) 1990
Twenty20 Cup Winners: (0) best – Semi-Finalist 2019

Chief Executive: Ryan Duckett, Derbyshire County Cricket Club, The Incora County Ground, Nottingham Road, Derby, DE21 6DA • Tel: 01332 388101 • Email: info@derbyshireccc.com • Web: www.derbyshireccc.com • Twitter: @DerbyshireCCC (64,941 followers)

Head of Cricket: David Houghton. **Assistant Coaches**: Ajmal Shahzad (bowling) and Mal Loye (batting). **T20 Head Coach**: Dominic Cork. **Captain**: B.A.Godleman. **Overseas Players**: B.R.McDermott (white ball only), D.J.Melton and B.Stanlake. **2021 Testimonial**: None. **Head Groundsman**: Neil Godrich. **Scorer**: John Brown. **Blast Team Name**: Derbyshire Falcons. ‡ New registration. NQ Not qualified for England.

AITCHISON, Benjamin William,.b Southport, Lancs 6 Jul 1999. RHB, RFM. Squad No 11. Debut (Derbyshire) 2020. Lancashire 2nd XI 2019. Cheshire 2018-19. HS 8 and BB 3-55 v Notts (Nottingham) 2020.

NQCOHEN, Michael Alexander Robert (Reddam House C), b Cape Town, South Africa 4 Aug 1998. LHB, LFM. Squad No 8. Western Province 2017-18 to 2018-19. Cape Cobras 2017-18. Nottinghamshire 2nd XI 2019. HS 30* and De BB 3-47 v Notts (Nottingham) 2020. BB 5-40 WP v SW Districts (Rondebosch) 2017-18. LO HS 16 WP v Northerns (Rondebosch) 2017-18. LO BB 1-17 WP v SW Districts (Rondebosch) 2017-18. T20 HS 7*. T20 BB 2-17.

CONNERS, Samuel (George Spencer Ac), b Nottingham 13 Feb 1999. 6'0". RHB, RM. Squad No 59. Debut (Derbyshire) 2019. Derbyshire 2nd XI debut 2016. England U19 2018. HS 21 v Leics (Leicester) 2020. BB 3-63 v Notts (Nottingham) 2020. LO HS 4 and LO BB 1-45 v Durham (Chester-le-St) 2019 (RLC). T20 HS 2*. T20 BB 2-38.

CRITCHLEY, Matthew James John (St Michael's HS, Chorley), b Preston, Lancs 13 Aug 1996. 6'2". RHB, LB. Squad No 20. Debut (Derbyshire) 2015; cap 2019. Derbyshire 2nd XI debut 2014. HS 137* v Northants (Derby) 2015. BB 6-73 v Leics (Leicester) 2020. LO HS 64* v Northants (Derby) 2019 (RLC). LO BB 4-48 v Northants (Derby) 2015 (RLC). T20 HS 72*. T20 BB 4-36.

DAL, Anuj Kailash (Durban HS; Nottingham HS), b Newcastle-upon-Tyne, Northumb 8 Jul 1996. 5'9". RHB, RM. Squad No 65. Debut (Derbyshire) 2018. Nottinghamshire 2nd XI 2013-17. HS 92 v Middx (Derby) 2019. BB 3-11 v Sussex (Derby) 2019. LO HS 52 v Lancs (Manchester) 2019 (RLC). T20 HS 35.

NQDu PLOOY, Jacobus Leus, b Pretoria, South Africa 12 Jan 1995. LHB, SLA. Squad No 76. Free State 2014-15 to 2017-18. Knights 2015-16. Northerns 2018-19. Titans 2018-19. Derbyshire debut 2019. HS 181 FS v Namibia (Windhoek) 2015-16. De HS 130 v Notts (Nottingham) 2020. BB 3-76 Northerns v WP (Pretoria, TU) 2018-19. De BB 2-24 v Glamorgan (Swansea) 2019. LO HS 155 Northerns v WP (Pretoria, TU) 2018-19. LO BB 3-19 Northerns v KZN (Pretoria, TU) 2018-19. T20 HS 70. T20 BB 4-15.

GODLEMAN, Billy Ashley (Islington Green S), b Islington, London 11 Feb 1989. 6'3''. LHB, LB. Squad No 1. Middlesex 2005-09. Essex 2010-12. Derbyshire debut 2013; cap 2015; captain 2016 to date. F-c Tour (MCC): Nepal 2019-20. 1000 runs (2); most – 1087 (2019). HS 227 v Glamorgan (Swansea) 2016. BB – . LO HS 137 v Warwks (Birmingham) 2018 (RLC). T20 HS 92.

GUEST, Brooke David (Kent Street Senior HS, Perth, WA; Murdoch U, Perth), b Whitworth Park, Manchester 14 May 1997. 5'11''. RHB, WK. Squad No 29. Lancashire 2018-19. Derbyshire debut 2020. Lancashire 2nd XI 2016-19. HS 17 La v Middx (Lord's) 2019. LO HS 36 v Worcs (Manchester) 2019 (RLC). T20 HS 22*.

HOSEIN, Harvey Richard (Denstone C), b Chesterfield 12 Aug 1996. 5'10''. RHB, WK. Squad No 16. Debut (Derbyshire) 2014, taking seven catches in an innings and UK record-equalling 11 in match v Surrey (Oval). Derbyshire 2nd XI debut 2010, aged 13y 287d. HS 138* v Leeds/Brad MCCU (Derby) 2019. CC HS 108 v Worcs (Worcester) 2016. LO HS 41* v Lancs (Manchester) 2019 (RLC). T20 HS 10*.

HUDSON-PRENTICE, Fynn Jake (Warden Park S, Cuckfield; Bede's S, Upper Dicker), b Haywards Heath, Sussex 12 Jan 1996. RHB, RMF. Squad No 33. Sussex 2015-16. Derbyshire debut 2019. HS 99 v Middx (Derby) 2019. BB 3-27 v Worcs (Kidderminster) 2019. LO HS 48 Sx v Kent (Hove) 2016 (RLC). LO BB – . T20 HS 31*. T20 BB 2-2.

HUGHES, Alex Lloyd (Ounsdale HS, Wolverhampton), b Wordsley, Staffs 29 Sep 1991. 5'10''. RHB, RM. Squad No 18. Debut (Derbyshire) 2013; cap 2017. HS 142 v Glos (Bristol) 2017. BB 4-46 v Glamorgan (Derby) 2014. LO HS 96* v Leics (Leicester) 2016 (RLC). LO BB 4-44 v Northants (Derby) 2019 (RLC). T20 HS 43*. T20 BB 4-42.

‡NQMcDERMOTT, Benjamin Reginald, b Caboolture, Queensland, Australia 12 Dec 1994. Son of C.J.McDermott (Queensland and Australia 1983-84 to 1995-96); younger brother of A.C.McDermott (Queensland 2009-10 to 2014-15). RHB, WK, occ RM. Squad No 47. Queensland 2014-15. Tasmania 2015-16 to date. Big Bash: BH 2013-14. MR 2015-16. HH 2016-17 to date. Joins Derbyshire for white-ball season. **IT20** (A): 12 (2018-19 to 2019-20); HS 32* v I (Melbourne) 2018-19. HS 107* Aus A v Indians (Sydney) 2020-21. BB – . LO HS 117 Tas v Q (Townsville) 2018-19. T20 HS 114.

McKIERNAN, Matthew Harry ('**Mattie**') (Lowton S; St John Rigby C, Wigan), b Billinge, Lancs 14 Jun 1994. 6'0''. RHB, LB. Squad No 21. Debut (Derbyshire) 2019. Cumberland 2016-17. HS 52 v Lancs (Liverpool) 2020. BB 2-3 v Notts (Nottingham) 2020. T20 HS 25. T20 BB 2-22.

MADSEN, Wayne Lee (Kearsney C, Durban; U of South Africa), b Durban, South Africa 2 Jan 1984. Nephew of M.B.Madsen (Natal 1967-68 to 1978-79), T.R.Madsen (Natal 1976-77 to 1989-90) and H.R.Fotheringham (Natal, Transvaal 1971-72 to 1989-90), cousin of G.S.Fotheringham (KwaZulu-Natal 2008-09 to 2009-10). 5'11". RHB, OB. Squad No 77. KwaZulu-Natal 2003-04 to 2007-08. Dolphins 2006-07 to 2007-08. Derbyshire debut 2009, scoring 170 v Glos (Cheltenham); cap 2011; captain 2012-15; testimonial 2017. Qualified for England by residence in February 2015. 1000 runs (5); most – 1292 (2016). HS 231* v Northants (Northampton) 2012. BB 3-45 KZN v EP (Pt Elizabeth) 2007-08. De BB 2-9 v Sussex (Hove) 2013. LO HS 138 v Hants (Derby) 2014 (RLC). LO BB 3-27 v Durham (Derby) 2013 (Y40). T20 HS 86*. T20 BB 2-20.

NQMELTON, Dustin Renton (Pretoria BHS; U of Pretoria), b Harare, Zimbabwe 11 Apr 1995. RHB, RFM. Squad No 13. Debut (Derbyshire) 2019. HS 11 v Lancs (Liverpool) 2020. BB 4-22 v Leics (Leicester) 2020. T20 BB 2-37.

POTTS, Nicholas James (De Ferrers Ac), b Burton-on-Trent, Staffs 17 Jul 2002. RHB, RFM. Derbyshire 2nd XI debut 2018. Awaiting 1st XI debut.

PRIESTLEY, Nils Oscar (Blessed Robert Sutton S; Abbotsholme SFC), b Sutton Coldfield, Warwks 18 Sep 2000. LHB, RM. Squad No 53. Derbyshire 2nd XI debut 2017. Awaiting 1st XI debut.

REECE, Luis Michael (St Michael's HS, Chorley; Leeds Met U), b Taunton, Somerset 4 Aug 1990. 6'1". LHB, LM. Squad No 10. Leeds/Bradford MCCU 2012-13. Lancashire 2013-15, no f-c appearances in 2016. Derbyshire debut 2017; cap 2019. MCC 2014. Unicorns 2011-12. HS 184 v Sussex (Derby) 2019. 50 wkts (1): 55 (2019). BB 7-20 v Glos (Derby) 2018. LO HS 128 v Worcs (Derby) 2019 (RLC). LO BB 4-35 Unicorns v Glos (Exmouth) 2011 (CB40). T20 HS 97*. T20 BB 3-33.

‡NQSTANLAKE, Billy, b Hervey Bay, Queensland, Australia 4 Nov 1994. RHB, RFM. Queensland 2015-16 to date. IPL: RCB 2017. SH 2018. Big Bash: AS 2015-16 to 2019-20. MS 2020-21. LOI (A): 7 (2016-17 to 2018-19); HS 2 and BB 3-35 v E (Manchester) 2018. IT20 (A): 19 (2016-17 to 2019-20); HS 7 v E (Birmingham) 2018; BB 4-8 v P (Harare) 2018. HS 4 Q v NSW (Brisbane) 2018-19. BB 3-50 Q v SA (Brisbane) 2015-16. LO HS 4* (twice). LO BB 4-24 Q v Tas (Hobart) 2020-21. T20 HS 7. T20 BB 4-8.

WOOD, Thomas Anthony (Heanor Gate Science C), b Derby 11 May 1994. 6'3". RHB, RM. Squad No 24. Debut (Derbyshire) 2016. HS 26 v Yorks (Leeds) 2020. LO HS 44 v Sri Lanka A (Derby) 2016. T20 HS 67.

A.P.Palladino and R.Rampaul left the staff without making a County 1st XI appearance in 2020.

DERBYSHIRE 2020

RESULTS SUMMARY

	Place	Won	Lost	Drew	NR
Bob Willis Trophy (North Group)	2nd	2	1	2	
Vitality Blast (North Group)	6th	1	7		2

BOB WILLIS TROPHY AVERAGES
BATTING AND FIELDING

Cap		M	I	NO	HS	Runs	Avge	100	50	Ct/St
	F.J.Hudson-Prentice	3	5	2	91*	145	48.33	–	1	1
2019	L.M.Reece	4	7	1	122	277	46.16	1	2	4
	M.A.Cohen	2	3	2	30*	43	43.00	–	–	–
	J.L.du Plooy	5	7	–	130	296	42.28	1	1	5
2019	M.J.J.Critchley	5	7	1	63	234	39.00	–	1	4
	A.K.Dal	4	4	1	78*	108	36.00	–	1	2
	H.R.Hosein	4	6	1	84	167	33.40	–	2	13/1
2011	W.L.Madsen	5	8	1	103	213	30.42	1	1	10
2015	B.A.Godleman	5	8	–	86	226	28.25	–	3	2
	M.H.McKiernan	2	4	–	52	103	25.75	–	1	3
	S.Conners	4	4	2	21	45	22.50	–	–	–
	D.R.Melton	3	3	1	11	11	5.50	–	–	–

Also played: B.W.Aitchison (3 matches) 8 (2 ct); E.Barnes (2) 4; B.D.Guest (1) did not bat; A.L.Hughes (2 – cap 2017) 27, 13; T.A.Wood (1) 26.

BOWLING

	O	M	R	W	Avge	Best	5wI	10wM
L.M.Reece	132.3	40	340	13	26.15	3-51	–	–
M.J.J.Critchley	128.4	14	457	17	26.88	6-73	1	–
M.A.Cohen	44.2	7	191	7	27.28	3-47	–	–
D.R.Melton	70	13	233	8	29.12	4-22	–	–
B.W.Aitchison	78	20	211	6	35.16	3-55	–	–
E.Barnes	32	6	107	3	35.66	2-24	–	–
S.Conners	94.2	23	328	9	36.44	3-63	–	–

Also bowled: A.K.Dal 43-10-95-2; J.L.du Plooy 9-1-41-2; F.J.Hudson-Prentice 34-8-105-1; A.L.Hughes 21-2-79-1; M.H.McKiernan 10.2-2-48-2; W.L.Madsen 1-0-4-0.

The First-Class Averages (pp 209–221) give the records of Derbyshire players in all first-class county matches.

DERBYSHIRE RECORDS

FIRST-CLASS CRICKET

Highest Total	For 801-8d		v	Somerset	Taunton	2007
	V 677-7d		by	Yorkshire	Leeds	2013
Lowest Total	For 16		v	Notts	Nottingham	1879
	V 23		by	Hampshire	Burton upon T	1958
Highest Innings	For 274	G.A.Davidson	v	Lancashire	Manchester	1896
	V 343*	P.A.Perrin	for	Essex	Chesterfield	1904

Highest Partnership for each Wicket

1st	333	L.M.Reece/B.A.Godleman	v	Northants	Derby	2017
2nd	417	K.J.Barnett/T.A.Tweats	v	Yorkshire	Derby	1997
3rd	316*	A.S.Rollins/K.J.Barnett	v	Leics	Leicester	1997
4th	328	P.Vaulkhard/D.Smith	v	Notts	Nottingham	1946
5th	302*†	J.E.Morris/D.G.Cork	v	Glos	Cheltenham	1993
6th	212	G.M.Lee/T.S.Worthington	v	Essex	Chesterfield	1932
7th	258	M.P.Dowman/D.G.Cork	v	Durham	Derby	2000
8th	198	K.M.Krikken/D.G.Cork	v	Lancashire	Manchester	1996
9th	283	A.Warren/J.Chapman	v	Warwicks	Blackwell	1910
10th	132	A.Hill/M.Jean-Jacques	v	Yorkshire	Sheffield	1986

   † 346 runs were added for this wicket in two separate partnerships

Best Bowling	For 10- 40	W.Bestwick	v	Glamorgan	Cardiff	1921
(Innings)	V 10- 45	R.L.Johnson	for	Middlesex	Derby	1994
Best Bowling	For 17-103	W.Mycroft	v	Hampshire	Southampton	1876
(Match)	V 16-101	G.Giffen	for	Australians	Derby	1886

Most Runs – Season	2165	D.B.Carr	(av 48.11)	1959
Most Runs – Career	23854	K.J.Barnett	(av 41.12)	1979-98
Most 100s – Season	8	P.N.Kirsten		1982
Most 100s – Career	53	K.J.Barnett		1979-98
Most Wkts – Season	168	T.B.Mitchell	(av 19.55)	1935
Most Wkts – Career	1670	H.L.Jackson	(av 17.11)	1947-63
Most Career W-K Dismissals	1304	R.W.Taylor	(1157 ct; 147 st)	1961-84
Most Career Catches in the Field	563	D.C.Morgan		1950-69

LIMITED-OVERS CRICKET

Highest Total	50ov	366-4		v	Comb Univs	Oxford	1991
	40ov	321-5		v	Essex	Leek	2013
	T20	222-5		v	Yorkshire	Leeds	2010
		222-5		v	Notts	Nottingham	2017
Lowest Total	50ov	73		v	Lancashire	Derby	1993
	40ov	60		v	Kent	Canterbury	2008
	T20	72		v	Leics	Derby	2013
Highest Innings	50ov	173*	M.J.Di Venuto	v	Derbys CB	Derby	2000
	40ov	141*	C.J.Adams	v	Kent	Chesterfield	1992
	T20	111	W.J.Durston	v	Notts	Nottingham	2010
Best Bowling	50ov	8-21	M.A.Holding	v	Sussex	Hove	1988
	40ov	6- 7	M.Hendrick	v	Notts	Nottingham	1972
	T20	5-27	T.Lungley	v	Leics	Leicester	2009

DURHAM

Formation of Present Club: 23 May 1882
Inaugural First-Class Match: 1992
Colours: Navy Blue, Yellow and Maroon
Badge: Coat of Arms of the County of Durham
County Champions: (3) 2008, 2009, 2013
Friends Provident Trophy Winners: (1) 2007
Royal London One-Day Cup Winners: (1) 2014
Twenty20 Cup Winners: (0); best – Finalist 2016

Chief Executive: Tim Bostock, Emirates Riverside, Chester-le-Street, Co Durham DH3 3QR • Tel: 0191 387 1717 • Email: marcoms@durhamcricket.co.uk • Web: www.durhamcricket.co.uk • Twitter: @DurhamCricket (79,488 followers)

Director of Cricket: Marcus North. **Lead High Performance Coach**: James Franklin. **Bowling Coach**: Neil Killeen. **Assistant Coaches**: Alan Walker and Will Gidman. **Captain**: S.G.Borthwick. **Overseas Players**: C.T.Bancroft D.G.Bedingham and W.A.Young. **2021 Testimonial**: None. **Head Groundsman**: Vic Demain. **Scorer**: William Dobson. **Blast Team Name**: Durham Jets. ‡ New registration. ^NQ Not qualified for England.

Durham initially awarded caps immediately after their players joined the staff but revised this policy in 1998, capping players on merit, past 'awards' having been nullified. Durham abolished both their capping and 'awards' systems after the 2005 season.

^NQ**BANCROFT, Cameron** Timothy (Aquinas C, Perth), b Attadale, Perth, Australia 19 Nov 1992. 6'0". RHB, RM, occ WK. Squad No 4. W Australia 2013-14 to date. Gloucestershire 2016-17; cap 2016. Durham debut 2019; captain 2019. Big Bash: PS 2014-15 to date. **Tests** (A): 10 (2017-18 to 2019); HS 82* v E (Brisbane) 2017-18. **IT20** (A): 1 (2015-16); HS 0* v I (Sydney) 2015-16. F-c Tours (A): E 2019; SA 2017-18; I 2015 (Aus A). HS 228* WA v SA (Perth) 2017-18. CC HS 206* Gs v Kent (Bristol) 2017. Du HS 158 v Sussex (Hove) 2019, sharing Du record 6th wkt partnership of 282 with E.J.H.Eckersley. BB 1-10 WA v Q (Brisbane) 2019-20. LO HS 176 WA v SA (Sydney, HO) 2015-16. T20 HS 87*.

^NQ**BEDINGHAM, David** Guy, b George, Cape Province, South Africa 22 Apr 1994. 5'9". RHB, OB, occ WK. Squad No 5. Western Province 2012-13 to 2019-20. Boland 2015-16 to 2018-19. Cape Cobras 2018-19 to 2019-20. Durham debut 2020. HS 147 Boland v Easterns (Paarl) 2017-18. Du HS 96 v Leics (Leicester) 2020. BB – . LO HS 104* Boland v Border (East London) 2017-18. LO BB – . T20 HS 73.

BORTHWICK, Scott George (Farringdon Community Sports C, Sunderland), b Sunderland 19 Apr 1990. 5'9". LHB, LBG. Squad No 16. Debut (Durham) 2009; rejoins in 2021 as captain. Wellington 2015-16 to 2016-17. Surrey 2017-20; cap 2018. **Tests**: 1 (2013-14); HS 4 and BB 3-33 v A (Sydney) 2013-14. **LOI**: 2 (2011 to 2011-12); HS 15 v Ire (Dublin) 2011; BB – . **IT20**: 1 (2011); HS 14 and BB 1-15 v WI (Oval) 2011. F-c Tours: A 2013-14; SL 2013-14 (EL). 1000 runs (5); most – 1390 (2015). HS 216 v Middx (Chester-le-St) 2014, sharing Du record 2nd wkt partnership of 274 with M.D.Stoneman. BB 6-70 v Surrey (Oval) 2013. LO HS 87 and LO BB 5-38 v Leics (Leicester) 2015 (RLC). T20 HS 62. T20 BB 4-18.

BURNHAM, Jack Tony Arthur (Deerness Valley CS, Durham), b Durham 18 Jan 1997. 6'1". RHB, RM. Squad No 8. Debut (Durham) 2015. Durham 2nd XI debut 2014. Northumberland 2015. HS 135 v Surrey (Oval) 2016. LO HS 45 v Derbys (Chester-le-St) 2019 (RLC). T20 HS 53*.

CAMPBELL, Jack Oliver Ian (Churcher's C, Petersfield; Durham U), b Portsmouth, Hants 11 Nov 1999. 6'7''. RHB, LMF. Squad No 21. Durham MCCU 2019. Durham debut 2019. Hampshire 2nd XI 2017. Kent 2nd XI 2018. Durham 2nd XI debut 2018. No 1st XI appearances in 2020. HS 2 Durham MCCU v Durham (Chester-le-St) 2019. Du HS 0* and BB 1-43 v Leics (Leicester) 2019.

CARSE, Brydon Alexander (Pearson HS, Pt Elizabeth), b Port Elizabeth, South Africa 31 Jul 1995. Son of J.A.Carse (Rhodesia, W Province, E Province, Northants, Border, Griqualand W 1977-78 to 1992-93). 6'1½''. RHB, RF. Squad No 99. Debut (Durham) 2016. F-c Tour (EL): A 2019-20. HS 77* v Northants (Chester-le-St) 2019, sharing Du record 8th wkt partnership of 154 with B.A.Raine. BB 6-26 v Middx (Lord's) 2019. LO HS 2 v Derbys (Chester-le-St) 2019 (RLC). LO BB 3-52 v Warwks (Birmingham) 2019 (RLC). T20 HS 35. T20 BB 1-11.

CLARK, Graham (St Benedict's Catholic HS, Whitehaven), b Whitehaven, Cumbria 16 Mar 1993. Younger brother of J.Clark (see SURREY). 6'1''. RHB, LB. Squad No 7. Debut (Durham) 2015. HS 109 v Glamorgan (Chester-le-St) 2017. BB 1-10 v Sussex (Arundel) 2018. LO HS 114 v Worcs (Worcester) 2017 (RLC). LO BB 3-18 v Leics (Leicester) 2018 (RLC). T20 HS 91*. T20 BB – .

COUGHLIN, Paul (St Robert of Newminster Catholic CS, Washington), b Sunderland 23 Oct 1992. Elder brother of J.Coughlin (Durham 2016-19); nephew of T.Harland (Durham 1974-78). 6'3''. RHB, RM. Squad No 23. Debut (Durham) 2012. Nottinghamshire in 2019. Northumberland 2011. F-c Tour (EL): WI 2017-18. HS 90 v Derbys (Chester-le-St) 2020. BB 5-49 (10-133 match) v Northants (Chester-le-St) 2017. LO HS 22 v Notts (Nottingham) 2017 (RLC) and 22 v Lancs (Chester-le-St) 2017 (RLC). LO BB 3-36 v Worcs (Worcester) 2017 (RLC). T20 HS 53. T20 BB 5-42.

DICKSON, Sean Robert, b Johannesburg, South Africa 2 Sep 1991. 5'10''. RHB, RM. Squad No 58. Northerns 2013-14 to 2014-15. Kent 2015-19. Durham debut 2020. UK passport holder; England qualified. HS 318 K v Northants (Beckenham) 2017, 2nd highest score in K history, sharing K record 2nd wkt partnership of 382 with J.L.Denly. Du HS 56 v Notts (Nottingham) 2020. LO BB 1-15 Northerns v GW (Centurion) 2014-15. CC BB – . LO HS 99 K v Middx (Lord's) 2016 (RLC). T20 HS 53. T20 BB 1-9.

ECKERSLEY, Edmund John Holden ('Ned') (St Benedict's GS, Ealing), b Oxford 9 Aug 1989. 6'0''. RHB, WK, occ OB. Squad No 66. Leicestershire 2011-18; cap 2013. Mountaineers 2011-12. Durham debut 2019; captain 2020. MCC 2013. 1000 runs (1): 1302 (2013). HS 158 Le v Derbys (Derby) 2017. Du HS 118 v Sussex (Hove) 2019, sharing Du record 6th wkt partnership of 282 with C.T.Bancroft. BB 2-29 Le v Lancs (Manchester) 2013. LO HS 108 Le v Yorks (Leicester) 2013 (Y40). T20 HS 43.

GIBSON, Oliver James (Q Elizabeth GS, Hexham; Derwentside SFC), b Northallerton, Yorks 7 Jul 2000. RHB, RFM. Durham 2nd XI debut 2018. Awaiting 1st XI debut.

ᴺᴼJONES, Michael Alexander (Ormskirk S; Myerscough C), b Ormskirk, Lancs 5 Jan 1998. 6'2''. RHB, OB. Squad No 10. Debut (Durham) 2018. Durham 2nd XI debut 2017. Derbyshire 2nd XI 2017. Leicestershire 2nd XI 2017. **LOI** (Scot): 8 (2017-18 to 2019-20); HS 87 v Ire (Dubai, ICCA) 2017-18. HS 82 v Notts (Nottingham) 2020. LO HS 87 (see LOI).

LEES, Alexander Zak (Holy Trinity SS, Halifax), b Halifax, Yorks 14 Apr 1993. 6'3''. LHB, LB. Squad No 19. Yorkshire 2010-18; cap 2014; captain (l-o) 2016. Durham debut 2018. MCC 2017. YC 2014. 1000 runs (2); most – 1199 (2016). HS 275* Y v Derbys (Chesterfield) 2013. Du HS 181 v Leics (Chester-le-St) 2019. BB 2-51 Y v Middx (Lord's) 2016. Du BB 1-12 v Yorks (Chester-le-St) 2020. LO HS 115 v Lancs (Gosforth) 2019 (RLC). T20 HS 77*.

POTTS, Matthew ('Matty') James (St Robert of Newminster Catholic S), b Sunderland 29 Oct 1998. 6'0". RHB, RM. Squad No 35. Debut (Durham) 2017. Durham 2nd XI debut 2016. England U19 2017. HS 53* v Derbys (Chester-le-St) 2017. BB 3-48 v Glamorgan (Chester-le-St) 2017. LO HS 30 v Yorks (Chester-le-St) 2018 (RLC). LO BB 4-62 v Northants (Chester-le-St) 2019 (RLC). T20 HS 12. T20 BB 3-8.

ᴺᴼPOYNTER, Stuart William (Teddington S), b Hammersmith, London 18 Oct 1990. Younger brother of A.D.Poynter (Middlesex and Ireland 2005-11). 5'9". RHB, WK. Squad No 90. Middlesex 2010. Ireland 2011 to date. Warwickshire 2013. Durham debut 2016. **Tests** (Ire): 1 (2018-19); HS 1 v Afg (Dehradun) 2018-19. **LOI** (Ire): 21 (2014 to 2018-19); HS 36 v SL (Dublin) 2016. **IT20** (Ire): 25 (2015 to 2018-19); HS 39 v Scotland (Dubai, DSC) 2016-17. F-c Tour (Ire): Z 2015-16. HS 170 v Derbys (Derby) 2018. LO HS 109 Ire v Sri Lanka A (Belfast) 2014. T20 HS 61*.

RAINE, Benjamin Alexander (St Aidan's RC SS, Sunderland) b Sunderland, 14 Sep 1991. 6'0". LHB, RMF. Squad No 44. Debut (Durham) 2011 – one game only. Leicestershire 2013-18; cap 2018. HS 82 v Northants (Chester-le-St) 2018, sharing Du record 8th wkt partnership of 154 with B.A.Carse. 50 wkts (2); most – 61 (2015). BB 6-27 v Sussex (Hove) 2019. LO HS 83 Le v Worcs (Worcester) 2018 (RLC). LO BB 3-31 Le v Northants (Northampton) 2018 (RLC). T20 HS 113 v Warwks (Birmingham) 2018 – Le record. T20 BB 3-7.

RUSHWORTH, Christopher (Castle View CS, Sunderland), b Sunderland 11 Jul 1986. Cousin of P.Mustard (Durham, Mountaineers, Auckland, Lancashire and Gloucestershire 2002-17). 6'2". RHB, RMF. Squad No 22. Debut (Durham) 2010; testimonial 2019. MCC 2013, 2015. Northumberland 2004-05. PCA 2015. HS 57 v Kent (Canterbury) 2017. 50 wkts (5); most – 88 (2015) – Du record. BB 9-52 (15-95 match – Du record) v Northants (Chester-le-St) 2014. Hat-trick v Hants (Southampton) 2015. LO HS 38* v Derbys (Chester-le-St) 2015 (RLC). LO BB 5-31 v Notts (Chester-le-St) 2010 (CB40). T20 HS 5. T20 BB 3-14.

SALISBURY, Matthew Edward Thomas (Shenfield HS; Anglia Ruskin U), b Chelmsford, Essex 18 Apr 1993. 6'0½". RHB, RMF. Squad No 32. Cambridge MCCU 2012-13. Essex 2014-15. Hampshire 2017. Durham debut 2018. Suffolk 2016. HS 37 v Warwks (Birmingham) 2018. BB 6-37 v Middx (Chester-le-St) 2018. LO HS 5* Ex v Leics (Chelmsford) 2014 (RLC). LO BB 4-55 Ex v Lancs (Chelmsford) 2014 (RLC). T20 HS 1*. T20 BB 2-19.

STEEL, Cameron Tate (Scotch C, Perth, Australia; Millfield S; Durham U), b San Francisco, USA 13 Sep 1995. 5'10". RHB, LB. Squad No 14. Durham MCCU 2014-16. Durham debut 2017. HS 224 v Leics (Leicester) 2017. BB 2-7 v Glamorgan (Cardiff) 2018. LO HS 77 v Notts (Nottingham) 2017 (RLC). LO BB – . T20 HS 37. T20 BB 2-60.

STOKES, Benjamin Andrew (Cockermouth S), b Christchurch, Canterbury, New Zealand 4 Jun 1991. 6'1". LHB, RFM. Squad No 38. Debut (Durham) 2010. IPL: RPS 2017. RR 2018 to date. Big Bash: MR 2014-15. YC 2013. *Wisden* 2015. PCA 2019. BBC Sports Personality of the Year 2019. OBE 2020. **ECB Test & LO Central Contract 2020-21. Tests**: 71 (2013-14 to 2020-21, 1 as captain); HS 258 v SA (Cape Town) 2015-16, setting E record fastest double century in 163 balls; BB 6-22 v WI (Lord's) 2017. **LOI**: 95 (2011 to 2019); HS 102* v A (Birmingham) 2017; BB 5-61 v A (Southampton) 2013. **IT20**: 29 (2011 to 2020-21); HS 47* v SA (Durban) 2019-20; BB 3-26 v NZ (Delhi) 2015-16. F-c Tours: A 2013-14; SA 2015-16, 2019-20; WI 2010-11 (EL), 2014-15, 2018-19; NZ 2017-18, 2019-20; I 2016-17, 2020-21; SL 2018-19; B 2016-17; UAE 2015-16 (v P). HS 258 (*see Tests*). Du HS 185 v Lancs (Chester-le-St) 2011, sharing Du record 4th wkt partnership of 331 with D.M.Benkenstein. BB 7-67 (10-121 match) v Sussex (Chester-le-St) 2014. LO HS 164 v Notts (Chester-le-St) 2016 (RLC) – Du record. LO BB 5-61 (*see LOI*). T20 HS 107*. T20 BB 4-16.

TREVASKIS, Liam (Q Elizabeth GS, Penrith), b Carlisle, Cumberland 18 Apr 1999. 5'8''. LHB, SLA. Squad No 80. Debut (Durham) 2017. Durham 2nd XI debut 2015. HS 64 v Leics (Leicester) 2019. BB 2-96 v Leics (Chester-le-St) 2019. LO HS 16 v Lancs (Gosforth) 2019 (RLC). LO BB 2-37 v Leics (Chester-le-St) 2019 (RLC). T20 HS 31*. T20 BB 4-16.

WOOD, Mark Andrew (Ashington HS; Newcastle C), b Ashington 11 Jan 1990. 5'11''. RHB, RF. Squad No 33. Debut (Durham) 2011. IPL: CSK 2018. Northumberland 2008-10. **ECB L-O Central Contract 2020-21. Tests**: 18 (2015 to 2020-21); HS 52 v NZ (Christchurch) 2017-18; BB 5-41 v WI (Gros Islet) 2018-19. **LOI**: 53 (2015 to 2020); HS 13 v A (Manchester) 2015; BB 4-33 v A (Birmingham) 2017. **IT20**: 11 (2015 to 2020); HS 5* v A (Hobart) 2017-18 and 5* v NZ (Wellington) 2017-18; BB 3-9 v WI (Basseterre) 2018-19. F-c Tours: SA 2014-15 (EL), 2019-20; WI 2018-19; NZ 2017-18; SL 2013-14 (EL), 2020-21; UAE 2015-16 (v P), 2018-19 (EL v P A). HS 72* v Kent (Chester-le-St) 2017. BB 6-46 v Derbys (Derby) 2018. LO HS 24 EL v Pakistan A (Abu Dhabi) 2018-19. LO BB 4-33 (*see LOI*). T20 HS 27*. T20 BB 4-25.

‡^{NQ}**YOUNG, Wil**liam Alexander, New Plymouth, New Zealand 22 Nov 1992. RHB, OB. Central Districts 2011-12 to date. Somerset 2nd XI 2018. Joins Durham for first part of CC season. **Tests** (NZ): 2 (2020-21); HS 43 v WI (Wellington) 2020-21. F-c Tours (NZ A) 1 2017-18; UAE 2018-19 (v P A). HS 162 CD v Auckland (Auckland) 2017-18. LO HS 136 NZ A v Pakistan A (Abu Dhabi) 2018-19. T20 HS 101.

RELEASED/RETIRED
(Having made a County 1st XI appearance in 2020)

^{NQ}**BEHARDIEN, Farhaan**, b Johannesburg, South Africa 9 Oct 1983. 5'8''. RHB, RFM. W Province 2004-05. Titans 2006-07 to 2019-20. Northerns 2007-08 to 2008-09. Knights 2020-21. IPL: KXIP 2016. Leicestershire 2016 (T20 only). Durham 2020 (T20 only). **LOI** (SA): 59 (2012-13 to 2017-18); HS 70 v NZ (Potchefstroom) 2015; BB 3-19 v SL (Pallekele) 2013. **IT20** (SA): 38 (2011-12 to 2018-19); HS 64* v E (Southampton) 2017; BB 2-15 v SL (Delhi) 2015-16. F-c Tours (SA A): A 2014; Ire 2012 (v SL A). HS 150* Titans v Eagles (Benoni) 2008-09. BB 3-48 WP v E Province (Pt Elizabeth) 2004-05 – on debut. LO HS 113* Titans v Lions (Centurion) 2013-14. LO BB 3-16 Northerns v KZN (Pretoria) 2008-09. T20 HS 72*. T20 BB 2-15.

HARTE, Gareth Jason (King Edward VII S), b Johannesburg, South Africa 15 Mar 1993. 5'9''. RHB, RM. Durham 2018-20. HS 114 v Derbys (Chester-le-St) 2018. BB 4-15 v Derbys (Chester-le-St) 2019. LO HS 51* v Warwks (Birmingham) 2019 (RLC). LO BB 2-35 v Notts (Chester-le-St) 2018 (RLC). T20 HS 11. T20 BB 1-11.

^{NQ}**RIMMINGTON, Nathan** John (Wellington C), b Redcliffe, Queensland, Australia 11 Nov 1982. 5'10''. RHB, RFM. Queensland 2005-06 to 2017-18 W Australia 2011-12 to 2016-17. Hampshire 2014. Durham 2018-19. Derbyshire 2015 (T20 only). IPL: KXIP 2011. Big Bash: PS 2011-12 to 2012-13. MR 2012-13 to 2016-17. HS 102* WA v NSW (Sydney) 2011-12. CC HS 92 v Leics (Leicester) 2019. BB 5-27 WA v Q (Perth) 2014-15. CC BB 4-42 v Lancs (Sedbergh) 2019. LO HS 55 WA v Tas (Sydney) 2014-15. LO BB 4-34 WA v SA (Perth) 2014-15. T20 HS 26. T20 BB 5-27.

STEEL, S. – *see LEICESTERSHIRE.*

WEIGHELL, William James (Stokesley S), b Middlesbrough, Yorks 28 Jan 1994. 6'4''. LHB, RMF. Durham 2015-19. Leicestershire 2020. Northumberland 2012-15. HS 84 v Kent (Chester-le-St) 2018. BB 7-32 v Leics (Chester-le-St) 2018. LO HS 23 v Lancs (Manchester) 2018 (RLC). LO BB 5-57 v Warwks (Birmingham) 2017 (RLC). T20 HS 28. T20 BB 3-28.

H.R.D.Adair, S.J.D.Bell, J.Coughlin and B.G.Whitehead left the staff without making a County 1st XI appearance in 2020.

DURHAM 2020

RESULTS SUMMARY

	Place	Won	Lost	Drew	NR
Bob Willis Trophy (North Group)	6th		2	3	
Vitality Blast (North Group)	4th	4	5		1

BOB WILLIS TROPHY AVERAGES
BATTING AND FIELDING

Cap		M	I	NO	HS	Runs	Avge	100	50	Ct/St
	A.Z.Lees	5	8	–	106	386	48.25	1	3	4
	G.J.Harte	5	8	2	72	250	41.66	–	1	–
	B.A.Raine	4	7	4	31	124	41.33	–	–	–
	D.G.Bedingham	5	8	–	96	253	31.62	–	2	3
	M.A.Jones	2	3	–	82	84	28.00	–	1	2
	E.J.H.Eckersley	5	8	2	78*	152	25.33	–	1	3
	B.A.Carse	3	5	–	41	100	20.00	–	–	–
	S.W.Poynter	2	3	–	50	58	19.33	–	1	–
	P.Coughlin	4	6	–	90	114	19.00	–	1	2
	J.T.A.Burnham	3	5	–	31	72	14.40	–	–	1
	S.R.Dickson	5	8	–	56	97	12.12	–	1	4
	C.Rushworth	4	7	2	25	54	10.80	–	–	–
	C.T.Steel	3	5	–	11	22	4.40	–	–	–
	M.J.Potts	2	3	–	10	10	3.33	–	–	1
	M.E.T.Salisbury	3	3	–	4	5	1.66	–	–	–

BOWLING

	O	M	R	W	Avge	Best	5wI	10wM
C.Rushworth	104	14	358	16	22.37	7-108	1	–
M.E.T.Salisbury	53.1	14	148	5	29.60	4- 57	–	–
B.A.Raine	105.1	25	308	9	34.22	3- 53	–	–
B.A.Carse	49	4	245	3	81.66	2-110	–	–
P.Coughlin	78.4	9	304	3	101.33	3- 46	–	–

Also bowled: G.J.Harte 50.4-5-206-2; A.Z.Lees 2-0-19-1; M.J.Potts 36-9-94-2; S.W.Poynter 4-0-21-0; C.T.Steel 2-0-8-1.

The First-Class Averages (pp 209–221) give the records of Durham players in all first-class county matches.

DURHAM RECORDS

FIRST-CLASS CRICKET

Highest Total	For 648-5d		v	Notts	Chester-le-St[2]	2009
	V 810-4d		by	Warwicks	Birmingham	1994
Lowest Total	For 61		v	Leics	Leicester	2018
	V 18		by	Durham MCCU	Chester-le-St[2]	2012
Highest Innings	For 273	M.L.Love	v	Hampshire	Chester-le-St[2]	2003
	V 501*	B.C.Lara	for	Warwicks	Birmingham	1994

Highest Partnership for each Wicket

1st	334*	S.Hutton/M.A.Roseberry	v	Oxford U	Oxford	1996
2nd	274	M.D.Stoneman/S.G.Borthwick	v	Middlesex	Chester-le-St[2]	2014
3rd	212	M.J.Di Venuto/D.M.Benkenstein	v	Essex	Chester-le-St[2]	2010
4th	331	B.A.Stokes/D.M.Benkenstein	v	Lancashire	Chester-le-St[2]	2011
5th	247	G.J.Muchall/I.D.Blackwell	v	Worcs	Worcester	2011
6th	282	C.T.Bancroft/E.J.H.Eckersley	v	Sussex	Hove	2019
7th	315	D.M.Benkenstein/O.D.Gibson	v	Yorkshire	Leeds	2006
8th	154	B.A.Raine/B.A.Carse	v	Yorkshire	Chester-le-St[2]	2019
9th	150	P.Mustard/P.Coughlin	v	Northants	Chester-le-St[2]	2014
10th	103	M.M.Betts/D.M.Cox	v	Sussex	Hove	1996

Best Bowling	For 10- 47	O.D.Gibson	v	Hampshire	Chester-le-St[2]	2007
(Innings)	V 9- 34	J.A.R.Harris	for	Middlesex	Lord's	2015
Best Bowling	For 15- 95	C.Rushworth	v	Northants	Chester-le-St[2]	2014
(Match)	V 13-103	J.A.R.Harris	for	Middlesex	Lord's	2015

Most Runs – Season	1654	M.J.Di Venuto	(av 78.76)	2009
Most Runs – Career	12030	P.D.Collingwood	(av 33.98)	1996-2018
Most 100s – Season	7	K.K.Jennings		2016
Most 100s – Career	25	P.D.Collingwood		1996-2018
Most Wkts – Season	80	O.D.Gibson	(av 20.75)	2007
Most Wkts – Career	527	G.Onions	(av 25.58)	2004-17
Most Career W-K Dismissals	638	P.Mustard	(619 ct; 19 st)	2002-16
Most Career Catches in the Field	246	P.D.Collingwood		1996-2018

LIMITED-OVERS CRICKET

Highest Total	50ov 353-8		v	Notts	Chester-le-St[2]	2014
	40ov 325-9		v	Surrey	The Oval	2011
	T20 225-2		v	Leics	Chester-le-St[2]	2010
Lowest Total	50ov 82		v	Worcs	Chester-le-St[1]	1968
	40ov 72		v	Warwicks	Birmingham	2002
	T20 78		v	Lancashire	Chester-le-St[2]	2009
Highest Innings	50ov 164	B.A.Stokes	v	Notts	Chester-le-St[2]	2014
	40ov 150*	B.A.Stokes	v	Warwicks	Birmingham	2011
	T20 108*	P.D.Collingwood	v	Worcs	Worcester	2017
Best Bowling	50ov 7-32	S.P.Davis	v	Lancashire	Chester-le-St[1]	1983
	40ov 6-31	N.Killeen	v	Derbyshire	Derby	2000
	T20 5- 6	P.D.Collingwood	v	Northants	Chester-le-St[2]	2011

[1] Chester-le-Street CC (Ropery Lane) [2] Emirates Riverside

ESSEX

Formation of Present Club: 14 January 1876
Inaugural First-Class Match: 1894
Colours: Blue, Gold and Red
Badge: Three Seaxes above Scroll bearing 'Essex'
County Champions: (8) 1979, 1983, 1984, 1986, 1991, 1992, 2017, 2019
NatWest/Friends Prov Trophy Winners: (3) 1985, 1997, 2008
Benson and Hedges Cup Winners: (2) 1979, 1998
Pro 40/National League (Div 1) Winners: (2) 2005, 2006
Sunday League Winners: (3) 1981, 1984, 1985
Twenty20 Cup Winners: (1) 2019
Bob Willis Trophy Winners: (1) 2020

Executive Chairman: John Faragher, The Cloudfm County Ground, New Writtle Street, Chelmsford CM2 0PG • Tel: 01245 252420 • Email: administration@essexcricket.org.uk • Web: www.essexcricket.org.uk • Twitter: @EssexCricket (106,800 followers)

Head Coach: Anthony McGrath. **Assistant Head Coach**: Andre Nel. **Captains**: T.Westley (f-c and 50 ov) and S.R.Harmer (T20). **Overseas Players**: S.R.Harmer and P.M.Siddle. **2021 Testimonial**: None. **Head Groundsman**: Stuart Kerrison. **Scorer**: Tony Choat. **Blast Team Name**: Essex Eagles. ‡ New registration. ^NQ Not qualified for England.

ALLISON, Benjamin Michael John (New Hall S; Chelmsford C), b Colchester 18 Dec 1999. RHB, RFM. Squad No 65. Gloucestershire 2019; cap 2019. Essex 2nd XI debut 2017. Bedfordshire 2018. Cambridgeshire 2019. HS 0 and BB 3-109 Gs v Derbys (Derby) 2019. T20 HS 1*. T20 BB 1-32.

BEARD, Aaron Paul (Boswells S, Chelmsford), b Chelmsford 15 Oct 1997. LHB, RFM. Squad No 14. Debut (Essex) 2016. England U19 2016 to 2016-17. HS 58* v Durham MCCU (Chelmsford) 2017. CC HS 41 v Yorks (Chelmsford) 2019. BB 4-21 v Middx (Chelmsford) 2020. LO HS 22* v Kent (Beckenham) 2019 (RLC). LO BB 3-51 v Glos (Chelmsford) 2019 (RLC). T20 HS 13. T20 BB 3-41.

BROWNE, Nicholas Lawrence Joseph (Trinity Catholic HS, Woodford Green), b Leytonstone 24 Mar 1991. 6'3½". LHB, LB. Squad No 10. Debut (Essex) 2013; cap 2015. MCC 2016. 1000 runs (3); most – 1262 (2016). HS 255 v Derbys (Chelmsford) 2016. BB – . LO HS 99 v Glamorgan (Chelmsford) 2016 (RLC). T20 HS 38.

BUTTLEMAN, William Edward Lewis (Felsted S), b Chelmsford 20 Apr 2000. Younger brother of J.E.L.Buttleman (Durham UCCE 2007-09). RHB, WK, occ OB. Squad No 9. Debut (Essex) 2019. Essex 2nd XI debut 2017. HS 0 v Yorks (Leeds) 2019 – only 1st XI appearance.

CHOPRA, Varun (Ilford County HS), b Barking 21 Jun 1987. 6'1". RHB, LB. Squad No 6. Debut (Essex) 2006, scoring 106 v Glos (Chelmsford) on CC debut; cap 2018. Warwickshire 2010-16; cap 2012; captain 2015. Tamil Union 2011-12. Sussex 2019. F-c Tour (EL): SL 2013-14. 1000 runs (3); most – 1203 (2011). HS 233* TU v Sinhalese (Colombo, PSS) 2011-12. CC HS 228 Wa v Worcs (Worcester) 2011 (in 2nd CC game of season, having scored 210 v Somerset in 1st). Ex HS 155 v Glos (Bristol) 2008. BB – . LO HS 160 v Somerset (Chelmsford) 2018 (RLC). T20 HS 116.

COOK, Sir Alastair Nathan (Bedford S), b Gloucester 25 Dec 1984. 6'3". LHB, OB. Squad No 26. Debut (Essex) 2003; cap 2005; benefit 2014. MCC 2004-07, 2015. YC 2005. *Wisden* 2011. Knighted in 2019 New Year's honours list. **Tests**: 161 (2005-06 to 2018, 59 as captain); 1000 runs (5); most – 1364 (2015); HS 294 v I (Birmingham) 2011. Scored 60 and 104* v I (Nagpur) 2005-06 on debut, and 71 and 147 in final Test v I (Oval) 2018. Second, after M.A.Taylor, to score 1000 runs in the calendar year of his debut. Finished career after appearing in world record 159 consecutive Tests. BB 1-6 v I (Nottingham) 2014. **LOI**: 92 (2006 to 2014-15, 69 as captain); HS 137 v P (Abu Dhabi) 2011-12. **IT20**: 4 (2007 to 2009-10); HS 26 v SA (Centurion) 2009-10. F-c Tours (C=Captain): A 2006-07, 2010-11, 2013-14C, 2017-18; SA 2009-10, 2015-16C; WI 2008-09 (Eng A), 2008-09, 2014-15C; NZ 2007-08, 2012-13C, 2017-18; I 2005-06, 2008-09, 2012-13C, 2016-17C; SL 2004-05 (Eng A), 2007-08, 2011-12; B 2009-10C, 2016-17C; UAE 2011-12 (v P), 2015-16C (v P). 1000 runs (8+1); most – 1466 (2005). HS 294 (*see Tests*). CC HS 195 v Northants (Northampton) 2005. BB 3-13 v Northants (Chelmsford) 2005. LO HS 137 (*see LOI*). BB – . T20 HS 100*.

COOK, Samuel James (Great Baddow HS & SFC; Loughborough U), b Chelmsford 4 Aug 1997. RHB, RFM. Squad No 16. Loughborough MCCU 2016-17. Essex debut 2017; cap 2020. MCC 2019. Essex 2nd XI debut 2014. HS 37* v Yorks (Leeds) 2019. BB 7-23 (12-65 match) v Kent (Canterbury) 2019. LO HS 6 v Middx (Chelmsford) 2019 (RLC). LO BB 3-37 v Surrey (Oval) 2019 (RLC). T20 HS 0*. T20 BB 2-25.

DAS, Robin James (Brentwood S), b Leytonstone 27 Feb 2002. RHB. Essex 2nd XI debut 2018. Awaiting f-c debut. T20 HS 7.

NQHARMER, Simon Ross, b Pretoria, South Africa 10 Feb 1993. RHB, OB. Squad No 11. Eastern Province 2009-10 to 2011-12. Warriors 2010-11 to 2018-19. Essex debut 2017; cap 2018; captain 2020 to date (T20 only). *Wisden* 2019. **Tests** (SA): 5 (2014-15 to 2015-16); HS 13 v I (Nagpur) 2015-16; BB 4-61 v I (Mohali) 2015-16. F-c Tours (SA): A 2014 (SA A); I 2015-16; B 2015; Ire 2012 (SA A). HS 102* v Surrey (Oval) 2018. 50 wkts (3+1); most – 86 (2019). BB 9-95 (14-172 match) v Middx (Chelmsford) 2017. LO HS 44* v Surrey (Oval) 2017 (RLC). LO BB 4-42 Warriors v Lions (Potchefstroom) 2011-12. T20 HS 43. T20 BB 4-19.

KALLEY, Eshun Singh (Barking Abbey S), b Ilford 23 Nov 2001. RHB, RM. Essex 2nd XI debut 2017. Awaiting 1st XI debut.

KHUSHI, Feroze Isa Nazir (Kelmscott S, Walthamstow; Leyton SFC), b Whipps Cross 23 Jun 1999. RHB. OB. Squad No 23. Debut (Essex) 2020. Essex 2nd XI debut 2015. Suffolk 2019. HS 66 v Surrey (Chelmsford) 2020. T20 HS 0.

LAWRENCE, Daniel William (Trinity Catholic HS, Woodford Green), b Whipps Cross 12 Jul 1997. 6'2". RHB, LB. Squad No 28. Debut (Essex) 2015; cap 2017. MCC 2019. Essex 2nd XI debut 2013. England U19 2015. **Tests**: 5 (2020-21); HS 73 v SL (Galle) 2020-21 – on debut; BB – . F-c Tours: A 2019-20 (EL); I 2020-21; SL 2020-21. 1000 runs (1): 1070 (2016). HS 161 v Surrey (Oval) 2015. BB 2-63 v MCC (Bridgetown) 2017-18. CC BB 1-5 v Kent (Chelmsford) 2016. LO HS 115 v Kent (Chelmsford) 2018 (RLC). LO BB 3-35 v Middx (Lord's) 2016 (RLC). T20 HS 86. T20 BB 3-21.

NIJJAR, Aron Stuart Singh (Ilford County HS), b Goodmayes 24 Sep 1994. LHB, SLA. Squad No 24. Debut (Essex) 2015. Suffolk 2014. HS 53 v Northants (Chelmsford) 2015. BB 2-28 v Cambridge MCCU (Cambridge) 2019. CC BB 2-33 v Lancs (Chelmsford) 2015. LO HS 21 v Yorks (Chelmsford) 2015 (RLC). LO BB 1-39 v Sussex (Hove) 2015 (RLC). T20 HS 5. T20 BB 3-22.

PEPPER, Michael-Kyle Steven (The Perse S), b Harlow 25 Jun 1998. Younger brother of C.A.Pepper (Cambridgeshire 2013-16). RHB, WK. Squad No 19. Debut (Essex) 2018. Essex 2nd XI debut 2017. Cambridgeshire 2014-19. HS 22 v Somerset (Chelmsford) 2018. T20 HS 34*.

PLOM, Jack Henry (Gable Hall S; S Essex C), b Basildon 27 Aug 1999. LHB, RFM. Squad No 77. Debut (Essex) 2018 – did not bat or bowl. Essex 2nd XI debut 2016. T20 HS 5. T20 BB 3-32.

PORTER, James Alexander (Oak Park HS, Newbury Park; Epping Forest C), b Leyton-stone 25 May 1993. 5'11½". RHB, RFM. Squad No 44. Debut (Essex) 2014, taking a wkt with his 5th ball; cap 2015. *Wisden* 2017. F-c Tours (EL): WI 2017-18; I 2018-19; UAE 2018-19 (v P A). HS 34 v Glamorgan (Cardiff) 2015. 50 wkts (5); most – 85 (2017). BB 7-41 (11-98 match) v Worcs (Chelmsford) 2018. LO HS 7* v Middx (Chelmsford) 2019 (RLC). LO BB 4-29 v Glamorgan (Chelmsford) 2018 (RLC). T20 HS 1*. T20 BB 4-20.

NOQUINN, Matthew Richard, b Auckland, New Zealand 28 Feb 1993. RHB, RMF. Squad No 94. Auckland 2012-13 to 2015-16. Essex debut 2016. UK passport. HS 50 Auckland v Canterbury (Auckland) 2013-14. Ex HS 16 v Notts (Chelmsford) 2018. BB 7-76 (11-163 match) v Glos (Cheltenham) 2016. LO HS 36 Auckland v CD (Auckland) 2013-14. LO BB 4-71 v Sussex (Hove) 2016 (RLC). T20 HS 8*. T20 BB 4-20.

RYMELL, Joshua Sean (Ipswich S; Colchester SFC), b Ipswich, Suffolk 4 Apr 2001. RHB. Essex 2nd XI debut 2017. Awaiting 1st XI debut.

NOSIDDLE, Peter Matthew, b Traralgon, Victoria, Australia 25 Nov 1984. 6'1½". RHB, RFM. Squad No 64. Victoria 2005-06 to date. Nottinghamshire 2014; cap 2014. Lancashire 2015. Essex debut 2018. Big Bash: MR 2013-14 to 2014-15. AS 2017-18 to date. **Tests** (A): 67 (2008-09 to 2019); HS 51 v I (Delhi) 2012-13; BB 6-54 v E (Brisbane) 2010-11. **LOI** (A): 20 (2008-09 to 2018-19); HS 10* v I (Melbourne) 2018-19; BB 3-55 v E (Centurion) 2009-10. **IT20** (A): 2 (2008-09 to 2010-11); HS 1* and BB 2-24 v NZ (Sydney) 2009-09. F-c Tours (A): E 2009, 2013, 2015, 2019; SA 2008-09, 2011-12, 2013-14; WI 2011-12; NZ 2015-16; I 2008-09 (Aus A), 2008-09, 2012-13; SL 2011; Z 2011 (Aus A); UAE 2014-15 (v P), 2018-19 (v P). HS 103* Aus A v Scotland (Edinburgh) 2013. CC HS 89 La v Northants (Northampton) 2015. Ex HS 60 v Yorks (Leeds) 2019. 50 wkts (0+1): 54 (2011-12). BB 8-54 Vic v SA (Adelaide) 2014-15. CC BB 6-104 v Surrey (Oval) 2019. LO HS 62 Vic v Q (N Sydney) 2017-18. LO BB 4-27 Vic v Tas (Hobart) 2008-09. T20 HS 11. T20 BB 5-16.

NOSNATER, Shane (St John's C, Harare), b Harare, Zimbabwe 24 Mar 1996. RHB, RM. Squad No 29. Netherlands 2016 to date. Awaiting Essex f-c debut. Essex 2nd XI debut 2017. **LOI** (Neth): 2 (2018); HS 12 and BB 1-41 v Nepal (Amstelveen) 2018. **IT20** (Neth): 13 (2018 to 2019-20); HS 10 and BB 3-42 v Scotland (Dublin) 2019. HS 50* and BB 5-88 Neth v Namibia (Dubai, ICCA) 2017-18. LO HS 23* Neth v Nepal (Kwekwe) 2017-18. LO BB 5-60 v Somerset (Chelmsford) 2018 (RLC). T20 HS 16*. T20 BB 3-42.

NOTen DOESCHATE, Ryan Neil (Fairbairn C; Cape Town U), b Port Elizabeth, South Africa 30 Jun 1980. 5'10½". RHB, RMF. Squad No 27. Debut (Essex) 2003; cap 2006; captain (l-o) 2014-15; captain 2016-19. EU passport – Dutch ancestry. Netherlands 2003 to 2009-10. Otago 2012-13. IPL: KKR 2011-15. Big Bash: AS 2014-15. **LOI** (Neth): 33 (2006 to 2010-11); HS 119 v E (Nagpur) 2010-11; BB 4-31 v Canada (Nairobi) 2006-07. **IT20** (Neth): 22 (2008 to 2019-20); HS 59 v Namibia (Dubai, ICCA) 2019-20; BB 3-23 v Scotland (Belfast) 2008. F-c Tours (Ne): SA 2006-07, 2007-08; K 2005-06, 2009-10; Ireland 2005. 1000 runs (1): 1226 (2016). HS 259* and BB 6-20 Neth v Canada (Pretoria) 2006. Ex HS 173* v Somerset (Chelmsford) 2018. Ex BB 6-57 v New Zealanders (Chelmsford) 2008. CC BB 5-13 v Hants (Chelmsford) 2010. LO HS 180 v Scotland (Chelmsford) 2013 (Y40) – Ex 40-over record, inc 15 sixes. LO BB 5-50 v Glos (Bristol) 2007 (FPT). T20 HS 121*. T20 BB 4-24.

WALTER, Paul Ian (Billericay S), b Basildon 28 May 1994. LHB, LMF. Squad No 22. Debut (Essex) 2016. HS 68* v West Indians (Chelmsford) 2017. CC HS 47 and BB 3-44 v Derbys (Derby) 2016. LO HS 25 v Surrey (Oval) 2019 (RLC). LO BB 4-37 v Middx (Chelmsford) 2017 (RLC). T20 HS 76. T20 BB 3-24.

WESTLEY, Thomas (Linton Village C; Hills Road SFC), b Cambridge 13 March 1989. 6'2''. RHB, OB. Squad No 21. Debut (Essex) 2007; cap 2013; captain 2020 to date. MCC 2007, 2009, 2016, 2019. Durham MCCU 2010-11. Cambridgeshire 2005. **Tests**: 5 (2017); HS 59 v SA (Oval) 2017. F-c Tours: SL 2016-17 (EL); Nepal 2019-20 (MCC). 1000 runs (1): 1435 (2016). HS 254 v Worcs (Chelmsford) 2016. BB 4-55 DU v Durham (Durham) 2010. CC BB 4-75 v Surrey (Colchester) 2015. LO HS 134 v Middx (Radlett) 2018 (RLC). LO BB 4-60 v Northants (Northampton) 2014 (RLC). T20 HS 109*. T20 BB 2-27.

WHEATER, Adam Jack Aubrey (Millfield S), b Whipps Cross 13 Feb 1990. 5'6''. RHB, WK. Squad No 31. Debut (Essex) 2008; cap 2020. Cambridge MCCU 2010. Matabeleland Tuskers 2010-11 to 2012-13. Badureliya Sports Club 2011-12. Northern Districts 2012-13. Hampshire 2013-16; cap 2016. HS 204* H v Warwks (Birmingham) 2016. Ex HS 164 v Northants (Chelmsford) 2011, sharing Ex record 6th wkt partnership of 253 with J.S.Foster. BB 1-86 v Leics (Leicester) 2012 – in contrived circumstances. LO HS 135 v Essex (Chelmsford) 2014 (RLC). T20 HS 78.

RELEASED/RETIRED

(Having made a County 1st XI appearance in 2020)

[NO]**DELPORT, Cameron** Scott (Kloof Senior S, Durban; Westville BHS), b Durban, South Africa 12 May 1989. 5'10''. LHB, RM. UK ancestry visa. KwaZulu-Natal 2008-09 to 2016-17. Dolphins 2008-09 to 2011-12. Leicestershire 2017 (white ball 2016-18). Essex 2019-20 (T20 only). Big Bash: ST 2014-15. Won Walter Lawrence Trophy in 2019 for 38-ball hundred v Surrey in T20. HS 163 KZN v Northerns (Centurion) 2010-11. CC HS 20 Le v Glamorgan (Leicester) 2017. BB 2-10 KZN v Northern Cape (Chatsworth) 2016-17. LO HS 169* Dolphins v Knights (Bloemfontein) 2014-15. LO BB 4-42 Dolphins v Titans (Durban) 2011-12. T20 HS 129. T20 BB 4-17. May return in 2021.

PATEL, R.K. – *see LEICESTERSHIRE.*

ESSEX 2020

RESULTS SUMMARY

	Place	Won	Lost	Drew	Tied	NR
Bob Willis Trophy (South Group)	Winners	4		2		
Vitality Blast (South Group)	5th	2	6		1	1

BOB WILLIS TROPHY AVERAGES
BATTING AND FIELDING

Cap		M	I	NO	HS	Runs	Avge	100	50	Ct/St
2020	A.J.A.Wheater	6	9	4	83*	291	58.20	–	2	17/3
2005	A.N.Cook	6	11	1	172	563	56.30	2	1	10
	P.I.Walter	5	9	2	46	266	38.00	–	–	2
2006	R.N.ten Doeschate	5	7	–	78	218	31.14	–	1	–
2017	D.W.Lawrence	4	6	1	60	144	28.80	–	1	–
	F.I.N.Khushi	4	5	–	66	125	25.00	–	1	5
2018	V.Chopra	2	4	–	41	89	22.25	–	–	4
2015	N.L.J.Browne	4	8	–	61	142	17.75	–	1	4
2013	T.Westley	6	11	1	51	172	17.20	–	1	3
2018	S.R.Harmer	6	9	1	32	111	13.87	–	–	10
	A.P.Beard	5	6	2	17	43	10.75	–	–	1
2015	J.A.Porter	6	8	4	13	30	7.50	–	–	3
2020	S.J.Cook	5	5	1	15*	26	6.50	–	–	–

Also batted: M.R.Quinn (2 matches) 0, 13.

BOWLING

	O	M	R	W	Avge	Best	5wI	10wM
S.R.Harmer	257.1	81	603	38	15.86	8-64	3	1
S.J.Cook	140	39	318	17	18.70	5-76	1	–
J.A.Porter	188.5	48	553	27	20.48	5-60	1	–
A.P.Beard	78.1	17	265	11	24.09	4-21	–	–
M.R.Quinn	55.3	10	156	3	52.00	1-19	–	–

Also bowled: D.W.Lawrence 2-1-2-0; R.N.ten Doeschate 6-0-14-1; P.I.Walter 15-1-53-0.

The First-Class Averages (pp 209–221) give the records of Essex players in all first-class county matches.

ESSEX RECORDS

FIRST-CLASS CRICKET

Highest Total	For 761-6d		v	Leics	Chelmsford	1990
	V 803-4d		by	Kent	Brentwood	1934
Lowest Total	For 20		v	Lancashire	Chelmsford	2013
	V 14		by	Surrey	Chelmsford	1983
Highest Innings	For 343*	P.A.Perrin	v	Derbyshire	Chesterfield	1904
	V 332	W.H.Ashdown	for	Kent	Brentwood	1934

Highest Partnership for each Wicket

1st	373	N.L.J.Browne/A.N.Cook	v	Middlesex	Chelmsford	2017
2nd	403	G.A.Gooch/P.J.Prichard	v	Leics	Chelmsford	1990
3rd	347*	M.E.Waugh/N.Hussain	v	Lancashire	Ilford	1992
4th	314	Salim Malik/N.Hussain	v	Surrey	The Oval	1991
5th	339	J.C.Mickleburgh/J.S.Foster	v	Durham	Chester-le-St[2]	2010
6th	253	A.J.A.Wheater/J.S.Foster	v	Northants	Chelmsford	2011
7th	261	J.W.H.T.Douglas/J.Freeman	v	Lancashire	Leyton	1914
8th	263	D.R.Wilcox/R.M.Taylor	v	Warwicks	Southend	1946
9th	251	J.W.H.T.Douglas/S.N.Hare	v	Derbyshire	Leyton	1921
10th	218	F.H.Vigar/T.P.B.Smith	v	Derbyshire	Chesterfield	1947

Best Bowling	For 10- 32	H.Pickett	v	Leics	Leyton	1895
(Innings)	V 10- 40	E.G.Dennett	for	Glos	Bristol	1906
Best Bowling	For 17-119	W.Mead	v	Hampshire	Southampton[1]	1895
(Match)	V 17- 56	C.W.L.Parker	for	Glos	Gloucester	1925

Most Runs – Season	2559	G.A.Gooch	(av 67.34)		1984
Most Runs – Career	30701	G.A.Gooch	(av 51.77)		1973-97
Most 100s – Season	9	J.O'Connor			1929, 1934
	9	D.J.Insole			1955
Most 100s – Career	94	G.A.Gooch			1973-97
Most Wkts – Season	172	T.P.B Smith	(av 27.13)		1947
Most Wkts – Career	1610	T.P.B.Smith	(av 26.68)		1929-51
Most Career W-K Dismissals	1231	B.Taylor	(1040 ct; 191 st)		1949-73
Most Career Catches in the Field	519	K.W.R.Fletcher			1962-88

LIMITED-OVERS CRICKET

Highest Total	50ov	391-5		v	Surrey	The Oval	2008
	40ov	368-7		v	Scotland	Chelmsford	2013
	T20	242-3		v	Sussex	Chelmsford	2008
Lowest Total	50ov	57		v	Lancashire	Lord's	1996
	40ov	69		v	Derbyshire	Chesterfield	1974
	T20	74		v	Middlesex	Chelmsford	2013
Highest Innings	50ov	201*	R.S.Bopara	v	Leics	Leicester	2008
	40ov	180	R.N.ten Doeschate	v	Scotland	Chelmsford	2013
	T20	152*	G.R.Napier	v	Sussex	Chelmsford	2008
Best Bowling	50ov	5- 8	J.K.Lever	v	Middlesex	Westcliff	1972
		5- 8	G.A.Gooch	v	Cheshire	Chester	1995
	40ov	8-26	K.D.Boyce	v	Lancashire	Manchester	1971
	T20	6-16	T.G.Southee	v	Glamorgan	Chelmsford	2011

GLAMORGAN

Formation of Present Club: 6 July 1888
Inaugural First-Class Match: 1921
Colours: Blue and Gold
Badge: Gold Daffodil
County Champions: (3) 1948, 1969, 1997
Pro 40/National League (Div 1) Winners: (2) 2002, 2004
Sunday League Winners: (1) 1993
Twenty20 Cup Winners: (0); best – Semi-Finalist 2004, 2017

GLAMORGAN

Chief Executive: Hugh Morris, Sophia Gardens, Cardiff, CF11 9XR • Tel: 02920 409380 • email: info@glamorgancricket.co.uk • Web: www.glamorgancricket.com • Twitter: @GlamCricket (73,407 followers)

Director of Cricket: Mark Wallace. **Head Coach:** Matthew Maynard. **2nd XI Coach:** Steve Watkin. **Player Development Manager:** Richard Almond. **Captain:** C.B.Cooke. **Vice-captain:** D.L.Lloyd. **Overseas Players:** C.A.Ingram, M.Labuschagne and M.G.Neser. **2021 Testimonial:** M.G.Hogan. **Head Groundsman:** Robin Saxton. **Scorer:** Andrew K.Hignell. ‡ New registration. ^{NQ} Not qualified for England.

CAREY, Lukas John (Pontarddulais CS; Gower SFC), b Carmarthen 17 Jul 1997. 6'0". RHB, RFM. Squad No 17. Debut (Glamorgan) 2016. Glamorgan 2nd XI debut 2014. Wales MC 2016. HS 62* v Derbys (Swansea) 2019. BB 4-54 v Middx (Cardiff) 2019. LO HS 39 v Somerset (Cardiff) 2019 (RLC). LO BB 2-57 v Somerset (Taunton) 2018 (RLC). T20 HS 5. T20 BB 1-15.

CARLSON, Kiran Shah (Whitchurch HS; Cardiff U), b Cardiff 16 May 1998. 5'8". RHB, OB. Squad No 5. Debut (Glamorgan) 2016. Cardiff MCCU 2019. Glamorgan 2nd XI debut 2015. Wales MC 2014. HS 191 v Glos (Cardiff) 2017. BB 5-28 v Northants (Northampton) 2016 – on debut. Youngest ever to score a century & take five wkts in an innings in a f-c career, aged 18y 119d. LO HS 63 v Somerset (Cardiff) 2017 (RLC). LO BB 1-30 v Middx (Radlett) 2017 (RLC). T20 HS 58.

COOKE, Christopher Barry (Bishops S, Cape Town; U of Cape Town), b Johannesburg, South Africa 30 May 1986. 5'11". RHB, WK. Squad No 46. W Province 2009-10. Glamorgan debut 2013; cap 2016; captain 2019 to date. HS 171 v Kent (Canterbury) 2014. LO HS 161 v Glos (Bristol) 2019 (RLC). T20 HS 72.

COOKE, Joseph Michael (Durham U), b Hemel Hempstead, Herts 30 May 1997. LHB, RMF. Squad No 57. Durham MCCU 2017-18. Glamorgan debut 2020. Sussex 2nd XI 2018-19. Glamorgan 2nd XI debut 2019. Hertfordshire 2014-18. HS 23 v Warwks (Cardiff) 2020. BB 1-26 DU v Warwks (Birmingham) 2018.

CULLEN, Thomas Nicholas (Aquinas C, Stockport; Cardiff Met U), b Perth, Australia 4 Jan 1992. RHB, WK. Squad No 54. Cardiff MCCU 2015-17. Glamorgan debut 2017. HS 63 v Northants (Northampton) 2019.

DOUTHWAITE, Daniel Alexander (Reed's S, Cobham), b Kingston-upon-Thames, Surrey 8 Feb 1997. RHB, RMF. Squad No 88. Cardiff MCCU 2019. Glamorgan debut 2019. Warwickshire 2018 (l-o only). Surrey 2nd XI 2015-16. Sussex 2nd XI 2016. HS 100* Cardiff MCCU v Sussex (Hove) 2019. Gm HS 86 v Northants (Northampton) 2020. BB 4-48 v Derbys (Derby) 2019. LO HS 52* v Sussex (Hove) 2019 (RLC). LO BB 3-43 Wa v West Indies A (Birmingham) 2018. T20 HS 24. T20 BB 1-7.

HEMPHREY, Charles Richard (Harvey GS, Folkestone), b Doncaster, Yorks 31 Aug 1990. RHB, OB. Squad No 22. Queensland 2014-15 to 2019-20. Glamorgan debut 2019. HS 118 Q v SA (Brisbane) 2014-15. Gm HS 75 v Derbys (Derby) 2019. BB 2-56 Q v SA (Adelaide) 2015-16. Gm BB 1-17 v Middx (Cardiff) 2019. LO HS 87 v Middx (Lord's) 2019 (RLC). LO BB 1-18 Q v Cricket Australia (Sydney, DO) 2015-16.

HOGAN, Michael Garry, b Newcastle, New South Wales, Australia 31 May 1981. British passport. 6'5". RHB, RFM. Squad No 31. W Australia 2009-10 to 2015-16. Glamorgan debut/cap 2013; captain 2018; testimonial 2020-21. Big Bash: HH 2011-12 to 2012-13. HS 57 v Lancs (Colwyn Bay) 2015. 50 wkts (3); most – 67 (2013). BB 7-92 v Glos (Bristol) 2013. LO HS 27 WA v Vic (Melbourne) 2011-12. LO BB 5-44 WA v Vic (Melbourne) 2010-11. T20 HS 17*. T20 BB 5-17.

HORTON, Alex Jack (St Edward's, Oxford), b 7 Jan 2004. RHB, WK. Squad No 12. Glamorgan 2nd XI debut 2019. Wales MC 2018-19. Awaiting 1st XI debut.

NQINGRAM, Colin Alexander, b Port Elizabeth, South Africa 3 Jul 1985. LHB, LB. Squad No 41. Free State 2004-05 to 2005-06. Eastern Province 2005-06 to 2008-09. Warriors 2006-07 to 2016-17. Somerset 2014. Glamorgan debut 2015; cap 2017; captain 2018-19 (T20 only). IPL: DD 2011. Big Bash: AS 2017-18 to 2018-19. HH 2020-21. **LOI** (SA): 31 (2010-11 to 2013-14); HS 124 v Z (Bloemfontein) 2010-11 – on debut; BB – . **IT20** (SA): 9 (2010-11 to 2011-12); HS 78 v I (Johannesburg) 2011-12. HS 190 EP v KZN (Port Elizabeth) 2008-09. Gm HS 155* v Notts (Cardiff) 2017. BB 4-16 EP v Boland (Port Elizabeth) 2005-06. Gm BB 3-90 v Essex (Chelmsford) 2015. LO HS 142 v Essex (Cardiff) 2017 (RLC). LO BB 4-39 v Middx (Radlett) 2017 (RLC). T20 HS 127*. T20 BB 4-32.

NQLABUSCHAGNE, Marnus, b Klerksdorp, South Africa 22 Jun 1994. RHB, LB/RM. Squad No 99. Queensland 2014-15 to date. Glamorgan debut 2019; cap 2019. Big Bash: BH 2016-17 to date. *Wisden* 2019. **Tests** (A): 18 (2018-19 to 2020-21); 1000 runs (1): 1104 (2019); HS 215 v NZ (Sydney) 2019-20; BB 3-45 v P (Abu Dhabi) 2018-19. **LOI** (A): 13 (2019-20 to 2020-21); HS 108 v SA (Potchefstroom) 2019-20; BB – . F-c Tours (A): E 2019; I 2018-19 (Aus A); UAE 2018-19 (v P). 1000 runs (1+1); most – 1530 (2019). HS 215 (*see Tests*). Gm HS 182 v Sussex (Hove) 2019, sharing Gm record 2nd wkt partnership of 291 with N.J.Selman. BB 3-45 (*see Tests*). Gm BB 3-52 v Middx (Radlett) 2019. LO HS 135 Q v SA (Brisbane) 2019-20. LO BB 3-46 v Somerset (Cardiff) 2019 (RLC). T20 HS 49. T20 BB 3-13.

LLOYD, David Liam (Darland HS; Shrewsbury S), b St Asaph, Denbighs 15 May 1992. 5'9". RHB, RM. Squad No 73. Debut (Glamorgan) 2012; cap 2019; captain 2020 (50 ov only). Wales MC 2010-11. HS 119 v Glos (Bristol) 2018. BB 3-36 v Northants (Swansea) 2016. LO HS 92 v Middx (Cardiff) 2018 (RLC). LO BB 5-53 v Kent (Swansea) 2017 (RLC). T20 HS 97*. T20 BB 2-13.

McILROY, Jamie Peter (Builth Wells HS), b Hereford 19 Jun 1994. RHB, LFM. Squad No 35. Glamorgan 2nd XI debut 2017. MCC YC 2018-19. Worcestershire 2nd XI 2018. Gloucestershire 2nd XI 2018. Herefordshire 2014-18. Awaiting 1st XI debut.

‡NQNESER, Michael Gertges, b Pretoria, South Africa 29 Mar 1990. 6'0". RHB, RMF. Queensland 2010-11 to date. IPL: KXIP 2013. Big Bash: BH 2011-12. AS 2012-13 to date. **LOI** (A): 2 (2018); HS 6 and BB 2-46 v E (Oval) 2018. F-c Tours (Aus A): E 2019; I 2018-19; UAE 2018-19. HS 121 Q v Tas (Adelaide) 2020-21. BB 6-57 Q v Tas (Hobart) 2017-18. LO HS 122 Q v WA (Sydney, DO) 2017-18. LO BB 4-41 Q v Tas (Perth) 2016-17. T20 HS 40*. T20 BB 3-24.

ROOT, William ('**Billy**') Thomas (Worksop C; Leeds Beckett U), b Sheffield, Yorks 5 Aug 1992. Younger brother of J.E.Root (*see YORKSHIRE*). LHB, OB. Squad No 7. Leeds/ Bradford MCCU 2015-16. Nottinghamshire 2015-18. Glamorgan debut 2019. Suffolk 2014. HS 229 v Northants (Northampton) 2019. BB 3-29 Nt v Sussex (Hove) 2017. Gm BB 2-63 v Northants (Cardiff) 2019. LO HS 113* v Surrey (Cardiff) 2019 (RLC). LO BB 2-36 v Middx (Lord's) 2019 (RLC). T20 HS 40. T20 BB – .

SALTER, Andrew Graham (Milford Haven SFC; Cardiff Met U), b Haverfordwest 1 Jun 1993. 5'9". RHB, OB. Squad No 21. Cardiff MCCU 2012-14. Glamorgan debut 2013. Wales MC 2010-11. HS 88 v Glos (Cardiff) 2017. BB 4-80 v Warwks (Birmingham) 2018. LO HS 51 v Pakistan A (Newport) 2016. LO BB 2-41 v Notts (Nottingham) 2012 (CB40) and 2-41 v Notts (Lord's) 2013 (Y40). T20 HS 39*. T20 BB 4-12.

SELMAN, Nicholas James (Matthew Flinders Anglican C, Buderim), b Brisbane, Australia 18 Oct 1995. 6'4". RHB, RM. Squad No 9. Debut (Glamorgan) 2016. HS 150 v Glos (Newport) 2019. BB 1-22 v Northants (Cardiff) 2019. LO HS 92 v Kent (Canterbury) 2018 (RLC). T20 HS 78.

SISODIYA, Prem (Clifton C; Cardiff Met U), b Cardiff 21 Sep 1998. RHB, SLA. Squad No 32. Debut (Glamorgan) 2018. Cardiff MCCU 2019. Wales MC 2017. HS 38 and CC BB 3-54 v Derbys (Swansea) 2018. BB 4-79 CfU v Somerset (Taunton) 2019. T20 HS 4*. T20 BB 3-26.

^{NQ}**SMITH, Ruaidhri** Alexander James (Llandaff Cathedral S; Shrewsbury S; Bristol U), b Glasgow, Scotland 5 Aug 1994. 6'1". RHB, RM. Squad No 20. Debut (Glamorgan) 2013. Scotland 2017. Wales MC 2010-16. **LOI** (Scot): 2 (2016); HS 10 and BB 1-34 v Afg (Edinburgh) 2016. **IT20** (Scot): 2 (2018-19); HS 9* v Netherlands (Al Amerat) 2018-19; BB – . HS 57* v Glos (Bristol) 2014. BB 5-87 v Durham (Cardiff) 2018. LO HS 14 v Hants (Swansea) 2018 (RLC). LO BB 4-7 v Oman (Al Amerat) 2018-19. T20 HS 22*. T20 BB 4-6.

TAYLOR, Callum Zinzan (The Southport S), b Newport, Monmouths 19 Jun 1998. RHB, OB. Squad No 4. Debut (Glamorgan) 2020, scoring 106 v Northants (Northampton). Glamorgan 2nd XI debut 2017. HS 106 (*see above*). Wales MC 2017. BB 1-20 v Northants (Northampton) 2020. T20 HS 23. T20 BB 2-9.

^{NQ}**van der GUGTEN, Timm**, b Hornsby, Sydney, Australia 25 Feb 1991. 6'1½". RHB, RFM. Squad No 64. New South Wales 2011-12. Netherlands 2012 to date. Glamorgan debut 2016; cap 2018. Big Bash: HH 2014-15. **LOI** (Neth): 4 (2011-12 to 2013); HS 2 (twice); BB 5-24 v Canada (King City, NW) 2013. **IT20** (Neth): 39 (2011-12 to 2019-20); HS 40* v PNG (Dubai, ICCA) 2019-20; BB 3-9 v Singapore (Dubai, ICCA) 2019-20. HS 60* v Glos (Cardiff) 2018. 50 wkts (1): 56 (2016). BB 7-42 v Kent (Cardiff) 2018. LO HS 36 Neth v Nepal (Amstelveen) 2016. LO BB 5-24 (*see LOI*). T20 HS 40*. T20 BB 5-21.

WALKER, Roman Isaac (Ysgol Bryn Alyn), b Wrexham 6 Aug 2000. RHB, RFM. Squad No 37. Glamorgan 2nd XI debut 2016. Wales MC 2018. Awaiting f-c debut. No 1st XI appearances in 2020. LO HS 7* v Sussex (Hove) 2019 (RLC). T20 HS 1. T20 BB 3-39.

RELEASED/RETIRED

(Having made a County 1st XI appearance in 2020)

BALBIRNIE, A. – *see IRELAND*.

BULL, Kieran Andrew (Q Elizabeth HS, Haverfordwest; Cardiff Met U), b Haverfordwest 5 Apr 1995. 6'2". RHB, OB. Glamorgan 2014-20. Cardiff MCCU 2015. Wales MC 2012-13. HS 31 v Glos (Swansea) 2015. BB 4-62 v Kent (Canterbury) 2014. LO HS – . LO BB 1-40 v Middx (Lord's) 2015 (RLC).

De LANGE, M. – *see SOMERSET*.

MORGAN, Alan Owen (Ysgol Gyfun yr Strade, Llanelli; Cardiff U), b Swansea 14 Apr 1994. 5'11". RHB, SLA. Cardiff MCCU 2014. Glamorgan 2016-20. Wales MC 2012-16. HS 103* v Worcs (Worcester) 2016. BB 2-37 v Northants (Northampton) 2016. LO HS 29 and LO BB 2-49 v Pakistan A (Newport) 2016. T20 HS 24. T20 BB – .

WAGG, Graham Grant (Ashlawn S, Rugby), b Rugby, Warwks 28 Apr 1983. 6'0". RHB, LM. Warwickshire 2002-04. Derbyshire 2006-10; cap 2007. Glamorgan 2011-20; cap 2013; testimonial 2019. F-c Tour (Eng A): I 2003-04. HS 200 v Surrey (Guildford) 2015. 50 wkts (2); most – 59 (2008). BB 6-29 v Surrey (Oval) 2014. LO HS 68 v Hants (Southampton) 2019 (RLC). LO BB 4-35 De v Durham (Derby) 2008 (FPT). T20 HS 62. T20 BB 5-14 v Worcs (Worcester) 2013 – Gm record.

C.R.Brown, C.A.J.Meschede left the staff without making a County 1st XI appearance in 2020.

GLAMORGAN 2020

RESULTS SUMMARY

	Place	Won	Lost	Drew	NR
Bob Willis Trophy (Central Group)	6th		2	3	
Vitality Blast (Central Group)	5th	4	5		1

BOB WILLIS TROPHY AVERAGES
BATTING AND FIELDING

Cap		M	I	NO	HS	Runs	Avge	100	50	Ct/St
	C.Z.Taylor	2	4	–	106	153	38.25	1	–	–
2019	M.de Lange	3	5	1	113	131	32.75	1	–	2
2016	C.B.Cooke	5	10	1	82	294	32.66	–	3	16/2
	W.T.Root	5	10	1	118	286	31.77	1	1	1
2013	M.G.Hogan	4	7	4	33*	78	26.00	–	–	1
	T.van der Gugten	4	7	3	30*	98	24.50	–	–	3
	N.J.Selman	5	10	–	73	215	21.50	–	2	10
2013	G.G.Wagg	3	6	1	54	100	20.00	–	1	3
	D.A.Douthwaite	5	10	1	86	160	17.77	–	1	3
	K.S.Carlson	4	8	–	79	109	13.62	–	1	2
	T.N.Cullen	3	6	–	26	80	13.33	–	–	6
	J.M.Cooke	2	4	–	23	48	12.00	–	–	1
	C.R.Hemphrey	3	6	–	20	62	10.33	–	–	3
	K.A.Bull	4	8	1	23	50	7.14	–	–	1

Also batted (1 match each): L.J.Carey 23, 11 (1 ct); A.O.Morgan 28, 0; R.A.J.Smith 23, 3.

BOWLING

	O	M	R	W	Avge	Best	5wI	10wM
R.A.J.Smith	14	4	41	3	13.66	3- 41	–	–
M.de Lange	81.2	17	218	9	24.22	4- 84	–	–
G.G.Wagg	73	14	272	11	24.72	3- 38	–	–
L.J.Carey	24.5	4	82	3	27.33	3- 54	–	–
T.van der Gugten	119	31	362	12	30.16	3- 45	–	–
D.A.Douthwaite	121.1	16	473	14	33.78	3- 42	–	–
M.G.Hogan	139	32	397	8	49.62	3- 59	–	–
K.A.Bull	102.3	4	462	9	51.33	3-112	–	–

Also bowled: K.S.Carlson 1-0-2-0; C.R.Hemphrey 9-0-37-0; A.O.Morgan 11.5-0-43-1; C.Z.Taylor 26-2-81-2.

The First-Class Averages (pp 209–221) give the records of Glamorgan players in all first-class county matches.

GLAMORGAN RECORDS

FIRST-CLASS CRICKET

Highest Total	For 718-3d		v	Sussex	Colwyn Bay	2000
	V 750		by	Northants	Cardiff	2019
Lowest Total	For 22		v	Lancashire	Liverpool	1924
	V 33		by	Leics	Ebbw Vale	1965
Highest Innings	For 309*	S.P.James	v	Sussex	Colwyn Bay	2000
	V 322*	M.B.Loye	for	Northants	Northampton	1998

Highest Partnership for each Wicket

1st	374	M.T.G.Elliott/S.P.James	v	Sussex	Colwyn Bay	2000
2nd	291	N.J.Selman/M.Labuschagne	v	Sussex	Hove	2019
3rd	313	D.E.Davies/W.E.Jones	v	Essex	Brentwood	1948
4th	425*	A.Dale/I.V.A.Richards	v	Middlesex	Cardiff	1993
5th	264	M.Robinson/S.W.Montgomery	v	Hampshire	Bournemouth	1949
6th	240	J.Allenby/M.A.Wallace	v	Surrey	The Oval	2009
7th	211	P.A.Cottey/O.D.Gibson	v	Leics	Swansea	1996
8th	202	D.Davies/J.J.Hills	v	Sussex	Eastbourne	1928
9th	203*	J.J.Hills/J.C.Clay	v	Worcs	Swansea	1929
10th	143	T.Davies/S.A.B.Daniels	v	Glos	Swansea	1982

Best Bowling	For 10- 51	J.Mercer	v	Worcs	Worcester	1936
(Innings)	V 10- 18	G.Geary	for	Leics	Pontypridd	1929
Best Bowling	For 17-212	J.C.Clay	v	Worcs	Swansea	1937
(Match)	V 16- 96	G.Geary	for	Leics	Pontypridd	1929

Most Runs – Season	2276	H.Morris	(av 55.51)		1990
Most Runs – Career	34056	A.Jones	(av 33.03)		1957-83
Most 100s – Season	10	H.Morris			1990
Most 100s – Career	54	M.P.Maynard			1985-2005
Most Wkts – Season	176	J.C.Clay	(av 17.34)		1937
Most Wkts – Career	2174	D.J.Shepherd	(av 20.95)		1950-72
Most Career W-K Dismissals	933	E.W.Jones	(840 ct; 93 st)		1961-83
Most Career Catches in the Field	656	P.M.Walker			1956-72

LIMITED-OVERS CRICKET

Highest Total	50ov	429	v	Surrey	The Oval	2002
	40ov	328-4	v	Lancashire	Colwyn Bay	2011
	T20	240-3	v	Surrey	The Oval	2015
Lowest Total	50ov	68	v	Lancashire	Manchester	1973
	40ov	42	v	Derbyshire	Swansea	1979
	T20	44	v	Surrey	The Oval	2019
Highest Innings	50ov	169*	J.A.Rudolph	v	Sussex	Hove	2014
	40ov	155*	J.H.Kallis	v	Surrey	Pontypridd	1999
	T20	116*	I.J.Thomas	v	Somerset	Taunton	2004
Best Bowling	50ov	6-20	S.D.Thomas	v	Comb Univs	Cardiff	1995
	40ov	7-16	S.D.Thomas	v	Surrey	Swansea	1998
	T20	5-14	G.G.Wagg	v	Worcs	Worcester	2013

GLOUCESTERSHIRE

Formation of Present Club: 1871
Inaugural First-Class Match: 1870
Colours: Blue, Gold, Brown, Silver, Green and Red
Badge: Coat of Arms of the City and County of Bristol
County Champions (since 1890): (0); best – 2nd 1930, 1931, 1947, 1959, 1969, 1986
Gillette/NatWest/C&G Trophy Winners: (5) 1973, 1999, 2000, 2003, 2004
Benson and Hedges Cup Winners: (3) 1977, 1999, 2000
Pro 40/National League (Div 1) Winners: (1) 2000
Royal London One-Day Cup Winners: (1) 2015
Twenty20 Cup Winners: (0); best – Finalist 2007

Chief Executive: Will Brown, Bristol County Ground, Nevil Road, Bristol BS7 9EJ • Tel: 0117 910 8000 • Email: reception@gloscc.co.uk • Web: www.gloscricket.co.uk • Twitter: @Gloscricket (67,152 followers)

Interim Head Coach: Ian Harvey. **Captain**: C.D.J.Dent (f-c) and J.M.R.Taylor (T20). **Vice-Captain**: J.M.R.Taylor. **Overseas Player**: D.J.Worrall. **2021 Testimonial**: None. **Head Groundsman**: Sean Williams. **Scorer**: Adrian Bull. ‡ New registration. ^NQ Not qualified for England.

Gloucestershire revised their capping policy in 2004 and now award players with their County Caps when they make their first-class debut.

BRACEY, James Robert (Filton CS), b Bristol 3 May 1997. Younger brother of S.N.Bracey (Cardiff MCCU 2014-15). 6'1". LHB, WK, occ RM. Squad No 25. Debut (Gloucestershire) 2016; cap 2016. Loughborough MCCU 2017-18. Gloucestershire 2nd XI debut 2015. F-c Tour (EL): A 2019-20. HS 156 v Glamorgan (Cardiff) 2017. BB – . LO HS 113* and LO BB 1-23 v Essex (Chelmsford) 2019 (RLC). T20 HS 64.

CHARLESWORTH, Ben Geoffrey (St Edward's S), b Oxford 19 Nov 2000. Son of G.M.Charlesworth (Griqualand W and Cambridge U 1989-90 to 1993). 6'2½". LHB, RM/OB. Squad No 64. Debut (Gloucestershire) 2018; cap 2018. Gloucestershire 2nd XI debut 2016. Oxfordshire 2016. England U19 2018 to 2018-19. HS 77* and BB 3-25 v Middx (Bristol) 2018. HS 77* v Northants (Bristol) 2019. LO HS 14 v Australia A (Bristol) 2019.

COCKBAIN, Ian Andrew (Maghull HS), b Bootle, Liverpool 17 Feb 1987. Son of I.Cockbain (Lancs and Minor Cos 1979-94). 6'0". RHB, RM. Squad No 28. Debut (Gloucestershire) 2011; cap 2011; testimonial 2019. HS 151* v Surrey (Bristol) 2014. BB 1-23 v Durham MCCU (Bristol) 2016. LO HS 108* v Middx (Lord's) 2017 (RLC). T20 HS 123.

DENT, Christopher David James (Backwell CS; Alton C), b Bristol 20 Jan 1991. 5'9". LHB, WK, occ SLA. Squad No 15. Debut (Gloucestershire) 2010; cap 2010; captain 2018 to date. 1000 runs (4); most – 1336 (2016). HS 268 v Glamorgan (Bristol) 2015. BB 2-21 v Sussex (Hove) 2016. LO HS 151* v Glamorgan (Cardiff) 2013 (Y40). LO BB 4-43 v Leics (Bristol) 2012 (CB40). T20 HS 87. T20 BB 1-4.

GOODMAN, Dominic Charles (Dr Challenor's GS), b Ashford, Kent 23 Oct 2000. 6'6". RHB, RM. Gloucestershire 2nd XI debut 2019. Awaiting 1st XI debut.

HAMMOND, Miles Arthur Halhead (St Edward's S, Oxford), b Cheltenham 11 Jan 1996. 5'11". LHB, OB. Squad No 88. Debut (Gloucestershire) 2013; cap 2013. F-c Tour (MCC): Nepal 2019-20. HS 123* v Middx (Bristol) 2018. BB 1-29 MCC v Nepal (Kirtipur) 2019-20. Gs BB 1-96 v Glamorgan (Bristol) 2013. LO HS 95 v Sussex (Eastbourne) 2019 (RLC). LO BB 2-18 v Northants (Northampton) 2015 (RLC). T20 HS 63. T20 BB – .

HANKINS, George Thomas (Millfield S), b Bath, Somerset 4 Jan 1997. Elder brother of H.J.Hankins (*see below*). 6'1½". RHB, OB. Squad No 21. Debut (Gloucestershire) 2016; cap 2016. Gloucestershire 2nd XI debut 2014. England U19 2016. HS 116 v Northants (Northampton) 2016. BB – . LO HS 92 v Kent (Beckenham) 2018 (RLC). T20 HS 14.

HANKINS, Harry John (Beechen Cliff S), b Bath, Somerset 24 Apr 1999. Younger brother of G.T.Hankins (*see above*). 6'2". RHB, RMF. Debut (Gloucestershire) 2019; cap 2019. Gloucestershire 2nd XI debut 2018. HS 9 v Derbys (Bristol) 2019 – only 1st XI appearance.

HIGGINS, Ryan Francis (Bradfield C), b Harare, Zimbabwe 6 Jan 1995. 5'10". RHB, RM. Squad No 29. Middlesex 2017. Gloucestershire debut/cap 2018. HS 199 v Leics (Leicester) 2019. 50 wkts (1): 50 (2019). BB 7-42 (11-96 match) v Warwks (Bristol) 2020. LO HS 81* v Surrey (Oval) 2018 (RLC). LO BB 4-50 ECB XI v India A (Leeds) 2018. T20 HS 77*. T20 BB 5-13.

HOWELL, Benny Alexander Cameron (The Oratory S), b Bordeaux, France 5 Oct 1988. Son of J.B.Howell (Warwickshire 2nd XI 1978). 5'11". RHB, RM. Squad No 13. Hampshire 2011. Gloucestershire debut/cap 2012. Big Bash: MR 2020-21. Berkshire 2007. HS 163 v Glamorgan (Cardiff) 2017. BB 5-57 v Leics (Leicester) 2013. LO HS 122 v Surrey (Croydon) 2011 (CB40). LO BB 3-37 v Yorks (Leeds) 2015 (RLC). T20 HS 57. T20 BB 5-18.

LACE, Thomas Cresswell (Millfield S), b Hammersmith, Middx 27 May 1998. 5'8". RHB, WK. Squad No 8. Derbyshire 2018-19 (on loan). Middlesex 2019. Gloucestershire debut/cap 2020. Middlesex 2nd XI 2015-18. HS 143 De v Glamorgan (Swansea) 2019. Gs HS 42 v Glamorgan (Cardiff) 2020. LO HS 48 De v Durham (Chester-le-St) 2019 (RLC).

PAYNE, David Alan (Lytchett Minster S), b Poole, Dorset, 15 Feb 1991. 6'2". RHB, LMF. Squad No 14. Debut (Gloucestershire) 2011; cap 2011. Dorset 2009. HS 67* v Glamorgan (Cardiff) 2016. BB 6-26 v Leics (Bristol) 2011. LO HS 36* v Glamorgan (Bristol) 2019 (RLC). LO BB 7-29 v Essex (Chelmsford) 2010 (CB40), inc 4 wkts in 4 balls and 6 wkts in 9 balls – Gs record. T20 HS 10. T20 BB 5-24.

PRICE, Oliver James (Magdalen Coll S), b Oxford 12 Jun 2001. Younger brother of T.J.Price (*see below*). 6'3". RHB, OB. Gloucestershire 2nd XI debut 2018. Oxfordshire 2018-19. Awaiting 1st XI debut.

PRICE, Thomas James (Magdalen Coll S), b Oxford 2 Jan 2000. Elder brother of O.J.Price (*see above*). 6'1". RHB, RM. Debut (Gloucestershire) 2020; cap 2020. Gloucestershire 2nd XI debut 2015. Oxfordshire 2018-19. HS 0 and BB 1-69 v Worcs (Bristol) 2020. LO HS 0. LO BB – .

SCOTT, George Frederick Buchan (Beechwood Park S; St Albans S; Leeds U), b Hemel Hempstead, Herts 6 Nov 1995. Younger brother of J.E.B.Scott (Hertfordshire 2013-18); elder brother of C.F.B.Scott (Durham MCCU 2019) and P.E.B.Scott (Hertfordshire 2014-17). 6'2". RHB, RM. Squad No 17. Leeds/Bradford MCCU 2015-16. Middlesex 2018-19. Gloucestershire debut/cap 2020. Hertfordshire 2011-14. HS 55 M v Leics (Lord's) 2019. Gs HS 44* and BB 2-34 v Warwks (Bristol) 2020. LO HS 63 M v Essex (Chelmsford) 2019 (RLC). LO BB 1-65 M v Lancs (Lord's) 2019 (RLC). T20 HS 38*. T20 BB 1-14.

SHAW, Joshua (Crofton HS, Wakefield; Skills Exchange C), b Wakefield, Yorks 3 Jan 1996. Son of C.Shaw (Yorkshire 1984-88). 6'1". RHB, RMF. Squad No 5. Debut (Gloucestershire) 2016 (on loan); cap 2016. Yorkshire 2016-19. HS 42 Y v Somerset (Leeds) 2018. Gs HS 38* v Worcs (Worcester) 2019. BB 5-79 v Sussex (Bristol) 2016. LO BB – . T20 HS 1. T20 BB 2-39.

SMITH, Thomas Michael John (Seaford Head Community C; Sussex Downs C), b Eastbourne, Sussex 29 Aug 1987. 5'9". RHB, SLA. Squad No 6. Sussex 2007-09. Surrey 2009 (l-o only). Middlesex 2010-13. Gloucestershire debut/cap 2013. HS 84 v Leics (Cheltenham) 2019. BB 4-35 v Kent (Canterbury) 2014. LO HS 65 Sy v Leics (Leicester) 2009 (P40). LO BB 4-26 v Sussex (Cheltenham) 2016 (RLC). T20 HS 36*. T20 BB 5-16 v Warwks (Birmingham) 2020 – Gs record.

TAYLOR, Jack Martin Robert (Chipping Norton S), b Banbury, Oxfordshire 12 Nov 1991. Elder brother of M.D.Taylor (*see below*). 5'11". RHB, OB. Squad No 10. Debut (Gloucestershire) 2010; cap 2010. Oxfordshire 2009-11. HS 156 v Northants (Cheltenham) 2015. BB 4-16 v Glamorgan (Bristol) 2016. LO HS 75 v Glamorgan (Bristol) 2019 (RLC). LO BB 4-38 v Hants (Bristol) 2014 (RLC). T20 HS 80. T20 BB 4-16.

TAYLOR, Matthew David (Chipping Norton S), b Banbury, Oxfordshire 8 Jul 1994. Younger brother of J.M.R.Taylor (*see above*). 6'0". RHB, LMF. Squad No 36. Debut (Gloucestershire) 2013; cap 2013. Oxfordshire 2011-12. HS 48 v Glamorgan (Bristol) 2018. BB 5-15 v Cardiff MCCU (Bristol) 2018. CC BB 5-57 v Lancs (Cheltenham) 2019. LO HS 16 v Kent (Canterbury) 2016 (RLC). LO BB 3-39 v Sussex (Eastbourne) 2019 (RLC). T20 HS 9*. T20 BB 3-16.

van BUUREN, Graeme Lourens, b Pretoria, South Africa 22 Aug 1990. 5'6". RHB, SLA. Squad No 12. Northerns 2009-10 to 2015-16. Titans 2012-13 to 2014-15. Gloucestershire debut/cap 2016. England resident since May 2019. HS 235 Northerns v EP (Centurion) 2014-15. Gs HS 172* v Worcs (Worcester) 2016. BB 4-12 Northerns v SW Districts (Oudtshoorn) 2012-13. Gs BB 4-18 v Durham MCCU (Bristol) 2017. CC BB 3-15 v Glamorgan (Bristol) 2016. LO HS 119* Northerns v EP (Pt Elizabeth, Grey HS) 2013-14. LO BB 5-35 Northerns v SW Districts (Pretoria) 2011-12. T20 HS 64. T20 BB 5-8.

‡**WARNER, Jared** David (Kettleborough Park HS; Silcoates SFC), b Wakefield, Yorks 14 Nov 1996. 6'1". RHB, RFM. Squad No 4. Sussex 2019 (on loan). Yorkshire 2020. Yorkshire 2nd XI 2015-19. England U19 2014-15 to 2015. HS 13* Sx v Middx (Hove) 2019. BB 3-35 Sx v Glamorgan (Hove) 2019. LO BB – .

ᴺQ**WORRALL, Daniel** James (Kardina International C; U of Melbourne), b Melbourne, Australia 10 Jul 1991. 6'0". RHB, RFM. S Australia 2012-13 to date. Gloucestershire debut 2018; cap 2018. Big Bash: MS 2013-14 to 2019-20. AS 2020-21. **LOI** (A): 3 (2016-17); HS 6* v SA (Centurion) 2016-17; BB 1-43 v SA (Benoni) 2016-17. HS 50 v Glamorgan (Bristol) 2018. BB 7-64 (10-148 match) SA v WA (Adelaide) 2018-19. Gs BB 4-45 v Sussex (Hove) 2018. LO HS 16 SA v Tas (N Sydney) 2017-18. LO BB 5-62 SA v Vic (Hobart) 2017-18. T20 HS 62*. T20 BB 4-23.

RELEASED/RETIRED

(Having made a County 1st XI appearance in 2020)

RODERICK, G.H. – *see WORCESTERSHIRE.*

G.S.Drissell and S.G.Whittingham left the staff without making a County 1st XI appearance in 2020.

GLOUCESTERSHIRE 2020

RESULTS SUMMARY

	Place	Won	Lost	Drew	NR
Bob Willis Trophy (Central Group)	5th	1	2	2	
Vitality Blast (Central Group)	SF	8	3		1

BOB WILLIS TROPHY AVERAGES
BATTING AND FIELDING

Cap†		M	I	NO	HS	Runs	Avge	100	50	Ct/St
2016	G.L.van Buuren	5	8	–	72	244	30.50	–	2	3
2018	R.F.Higgins	5	8	1	51	173	24.71	–	1	2
2010	C.D.J.Dent	4	7	–	92	170	24.28	–	2	4
2020	G.F.B.Scott	4	6	2	44*	87	21.75	–	–	–
2020	T.C.Lace	3	4	–	42	73	18.25	–	–	1
2010	J.M.R.Taylor	2	4	–	34	71	17.75	–	–	1
2013	G.H.Roderick	4	7	1	39	101	16.83	–	–	12
2016	G.T.Hankins	5	8	–	69	130	16.25	–	1	7
2018	B.G.Charlesworth	4	6	–	51	78	13.00	–	1	–
2013	M.D.Taylor	5	7	2	19*	43	8.60	–	–	–
2016	J.Shaw	5	7	–	21	50	7.14	–	–	–
2011	D.A.Payne	4	5	1	14	24	6.00	–	–	–

Also batted: J.R.Bracey (1 match – cap 2016) 4; M.A.H.Hammond (1 – cap 2013) 14, 9 (1 ct); T.J.Price (1 – cap 2020) 0, 0; T.M.J.Smith (2 – cap 2013) 24*, 6.

BOWLING

	O	M	R	W	Avge	Best	5wI	10wM
D.A.Payne	95	29	199	14	14.21	5-31	1	–
R.F.Higgins	148.4	41	391	17	23.00	7-42	1	1
M.D.Taylor	115	22	330	11	30.00	3-43	–	–
J.Shaw	99.5	17	328	8	41.00	3-13	–	–
G.F.B.Scott	44	9	129	3	43.00	2-34	–	–

Also bowled: B.G.Charlesworth 27-6-103-1; T.J.Price 18-1-80-1; T.M.J.Smith 5-0-10-0; J.M.R.Taylor 0.1-0-4-0; G.L.van Buuren 21-5-60-1.

The First-Class Averages (pp 209–221) give the records of Gloucestershire players in all first-class county matches.
† Gloucestershire revised their capping policy in 2004 and now award players with their County Caps when they make their first-class debut.

GLOUCESTERSHIRE RECORDS

FIRST-CLASS CRICKET

Highest Total	For 695-9d		v	Middlesex	Gloucester	2004
	V 774-7d		by	Australians	Bristol	1948
Lowest Total	For 17		v	Australians	Cheltenham	1896
	V 12		by	Northants	Gloucester	1907
Highest Innings	For 341	C.M.Spearman	v	Middlesex	Gloucester	2004
	V 319	C.J.L.Rogers	for	Northants	Northampton	2006

Highest Partnership for each Wicket

1st	395	D.M.Young/R.B.Nicholls	v	Oxford U	Oxford	1962
2nd	256	C.T.M.Pugh/T.W.Graveney	v	Derbyshire	Chesterfield	1960
3rd	392	G.H.Roderick/A.P.R.Gidman	v	Leics	Bristol	2014
4th	321	W.R.Hammond/W.L.Neale	v	Leics	Gloucester	1937
5th	261	W.G.Grace/W.O.Moberley	v	Yorkshire	Cheltenham	1876
6th	320	G.L.Jessop/J.H.Board	v	Sussex	Hove	1903
7th	248	W.G.Grace/E.L.Thomas	v	Sussex	Hove	1896
8th	239	W.R.Hammond/A.E.Wilson	v	Lancashire	Bristol	1938
9th	193	W.G.Grace/S.A.P.Kitcat	v	Sussex	Bristol	1896
10th	137	C.N.Miles/L.C.Norwell	v	Worcs	Cheltenham	2014

Best Bowling	For 10-40	E.G.Dennett	v	Essex	Bristol	1906
(Innings)	V 10-66	A.A.Mailey	for	Australians	Cheltenham	1921
	10-66	K.Smales	for	Notts	Stroud	1956
Best Bowling	For 17-56	C.W.L.Parker	v	Essex	Gloucester	1925
(Match)	V 15-87	A.J.Conway	for	Worcs	Moreton-in-M	1914

Most Runs – Season	2860	W.R.Hammond	(av 69.75)		1933
Most Runs – Career	33664	W.R.Hammond	(av 57.05)		1920-51
Most 100s – Season	13	W.R.Hammond			1938
Most 100s – Career	113	W.R.Hammond			1920-51
Most Wkts – Season	222	T.W.J.Goddard	(av 16.80)		1937
	222	T.W.J.Goddard	(av 16.37)		1947
Most Wkts – Career	3170	C.W.L.Parker	(av 19.43)		1903-35
Most Career W-K Dismissals	1054	R.C.Russell	(950 ct; 104 st)		1981-2004
Most Career Catches in the Field	719	C.A.Milton			1948-74

LIMITED-OVERS CRICKET

Highest Total	50ov	401-7		v	Bucks	Wing	2003
	40ov	344-6		v	Northants	Cheltenham	2001
	T20	254-3		v	Middlesex	Uxbridge	2011
Lowest Total	50ov	82		v	Notts	Bristol	1987
	40ov	49		v	Middlesex	Bristol	1978
	T20	68		v	Hampshire	Bristol	2010
Highest Innings	50ov	177	A.J.Wright	v	Scotland	Bristol	1997
	40ov	153	C.M.Spearman	v	Warwicks	Gloucester	2003
	T20	126*	M.Klinger	v	Essex	Bristol	2015
Best Bowling	50ov	6-13	M.J.Procter	v	Hampshire	Southampton[1]	1977
	40ov	7-29	D.A.Payne	v	Essex	Chelmsford	2010
	T20	5-16	T.M.J.Smaith	v	Warwicks	Birmingham	2020

HAMPSHIRE

Formation of Present Club: 12 August 1863
Inaugural First-Class Match: 1864
Colours: Blue, Gold and White
Badge: Tudor Rose and Crown
County Champions: (2) 1961, 1973
NatWest/C&G/FP Trophy Winners: (3) 1991, 2005, 2009
Benson and Hedges Cup Winners: (2) 1988, 1992
Sunday League Winners: (3) 1975, 1978, 1986
Clydesdale Bank Winners: (1) 2012
Royal London One-Day Cup: (1) 2018
Twenty20 Cup Winners: (2) 2010, 2012

HAMPSHIRE
CRICKET

CEO: David Mann, The Ageas Bowl, Botley Road, West End, Southampton SO30 3XH •
Tel: 023 8047 2002 • Email: enquiries@ageasbowl.com • Web: www.ageasbowl.com •
Twitter: @hantscricket (91,288 followers)

Cricket Operations Manager: Tim Tremlett. **Director of Cricket**: Giles White. **1st XI
Manager**: Adrian Birrell. **Assistant Coach**: Alfonso Thomas. **Captain**: J.M.Vince.
Overseas Players: K.J.Abbott and Mohammad Abbas. **2021 Testimonial**: None. **Head
Groundsman**: Simon Lee. **Scorer**: Kevin Baker. ‡ New registration. NQ Not qualified for
England.

NQ**ABBOTT, Kyle** John (Kearnsey C, KZN), b Empangeni, South Africa 18 Jun 1987.
6'3½". RHB, RFM. Squad No 11. KwaZulu-Natal 2008-09 to 2009-10. Dolphins 2008-09
to 2014-15. Hampshire debut 2014; cap 2017. Worcestershire 2016. IPL: KXIP 2016.
Middlesex 2015 (T20 only). **Tests** (SA): 11 (2012-13 to 2016-17); HS 17 v A (Adelaide)
2016-17; BB 7-29 v P (Centurion) 2012-13. **LOI** (SA): 28 (2012-13 to 2016-17); HS 23 v Z
(Bulawayo) 2014; BB 4-21 v Ire (Canberra) 2014-15. **IT20** (SA): 21 (2012-13 to 2015-16);
HS 9* v NZ (Centurion) 2015; BB 3-20 v B (Dhaka) 2015. F-c Tours (SA): A 2016-17; I
2015-16. HS 97* v Lancs (Manchester) 2017. 50 wkts (3+1): 72 (2019). BB 9-40 (17-86
match) v Somerset (Southampton) 2019 – 4th best match figures in CC history. Hat-trick v
Worcs (Worcester) 2018. LO HS 56 v Surrey (Oval) 2017 (RLC). LO BB 4-21 (see LOI).
T20 HS 30. T20 BB 5-14.

ALSOP, Thomas Philip (Lavington S), b High Wycombe, Bucks 26 Nov 1995. Younger
brother of O.J.Alsop (Wiltshire 2010-12). 5'11". LHB, WK, occ SLA. Squad No 9. Debut
(Hampshire) 2014. MCC 2017. F-c Tours (EL): SL 2016-17. UAE 2016-17 (v Afg). HS 150
v Warwks (Birmingham) 2019. BB 2-59 v Yorks (Leeds) 2016. LO HS 130* v Glamorgan
(Southampton) 2019 (RLC). T20 HS 85.

BARKER, Keith Hubert Douglas (Moorhead HS; Fulwood C, Preston), b Manchester
21 Oct 1986. Son of K.H.Barker (British Guiana 1960-61 to 1963-64). Played football for
Blackburn Rovers and Rochdale. 6'3". LHB, LMF. Squad No 10. Warwickshire 2009-18;
cap 2013. Hampshire debut 2019. HS 125 Wa v Surrey (Guildford) 2013. H HS 64 v
Yorks (Southampton) 2019. 50 wkts (3); most – 62 (2016). BB 6-40 Wa v Somerset
(Taunton) 2012. H BB 5-48 v Kent (Canterbury) 2019. LO HS 56 Wa v Scotland
(Birmingham) 2011 (CB40). LO BB 4-33 Wa v Scotland (Birmingham) 2010 (CB40).
T20 HS 46. T20 BB 4-19.

CRANE, Mason Sydney (Lancing C), b Shoreham-by-Sea, Sussex 18 Feb 1997. 5'7". RHB, LB. Squad No 32. Debut (Hampshire) 2015. NSW 2016-17. MCC 2017. Hampshire 2nd XI debut 2013. **Test**: 1 (2017-18); HS 4 and BB 1-193 v A (Sydney) 2017-18. **IT20**: 2 (2017); HS – ; BB 1-38 v SA (Cardiff) 2017. F-c Tours: A 2017-18; WI 2017-18 (EL). HS 29 v Somerset (Taunton) 2017. BB 5-35 v Warwks (Southampton) 2015. LO HS 28* v Somerset (Lord's) 2019 (RLC). LO BB 4-30 v Middx (Southampton) 2015 (RLC). T20 HS 12*. T20 BB 3-15.

CURRIE, Scott William (St Edward's RC & C of E S), b Poole, Dorset 2 May 2001. Younger brother of B.J.Currie (Dorset 2016 to date). 6'5". RHB, RMF. Squad No 44. Debut (Hampshire) 2020. Hampshire 2nd XI debut 2017-19. HS 38 and BB 3-42 v Kent (Canterbury) 2020. T20 HS 2. T20 BB 1-28.

DALE, Ajeet Singh (Wellington C), b Slough, Berks 3 Jul 2000. 6'1". RHB, RFM. Squad No 39. Debut (Hampshire) 2020. Hampshire 2nd XI debut 2018. HS 6 v Kent (Canterbury) 2020. BB 3-20 v Sussex (Hove) 2020.

DAWSON, Liam Andrew (John Bentley S, Calne), b Swindon, Wilts 1 Mar 1990. 5'8". RHB, SLA. Squad No 8. Debut (Hampshire) 2007; cap 2013. Mountaineers 2011-12. Essex 2015 (on loan). Wiltshire 2006-07. **Tests**: 3 (2016-17 to 2017); HS 66* v I (Chennai) 2016-17; BB 2-34 v SA (Lord's) 2017. **LOI**: 3 (2016 to 2018-19); HS 10 and BB 2-70 v P (Cardiff) 2016. **IT20**: 6 (2016 to 2017-18); HS 10 v NZ (Hamilton) 2017-18; BB 3-27 v SL (Southampton) 2016. F-c Tour: I 2016-17. HS 169 v Somerset (Southampton) 2011. BB 7-51 Mountaineers v ME (Mutare) 2011-12 (also scored 110* in same match). H BB 5-29 v Leics (Southampton) 2012. LO HS 113* SJD v Kalabagan (Savar) 2014-15. LO BB 6-47 v Sussex (Southampton) 2015 (RLC). T20 HS 82. T20 BB 5-17.

DONALD, Aneurin Henry Thomas (Pontarddulais CS), b Swansea, Glamorgan 20 Dec 1996. 6'2". RHB, OB. Squad No 12. Glamorgan 2014-18. Hampshire debut 2019. Wales MC 2012. No 1st XI appearances in 2020 due to injury. 1000 runs (1): 1088 (2016). HS 234 Gm v Derbys (Colwyn Bay) 2016, in 123 balls, equalling world record for fastest 200, inc 15 sixes, going from 0-127* between lunch and tea, and 127-234 after tea. H HS 173 v Warwks (Southampton) 2019, sharing H record 5th wkt partnership of 262 with I.G.Holland. LO HS 57 v Somerset (Taunton) 2019 (RLC). T20 HS 76.

FULLER, James Kerr (Otago U, NZ), b Cape Town, South Africa 24 Jan 1990. UK passport. 6'3". RHB, RFM. Squad No 26. Otago 2009-10 to 2012-13. Gloucestershire 2011-15; cap 2011. Middlesex 2016-18. Hampshire debut 2019. HS 93 M v Somerset (Taunton) 2016. H HS 54* v Yorks (Leeds) 2019. BB 6-24 (10-79 match) Otago v Wellington (Dunedin) 2012-13. CC BB 6-47 Gs v Surrey (Oval) 2014. H BB 4-17 v Surrey (Arundel) 2020. Hat-tricks (2): Gs v Worcs (Cheltenham) 2013; v Surrey (Arundel) 2020. LO HS 55* v Somerset (Lord's) 2019 (RLC). LO BB 6-35 M v Netherlands (Amstelveen) 2012 (CB40). T20 HS 53*. T20 BB 6-28 M v Hants (Southampton) 2018 – M record.

HOLLAND, Ian Gabriel (Ringwood Secondary C, Melbourne), b Stevens Point, Wisconsin, USA 3 Oct 1990. 6'0". RHB, RMF. Squad No 22. England qualified at the start of the 2020 season. Victoria 2015-16. Hampshire debut 2017. **LOI** (USA): 8 (2019-20); HS 75 v Nepal (Kirtipur) 2019-20; BB 3-11 v UAE (Dubai, ICCA) 2019-20. HS 143 v Warwks (Southampton) 2019, sharing H record 5th wkt partnership of 262 with A.H.T.Donald. BB 4-16 v Somerset (Southampton) 2017. LO HS 75 (see LOI). LO BB 3-11 (see LOI). T20 HS 65. T20 BB 1-25.

McMANUS, Lewis David (Clayesmore S, Bournemouth), b Poole, Dorset 9 Oct 1994. 5'10". RHB, WK. Squad No 18. Debut (Hampshire) 2015. Dorset 2011-13. HS 132* v Surrey (Southampton) 2016. LO HS 47 v Barbados (Bridgetown) 2017-18. T20 HS 59.

MIDDLETON, Fletcha Scott (Wyvern C), b Winchester 21 Jan 2002. Son of T.C.Middleton (Hampshire 1984-95). 5'8½". RHB, OB. Hampshire 2nd XI debut 2018. Awaiting 1st XI debut.

‡**NQMOHAMMAD ABBAS**, b Sialkot, Pakistan 10 Mar 1990. 5'11". RHB, RMF. Sialkot 2008-09 to 2012-13. KRL 2015-16 to 2016-17. SNGPL 2017-18 to 2018-19. Leicestershire 2018-19; cap 2018. Southern Punjab 2019-20 to date. **Tests** (P): 23 (2017 to 2020-21); HS 29 v A (Adelaide) 2019-20; BB 5-33 v A (Abu Dhabi) 2018-19. **LOI** (P): 3 (2018-19); HS – ; BB 1-44 v A (Sharjah) 2018-19. F-c Tours (P): E 2018, 2020; A 2019-20; SA 2018-19; WI 2017; NZ 2020-21; Ire 2018. HS 40 and BB 8-46 (14-93 match) KRL v Karachi Whites (Karachi) 2016-17. CC HS 32* Le v Sussex (Hove) 2018. 50 wkts (1+2); most – 71 (2016-17). CC BB 6-48 Le v Kent (Leicester) 2018. LO HS 15* KRL v HB (Karachi) 2016-17. LO BB 4-31 KRL v SNGPL (Karachi) 2016-17. T20 HS 15*. T20 BB 3-22.

NORTHEAST, Sam Alexander (Harrow S), b Ashford, Kent 16 Oct 1989. 5'11". RHB, LB. Squad No 17. Kent 2007-17; cap 2012; captain 2016-17. Hampshire debut 2018; cap 2019. MCC 2013, 2018. 1000 runs (4); most – 1402 (2016). HS 191 K v Derbys (Canterbury) 2016. H HS 169 v Essex (Southampton) 2019. BB 1-60 K v Glos (Cheltenham) 2013. LO HS 132 K v Somerset (Taunton) 2014 (RLC). T20 HS 114.

ORGAN, Felix Spencer (Canford S), b Sydney, Australia 2 Jun 1999. 5'9". RHB, OB. Squad No 3. Debut (Hampshire) 2017. Hampshire 2nd XI debut 2015. HS 100 v Kent (Southampton) 2019. BB 5-25 v Surrey (Southampton) 2019. LO HS 0. LO BB 1-6 v CC&C (Lucas Street) 2017-18. T20 HS 9. T20 BB 2-21.

SCRIVEN, Thomas Antony Rhys (Magdalen Coll S), b Oxford 18 Nov 1998. 6'0½". RHB, RMF. Squad No 33. Debut (Hampshire) 2020. Hampshire 2nd XI debut 2016. HS 68 and BB 2-24 v Kent (Canterbury) 2020. T20 HS 2. T20 BB – .

STEVENSON, Ryan Anthony (King Edward VI Community C), b Torquay, Devon 2 Apr 1992. 6'2". RHB, RMF. Squad No 47. Debut (Hampshire) 2015. Devon 2015. HS 51 v Surrey (Oval) 2019. BB 4-70 v Middx (Radlett) 2020. LO HS 0. LO BB 1-28 v Essex (Southampton) 2016 (RLC). T20 HS 17. T20 BB 2-28.

TAYLOR, Bradley Jacob (Eggar's S, Alton), b Winchester 14 Mar 1997. 5'11". RHB, OB. Squad No 93. Debut (Hampshire) 2013. Hampshire 2nd XI debut 2013. England U19 2014 to 2014-15. No 1st XI appearances in 2020. HS 36 v Cardiff MCCU (Southampton) 2016. CC HS 20 and BB 4-64 v Lancs (Southport) 2013. LO HS 69 v CC&C (Bridgetown) 2017-18. LO BB 4-26 v CC&C (Lucas Street) 2017-18. T20 HS 9*. T20 BB 2-20.

VINCE, James Michael (Warminster S), b Cuckfield, Sussex 14 Mar 1991. 6'2". RHB, RM. Squad No 14. Debut (Hampshire) 2009; cap 2013; captain 2016 to date. Wiltshire 2007-08. Big Bash: ST 2016-17 to 2017-18. SS 2018-19 to date. **Tests**: 13 (2016 to 2017-18); HS 83 v A (Brisbane) 2017-18; BB – . **LOI**: 16 (2015 to 2020); HS 51 v SL (Cardiff) 2016; BB 1-18 v Ire (Southampton) 2020. **IT20**: 12 (2015-16 to 2019-20); HS 59 v NZ (Christchurch) 2019-20. F-c Tours: A 2017-18; SA 2014-15 (EL); NZ 2017-18; SL 2013-14 (EL). 1000 runs (2); most – 1525 (2014). HS 240 v Essex (Southampton) 2014. BB 5-41 v Loughborough MCCU (Southampton) 2013. CC BB 2-2 v Lancs (Southport) 2013. LO HS 190 v Glos (Southampton) 2019 (RLC) – H record. LO BB 1-18 EL v Australia A (Sydney) 2012-13. T20 HS 107*. T20 BB 1-5.

WEATHERLEY, Joe James (King Edward VI S, Southampton), b Winchester 19 Jan 1997. 6'1". RHB, OB. Squad No 5. Debut (Hampshire) 2016. Kent 2017 (on loan). Hampshire 2nd XI debut 2014. England U19 2014-15. HS 126* v Lancs (Manchester) 2018. BB 1-2 v Notts (Southampton) 2018. LO HS 105* v Kent (Southampton) 2018 (RLC). LO BB 4-25 v T&T (Cave Hill) 2017-18. T20 HS 68. T20 BB – .

[NQ]**WHEAL, Brad**ley Thomas James (Clifton C), b Durban, South Africa 28 Aug 1996. 5'9". RHB, RMF. Squad No 58. Debut (Hampshire) 2015. **LOI** (Scot): 13 (2015-16 to 2019); HS 14 v Ire (Harare) 2017-18; BB 3-34 v WI (Harare) 2017-18. **IT20** (Scot): 5 (2015-16 to 2016-17); HS 2* and BB 3-20 v Hong Kong (Mong Kok) 2015-16. HS 25* v Somerset (Taunton) 2018. BB 6-51 v Notts (Nottingham) 2016. LO HS 18* v CC&C (Bridgetown) 2017-18. LO BB 4-38 v Kent (Southampton) 2016 (RLC). T20 HS 16. T20 BB 3-20.

WOOD, Christopher Philip (Alton C), b Basingstoke 27 June 1990. 6'2". RHB, LM. Squad No 25. Debut (Hampshire) 2010; cap 2018. HS 105* v Leics (Leicester) 2012. BB 5-39 v Kent (Canterbury) 2014. LO HS 41 v Essex (Southampton) 2013 (Y40). LO BB 5-22 v Glamorgan (Cardiff) 2012 (CB40). T20 HS 27. T20 BB 5-32.

RELEASED/RETIRED

(Having made a County 1st XI appearance in 2020)

CAME, Harry Robert Charles (Bradfield C), b Basingstoke 27 Aug 1998. Son of P.R.C.Came (Hampshire 2nd XI 1986-87); grandson of K.C.Came (Free Foresters 1957); great-grandson of R.W.V.Robins (Middlesex, Cambridge U & England 1925-58). 5'9". RHB, OB. Hampshire 2019-20. Hampshire 2nd XI debut 2017. Kent 2nd XI 2017-18. HS 25 v Sussex (Hove) 2020.

HARRISON, Calvin Grant (King's C, Taunton; Oxford Brookes U), b Durban, S Africa 29 Apr 1998. RHB, LBG. Oxford MCCU 2019. Hampshire 2020 (T20 only). Somerset 2nd XI 2015-17. Warwickshire 2nd XI 2017. Surrey 2nd XI 2018. Gloucestershire 2nd XI 2018-19. Hampshire 2nd XI 2019. HS 37* and BB 1-30 OU v Middx (Northwood) 2019. T20 HS 2*. T20 BB 1-39.

[NQ]**MUNSEY, Henry George** (Loretto S), b Oxford 22 Feb 1993. LHB, RMF. Northamptonshire 2015. Scotland 2017 to 2017-18. Leicestershire 2019 (l-o only). Hampshire 2020 (T20 only). **LOI** (Scot): 25 (2016-17 to 2019-20); HS 61 v SL (Edinburgh) 2019. **IT20** (Scot): 38 (2015 to 2019-20); HS 127* v Neth (Dublin) 2019. HS 100* Scot v Namibia (Alloway) 2017. LO HS 96 Scot v Oman (Al Amerat) 2018-19. T20 HS 127*.

[NQ]**SHAHEEN** Shah **AFRIDI**, b Khyber Agency, Pakistan 6 Apr 2000. 6'4½". LHB, LFM. Khan Research Laboratories 2017-18. Northern Areas 2019-20. Hampshire 2020 (T20 only). **Tests** (P): 15 (2018-19 to 2020-21); HS 14 v SA (Cape Town) 2018-19; BB 5-77 v SL (Karachi) 2019-20. **LOI** (P): 22 (2018-19 to 2020-21); HS 19* v E (Leeds) 2019; BB 6-35 v B (Lord's) 2019. **IT20** (P): 21 (2017-18 to 2020-21); HS 10* v NZ (Auckland) 2020-21; BB 3-20 v NZ (Dubai, DSC) 2018-19. F-c Tours (P): E 2020; A 2019-20; SA 2018-19; NZ 2020-21. HS 25 P v Australia A (Perth, OS) 2019-20. BB 8-39 KRL v Rawalpindi (Rawalpindi) 2017-18 – on f-c debut, aged 17y 174d. LO HS 19* (*see LOI*). LO BB 6-35 (*see LOI*). T20 HS 14. T20 BB 6-19 v Middx (Southampton) 2020 – H record.

F.H.Edwards, R.R.Rossouw and O.C.Soames left the staff without making a County 1st XI appearance in 2020.

HAMPSHIRE 2020

RESULTS SUMMARY

	Place	Won	Lost	Drew	NR
Bob Willis Trophy (South Group)	4th	2	2	1	
Vitality Blast (South Group)	6th	2	7		1

BOB WILLIS TROPHY AVERAGES
BATTING AND FIELDING

Cap		M	I	NO	HS	Runs	Avge	100	50	Ct/St
	J.J.Weatherley	5	7	1	98	263	43.83	–	2	2
	K.H.D.Barker	2	4	2	28*	63	31.50	–	–	1
	T.A.R.Scriven	2	3	–	68	84	28.00	–	1	1
2019	S.A.Northeast	5	7	–	81	181	25.85	–	2	–
	B.T.J.Wheal	3	3	2	14*	24	24.00	–	–	–
	T.P.Alsop	5	7	–	87	164	23.42	–	1	5
	L.D.McManus	5	7	–	50	142	20.28	–	1	11/2
	I.G.Holland	5	7	–	42	115	16.42	–	–	4
	J.K.Fuller	4	5	1	30	61	15.25	–	–	2
	H.R.C.Came	4	5	–	25	49	9.80	–	–	1
	F.S.Organ	5	7	–	16	60	8.57	–	–	1
	M.S.Crane	4	5	1	25*	33	8.25	–	–	–
	A.S.Dale	2	4	1	6	7	2.33	–	–	–

Also batted: S.W.Currie (1 match) 38, 0 (2 ct); L.A.Dawson (1 – cap 2013) 43* (3 ct); R.A.Stevenson (2) 0.

BOWLING

	O	M	R	W	Avge	Best	5wI	10wM
F.S.Organ	27	3	90	7	12.85	4-42	–	–
M.S.Crane	60.4	8	190	14	13.57	3-19	–	–
I.G.Holland	129	41	297	17	17.47	6-60	1	–
A.S.Dale	21	4	73	4	18.25	3-20	–	–
S.W.Currie	17	4	58	3	19.33	3-42	–	–
R.A.Stevenson	32	8	103	5	20.60	4-70	–	–
T.A.R.Scriven	21	3	79	3	26.33	2-24	–	–
K.H.D.Barker	66	13	201	7	28.71	2-44	–	–
J.K.Fuller	70	12	293	9	32.55	4-17	–	–
B.T.J.Wheal	61	21	203	5	40.60	2-11	–	–

Also bowled: L.A.Dawson 16.5-5-39-2.

The First-Class Averages (pp 209–221) give the records of Hampshire players in all first-class county matches.

HAMPSHIRE RECORDS

FIRST-CLASS CRICKET

Highest Total	For 714-5d		v	Notts	Southampton[2]	2005
	V 742		by	Surrey	The Oval	1909
Lowest Total	For 15		v	Warwicks	Birmingham	1922
	V 23		by	Yorkshire	Middlesbrough	1965
Highest Innings	For 316	R.H.Moore	v	Warwicks	Bournemouth	1937
	V 303*	G.A.Hick	for	Worcs	Southampton[1]	1997

Highest Partnership for each Wicket

1st	347	V.P.Terry/C.L.Smith	v	Warwicks	Birmingham	1987
2nd	373	J.H.K.Adams/M.A.Carberry	v	Somerset	Taunton	2011
3rd	523	M.A.Carberry/N.D.McKenzie	v	Yorkshire	Southampton[2]	2011
4th	367	J.H.K.Adams/S.M.Ervine	v	Warwicks	Southampton[2]	2017
5th	262	I.G.Holland/A.H.T.Donald	v	Warwicks	Southampton[2]	2019
6th	411	R.M.Poore/E.G.Wynyard	v	Somerset	Taunton	1899
7th	325	G.Brown/C.H.Abercrombie	v	Essex	Leyton	1913
8th	257	N.Pothas/A.J.Bichel	v	Glos	Cheltenham	2005
9th	230	D.A.Livingstone/A.T.Castell	v	Surrey	Southampton[1]	1962
10th	192	H.A.W.Bowell/W.H.Livsey	v	Worcs	Bournemouth	1921

Best Bowling	For	9- 25	R.M.H.Cottam	v	Lancashire	Manchester	1965
(Innings)	V	10- 46	W.Hickton	for	Lancashire	Manchester	1870
Best Bowling	For	17- 86	K.J.Abbott	v	Somerset	Southampton[2]	2019
(Match)	V	17-103	W.Mycroft	for	Derbyshire	Southampton	1876

Most Runs – Season	2854	C.P.Mead	(av 79.27)	1928
Most Runs – Career	48892	C.P.Mead	(av 48.84)	1905-36
Most 100s – Season	12	C.P.Mead		1928
Most 100s – Career	.138	C.P.Mead		1905-36
Most Wkts – Season	190	A.S.Kennedy	(av 15.61)	1922
Most Wkts – Career	2669	D.Shackleton	(av 18.23)	1948-69
Most Career W-K Dismissals	700	R.J.Parks	(630 ct; 70 st)	1980-92
Most Career Catches in the Field	629	C.P.Mead		1905-36

LIMITED-OVERS CRICKET

Highest Total	50ov	371-4		v	Glamorgan	Southampton[1]	1975
	40ov	353-8		v	Middlesex	Lord's	2005
	T20	249-8		v	Derbyshire	Derby	2017
Lowest Total	50ov	50		v	Yorkshire	Leeds	1991
	40ov	43		v	Essex	Basingstoke	1972
	T20	85		v	Sussex	Southampton[2]	2008
Highest Innings	50ov	190	J.M.Vince	v	Glos	Southampton[2]	2019
	40ov	172	C.G.Greenidge	v	Surrey	Southampton[1]	1987
	T20	124*	M.J.Lumb	v	Essex	Southampton[2]	2009
Best Bowling	50ov	7-30	P.J.Sainsbury	v	Norfolk	Southampton[1]	1965
	40ov	6-20	T.E.Jesty	v	Glamorgan	Cardiff	1975
	T20	6-19	Shaheen Shah Afridi	v	Middlesex	Southampton[2]	2020

[1] County Ground (Northlands Road) [2] Ageas Bowl

KENT

Formation of Present Club: 1 March 1859
Substantial Reorganisation: 6 December 1870
Inaugural First-Class Match: 1864
Colours: Maroon and White
Badge: White Horse on a Red Ground
County Champions: (6) 1906, 1909, 1910, 1913, 1970, 1978
Joint Champions: (1) 1977
Gillette Cup Winners: (2) 1967, 1974
Benson and Hedges Cup Winners: (3) 1973, 1976, 1978
Pro 40/National League (Div 1) Winners: (1) 2001
Sunday League Winners: (4) 1972, 1973, 1976, 1995
Twenty20 Cup Winners: (1) 2007

Cricket Chief Executive: Simon Storey, The Spitfire Ground, Old Dover Road, Canterbury, CT1 3NZ • Tel: 01227 456886 • • Email: feedback@kentcricket.co.uk • Web: www.kentcricket.co.uk • Twitter: @kentcricket (92,551 followers)

Director of Cricket: Paul Downton. **Head Coach**: Matt Walker. **Batting Coach**: Michael Yardy. **Bowling Coach**: Simon Cook. **Captain**: S.W.Billings. **Vice-Captain**: J.L.Denly. **Overseas Player**: M.L.Cummins. **2021 Testimonial**: None. **Head Groundsman**: Adrian Llong. **Scorers**: Lorne Hart and Andy Bateup. **Blast Team Name**: Kent Spitfires. ‡ New registration. ^NQ Not qualified for England.

BELL-DRUMMOND, Daniel James (Millfield S), b Lewisham, London 4 Aug 1993. 5'10". RHB, RMF. Squad No 23. Debut (Kent) 2011; cap 2015. MCC 2014, 2018. 1000 runs (1): 1058 (2014). HS 206* v Loughborough MCCU (Canterbury) 2016. CC HS 166 v Warwks (Canterbury) 2019. BB 2-6 v Loughborough MCCU (Canterbury) 2019. CC BB 2-7 v Yorks (Leeds) 2019. LO HS 171* EL v Sri Lanka A (Canterbury) 2016. LO BB 2-22 v Surrey (Oval) 2019 (RLC). T20 HS 112*. T20 BB 2-19.

BILLINGS, Samuel William (Haileybury S; Loughborough U), b Pembury 15 Jun 1991. 5'11". RHB, WK. Squad No 7. Loughborough MCCU 2011, scoring 131 v Northants (Loughborough) on f-c debut. Kent debut 2011; cap 2015; captain 2018 to date. MCC 2015. IPL: DD 2016-17. CSK 2018-19. Big Bash: SS 2016-17 to 2017-18. ST 2020-21. **LOI**: 21 (2015 to 2020); HS 118 v A (Manchester) 2020. **IT20**: 30 (2015 to 2020); HS 87 v WI (Basseterre) 2018-19 – world record IT20 score by a No 6 batsman. F-c Tours (EL): I 2018-19; UAE 2018-19 (v P). HS 171 v Glos (Bristol) 2016. LO HS 175 EL v Pakistan A (Canterbury) 2016. T20 HS 95*.

BLAKE, Alexander James (Hayes SS; Leeds Met U), b Farnborough 25 Jan 1989. 6'1". LHB, RMF. Squad No 10. Debut (Kent) 2008; cap 2017. Leeds/Bradford UCCE 2009-11 (not f-c). HS 105* v Yorks (Leeds) 2010. BB 2-9 v Pakistanis (Canterbury) 2010. CC BB 1-60 v Hants (Southampton) 2010. LO HS 116 v Somerset (Taunton) 2017 (RLC). LO BB 2-13 v Yorks (Leeds) 2011 (CB40). T20 HS 71*. T20 BB 1-17.

COX, Jordan Matthew (Felsted S), b Margate 21 Oct 2000. 5'8". RHB, WK. Squad No 22. Debut (Kent) 2019. Kent 2nd XI debut 2017. England U19 2018-19. HS 238* v Sussex (Canterbury) 2020, sharing K record 2nd wkt partnership of 423 with J.A.Leaning. LO HS 21 v Pakistanis (Beckenham) 2019. T20 HS 39*.

CRAWLEY, Zak (Tonbridge S), b Bromley 3 Feb 1998. 6'6''. RHB, RM. Squad No 16. Debut (Kent) 2017; cap 2019. YC 2020. **ECB Test Central Contract 2020-21. Tests**: 12 (2019-20 to 2020-21); HS 267 v P (Southampton) 2020. F-c Tours: SA 2019-20; NZ 2019-20; I 2020-21; SL 2019-20, 2020-21. HS (*see Tests*). K HS 168 v Glamorgan (Canterbury) 2018. LO HS 120 v Middx (Canterbury) 2019 (RL). T20 HS 108*.

‡**NQ**CUMMINS, Miguel** Lamar, b St Michael, Barbados 5 Sep 1990. 6'2''. LHB, RF. Squad No 41. Barbados 2011-12 to2018-19. Sagicor HPC 2014. Worcestershire 2016. Middlesex 2019-20. **Tests** (WI): 14 (2016 to 2019); HS 24* v I (Kingston) 2016; BB 6-48 v I (Gros Islet) 2016. **LOI** (WI): 11 (2013-14 to 2017); HS 5 v Afg (Gros Islet) 2017; BB 3-82 v E (Bristol) 2017. F-c Tours (WI): E 2017; NZ 2017-18; I 2013-14 (WIA); SL 2014-15 (WIA); UAE (v P) 2016-17. HS 29* Barbados v Leeward Is (Basseterre) 2015-16. CC HS 25 and CC BB 7-84 (12-166 match) Wo v Sussex (Hove) 2016. CC HS 25 M v Sussex (Radlett) 2020. BB 7-45 Barbados v T&T (Port of Spain) 2012-13. LO HS 20 Barbados v CC&C (Cave Hill) 2018-19. LO BB 4-27 Barbados v Windward Is (Bridgetown) 2017-18. T20 HS 10. T20 BB 3-19.

DENLY, Joseph Liam (Chaucer TC), b Canterbury 16 Mar 1986. 6'0''. RHB, LB. Squad No 6. Kent debut 2004; cap 2008; testimonial 2019. Middlesex 2012-14; cap 2012. Big Bash: BH 2020-21. MCC 2013. PCA 2018. **Tests**: 15 (2018-19 to 2020); HS 94 v A (Oval) 2019; BB 2-42 v SA (Cape Town) 2019-20. **LOI**: 16 (2009 to 2019); HS 87 v SA (Cape Town) 2019-20; BB 1-24 v Ire (Dublin) 2019. **IT20**: 13 (2009 to 2020); HS 30 v WI (Gros Islet) 2018-19; BB 4-19 v SL (Colombo, RPS) 2018-19. F-c Tours: SA 2019-20; WI 2018-19; NZ 2008-09 (Eng A), 2019-20; I 2007-08 (Eng A); SL 2019-20. 1000 runs (4); most – 1266 (2017). HS 227 v Worcs (Worcester) 2017. BB 4-36 v Derbys (Derby) 2018. LO HS 150* v Glamorgan (Canterbury) 2018 (RLC) – K record. LO BB 4-35 v Jamaica (North Sound) 2017-18. T20 HS 127 v Essex (Chelmsford) 2017 – K record. T20 BB 4-19.

GILCHRIST, Nathan Nicholas (St Stithian's C; King's C, Taunton), b Harare, Zimbabwe 11 Jun 2000. 6'5''. RHB, RFM. Squad No 17. Debut (Kent) 2020. Somerset 2nd XI 2016-19. HS 25 v Surrey (Oval) 2020.

GROENEWALD, Timothy Duncan (Maritzburg C; South Africa U), b Pietermaritzburg, South Africa 10 Jan 1984. 6'0''. RHB, RFM. Squad No 12. Debut Cambridge UCCE 2006. Warwickshire 2006-08. Derbyshire 2009-14; cap 2011. Somerset 2014-19; cap 2016. Kent debut 2020. HS 78 Wa v Bangladesh A (Birmingham) 2008. CC HS 76 Wa v Durham (Chester-le-St) 2006. K HS – . BB 6-50 De v Surrey (Croydon) 2009. K BB 1-53 v Sussex (Canterbury) 2020. Hat-trick De v Essex (Chelmsford) 2014. LO HS 57 Sm v Warwks (Birmingham) 2014 (RLC). LO BB 4-22 De v Worcs (Worcester) 2011 (CB40). T20 HS 41. T20 BB 4-21.

HAMIDULLAH QADRI (Derby Moor S; Chellaston Ac), b Kandahar, Afghanistan 5 Dec 2000. 5'9''. RHB, OB. Squad No 75. Derbyshire 2017-19, taking 5-60 v Glamorgan (Cardiff), the youngest to take 5 wkts on CC debut, and the first born this century to play f-c cricket in England. Kent debut 2020. England U19 2018-19. HS 17* De v Lancs (Manchester) 2019. K HS 5 v Middx (Canterbury) 2020. BB 5-60 (*see above*). K BB 1-24 v Essex (Chelmsford) 2020. LO HS 4 De v Notts (Nottingham) 2018 (RLC). LO BB 1-31 De v Northants (Northampton) 2018 (RLC). T20 BB – .

KLAASSEN, Frederick Jack (Sacred Heart C, Auckland, NZ), b Haywards Heath, Sussex 13 Nov 1992. 6'4''. RHB, LMF. Squad No 18. Debut (Kent) 2019. **LOI** (Neth): 4 (2018 to 2019); HS 13 v Nepal (Amstelveen) 2018; BB 3-30 v Nepal (Amstelveen) 2018 – separate matches. **IT20** (Neth): 21 (2018 to 2019); HS 13 v Z (Rotterdam) 2019; BB 3-31 v Ire (Al Amerat) 2018-19. HS 14* v Loughborough MCCU (Canterbury) 2019. CC HS 13 v Yorks (Canterbury) 2019. BB 4-44 v Middx (Canterbury) 2020. LO HS 13 (*see LOI*). LO BB 3-30 (*see LOI*). T20 HS 13. T20 BB 3-31.

NQKUHN, Heino Gunther, b Piet Relief, Mpumalanga, South Africa 1 Apr 1984. 5'10". RHB, WK. Squad No 4. Northerns 2004-05 to 2015-16. Titans 2005-06 to 2018-19. Kent debut/cap 2018. **Tests** (SA): 4 (2017); HS 34 v E (Nottingham) 2017. **IT20** (SA): 7 (2009-10 to 2016-17); HS 29 v SL (Johannesburg) 2016-17. F-c Tours (SAA): E 2017 (SA); A 2014; SL 2010; Z 2016; Ire 2012. 1000 runs (0+1): 1159 (2015-16). HS 244* Titans v Lions (Benoni) 2014-15. Scored 200* SAA v Hants (Southampton) 2017 on UK debut. K HS 140 v Essex (Chelmsford) 2020. LO HS 141* SAA v Bangladesh A (Benoni) 2011. T20 HS 83*.

LEANING, Jack Andrew (Archbishop Holgate's S, York; York C), b Bristol, Glos 18 Oct 1993. 5'10". RHB, RMF. Squad No 34. Yorkshire 2013-19; cap 2016. Kent debut 2020. YC 2015. HS 220* v Sussex (Canterbury) 2020, sharing K record 2nd wkt partnership of 423 with J.M.Cox. BB 2-20 Y v Hants (Southampton) 2019. K BB – . LO HS 131* Y v Leics (Leicester) 2016 (RLC). LO BB 5-22 Y v Unicorns (Leeds) 2013 (Y40). T20 HS 64. T20 BB 1-15.

MILNES, Matthew Edward (West Bridgford CS; Durham U), b Nottingham 29 Jul 1994. 6'1". RHB, RMF. Squad No 8. Durham MCCU 2014. Nottinghamshire 2018. Kent debut 2019. MCC Univs 2015. HS 43 Nt v Yorks (Nottingham) 2018 and 43 v Surrey (Oval) 2020. 50 wkts (1): 58 (2019). BB 5-68 v Notts (Tunbridge W) 2019. LO HS 26 and LO BB 5-79 v Hants (Canterbury) 2019 (RLC). T20 HS 3. T20 BB 3-19.

O'RIORDAN, Marcus Kevin (Tonbridge S), b Pembury 25 Jan 1998. 5'10". RHB, OB. Squad No 55. Debut (Kent) 2019. Kent 2nd XI debut 2014. HS 52* v Hants (Canterbury) 2020. BB 3-50 v Sussex (Canterbury) 2020. T20 HS – .

PODMORE, Harry William (Twyford HS), b Hammersmith, London 23 Jul 1994. 6'3". RHB, RMF. Squad No 1. Glamorgan 2016-17 (on loan). Middlesex 2016 to 2016-17. Derbyshire 2017 (on loan). Kent debut 2018; cap 2019. HS 66* De v Sussex (Hove) 2017. K HS 54* v Essex (Canterbury) 2019. 50 wkts (1): 54 (2019). BB 6-36 v Middx (Canterbury) 2018. LO HS 40 v Hants (Canterbury) 2019 (RLC). LO BB 4-57 v Notts (Nottingham) 2018 (RLC). T20 HS 9. T20 BB 3-13.

QAYYUM, Imran (Villiers HS, Southall; Greenford SFC; City U), b Ealing, Middx 23 May 1993. 6'0". RHB, SLA. Squad No 11. Debut (Kent) 2016. HS 39 v Leics (Canterbury) 2018. BB 3-158 v Northants (Northampton) 2016. LO HS 26* v Pakistanis (Beckenham) 2019. LO BB 4-33 v USA (North Sound) 2017-18. T20 HS 21*. T20 BB 5-21.

ROBINSON, Oliver Graham (Hurtsmere S, Greenwich), b Sidcup 1 Dec 1998. 5'8". RHB, WK, occ RM. Squad No 21. Debut (Kent) 2018. Kent 2nd XI debut 2015. England U19 2017 to 2018. HS 143 v Warwks (Birmingham) 2019. LO HS 49 v Pakistanis (Beckenham) 2019. T20 HS 53.

STEVENS, Darren Ian (Hinckley C), b Leicester 30 Apr 1976. 5'11". RHB, RM. Squad No 3. Leicestershire 1997-2004; cap 2002. Kent debut/cap 2005; benefit 2016. MCC 2002. F-c Tour (ECB Acad): SL 2002-03. 1000 runs (3); most – 1304 (2013). HS 237 v Yorks (Leeds) 2019, sharing K record 6th wkt partnership of 346 with S.W.Billings. 50 wkts (4); most – 63 (2017). BB 8-75 v Leics (Canterbury) 2017. LO HS 147 v Glamorgan (Swansea) 2017 (RLC). LO BB 6-25 v Surrey (Beckenham) 2018 (RLC). T20 HS 90. T20 BB 4-14.

NQSTEWART, Grant (All Saints C, Maitland; U of Newcastle), b Kalgoorlie, W Australia 19 Feb 1994. 6'2". RHB, RMF. Squad No 9. UK qualified due to Italian mother. Debut (Kent) 2017. HS 103 and BB 6-22 v Middx (Canterbury) 2018. LO HS 44 v USA (North Sound) 2017-18. LO BB 3-17 v Guyana (Coolidge) 2017-18. T20 HS 21*. T20 BB 2-23.

(Having made a County 1st XI appearance in 2020)

HAGGETT, Calum John (Millfield S), b Taunton, Somerset 30 Oct 1990. 6'3''. LHB,
RMF. Kent 2013-18. HS 80 v Surrey (Oval) 2015. BB 4-15 v Derbys (Derby) 2016. LO HS
45 v Leeward Is (Coolidge) 2016-17. LO BB 4-59 v Windward Is (Coolidge) 2016-17. T20
HS 20. T20 BB 2-12.

THOMAS, Ivan Alfred Astley (John Roan S, Blackheath; Leeds U), b Greenwich, London
25 Sep 1991. 6'4''. RHB, RMF. Leeds/Bradford MCCU 2012-14. Kent 2012-20. HS 13 v
Australians (Canterbury) 2015. CC HS 7* v Glos (Bristol) 2015. BB 5-91 v Leics
(Leicester) 2018. LO HS 6 v Guyana (North Sound) 2017-18. LO BB 4-30 v Jamaica (North
Sound) 2017-18. T20 HS 3*. T20 BB 2-42.

A.P.Rouse left the staff without making a County 1st XI appearance in 2020.

COUNTY CAPS AWARDED IN 2020

Derbyshire	–
Durham	–
Essex	S.J.Cook, A.J.A.Wheater
Glamorgan	–
Gloucestershire	T.C.Lace, T.J.Price, G.F.B.Scott
Hampshire	–
Kent	–
Lancashire	–
Leicestershire	–
Middlesex	–
Northamptonshire	L.A.Procter
Nottinghamshire	H.Hameed
Somerset	–
Surrey	–
Sussex	–
Warwickshire	W.M.H.Rhodes, O.P.Stone
Worcestershire (colours)	J.D.Libby
Yorkshire	D.J.Malan, D.Olivier

*Durham abolished their capping system after 2005. Gloucestershire award caps on
first-class debut. Worcestershire award club colours on Championship debut. Glamorgan's
capping system is now based on a player's number of appearances and not on his
performances.*

KENT 2020

RESULTS SUMMARY

	Place	Won	Lost	Drew	Tied	NR
Bob Willis Trophy (South Group)	2nd	3	1	1		
Vitality Blast (South Group)	QF	5	4		1	1

BOB WILLIS TROPHY AVERAGES
BATTING AND FIELDING

Cap		M	I	NO	HS	Runs	Avge	100	50	Ct/St
2018	H.G.Kuhn	2	4	1	140	202	67.33	1	–	5
	J.M.Cox	4	6	1	238*	324	64.80	1	–	6
	M.K.O'Riordan	5	8	3	52*	216	43.20	–	1	1
	J.A.Leaning	5	8	1	220*	279	39.85	1	–	9
2019	H.W.Podmore	3	3	1	47	79	39.50	–	–	2
2015	D.J.Bell-Drummond	5	9	1	45	185	23.12	–	–	3
	O.G.Robinson	5	6	–	78	138	23.00	–	1	22
	G.Stewart	4	6	–	58	129	21.50	–	1	–
	M.E.Milnes	4	6	–	43	96	16.00	–	–	1
2005	D.I.Stevens	5	6	–	36	77	12.83	–	–	3
	Hamidullah Qadri	4	5	2	5	11	3.66	–	–	–

Also played: S.W.Billings (2 matches – cap 2015) 20 (2 ct); Z.Crawley (1 – cap 2019) 0, 105 (1 ct); J.L.Denly (1 – cap 2008) 89 (1 ct); N.N.Gilchrist (1) 25, 13; T.D.Groenewald (1) did not bat; F.J.Klaassen (1) 0* (1 ct); I.A.A.Thomas (2) 0, 3*.

BOWLING

	O	M	R	W	Avge	Best	5wI	10wM
D.I.Stevens	209	64	452	29	15.58	5-37	3	–
H.W.Podmore	117.3	30	307	19	16.15	5-43	1	–
F.J.Klaassen	27	6	80	4	20.00	4-44	–	–
M.E.Milnes	119.3	29	355	15	23.66	4-46	–	–
M.K.O'Riordan	62.1	5	255	8	31.87	3-50	–	–
I.A.A.Thomas	30	3	136	4	34.00	4-32	–	–
G.Stewart	95.5	19	299	5	59.80	3-48	–	–

Also bowled: D.J.Bell-Drummond 5-0-22-0; J.L.Denly 2-0-12-0; N.N.Gilchrist 9-1-52-0; T.D.Groenewald 28-5-119-2; Hamidullah Qadri 38.4-7-104-1; J.A.Leaning 2-1-2-0.

The First-Class Averages (pp 209–221) give the records of Kent players in all first-class county matches, with the exception of Z.Crawley and J.L.Denly, whose first-class figures for Kent are as above.

KENT RECORDS

FIRST-CLASS CRICKET

Highest Total	For 803-4d		v	Essex	Brentwood	1934
	V 676		by	Australians	Canterbury	1921
Lowest Total	For 18		v	Sussex	Gravesend	1867
	V 16		by	Warwicks	Tonbridge	1913
Highest Innings	For 332	W.H.Ashdown	v	Essex	Brentwood	1934
	V 344	W.G.Grace	for	MCC	Canterbury	1876

Highest Partnership for each Wicket

1st	300	N.R.Taylor/M.R.Benson	v	Derbyshire	Canterbury	1991
2nd	423	J.M.Cox/J.A.Leaning	v	Sussex	Canterbury	2020
3rd	323	R.W.T.Key/M.van Jaarsveld	v	Surrey	Tunbridge Wells	2005
4th	368	P.A.de Silva/G.R.Cowdrey	v	Derbyshire	Maidstone	1995
5th	277	F.E.Woolley/L.E.G.Ames	v	N Zealanders	Canterbury	1931
6th	346	S.W.Billings/D.I.Stevens	v	Yorkshire	Leeds	2019
7th	248	A.P.Day/E.Humphreys	v	Somerset	Taunton	1908
8th	222	S.A.Northeast/J.C.Tredwell	v	Essex	Chelmsford	2016
9th	171	M.A.Ealham/P.A.Strang	v	Notts	Nottingham	1997
10th	235	F.E.Woolley/A.Fielder	v	Worcs	Stourbridge	1909

Best Bowling	For	10- 30	C.Blythe	v	Northants	Northampton	1907
(Innings)	V	10- 48	C.H.G.Bland	for	Sussex	Tonbridge	1899
Best Bowling	For	17- 48	C.Blythe	v	Northants	Northampton	1907
(Match)	V	17-106	T.W.J.Goddard	for	Glos	Bristol	1939

Most Runs – Season	2894	F.E.Woolley	(av 59.06)	1928
Most Runs – Career	47868	F.E.Woolley	(av 41.77)	1906-38
Most 100s – Season	10	F.E.Woolley		1928, 1934
Most 100s – Career	122	F.E.Woolley		1906-38
Most Wkts – Season	262	A.P.Freeman	(av 14.74)	1933
Most Wkts – Career	3340	A.P.Freeman	(av 17.64)	1914-36
Most Career W-K Dismissals	1253	F.H.Huish	(901 ct; 352 st)	1895-1914
Most Career Catches in the Field	773	F.E.Woolley		1906-38

LIMITED-OVERS CRICKET

Highest Total	50ov	384-6		v	Berkshire	Finchampstead	1994
		384-8		v	Surrey	Beckenham	2018
	40ov	337-7		v	Sussex	Canterbury	2013
	T20	231-7		v	Surrey	The Oval	2015
		231-5		v	Somerset	Canterbury	2018
Lowest Total	50ov	60		v	Somerset	Taunton	1979
	40ov	83		v	Middlesex	Lord's	1984
	T20	72		v	Hampshire	Southampton[2]	2011
Highest Innings	50ov	150*	J.L.Denly	v	Glamorgan	Canterbury	2018
	40ov	146	A.Symonds	v	Lancashire	Tunbridge Wells	2004
	T20	127	J.L.Denly	v	Essex	Chelmsford	2017
Best Bowling	50ov	8-31	D.L.Underwood	v	Scotland	Edinburgh	1987
	40ov	6- 9	R.A.Woolmer	v	Derbyshire	Chesterfield	1979
	T20	5-11	A.F.Milne	v	Somerset	Taunton	2017

LANCASHIRE

Formation of Present Club: 12 January 1864
Inaugural First-Class Match: 1865
Colours: Red, Green and Blue
Badge: Red Rose
County Champions (since 1890): (8) 1897, 1904, 1926, 1927, 1928, 1930, 1934, 2011
Joint Champions: (1) 1950
Gillette/NatWest Trophy Winners: (7) 1970, 1971, 1972, 1975, 1990, 1996, 1998
Benson and Hedges Cup Winners: (4) 1984, 1990, 1995, 1996
Pro 40/National League (Div 1) Winners: (1) 1999.
Sunday League Winners: (4) 1969, 1970, 1989, 1998
Twenty20 Cup Winners: (1) 2015

Chief Executive: Daniel Gidney, Emirates Old Trafford, Talbot Road, Manchester M16 0PX • Tel: 0161 282 4000 • Email: enquiries@lancashirecricket.co.uk • Web: www.lancashirecricket.co.uk • Twitter: @lancscricket (117,463 followers)

Director of Cricket: Paul Allott. **Head Coach**: Glen Chapple. **Assistant Coach/Development Director**: Mark Chilton. **Bowling Coach**: Graham Onions. **Captain**: D.J.Vilas. **Overseas Player**: D.J.Vilas. **2021 Testimonial**: S.D.Parry. **Head Groundsman**: Matthew Merchant. **Scorer**: Chris Rimmer. **Blast Team Name**: Lancashire Lightning. ‡ New registration. ^{NQ} Not qualified for England.

ANDERSON, James Michael (St Theodore RC HS and SFC, Burnley), b Burnley 30 Jul 1982. 6'2". LHB, RFM. Squad No 9. Debut (Lancashire) 2002; cap 2003; benefit 2012. Auckland 2007-08. YC 2003. *Wisden* 2008. OBE 2015. **ECB Test Central Contract 2020-21. Tests**: 160 (2003 to 2020-21); HS 81 v I (Nottingham) 2014, sharing a world Test record 10th wkt partnership of 198 with J.E.Root; 50 wkts (3); most – 57 (2010); BB 7-42 v WI (Lord's) 2017. **LOI**: 194 (2002-03 to 2014-15); HS 28 v NZ (Southampton) 2013; BB 5-23 v SA (Port Elizabeth) 2009-10. Hat-trick v P (Oval) 2003 – 1st for E in 373 LOI. **IT20**: 19 (2006-07 to 2009); HS 1* v A (Sydney) 2006-07; BB 3-23 v Netherlands (Lord's) 2009. F-c Tours: A 2006-07, 2010-11, 2013-14, 2017-18; SA 2004-05, 2009-10, 2015-16, 2019-20; WI 2003-04, 2005-06 (Eng A) *(part)*, 2008-09, 2014-15, 2018-19; NZ 2007-08, 2012-13, 2017-18; I 2005-06 *(part)*, 2008-09, 2012-13, 2016-17, 2020-21; SL 2003-04, 2007-08, 2011-12, 2018-19, 2020-21; UAE 2011-12 (v P), 2015-16 (v P). HS 81 *(see Tests)*. La HS 42 v Surrey (Manchester) 2015. 50 wkts (4); most – 60 (2005, 2017). BB 7-42 *(see Tests)*. La BB 7-77 v Essex (Chelmsford) 2015. Hat-trick v Essex (Manchester) 2003. LO HS 28 *(see LOI)*. LO BB 5-23 *(see LOI)*. T20 HS 16. T20 BB 3-23.

BAILEY, Thomas Ernest (Our Lady's Catholic HS, Preston), b Preston 21 Apr 1991. 6'4". RHB, RMF. Squad No 8. Debut (Lancashire) 2012; cap 2018. F-c Tour (EL): I 2018-19. HS 68 v Northants (Manchester) 2019. 50 wkts (1): 65 (2018). BB 5-12 v Leics (Leicester) 2015. LO HS 33 v Yorks (Manchester) 2018 (RLC). LO BB 3-31 v Middx (Blackpool) 2015 (RLC). T20 HS 10. T20 BB 5-17.

BALDERSON, George Philip (Cheadle Hulme HS), b Manchester 11 Oct 2000. 5'11". LHB, RM. Squad No 10. Debut (Lancashire) 2020. Lancashire 2nd XI debut 2018. England U19 2018-19. HS 61* and BB 3-63 v Derbys (Liverpool) 2020.

‡**BLATHERWICK, Jack** Morgan (Holgate Ac, Hucknall; Central C, Nottingham), b Nottingham 4 June 1998. 6'2". RHB, RMF. Squad No 4. Nottinghamshire 2019. Nottinghamshire 2nd XI 2016-19. England U19 2017. HS 4* Nt v Warwks (Nottingham) 2019. BB 1-82 Nt v Surrey (Oval) 2019. LO HS 3* Nt v Warwks (Nottingham) 2018 (RLC). LO BB 1-55 Nh v Australia A (Northampton) 2019.

BOHANNON, Joshua James (Harper Green HS), b Bolton 9 Apr 1997. 5'8". RHB, RM. Squad No 20. Debut (Lancashire) 2018. Lancashire 2nd XI debut 2014. HS 174 v Derbys (Manchester) 2019. BB 3-46 v Hants (Southampton) 2018. LO HS 55* v Yorks (Leeds) 2019 (RLC). LO BB 1-33 v Notts (Nottingham) 2019. T20 HS 23.

BURROWS, George Davidson (Liverpool John Moores U), b Wigan 22 Jun 1998. 6'5". RHB, RFM. Squad No 21. Debut (Lancashire) 2020. Lancashire 2nd XI debut 2017. HS 1 and BB 2-20 v Derbys (Liverpool) 2020.

BUTTLER, Joseph Charles (King's C, Taunton), b Taunton, Somerset 8 Sep 1990. 6'0". RHB, WK. Squad No 6. Somerset 2009-13; cap 2013. Lancashire debut 2014; *cap 2018*. IPL: MI 2016-17. RR 2018 to date. Big Bash: MR 2013-14. ST 2017-18 to 2018-19. *Wisden* 2018. MBE 2020. **ECB Test & L-O Central Contract 2020-21.** Tests: 50 (2014 to 2020-21); HS 152 v P (Southampton) 2020. **LOI**: 145 (2011-12 to 2020); HS 150 v WI (St George's) 2018-19. **IT20**: 74 (2011 to 2020-21); HS 77* v A (Southampton) 2020. F-c Tours: SA 2019-20; WI 2015, 2018-19; NZ 2019-20; I 2016-17, 2020-21; SL 2018-19, 2019-20, 2020-21; UAE 2015-16 (v P). HS 144 Sm v Hants (Southampton) 2010. La HS 100* v Durham (Chester-le-St) 2014. BB – . LO HS 150 (*see LOI*). T20 HS 95*.

CROFT, Steven John (Highfield HS, Blackpool; Myerscough C), b Blackpool 11 Oct 1984. 5'10". RHB, OB. Squad No 15. Debut (Lancashire) 2005; cap 2010; captain 2017; testimonial 2018. Auckland 2008-09. HS 156 v Northants (Manchester) 2014. BB 6-41 v Worcs (Manchester) 2012. LO HS 127 v Warwks (Birmingham) 2017 (RLC). LO BB 4-24 v Scotland (Manchester) 2008 (FPT). T20 HS 94*. T20 BB 3-6.

DAVIES, Alexander Luke (Queen Elizabeth GS, Blackburn), b Darwen 23 Aug 1994. 5'7". RHB, WK. Squad No 17. Debut (Lancashire) 2012; cap 2017. F-c Tour (EL): WI 2017-18. 1000 runs (1): 1046 (2017). HS 147 v Northants (Northampton) 2019. LO HS 147 v Durham (Manchester) 2018 (RLC). T20 HS 94*.

GLEESON, Richard James (Baines HS), b Blackpool, Lancs 2 Dec 1987. 6'3". RHB, RFM. Squad No 11. Northamptonshire 2015-18. Lancashire debut 2018. MCC 2018. Big Bash: MR 2019-20. Cumberland 2010-15. F-c Tour (EL): WI 2017-18. HS 31 Nh v Glos (Bristol) 2016. La HS 11 v Leics (Liverpool) 2019. BB 6-43 v Leics (Leicester) 2019. Hat-trick MCC v Essex (Bridgetown) 2017-18. LO HS 13 EL v West Indies A (Coolidge) 2017-18. LO BB 5-47 Nh v Worcs (Worcester) 2016 (RLC). T20 HS 7*. T20 BB 3-12.

HARTLEY, Tom William (Merchant Taylors S), b Ormskirk 3 May 1999. 6'3". LHB, SLA. Squad No 2. Debut (Lancashire) 2020. Lancashire 2nd XI debut 2016. HS 13* v Notts (Nottingham) 2020. BB 3-79 v Derbys (Liverpool) 2020. T20 HS 4. T20 BB 2-21.

HURT, Liam Jack (Balshaw's CE HS, Leyland), b Preston 15 Mar 1994. 6'4". RHB, RMF. Squad No 22. Debut (Lancashire) 2019. Leicestershire 2015 (l-o only). HS 38 v Leics (Leicester) 2019. BB 4-27 v Durham (Chester-le-St) 2020. LO HS 15* v Yorks (Leeds) 2019 (RLC). LO BB 2-24 v Leics (Manchester) 2019 (RLC). T20 HS 0. T20 BB 2-29.

JENNINGS, Keaton Kent (King Edward VII S, Johannesburg), b Johannesburg, South Africa 19 Jun 1992. Son of R.V.Jennings (Transvaal 1973-74 to 1992-93), brother of D.Jennings (Gauteng and Easterns 1999 to 2003-04), nephew of K.E.Jennings (Northern Transvaal 1981-82 to 1982-83). 6'4". LHB, RM. Squad No 1. Gauteng 2011-12. Durham 2012-17; captain 2017 (1-o only). Lancashire debut/cap 2018. **Tests**: 17 (2016-17 to 2018-19); HS 146* v SL (Galle) 2018-19; scored 112 v I (Mumbai) on debut; BB – . F-c Tours (C=Captain): A 2019-20 (EL)C; WI 2017-18 (EL)C, 2018-19; I 2016-17; SL 2016-17 (EL), 2018-19. 1000 runs (1): 1602 (2016), inc seven hundreds (Du record). HS 221* Du v Yorks (Chester-le-St) 2016. La HS 177 v Worcs (Worcester) 2018. BB 3-37 Du v Sussex (Chester-le-St) 2017. La BB 1-8 v Durham (Sedbergh) 2019. LO HS 139 Du v Warwks (Birmingham) 2017 (RLC). LO BB 2-19 v Worcs (Worcester) 2018 (RLC). T20 HS 108 v Durham (Chester-le-St) 2020 – La record. T20 BB 4-37.

JONES, Robert Peter (Bridgewater HS), b Warrington, Cheshire 3 Nov 1995. 5'10". RHB, LB. Squad No 12. Debut (Lancashire) 2016. Cheshire 2014. HS 122 v Middx (Lord's) 2019. BB 1-18 v Worcs (Worcester) 2018. LO HS 65 v Yorks (Leeds) 2019 (RLC). LO BB 1-3 v Leics (Manchester) 2019 (RLC). T20 HS 38*.

LAMB, Daniel John (St Michael's HS, Chorley; Cardinal Newman C, Preston), b Preston 7 Sep 1995. 6'0". RHB, RMF. Squad No 26. Debut (Lancashire) 2018. HS 50* v Derbys (Liverpool) 2020. BB 4-55 v Yorks (Leeds) 2019. LO HS 4* and LO BB 2-51 v Durham (Chester-le-St) 2017 (RLC). T20 HS 29*. T20 BB 3-30.

LAVELLE, George Isaac Davies (Merchant Taylors S), b Ormskirk 24 Mar 2000. 5'8". RHB. WK. Squad No 24. Debut (Lancashire) 2020. Lancashire 2nd XI debut 2017. England U19 2018. HS 13 v Derbys (Liverpool) 2020. T20 HS 12.

LIVINGSTONE, Liam Stephen (Chetwynde S, Barrow-in-Furness), b Barrow-in-Furness, Cumberland 4 Aug 1993. 6'1". RHB. LB. Squad No 7. Debut (Lancashire) 2016; cap 2017; captain 2018. IPL: RR 2019. Big Bash: PS 2019-20 to date. **IT20**: 2 (2017); HS 16 v SA (Taunton) 2017. F-c Tours (EL): WI 2017-18; SL 2016-17. HS 224 v Warwks (Manchester) 2017. BB 6-52 v Surrey (Manchester) 2017. LO HS 129 EL v South Africa A (Northampton) 2017. LO BB 3-51 v Yorks (Manchester) 2016 (RLC). T20 HS 100. T20 BB 4-17.

MAHMOOD, Saqib (Matthew Moss HS, Rochdale), b Birmingham, Warwks 25 Feb 1997. 6'3". RHB, RFM. Squad No 25. Debut (Lancashire) 2016. **LOI**: 4 (2019-20 to 2020); HS 12 v Ire (Southampton) 2020; BB 2-36 v Ire (Southampton) 2020 – separate matches. **IT20**: 6 (2019-20 to 2020); HS 4 v NZ (Wellington) 2019-20; BB 1-20 v NZ (Auckland) 2019-20. F-c Tour (EL): WI 2017-18. HS 34 v Middx (Manchester) 2019. BB 4-48 v Glos (Cheltenham) 2019. LO HS 45 v Warwks (Birmingham) 2019 (RLC). LO BB 6-37 v Northants (Manchester) 2019 (RLC). T20 HS 6. T20 BB 4-14.

MORLEY, Jack Peter (Siddal Moor Sports C), b Rochdale 25 Jun 2001. 5'10". LHB, SLA. Squad No 18. Debut (Lancashire) 2020. Lancashire 2nd XI debut 2018. England U19 2018-19. HS 3 and BB 4-62 v Derbys (Liverpool) 2020 – only 1st XI game.

MOULTON, Edwin Henry Taylor (Bishop Rawstone C of E Ac; Myerscough C), Preston 18 Apr 1999. RHB, RMF. Squad No 27. Debut (Lancashire) 2020. Lancashire 2nd XI debut 2017. HS 0. BB – .

PARKINSON, Matthew William (Bolton S), b Bolton 24 Oct 1996. Twin brother of C.F.Parkinson (*see LEICESTERSHIRE*). 6'0". RHB, LB. Squad No 28. Debut (Lancashire) 2016; cap 2019. Lancashire 2nd XI debut 2013. Staffordshire 2014. England U19 2015. **LOI:** 2 (2019-20); HS – ; BB – . **IT20:** 2 (2019-20); HS – ; BB 4-47 v NZ (Napier) 2019-20. F-c Tour: SL 2019-20. HS 22 E v SLPB (Colombo, PSS) 2019-20. La HS 14 v Middx (Manchester) 2019. BB 6-23 (10-165 match) v Sussex (Manchester) 2019. LO HS 15* EL v West Indies A (Coolidge) 2017-18. LO BB 5-51 v Worcs (Manchester) 2019 (RLC). T20 HS 7*. T20 BB 4-23.

SHAH, Syed Mohammed Owais (Bellahouston Ac, Glasgow; Myerscough C), b Glasgow, Scotland 1 Oct 1998. Elder brother of S.M.U.Shah (Scotland U19). 5'10". LHB, LB. Squad No 19. Lancashire 2nd XI debut 2019. Awaiting 1st XI debut.

NQ**VILAS, Dane** James, b Johannesburg, South Africa 10 Jun 1985. 6'2". RHB, WK. Squad No 33. Gauteng 2006-07 to 2009-10. Lions 2008-09 to 2009-10. W Province 2010-11. Cape Cobras 2011-12 to 2016-17. Lancashire debut 2017; cap 2018; captain 2019 to date. Dolphins 2017-18 to 2018-19. **Tests** (SA): 6 (2015 to 2015-16); HS 26 v E (Johannesburg) 2015-16. **IT20** (SA): 1 (2011-12); HS – . F-c Tours (SA): A 2016 (SA A), I 2015 (SA A), 2015-16; Z 2016 (SA A), B 2015. 1000 runs (1): 1036 (2019). HS 266 v Glamorgan (Colwyn B) 2019. LO HS 166 v Notts (Nottingham) 2019 (RLC). T20 HS 75*.

‡**WELLS, Luke** William Peter (St Bede's S, Upper Dicker), b Eastbourne, E Sussex 29 Dec 1990. Son of A.P.Wells (Border, Kent, Sussex and England 1981-2000); elder brother of D.A.C.Wells (Oxford MCCU 2017); nephew of C.M.Wells (Border, Derbyshire, Sussex and WP 1979-96). 6'4". LHB, LB. Squad No 3. Sussex 2010-19; cap 2016. Colombo CC 2011-12. 1000 runs (2); most – 1292 (2017). HS 258 Sx v Durham (Hove) 2017. BB 5-63 Sx v Glamorgan (Hove) 2019. LO HS 62 Sx v Kent (Hove) 2018 (RLC). BB 3-19 Sx v Netherlands (Amstelveen) 2011 (CB40). T20 HS 11.

WOOD, Luke (Portland CS, Worksop), b Sheffield, Yorks 2 Aug 1995. 5'9". LHB, LFM. Squad No 14. Nottinghamshire 2014-19. Worcestershire 2018 (on loan). Northamptonshire 2019 (on loan). Lancashire debut 2020. HS 100 Nt v Sussex (Nottingham) 2015. La HS 46 and La BB 2-31 v Durham (Chester-le-St) 2020. BB 5-40 Nt v Cambridge MCCU (Cambridge) 2016. CC BB 5-67 Nt v Yorks (Scarborough) 2019. LO HS 52 Nt v Leics (Leicester) 2016 (RLC). LO BB 2-36 Nt v Worcs (Worcester) 2019 (RLC). T20 HS 11. T20 BB 3-16.

RELEASED/RETIRED

(Having made a County 1st XI appearance in 2020)

GUEST, B.D. – *see DERBYSHIRE.*

PARRY, Stephen David (Audenshaw HS), b Manchester 12 Jan 1986. 6'0". RHB, SLA. Lancashire 2007-19, taking 5-23 v Durham U (Durham) on debut; cap 2015; testimonial 2020-21. MCC 2019. Cumberland 2005-06. Big Bash: BH 2014-15. **LOI:** 2 (2013-14); HS – ; BB 3-32 v WI (North Sound) 2013-14. **IT20:** 5 (2013-14 to 2015-16); HS 1 v Netherlands (Chittagong) 2013-14; BB 2-33 v P (Dubai, DSC) 2015-16. HS 44 v Somerset (Manchester) 2017. BB 5-23 (*see above*). LO BB 5-45 v Middx (Southport) 2017. LO HS 31 v Essex (Chelmsford) 2009 (FPT). LO BB 5-17 v Surrey (Manchester) 2013 (Y40). T20 HS 15*. T20 BB 5-13 v Worcs (Manchester) 2016 – La record.

J.P.Faulkner, T.J.Lester and G.J.Maxwell left the staff without making a County 1st XI appearance in 2020.

LANCASHIRE 2020

RESULTS SUMMARY

	Place	Won	Lost	Drew	NR
Bob Willis Trophy (North Group)	3rd	2	1	2	
Vitality Blast (North Group)	SF	6	4		2

BOB WILLIS TROPHY AVERAGES
BATTING AND FIELDING

Cap		M	I	NO	HS	Runs	Avge	100	50	Ct/St
2010	S.J.Croft	4	5	2	63	199	66.33	–	3	6
2017	A.L.Davies	5	8	1	86	337	48.14	–	4	7
	J.J.Bohannon	5	7	–	94	257	36.71	–	2	4
2018	D.J.Vilas	5	7	–	90	247	35.28	–	1	5
	T.W.Hartley	4	4	3	13*	35	35.00	–	–	2
	D.J.Lamb	3	4	1	50*	104	34.66	–	1	1
	G.P.Balderson	5	7	2	61*	156	31.20	–	1	–
2018	K.K.Jennings	5	8	1	81	182	26.00	–	1	8
2018	T.E.Bailey	4	4	1	38*	47	15.66	–	–	–
	R.P.Jones	3	5	–	23	77	15.40	–	–	3

Also batted: G.D.Burrows (2 matches) 1; R.J.Gleeson (1) 6; L.J.Hurt (2) 2, 1;
G.I.D.Lavelle (1) 13, 7 (2 ct); L.S.Livingstone (2 – cap 2017) 23, 14 (1 ct); J.P.Morley (1) 3;
E.H.T.Moulton (1) 0, 0; L.Wood (2) 46, 6.

BOWLING

	O	M	R	W	Avge	Best	5wI	10wM
J.P.Morley	40	15	71	5	14.20	4-62	–	–
D.J.Lamb	68.1	13	203	12	16.91	4-55	–	–
R.J.Gleeson	18	4	52	3	17.33	3-32	–	–
L.S.Livingstone	21.3	2	92	5	18.40	3-79	–	–
T.E.Bailey	111.4	44	282	13	21.69	3-11	–	–
L.J.Hurt	48	6	182	7	26.00	4-27	–	–
G.D.Burrows	40	8	127	4	31.75	2-20	–	–
G.P.Balderson	104	23	296	9	32.88	3-63	–	–
L.Wood	44	8	118	3	39.33	2-31	–	–
T.W.Hartley	111	28	324	6	54.00	3-79	–	–

Also bowled: S.J.Croft 1-0-6-0; R.P.Jones 3-2-4-0; K.K.Jennings 15-3-28-1;
E.H.T.Moulton 27-4-110-0.

The First-Class Averages (pp 209–221) give the records of Lancashire players in all
first-class county matches.

LANCASHIRE RECORDS

FIRST-CLASS CRICKET

Highest Total	For 863		v	Surrey	The Oval	1990
	V 707-9d		by	Surrey	The Oval	1990
Lowest Total	For 25		v	Derbyshire	Manchester	1871
	V 20		by	Essex	Chelmsford	2013
Highest Innings	For 424	A.C.MacLaren	v	Somerset	Taunton	1895
	V 315*	T.W.Hayward	for	Surrey	The Oval	1898

Highest Partnership for each Wicket

1st	368	A.C.MacLaren/R.H.Spooner	v	Glos	Liverpool	1903
2nd	371	F.B.Watson/G.E.Tyldesley	v	Surrey	Manchester	1928
3rd	501	A.N.Petersen/A.G.Prince	v	Glamorgan	Colwyn Bay	2015
4th	358	S.P.Titchard/G.D.Lloyd	v	Essex	Chelmsford	1996
5th	360	S.G.Law/C.L.Hooper	v	Warwicks	Birmingham	2003
6th	278	J.Iddon/H.R.W.Butterworth	v	Sussex	Manchester	1932
7th	248	G.D.Lloyd/I.D.Austin	v	Yorkshire	Leeds	1997
8th	158	J.Lyon/R.M.Ratcliffe	v	Warwicks	Manchester	1979
9th	142	L.O.S.Poidevin/A.Kermode	v	Sussex	Eastbourne	1907
10th	173	J.Briggs/R.Pilling	v	Surrey	Liverpool	1885

Best Bowling	For 10-46	W.Hickton	v	Hampshire	Manchester	1870
(Innings)	V 10-40	G.O.B.Allen	for	Middlesex	Lord's	1929
Best Bowling	For 17-91	H.Dean	v	Yorkshire	Liverpool	1913
(Match)	V 16-65	G.Giffen	for	Australians	Manchester	1886

Most Runs – Season	2633	J.T.Tyldesley	(av 56.02)		1901
Most Runs – Career	34222	G.E.Tyldesley	(av 45.20)		1909-36
Most 100s – Season	11	C.Hallows			1928
Most 100s – Career	90	G.E.Tyldesley			1909-36
Most Wkts – Season	198	E.A.McDonald	(av 18.55)		1925
Most Wkts – Career	1816	J.B.Statham	(av 15.12)		1950-68
Most Career W-K Dismissals	925	G.Duckworth	(635 ct; 290 st)		1923-38
Most Career Catches in the Field	556	K.J.Grieves			1949-64

LIMITED-OVERS CRICKET

Highest Total	50ov	406-9		v	Notts	Nottingham	2019
	40ov	324-4		v	Worcs	Worcester	2012
	T20	231-4		v	Yorkshire	Manchester	2015
Lowest Total	50ov	59		v	Worcs	Worcester	1963
	40ov	68		v	Yorkshire	Leeds	2000
		68		v	Surrey	The Oval	2002
	T20	83		v	Durham	Manchester	2020
Highest Innings	50ov	166	D.J.Vilas	v	Notts	Nottingham	2019
	40ov	143	A.Flintoff	v	Essex	Chelmsford	1999
	T20	108	K.K.Jennings	v	Durham	Chester-le-St[2]	2020
Best Bowling	50ov	6-10	C.E.H.Croft	v	Scotland	Manchester	1982
	40ov	6-25	G.Chapple	v	Yorkshire	Leeds	1998
	T20	5-13	S.D.Parry	v	Worcs	Manchester	2016

LEICESTERSHIRE

Formation of Present Club: 25 March 1879
Inaugural First-Class Match: 1894
Colours: Dark Green and Scarlet
Badge: Gold Running Fox on Green Ground
County Champions: (3) 1975, 1996, 1998
Benson and Hedges Cup Winners: (3) 1972, 1975, 1985
Sunday League Champions: (2) 1974, 1977
Twenty20 Cup Winners: (3) 2004, 2006, 2011

Chief Executive: Sean Jarvis, Uptonsteel County Ground, Grace Road, Leicester LE2 8EB
• Tel: 0116 283 2128 • Email: enquiries@leicestershireccc.co.uk • Web:
www.leicestershireccc.co.uk • Twitter: @leicsccc (64,095 followers)

Head Coach: Paul Nixon. **Assistant Coach**: Tom Smith. **Captain**: C.N.Ackermann.
Vice-captain: C.F.Parkinson. **Overseas Players**: C.N.Ackermann, M.S.Harris,
P.W.A.Mulder and Naveen-ul-Haq (T20 only). **2021 Testimonial**: None. **Head
Groundsman**: Andy Ward. **Scorer**: Paul Rogers. **Blast Team Name**: Leicestershire Foxes.
‡ New registration. ^{NQ} Not qualified for England.

^{NQ}**ACKERMANN, Colin** Neil (Grey HS, Port Elizabeth; U of SA), b George, South Africa
4 Apr 1991. RHB, OB. Squad No 48. Eastern Province 2010-11 to 2015-16. Warriors
2013-14 to 2018-19. Leicestershire debut 2017; cap 2019; captain 2020 to date (T20 only in
2020). **IT20** (Neth): 11 (2019-20); HS 43* and BB 1-6 v Bermuda (Dubai, DSC) 2019-20.
1000 runs (0+1): 1200 (2013-14). HS 196* v Middx (Leicester) 2018. BB 5-69 v Sussex
(Hove) 2019. LO HS 152* v Worcs (Leicester) 2019 (RLC). LO BB 4-48 Warriors v
Dolphins (Durban) 2017-18. T20 HS 79*. T20 BB 7-18 v Warwks (Leicester) 2019 – world
record T20 figures.

AZAD, Mohammad Hasan (Fernwood S, Nottingham; Bilborough SFC; Loughborough U),
b Quetta, Pakistan 7 Jan 1994. Son of Imran Azad (Public Works 1986-87). LHB, OB.
Squad No 42. Loughborough MCCU 2015-16. Leicestershire debut 2019, scoring 139 v
Loughborough MCCU (Leicester), sharing then Le record 2nd wkt partnership of 309 with
A.Javid. 1000 runs (1): 1189 (2019). HS 139 (*see above*). CC HS 137 v Glos (Leicester)
2019, sharing Le record 2nd wkt partnership of 320 with N.J.Dexter. BB 1-15 v Durham
(Leicester) 2020.

‡**BARNES, Ed**ward (King James S, Knaresborough), b York 26 Nov 1997. 6'0". RHB,
RFM. Squad No 62. Derbyshire 2020. Yorkshire 2nd XI 2016-19. England U19 2016. HS 4
and BB 2-24 De v Leics (Leicester) 2020. T20 HS – . T20 BB 2-27.

BATES, Samuel David (Groby C; Gateway C), b Leicester 14 Sep 1999. 6'3". LHB, WK.
Squad No 14. Leicestershire 2nd XI debut 2018. Awaiting 1st XI debut.

BOWLEY, Nathan John (Woodvale S, Loughborough; Loughborough C), b Nottingham
3 Aug 2001. LHB, OB. Squad No 33. Leicestershire 2nd XI debut 2018. Awaiting 1st XI
debut.

DAVIS, William Samuel (Stafford GS), b 6 Mar 1996. 6'1". RHB, RFM. Squad No 44.
Derbyshire 2015-18. Leicestershire debut 2019. HS 39* v Glamorgan (Cardiff) 2019. BB
7-146 De v Glamorgan (Colwyn Bay) 2016. Le BB 4-73 v Northants (Leicester) 2019. LO
HS 15* v Durham (Chester-le-St) 2019 (RLC). LO BB 1-60 v Worcs (Leicester) 2019
(RLC). T20 HS 4*. T20 BB 3-24.

DEARDEN, Harry Edward (Tottington HS), b Bury, Lancs 7 May 1997. LHB, OB. Squad No 5. Debut (Leicestershire) 2016. Lancashire 2nd XI 2014-15. Cheshire 2016. HS 87 v Glamorgan (Leicester) 2017. BB 1-0 v Kent (Leicester) 2017. LO HS 91 v Worcs (Leicester) 2019 (RLC). T20 HS 61.

EVANS, Huw Alexander (Bedford Modern S; Loughborough U), b Bedford 9 Aug 2000. 6'3". LHB, RFM. Squad No 72. Loughborough MCCU 2019. Leicestershire debut 2019. Leicestershire 2nd XI debut 2018. Bedfordshire 2017. HS 15 and Le BB 2-59 v Yorks (Leeds) 2020. BB 3-49 LU v Kent (Canterbury) 2019.

EVANS, Samuel Thomas (Lancaster S, Leicester; Wyggeston & QE I C; Leicester U), b Leicester 20 Dec 1997. 5'8". RHB, OB. Squad No 21. Loughborough MCCU 2017-18. Leicestershire debut 2017. Leicestershire 2nd XI debut 2015. HS 114 LU v Northants (Northampton) 2017. Le HS 85 v Durham (Leicester) 2020. BB – . LO HS 20 v India A (Leicester) 2018.

GRIFFITHS, Gavin Timothy (St Mary's C, Crosby), b Ormskirk, Lancs 19 Nov 1993. 6'2". RHB, RMF. Squad No 93. Debut (Leicestershire) 2017. Lancashire 2014-15 (l-o only). Hampshire 2016 (T20 only). HS 40 v Middx (Leicester) 2018. BB 6-49 (10-83 match) v Durham (Chester-le-St) 2018. Le BB 15* v Notts (Leicester) 2018 (RLC). LO BB 4-30 v Northants (Northampton) 2018 (RLC). T20 HS 11. T20 BB 4-35.

‡^{NO}**HARRIS, Marcus** Sinclair, b Perth, W Australia 21 July 1992. LHB, OB. W Australia 2010-11 to 2015-16. Victoria 2016-17 to date. Big Bash: PS 2014-15 to 2015-16. MR 2016-17 to 2019-20. **Tests** (A): 10 (2018-19 to 2020-21); HS 79 v I (Sydney) 2018-19. HS 250* Vic v NSW (Melbourne) 2018-19. BB – . LO HS 84 Cricket Aus v Tas (Sydney, BO) 2015-16. T20 HS 85.

HILL, Lewis John (Hastings HS, Hinckley; John Cleveland C), b Leicester 5 Oct 1990. 5'7½". RHB, WK, occ RM. Squad No 23. Debut (Leicestershire) 2015. Unicorns 2012-13. HS 126 v Surrey (Oval) 2015. LO HS 118 v Worcs (Leicester) 2019 (RLC). T20 HS 58.

^{NO}**KLEIN, Dieter** (Hoerskool, Lichtenburg), b Lichtenburg, South Africa 31 Oct 1988. 5'10". RHB, LMF. Squad No 77. North West 2007-08 to 2015-16. Lions 2012-13 to 2013-14. Leicestershire debut 2016. **IT20** (Ger): 2 (2019-20); HS 31* and BB 1-12 v Spain (Almeria) 2019-20. HS 94 v Glamorgan (Cardiff) 2018. BB 8-72 NW v Northerns (Potchefstroom) 2014-15. Le BB 6-80 v Northants (Northampton) 2017. LO HS 46 v Durham (Chester-le-St) 2019 (RLC). LO BB 5-35 NW v Northerns (Pretoria) 2012-13. T20 HS 31*. T20 BB 3-20.

LILLEY, Arron Mark (Mossley Hollins HS; Ashton SFC), b Tameside, Lancs 1 Apr 1991. 6'1". RHB, OB. Squad No 7. Lancashire 2013-18. Leicestershire debut 2019. White-ball contract in 2021. HS 63 and BB 5-23 La v Derbys (Southport) 2015. Le HS 13 and Le BB 3-21 v Yorks (Leeds) 2020. LO HS 25 v Yorks (Leeds) 2019 (RLC). LO BB 4-30 La v Derbys (Manchester) 2013 (Y40). T20 HS 69. T20 BB 3-31.

MIKE, Benjamin Wentworth Munro (Loughborough GS), b Nottingham 24 Aug 1998. Son of G.W.Mike (Nottinghamshire 1989-96). 6'1". RHB, RM. Squad No 8. Debut (Leicestershire) 2018. Warwickshire 2019 (on loan). Leicestershire 2nd XI debut 2017. HS 72 Wa v Hants (Southampton) 2019. Le HS 51* v Notts (Leicester) 2020. BB 5-37 (9-94 match) v Sussex (Hove) 2018 – on debut. LO HS 41 and LO BB 1-47 v Northants (Leicester) 2019 (RLC). T20 HS 37. T20 BB 3-38.

‡**NQMULDER**, Peter Willem Adriaan (**'Wiaan'**), b Johannesburg, South Africa 19 Feb 1998. RHB, RM. Lions 2016-17 to date. Gauteng 2017-18 to 2018-19. Kent 2019. **Tests** (SA): 4 (2018-19 to 2020-21); HS 36 v SL (Centurion) 2020-21; BB 3-25 v SL (Johannesburg) 2020-21. **LOI** (SA): 10 (2017-18 to 2018-19); HS 19* v SL (Dambulla) 2018; BB 2-59 v SL (Colombo, RPS) 2018. F-c Tours (SA): E 2017 (SA A); P 2020-21. HS 146 Lions v Knights (Bloemfontein) 2018-19. CC HS 68* and CC BB 4-118 K v Surrey (Beckenham) 2019. BB 7-25 Lions v Dolphins (Potchefstroom) 2016-17. LO HS 66 SA A v India A (Pretoria) 2017. LO BB 3-32 Lions v Knights (Potchefstroom) 2017-18. T20 HS 63. T20 BB 2-13.

‡**NQNAVEEN-UL-HAQ** Murid, b Logar, Afghanistan 23 Sep 1999. RHB, RMF. Kabul Region 2017-18 to 2018-19. **LOI** (Afg): 7 (2016 to 2020-21); HS 10* v Ire (Abu Dhabi) 2020-21; BB 4-42 v Ire (Abu Dhabi) 2020-21 – separate matches. **IT20** (Afg): 5 (2019 to 2019-20); HS 5 v WI (Lucknow) 2019-20; BB 3-21 v Ire (Greater Noida) 2019-20. HS 34 Kabul v Mis Ainak (Asadabad) 2017-18. BB 8-35 Kabul v Mis Ainak (Kabul) 2018-19. LO HS 30 Kabul v Band-e-Amir (Kabul) 2018. LO BB 5-40 Afg A v Bangladesh A (Savar) 2019. T20 HS 20*. T20 BB 4-14.

PARKINSON, Callum Francis (Bolton S), b Bolton, Lancs 24 Oct 1996. Twin brother of M.W.Parkinson (*see LANCASHIRE*). 5'8". RHB, SLA. Squad No 10. Derbyshire 2016. Leicestershire debut 2017. Staffordshire 2015-16. HS 75 v Kent (Canterbury) 2017. BB 8-148 (10-185 match) v Worcs (Worcester) 2017. LO HS 52* v Notts (Leicester) 2018 (RLC). LO BB 1-34 v Derbys (Derby) 2018 (RLC). T20 HS 27*. T20 BB 4-20.

PATEL, Rishi Ketan (Brentwood S), b Chigwell, Essex 26 Jul 1998. 6'2". RHB, LB. Squad No 26. Cambridge MCCU 2019. Essex 2019. Leicestershire debut 2020. Essex 2nd XI 2015-19. Hertfordshire 2019. HS 35 Ex v Yorks (Chelmsford) 2019. Le HS 19 v Yorks (Leeds) 2020. LO HS 35 Ex v Hants (Chelmsford) 2019 (RLC).

RHODES, George Harry (Chase HS & SFC, Malvern), b Birmingham 26 Oct 1993. Son of S.J.Rhodes (Yorkshire, Worcestershire & England 1981-2004) and grandson of W.E.Rhodes (Nottinghamshire 1961-64). 6'0". RHB, OB. Squad No 34. Worcestershire 2016-19. Leicestershire debut 2019. HS 61* v Northants (Leicester) 2019. BB 2-83 Wo v Kent (Canterbury) 2016. Le BB – . LO HS 106 Wo v Yorks (Worcester) 2019 (RLC). LO BB 2-34 Wo v Yorks (Leeds) 2016 (RLC). T20 HS 30*. T20 BB 4-13.

‡**STEEL, Scott** (Belmont Community S), b Durham 20 Apr 1999. 6'0". RHB, OB. Squad No 55. Durham 2019. Durham 2nd XI 2016-19. Northumberland 2017. HS 39 Du v Middx (Lord's) 2019. BB – . LO HS 68 Du v Northants (Chester-le-St) 2019 (RLC) and 68 Du v Yorks (Leeds) 2019 (RLC). LO BB 1-38 Du v Derbys (Chester-le-St) 2019 (RLC). T20 HS 70. T20 BB 3-20.

SWINDELLS, Harry John (Brockington C; Lutterworth C), b Leicester 21 Feb 1999. 5'7". RHB, WK. Squad No 28. Debut (Leicestershire) 2019. Leicestershire 2nd XI debut 2015. England U19 2017. HS 52* v Notts (Leicester) 2020. LO HS 28 v India A (Leicester) 2018. T20 HS 63.

WELCH, Nicholas Roy (St John's C, Harare; Loughborough U), b Harare, Zimbabwe 5 Feb 1998. 5'11". RHB, LBG. Squad No 67. Mashonaland Eagles 2013-14. Loughborough MCCU 2019. Sussex 2nd XI 2016-19. Northamptonshire 2nd XI 2017. Surrey 2nd XI 2017-19. Essex 2nd XI 2017. Leicestershire 2nd XI debut 2019. HS 83 ME v SR (Harare) 2013-14. LO HS 52 ME v MT (Bulawayo) 2013-14. T20 HS 43.

WRIGHT, Christopher Julian Clement (Eggars S, Alton; Anglia Ruskin U), b Chipping Norton, Oxon 14 Jul 1985. 6'3". RHB, RFM. Squad No 31. Cambridge UCCE 2004-05. Middlesex 2004-07. Tamil Union 2005-06. Essex 2008-11. Warwickshire 2011-18; cap 2013. Leicestershire debut 2019. F-c Tour (MCC): Nepal 2019-20. HS 77 Ex v Cambridge MCCU (Cambridge) 2011. CC HS 72 Wa v Derbys (Birmingham) 2018. Le HS 60 v Glamorgan (Cardiff) 2019. 50 wkts (2); most – 67 (2012). BB 6-22 Ex v Leics (Leicester) 2008. Le BB 5-30 v Durham (Leicester) 2019. LO HS 42 Ex v Glos (Cheltenham) 2011 (CB40). LO BB 4-20 Ex v Unicorns (Chelmsford) 2011 (CB40). T20 HS 6*. T20 BB 4-24.

RELEASED/RETIRED

(Having made a County 1st XI appearance in 2020)

DELANY, G.J. – *see IRELAND.*

TAYLOR, T.A.I. – *see NORTHAMPTONSHIRE.*

M.J.Cosgrove and P.J.Horton left the staff without making a County 1st XI appearance in 2020.

LEICESTERSHIRE 2020

RESULTS SUMMARY

	Place	Won	Lost	Drew	Tied	NR
Bob Willis Trophy (North Group)	5th	1	2	2		
Vitality Blast (North Group)	QF	4	3		1	3

BOB WILLIS TROPHY AVERAGES
BATTING AND FIELDING

Cap		M	I	NO	HS	Runs	Avge	100	50	Ct/St
2019	C.N.Ackermann	5	9	2	94	379	54.14	–	4	6
	B.T.Slater	2	4	–	172	197	49.25	1	–	4
	T.A.I.Taylor	3	3	1	57	78	39.00	–	1	1
	H.J.Swindells	5	7	2	52*	188	37.60	–	1	11
	S.T.Evans	3	5	–	85	148	29.60	–	1	3
	H.E.Dearden	5	9	–	70	234	26.00	–	1	1
	G.T.Griffiths	3	3	2	11*	23	23.00	–	–	1
	C.F.Parkinson	3	3	1	21	42	21.00	–	–	–
	B.W.M.Mike	4	6	1	51*	99	19.80	–	1	2
	M.H.Azad	5	8	–	58	144	18.00	–	1	3
	G.H.Rhodes	4	7	2	22*	83	16.60	–	–	4
	D.Klein	4	5	1	27	53	13.25	–	–	–
	H.A.Evans	2	3	–	15	16	5.33	–	–	1

Also batted: W.S.Davis (2 matches) 20, 8; A.M.Lilley (1) 5, 13 (1 ct); R.K.Patel (1) 19, 5; W.J.Weighell (1) 23; C.J.C.Wright (2) 10*, 23.

BOWLING

	O	M	R	W	Avge	Best	5wI	10wM
A.M.Lilley	6	1	21	3	7.00	3-21	–	–
C.N.Ackermann	35	12	92	4	23.00	2-24	–	–
C.F.Parkinson	79.3	22	192	8	24.00	3-30	–	–
C.J.C.Wright	57	21	141	5	28.20	2-39	–	–
B.W.M.Mike	88.1	13	279	9	31.00	4-39	–	–
W.S.Davis	30	6	106	3	35.33	2-75	–	–
G.T.Griffiths	61.5	13	181	5	36.20	3-52	–	–
D.Klein	95	10	332	9	36.88	3-44	–	–
T.A.I.Taylor	93	25	247	6	41.16	2-49	–	–
H.A.Evans	35.2	7	140	3	46.66	2-59	–	–

Also bowled: M.H.Azad 2.1-0-15-1; S.T.Evans 3-0-22-0; W.J.Weighell 6-0-29-0.

The First-Class Averages (pp 209–221) give the records of Leicestershire players in all first-class county matches, with the exception of B.T.Slater, whose first-class figures for Leicestershire are as above.

LEICESTERSHIRE RECORDS

FIRST-CLASS CRICKET

Highest Total	For 701-4d		v	Worcs	Worcester	1906
	V 761-6d		by	Essex	Chelmsford	1990
Lowest Total	For 25		v	Kent	Leicester	1912
	V 24		by	Glamorgan	Leicester	1971
	24		by	Oxford U	Oxford	1985
Highest Innings	For 309*	H.D.Ackerman	v	Glamorgan	Cardiff	2006
	V 355*	K.P.Pietersen	for	Surrey	The Oval	2015

Highest Partnership for each Wicket

1st	390	B.Dudleston/J.F.Steele	v	Derbyshire	Leicester	1979
2nd	320	M.H.Azad/N.J.Dexter	v	Glos	Leicester	2019
3rd	436*	D.L.Maddy/B.J.Hodge	v	L'boro UCCE	Leicester	2003
4th	360*	J.W.A.Taylor/A.B.McDonald	v	Middlesex	Leicester	2010
5th	330	J.W.A.Taylor/S.J.Thakor	v	L'boro MCCU	Leicester	2011
6th	284	P.V.Simmons/P.A.Nixon	v	Durham	Chester-le-St[2]	1996
7th	219*	J.D.R.Benson/P.Whitticase	v	Hampshire	Bournemouth	1991
8th	195	J.W.A.Taylor/J.K.H.Naik	v	Derbyshire	Leicester	2009
9th	160	R.T.Crawford/ W.W.Odell	v	Worcs	Leicester	1902
10th	228	R.Illingworth/K.Higgs	v	Northants	Leicester	1977

Best Bowling	For 10- 18	G.Geary	v	Glamorgan	Pontypridd	1929
(Innings)	V 10- 32	H.Pickett	for	Essex	Leyton	1895
Best Bowling	For 16- 96	G.Geary	v	Glamorgan	Pontypridd	1929
(Match)	V 16-102	C.Blythe	for	Kent	Leicester	1909

Most Runs – Season	2446	L.G.Berry	(av 52.04)	1937
Most Runs – Career	30143	L.G.Berry	(av 30.32)	1924-51
Most 100s – Season	7	L.G.Berry		1937
	7	W.Watson		1959
	7	B.F.Davison		1982
Most 100s – Career	45	L.G.Berry		1924-51
Most Wkts – Season	170	J.E.Walsh	(av 18.96)	1948
Most Wkts – Career	2131	W.E.Astill	(av 23.18)	1906-39
Most Career W-K Dismissals	905	R.W.Tolchard	(794 ct; 111 st)	1965-83
Most Career Catches in the Field	426	M.R.Hallam		1950-70

LIMITED-OVERS CRICKET

Highest Total	50ov	406-5		v	Berkshire	Leicester	1996
	40ov	344-4		v	Durham	Chester-le-St[2]	1996
	T20	229-5		v	Warwicks	Birmingham	2018
Lowest Total	50ov	56		v	Northants	Leicester	1964
		56		v	Minor Cos	Wellington	1982
	40ov	36		v	Sussex	Leicester	1973
	T20	90		v	Notts	Nottingham	2014
Highest Innings	50ov	201	V.J.Wells	v	Berkshire	Leicester	1996
	40ov	154*	B.J.Hodge	v	Sussex	Horsham	2004
	T20	113	B.A.Raine	v	Warwicks	Birmingham	2018
Best Bowling	50ov	6-16	C.M.Willoughby	v	Somerset	Leicester	2005
	40ov	6-17	K.Higgs	v	Glamorgan	Leicester	1973
	T20	7-18	C.N.Ackermann	v	Warwicks	Leicester	2019

MIDDLESEX

Formation of Present Club: 2 February 1864
Inaugural First-Class Match: 1864
Colours: Blue
Badge: Three Seaxes
County Champions (since 1890): (11) 1903, 1920, 1921, 1947, 1976, 1980, 1982, 1985, 1990, 1993, 2016
Joint Champions: (2) 1949, 1977
Gillette/NatWest Trophy Winners: (4) 1977, 1980, 1984, 1988
Benson and Hedges Cup Winners: (2) 1983, 1986
Sunday League Winners: (1) 1992
Twenty20 Cup Winners: (1) 2008

Chief Executive: Richard Goatley, Lord's Cricket Ground, London NW8 8QN • Tel: 020 7289 1300 • Email: enquiries@middlesexccc.com • Web: www.middlesexccc.com • Twitter: @Middlesex_CCC (84,417 followers)

Managing Director of Cricket: Angus Fraser MBE. **Head Coach**: Stuart Law. **Assistant Coaches**: Nic Pothas and Alan Coleman. **T20 Bowling Coach**: Dimitri Mascarenhas. **Captains**: P.S.P.Handscomb (f-c and l-o) and E.J.G.Morgan (T20). **Overseas Players**: P.S.P.Handscomb, M.R.Marsh (T20 only) and Mujeeb Zadran (T20 only). **2021 Testimonial**: None. **Head Groundsman**: Karl McDermott. **Scorer**: Don Shelley. ‡ New registration. NQ Not qualified for England.

ANDERSSON, Martin Kristoffer (Reading Blue Coat S), b Reading, Berks 6 Sep 1996. 6'1". RHB, RM. Squad No 24. Debut (Leeds/Bradford MCCU) 2017. Derbyshire 2018 (on loan). Middlesex debut 2018. Middlesex 2nd XI debut 2013. Berkshire 2015-16. HS 92 v Hants (Radlett) 2020. BB 4-25 De v Glamorgan (Derby) 2018. M BB 4-38 v Essex (Chelmsford) 2020. T20 HS 24. T20 BB – .

BAMBER, Ethan Read (Mill Hill S), b Westminster 17 Dec 1998. 5'11". RHB, RMF. Squad No 54. Debut (Middlesex) 2018. Gloucestershire 2019 (on loan). Middlesex 2nd XI debut 2015. Berkshire 2017. HS 27* v Glos (Bristol) 2018. BB 5-93 v Derbys (Lord's) 2019. T20 HS 0*. T20 BB 1-38.

CRACKNELL, Joseph Benjamin (London Oratory S), b Enfield 16 Mar 2000. 5'9". RHB, WK. Squad No 48. Middlesex 2nd XI debut 2017. Berkshire 2018. Awaiting f-c debut. T20 HS 50.

CULLEN, Blake Carlton (Hampton S), b Hounslow 19 Feb 2002. 6'1". RHB, RMF. Squad No 19. Debut (Middlesex) 2020. Middlesex 2nd XI debut 2017, aged 15y 142d. HS 34 and BB 2-51 v Sussex (Radlett) 2020.

DAVIES, Jack Leo Benjamin (Wellington C), b Reading, Berks 30 Mar 2000. Son of A.G.Davies (Cambridge U 1982-89). 5'10". LHB, WK. Squad No 23. Debut (Middlesex) 2020. Middlesex 2nd XI debut 2017. Berkshire 2017-19. England U19 2018. HS 13 v Kent (Canterbury) 2020. T20 HS 23.

De CAIRES, Joshua Michael (St Albans S; Leeds U), b Paddington 25 Apr 2002. Son of M.A.Atherton (Lancashire, Cambridge U & England 1987-2001); great grandson of F.I.de Caires (British Guiana & West Indies 1928/29-1938). 6'0". RHB, RM. Squad No 99. Middlesex 2nd XI debut 2017. Awaiting 1st XI debut.

ESKINAZI, Stephen Sean (Christ Church GS, Claremont; U of WA), b Johannesburg, South Africa 28 Mar 1994. 6'2". RHB, WK. Squad No 28. Debut (Middlesex) 2015; cap 2018; captain 2020. UK passport. HS 179 v Warwks (Birmingham) 2017. LO HS 107* v Glos (Lord's) 2019 (RLC). T20 HS 84.

FINN, Steven Thomas (Parmiter's S, Garston), b Watford, Herts 4 Apr 1989. 6'7½". RHB, RFM. Squad No 9. Debut (Middlesex) 2005; cap 2009. Otago 2011-12. YC 2010. **Tests**: 36 (2009-10 to 2016-17); HS 56 v NZ (Dunedin) 2012-13; BB 6-79 v A (Birmingham) 2015. **LOI**: 69 (2010-11 to 2017); HS 35 v A (Brisbane) 2010-11; BB 5-33 v I (Brisbane) 2014-15. **IT20**: 21 (2011 to 2015); HS 8* v I (Colombo, RPS) 2012-13; BB 3-16 v NZ (Pallekele) 2012-13. F-c Tours: A 2010-11, 2013-14; SA 2015-16; NZ 2012-13; I 2012-13; SL 2011-12; B 2009-10, 2016-17; UAE 2011-12 (v P). HS 56 (*see Tests*) and 56 v Sussex (Hove) 2019. 50 wkts (2); most – 64 (2010). BB 9-37 (14-106 match) v Worcs (Worcester) 2010. LO HS 42* v Glamorgan (Cardiff) 2014 (RLC). LO BB (*see LOI*) and 5-33 v Derbys (Lord's) 2011 (CB40). T20 HS 8*. T20 BB 5-16.

GUBBINS, Nicholas Richard Trail (Radley C; Leeds U), b Richmond, Surrey 31 Dec 1993. 6'0½". LHB, LB. Squad No 18. Leeds/Bradford MCCU 2013-15. Middlesex debut 2014; cap 2016. F-c Tours (EL): WI 2017-18; SL 2016-17; UAE 2016-17 (v Afg), 2018-19 (v PA). 1000 runs (1): 1409 (2016). HS 201* v Lancs (Lord's) 2016. BB – . LO HS 141 v Sussex (Hove) 2015 (RLC). T20 HS 75.

‡**[NQ]HANDSCOMB, Peter** Stephen Patrick (Mt Waverley SC; Deakin U, Melbourne), b Melbourne, Australia 26 Apr 1991. RHB, WK. Squad No 29. British passport (English parents). Victoria 2011-12 to date. Gloucestershire 2015; cap 2015. Yorkshire 2017. Durham 2019. Joins Middlesex in 2021 as f-c and 50-over captain. IPL: RPS 2017. Big Bash: MS 2012-13 to 2019-20. HH 2020-21. **Tests** (A): 16 (2016-17 to 2018-19); HS 110 v P (Sydney) 2016-17. **LOI** (A): 22 (2016-17 to 2019); HS 117 v I (Mohali) 2018-19. **IT20** (A): 2 (2018-19); HS 20* v I (Bengaluru) 2018-19. F-c Tours (A): SA 2017-18; I 2015 (Aus A), 2016-17, 2018-19; B 2017. HS 215 Vic v NSW (Sydney) 2016-17. CC HS 101* Y v Lancs (Manchester) 2017. LO HS 140 Y v Derbys (Leeds) 2017 (RLC). T20 HS 103*.

HARRIS, James Alexander Russell (Pontardulais CS; Gorseinon S), b Morriston, Swansea, Glamorgan 16 May 1990. 6'0". RHB, RMF. Squad No 5. Glamorgan 2007-14, making debut aged 16y 351d – youngest Gm player to take a f-c wicket; cap 2010. Middlesex debut 2013; cap 2015. Kent 2017 (on loan). MCC 2016. Wales MC 2005-08. F-c Tours (EL): WI 2010-11; SL 2013-14. HS 87* Gm v Notts (Swansea) 2007. M HS 80 v Sussex (Lord's) 2019. 50 wkts (3); most – 73 (2015). BB 9-34 (13-103 match) v Durham (Lord's) 2015 – record innings and match analysis v Durham. Took 12-118 in match for Gm v Glos (Bristol) 2007 – youngest (17y 3d) to take 10 wickets in any CC match. LO HS 117 v Lancs (Lord's) 2019 (RLC). LO BB 4-38 v Glamorgan (Lord's) 2015 (RLC). T20 HS 18. T20 BB 4-23.

HELM, Thomas George (Misbourne S, Gt Missenden), b Stoke Mandeville Hospital, Bucks 7 May 1994. 6'4". RHB, RMF. Squad No 7. Debut (Middlesex) 2013; cap 2019. Glamorgan 2014 (on loan). Buckinghamshire 2011. F-c Tour (EL): SL 2016-17. HS 52 v Derbys (Derby) 2018. BB 5-36 v Worcs (Worcester) 2019. LO HS 30 v Surrey (Lord's) 2018 (RLC). LO BB 5-33 EL v Sri Lanka A (Colombo, CCC) 2016-17. T20 HS 28*. T20 BB 5-11.

HOLDEN, Max David Edward (Sawston Village C; Hills Road SFC, Cambridge), b Cambridge 18 Dec 1997. 5'11". LHB, OB. Squad No 4. Northamptonshire 2017 (on loan). Middlesex debut 2017. Middlesex 2nd XI debut 2013. England U19 2014-15 to 2016-17. F-c Tour (EL): I 2018-19. HS 153 and BB 2-59 Nh v Kent (Beckenham) 2017. M HS 119* v Derbys (Lord's) 2018. M BB 1-15 v Leics (Leicester) 2018. LO HS 166 v Kent (Canterbury) 2019 (RLC) – M record. LO BB 1-29 v Australians (Lord's) 2018. T20 HS 102*. T20 BB – .

HOLLMAN, Luke Barnaby Kurt (Acland Burghley S), b Islington 16 Sep 2000. 6'2". LHB, LB. Squad No 56. Middlesex 2nd XI debut 2017. Berkshire 2019. England U19 2018 to 2018-19. Awaiting f-c debut. T20 HS 46. T20 BB 3-18.

‡ᴺᵠ**MARSH, Mitchell** Ross, b Attadale, Perth, W Australia 20 Oct 1991. Son of G.R.Marsh (W Australia and Australia 1977-78 to 1993-94) and younger brother of S.E.Marsh (W Australia, Yorkshire, Glamorgan & Australia 2000-01 to date). 6'3". RHB, RMF. Squad No 8. W Australia 2009-10 to date. IPL: DC 2009-10. PW 2011-13. RPS 2016. SH 2020-21. Big Bash: PS 2011-12 to date. **Tests** (A): 32 (2014-15 to 2019); HS 181 v E (Perth) 2017-18; BB 5-46 v E (Oval) 2019. **LOI** (A): 60 (2011-12 to 2020); HS 102* v I (Sydney) 2015-16; BB 5-33 v E (Melbourne) 2014-15. **IT20** (A): 20 (2011-12 to 2020-21); HS 45 v NZ (Christchurch) 2020-21; BB 2-6 v P (Dubai, DSC) 2018-19. F-c Tours (A): E 2015, 2019; SA 2013 (Aus A), 2017-18; WI 2015; NZ 2015-16; I 2016-17, 2018-19; SL 2016; Z 2011 (Aus A); UAE 2014-15, 2018-19 (v P). HS 211 Aus A v India A (Brisbane, AB) 2014. BB 6-84 WA v Q (Perth) 2011-12. LO HS 124 WA v SA (Sydney, DO) 2017-18. LO BB 5-33 (see *LOI*). T20 HS 93*. T20 BB 4-6.

MORGAN, Eoin Joseph Gerard (Catholic University S), b Dublin, Ireland 10 Sep 1986. 6'0". LHB, RM. Squad No 16. UK passport. Ireland 2004 to 2007-08. Middlesex debut 2006; cap 2008; l-o captain 2014-15; T20 captain 2020 to date. IPL: RCB 2009-10. KKR 2011 to date. SH 2015-16. KXIP 2017. Big Bash: ST 2013-14 to 2016-17. *Wisden* 2010. CBE 2020. **ECB L-O Central Contract 2020-21. Tests**: 16 (2010 to 2011-12); HS 130 v P (Nottingham) 2010. **LOI** (E/Ire): 242 (23 for Ire 2006 to 2008-09; 219 for E 2009 to 2020, 120 as captain); HS 148 v Afg (Manchester) 2019, inc world record 17 sixes. **IT20**: 97 (2009 to 2020-21, 54 as captain); HS 91 v NZ (Napier) 2019-20. F-c Tours (Ire): A 2010-11 (E); NZ 2008-09 (Aus A); Namibia 2005-06; UAE 2006-07, 2007-08, 2011-12 (v P). 1000 runs (1): 1085 (2008). HS 209* v UAE (Abu Dhabi) 2006-07. M HS 191 v Notts (Nottingham) 2014. BB 2-24 v Notts (Lord's) 2007. LO HS 161 v Kent (Canterbury) 2009 (FPT). LO BB – . T20 HS 91.

ᴺᵠ**MUJEEB ZADRAN** (also known as Mujeeb Ur Rahman), b Khost, Afghanistan 28 Mar 2001. 5'11". RHB, OB. Squad No 88. Afghanistan 2018. Hampshire 2018 (T20 only). Middlesex debut 2019 (T20 only). IPL: KXIP 2018 to date. Big Bash: BH 2018-19 to date. **Tests** (Afg): 1 (2018); HS 15 and BB 1-75 v I (Bengaluru) 2018. **LOI** (Afg): 43 (2017-18 to 2020-21); HS 18* v Ire (Abu Dhabi) 2020-21; BB 5-50 v Z (Sharjah) 2017-18. **IT20** (Afg): 19 (2017-18 to 2019-20); HS 8* v WI (Lucknow) 2019-20; BB 4-15 v B (Dhaka) 2019-20. F-c Tour (Afg): I 2018. HS 15 (see *Tests*). BB 1-75 (see *Tests*). LO HS 18* (see *LOI*). LO BB 5-50 (see *LOI*). T20 HS 27. T20 BB 5-15.

ᴺᵠ**MURTAGH, Tim**othy James (John Fisher S; St Mary's C), b Lambeth, London 2 Aug 1981. Elder brother of C.P.Murtagh (Loughborough UCCE and Surrey 2005-09), nephew of A.J.Murtagh (Hampshire and EP 1973-77). 6'0". LHB, RMF. Squad No 34. British U 2000-03. Surrey 2001-06. Middlesex debut 2007; cap 2008; benefit 2015. Ireland 2012-13 to 2019. MCC 2010. **Tests** (Ire): 3 (2018 to 2019); HS 54* v Afg (Dehradun) 2018-19; BB 5-13 v E (Lord's) 2019. **LOI** (Ire): 58 (2012 to 2019); HS 23* v Scotland (Belfast) 2013; BB 5-21 v Z (Belfast) 2019. **IT20** (Ire): 14 (2012 to 2015-16); HS 12* v UAE (Abu Dhabi) 2015-16; BB 3-23 v PNG (Townsville) 2015-16. HS 74* Sy v Middx (Oval) 2004 and 74* Sy v Warwks (Croydon) 2005. M HS 55 v Leics (Leicester) 2011, sharing M record 9th wkt partnership of 172 with G.K.Berg. 50 wkts (8); most – 85 (2011). BB 7-82 v Derbys (Derby) 2009. LO HS 35* v Surrey (Lord's) 2008 (FPT). LO BB 5-21 (see *LOI*). T20 HS 40*. T20 BB 6-24 Sy v Middx (Lord's) 2005 – Sy record.

ROBSON, Sam David (Marcellin C, Randwick), b Paddington, Sydney, Australia 1 Jul 1989. Elder brother of A.J.Robson Leicestershire, Sussex and Durham 2013-19). 6'0". RHB, LB. Squad No 12. Qualified for England in April 2013. Debut (Middlesex) 2009; cap 2013. **Tests**: 7 (2014); HS 127 v SL (Leeds) 2014. F-c Tours (EL): SA 2014-15; SL 2013-14. 1000 runs (2); most – 1180 (2013). HS 231* v Warwks (Lord's) 2013. BB 2-0 v Surrey (Oval) 2020. LO HS 106 v Somerset (Radlett) 2019 (RLC). LO BB 1-27 v Glamorgan (Lord's) 2019 (RLC). T20 HS 28*. T20 BB 3-31.

ROLAND-JONES, Tobias Skelton ('**Toby**') (Hampton S; Leeds U), b Ashford 29 Jan 1988. 6'4". RHB, RFM. Squad No 21. Debut (Middlesex) 2010; cap 2012. MCC 2011. *Wisden* 2016. Leeds/Bradford UCCE 2009 (not f-c). No 1st XI appearances in 2020. **Tests:** 4 (2017); HS 25 and BB 5-57 v SA (Oval) 2017. **LOI:** 1 (2017); HS 37* and BB 1-34 v SA (Lord's) 2017. F-c Tours (EL): WI 2017-18; SL 2016-17; UAE 2016-17 (v Afg). HS 103* v Yorks (Lord's) 2015. 50 wkts (2); most – 64 (2012). BB 7-52 (10-79 match) v Glos (Northwood) 2019. Hat-tricks (2): v Derbys (Lord's) 2013, and v Yorks (Lord's) 2016 – at end of match to secure the Championship. LO HS 65 v Glos (Lord's) 2017 (RLC). LO BB 4-10 v Hants (Southampton) 2017 (RLC). T20 HS 40. T20 BB 5-21.

SIMPSON, John Andrew (St Gabriel's RC HS), b Bury, Lancs 13 Jul 1988. 5'10". LHB, WK. Squad No 20. Debut (Middlesex) 2009; cap 2011. MCC 2018. Cumberland 2007. HS 167* v Lancs (Manchester) 2019. LO HS 82* v Sussex (Lord's) 2017 (RLC). T20 HS 84*.

SOWTER, Nathan Adam (Hill Sport HS, NSW), b Penrith, NSW, Australia 12 Oct 1992. 5'10". RHB, LB. Squad No 72. Debut (Middlesex) 2017. HS 57* v Glamorgan (Cardiff) 2019. BB 3-42 v Lancs (Manchester) 2017. LO HS 31 v Surrey (Oval) 2019 (RLC). LO BB 6-62 v Essex (Chelmsford) 2019 (RLC). T20 HS 13*. T20 BB 4-23.

WALALLAWITA, Thilan Nipuna (Oaklands S), b Colombo, Sri Lanka 23 Jun 1998. 5'9". LHB, SLA. Squad No 32. Moved to UK in 2004. Debut (Middlesex) 2020. Middlesex 2nd XI debut 2015. HS 11 v Kent (Canterbury) 2020. BB 3-28 v Hants (Radlett) 2020. T20 HS 0. T20 BB 3-19.

WHITE, Robert George (Harrow S; Loughborough U), b Ealing 15 Sep 1995. 5'9". RHB, WK, occ RM. Squad No 14. Loughborough MCCU 2015-17. Middlesex debut 2018. Essex 2019 (on loan). HS 99 v Kent (Canterbury) 2020. LO HS 21* Ex v Sussex (Chelmsford) 2019 (RLC). T20 HS 11*.

RELEASED/RETIRED

(Having made a County 1st XI appearance in 2020)

CUMMINS, M.L. – *see KENT.*

LACE, T.C. – *see GLOUCESTERSHIRE.*

LINCOLN, Daniel John (Edgbarrow S, Crowthorne), b Frimley, Surrey 26 May 1995. 6'1". RHB, RM. Awaiting f-c debut. Berkshire 2012-19. Played as a goalkeeper for Reading and Arsenal junior sides, and as 12th man for England in 2019 Ashes. T20 HS 30.

MIDDLESEX 2020

RESULTS SUMMARY

	Place	Won	Lost	Drew	Tied	NR
Bob Willis Trophy (South Group)	3rd	2	2	1		
Vitality Blast (South Group)	4th	3	5		1	1

BOB WILLIS TROPHY AVERAGES
BATTING AND FIELDING

Cap		M	I	NO	HS	Runs	Avge	100	50	Ct/St
2016	N.R.T.Gubbins	4	8	–	192	350	43.75	1	1	1
2011	J.A.Simpson	5	9	2	53	250	35.71	–	1	19/1
	R.G.White	3	5	–	99	176	35.20	–	1	1
	M.D.E.Holden	5	10	–	72	299	29.90	–	1	4
	M.K.Andersson	5	9	1	92	227	28.37	–	2	3
2015	J.A.R.Harris	4	7	2	41	128	25.60	–	–	–
2013	S.D.Robson	5	10	1	82*	215	23.88	–	1	8
2018	S.S.Eskinazi	5	10	1	29	151	16.77	–	–	7
	B.C.Cullen	2	3	–	34	49	16.33	–	–	1
	N.A.Sowter	2	4	2	20	25	12.50	–	–	5
2008	T.J.Murtagh	4	5	2	11*	26	8.66	–	–	1
	T.N.Walallawita	5	6	2	11	22	5.50	–	–	–

Also batted: E.R.Bamber (1 match) 24*; M.L.Cummins (3) 1, 25; J.L.B.Davies (1) 13; T.G.Helm (1) 28, 1.

BOWLING

	O	M	R	W	Avge	Best	5wI	10wM
T.J.Murtagh	145.5	48	318	25	12.72	5-34	2	–
M.K.Andersson	75.5	15	250	14	17.85	4-38	–	–
M.L.Cummins	92.1	28	269	13	20.69	5-62	1	–
J.A.R.Harris	89	19	284	9	31.55	2-46	–	–
B.C.Cullen	30	5	110	3	36.66	2-51	–	–
N.A.Sowter	52.5	16	120	3	40.00	1- 4	–	–
T.N.Walallawita	88.2	28	245	6	40.83	3-28	–	–

Also bowled: E.R.Bamber 21-6-79-1; N.R.T.Gubbins 1.3-0-2-0; T.G.Helm 24.3-7-66-1; S.D.Robson 4-3-6-2.

The First-Class Averages (pp 209–221) give the records of Middlesex players in all first-class county matches.

MIDDLESEX RECORDS

FIRST-CLASS CRICKET

Highest Total	For 642-3d		v	Hampshire	Southampton[1]	1923
	V 850-7d		by	Somerset	Taunton	2007
Lowest Total	For 20		v	MCC	Lord's	1864
	V 31		by	Glos	Bristol	1924
Highest Innings	For 331*	J.D.B.Robertson	v	Worcs	Worcester	1949
	V 341	C.M.Spearman	for	Glos	Gloucester	2004

Highest Partnership for each Wicket

1st	372	M.W.Gatting/J.L.Langer	v	Essex	Southgate	1998
2nd	380	F.A.Tarrant/J.W.Hearne	v	Lancashire	Lord's	1914
3rd	424*	W.J.Edrich/D.C.S.Compton	v	Somerset	Lord's	1948
4th	325	J.W.Hearne/E.H.Hendren	v	Hampshire	Lord's	1919
5th	338	R.S.Lucas/T.C.O'Brien	v	Sussex	Hove	1895
6th	270	J.D.Carr/P.N.Weekes	v	Glos	Lord's	1994
7th	271*	E.H.Hendren/F.T.Mann	v	Notts	Nottingham	1925
8th	182*	M.H.C.Doll/H.R.Murrell	v	Notts	Lord's	1913
9th	172	G.K.Berg/T.J.Murtagh	v	Leics	Leicester	2011
10th	230	R.W.Nicholls/W.Roche	v	Kent	Lord's	1899

Best Bowling	For 10- 40	G.O.B.Allen	v	Lancashire	Lord's	1929
(Innings)	V 9- 38	R.C.R-Glasgow†	for	Somerset	Lord's	1924
Best Bowling	For 16-114	G.Burton	v	Yorkshire	Sheffield	1888
(Match)	16-114	J.T.Hearne	v	Lancashire	Manchester	1898
	V 16-100	J.E.B.B.P.Q.C.Dwyer	for	Sussex	Hove	1906

Most Runs – Season	2669	E.H.Hendren	(av 83.41)		1923
Most Runs – Career	40302	E.H.Hendren	(av 48.81)		1907-37
Most 100s – Season	13	D.C.S.Compton			1947
Most 100s – Career	119	E.H.Hendren			1907-37
Most Wkts – Season	158	F.J.Titmus	(av 14.63)		1955
Most Wkts – Career	2361	F.J.Titmus	(av 21.27)		1949-82
Most Career W-K Dismissals	1223	J.T.Murray	(1024 ct; 199 st)		1952-75
Most Career Catches in the Field	561	E.H.Hendren			1907-37

LIMITED-OVERS CRICKET

Highest Total	50ov	380-5	v	Kent	Canterbury	2019
	40ov	350-6	v	Lancashire	Lord's	2012
	T20	227-4	v	Somerset	Taunton	2019
Lowest Total	50ov	41	v	Essex	Westcliff	1972
	40ov	23	v	Yorkshire	Leeds	1974
	T20	92	v	Surrey	Lords	2013
Highest Innings	50ov	166	M.D.E.Holden	v	Kent	Canterbury	2019
	40ov	147*	M.R.Ramprakash	v	Worcs	Lord's	1990
	T20	129	D.T.Christian	v	Kent	Canterbury	2014
Best Bowling	50ov	7-12	W.W.Daniel	v	Minor Cos E	Ipswich	1978
	40ov	6- 6	R.W.Hooker	v	Surrey	Lord's	1969
	T20	6-28	J.K.Fuller	v	Hampshire	Southampton[2]	2018

† R.C.Robertson-Glasgow

NORTHAMPTONSHIRE

Formation of Present Club: 31 July 1878
Inaugural First-Class Match: 1905
Colours: Maroon
Badge: Tudor Rose
County Champions: (0); best – 2nd 1912, 1957, 1965, 1976
Gillette/NatWest/C&G/FP Trophy Winners: (2) 1976, 1992
Benson and Hedges Cup Winners: (1) 1980
Twenty20 Cup Winners: (2) 2013, 2016

est. 1878
NORTHAMPTONSHIRE
COUNTY CRICKET CLUB

Chief Executive: Ray Payne, County Ground, Abington Avenue, Northampton, NN1 4PR •
Tel: 01604 514455 • Email: info@nccc.co.uk • Web: www.nccc.co.uk • Twitter:
@NorthantsCCC (63,242 followers)

Head Coach: David Ripley. **Assistant Coach/Batting Lead**: John Sadler. **Bowling Lead**:
Chris Liddle. **Captains**: A.M.Rossington (f-c) and J.J.Cobb (T20). **Overseas Players**:
Mohammad Nabi (T20 only) and W.D.Parnell. **2021 Testimonial**: A.G.Wakely. **Head
Groundsman**: Craig Harvey. **Scorer**: Tony Kingston. **Blast Team Name**: Northamptonshire
Steelbacks. ‡ New registration. ᴺᴼ Not qualified for England.

BERG, Gareth Kyle (South African College S), b Cape Town, South Africa 18 Jan 1981.
6'0". RHB, RMF. Squad No 13. England qualified through residency. Middlesex 2008-14;
cap 2010. Hampshire 2015-19; cap 2016. Northamptonshire debut 2019. Italy 2011-12 to
date (l-o and T20 only). HS 130* M v Leics (Leicester) 2011, sharing M record 9th wkt
partnership of 172 with T.J.Murtagh. Nh HS 45 v Worcs (Northampton) 2020. BB 6-56 H v
Yorks (Southampton) 2016. Nh BB 4-64 v Somerset (Northampton) 2020. LO HS 75 M v
Glamorgan (Lord's) 2013 (Y40). LO BB 5-26 H v Lancs (Southampton) 2019 (RLC). T20
HS 90. T20 BB 4-20.

BUCK, Nathan Liam (Newbridge HS; Ashby S), b Leicester 26 Apr 1991. 6'2" RHB,
RMF. Squad No 11. Leicestershire 2009-14; cap 2011. Lancashire 2015-16.
Northamptonshire debut 2017. F-c Tour (EL): WI 2010-11. HS 53 v Glamorgan (Cardiff)
2019. BB 6-34 v Durham (Chester-le-St) 2017. LO HS 21 Le v Glamorgan (Leicester) 2009
(P40). LO BB 4-39 EL v Sri Lanka A (Dambulla) 2011-12. T20 HS 16*. T20 BB 4-26.

COBB, Joshua James (Oakham S), b Leicester 17 Aug 1990. Son of R.A.Cobb (Leics and
N Transvaal 1980-89). 5'11½". RHB, OB. Squad No 4. Leicestershire 2007-14; l-o captain
2014. Northamptonshire debut 2015; cap 2018; captain 2020 to date (white ball only). HS
148* Le v Middx (Lord's) 2008. Nh HS 139 v Durham MCCU (Northampton) 2019. BB
2-11 Le v Glos (Leicester) 2008. Nh BB 2-44 v Loughborough MCCU (Northampton)
2017. LO HS 146* v Pakistanis (Northampton) 2019. LO BB 3-34 Le v Glos (Leicester)
2013 (Y40). T20 HS 103. T20 BB 4-22.

CURRAN, Benjamin Jack (Wellington C), b Northampton 7 Jun 1996. Son of K.M.Curran
(Glos, Natal, Northants, Boland and Zimbabwe 1980-81 to 1999); grandson of K.P.Curran
(Rhodesia 1947-48 to 1954-55); younger brother of T.K.Curran (*see SURREY*) and elder
brother of S.M.Curran (*see SURREY*). 5'8". LHB, OB. Squad No 57. Debut
(Northamptonshire) 2018. Nottinghamshire 2nd XI 2016. Surrey 2nd XI 2016.
Warwickshire 2nd XI 2017. Leicestershire 2nd XI 2017. HS 83* v Sussex (Northampton)
2018. LO HS 69 v Leics (Leicester) 2019 (RLC). T20 HS 29.

132

GAY, Emilio Nico (Bedford S), b Bedford May 2000. 6'2''. LHB, RM. Squad No 19. Debut (Northamptonshire) 2019. Northamptonshire 2nd XI debut 2018. HS 77* v Glamorgan (Northampton) 2020.

NQGLOVER, Brandon Dale (St Stithians C), b Johannesburg, South Africa 3 Apr 1997. 6'2½''. RHB, RFM. Squad No 20. Boland 2016-17 to 2018-19. **LOI** (Neth): 1 (2019); HS – ; BB 1-37 v Z (Deventer) 2019. **IT20** (Neth): 19 (2019 to 2019-20); HS 1* (twice); BB 4-12 v UAE (Dubai, DSC) 2019-20. HS 12* Boland v Gauteng (Paarl) 2018-19. Nh HS 0. BB 4-83 Boland v FS (Bloemfontein) 2017-18. Nh BB 2-45 v Somerset (Northampton) 2020. LO HS 27 Boland v Easterns (Benoni) 2017-18. LO BB 2-60 Boland v Namibia (Paarl) 2016-17. T20 HS 1*. T20 BB 4-12.

KEOGH, Robert Ian (Queensbury S; Dunstable C), b Luton, Beds 21 Oct 1991. 5'11''. RHB, OB. Squad No 21. Debut (Northamptonshire) 2012; cap 2019. Bedfordshire 2009-10. HS 221 v Hants (Southampton) 2013. BB 9-52 (13-125 match) v Glamorgan (Northampton) 2016. LO HS 134 v Durham (Northampton) 2016 (RLC). LO BB 2-26 v Yorks (Leeds) 2018 (RLC). T20 HS 59*. T20 BB 3-30.

KERRIGAN, Simon Christopher (Corpus Christi RC HS, Preston), b Preston, Lancs 10 May 1989. 5'9''. RHB, SLA. Squad No 10. Lancashire 2010-17; cap 2013. Northamptonshire debut 2017. MCC 2013. **Tests**: 1 (2013); HS 1* and BB – v A (Oval) 2013. F-c Tour (EL): SL 2013-14. HS 62* La v Hants (Southport) 2013. Nh HS 62 v Glamorgan (Cardiff) 2017. 50 wkts (2); most – 58 (2013). BB 9-51 (12-192 match) La v Hants (Liverpool) 2011. Nh BB 4-62 v Leics (Leicester) 2017. LO HS 10 La v Middx (Lord's) 2012 (CB40). LO BB 3-21 EL v Sri Lanka A (Northampton) 2011. T20 HS 4*. T20 BB 3-17.

NQLEVI, Richard Ernst, b Johannesburg, South Africa 14 Jan 1988. 5'11''. RHB, RM. Squad No 88. W Province 2006-07 to 2016-17. Cape Cobras 2008-09 to 2015-16. Northamptonshire debut 2014; cap 2017. IPL: MI 2012. **IT20** (SA): 13 (2011-12 to 2012-13); HS 117* v NZ (Hamilton) 2011-12. HS 168 v Essex (Northampton) 2015. LO HS 166 Cobras v Titans (Paarl) 2012-13. T20 HS 117*.

‡NQMOHAMMAD NABI Eisakhil, b Peshawar, Pakistan 7 Mar 1985. 6'3''. RHB, OB. Pakistan Customs 2007-08 to 2009-10. MCC 2007-11. Afghanistan 2009 to date. IPL: SH 2017-18 to date. Big Bash: MR 2017-18 to date. Leicestershire 2018 (T20 only). Kent 2019 (T20 only). **Tests** (Afg): 3 (2018 to 2019); HS 24 v I (Bengaluru) 2018; BB 3-36 v Ire (Dehradun) 2018-19. **LOI** (Afg): 127 (2009 to 2020-21); HS 116 v Z (Bulawayo) 2015-16; BB 4-30 v Ire (Greater Noida) 2016-17 and 4-30 v SL (Cardiff) 2019. **IT20** (Afg): 78 (2009-10 to 2019-20); HS 89 v Ire (Greater Noida) 2016-17; BB 4-10 v Ire (Dubai, DSC) 2016-17. HS 117 Afg v UAE (Sharjah) 2011-12. BB 6-33 Afg v Namibia (Windhoek) 2013. LO HS 146 MSC v PDSC (Bogra) 2013-14. LO BB 5-12 Afg v Namibia (Windhoek) 2013. T20 HS 89. T20 BB 5-15.

‡NQPARNELL, Wayne Dillon (Grey HS), b Port Elizabeth, South Africa 30 Jul 1989. 6'2''. LHB, LFM. E Province 2006-07 to 2010-11. Warriors 2008-09 to 2014-15. Kent 2009-11. Sussex 2011. Cape Cobras 2015-16 to 2016-17. Worcestershire 2018-19. IPL: PW 2011-13. DD 2014. Glamorgan 2015 (T20 only). **Tests** (SA): 6 (2009-10 to 2017-18); HS 23 and BB 4-51 v SL (Johannesburg) 2016-17. **LOI** (SA): 65 (2008-09 to 2017); HS 56 v P (Sharjah) 2013-14; BB 5-48 v E (Cape Town) 2009-10. **IT20** (SA): 40 (2008-09 to 2017); HS 29* v A (Johannesburg) 2011-12; BB 4-13 v WI (Oval) 2009. F-c Tours (SA A): A 2016; I 2009-10 (SA), 2015; Ire 2012. HS 111* Cobras v Warriors (Paarl) 2015-16. CC HS 90 K v Glamorgan (Canterbury) 2009. BB 7-51 Cobras v Dolphins (Cape Town) 2015-16. CC BB 5-47 Wo v Lancs (Manchester) 2019. LO HS 129 Warriors v Lions (Potchefstroom) 2013-14. LO BB 6-51 Warriors v Knights (Kimberley) 2013-14. T20 HS 99. T20 BB 4-13.

PROCTER, Luke Anthony (Counthill S, Oldham), b Oldham, Lancs 24 June 1988. 5'11". LHB, RM. Squad No 2. Lancashire 2010-17. Northamptonshire debut 2017; cap 2020. Cumberland 2007. HS 137 v Hants (Manchester) 2016. Nh HS 112* v Warwks (Birmingham) 2020. BB 7-71 La v Surrey (Liverpool) 2012. Nh BB 5-33 v Durham (Chester-le-St) 2017. LO HS 97 v West Indies A (Manchester) 2010. LO BB 3-29 v Unicorns (Colwyn Bay) 2010 (CB40). T20 HS 25*. T20 BB 3-22.

ROSSINGTON, Adam Matthew (Mill Hill S), b Edgware, Middx 5 May 1993. 5'11". RHB, WK, occ RM. Squad No 7. Middlesex 2010-14. Northamptonshire debut 2014; cap 2019; captain 2020. HS 138* v Sussex (Arundel) 2016. Won 2013 Walter Lawrence Trophy with 55-ball century v Cambridge MCCU (Cambridge). LO HS 97 v Notts (Nottingham) 2016 (RLC). T20 HS 85.

SANDERSON, Ben William (Ecclesfield CS; Sheffield C), b Sheffield, Yorks 3 Jan 1989. 6'0". RHB, RMF. Squad No 26. Yorkshire 2008-10. Northamptonshire debut 2015; cap 2018. Shropshire 2013-15. HS 42 v Kent (Canterbury) 2015. 50 wkts (3); most – 61 (2019). BB 8-73 v Glos (Northampton) 2016. LO HS 31 v Derbys (Derby) 2019 (RLC). LO BB 3-36 v Durham (Chester-le-St) 2017 (RLC). T20 HS 12*. T20 BB 4-21.

TAYLOR, Thomas Alex Ian (Trentham HS, Stoke-on-Trent), b Stoke-on-Trent, Staffs 21 Dec 1994. Elder brother of J.P.A.Taylor (*see SURREY*). 6'2". RHB, RMF. Squad No 12. Derbyshire 2014-17. Leicestershire 2018-20. Northamptonshire debut 2020 (T20 only). HS 80 De v Kent (Derby) 2016. BB 6-47 (10-122 match) Le v Sussex (Hove) 2019. LO HS 98* Le v Warwks (Leicester) 2019 (RLC). LO BB 3-48 De v Worcs (Worcester) 2014 (RLC). T20 HS 50*. T20 BB 2-38.

THURSTON, Charles Oliver (Bedford S; Loughborough U), b Cambridge 17 Aug 1996. 5'11½". RHB, RM. Squad No 96. Loughborough MCCU 2016-18. Northamptonshire debut 2018. Bedfordshire 2014-17. Middlesex 2nd XI 2013-14. Northamptonshire 2nd XI debut 2015. HS 126 LU v Northants (Northampton) 2017. Nh HS 115 v Glamorgan (Northampton) 2020. BB – . LO HS 53 v Yorks (Leeds) 2018 (RLC). T20 HS 41.

[NQ]**VASCONCELOS, Ricardo** Surrador (St Stithians C), b Johannesburg, South Africa 27 Oct 1997. 5'5". LHB, WK. Squad No 27. Boland 2016-17 to 2017-18. Northamptonshire debut 2018. South Africa U19 2016. Portuguese passport. HS 184 v Glamorgan (Cardiff) 2019. LO HS 112 v Yorks (Northampton) 2019 (RLC). T20 HS 45*.

WAKELY, Alexander George (Bedford S), b Hammersmith, London 3 Nov 1988. 6'2". RHB, RM. Squad No 8. Debut (Northamptonshire) 2007; cap 2012; captain 2015-19; testimonial 2020-21. Bedfordshire 2004-05. HS 123 v Leics (Northampton) 2015. BB 2-62 v Somerset (Taunton) 2007. LO HS 109* v Lancs (Liverpool) 2017 (RLC). LO BB 2-14 v Lancs (Northampton) 2007 (P40). T20 HS 64. T20 BB – .

WHITE, Curtley-Jack (Ullswater Comm C; Queen Elizabeth GS, Penrith), b Kendal, Cumberland 19 Feb 1992. 6'2". LHB, RFM. Squad No 9. Debut (Northamptonshire) 2020. Cumberland 2013. Cheshire 2016-17. HS 7* v Worcs (Northampton) 2020. BB 4-35 v Glamorgan (Northampton) 2020.

WHITE, Graeme Geoffrey (Stowe S), b Milton Keynes, Bucks 18 Apr 1987. 5'11". RHB, SLA. Squad No 87. Debut (Northamptonshire) 2006. Nottinghamshire 2010-13. HS 65 v Glamorgan (Colwyn Bay) 2007. BB 6-44 v Glamorgan (Northampton) 2016. LO HS 41* v Yorks (Leeds) 2018 (RLC). LO BB 6-37 v Lancs (Northampton) 2016 (RLC). T20 HS 37*. T20 BB 5-22 Nt v Lancs (Nottingham) 2013 – Nt record.

ZAIB, Saif Ali (RGS High Wycombe), b High Wycombe, Bucks 22 May 1998. 5'7½". LHB, SLA. Squad No 18. Debut (Northamptonshire) 2015. Northamptonshire 2nd XI debut 2013, aged 15y 90d. HS 65* v Glamorgan (Swansea) 2016. BB 6-115 v Loughborough MCCU (Northampton) 2017 CC BB 5-148 v Leics (Northampton) 2016. LO HS 17 and LO BB 2-22 v South Africans (Northampton) 2017. T20 HS 30. T20 BB 1-20.

RELEASED/RETIRED

(Having made a County 1st XI appearance in 2020, even if not formally contracted. Some may return in 2021.)

GOULDSTONE, Harry Oliver Michael (Bedford S), b Kettering 26 Mar 2001. RHB, WK. Northamptonshire 2020 – did not bat or bowl. Northamptonshire 2nd XI debut 2019.

HUTTON, B.A. – *see NOTTINGHAMSHIRE.*

^{NQ}**MUZARABANI, Blessing** (Churchill S), b Harare, Zimbabwe 2 Oct 1996. Younger brother of T.Muzarabani (Centrals, MWR, SR, ME, HME 2006-07 to 2017-18). 6'6". RHB, RMF. Rising Stars 2017-18. Northamptonshire 2019-20. Eagles 2019-20. Southern Rocks 2020-21. **Tests** (Z): 2 (2017-18 to 2020-21); HS 12* and BB 4-48 v Afg (Abu Dhabi) 2020-21. **LOI** (Z): 21 (2017-18 to 2020-21); HS 17 v P (Rawalpindi) 2020-21; BB 5-49 v P (Rawalpindi) 2020-21 – separate matches. **IT20** (Z): 9 (2017-18 to 2020-21); HS 5* v P (Rawalpindi) 2020-21; BB 3-21 v A (Harare) 2018. HS 23 Eagles v Rhinos (Harare) 2019-20. Nh HS 15 and Nh BB 4-29 v Worcs (Northampton) 2020. BB 5-32 RS v BMT (Kwekwe) 2017-18. Nh BB 2-29 v Durham MCCU (Northampton) 2019. LO HS 18 v Derbys (Derby) 2019 (RLC). LO BB 5-49 (*see LOI*). T20 HS 9. T20 BB 3-21.

SOLE, Thomas Barclay (Merchiston Castle S; Cardiff Met U), b Edinburgh, Scotland 12 Jun 1996. Younger brother of C.B.Sole (Scotland 2016 to 2017-18); son of D.M.B.Sole (Scotland Grand Slam-winning rugby union captain); nephew of C.R.Trembath (Gloucestershire 1982-84). RHB, OB. Awaiting f-c debut. **LOI** (Scot): 10 (2017-18 to 2019); HS 20 v Ire (Dubai, ICCA) 2017-18; BB 4-15 v Hong Kong (Bulawayo) 2017-18. **IT20** (Scot): 9 (2019 to 2019-20); HS 33* v Kenya (Dubai, ICCA) 2019-20; BB 2-15 v Neth (Dublin) 2019. LO HS 54 v S Africans (Northampton) 2017. LO BB 4-15 (*see LOI*). T20 HS 41*. T20 BB 2-15.

STIRLING, P.R. – *see IRELAND.*

Faheem Ashraf and R.I.Newton left the staff without making a County 1st XI appearance in 2020.

NORTHAMPTONSHIRE 2020

RESULTS SUMMARY

	Place	Won	Lost	Drew	NR
Bob Willis Trophy (Central Group)	4th	1	2	2	
Vitality Blast (Central Group)	QF	5	5		1

BOB WILLIS TROPHY AVERAGES
BATTING AND FIELDING

Cap		M	I	NO	HS	Runs	Avge	100	50	Ct/St
2020	L.A.Procter	4	6	2	112*	200	50.00	1	–	1
	C.O.Thurston	5	8	–	115	357	44.62	1	2	2
2019	A.M.Rossington	3	6	1	135*	196	39.20	1	–	8
	R.S.Vasconcelos	5	8	–	58	222	31.71	–	2	13/1
	N.L.Buck	2	3	1	32	61	30.50	–	–	5
	B.J.Curran	4	8	–	82	238	29.75	–	2	5
	E.N.Gay	4	6	1	77*	121	24.20	–	1	4
	G.K.Berg	2	4	–	45	63	15.75	–	–	3
2019	R.I.Keogh	4	6	–	31	80	13.33	–	–	1
	B.Muzurabani	4	5	2	15	27	9.00	–	–	1
2018	B.W.Sanderson	2	3	–	23	23	7.66	–	–	–
	S.A.Zaib	4	5	–	23	36	7.20	–	–	2
	C.J.White	4	4	2	7*	9	4.50	–	–	–

Also played: B.D.Glover (1 match) 0, 0; H.O.M.Gouldstone (1) did not bat (1 ct); B.A.Hutton (2) 9 (1 ct); S.C.Kerrigan (2) 1 (1 ct); R.E.Levi (1 – cap 2017) 11, 8 (1 ct); A.G.Wakely (1 – cap 2012) 9, 2 (1 ct).

BOWLING

	O	M	R	W	Avge	Best	5wI	10wM
B.W.Sanderson	55.1	14	166	11	15.09	5-28	1	–
N.L.Buck	64	21	173	9	19.22	3-42	–	–
C.J.White	88	20	260	13	20.00	4-35	–	–
S.A.Zaib	28	5	84	4	21.00	2-11	–	–
B.A.Hutton	39	8	136	6	22.66	4-77	–	–
B.D.Glover	24	5	94	4	23.50	2-45	–	–
B.Muzurabani	70.5	17	278	11	25.27	4-29	–	–
S.C.Kerrigan	23.3	4	89	3	29.66	2-54	–	–
G.K.Berg	47	9	203	6	33.83	4-64	–	–

Also bowled: R.I.Keogh 38-10-112-1; L.J.Procter 30-5-130-2.

The First-Class Averages (pp 209–221) give the records of Northamptonshire players in all first-class county matches.

NORTHAMPTONSHIRE RECORDS

FIRST-CLASS CRICKET

Highest Total	For 781-7d		v	Notts	Northampton	1995
	V 701-7d		by	Kent	Beckenham	2017
Lowest Total	For 12		v	Glos	Gloucester	1907
	V 33		by	Lancashire	Northampton	1977
Highest Innings	For 331*	M.E.K.Hussey	v	Somerset	Taunton	2003
	V 333	K.S.Duleepsinhji	for	Sussex	Hove	1930

Highest Partnership for each Wicket

1st	375	R.A.White/M.J.Powell	v	Glos	Northampton	2002
2nd	344	G.Cook/R.J.Boyd-Moss	v	Lancashire	Northampton	1986
3rd	393	A.Fordham/A.J.Lamb	v	Yorkshire	Leeds	1990
4th	370	R.T.Virgin/P.Willey	v	Somerset	Northampton	1976
5th	401	M.B.Loye/D.Ripley	v	Glamorgan	Northampton	1998
6th	376	R.Subba Row/A.Lightfoot	v	Surrey	The Oval	1958
7th	293	D.J.G.Sales/D.Ripley	v	Essex	Northampton	1999
8th	179	A.J.Hall/J.D.Middlebrook	v	Surrey	The Oval	2011
9th	156	R.Subba Row/S.Starkie	v	Lancashire	Northampton	1955
10th	148	B.W.Bellamy/J.V.Murdin	v	Glamorgan	Northampton	1925

Best Bowling	For	10-127	V.W.C.Jupp	v	Kent	Tunbridge W	1932
(Innings)	V	10- 30	C.Blythe	for	Kent	Northampton	1907
Best Bowling	For	15- 31	G.E.Tribe	v	Yorkshire	Northampton	1958
(Match)	V	17- 48	C.Blythe	for	Kent	Northampton	1907

Most Runs – Season	2198	D.Brookes	(av 51.11)	1952
Most Runs – Career	28980	D.Brookes	(av 36.13)	1934-59
Most 100s – Season	8	R.A.Haywood		1921
Most 100s – Career	67	D.Brookes		1934-59
Most Wkts – Season	175	G.E.Tribe	(av 18.70)	1955
Most Wkts – Career	1102	E.W.Clark	(av 21.26)	1922-47
Most Career W-K Dismissals	810	K.V.Andrew	(653 ct; 157 st)	1953-66
Most Career Catches in the Field	469	D.S.Steele		1963-84

LIMITED-OVERS CRICKET

Highest Total	50ov	425		v	Notts	Nottingham	2016
	40ov	324-6		v	Warwicks	Birmingham	2013
	T20	231-5		v	Warwicks	Birmingham	2018
Lowest Total	50ov	62		v	Leics	Leicester	1974
	40ov	41		v	Middlesex	Northampton	1972
	T20	47		v	Durham	Chester-le-St[2]	2011
Highest Innings	50ov	161	D.J.G.Sales	v	Yorkshire	Northampton	2006
	40ov	172*	W.Larkins	v	Warwicks	Luton	1983
	T20	111*	L.Klusener	v	Worcs	Kidderminster	2007
Best Bowling	50ov	7-10	C.Pietersen	v	Denmark	Brondby	2005
	40ov	7-39	A.Hodgson	v	Somerset	Northampton	1976
	T20	6-21	A.J.Hall	v	Worcs	Northampton	2008

NOTTINGHAMSHIRE

Formation of Present Club: March/April 1841
Substantial Reorganisation: 11 December 1866
Inaugural First-Class Match: 1864
Colours: Green and Gold
County Champions (since 1890): (6) 1907, 1929, 1981, 1987, 2005, 2010
NatWest Trophy Winners: (1) 1987
Benson and Hedges Cup Winners: (1) 1989
Sunday League Winners: (1) 1991
Yorkshire Bank 40 Winners: (1) 2013
Royal London Cup Winners: (1) 2017
Twenty20 Cup Winners: (2) 2017, 2020

Chief Executive: Lisa Pursehouse, Trent Bridge, West Bridgford, Nottingham NG2 6AG • Tel: 0115 982 3000 • Email: questions@nottsccc.co.uk • Web: www.trentbridge.co.uk • Twitter: @TrentBridge (89,367 followers)

Director of Cricket: Mick Newell. **Head Coach**: Peter Moores. **Assistant Head Coach**: Paul Franks. **Assistant Coach**: Kevin Shine. **Captains**: S.J.Mullaney (f-c) and H.Hameed (l-o) and D.T.Christian (T20). **Vice-captain**: H.Hameed. **Overseas Players**: D.T.Christian (T20 only) and D.Paterson. **2021 Testimonial**: None. **Head Groundsman**: Steve Birks. **Scorer**: Roger Marshall and Anne Cusworth. **Blast Team Name**: Nottinghamshire Outlaws. ‡ New registration. ^{NQ} Not qualified for England.

BALL, Jacob Timothy (**'Jake'**) (Meden CS), b Mansfield 14 Mar 1991. Nephew of B.N.French (Notts and England 1976-95). 6'0". RHB, RFM. Squad No 28. Debut (Nottinghamshire) 2011; cap 2016. MCC 2016. Big Bash: SS 2020-21. **Tests**: 4 (2016 to 2017-18); HS 31 and BB 1-47 v I (Mumbai) 2016-17. **LOI**: 18 (2016-17 to 2018); HS 28 v B (Dhaka) 2016-17; BB 5-51 v B (Dhaka) 2016-17 – different games. **IT20**: 2 (2018); HS – ; BB 1-39 v I (Bristol) 2018. F-c Tours: A 2017-18; I 2016-17. HS 49* v Warwks (Nottingham) 2015. 50 wkts (1): 54 (2016). BB 6-49 v Sussex (Nottingham) 2015. Hat-trick v Middx (Nottingham) 2016. LO HS 28 (*see LOI*). BB 5-51 (*see LOI*). T20 HS 8*. T20 BB 3-25.

BARBER, Thomas Edward (Bournemouth GS), b Poole, Dorset 31 May 1994. 6'3". RHB, LFM. Squad No 18. Middlesex 2018. Nottinghamshire debut 2020. Hampshire 2014 (l-o only). Dorset 2016. HS 3 M v Sussex (Hove) 2018. Nt HS 2* and BB 3-42 v Lancs (Nottingham) 2020. LO HS 1 South v North (Cave Hill) 2017-18. LO BB 3-62 M v Australians (Lord's) 2018. T20 HS 2. T20 BB 4-28.

BROAD, Stuart Christopher John (Oakham S), b Nottingham 24 Jun 1986. Son of B.C.Broad (Glos, Notts, OFS and England 1979-94). 6'6". LHB, RFM. Squad No 8. Debut (Leicestershire) 2005; cap 2007. Nottinghamshire debut/cap 2008; testimonial 2019. MCC 2019. Big Bash: HH 2016-17. YC 2006. *Wisden* 2009. **ECB Test Central Contract 2020-21. Tests:** 146 (2007-08 to 2020-21); HS 169 v P (Lord's) 2010, sharing in record Test and UK f-c 8th wkt partnership of 332 with I.J.L.Trott; 50 wkts (2); most – 62 (2013); BB 8-15 v A (Nottingham) 2015. Hat-tricks (2): v I (Nottingham) 2011, and v SL (Leeds) 2014. **LOI:** 121 (2006 to 2015-16, 3 as captain); HS 45* v I (Manchester) 2007; BB 5-23 v SA (Nottingham) 2008. **IT20:** 56 (2006 to 2013-14, 27 as captain); HS 18* v SA (Chester-le-St) 2012 and 18* v A (Melbourne) 2013-14; BB 4-24 v NZ (Auckland) 2012-13. F-c Tours: A 2010-11, 2013-14, 2017-18; SA 2009-10, 2015-16, 2019-20; WI 2005-06 (Eng A), 2008-09, 2014-15, 2018-19; NZ 2007-08, 2012-13, 2017-18, 2019-20; I 2008-09, 2012-13, 2016-17, 2020-21; SL 2007-08, 2011-12, 2018-19, 2020-21; B 2006-07 (Eng A), 2009-10, 2016-17; UAE 2011-12 (v P), 2015-16 (v P). HS 169 (*see Tests*). HS 91* Le v Derbys (Leicester) 2007. Nt HS 60 v Worcs (Nottingham) 2009. BB 8-15 (*see Tests*). CC BB 8-52 (11-131 match) Nt v Warwks (Birmingham) 2010. LO HS 45* (*see LOI*). LO BB 5-23 (*see LOI*). T20 HS 18*. T20 BB 4-24.

BUDINGER, Soloman George (Southport S), b Colchester, Essex 21 Aug 1999. LHB, OB, occ WK. Squad No 1. Sussex 2nd XI 2016-17. Nottinghamshire 2nd XI debut 2018. Awaiting 1st XI debut.

CARTER, Matthew (Branston S), b Lincoln 26 May 1996. Younger brother of A.Carter (*see WORCESTERSHIRE*). RHB, OB. Squad No 20. Debut (Nottinghamshire) 2015, taking 7-56 v Somerset (Taunton) – the best debut figures for Nt since 1914. Nottinghamshire 2nd XI debut 2013. Lincolnshire 2013-17. HS 33 v Sussex (Hove) 2017. BB 7-56 (10-195 match) (*see above*). LO HS 21* v Warwks (Birmingham) 2019 (RLC). LO BB 4-40 v Warwks (Nottingham) 2018 (RLC). T20 HS 16*. T20 BB 3-14.

CHAPPELL, Zachariah John ('**Zak**') (Stamford S), b Grantham, Lincs 21 Aug 1996. 6'4''. RHB, RFM. Squad No 32. Leicestershire 2015-18. Nottinghamshire debut 2019. HS 96 Le v Derbys (Derby) 2015. Nt HS 29 v Warwks (Nottingham) 2019. BB 6-44 Le v Northants (Northampton) 2018. Nt BB 4-59 v Yorks (Nottingham) 2020. LO HS 59* Le v Durham (Gosforth) 2017 (RLC). LO BB 3-45 Le v Durham (Leicester) 2018 (RLC). T20 HS 16. T20 BB 3-23.

^{NO}CHRISTIAN, Daniel Trevor, b Camperdown, NSW, Australia 4 May 1983. RHB, RFM. Squad No 54. S Australia 2007-08 to 2012-13. Hampshire 2010. Gloucestershire 2013; cap 2013. Victoria 2013-14 to 2017-18. Nottinghamshire debut 2016, having joined in 2015 for l-o and T20 only; cap 2015; captain 2016 to date (T20 only). IPL: DC 2011-12. RCB 2013. RPS 2017. DD 2018. Big Bash: BH 2011-12 to 2014-15. HH 2015-16 to 2017-18. MR 2018-19 to 2019-20. SS 2020-21. **LOI** (A): 19 (2011-12 to 2013-14); HS 39 v I (Adelaide) 2011-12; BB 5-31 v SL (Melbourne) 2011-12. **IT20** (A): 16 (2009-10 to 2017-18); HS 9 v I (Ranchi) 2017-18; BB 3-27 v WI (Gros Islet) 2011-12. HS 131* SA v NSW (Adelaide) 2011-12. CC HS 36 and CC BB 2-115 H v Somerset (Taunton) 2010. Nt HS 31 v Hants (Southampton) 2016. BB 5-24 SA v WA (Perth) (2009-10). Nt BB 1-22 v Warwks (Birmingham) 2016. LO HS 117 Vic v NSW (Sydney) 2013-14. LO BB 6-48 SA v Vic (Geelong) 2010-11. T20 HS 129 M v Kent (Canterbury) 2014 – M record. T20 BB 5-14.

CLARKE, Joe Michael (Llanfyllin HS), b Shrewsbury, Shrops 26 May 1996. 5'11''. RHB, WK. Squad No 33. Worcestershire 2015-18. Nottinghamshire debut 2019. MCC 2017. Shropshire 2012-13. England U19 2014. F-c Tours (EL): WI 2017-18; UAE 2016-17 (v Afg). 1000 runs (1): 1325 (2016). HS 194 Wo v Derbys (Worcester) 2016. Nt HS 133 v Durham (Nottingham) 2020. BB – . LO HS 139 v Lancs (Nottingham) 2019 (RLC). T20 HS 124*.

COMPTON, Benjamin Garnet (Clifton C, Durban), b Durban, S Africa 29 Mar 1994. Son of P.M.D.Compton (Natal 1979-80); grandson of D.S.C.Compton (Middlesex and England 1936-58); cousin of N.R.D.Compton (Middlesex, Somerset, ME, Worcs and England 2004-17). LHB, OB. Squad No 7. Debut (Nottinghamshire) 2019. No 1st XI appearances in 2020. HS 16* v Surrey (Oval) 2019.

DUCKETT, Ben Matthew (Stowe S), b Farnborough, Kent 17 Oct 1994. 5'7". LHB, WK, occ OB. Squad No 17. Northamptonshire 2013-18; cap 2016. Nottinghamshire debut 2018; cap 2019. MCC 2017. Big Bash: HH 2018-19. PCA 2016. YC 2016. *Wisden* 2016. **Tests**: 4 (2016-17); HS 56 v B (Dhaka) 2016-17. **LOI**: 3 (2016-17); HS 63 v B (Chittagong) 2016-17. **IT20**: 1 (2019); HS 9 v P (Cardiff) 2019. F-c Tours: I 2016-17; B 2016-17. 1000 runs (2); most – 1338 (2016). HS 282* Nh v Sussex (Northampton) 2016. Nt HS 216 v Cambridge MCCU (Cambridge) 2019. BB 1-21 Nh v Kent (Beckenham) 2017. LO HS 220* EL v Sri Lanka A (Canterbury) 2016. T20 HS 96.

EVISON, Joseph David Michael (Stamford S), b Peterborough, Cambs 14 Nov 2001. Son of G.M.Evison (Lincolnshire 1993-97); younger brother of S.H.G.Evison (Lincolnshire 2017-18). RHB, RM. Squad No 90. Debut (Nottinghamshire) 2019. Nottinghamshire 2nd XI debut 2017. HS 45 v Warwks (Nottingham) 2019.

FLETCHER, Luke Jack (Henry Mellish S, Nottingham), b Nottingham 18 Sep 1988. 6'6". RHB, RMF. Squad No 19. Debut (Nottinghamshire) 2008; cap 2014. Surrey 2015 (on loan). Derbyshire 2016 (on loan). HS 92 v Hants (Southampton) 2009 and 92 v Durham (Chester-le-St) 2017. BB 5-27 v Worcs (Worcester) 2018. LO HS 53* v Kent (Nottingham) 2018 (RLC). LO BB 5-56 v Derbys (Derby) 2019 (RLC). T20 HS 27. T20 BB 5-43.

GURNEY, Harry Frederick (Garendon HS; Loughborough GS; Leeds U), b Nottingham 25 Oct 1986. 6'2". RHB, LFM. Squad No 11. Leicestershire 2007-11. Nottinghamshire debut 2012; cap 2014. MCC 2014. Bradford/Leeds UCCE 2006-07 (not f-c). IPL: KKR 2019. Big Bash: MR 2018-19 to date. No 1st XI appearances in 2020 due to injury. **LOI**: 10 (2014 to 2014-15); HS 6* v SL (Colombo, RPS) 2014-15; BB 4-55 v SL (Lord's) 2014. **IT20**: 2 (2014); BB 2-26 v SL (Oval) 2014. HS 42* v Sussex (Hove) 2017. BB 6-25 v Lancs (Manchester) 2018. Hat-trick v Sussex (Hove) 2013. LO HS 13* v Durham (Chester-le-St) 2012 (CB40). LO BB 5-24 Le v Hants (Leicester) 2010 (CB40). T20 HS 6. T20 BB 5-30.

HALES, Alexander Daniel (Chesham HS), b Hillingdon, Middx 3 Jan 1989. 6'5". RHB, OB, occ WK. Squad No 10. Debut (Nottinghamshire) 2008; cap 2011. Agreed white-ball-only contract in 2018. Worcestershire 2014 (1 game, on loan). Buckinghamshire 2006-07. IPL: SH 2018. Big Bash: MR 2012-13. AS 2013-14. HH 2014-15. ST 2019-20 to date. **Tests**: 11 (2015-16 to 2016); HS 94 v SL (Lord's) 2016; BB – . **LOI**: 70 (2014 to 2018-19); HS 171 v P (Nottingham) 2016. **IT20**: 60 (2011 to 2018-19); HS 116* v SL (Chittagong) 2013-14 – E record. 1000 runs (3); most – 1127 (2011). HS 236 v Yorks (Nottingham) 2015. BB 2-63 v Yorks (Nottingham) 2009. LO HS 187* v Surrey (Lord's) 2017 (RLC) – Nt record. T20 HS 116*.

HAMEED, Haseeb (Bolton S), b Bolton, Lancs 17 Jan 1997. 6'2". RHB, LB. Squad No 99. Lancashire 2015-19; cap 2016. Nottinghamshire debut/cap 2020. Lancashire 2nd XI debut 2013. England U19 2014-15 to 2015. **Tests**: 3 (2016-17); HS 82 v I (Rajkot) 2016-17 – on debut. F-c Tours: WI 2017-18 (EL); I 2016-17; SL 2016-17 (EL). 1000 runs (1): 1198 (2016). HS 122 La v Notts (Nottingham) 2016. Nt HS 87 v Leics (Leicester) 2020. BB – . LO HS 88 La v Leics (Manchester) 2017 (RLC).

HUTTON, Brett Alan (Worksop C), b Doncaster, Yorks 6 Feb 1993. 6'2''. RHB, RM. Squad No 16. Debut (Nottinghamshire) 2011. Northamptonshire 2018-20. HS 74 v Durham (Nottingham) 2016. BB 8-57 Nh v Glos (Northampton) 2018. Nt BB 5-29 v Durham (Nottingham) 2015. LO HS 34* Nh v Leics (Northampton) 2018 (RLC). LO BB 3-72 v Kent (Nottingham) 2015 (RLC). T20 HS 18*. T20 BB 2-28.

JAMES, Lyndon Wallace (Oakham S), b Worksop 27 Dec 1998. RHB, RMF. Squad No 45. Debut (Nottinghamshire) 2018. Nottinghamshire 2nd XI debut 2017. HS 36* v Leics (Leicester) 2020. BB 3-54 v Essex (Nottingham) 2018. LO HS 0.

MOORES, Thomas James (Loughborough GS), b Brighton, Sussex 4 Sep 1996. Son of P.Moores (Worcestershire, Sussex & OFS 1983-98); nephew of S.Moores (Cheshire 1995). LHB, WK. Squad No 23. Lancashire 2016 (on loan). Nottinghamshire debut 2016. Nottinghamshire 2nd XI debut 2014. HS 106 v Yorks (Nottingham) 2020. LO HS 76 v Leics (Leicester) 2018 (RLC). T20 HS 80*.

MULLANEY, Steven John (St Mary's RC S, Astley), b Warrington, Cheshire 19 Nov 1986. 5'9''. RHB, RM. Squad No 5. Lancashire 2006-08. Nottinghamshire debut 2010, scoring 100* v Hants (Southampton); cap 2013; captain 2018 to date. F-c Tour (EL): I 2018-19. 1000 runs (1): 1148 (2016). HS 179 v Warwks (Nottingham) 2017. BB 5-32 v Glos (Nottingham) 2017. LO HS 124 v Durham (Chester-le-St) 2018 (RLC). LO BB 4-29 v Kent (Nottingham) 2013 (Y40). T20 HS 55. T20 BB 4-19.

PATEL, Samit Rohit (Worksop C), b Leicester 30 Nov 1984. Elder brother of A.Patel (Derbyshire and Notts 2007-11). 5'8''. RHB, SLA. Squad No 21. Debut (Nottinghamshire) 2002; cap 2008; testimonial 2017. Glamorgan 2016 (on loan). MCC 2014, 2016. PCA 2017. **Tests**: 6 (2011-12 to 2015-16); HS 42 v P (Sharjah) 2015-16; BB 2-27 v SL (Galle) 2011-12. **LOI**: 36 (2008 to 2012-13); HS 70* v I (Mohali) 2011-12; BB 5-41 v SA (Oval) 2008. **IT20**: 18 (2011 to 2012-13); HS 67 v SL (Pallekele) 2012-13; BB 2-6 v Afg (Colombo, RPS) 2012-13. F-c Tours: NZ 2008-09 (Eng A); I 2012-13; SL 2011-12; UAE 2015-16 (v P). 1000 runs (2); most – 1125 (2014). HS 257* v Glos (Bristol) 2017. BB 7-68 (11-111 match) v Hants (Southampton) 2011. LO HS 136* v Northants (Northampton) 2019 (RLC). LO BB 6-13 v Ireland (Dublin) 2009 (FPT). T20 HS 90*. T20 BB 4-5.

‡[NQ]**PATERSON, Dane**, b Cape Town, South Africa 4 Apr 1989. RHB, RFM. Squad No 4. Western Province 2009-10 to 2014-15. Dolphins 2010-11 to 2012-13. KwaZulu-Natal 2011-12 to 2012-13. Cape Cobras 2013-14 to 2019-20. **Tests** (SA): 2 (2019-20); HS 39* v E (Port Elizabeth) 2019-20; BB 2-86 v E (Johannesburg) 2019-20. **LOI** (SA): 4 (2017-18 to 2018-19); HS – ; BB 3-44 v B (East London) 2017-18. **IT20** (SA): (2016-17 to 2018-19); HS 4* v E (Taunton) 2017; BB 4-32 v E (Cardiff) 2017. F-c Tour (SA A): E 2017. HS 59 KZN v FS (Bloemfontein) 2012-13. BB 7-20 (10-62 match) WP v FS (Rondebosch) 2013-14. LO HS 29 Cape Cobras v Dolphins (Cape Town) 2017-18. LO BB 5-19 SA A v India A (Bangalore) 2018. T20 HS 24*. T20 BB 4-24.

PATTERSON-WHITE, Liam Anthony (Worksop C), b Sunderland, Co Durham 8 Nov 1998. LHB, SLA. Squad No 22. Debut (Nottinghamshire) 2019. Nottinghamshire 2nd XI debut 2016. England U19 2016-17. No 1st XI appearances in 2020. HS 58* v Yorks (Scarborough) 2019. BB 5-73 v Somerset (Taunton) 2019 – on debut.

‡**PETTMAN, Toby** Henry Somerville (Tonbridge S; Jesus C, Oxford), b Kingston-upon-Thames, Surrey 11 May 1998. 6'7''. RHB, RFM. Squad No 15. Oxford University 2017-20. HS 54* OU v Cambridge U (Oxford) 2018. BB 5-19 OU v Cambridge (Cambridge) 2019.

‡[NQ]**SCHADENDORF, Dane** J., b Harare, Zimbabwe 31 Jul 2002. RHB, WK. Squad No 89. Zimbabwe U19 2019-20.

SLATER, Benjamin Thomas (Netherthorpe S; Leeds Met U), b Chesterfield, Derbys 26 Aug 1991. 5'10". LHB, OB. Squad No 26. Debut (Leeds/Bradford MCCU) 2012. Southern Rocks 2012-13. Derbyshire 2013-18. Nottinghamshire debut 2018. Leicestershire 2020 (on loan). HS 172 Le v Lancs (Worcester) 2020. Nt HS 142 v Lancs (Nottingham) 2020. BB – . LO HS 148* De v Northants (Northampton) 2016 (RLC). T20 HS 57.

TREGO, Peter David (Wyvern CS, W-s-M), b Weston-super-Mare, Somerset 12 Jun 1981. 6'0". RHB, RMF. Squad No 77. Somerset 2000-18; cap 2007; benefit 2015. Kent 2003. Middlesex 2005. C Districts 2013-14. Nottinghamshire debut 2020. MCC 2013, 2019. Herefordshire 2005. 1000 runs (1): 1070 (2016). HS 154* Sm v Lancs (Manchester) 2016, sharing Sm record 8th wkt partnership of 236 with R.C.Davies. Nt HS 39 v Yorks (Nottingham) 2020. 50 wkts (1): 50 (2012). BB 7-84 (11-153 match) Sm v Yorks (Leeds) 2014. Nt BB 3-33 v Lancs (Nottingham) 2020. LO HS 147 Sm v Glamorgan (Taunton) 2010 (CB40). LO BB 5-40 EL v West Indies A (Worcester) 2010. T20 HS 94*. T20 BB 4-27.

RELEASED/RETIRED

(Having made a County 1st XI appearance in 2020)

BLATHERWICK, J.M. – *see LANCASHIRE.*

[NQ]**IMAD WASIM**, b Swansea, Glamorgan 18 Dec 1988. LHB, SLA. Islamabad 2006-07 to 2017-18. Federal Areas 2008-09 to 2011-12. Islamabad Leopards 2014-15. Northern Areas 2019-20. Nottinghamshire 2019-20 (T20 only). Big Bash: MR 2020-21. **LOI** (P): 55 (2015 to 2020-21, 2 as captain); HS 63* v E (Lord's) 2016; BB 5-14 v Ire (Dublin) 2016. **IT20** (P): 49 (2015 to 2020-21); HS 47 v SL (Lahore) 2019-20; BB 5-14 v WI (Dubai, DSC) 2016-17. F-c Tour (PA): SL 2015. HS 207 Leopards v Multan Tigers (Multan) 2014-15. BB 8-81 (12-104 match) Islamabad v Multan (Karachi) 2013-14. LO HS 117* P v Kent (Beckenham) 2019. LO BB 5-14 (see LOI). T20 HS 64. T20 BB 5-14.

NASH, Christopher David (Collyer's SFC; Loughborough U), b Cuckfield, Sussex 19 May 1983. 5'11". RHB, OB. Sussex 2002-17; cap 2008; testimonial 2017. Nottinghamshire 2018-20. Loughborough UCCE 2003-04. British U 2004. 1000 runs (4); most – 1321 (2009). HS 184 Sx v Leics (Leicester) 2010. Nt HS 139 v Worcs (Nottingham) 2018. BB 4-12 Sx v Glamorgan (Cardiff) 2010. Nt BB 3-20 v Yorks (Nottingham) 2020. LO HS 124* Sx v Kent (Canterbury) 2011 (CB40). LO BB 4-40 Sx v Yorks (Hove) 2009 (FPT). T20 HS 112*. T20 BB 4-7.

NOTTINGHAMSHIRE 2020

RESULTS SUMMARY

	Place	Won	Lost	Drew	Tied	NR
Bob Willis Trophy (North Group)	4th	2	3			
Vitality Blast (North Group)	Winners 9	1		1	2	

BOB WILLIS TROPHY AVERAGES
BATTING AND FIELDING

Cap		M	I	NO	HS	Runs	Avge	100	50	Ct/St
	B.T.Slater	3	3	–	142	228	76.00	1	1	2
2019	B.M.Duckett	5	8	1	150	394	56.28	2	–	3
2020	H.Hameed	5	7	–	87	272	38.85	–	3	8
	J.M.Clarke	5	8	1	133	263	37.57	1	1	–
2013	S.J.Mullaney	5	7	–	67	235	33.57	–	2	10
2008	S.R.Patel	5	7	–	80	210	30.00	–	2	2
	T.J.Moores	5	7	–	106	207	29.57	1	–	15/1
	C.D.Nash	2	4	–	59	78	19.50	–	1	1
	M.Carter	3	4	1	22	50	16.66	–	–	3
	P.D.Trego	5	8	–	39	116	14.50	–	–	1
2016	J.T.Ball	3	5	1	34	56	14.00	–	–	3
	Z.J.Chappell	4	4	1	1	1	0.33	–	–	3
	T.E.Barber	3	3	3	2*			–	–	–

Also batted: J.D.M.Evison (1 match) 38, 31 (1 ct); L.W.James (1) 36* (1 ct).

BOWLING

	O	M	R	W	Avge	Best	5wI	10wM
C.D.Nash	11.2	1	38	3	12.66	3-20	–	–
J.D.M.Evison	22.5	4	74	4	18.50	3-38	–	–
M.Carter	149.2	54	263	11	23.90	4-76	–	–
P.D.Trego	134.3	44	342	12	28.50	3-33	–	–
Z.J.Chappell	131.2	30	431	15	28.73	4-59	–	–
S.R.Patel	156.2	36	388	13	29.84	4-80	–	–
J.T.Ball	112.5	30	336	10	33.60	3-71	–	–
T.E.Barber	79	9	289	7	41.28	3-42	–	–
S.J.Mullaney	80	22	183	4	45.75	1-23	–	–

Also bowled: B.M.Duckett 1-0-2-0; L.W.James 16-2-55-1.

The First-Class Averages (pp 209–221) give the records of Nottinghamshire players in all first-class county matches, with the exception of B.T.Slater, whose first-class figures for Nottinghamshire are as above.

NOTTINGHAMSHIRE RECORDS

FIRST-CLASS CRICKET

Highest Total	For 791		v	Essex	Chelmsford	2007
	V 781-7d		by	Northants	Northampton	1995
Lowest Total	For 13		v	Yorkshire	Nottingham	1901
	V 16		by	Derbyshire	Nottingham	1879
	16		by	Surrey	The Oval	1880
Highest Innings	For 312*	W.W.Keeton	v	Middlesex	The Oval	1939
	V 345	C.G.Macartney	for	Australians	Nottingham	1921

Highest Partnership for each Wicket

1st	406*	D.J.Bicknell/G.E.Welton	v	Warwicks	Birmingham	2000
2nd	398	A.Shrewsbury/W.Gunn	v	Sussex	Nottingham	1890
3rd	367	W.Gunn/J.R.Gunn	v	Leics	Nottingham	1903
4th	361	A.O.Jones/J.R.Gunn	v	Essex	Leyton	1905
5th	359	D.J.Hussey/C.M.W.Read	v	Essex	Nottingham	2007
6th	372*	K.P.Pietersen/J.E.Morris	v	Derbyshire	Derby	2001
7th	301	C.C.Lewis/B.N.French	v	Durham	Chester-le-St[2]	1993
8th	220	G.F.H.Heane/R.Winrow	v	Somerset	Nottingham	1935
9th	170	J.C.Adams/K.P.Evans	v	Somerset	Taunton	1994
10th	152	E.B.Alletson/W.Riley	v	Sussex	Hove	1911
	152	U.Afzaal/A.J.Harris	v	Worcs	Nottingham	2000

Best Bowling	For	10-66	K.Smales	v	Glos	Stroud	1956
(Innings)	V	10-10	H.Verity	for	Yorkshire	Leeds	1932
Best Bowling	For	17-89	F.C.L.Matthews	v	Northants	Nottingham	1923
(Match)	V	17-89	W.G.Grace	for	Glos	Cheltenham	1877

Most Runs – Season	2620	W.W.Whysall	(av 53.46)	1929
Most Runs – Career	31592	G.Gunn	(av 35.69)	1902-32
Most 100s – Season	9	W.W.Whysall		1928
	9	M.J.Harris		1971
	9	B.C.Broad		1990
Most 100s – Career	65	J.Hardstaff jr		1930-55
Most Wkts – Season	181	B.Dooland	(av 14.96)	1954
Most Wkts – Career	1653	T.G.Wass	(av 20.34)	1896-1920
Most Career W-K Dismissals	983	C.M.W.Read	(939 ct; 44 st)	1998-2017
Most Career Catches in the Field	466	A.O.Jones		1892-1914

LIMITED-OVERS CRICKET

Highest Total	50ov	445-8		v	Northants	Nottingham	2016
	40ov	296-7		v	Somerset	Taunton	2002
	T20	227-3		v	Derbyshire	Nottingham	2017
Lowest Total	50ov	74		v	Leics	Leicester	1987
	40ov	57		v	Glos	Nottingham	2009
	T20	91		v	Lancashire	Manchester	2006
Highest Innings	50ov	187*	A.D.Hales	v	Surrey	Lord's	2017
	40ov	150*	A.D.Hales	v	Worcs	Nottingham	2009
	T20	113*	D.T.Christian	v	Northants	Northampton	2018
Best Bowling	50ov	6-10	K.P.Evans	v	Northumb	Jesmond	1994
	40ov	6-12	R.J.Hadlee	v	Lancashire	Nottingham	1980
	T20	5-22	G.G.White	v	Lancashire	Nottingham	2013

SOMERSET

Formation of Present Club: 18 August 1875
Inaugural First-Class Match: 1882
Colours: Black, White and Maroon
Badge: Somerset Dragon
County Champions: (0); best – 2nd (Div 1) 2001, 2010, 2012, 2016, 2018, 2019

SOMERSET CCC

Gillette/NatWest/C&G Trophy Winners: (3) 1979, 1983, 2001
Benson and Hedges Cup Winners: (2) 1981, 1982
Sunday League Winners: (1) 1979
Royal London One-Day Cup Winners: (1) 2019
Twenty20 Cup Winners: (1) 2005

Chief Executive: Gordon Hollins, Cooper Associates County Ground, Taunton TA1 1JT • Tel: 01823 425301 • Email: enquiries@somersetcountycc.co.uk • Web: www.somerset-countycc.co.uk • Twitter: @SomersetCCC (142,947 followers)

Director of Cricket: Andy Hurry. **Head Coach:** Jason Kerr. **Assistant Coaches:** Greg Kennis, Steve Kirby and Paul Tweddle. **Captains:** T.B.Abell (f-c) and L.Gregory (T20). **Overseas Player:** M.de Lange. **2021 Testimonial:** None. **Groundsman:** Scott Hawkins. **Scorer:** Polly Rhodes. ‡ New registration. ^{NQ} Not qualified for England.

ABELL, Thomas Benjamin (Taunton S; Exeter U), b Taunton 5 Mar 1994. 5'10". RHB, RM. Squad No 28. Debut (Somerset) 2014; captain 2017 to date; cap 2018. MCC 2019. F-c Tour (EL): A 2019-20. HS 135 v Lancs (Manchester) 2016. BB 4-39 v Warwks (Birmingham) 2019. Hat-trick v Notts (Nottingham) 2018. LO HS 106 v Sussex (Taunton) 2016 (RLC). LO BB 2-19 v Hants (Lord's) 2019 (RLC). T20 HS 101*. T20 BB 1-11.

ALDRIDGE, Kasey Luke (Millfield S), b Bristol 24 Dec 2000. RHB, RMF. Squad No 5. Somerset 2nd XI debut 2019. Devon 2019. England U19 2018-19. Awaiting 1st XI debut.

BANTON, Thomas (Bromsgrove S), b Chiltern, Bucks 11 Nov 1998. Son of C.Banton (Nottinghamshire 1995). 6'2". RHB, WK. Squad No 18. Debut (Somerset) 2018. Warwickshire 2nd XI 2015. Somerset 2nd XI debut 2016. England U19 2018. **LOI:** 6 (2019-20 to 2020); HS 58 v Ire (Southampton) 2020. **IT20:** 9 (2019-20 to 2020); HS 71 v P (Manchester) 2020. HS 79 v Hants (Taunton) 2019. LO HS 112 v Worcs (Worcester) 2019 (RLC). T20 HS 100.

BARTLETT, George Anthony (Millfield S), b Frimley, Surrey 14 Mar 1998. 6'0". RHB, OB. Squad No 14. Debut (Somerset) 2017. Somerset 2nd XI debut 2015. England U19 2016 to 2017. HS 137 v Surrey (Guildford) 2019. BB – . LO HS 57* v Surrey (Taunton) 2019 (RLC). T20 HS 24.

BROOKS, Jack Alexander (Wheatley Park S), b Oxford 4 Jun 1984. 6'2". RHB, RFM. Squad No 70. Northamptonshire 2009-12; cap 2012. Yorkshire 2013-18; cap 2013. Somerset debut 2019. Oxfordshire 2004-09. F-c Tour (EL): SA 2014-15. HS 109* Y v Lancs (Manchester) 2017. Sm HS 72 v Glamorgan (Taunton) 2020. 50 wkts (4); most – 71 (2014). BB 6-65 Y v Middx (Lord's) 2016. Sm BB 5-33 v Surrey (Guildford) 2019. LO HS 10 Nh v Middx (Uxbridge) 2009 (P40). LO BB 3-30 Y v Hants (Southampton) 2014 (RLC). T20 HS 33*. T20 BB 5-21.

BYROM, Edward James (St John's C, Harare), b Harare, Zimbabwe 17 Jun 1997. 5'11". LHB, OB. Squad No 97. Irish passport. Debut (Somerset) 2017. Rising Stars 2017-18. Somerset 2nd XI debut 2015. HS 152 RS v MT (Kwekwe) 2017-18. Sm HS 117 v Essex (Lord's) 2020. BB – . T20 HS 54*.

^{NQ}DAVEY, Joshua Henry (Culford S), b Aberdeen, Scotland 3 Aug 1990. 5'11". RHB, RMF. Squad No 38. Middlesex 2010-12. Scotland 2011-12 to 2016. Somerset debut 2015. Suffolk 2014. **LOI** (Scot): 31 (2010 to 2019-20); HS 64 v Afg (Sharjah) 2012-13; BB 6-28 v Afg (Abu Dhabi) 2014-15 – Scot record. **IT20** (Scot): 21 (2012 to 2019-20); HS 24 v Z (Nagpur) 2015-16; BB 4-34 v Netherlands (Abu Dhabi) 2016-17. HS 72 M v Oxford MCCU (Oxford) 2010 – on debut. CC HS 61 M v Glos (Bristol) 2010. Sm HS 47 v Middx (Lord's) 2017. BB 5-21 v Yorks (Taunton) 2019. LO HS 91 Scot v Warwks (Birmingham) 2011 (CB40). LO BB 6-28 (*see LOI*). T20 HS 24. T20 BB 4-34.

DAVIES, Steven Michael (King Charles I S, Kidderminster), b Bromsgrove, Worcs 17 Jun 1986. 5'10". LHB, WK. Squad No 11. Worcestershire 2005-09. Surrey 2010-16; cap 2011. Somerset debut/cap 2017. MCC 2006-07, 2011. **LOI**: 8 (2009-10 to 2010-11); HS 87 v P (Chester-le-St) 2010. **IT20**: 5 (2008-09 to 2010-11); HS 33 v P (Cardiff) 2010. F-c Tours: A 2010-11; B 2006-07 (Eng A); UAE 2011-12 (v P). 1000 runs (6); most – 1147 (2016). HS 200* Sy v Glamorgan (Cardiff) 2015. Sm HS 142 v Surrey (Taunton) 2017. LO HS 127* Sy v Hants (Oval) 2013 (Y40). T20 HS 99*.

‡^{NQ}De LANGE, Marchant, b Tzaneen, South Africa 13 Oct 1990. RHB, RF. Squad No 90. Easterns 2010-11 to 2015-16. Titans 2010-11 to 2015-16. Knights 2016-17 to 2017-18. Free State 2016-17. Glamorgan 2017-20; cap 2019. IPL: KKR 2012. MI 2014-15. **Tests** (SA): 2 (2011-12); HS 9 and BB 7-81 v SL (Durban) 2011-12 – on debut. **LOI** (SA): 4 (2011-12 to 2015-16); HS – ; BB 4-46 v NZ (Auckland) 2011-12. **IT20** (SA): 6 (2011-12 to 2015-16); HS – ; BB 2-26 v WI (Durban) 2014-15. F-c Tours (SA): A 2014 (SA A); NZ 2011-12. HS 113 Gm v Northants (Northampton) 2020. BB 7-23 Knights v Titans (Centurion) 2016-17. CC BB 5-62 Gm v Glos (Bristol) 2018. LO HS 58* Gm v Surrey (Cardiff) 2019 (RLC). LO BB 5-49 Gm v Hants (Southampton) 2017 (RLC). T20 HS 28*. T20 BB 4-23.

GOLDSWORTHY, Lewis Peter (Cambourne Science & Int Ac), b Truro, Cornwall 8 Jan 2001. RHB, SLA. Squad No 44. Somerset 2nd XI debut 2017. Cornwall 2017-19. England U19 2018-19. Awaiting f-c debut. T20 HS 38*. T20 BB 2-21.

GREEN, Benjamin George Frederick (Exeter S), b Exeter, Devon 28 Sep 1997. 6'2". RHB, RFM. Squad No 54. Debut (Somerset) 2018. Somerset 2nd XI debut 2014. Devon 2014-18. England U19 2014-15 to 2017. HS 54 v Glamorgan (Taunton) 2020. BB 1-8 v Hants (Southampton) 2018. LO HS 26* v Kent (Canterbury) 2018 (RLC). LO BB 1-52 v Hants (Southampton) 2018 (RLC). T20 HS 14. T20 BB 4-26.

GREGORY, Lewis (Hele's S, Plympton), b Plymouth, Devon 24 May 1992. 6'0". RHB, RMF. Squad No 24. Debut (Somerset) 2011; cap 2015; T20 captain 2018 to date. MCC 2017. Devon 2008. Big Bash: BH 2020-21. **IT20**: 8 (2019-20 to 2020); HS 15 and BB 1-10 v NZ (Wellington) 2019-20. HS 137 v Middx (Lord's) 2017. 50 wkts (1): 59 (2019). BB 6-32 (11-53 match) v Kent (Canterbury) 2019. LO HS 105* v Durham (Taunton) 2014 (RLC). LO BB 4-23 v Essex (Chelmsford) 2016 (RLC). T20 HS 76*. T20 BB 4-15.

HILDRETH, James Charles (Millfield S), b Milton Keynes, Bucks 9 Sep 1984. 5'10", RHB, RMF. Squad No 25. Debut (Somerset) 2003; cap 2007; testimonial 2017. MCC 2015. F-c Tour (EL): WI 2010-11. 1000 runs (7); most – 1620 (2015). HS 303* v Warwks (Taunton) 2009. BB 2-39 v Hants (Taunton) 2004. LO HS 159 v Glamorgan (Taunton) 2018 (RLC). LO BB 2-26 v Worcs (Worcester) 2008 (FPT). T20 HS 107*. T20 BB 3-24.

LAMMONBY, Thomas Alexander (Exeter S), b Exeter, Devon 2 Jun 2000. LHB, LM. Squad No 15. Debut (Somerset) 2020. Somerset 2nd XI debut 2015. Devon 2016-18. England U19 2018-19. HS 116 v Essex (Lord's) 2020. BB 1-4 v Glos (Taunton) 2020. T20 HS 43*. T20 BB 2-32.

146

LEACH, Matthew **Jack** (Bishop Fox's Community S, Taunton; Richard Huish C; UWIC), b Taunton 22 Jun 1991. 6'0''. LHB, SLA. Squad No 17. Cardiff MCCU 2012. Somerset debut 2012; cap 2017. MCC 2017. Dorset 2011. **ECB Incremental Contract 2020-21. Tests**: 16 (2017-18 to 2020-21); HS 92 v Ire (Lord's) 2019; BB 5-83 v SL (Pallekele) 2018-19. F-c Tours: WI 2017-18 (EL); NZ 2017-18, 2019-20; I 2020-21; SL 2016-17 (EL), 2018-19, 2019-20, 2020-21; UAE 2016-17 (v Afg)(EL). HS 92 (*see* Tests). Sm HS 66 v Lancs (Manchester) 2018. 50 wkts (2); most – 68 (2016). BB 8-85 (10-112 match) v Essex (Taunton) 2018. LO HS 18 v Surrey (Oval) 2014 (RLC). LO BB 3-7 EL v UAE (Dubai, DSC) 2016-17.

LEONARD, Edward Owen ('**Ned**') (Millfield S), b Hammersmith, Middx 15 Aug 2002. RHB, RMF. Squad No 19. Somerset 2nd XI debut 2018. Awaiting 1st XI debut.

OVERTON, Craig (West Buckland S), b Barnstaple, Devon 10 Apr 1994. Twin brother of Jamie Overton (*see* SURREY). 6'5''. RHB, RMF. Squad No 7. Debut (Somerset) 2012; cap 2016. MCC 2017. Devon 2010-11. **Tests**: 4 (2017-18 to 2019); HS 41* and BB 3-105 v A (Adelaide) 2017-18. F-c Tours: A 2017-18, 2019-20 (EL); NZ 2017-18. HS 138 v Hants (Taunton) 2016. BB 6-24 v Cardiff MCCU (Taunton) 2019. CC BB 6-74 v Warwks (Birmingham) 2015. LO HS 66* and LO BB 5-18 v Kent (Taunton) 2019 (RLC). T20 HS 35*. T20 BB 3-17.

SALE, Oliver Richard Trethowan (Sherborne S), b Newcastle-under-Lyme, Staffs 30 Sep 1995. 6'1''. RHB, RFM. Squad No 82. Awaiting f-c debut. T20 HS 14*. T20 BB 3-32.

SMEED, William Conrad Francis (King's C, Taunton), b Cambridge 26 Oct 2001. RHB, OB. Squad No 23. Somerset 2nd XI debut 2017. Awaiting f-c debut. T20 HS 82.

NQVAN DER MERWE, Roelof Erasmus (Pretoria HS), b Johannesburg, South Africa 31 Dec 1984. RHB, SLA. Squad No 52. Northerns 2006-07 to 2013-14. Titans 2007-08 to 2014-15. Netherlands 2015 to 2017-18. Somerset debut 2016; cap 2018. IPL: RCB 2009 to 2009-10. DD 2011-13. Big Bash: BH 2011-12. **LOI** (SA/Neth): 15 (13 for SA 2008-09 to 2010; 2 for Neth 2019); HS 57 v Z (Deventer) 2019; BB 3-27 v Z (Centurion) 2009-10. **IT20** (SA/Neth): 43 (13 for SA 2008-09 to 2010; 30 for Neth 2015 to 2019-20); HS 75* v Z (Rotterdam) 2019; BB 4-35 v Z (Rotterdam) 2019 – separate matches. HS 205* Titans v Warriors (Benoni) 2014-15. Sm HS 102* v Hants (Taunton) 2016. BB 4-22 v Middx (Taunton) 2017. LO HS 165* v Surrey (Taunton) 2017 (RLC). LO BB 5-26 Titans v Knights (Centurion) 2012-13. T20 HS 89*. T20 BB 5-32.

WALLER, Maximilian Thomas Charles (Millfield S; Bournemouth U), b Salisbury, Wiltshire 3 March 1988. 6'0''. RHB, LB. Squad No 10. Debut (Somerset) 2009. Dorset 2007-08. HS 28 v Hants (Southampton) 2009. BB 3-33 v Cardiff MCCU (Taunton Vale) 2012. CC BB 2-27 v Sussex (Hove) 2009. LO HS 25* v Glamorgan (Taunton) 2013 (Y40). LO BB 3-37 v Glos (Bristol) 2017 (RLC). T20 HS 17. T20 BB 4-16.

YOUNG, Samuel Jack (Millfield S), b Plymouth, Devon 30 Jul 2000. RHB, OB. Squad No 77. Somerset 2nd XI debut 2018. Awaiting 1st XI debut.

(Having made a County 1st XI appearance in 2020)

^{NO}**BABAR AZAM**, Mohammad, b Lahore, Pakistan 15 Oct 1994. RHB, OB. ZT Bank 2010-11 to 2013-14. Islamabad 2012-13. State Bank of Pak 2014-15. SSGC 2015-16 to 2017-18. Somerset 2019. Central Punjab 2019-20. **Tests** (P): 31 (2016-17 to 2020-21); HS 143 v B (Rawalpindi) 2019-20. **LOI** (P): 77 (2015 to 2020-21); HS 125* v WI (Providence) 2017. **IT20** (P): 47 (2016 to 2020-21); HS 97* v WI (Karachi) 2017-18. F-c Tours (P): E 2016 (P A), 2018, 2020; A 2016-17, 2019-20; SA 2018-19; WI 2016-17; NZ 2016-17; Ire 2018. HS 266 State Bank v HB (Faisalabad) 2014-15. Sm HS 40 Warwks (Birmingham) 2019. BB 1-13 ZT v UB (Islamabad) 2012-13. LO HS 142* State Bank v Karachi Dolphins (Karachi) 2014-15. LO BB 2-20 P A v Glamorgan (Newport) 2016. T20 HS 114*. T20 BB 2-20.

BESS, D.M. – *see YORKSHIRE.*

OVERTON, J. – *see SURREY.*

N.N.Gilchrist left the staff without making a County 1st XI appearance in 2020.

SOMERSET 2020

RESULTS SUMMARY

	Place	Won	Lost	Drew	NR
Bob Willis Trophy (Central Group)	Finalist 4			2	
Vitality Blast (Central Group)	4th	4	5		1

BOB WILLIS TROPHY AVERAGES
BATTING AND FIELDING

Cap		M	I	NO	HS	Runs	Avge	100	50	Ct/St
	T.A.Lammonby	6	11	2	116	459	51.00	3	–	4
2017	S.M.Davies	6	10	2	123*	320	40.00	1	1	19
2018	T.B.Abell	6	11	1	119	386	38.60	2	1	5
2019	J.Overton	4	6	–	120	206	34.33	1	1	7
	G.A.Bartlett	4	6	1	100*	160	32.00	1	–	2
2016	C.Overton	6	10	–	66	248	31.00	–	2	7
	J.A.Brooks	5	7	2	72	139	27.80	–	1	1
	B.G.F.Green	3	5	–	54	127	25.40	–	1	–
	E.J.Byrom	6	11	–	117	271	24.63	1	–	3
2007	J.C.Hildreth	4	6	–	45	124	20.66	–	–	10
	J.H.Davey	6	9	3	28	113	18.83	–	–	1
2015	L.Gregory	3	5	–	37	78	15.60	–	–	1
2018	R.E.van der Merwe	4	6	1	30	57	11.40	–	–	4
	T.Banton	2	3	–	18	33	11.00	–	–	–
2017	M.J.Leach	2	3	–	21	29	9.66	–	–	1

BOWLING

	O	M	R	W	Avge	Best	5wI	10wM
J.Overton	68.1	24	186	15	12.40	5-48	1	–
C.Overton	196.2	66	403	30	13.43	5-26	2	–
J.H.Davey	150.2	55	331	24	13.79	4-25	–	–
T.B.Abell	16.2	5	50	3	16.66	3- 4	–	–
L.Gregory	102.3	22	318	18	17.66	6-72	1	–
J.A.Brooks	89.5	23	254	13	19.53	4-40	–	–
M.J.Leach	52	17	112	3	37.33	3-38	–	–

Also bowled: E.J.Byrom 1-0-4-0; T.A.Lammonby 12-3-38-2; R.E.van der Merwe 6-2-8-1.

The First-Class Averages (pp 209–221) give the records of Somerset players in all first-class county matches, with the exception of J.Overton, whose first-class figures for Somerset are as above.

SOMERSET RECORDS

FIRST-CLASS CRICKET

Highest Total	For	850-7d		v	Middlesex	Taunton	2007
	V	811		by	Surrey	The Oval	1899
Lowest Total	For	25		v	Glos	Bristol	1947
	V	22		by	Glos	Bristol	1920
Highest Innings	For	342	J.L.Langer	v	Surrey	Guildford	2006
	V	424	A.C.MacLaren	for	Lancashire	Taunton	1895

Highest Partnership for each Wicket

1st	346	L.C.H.Palairet/ H.T.Hewett	v	Yorkshire	Taunton	1892
2nd	450	N.R.D.Compton/J.C.Hildreth	v	Cardiff MCCU	Taunton Vale	2012
3rd	319	P.M.Roebuck/M.D.Crowe	v	Leics	Taunton	1984
4th	310	P.W.Denning/I.T.Botham	v	Glos	Taunton	1980
5th	320	J.D.Francis/I.D.Blackwell	v	Durham UCCE	Taunton	2005
6th	265	W.E.Alley/K.E.Palmer	v	Northants	Northampton	1961
7th	279	R.J.Harden/G.D.Rose	v	Sussex	Taunton	1997
8th	236	P.D.Trego/R.C.Davies	v	Lancashire	Manchester	2016
9th	183	C.H.M.Greetham/H.W.Stephenson	v	Leics	Weston-s-Mare	1963
	183	C.J.Tavaré/N.A.Mallender	v	Sussex	Hove	1990
10th	163	I.D.Blackwell/N.A.M.McLean	v	Derbyshire	Taunton	2003

Best Bowling	For	10-49	E.J.Tyler	v	Surrey	Taunton	1895
(Innings)	V	10-35	A.Drake	for	Yorkshire	Weston-s-Mare	1914
Best Bowling	For	16-83	J.C.White	v	Worcs	Bath	1919
(Match)	V	17-86	K.J.Abbott	for	Hampshire	Southampton[2]	2019

Most Runs – Season	2761	W.E.Alley	(av 58.74)	1961
Most Runs – Career	21142	H.Gimblett	(av 36.96)	1935-54
Most 100s – Season	11	S.J.Cook		1991
Most 100s – Career	52	M.E.Trescothick		1993-2018
Most Wkts – Season	169	A.W.Wellard	(av 19.24)	1938
Most Wkts – Career	2165	J.C.White	(av 18.03)	1909-37
Most Career W-K Dismissals	1007	H.W.Stephenson	(698 ct; 309 st)	1948-64
Most Career Catches in the Field	443	M.E.Trescothick		1993-2019

LIMITED-OVERS CRICKET

Highest Total	50ov	413-4		v	Devon	Torquay	1990
	40ov	377-9		v	Sussex	Hove	2003
	T20	250-3		v	Glos	Taunton	2006
Lowest Total	50ov	58		v	Middlesex	Southgate	2000
	40ov	58		v	Essex	Chelmsford	1977
	T20	82		v	Kent	Taunton	2010
Highest Innings	50ov	177	S.J.Cook	v	Sussex	Hove	1990
	40ov	184	M.E.Trescothick	v	Glos	Taunton	2008
	T20	151*	C.H.Gayle	v	Kent	Taunton	2015
Best Bowling	50ov	8-66	S.R.G.Francis	v	Derbyshire	Derby	2004
	40ov	6-16	Abdur Rehman	v	Notts	Taunton	2012
	T20	6- 5	A.V.Suppiah	v	Glamorgan	Cardiff	2011

SURREY

Formation of Present Club: 22 August 1845
Inaugural First-Class Match: 1864
Colours: Chocolate
Badge: Prince of Wales' Feathers
County Champions (since 1890): (19) 1890, 1891, 1892, 1894, 1895, 1899, 1914, 1952, 1953, 1954, 1955, 1956, 1957, 1958, 1971, 1999, 2000, 2002, 2018
Joint Champions: (1) 1950
NatWest Trophy Winners: (1) 1982
Benson and Hedges Cup Winners: (3) 1974, 1997, 2001
Pro 40/National League (Div 1) Winners: (1) 2003
Sunday League Winners: (1) 1996
Clydesdale Bank 40 Winners: (1) 2011
Twenty20 Cup Winners: (1) 2003

Chief Executive: Richard Gould, The Kia Oval, London, SE11 5SS • Tel: 0203 946 0100 • Email: enquiries@surreycricket.com • Web: www.kiaoval.com • Twitter: @surreycricket (98,536 followers)

Director of Cricket: Alec Stewart. **Head Coach**: Vikram Solanki. **Assistant Coach**: Richard Johnson. **Captain**: R.J.Burns. **Overseas Players**: H.M.Amla and K.A.J.Roach. **2021 Testimonial**: R.Clarke. **Head Groundsman**: Lee Fortiss. **Scorer**: Debbie Beesley. ‡ New registration. ^NQ Not qualified for England.

^NQ**AMLA, Hashim** Mahomed, b Durban, South Africa 31 Mar 1983. Younger brother of A.M.Amla (Natal B, KZN, Dolphins 1997-98 to 2012-13). 6'0''. RHB, RM/OB. Squad No 1. KZN 1999-00 to 2003-04. Dolphins 2004-05 to 2011-12. Essex 2009. Nottinghamshire 2010; cap 2010. Surrey debut 2013. Derbyshire 2015. Cape Cobras 2015-16 to 2018-19. Hampshire 2018. IPL: KXIP 2016-17. *Wisden* 2012. **Tests** (SA): 124 (2004-05 to 2018-19, 14 as captain); 1000 runs (3); most – 1249 (2010); HS 311* v E (Oval) 2012; BB – . **LOI** (SA): 181 (2007-08 to 2019, 9 as captain); 1000 runs (2); most – 1062 (2015); HS 159 v Ire (Canberra) 2014-15. **IT20** (SA): 44 (2008-09 to 2018, 2 as captain); HS 97* v A (Cape Town) 2015-16. F-c Tours (SA) (C=Captain): E 2008, 2012, 2017; A 2008-09, 2012-13, 2016-17; WI 2010; NZ 2011-12, 2016-17; I 2004-05, 2007-08 (SA A), 2007-08, 2009-10, 2015-16C; P 2007-08; SL 2005-06 (SA A), 2006, 2014C; Z 2004 (SA A), 2007 (SA A), 2014C; A/B 2007-08, 2015C; UAE 2010-11, 2013-14 (v P). 1000 runs (0+2); most – 1126 (2005-06). HS 311* (*see Tests*). CC HS 181 Ex v Glamorgan (Chelmsford) 2009 – on debut. Sy HS 151 v Yorks (Oval) 2013. BB 1-10 SA A v India A (Kimberley) 2001-02. LO HS 159 (*see LOI*). T20 HS 104*.

ATKINSON, Angus ('Gus') Alexander Patrick (Bradfield C), b Chelsea, Middx 19 Jan 1998. 6'2''. RHB, RM. Squad No 37. Debut (Surrey) 2020. Surrey 2nd XI debut 2016. HS 15 and BB 2-57 v Essex (Chelmsford) 2020. T20 HS 14. T20 BB 2-18.

BATTY, Gareth Jon (Bingley GS), b Bradford, Yorks 13 Oct 1977. Younger brother of J.D.Batty (Yorkshire and Somerset 1989-96). 5'11''. RHB, OB. Squad No 13. Yorkshire 1997. Surrey debut 1999; cap 2011; captain 2015-17; testimonial 2017. Worcestershire 2002-09. MCC 2012. **Tests**: 9 (2003-04 to 2016-17); HS 38 v SL (Kandy) 2003-04; BB 3-55 v SL (Galle) 2003-04. Took wicket with his third ball in Test cricket. **LOI**: 10 (2002-03 to 2008-09); HS 17 v WI (Bridgetown) 2008-09; BB 2-40 v WI (Gros Islet) 2003-04. **IT20**: 1 (2008-09); HS 4 v WI (Port of Spain) 2008-09. F-c Tours: WI 2003-04, 2005-06; NZ 2008-09 (Eng A); I 2016-17; SL 2002-03 (ECB Acad), 2003-04; B 2003-04, 2016-17. SA v WI 133 Wo v Surrey (Oval) 2004. Sy HS 110* v Hants (Southampton) 2016, sharing Sy record 8th wkt partnership of 222* with B.T.Foakes. 50 wkts (2); most – 60 (2003). BB 8-64 (10-111 match) v Warwks (Birmingham) 2019. Hat-tricks (2): v Derbys (Oval) 2015 and v Warwks (Birmingham) 2019. LO HS 83* v Yorks (Oval) 2001 (NL). LO BB 5-35 Wo v Hants (Southampton) 2009 (FPT). T20 HS 87. T20 BB 4-13.

BURNS, Rory Joseph (City of London Freemens S), b Epsom 26 Aug 1990. 5'10". LHB, WK, occ RM. Squad No 17. Debut (Surrey) 2011; cap 2014; captain 2018 to date. MCC 2016. MCC Univs 2010. *Wisden* 2018. **ECB Test Central Contract 2020-21. Tests**: 23 (2018-19 to 2020-21); HS 133 v A (Birmingham) 2019. 1000 runs (6); most – 1402 (2018). HS 219* v Hants (Oval) 2017. BB 1-18 v Middx (Lord's) 2013. LO HS 95 v Glos (Bristol) 2015 (RLC). T20 HS 56*.

CLARK, Jordan (Sedbergh S), b Whitehaven, Cumbria 14 Oct 1990. Elder brother of G.Clark (see *DURHAM*). 6'4". RHB, RMF, occ WK. Squad No 8. Lancashire 2015-18. Surrey debut 2019. Big Bash: HH 2018-19. HS 140 La v Surrey (Oval) 2017. Sy HS 54 v Notts (Nottingham) 2019. BB 5-58 La v Yorks (Manchester) 2018. Sy BB 5-77 v Yorks (Scarborough) 2019. Hat-trick La v Yorks (Manchester) 2018, dismissing J.E.Root, K.S.Williamson and J.M.Bairstow. LO HS 79* and LO BB 4-34 La v Worcs (Manchester) 2017 (RLC). T20 HS 60. T20 BB 4-22.

CLARKE, Rikki (Broadwater SS; Godalming C), b Orsett, Essex 29 Sep 1981. 6'4". RHB, RMF. Squad No 81. Debut (Surrey) 2002, scoring 107* v Cambridge U (Cambridge); cap 2005; testimonial 2021. Derbyshire cap/captain 2008. Warwickshire 2008-17; cap 2011. MCC 2006, 2016. YC 2002. **Tests**: 2 (2003-04); HS 55 and BB 2-7 v B (Chittagong) 2003-04. **LOI**: 20 (2003 to 2006); HS 39 v P (Lord's) 2006; BB 2-28 v B (Dhaka) 2003-04. F-c Tours: WI 2003-04, 2005-06; SL 2002-03 (ECB Acad), 2004-05; B 2003-04. 1000 runs (1): 1027 (2006). HS 214 v Somerset (Guildford) 2006. BB 7-55 v Somerset (Oval) 2017. Took seven catches in an innings Wa v Lancs (Liverpool) 2011 to equal world record. LO HS 98* v Derbys (Derby) 2002 (NL). LO BB 5-26 Wa v Worcs (Birmingham) 2016 (RLC). T20 HS 79*. T20 BB 4-16.

CURRAN, Samuel Matthew (Wellington C), b Northampton 3 Jun 1998. Son of K.M.Curran (Glos, Natal, Northants, Boland and Zimbabwe 1980-81 to 1999), grandson of K.P.Curran (Rhodesia 1947-48 to 1954-55), younger brother of T.K.Curran (see *below*) and B.J.Curran (see *NORTHAMPTONSHIRE*). 5'9". LHB, LMF. Squad No 58. Debut (Surrey) 2015, taking 5-101 v Kent (Oval); cap 2018. Surrey 2nd XI debut 2013. YC 2018. *Wisden* 2018. **ECB Test Central Contract 2020-21. Tests**: 21 (2018 to 2020-21); HS 78 v I (Southampton) 2018; BB 4-58 v SA (Centurion) 2019-20. **LOI**: 5 (2018 to 2020); HS 15 v A (Manchester) 2018; BB 3-35 v A (Manchester) 2020. **IT20**: 8 (2019-20 to 2020-21); HS 24 v NZ (Auckland) 2019-20; BB 3-28 v SA (Cape Town) 2020-21. F-c Tours: SA 2019-20; WI 2018-19; NZ 2019-20; BB 4-36 v WI (Gros Islet) 2018-19, 2019-20, 2020-21; UAE 2016-17 (v Afg)(EL). HS 96 v Lancs (Oval) 2016. BB 7-58 v Durham (Chester-le-St) 2016. LO HS 57 v Glos (Oval) 2016 (RLC). LO BB 4-32 v Northants (Oval) 2015 (RLC). T20 HS 55*. T20 BB 4-11.

CURRAN, Thomas Kevin (Hilton C, Durban), b Cape Town, South Africa 12 Mar 1995. Son of K.M.Curran (Glos, Natal, Northants, Boland and Zimbabwe 1980-81 to 1999), grandson of K.P.Curran (Rhodesia 1947-48 to 1954-55), elder brother of S.M.Curran (see *above*) and B.J.Curran (see *NORTHAMPTONSHIRE*). 6'0". RHB, RFM. Squad No 59. Debut (Surrey) 2014; cap 2016. IPL: KKR 2018. RR 2020-21. Big Bash: SS 2018-19 to 2019-20. **ECB L-O Central Contract 2020-21. Tests**: 2 (2017-18); HS 39 v A (Sydney) 2017-18; BB 1-65 v A (Melbourne) 2017-18. **LOI**: 24 (2017 to 2020); HS 47* v Ire (Dublin) 2019; BB 5-35 v A (Perth) 2017-18. **IT20**: 27 (2017 to 2020-21); HS 14* v NZ (Nelson) 2019-20; BB 4-36 v WI (Gros Islet) 2018-19. F-c Tours: A 2017-18; SL 2016-17 (EL); UAE 2016-17 (v Afg)(EL). HS 60 v Leics (Leicester) 2015. 50 wkts (1): 76 (2015). BB 7-20 v Glos (Oval) 2015. LO HS 47* (see *LOI*). LO BB 5-16 EL v UAE (Dubai, DSC) 2016-17. T20 HS 62. T20 BB 4-22.

DERNBACH, Jade Winston (St John the Baptist S, Woking), b Johannesburg, South Africa 3 Mar 1986. 6'1½". RHB, RFM. Squad No 16. Italian passport. UK resident since 1998. Debut (Surrey) 2003; cap 2011; captain 2018-19 (T20 only); testimonial 2019. Big Bash: MS 2011-12. No 1st XI appearances in 2020 due to injury. **LOI**: 24 (2011 to 2013); HS 5 v SL (Leeds) 2011; BB 4-45 v P (Dubai) 2011-12. **IT20**: 34 (2011 to 2013-14); HS 12 v I (Colombo, RPS) 2012-13; BB 4-22 v I (Manchester) 2011. F-c Tour (EL): WI 2010-11. HS 56* v Northants (Northampton) 2010. 50 wkts (1): 51 (2010). BB 6-47 v Leics (Leicester) 2009. LO HS 31 v Somerset (Taunton) 2010 (CB40). LO BB 6-35 v Glos (Lord's) 2015 (RLC). T20 HS 24*. T20 BB 4-22.

DUNN, Matthew Peter (Bearwood C, Wokingham), b Egham 5 May 1992. 6'1". LHB, RFM. Squad No 4. Debut (Surrey) 2010. MCC 2015. HS 31* v Kent (Guildford) 2014. BB 5-43 v Somerset (Guildford) 2019. LO HS – . LO BB 2-32 Eng Dev XI v Sri Lanka A (Manchester) 2011. T20 HS 2. BB 3-8.

EVANS, Laurie John (Whitgift S; The John Fisher S; St Mary's C, Durham U), b Lambeth, London 12 Oct 1987. 6'0". RHB, RM. Squad No 10. Durham UCCE 2007. MCC 2007. Surrey debut 2009. Warwickshire 2010-16. Northamptonshire 2016 (on loan). Sussex 2017-19. HS 213* and BB 1-29 Wa v Sussex (Birmingham) 2015, sharing Wa 6th wkt record partnership of 327 with T.R.Ambrose. Sy HS 98 and Sy BB 1-30 v Bangladeshis (Oval) 2010. LO HS 134* Sx v Kent (Canterbury) 2017 (RLC). LO BB 1-29 Sx v Middx (Lord's) 2019 (RLC). T20 HS 108*. T20 BB 1-5.

FOAKES, Benjamin Thomas (Tendring TC), b Colchester, Essex 15 Feb 1993. 6'1". RHB, WK. Squad No 7. Essex 2011-14. Surrey debut 2015; cap 2016. MCC 2016. **Tests**: 8 (2018-19 to 2020-21); HS 107 v SL (Galle) 2018-19 – on debut. F-c Tours: WI 2017-18 (EL), 2018-19; I 2020-21; SL 2013-14 (EL), 2016-17 (EL), 2018-19; UAE 2016-17 (v Afg)(EL). HS 141* v Hants (Southampton) 2016, sharing Sy record 8th wkt partnership of 222* with G.J.Batty. LO HS 92 v Somerset (Taunton) 2016 (RLC). T20 HS 75*.

JACKS, William George (St George's C, Weybridge), b Chertsey 21 Nov 1998. 6'1". RHB, OB. Squad No 9. Debut (Surrey) 2018. Big Bash: HH 2020-21. Surrey 2nd XI debut 2016. England U19 2016-17 to 2017. F-c Tour (EL): I 2018-19. HS 120 v Kent (Beckenham) 2019. BB – . LO HS 121 v Glos (Oval) 2018 (RLC). LO BB 2-32 v Middx (Oval) 2019 (RLC). T20 HS 65. T20 BB 4-15.

KIMBER, Nicholas John Henry (William Farr C of E S), b Lincoln 16 Jan 2001. Younger brother of L.P.J.Kimber (Loughborough MCCU 2019) and J.F.Kimber (Lincolnshire 2016-18). 5'11". RHB, RMF. Squad No 12. Nottinghamshire 2nd XI 2019. Awaiting 1st XI debut.

McKERR, Conor (St John's C, Johannesburg), b Johannesburg, South Africa 19 Jan 1998. 6'6". RHB, RFM. Squad No 3. UK passport, qualified for England in March 2020. Derbyshire 2017 (on loan), taking wkt of J.D.Libby with 4th ball in f-c cricket. Surrey debut 2017. Surrey 2nd XI debut 2016. No 1st XI appearances in 2020. HS 29 v Yorks (Oval) 2018. BB 5-54 (10-141 match) De v Northants (Northampton) 2017. Sy BB 4-26 v Notts (Oval) 2018. LO HS 26* v Glamorgan (Cardiff) 2019 (RLC). LO BB 3-56 v Somerset (Taunton) 2019 (RLC).

MORIARTY, Daniel Thornhill (Rondesbosch Boys' HS), b Reigate 2 Dec 1999. 6'0". LHB, SLA. Squad No 21. Debut (Surrey) 2020, taking 5-64 v Middx (Oval). Surrey 2nd XI debut 2019. Essex 2nd XI 2019. MCC YC 2019. South Africa U19 2016. HS 1 and BB 6-70 (11-224 match) v Sussex (Oval) 2020. T20 HS – . T20 BB 3-25.

153

OVERTON, Jamie (West Buckland S), b Barnstaple, Devon 10 Apr 1994. Twin brother of Craig Overton (*see* SOMERSET). 6'5''. RHB, RFM. Squad No 88. Somerset 2012-20; cap 2019. Northamptonshire 2019 (on loan). Surrey debut 2020. Devon 2011. F-c Tour (EL): UAE 2018-19 (v PA). HS 120 Sm v Warwks (Birmingham) 2020. Sy HS 55 v Sussex (Oval) 2020. BB 6-95 v Middx (Taunton) 2013. Sy BB – . Hat-trick Sm v Notts (Nottingham) 2018. LO HS 40* Sm v Glos (Taunton) 2016 (RLC). LO BB 4-42 Sm v Durham (Chester-le-St) 2012 (CB40). T20 HS 40*. T20 BB 5-47.

PATEL, Ryan Samir (Whitgift S), b Sutton 26 Oct 1997. 5'10''. LHB, RMF. Squad No 26. Debut (Surrey) 2017. Surrey 2nd XI debut 2014. England U19 2017. HS 100* v Essex (Oval) 2019. BB 6-5 v Somerset (Guildford) 2018. LO HS 41* v Somerset (Taunton) 2019 (RLC). LO BB 2-65 v Hants (Oval) 2019 (RLC). T20 HS 5*. T20 BB – .

PLUNKETT, Liam Edward (Nunthorpe SS; Teesside Tertiary C), b Middlesbrough, Yorks 6 Apr 1985. 6'3''. RHB, RFM. Squad No 28. Durham 2003-12. Dolphins 2007-08. Yorkshire 2013-17; cap 2013. Surrey debut 2019. MCC 2017. IPL: DD 2018. Big Bash: MS 2018-19. **Tests**: 13 (2005-06 to 2014); HS 55* v I (Lord's) 2014; BB 5-64 v SL (Leeds) 2014. **LOI**: 89 (2005-06 to 2019); HS 56 v P (Lahore) 2005-06; BB 5-52 v WI (Bristol) 2017. **IT20**: 22 (2006 to 2018-19); HS 18 v WI (Chester-le-St) 2011; BB 3-21 v P (Dubai, DSC) 2015-16. F-c Tours (EL): SA 2014-15; WI 2010-11; NZ 2008-09; I 2005-06 (E), 2007-08; P 2005-06 (E); SL 2013-14. HS 126 Y v Hants (Leeds) 2016. Sy HS 2 v Essex (Chelmsford) 2019. 50 wkts (3); most – 60 (2009). BB 6-33 Y v Leeds/Bradford MCCU (Leeds) 2013 on Y debut. CC BB 6-63 (11-119 match) Du v Worcs (Chester-le-St) 2009. Sy BB 1-85 v Essex (Oval) 2019. LO HS 72 Du v Somerset (Chester-le-St) 2008 (P40). LO BB 5-52 (*see LOI*). T20 HS 41. T20 BB 5-31.

POPE, Oliver John Douglas (Cranleigh S), b Chelsea, Middx 2 Jan 1998. 5'9''. RHB, WK. Squad No 32. Debut (Surrey) 2017; cap 2018. Surrey 2nd XI debut 2015. England U19 2016 to 2016-17. **ECB Test Central Contract 2020-21. Tests**: 17 (2018 to 2020-21); HS 135* v SA (Port Elizabeth) 2019-20. F-c Tours: SA 2019-20; NZ 2019-20; I 2018-19 (EL), 2020-21; SL 2019-20. 1000 runs (1): 1098 (2018). HS 251 v MCC (Dubai, ICCA) 2018-19. CC HS 221* v Hants (Oval) 2019. LO HS 93* EL v Pakistan A (Abu Dhabi) 2018-19. T20 HS 48.

REIFER, Nico (Queen's C, Bridgetown; Whitgift S), b Bridgetown, Barbados 11 Nov 2000. 5'11''. RHB, RM. Squad No 27. Surrey 2nd XI debut 2018. Awaiting 1st XI debut.

ROACH, Kemar Andre Jamal, b St Lucy, Barbados 30 Jun 1988. RHB, RFM. Squad No 66. Barbados 2007-08 to date. Worcestershire 2011. IPL: DC 2009-10. Big Bash: BH 2012-13 to 2013-14. **Tests** (WI): 61 (2009 to 2020-21); HS 41 v NZ (Kingston) 2012; BB 6-48 v B (St George's) 2009. **LOI** (WI): 92 (2008 to 2019); HS 34 v I (Port of Spain) 2013; BB 6-27 v Netherlands (Delhi) 2010-11. **IT20** (WI): 11 (2008 to 2012-13); HS 3* and BB 2-25 v SA (North Sound) 2010. F-c Tours (WI): E 2012, 2017, 2020; A 2009-10, 2015-16; SA 2014-15; NZ 2008-09, 2017-18, 2020-21; I 2011-12, 2019-20 (v Afg); SL 2010-11, 2015-16; Z 2017-18; B 2011-12, 2018-19, 2020-21. HS 53 Barbados v Leeward Is (Basseterre) 2015-16. CC HS 6 and CC BB 3-44 Wo v Lancs (Worcester) 2011. BB 7-23 Barbados v CC&C (Charlestown) 2009-10. LO HS (*see LOI*). LO BB (*see LOI*). T20 HS 12. T20 BB 3-18.

ROY, Jason Jonathan (Whitgift S), b Durban, South Africa 21 Jul 1990. 6'0''. RHB, RM. Squad No 20. Debut (Surrey) 2010; cap 2014. IPL: GL 2017. DD 2018. Big Bash: ST 2014-15. SS 2016-17 to 2017-18. PS 2020-21. **ECB L-O Central Contract 2020-21. Tests**: 5 (2019); HS 72 v Ire (Lord's) 2019. **LOI**: 93 (2015 to 2020); HS 180 v A (Melbourne) 2017-18 – E record. **IT20**: 38 (2014 to 2020-21); HS 78 v NZ (Delhi) 2015-16. 1000 runs (1): 1078 (2014). HS 143 v Lancs (Oval) 2015. BB 3-9 v Glos (Bristol) 2014. LO HS 180 (*see LOI*). LO BB – . T20 HS 122*. T20 BB 1-23.

154

SMITH, Jamie Luke (Whitgift S), b Epsom 12 Jul 2000. 5'10". RHB, WK. Squad No 11. Debut (Surrey) 2019, scoring 127 v MCC (Dubai, ICCA). Surrey 2nd XI debut. England U19 2018-19. HS 127 (*see above*). CC HS 80 v Middx (Oval) 2020. LO HS 40 v Somerset (Taunton) 2019 (RLC). T20 HS 38*.

STONEMAN, Mark Daniel (Whickham CS), b Newcastle upon Tyne, Northumb 26 Jun 1987. 5'10". LHB, OB. Squad No 23. Durham 2007-16; captain (l-o only) 2015-16. Surrey debut 2017; cap 2018. **Tests:** 11 (2017 to 2018); HS 60 v NZ (Christchurch) 2017-18. F-c Tour: A 2017-18; NZ 2017-18. 1000 runs (5); most – 1481 (2017). HS 197 v Essex (Guildford) 2017. BB – . LO HS 144* v Notts (Lord's) 2017 (RLC). LO BB 1-8 Du v Derbys (Derby) 2016 (RLC). T20 HS 89*.

TAYLOR, James Philip Arthur (Trentham HS), b Stoke-on-Trent, Staffs 19 Jan 2001. Younger brother of T.A.I.Taylor (*see NORTHAMPTONSHIRE*). 6'3". RHB, RM. Squad No 25. Derbyshire 2017-19. Surrey debut 2020. Derbyshire 2nd XI 2016-19. HS 22 and Sy BB 2-31 v Essex (Chelmsford) 2020. BB 3-26 De v Leeds/Brad MCCU (Derby) 2019. LO HS 6* and LO BB 2-66 De v Australia A (Derby) 2019. T20 HS 3. T20 BB 1-6.

TOPLEY, Reece James William (Royal Hospital S, Ipswich), b Ipswich, Suffolk 21 February 1994. Son of T.D.Topley (Surrey, Essex, GW 1985-94) and nephew of P.A.Topley (Kent 1972-75). 6'7". RHB, LFM. Squad No 24. Essex 2011-15; cap 2013. Hampshire 2016-17. Sussex 2019. Surrey debut 2020 (T20 only). **LOI:** 11 (2015 to 2020); HS 6 v A (Manchester) 2015; BB 4-50 v SA (Port Elizabeth) 2015-16. **IT20:** 6 (2015 to 2015-16); HS 1* v SA (Johannesburg) 2015-16; BB 3-24 v P (Dubai, DSC) 2015-16. F-c Tour (EL): SL 2013-14. HS 16 H v Yorks (Southampton) 2017. BB 6-29 (11-85 match) Ex v Worcs (Chelmsford) 2013. LO HS 19 Ex v Somerset (Taunton) 2011 (CB40). LO BB 4-16 EL v West Indies A (Northampton) 2018. T20 HS 5*. T20 BB 4-20.

VIRDI, Guramar Singh ('**Amar**') (Guru Nanak Sikh Ac, Hayes), b Chiswick, Middx 19 Jul 1998. 5'10". RHB, OB. Squad No 19. Debut (Surrey) 2017. Surrey 2nd XI debut 2016. England U19 2016 to 2017. HS 21* v Somerset (Taunton) 2018. BB 8-61 (14-139 match) v Notts (Nottingham) 2019.

RELEASED/RETIRED

(Having made a County 1st XI appearance in 2020)

BORTHWICK, S.G. – *see DURHAM.*

[NQ]**MORKEL, Morne** (Hoerskool, Vereeniging), b Vereeniging, South Africa 6 Oct 1984. Younger brother of J.A.Morkel (Easterns, Titans, Durham and South Africa 1999-00 to 2015-16). 6'4". LHB, RF. Easterns 2003-04 to 2017-18. Titans 2004-05 to 2017-18. Yorkshire 2008 (1 match). Surrey 2018-20; cap 2018. IPL: RR 2009 to 2009-10. DD 2011-13. KKR 2014-16. Big Bash: PS 2019-20. BH 2020-21. Kent 2007 (T20 only). **Tests** (SA): 86 (2006-07 to 2017-18); HS 40 v A (Sydney) 2008-09 and 40 v NZ (Wellington) 2016-17; BB 6-23 v NZ (Wellington) 2011-12. **LOI** (SA): 114 (+ 3 Africa XI 2007) (2007 to 2017-18); HS 32* v WI (Bridgetown) 2016; BB 5-21 v A (Perth) 2014-15. **IT20** (SA): 41 (+ 3 World XI 2017) (2007 to 2017); HS 8* v P (Johannesburg) 2013-14; BB 4-17 v NZ (Durban) 2007. F-c Tours (SA): E 2008, 2012, 2017; A 2008-09, 2012-13; WI 2010; NZ 2011-12, 2016-17; I 2007-08, 2009-10, 2015-16; SL 2014; Z 2014; B 2007-08, 2015; UAE (v P) 2010-11, 2013-14. HS 82* (and 11-56 match) Titans v Warriors (E London) 2006-07. Sy HS 33 v Hants (Arundel) 2020. 50 wkts (1): 63 (2018). BB 6-23 (*see Tests*). Sy BB 6-57 v Lancs (Oval) 2018. LO HS 35 Easterns v Northerns (Pretoria) 2005-06. LO BB 5-21 (*see LOI*). T20 HS 23*. T20 BB 4-17.

SURREY 2020

RESULTS SUMMARY

	Place	Won	Lost	Drew	Tied	NR
Bob Willis Trophy (South Group)	5th	1	4			
Vitality Blast (South Group)	Finalist	9	2		1	1

BOB WILLIS TROPHY AVERAGES
BATTING AND FIELDING

Cap		M	I	NO	HS	Runs	Avge	100	50	Ct/St
2016	B.T.Foakes	2	4	1	118	227	75.66	1	1	4/1
	W.G.Jacks	5	10	2	84*	248	31.00	–	2	6
	J.L.Smith	5	10	1	80	274	30.44	–	1	8
	L.J.Evans	3	6	–	65	172	28.66	–	1	1
2018	S.G.Borthwick	5	10	–	92	192	19.20	–	2	5
2005	R.Clarke	3	6	–	30	91	15.16	–	–	4
2018	M.D.Stoneman	4	8	–	45	106	13.25	–	–	1
	R.S.Patel	3	6	–	44	78	13.00	–	–	5
	J.P.A.Taylor	3	5	1	22	34	8.50	–	–	1
	A.W.Finch	3	5	1	10	29	7.25	–	–	1
	M.P.Dunn	3	6	1	12	28	5.60	–	–	2
	A.A.P.Atkinson	2	4	–	15	21	5.25	–	–	–
	G.S.Virdi	5	9	4	12	26	5.20	–	–	1
	D.T.Moriarty	2	3	–	1	1	0.33	–	–	–

Also batted (1 match each): H.M.Amla 26, 18 (1 ct); R.J.Burns (cap 2014) 103, 52 (2 ct); J.Clark 1, 7; S.M.Curran (cap 2018) 21, 14; M.Morkel (cap 2018) 33, 0; J.Overton 55 (2 ct); J.J.Roy (cap 2014) 4, 14 (1 ct).

BOWLING

	O	M	R	W	Avge	Best	5wI	10wM
R.Clarke	88	23	190	13	14.61	5- 20	1	–
S.M.Curran	39.5	7	124	7	17.71	4- 39	–	–
D.T.Moriarty	98.2	15	342	17	20.11	6- 70	3	1
G.S.Virdi	179	26	570	22	25.90	6-101	1	–
A.W.Finch	74.1	9	215	8	26.87	4- 38	–	–
A.A.P.Atkinson	35.4	5	128	4	32.00	2- 57	–	–
J.P.A.Taylor	46	6	171	4	42.75	2- 31	–	–
M.P.Dunn	70.4	16	239	5	47.80	3- 53	–	–

Also bowled: S.G.Borthwick 43-3-161-2; J.Clark 11-3-30-0; W.G.Jacks 6-0-17-0; M.Morkel 14-7-28-0; J.Overton 21-3-70-0; R.S.Patel 14-1-72-0.

The First-Class Averages (pp 209–221) give the records of Surrey players in all first-class county matches, with the exception of R.J.Burns, S.M.Curran and J.Overton, whose first-class figures for Surrey are as above.

SURREY RECORDS

FIRST-CLASS CRICKET

Highest Total	For 811		v	Somerset	The Oval	1899
	V 863		by	Lancashire	The Oval	1990
Lowest Total	For 14		v	Essex	Chelmsford	1983
	V 16		by	MCC	Lord's	1872
Highest Innings	For 357*	R.Abel	v	Somerset	The Oval	1899
	V 366	N.H.Fairbrother	for	Lancashire	The Oval	1990

Highest Partnership for each Wicket

1st	428	J.B.Hobbs/A.Sandham	v	Oxford U	The Oval	1926
2nd	371	J.B.Hobbs/E.G.Hayes	v	Hampshire	The Oval	1909
3rd	413	D.J.Bicknell/D.M.Ward	v	Kent	Canterbury	1990
4th	448	R.Abel/T.W.Hayward	v	Yorkshire	The Oval	1899
5th	318	M.R.Ramprakash/Azhar Mahmood	v	Middlesex	The Oval	2005
6th	298	A.Sandham/H.S.Harrison	v	Sussex	The Oval	1913
7th	262	C.J.Richards/K.T.Medlycott	v	Kent	The Oval	1987
8th	222*	B.T.Foakes/G.J.Batty	v	Hampshire	Southampton[2]	2016
9th	168	E.R.T.Holmes/E.W.J.Brooks	v	Hampshire	The Oval	1936
10th	173	A.Ducat/A.Sandham	v	Essex	Leyton	1921

Best Bowling	For	10-43	T.Rushby	v	Somerset	Taunton	1921
(Innings)	V	10-28	W.P.Howell	for	Australians	The Oval	1899
Best Bowling	For	16-83	G.A.R.Lock	v	Kent	Blackheath	1956
(Match)	V	15-57	W.P.Howell	for	Australians	The Oval	1899

Most Runs – Season	3246	T.W.Hayward	(av 72.13)	1906
Most Runs – Career	43554	J.B.Hobbs	(av 49.72)	1905-34
Most 100s – Season	13	T.W.Hayward		1906
	13	J.B.Hobbs		1925
Most 100s – Career	144	J.B.Hobbs		1905-34
Most Wkts – Season	252	T.Richardson	(av 13.94)	1895
Most Wkts – Career	1775	T.Richardson	(av 17.87)	1892-1904
Most Career W-K Dismissals	1221	H.Strudwick	(1035 ct; 186 st)	1902-27
Most Career Catches in the Field	605	M.J.Stewart		1954-72

LIMITED-OVERS CRICKET

Highest Total	50ov	496-4		v	Glos	The Oval	2007
	40ov	386-3		v	Glamorgan	The Oval	2010
	T20	250-6		v	Kent	Canterbury	2018
Lowest Total	50ov	74		v	Kent	The Oval	1967
	40ov	64		v	Worcs	Worcester	1978
	T20	88		v	Kent	The Oval	2012
Highest Innings	50ov	268	A.D.Brown	v	Glamorgan	The Oval	2002
	40ov	203	A.D.Brown	v	Hampshire	Guildford	1997
	T20	131*	A.J.Finch	v	Sussex	Hove	2018
Best Bowling	50ov	7-33	R.D.Jackman	v	Yorkshire	Harrogate	1970
	40ov	7-30	M.P.Bicknell	v	Glamorgan	The Oval	1999
	T20	6-24	T.J.Murtagh	v	Middlesex	Lord's	2005

SUSSEX

Formation of Present Club: 1 March 1839
Substantial Reorganisation: August 1857
Inaugural First-Class Match: 1864
Colours: Dark Blue, Light Blue and Gold
Badge: County Arms of Six Martlets
County Champions: (3) 2003, 2006, 2007
Gillette/NatWest/C&G Trophy Winners: (5) 1963, 1964, 1978, 1986, 2006
Pro 40/National League (Div 1) Winners: (2) 2008, 2009
Sunday League Winners: (1) 1982
Twenty20 Cup Winners: (1) 2009

Chief Executive: Rob Andrew, The 1st Central County Ground, Eaton Road, Hove BN3 3AN • ' Tel: 01273 827100 • Email: info@sussexcricket.co.uk • Web: www.sussexcricket.co.uk • Twitter: @SussexCCC (100,484 followers)

Director of Cricket: Keith Greenfield. **Head Coach**: Ian Salisbury. **Lead Batting Coach**: Jason Swift. **T20 Head Coach**: James Kirtley. **Captains**: B.C.Brown (f-c and l-o) and L.J.Wright (T20). **Overseas Players**: T.M.Head, Rashid Khan (T20 only), S.van Zyl and D.Wiese (T20 only). **2021 Testimonial**: None. **Head Groundsman**: Ben Gibson. **Scorer**: Graham Irwin. **Vitality Blast Name**: Sussex Sharks. ‡ New registration. NQ Not qualified for England.

ARCHER, Jofra Chioke (Christchurch Foundation), b Bridgetown, Barbados 1 Apr 1995. 6'3". RHB, RF. Squad No 22. Debut (Sussex) 2016; cap 2017. IPL: RR 2018 to date. Big Bash: HH 2017-18 to 2018-19. *Wisden* 2019. **ECB Test & L-O Central Contract 2020-21. Tests**: 13 (2019 to 2020-21); HS 30 v NZ (Mt Maunganui) 2019-20; BB 6-45 v A (Leeds) 2019. **LOI**: 17 (2019 to 2020); HS 8* v A (Manchester) 2020; BB 3-27 v SA (Oval) 2019. **IT20**: 8 (2019 to 2020-21); HS – ; BB 3-23 v I (Ahmedabad) 2020-21. F-c Tours: SA 2019-20; NZ 2019-20; I 2020-21. HS 81* v Northants (Northampton) 2017. 50 wkts (1): 61 (2017). BB 7-67 v Kent (Hove) 2017. LO HS 45 v Essex (Chelmsford) 2017 (RLC). LO BB 5-42 v Somerset (Taunton) 2016 (RLC). T20 HS 36. T20 BB 4-18.

ATKINS, Jamie Ardley (Eastbourne C), b Redhill, Surrey 20 May 2002. 6'6". RHB, RMF. Squad No 32. Awaiting 1st XI debut.

BEER, William Andrew Thomas (Reigate GS; Collyer's C, Horsham), b Crawley 8 Oct 1988. 5'10". RHB, LB. Squad No 18. Debut (Sussex) 2008. HS 97 v Glos (Arundel) 2019. BB 6-29 (11-91 match) v South Africa A (Arundel) 2017. CC BB 3-31 v Worcs (Worcester) 2010. LO HS 75 v Essex (Chelmsford) 2019 (RLC). LO BB 3-27 v Warwks (Hove) 2012 (CB40). T20 HS 37. T20 BB 3-14.

BOPARA, Ravinder Singh (Brampton Manor S; Barking Abbey Sports C), b Newham, London 4 May 1985. 5'8". RHB, RM. Squad No 23. Essex 2002-19; cap 2005; benefit 2015; captain (l-o only) 2016. Auckland 2009-10. Dolphins 2010-11. Sussex debut 2020 (T20 only). MCC 2006, 2008. IPL: KXIP 2009 to 2009-10. SH 2015. Big Bash: SS 2013-14. YC 2008. **Tests**: 13 (2007-08 to 2012); HS 143 v WI (Lord's) 2009; BB 1-39 v SL (Galle) 2007-08. **LOI**: 120 (2006-07 to 2014-15); HS 101* v Ire (Dublin) 2013; BB 4-38 v B (Birmingham) 2010. **IT20**: 38 (2008 to 2014); HS 65* v A (Hobart) 2013-14; BB 4-10 v WI (Oval) 2011. F-c Tours: WI 2008-09, 2010-11 (EL); SL 2007-08, 2011-12. 1000 runs (1): 1256 (2008). HS 229 Ex v Northants (Chelmsford) 2007. BB 5-49 Ex v Derbys (Chelmsford) 2016. LO HS 201* Ex v Leics (Leicester) 2008 (FPT) – Ex record. LO BB 5-63 Dolphins v Warriors (Pietermaritzburg) 2010-11. T20 HS 105*. T20 BB 6-16.

BROWN, Ben Christopher (Ardingly C), b Crawley 23 Nov 1988. 5'8". RHB, WK. Squad No 26. Debut (Sussex) 2007; cap 2014; captain 2017 to date. 1000 runs (2); most – 1031 (2015, 2018). HS 163 v Durham (Hove) 2014. BB 1-48 v Essex (Colchester) 2016. LO HS 73* v Kent (Hove) 2018 (RLC). T20 HS 68.

CARSON, Jack Joshua (Bainbridge Ac; Hurstpierpoint C), b Craigavon, Co Armagh 3 Dec 2000. 6'2". RHB, OB. Squad No 16. Debut (Sussex) 2020. Sussex 2nd XI debut 2018. HS 21 and BB 5-93 v Surrey (Oval) 2020.

CLARK, Thomas Geoffrey Reeves (Ardingly C), b Haywards Heath 27 Feb 2001. 6'2". LHB, RM. Squad No 27. Debut (Sussex) 2019. Sussex 2nd XI debut 2017. HS 65 v Kent (Canterbury) 2020.

CLAYDON, Mitchell Eric (Westfield Sports HS, Sydney), b Fairfield, NSW, Australia 25 Nov 1982. 6'4". LHB, RMF. Squad No 4. Yorkshire 2005-06. Durham 2007-13. Canterbury 2010-11. Kent 2013-19; cap 2016. Sussex debut 2020. HS 77 K v Leics (Leicester) 2014. Sx HS 24 v Kent (Canterbury) 2020. 50 wkts (2); most – 59 (2014). BB 6-104 Du v Somerset (Taunton) 2011. Sx BB 3-23 v Middx (Radlett) 2020. LO HS 19 Du v Glos (Bristol) 2009 (FPT) and 19 K v Middx (Canterbury) 2017 (RLC). LO BB 5-31 K v Guyana (North Sound) 2017-18. T20 HS 19. T20 BB 5-26.

COLES, James Matthew (Magdalen Coll S), b Aylesbury, Bucks 2 Apr 2004. RHB, SLA. Squad No 30. Debut (Sussex) 2020, aged 16y 157d – youngest ever player for the county. HS 11 and BB 2-32 v Surrey (Oval) 2020 – only 1st XI appearance.

CROCOMBE, Henry Thomas (Bede's S, Upper Dicker), b Eastbourne 20 Sep 2001. 6'2". RHB, RMF. Squad No 14. Debut (Sussex) 2020. Sussex 2nd XI debut 2018. HS 15 v Kent (Canterbury) 2020. BB 2-36 v Surrey (Oval) 2020.

GARTON, George Henry Simmons (Hurstpierpoint C), b Brighton 15 Apr 1997. 5'10½". LHB, LF. Squad No 15. Debut (Sussex) 2016. Sussex 2nd XI debut 2014. HS 59* v Worcs (Hove) 2019. BB 5-26 v Essex (Hove) 2020. LO HS 38 v Essex (Chelmsford) 2019 (RLC). LO BB 4-43 EL v Sri Lanka A (Canterbury) 2016. T20 HS 34*. T20 BB 4-16.

HAINES, Thomas Jacob (Tanbridge House S, Horsham; Hurstpierpoint C), b Crawley 28 Oct 1998. 5'10". LHB, RM. Squad No 20. Debut (Sussex) 2016. Sussex 2nd XI debut 2014. HS 124 v Durham (Arundel) 2018. BB 1-9 v Durham (Chester-le-St) 2019.

‡NQ**HEAD, Travis** Michael, b Adelaide, Australia 29 Dec 1993. 5'9". LHB, OB. Squad No 62. S Australia 2011-12 to date. Yorkshire 2016. Worcestershire 2018. IPL: RCB 2016-17. Big Bash: AS 2012-13 to date. **Tests (A):** 19 (2018-19 to 2020-21); HS 161 v SL (Canberra) 2018-19; BB – . **LOI** (A): 42 (2016 to 2018-19); HS 128 v P (Adelaide) 2016-17; BB 2-22 v SL (Pallekele) 2016. **IT20** (A): 16 (2015-16 to 2018); HS 48* v I (Guwahati) 2017-18; BB 1-16 v SL (Adelaide) 2016-17. F-c Tours (A): E 2019; I 2015 (Aus A), 2018-19 (Aus A); UAE 2018-19 (v P). HS 223 SA v WA (Perth) 2020-21. CC HS 62 Wo v Essex (Worcester) 2018. BB 3-42 SA v NSW (Adelaide) 2015-16. LO HS 202 SA v WA (Sydney) 2015-16. LO BB 2-9 SA v NSW (Brisbane) 2014-15. T20 HS 101*. T20 BB 3-16.

‡**HUNT, Sean** Frank (Howard of Eggingham S), b Guildford, Surrey 7 Dec 2001. RHB, LMF. Squad No 21. Surrey 2nd XI 2019. Awaiting 1st XI debut.

JORDAN, Christopher James (Comber Mere S, Barbados; Dulwich C), b Christ Church, Barbados 4 Oct 1988. 6'1". RHB, RFM. Squad No 8. Surrey 2007-12. Barbados 2011-12 to 2012-13. Sussex debut 2013; cap 2014. IPL: RCB 2017-18. KXIP 2020-21. Big Bash: AS 2016-17. ST 2018-19. PS 2019-20. **ECB Incremental Contract 2020-21. Tests:** 8 (2014 to 2014-15); HS 35 v SL (Lord's) 2014; BB 4-18 v I (Oval) 2014. **LOI:** 34 (2013 to 2019-20); HS 38* v SL (Oval) 2014; BB 5-29 v SL (Manchester) 2014. **IT20:** 55 (2013-14 to 2020-21); HS 36 v NZ (Wellington) 2019-20; BB 4-6 v WI (Basseterre) 2018-19 – E record. F-c Tour: WI 2014-15. HS 166 v Northants (Northampton) 2019. 50 wkts (1): 61 (2013). BB 7-43 Barbados v CC&C (Bridgetown) 2012-13. Sx BB 6-48 v Yorks (Leeds) 2013. LO HS 55 v Surrey (Guildford) 2016 (RLC). LO BB 5-28 v Middx (Hove) 2016 (RLC). T20 HS 45*. T20 BB 4-6.

MEAKER, Stuart Christopher (Cranleigh S), b Durban, South Africa 21 Jan 1989. Moved to UK in 2001. 6'1". RHB, RFM. Squad No 12. Surrey 2008-18; cap 2012. Auckland 2017-18. Sussex debut 2020. **LOI:** 2 (2011-12); HS 1 (twice); BB 1-45 v I (Mumbai) 2011-12. **IT20:** 2 (2012-13); BB 1-28 v I (Pune) 2013-14. F-c Tour: I 2012-13. HS 94 Sy v Bangladeshis (Oval) 2010. CC HS 72 Sy v Essex (Colchester) 2009. Sx HS 42 v Surrey (Oval) 2020. 50 wkts (1): 51 (2012). BB 8-52 (11-167 match) Sy v Somerset (Oval) 2012. Sx HS BB 1-17 v Essex (Hove) 2020. LO HS 50 v Glamorgan (Cardiff) 2019 (RLC). LO BB 4-37 Sy v Kent (Oval) 2017 (RLC). T20 HS 17. T20 BB 4-30.

MILLS, Tymal Solomon (Mildenhall TC), b Dewsbury, Yorks 12 Aug 1992. 6'1". RHB, LF. Squad No 7. Essex 2011-14. Sussex debut 2015; has played T20 only since start of 2016. IPL: RCB 2017. Big Bash: BH 2016-17. HH 2017-18. **IT20:** 4 (+1 ICC World XI 2018) (2016 to 2016-17); HS 0; BB 1-27 v I (Kanpur) 2016-17. F-c Tour (EL): SL 2013-14. HS 31* EL v Sri Lanka A (Colombo, RPS) 2013-14. CC HS 30 Ex v Kent (Canterbury) 2014. Sx HS 8 v Worcs (Hove) 2015. BB 4-25 Ex v Glamorgan (Cardiff) 2012. Sx BB 2-28 v Hants (Southampton) 2015. LO HS 3* v Notts (Hove) 2015 (RLC). LO BB 3-23 Ex v Durham (Chelmsford) 2013 (Y40). T20 HS 10. T20 BB 4-22.

NQRASHID KHAN Arman, b Nangarhar, Afghanistan 20 Sep 1998. RHB, LBG. Squad No 1. Afghanistan 2016-17 to date. Sussex debut 2018 (T20 only). IPL: SH 2017 to date. Big Bash: AS 2017-18 to date. **Tests** (Afg): 4 (2018 to 2019-20); HS 51 and BB 6-49 (11-104 match) v B (Chittagong) 2019. **LOI** (Afg): 74 (2015-16 to 2020-21); HS 60* v Ire (Belfast) 2016; BB 7-18 v WI (Gros Islet) 2017 – 4th best analysis in all LOI. **IT20** (Afg): 48 (2015-16 to 2019-20); HS 33 v WI (Basseterre) 2017; BB 5-3 v Ire (Greater Noida) 2016-17. HS 52 and BB 8-74 (12-122 match) Afg v EL (Abu Dhabi) 2016-17. LO HS 60* (*see LOI*). LO BB 7-18 (*see LOI*). T20 HS 56*. T20 BB 5-3.

RAWLINS, Delray Millard Wendell (Bede's S, Upper Dicker), b Bermuda 14 Sep 1997. 6'1". LHB, SLA. Squad No 9. Debut (Sussex) 2017. MCC 2018. Bermuda (l-o and T20) 2019 to date. Sussex 2nd XI debut 2015. Oxfordshire 2017. England U19 2016-17. **IT20** (Ber): 11 (2019 to 2019-20); HS 63 v USA (Hamilton) 2019; BB 2-22 v USA (Hamilton) 2019 – separate matches. HS 100 v Lancs (Manchester) 2019. BB 3-19 v Durham (Hove) 2019. LO HS 53 South v North (Bridgetown) 2017-18 and 53 Bermuda v Uganda (Al Amerat) 2019-20. LO BB 1-27 Bermuda v Italy (Al Amerat) 2019-20. T20 HS 69. T20 BB 3-21.

ROBINSON, Oliver Edward (King's S, Canterbury), b Margate, Kent 1 Dec 1993. 6'1". RHB, RMF/OB. Squad No 25. Debut (Sussex) 2015; cap 2019. F-c Tour (EL): A 2019-20. HS 110 v Durham (Chester-le-St) 2015, on debut, sharing Sx record 10th wkt partnership of 164 with M.E.Hobden (Hove) 2015; most – 81 (2018). BB 8-34 (14-135 match) v Middx (Hove) 2019. LO HS 30 v Kent (Canterbury) 2015 (RLC). LO BB 3-31 v Kent (Hove) 2018 (RLC). T20 HS 18*. T20 BB 4-15.

SALT, Philip Dean (Reed's S, Cobham), b Bodelwyddan, Denbighs 28 Aug 1996. 5'10". RHB, OB. Squad No 28. Debut (Sussex) 2013. Sussex 2nd XI debut 2014. Big Bash: AS 2019-20 to date. HS 148 v Derbys (Hove) 2018. BB 1-32 v Warwks (Hove) 2018. LO HS 137* v Kent (Beckenham) 2019 (RLC). T20 HS 78*.

THOMASON, Aaron Dean (Barr Beacon S, Walsall), b Birmingham 26 Jun 1997. 5'10". RHB, RMF. Squad No 24. Debut (Sussex) 2019. Warwickshire (l-o and T20 only) 2014-19. Warwickshire 2nd XI 2014-18. England U19 2015. HS 90 v Worcs (Kidderminster) 2019 – on debut. BB 2-107 v Australia A (Arundel) 2019. LO BB 1-33 v Northants (Hove) 2019. LO HS 28 Wa v Durham (Birmingham) 2017 (RLC). LO BB 4-45 Wa v Notts (Nottingham) 2018 (RLC). T20 HS 47. T20 BB 3-33.

[NQ]**VAN ZYL, Stiaan**, b Cape Town, South Africa 19 Sep 1987. 5'11½". LHB, RM. Squad No 74. Boland 2006-07 to 2010-11. Cape Cobras 2007-08 to 2017-18. W Province 2014-15 to 2016-17. Sussex debut 2017; cap 2019. **Tests** (SA): 12 (2014-15 to 2016); HS 101* v WI (Centurion) 2014-15 – on debut; BB 3-20 v E (Durban) 2015-16. F-c Tours (SA): A 2016 (SA A), I 2015 (SA A), 2015-16; SL 2010 (SA A); B 2010 (SA A), 2015; Ire 2012 (SA A). 1000 runs (1): 1023 (2017). HS 228 Cobras v Lions (Paarl) 2017-18. Sx 173 v Middx (Lord's) 2019. BB 5-32 Boland v Northerns (Paarl) 2010-11. Sx BB 3-16 v Glos (Hove) 2018. LO HS 114* Cobras v Eagles (Kimberley) 2009-10. LO BB 4-24 Boland v Gauteng (Stellenbosch) 2010-11. T20 HS 86*. T20 BB 2-14.

[NQ]**WIESE, David** (Witbank HS), b Roodepoort, South Africa 18 May 1985. 6'3". RHB, RMF. Squad No 96. Easterns 2005-06 to 2011-12. Titans 2009-10 to 2016-17. Sussex debut/cap 2016. IPL: RCB 2015-16. **LOI** (SA): 6 (2015 to 2015-16); HS 41* and BB 3-50 v E (Cape Town) 2015-16. **IT20** (SA): 20 (2013 to 2015-16); HS 28 v WI (Nagpur) 2015-16; BB 5-23 v WI (Durban) 2014-15. F-c Tour (SA A): A 2014. HS 208 Easterns v GW (Benoni) 2008-09. Sx HS 139 v Cardiff MCCU (Hove) 2019. CC HS 106 v Warwks (Birmingham) 2018. BB 6-58 Titans v Knights (Centurion) 2014-15. Sx BB 5-26 v Middx (Lord's) 2019. LO HS 171 v Hants (Southampton) 2019 (RLC) – Sx record. LO BB 5-25 Easterns v Boland (Benoni) 2010-11. T20 HS 79*. T20 BB 5-19.

WRIGHT, Luke James (Belvoir HS; Ratcliffe C; Loughborough U), b Grantham, Lincs 7 Mar 1985. Younger brother of A.S.Wright (Leicestershire 2001-02). 5'11". RHB, RMF. Squad No 10. Leicestershire 2003 (one f-c match). Sussex debut 2004; cap 2007; T20 captain & benefit 2016; captain 2016-17; captain 2020 to date (T20 only). IPL: PW 2012-13. Big Bash: MS 2011-12 to 2017-18. **LOI**: 50 (2007 to 2013-14); HS 52 v NZ (Birmingham) 2008; BB 2-34 v NZ (Bristol) 2008 and 2-34 v A (Southampton) 2010. **IT20**: 51 (2007-08 to 2013-14); HS 99* v Afg (Colombo, RPS) 2012-13; BB 2-24 v NZ (Hamilton) 2012-13. F-c Tour (EL): NZ 2008-09. 1000 runs (1): 1220 (2015). HS 226* v Worcs (Worcester) 2015, sharing Sx record 6th wkt partnership of 335 with B.C.Brown. BB 5-65 v Derbys (Derby) 2010. LO HS 166 v Middx (Lord's) 2019 (RLC). LO BB 4-12 v Middx (Hove) 2004 (NL). T20 HS 153* v Essex (Chelmsford) 2014 – Sx record. T20 BB 3-17.

RELEASED/RETIRED

(Having made a County 1st XI appearance in 2020)

BRIGGS, D.R. – see WARWICKSHIRE.

FINCH, Harry Zachariah (St Richard's Catholic C, Bexhill; Eastbourne C), b Hastings 10 Feb 1995. 5'8". RHB, RM. Sussex 2013-20. HS 135* and BB 1-9 v Leeds/Bradford MCCU (Hove) 2016. CC HS 103 v Middx (Hove) 2018. CC BB 1-30 v Northants (Arundel) 2016. LO HS 108 v Hants (Hove) 2018 (RLC). LO BB – . T20 HS 35*.

[NQ]**MacLEOD, Calum** Scott (Hillpark S, Glasgow), b Glasgow, Scotland 15 Nov 1988. 6'0". RHB, RMF. Scotland 2007 to date. Warwickshire 2008-09. Durham 2014-16. Derbyshire 2018 (T20 only). Sussex 2020 (T20 only). **LOI** (Scot): 66 (2008 to 2019-20); HS 175 v Canada (Christchurch) 2013-14; BB 2-26 v Kenya (Aberdeen) 2013. **IT20** (Scot): 49 (2009 to 2019-20); HS 74 v Bermuda (Dubai, DSC) 2019-20; BB 2-17 v Kenya (Aberdeen) 2013. F-c Tours (Scot): UAE 2011-12, 2012-13; Namibia 2011-12. HS 84 Du v Lancs (Manchester) 2014. BB 4-66 Scot v Canada (Aberdeen) 2009. LO HS 175 (see LOI). LO BB 3-37 Scot v UAE (Queenstown) 2013-14. T20 HS 104*. T20 BB 2-17.

SHEFFIELD, William Arthur (Aldridge Ac, Saltdean), b Haywards Heath 26 Aug 2000. 6'4". LHB, LMF. Sussex 2020. Sussex 2nd XI 2018-19. HS 6 and BB 1-45 v Middx (Radlett) 2020 – only 1st XI appearance.

WELLS, L.W.P. – see LANCASHIRE.

E.O.Hooper left the staff without making a County 1st XI appearance in 2020.

SUSSEX 2020

RESULTS SUMMARY

	Place	Won	Lost	Drew	NR
Bob Willis Trophy (South Group)	6th	1	4		
Vitality Blast (South Group)	QF	6	4		1

BOB WILLIS TROPHY AVERAGES
BATTING AND FIELDING

Cap		M	I	NO	HS	Runs	Avge	100	50	Ct/St
	P.D.Salt	4	8	–	80	290	36.25	–	3	6
	T.J.Haines	5	10	1	117	249	27.66	1	–	1
2014	B.C.Brown	5	10	–	98	270	27.00	–	2	10/1
	H.Z.Finch	5	10	–	69	259	25.90	–	2	6
	D.M.W.Rawlins	5	10	–	65	252	25.20	–	1	–
	S.C.Meaker	3	6	1	42	106	21.20	–	–	–
	A.D.Thomason	3	6	–	49	111	18.50	–	–	1
	G.H.S.Garton	4	8	1	54*	109	15.57	–	1	4
	M.E.Claydon	4	8	3	24	77	15.40	–	–	–
2019	O.E.Robinson	2	4	–	23	56	14.00	–	–	–
	T.G.R.Clark	4	8	–	65	110	13.75	–	1	2
	H.T.Crocombe	4	8	4	15	45	11.25	–	–	1
	J.J.Carson	4	8	–	21	57	7.12	–	–	1

Also played (1 match each): J.M.Coles 11, 10; W.A.Sheffield 6, 1; D.Wiese (cap 2016) 57, 4 (1 ct).

BOWLING

	O	M	R	W	Avge	Best	5wI	10wM
J.M.Coles	13	0	35	3	11.66	2-32	–	–
O.E.Robinson	73.1	22	175	14	12.50	5-29	1	–
J.J.Carson	108.1	17	340	15	22.66	5-93	1	–
G.H.S.Garton	70.3	13	282	12	23.50	5-26	1	–
M.E.Claydon	102	25	294	11	26.72	3-23	–	–
H.T.Crocombe	71	13	245	3	81.66	2-36	–	–
D.M.W.Rawlins	69.5	8	261	3	87.00	1-14	–	–

Also bowled: T.J.Haines 25-3-72-2; S.C.Meaker 46.5-5-225-2; W.A.Sheffield 15-0-54-1; D.Wiese 13-3-32-1.

The First-Class Averages (pp 209–221) give the records of Sussex players in all first-class county matches.

SUSSEX RECORDS

FIRST-CLASS CRICKET

Highest Total	For 742-5d		v	Somerset	Taunton	2009
	V 726		by	Notts	Nottingham	1895
Lowest Total	For 19		v	Surrey	Godalming	1830
	19		v	Notts	Hove	1873
	V 18		by	Kent	Gravesend	1867
Highest Innings	For 344*	M.W.Goodwin	v	Somerset	Taunton	2009
	V 322	E.Paynter	for	Lancashire	Hove	1937

Highest Partnership for each Wicket

1st	490	E.H.Bowley/J.G.Langridge	v	Middlesex	Hove	1933
2nd	385	E.H.Bowley/M.W.Tate	v	Northants	Hove	1921
3rd	385*	M.H.Yardy/M.W.Goodwin	v	Warwicks	Hove	2006
4th	363	M.W.Goodwin/C.D.Hopkinson	v	Somerset	Taunton	2009
5th	297	J.H.Parks/H.W.Parks	v	Hampshire	Portsmouth	1937
6th	335	L.J.Wright/B.C.Brown	v	Durham	Hove	2014
7th	344	K.S.Ranjitsinhji/W.Newham	v	Essex	Leyton	1902
8th	291	R.S.C.Martin-Jenkins/M.J.G.Davis	v	Somerset	Taunton	2002
9th	178	H.W.Parks/A.F.Wensley	v	Derbyshire	Horsham	1930
10th	164	O.E.Robinson/M.E.Hobden	v	Durham	Chester-le-St[2]	2015

Best Bowling	For 10- 48	C.H.G.Bland	v	Kent	Tonbridge	1899
(Innings)	V 9- 11	A.P.Freeman	for	Kent	Hove	1922
Best Bowling	For 17-106	G.R.Cox	v	Warwicks	Horsham	1926
(Match)	V 17- 67	A.P.Freeman	for	Kent	Hove	1922

Most Runs – Season	2850	J.G.Langridge	(av 64.77)	1949
Most Runs – Career	34150	J.G.Langridge	(av 37.69)	1928-55
Most 100s – Season	12	J.G.Langridge		1949
Most 100s – Career	76	J.G.Langridge		1928-55
Most Wkts – Season	198	M.W.Tate	(av 13.47)	1925
Most Wkts – Career	2211	M.W.Tate	(av 17.41)	1912-37
Most Career W-K Dismissals	1176	H.R.Butt	(911 ct; 265 st)	1890-1912
Most Career Catches in the Field	779	J.G.Langridge		1928-55

LIMITED-OVERS CRICKET

Highest Total	50ov	384-9	v	Ireland	Belfast	1996
	40ov	399-4	v	Worcs	Horsham	2011
	T20	242-5	v	Glos	Bristol	2016
Lowest Total	50ov	49	v	Derbyshire	Chesterfield	1969
	40ov	59	v	Glamorgan	Hove	1996
	T20	67	v	Hampshire	Hove	2004
Highest Innings	50ov	171	D.Wiese	v	Hampshire	Southampton[2]	2019
	40ov	163	C.J.Adams	v	Middlesex	Arundel	1999
	T20	153*	L.J.Wright	v	Essex	Chelmsford	2014
Best Bowling	50ov	6- 9	A.I.C.Dodemaide	v	Ireland	Downpatrick	1990
	40ov	7-41	A.N.Jones	v	Notts	Nottingham	1986
	T20	5-11	Mushtaq Ahmed	v	Essex	Hove	2005

WARWICKSHIRE

Formation of Present Club: 8 April 1882
Substantial Reorganisation: 19 January 1884
Inaugural First-Class Match: 1894
Colours: Dark Blue, Gold and Silver
Badge: Bear and Ragged Staff
County Champions: (7) 1911, 1951, 1972, 1994, 1995, 2004, 2012
Gillette/NatWest Trophy Winners: (5) 1966, 1968, 1989, 1993, 1995
Benson and Hedges Cup Winners: (2) 1994, 2002
Sunday League Winners: (3) 1980, 1994, 1997
Clydesdale Bank 40 Winners: (1) 2010
Royal London Cup Winners: (1) 2015
Twenty20 Cup Winners: (1) 2014

Chief Executive: Stuart Cain, Edgbaston Stadium, Edgbaston, Birmingham, B5 7QU • Tel: 0121 369 1994 • Email: enquiries@edgbaston.com • Web: www.edgbaston.com • Twitter: @WarwickshireCCC (70,735 followers)

Director of Cricket: Paul Farbrace. **1st Team Coach**: Mark Robinson. **Batting Coach**: Tony Frost. **Bowling Coach**: Graeme Welch. **Captain**: W.H.M.Rhodes. **Vice-Captain**: D.P.Sibley. **Overseas Players**: C.R.Brathwaite (T20 only) and P.J.Malan. **2021 Testimonial**: None. **Head Groundsman**: Gary Barwell. **Scorer**: Mel Smith. **T20 Blast Name**: Birmingham Bears. ‡ New registration. ^{NQ} Not qualified for England.

BETHELL, Jacob Graham (Rugby S), b Barbados 23 Oct 2003. LHB, SLA. Squad No 2. Warwickshire 2nd XI debut 2019. Awaiting 1st XI debut.

‡^{NQ}**BRATHWAITE, Carlos** Ricardo, b Christ Church, Barbados 18 Jul 1988. RHB, RFM. CC&C 2010-11. Barbados 2011-12 to 2015-16. Sagicor HPC 2014. Kent 2018 (T20 only). IPL: DD 2016-17. SH 2018. KKR 2019. Big Bash: ST 2017-18 to date. **Tests** (WI): 3 (2015-16 to 2016); HS 69 v A (Sydney) 2015-16; BB 1-30 v A (Melbourne) 2015-16. **LOI** (WI): 44 (2011-12 to 2019); HS 101 v NZ (Manchester) 2019; BB 5-27 v PNG (Harare) 2017-18. **IT20** (WI): 41 (2011-12 to 2019); HS 37* v P (Port of Spain) 2016-17; BB 3-20 v E (Chester-le-St) 2017. F-c Tours (WI): A 2015-16; SL 2014-15 (WI A). HS 109 Bar v T&T (Bridgetown) 2013-14. BB 7-90 CC&C v T&T (St Augustine) 2010-11 – on debut. LO HS 113 WI v SL Board Pres (Colombo, CC) 2015-16. LO BB 5-27 (*see LOI*). T20 HS 64*. T20 BB 4-15.

BRESNAN, Timothy Thomas (Castleford HS and TC; Pontefract New C), b Pontefract, Yorks 28 Feb 1985. 6'0". RHB, RFM. Squad No 3. Yorkshire 2003-19; cap 2006; benefit 2014. Warwickshire debut 2020. MCC 2006, 2009. Big Bash: HH 2014-15. PS 2016-17 to 2017-18. *Wisden* 2011. **Tests**: 23 (2009 to 2013-14); HS 91 v B (Dhaka) 2009-10; BB 5-48 v I (Nottingham) 2011. **LOI**: 85 (2006 to 2015); HS 80 v SA (Centurion) 2009-10; BB 5-48 v I (Bangalore) 2010-11. **IT20**: 34 (2006 to 2013-14); HS 47* v WI (Bridgetown) 2013-14; BB 3-10 v P (Cardiff) 2010. F-c Tours: A 2010-11, 2013-14; I 2012-13; SL 2011-12; B 2006-07 (Eng A), 2009-10. HS 169* Y v Durham (Chester-le-St) 2015, sharing Y record 7th wkt partnership of 366* with J.M.Bairstow. Wa HS 105 v Northants (Birmingham) 2020 – on debut. BB 5-28 v Hants (Leeds) 2018. Wa BB 4-99 v Somerset (Birmingham) 2020. LO HS 95* Y v Notts (Scarborough) 2016 (RLC). BB 5-48 (*see LOI*). T20 HS 51. T20 BB 6-19 Y v Lancs (Leeds) 2017 – Y record.

‡**BRIGGS, Danny** Richard (Isle of Wight C), b Newport, IoW, 30 Apr 1991. 6'2". RHB, SLA. Squad No 14. Hampshire 2009-15; cap 2012. Sussex 2016-19. Big Bash: AS 2020-21. **LOI:** 1 (2011-12); BB 2-39 v P (Dubai) 2011-12. **IT20:** 7 (2012 to 2013-14); HS 0*; BB 2-25 v A (Chester-le-St) 2013. F-c Tours (EL): WI 2010-11; I 2018-19. HS 120* v South Africa A (Arundel) 2017. CC HS 54 H v Glos (Bristol) 2013. BB 6-45 EL v Windward Is (Roseau) 2010-11. CC BB 6-65 H v Notts (Southampton) 2011. LO HS 37* Sx v Essex (Chelmsford) 2019 (RLC). LO BB 4-32 H v Glamorgan (Cardiff) 2012 (CB40). T20 HS 35*. T20 BB 5-19.

BROOKES, Ethan Alexander (Solihull S & SFC), b Solihull 23 May 2001. Younger brother of H.J.H.Brookes (*see below*). 6'1". RHB, RMF. Squad No 77. Debut (Warwickshire) 2019. Warwickshire 2nd XI debut 2018. Staffordshire 2019. HS 15* v Glamorgan (Cardiff) 2020. BB – .

BROOKES, Henry James Hamilton (Tudor Grange Acad, Solihull), b Solihull 21 Aug 1999. Elder brother of E.A.Brookes (*see above*). 6'3". RHB, RMF. Squad No 10. Debut (Warwickshire) 2017. Warwickshire 2nd XI debut 2016. England U19 2016-17 to 2017. HS 84 v Kent (Birmingham) 2019. BB 4-54 v Northants (Birmingham) 2018. LO HS 12* v Derbys (Derby) 2019 (RLC). LO BB 3-50 v Yorks (Birmingham) 2019 (RLC). T20 HS 31*. T20 BB 3-26.

BURGESS, Michael Gregory Kerran (Cranleigh S; Loughborough U), b Epsom, Surrey 8 Jul 1994. 6'1". RHB, WK, occ RM. Squad No 61. Loughborough MCCU 2014-15. Leicestershire 2016. Sussex 2017-19. Warwickshire debut 2019. HS 146 Sx v Notts (Hove) 2017. Wa HS 64 v Essex (Chelmsford) 2019. BB – . LO HS 58 Sx v Glamorgan (Cardiff) 2018 (RLC). T20 HS 56.

FURRER, George William (Barker C; U of New South Wales) b London 10 Oct 1998. 6'5". RHB, LFM. Squad No 13. Warwickshire 2nd XI debut 2019. Awaiting 1st XI debut.

GARRETT, George Anthony (Shrewsbury S), Harpenden, Herts 4 Mar 2000. 6'3". RHB, RM. Squad No 44. Debut (Warwickshire) 2019. Warwickshire 2nd XI debut 2019. No 1st XI appearances in 2020. HS 24 v Essex (Birmingham) 2019. BB 2-53 v Notts (Nottingham) 2019. T20 BB 1-19.

HAIN, Samuel Robert (Southport S, Gold Coast), b Hong Kong 16 July 1995. 5'10". RHB, OB. Squad No 16. Debut (Warwickshire) 2014; cap 2018. MCC 2018. UK passport (British parents). HS 208 v Northants (Birmingham) 2014. BB – . LO HS 161* v Worcs (Worcester) 2019 (RLC). T20 HS 95.

HANNON-DALBY, Oliver James (Brooksbank S, Leeds Met U), b Halifax, Yorkshire 20 Jun 1989. 6'7". LHB, RMF. Squad No 20. Yorkshire 2008-12. Warwickshire debut 2013; cap 2019. F-c Tour (MCC): Nepal 2019-20. HS 40 v Somerset (Taunton) 2014. BB 6-33 (12-110 match) v Glos (Bristol) 2020. LO HS 21* Y v Warwks (Scarborough) 2012 (CB40). LO BB 5-27 v Glamorgan (Birmingham) 2015 (RLC). T20 HS 14*. T20 BB 4-20.

HOSE, Adam John (Carisbrooke S), b Newport, IoW 25 Oct 1992. 6'2". RHB, RMF. Squad No 21. Somerset 2016-17. Warwickshire debut 2018. HS 111 v Notts (Birmingham) 2019. LO HS 101* Sm v Glos (Bristol) 2017 (RLC). T20 HS 119.

JOHAL, Manraj Singh (Sandwell C; Oldbury Ac), b Birmingham 12 Oct 2001. 6'0". RHB, RFM. Squad No 5. Awaiting 1st XI debut. Staffordshire 2019.

KELLEY, Vikai Viran, b Wolverhampton, Staffs 2 Sep 2002. RHB, WK. Warwickshire debut 2020 (T20 only). Awaiting f-c debut. T20 HS 5.

LAMB, Matthew James (North Bromsgrove HS; Bromsgrove S), b Wolverhampton, Staffs 19 July 1996. 6'1''. RHB, RM. Squad No 7. Debut (Warwickshire) 2016. Warwickshire 2nd XI debut 2015. HS 173 and BB 1-15 v Essex (Birmingham) 2019. LO HS 47 v West Indies A (Birmingham) 2018. LO BB – . T20 HS 35.

LINTOTT, Jacob ('Jake') Benedict (Queen's C, Taunton), b Taunton, Somerset 22 Apr 1993. 5'11''. RHB, SLA. Squad No 23. Hampshire 2017 (T20 only). Gloucestershire 2018 (T20 only). Warwickshire debut 2020 (T20 only). Dorset 2011-15. Wiltshire 2016-19. Awaiting f-c debut. T20 HS 12. T20 BB 3-11.

‡NOMALAN, Pieter Jacobus (Waterkloof Hoer S), b Nelspruit, South Africa 13 Aug 1989. Elder brother of J.N.Malan (North West, Cape Cobras & South Africa 2015-15 to date) and A.J.Malan (Northerns, North West, W Province & Cape Cobras 2010-11 to 2019-20). RHB, RMF. Squad No 31. Northerns 2006-07 to 2012-13. Titans 2008-09 to 2012-13. Western Province 2013-14 to 2019-20. Cape Cobras 2014-15 to date. **Tests** (SA): 3 (2019-20); HS 84 v E (Cape Town) 2019-20; BB – . F-c Tours (SA A): I 2018, 2019. 1000 runs (0+2); most – 1114 (2017-18). HS 211* WP v Namibia (Walvis Bay) 2016-17. BB 5-35 WP v EP (Port Elizabeth) 2017-18. LO HS 169* Northerns v WP (Pretoria) 2008-09. LO BB – . T20 HS 140*. T20 BB 2-30.

MILES, Craig Neil (Bradon Forest S, Swindon; Filton C, Bristol), b Swindon, Wilts 20 July 1994. Brother of A.J.Miles (Cardiff MCCU 2012). 6'4''. RHB, RMF. Squad No 18. Gloucestershire 2011-18; cap 2011. Warwickshire debut 2019. HS 62* Gs v Worcs (Cheltenham) 2014. Wa HS 27 v Yorks (York) 2019. 50 wkts (3); most – 58 (2018). BB 6-63 Gs v Northants (Northampton) 2015. Wa BB 5-91 v Surrey (Oval) 2019. Hat-trick Gs v Essex (Cheltenham) 2016. LO HS 31 v Leics (Leicester) 2019 (RLC). LO BB 4-29 Gs v Yorks (Scarborough) 2015 (RLC). T20 HS 8. T20 BB 3-25.

MOUSLEY, Daniel Richard (Bablake S, Coventry), b Birmingham 8 Jul 2001. 5'11''. LHB, OB. Squad No 80. Debut (Warwickshire) 2019. Staffordshire 2019. England U19 2018-19. HS 71 v Glamorgan (Cardiff) 2020. BB – . T20 HS 58*. T20 BB 1-9.

NORWELL, Liam Connor (Redruth SS), b Bournemouth, Dorset 27 Dec 1991. 6'3''. RHB, RMF. Squad No 24. Gloucestershire 2011-18, taking 6-46 v Derbys (Bristol) on debut; cap 2011. Warwickshire debut 2019. HS 102 Gs v Derbys (Bristol) 2016. Wa HS 64 v Surrey (Birmingham) 2019. 50 wkts (2); most – 68 (2015). BB 8-43 (10-95 match) Gs v Leics (Leicester) 2017. Wa BB 7-41 v Somerset (Taunton) 2019. LO HS 16 Gs v Somerset (Bristol) 2017 (RLC). LO BB 6-52 Gs v Leics (Leicester) 2012 (CB40). T20 HS 2*. T20 BB 3-27.

POLLOCK, Edward John (RGS Worcester; Shrewsbury S; Collingwood C, Durham U), b High Wycombe, Bucks 10 Jul 1995. Son of A.J.Pollock (Cambridge U 1982-84); younger brother of A.W.Pollock (Cambridge MCCU & U 2013-15). 5'10''. LHB, OB. Squad No 28. Durham MCCU 2015-17. Awaiting Warwickshire f-c debut. Herefordshire 2014-16. HS 52 DU v Glos (Bristol) 2017. LO HS 57 v Leics (Leicester) 2019 (RLC). T20 HS 77.

RHODES, William Michael Henry (Cottingham HS, Cottingham SFC, Hull), b Nottingham 2 Mar 1995. 6'2''. LHB, RMF. Squad No 35. Yorkshire 2014-15 to 2016. Essex 2016 (on loan). Warwickshire debut 2018; cap 2020; captain 2020 to date. MCC 2019. F-c Tour (MCC): Nepal 2019-20. HS 207 v Worcs (Worcester) 2020. BB 5-17 v Essex (Chelmsford) 2019. LO HS 69 v Worcs (Birmingham) 2018 (RLC) and 69 v West Indies A (Birmingham) 2018. LO BB 2-22 Y v Essex (Chelmsford) 2015 (RLC). T20 HS 46. T20 BB 3-27.

SIBLEY, Dominic Peter (Whitgift S, Croydon), b Epsom, Surrey 5 Sep 1995. 6'2". RHB, OB. Squad No 45. Surrey 2013-17. Warwickshire debut 2017; cap 2019. MCC 2019. **ECB Test Central Contract 2020-21. Tests**: 18 (2019-20); HS 133* v SA (Cape Town) 2019-20. F-c Tours: SA 2019-20; NZ 2019-20; I 2020-21; SL 2019-20, 2020-21. 1000 runs (1): 1428 (2019). HS 244 v Kent (Canterbury) 2019. BB 2-103 Sy v Hants (Southampton) 2016. Wa BB – . LO HS 115 v West Indies A (Birmingham) 2018. LO BB 1-20 Sy v Essex (Chelmsford) 2016 (RLC). T20 HS 74*. T20 BB 2-33.

SIDEBOTTOM, Ryan Nathan, b Shepparton, Victoria, Australia 14 Aug 1989. UK passport. 6'0". RHB, RMF. Squad No 22. Victoria 2012-13. Warwickshire debut 2017. HS 27* v Kent (Birmingham) 2019. BB 6-35 (10-96 match) v Northants (Northampton) 2018.

STONE, Oliver Peter (Thorpe St Andrew HS), b Norwich, Norfolk 9 Oct 1993. 6'1". RHB, RF. Squad No 6. Northamptonshire 2012-16. Warwickshire debut 2017; cap 2020. Norfolk 2011. **Tests**: 2 (2019 to 2020-21); HS 19 and BB 3-29 v Ire (Lord's) 2019. **LOI**: 4 (2018-19); HS 9* and BB 1-23 v SL (Dambulla) 2018-19. HS 60 Nh v Kent (Northampton) 2016. Wa HS 42* v Glamorgan (Colwyn Bay) 2018. BB 8-80 v Sussex (Birmingham) 2018. LO HS 24* Nh v Derbys (Derby) 2015 (RLC). LO BB 4-71 v Worcs (Birmingham) 2018 (RLC). T20 HS 22*. T20 BB 3-22.

THOMSON, Alexander Thomas (Kings S, Macclesfield; Denstone C; Cardiff Met U), b Macclesfield, Cheshire 30 Oct 1993. 6'2". RHB, OB. Squad No 29. Cardiff MCCU 2014-16. Warwickshire debut 2017. Staffordshire 2013-16. F-c Tour (MCC): Nepal 2019-20. HS 46 and Wa BB 2-3 v Northants (Birmingham) 2020. BB 6-138 CfU v Hants (Southampton) 2016. LO HS 68* v Derbys (Derby) 2019 (RLC). LO BB 3-27 v Lancs (Birmingham) 2019 (RLC). T20 HS 14. T20 BB 4-35.

WOAKES, Christopher Roger (Barr Beacon Language S, Walsall), b Birmingham 2 March 1989. 6'2". RHB, RFM. Squad No 19. Debut (Warwickshire) 2006; cap 2009. Wellington 2012-13. MCC 2009. IPL: KKR 2017. RCB 2018. Big Bash: ST 2013-14. Herefordshire 2006-07. *Wisden* 2016. PCA 2020. **ECB Test & LO Central Contract 2020-21. Tests**: 38 (2013 to 2020); HS 137* v I (Lord's) 2018; BB 6-17 v Ire (Lord's) 2019. **LOI**: 104 (2010-11 to 2020); HS 95* v SL (Nottingham) 2016; BB 6-45 v A (Brisbane) 2010-11. **IT20**: 8 (2010-11 to 2015-16); HS 37 v P (Sharjah) 2015-16; BB 2-40 v P (Dubai, DSC) 2015-16. F-c Tours: A 2017-18; SA 2015-16, 2019-20; WI 2010-11 (EL); NZ 2017-18, 2019-20; I 2016-17; SL 2013-14 (EL), 2019-20; B 2016-17; UAE 2015-16 (v P). HS 152* v Derbys (Derby) 2013. 50 wkts (3); most – 59 (2016). BB 9-36 v Durham (Birmingham) 2016. LO HS 95* (*see LOI*). LO BB 6-45 (*see LOI*). T20 HS 57*. T20 BB 4-21.

YATES, Robert Michael (Warwick S), b Solihull 19 Sep 1999. 6'0". LHB, OB. Squad No 17. Debut (Warwickshire) 2019. Warwickshire 2nd XI debut 2017. Staffordshire 2018. HS 141 v Somerset (Birmingham) 2019. BB – . LO HS 66 v Leics (Leicester) 2019. T20 HS 37.

(Having made a County 1st XI appearance in 2020)

BELL, Ian Ronald (Princethorpe C), b Walsgrave-on-Sowe 11 Apr 1982. 5'9''. RHB, RM. Warwickshire 1999-2020; cap 2001; benefit 2011; captain 2016-17. MCC 2004, 2016. YC 2004. MBE 2005. *Wisden* 2007. **Tests**: 118 (2004 to 2015-16); 1000 runs (1): 1005 (2013); HS 235 v I (Oval) 2011; BB 1-33 v P (Faisalabad) 2005-06. **LOI**: 161 (2004-05 to 2014-15); 1000 runs (1): 1080 (2007); HS 141 v A (Hobart) 2014-15; BB 3-9 v Z (Bulawayo) 2004-05 – taking a wicket with his third ball in LOI. **IT20**: 8 (2006 to 2014); HS 60* v NZ (Manchester) 2008. F-c Tours: A 2006-07, 2010-11, 2013-14; SA 2009-10; WI 2000-01 (Eng A), 2008-09, 2014-15; NZ 2007-08, 2012-13; I 2005-06, 2008-09, 2012-13; P 2005-06; SL 2002-03 (ECB Acad), 2004-05, 2007-08, 2011-12; B 2009-10; UAE 2011-12 (v P), 2015-16 (v P). 1000 runs (5); most – 1714 (2004). HS 262* v Sussex (Horsham) 2004. BB 4-4 v Middx (Lord's) 2004. LO HS 158 EL v India A (Worcester) 2010. LO BB 5-41 v Essex (Chelmsford) 2003 (NL). T20 HS 131. T20 BB 1-12.

[NO]**PATEL, Jeetan** Shashi, b Wellington, New Zealand 7 May 1980. 5'10''. RHB, OB. Wellington 1999-00 to 2018-19. Warwickshire 2009-19; cap 2012; captain 2018-19. *Wisden* 2014. **Tests** (NZ): 24 (2006-07 to 2016-17); HS 47 v I (Kolkata) 2016-17; BB 5-110 v WI (Napier) 2008-09. **LOI** (NZ): 43 (2005 to 2017); HS 34 v SL (Kingston) 2006-07; BB 3-11 v SA (Mumbai, BS) 2006-07. **IT20** (NZ): 11 (2005-06 to 2008-09); HS 5 v E (Auckland) 2007-08; BB 3-20 v SA (Johannesburg) 2005-06. F-c Tours (NZ): E 2008; SA 2005-06, 2012-13; I 2010-11, 2012, 2016-17; SL 2009, 2012-13; Z 2010-11, 2011-12; B 2008-09. HS 120 v Yorks (Birmingham) 2009. 50 wkts (7); most – 69 (2016). BB 8-36 (12-89 match) v Surrey (Birmingham) 2019. LO HS 50 v Kent (Birmingham) 2013 (Y40). LO BB 5-43 v Somerset (Birmingham) 2016 (RLC). T20 HS 34*. T20 BB 4-11.

T.R.Ambrose and L.Banks left the staff without making a County 1st XI appearance in 2020.

WARWICKSHIRE 2020

RESULTS SUMMARY

	Place	Won	Lost	Drew	NR
Bob Willis Trophy (Central Group)	3rd		1	4	
Vitality Blast (Central Group)	3rd	5	4		1

BOB WILLIS TROPHY AVERAGES
BATTING AND FIELDING

Cap		M	I	NO	HS	Runs	Avge	100	50	Ct/St
	T.T.Bresnan	4	6	2	105	214	53.50	1	–	5
2020	W.M.H.Rhodes	5	9	1	207	423	52.87	1	–	2
	D.R.Mousley	2	3	–	71	149	49.66	–	1	1
	M.J.Lamb	3	4	–	65	101	25.25	–	1	1
2001	I.R.Bell	5	8	–	90	184	23.00	–	2	5
2018	S.R.Hain	5	8	–	65	146	18.25	–	2	5
	A.T.Thomson	5	8	–	46	146	18.25	–	–	1
	R.M.Yates	5	9	1	88	137	17.12	–	1	2
	M.G.K.Burgess	5	8	–	39	135	16.87	–	–	15/1
2019	O.J.Hannon-Dalby	5	7	3	19	43	10.75	–	–	1
	C.N.Miles	3	5	2	13*	27	9.00	–	–	–
	H.J.H.Brookes	2	4	–	12	23	5.75	–	–	1

Also batted: E.A.Brookes (1 match) 6, 15*; L.C.Norwell (1) 12, 7*; R.N.Sidebottom (3) 0*, 13*; O.P.Stone (1 – cap 2020) 36* (1 ct).

BOWLING

	O	M	R	W	Avge	Best	5wI	10wM
O.P.Stone	17	3	49	4	12.25	4-39	–	–
O.J.Hannon-Dalby	196.3	53	523	25	20.92	6-33	2	1
L.C.Norwell	44	10	95	4	23.75	4-43	–	–
W.M.H.Rhodes	79.4	16	245	10	24.50	4-46	–	–
T.T.Bresnan	116	36	275	10	27.50	4-99	–	–
R.N.Sidebottom	88	12	331	8	41.37	3-37	–	–
C.N.Miles	74	17	265	4	66.25	1-51	–	–
A.T.Thomson	100	14	276	4	69.00	2- 3	–	–

Also bowled: E.A.Brookes 3-1-13-0; H.J.H.Brookes 51-6-203-2; D.R.Mousley 9-1-37-0; R.M.Yates 22-9-37-0.

The First-Class Averages (pp 209–221) give the records of Warwickshire players in all first-class county matches.

WARWICKSHIRE RECORDS

FIRST-CLASS CRICKET

Highest Total	For	810-4d		v	Durham	Birmingham	1994
	V	887		by	Yorkshire	Birmingham	1896
Lowest Total	For	16		v	Kent	Tonbridge	1913
	V	15		by	Hampshire	Birmingham	1922
Highest Innings	For	501*	B.C.Lara	v	Durham	Birmingham	1994
	V	322	I.V.A.Richards	for	Somerset	Taunton	1985

Highest Partnership for each Wicket

1st	377*	N.F.Horner/K.Ibadulla	v	Surrey	The Oval	1960
2nd	465*	J.A.Jameson/R.B.Kanhai	v	Glos	Birmingham	1974
3rd	327	S.P.Kinneir/W.G.Quaife	v	Lancashire	Birmingham	1901
4th	470	A.I.Kallicharran/G.W.Humpage	v	Lancashire	Southport	1982
5th	335	J.O.Troughton/T.R.Ambrose	v	Hampshire	Birmingham	2009
6th	327	L.J.Evans/T.R.Ambrose	v	Sussex	Birmingham	2015
7th	289*	I.R.Bell/T.Frost	v	Sussex	Horsham	2004
8th	228	A.J.W.Croom/R.E.S.Wyatt	v	Worcs	Dudley	1925
9th	233	I.J.L.Trott/J.S.Patel	v	Yorkshire	Birmingham	2009
10th	214	N.V.Knight/A.Richardson	v	Hampshire	Birmingham	2002

Best Bowling	For	10-41	J.D.Bannister	v	Comb Servs	Birmingham	1959
(Innings)	V	10-36	H.Verity	for	Yorkshire	Leeds	1931
Best Bowling	For	15-76	S.Hargreave	v	Surrey	The Oval	1903
(Match)	V	17-92	A.P.Freeman	for	Kent	Folkestone	1932

Most Runs – Season	2417	M.J.K.Smith	(av 60.42)	1959
Most Runs – Career	35146	D.L.Amiss	(av 41.64)	1960-87
Most 100s – Season	9	A.I.Kallicharran		1984
	9	B.C.Lara		1994
Most 100s – Career	78	D.L.Amiss		1960-87
Most Wkts – Season	180	W.E.Hollies	(av 15.13)	1946
Most Wkts – Career	2201	W.E.Hollies	(av 20.45)	1932-57
Most Career W-K Dismissals	800	E.J.Smith	(662 ct; 138 st)	1904-30
Most Career Catches in the Field	422	M.J.K.Smith		1956-75

LIMITED-OVERS CRICKET

Highest Total	50ov	392-5		v	Oxfordshire	Birmingham	1984
	40ov	321-7		v	Leics	Birmingham	2010
	T20	242-2		v	Derbyshire	Birmingham	2015
Lowest Total	50ov	94		v	Glos	Bristol	2000
	40ov	59		v	Yorkshire	Leeds	2001
	T20	73		v	Somerset	Taunton	2013
Highest Innings	50ov	206	A.I.Kallicharran	v	Oxfordshire	Birmingham	1984
	40ov	137	I.R.Bell	v	Yorkshire	Birmingham	2005
	T20	158*	B.B.McCullum	v	Derbyshire	Birmingham	2015
Best Bowling	50ov	7-32	R.G.D.Willis	v	Yorkshire	Birmingham	1981
	40ov	6-15	A.A.Donald	v	Yorkshire	Birmingham	1995
	T20	5-19	N.M.Carter	v	Worcs	Birmingham	2005

WORCESTERSHIRE

Formation of Present Club: 11 March 1865
Inaugural First-Class Match: 1899
Colours: Dark Green and Black
Badge: Shield Argent a Fess between three Pears Sable
County Championships: (5) 1964, 1965, 1974, 1988, 1989
NatWest Trophy Winners: (1) 1994
Benson and Hedges Cup Winners: (1) 1991
Pro 40/National League (Div 1) Winners: (1) 2007
Sunday League Winners: (3) 1971, 1987, 1988
Twenty20 Cup Winners: (1) 2018

Chief Executive: tba, County Ground, Blackfinch New Road, Worcester, WR2 4QQ • Tel: 01905 748474 Email: info@wccc.co.uk • Web: www.wccc.co.uk • Twitter: @WorcsCCC (80,168 followers)

Head of Player and Coaches Development: Kevin Sharp. **Head Coach**: Alex Gidman. **Asst/ Bowling Coach**: Alan Richardson. **Captains**: J.Leach (f-c and l-o) and M.M.Ali (T20). **Overseas Players**: B.J.Dwarshuis (T20 only). **2021 Testimonial**: none. **Head Groundsman**: Tim Packwood. **Scorer**: Sue Drinkwater. **Vitality Blast Name**: Worcestershire Rapids. ‡ New registration. ^{NQ} Not qualified for England.

Worcestershire revised their capping policy in 2002 and now award players with their County Colours when they make their Championship debut.

ALI, Moeen Munir (Moseley S), b Birmingham, Warwks 18 Jun 1987. Brother of A.K.Ali (Worcs, Glos and Leics 2000-12), cousin of Kabir Ali (Worcs, Rajasthan, Hants and Lancs 1999-2014). 6'0". LHB, OB. Squad No 8. Warwickshire debut 2005-06. Worcestershire debut 2007; captain 2020 to date (T20 only). Moors SC 2011-12. MT 2012-13. MCC 2012. IPL: RCB 2018 to date. PCA 2013. *Wisden* 2014. ECB L-O Central Contract 2020-21. Tests: 61 (2014 to 2020-21); 1000 runs (1): 1078 (2016); HS 155* v SL (Chester-le-St) 2016; BB 6-53 v SA (Lord's) 2017. Hat-trick v SA (Oval) 2017. LOI: 106 (2013-14 to 2020); HS 128 v Scotland (Christchurch) 2014-15; BB 4-46 v A (Manchester) 2018. IT20: 34 (2013-14 to 2020); HS 72* v A (Cardiff) 2015; BB 2-21 v I (Kanpur) 2016-17. F-c Tours: A 2017-18; SA 2015-16; WI 2014-15, 2018-19; NZ 2017-18; I 2016-17, 2020-21; SL 2013-14 (EL), 2018-19; B 2016-17; UAE 2015-16 (v P). 1000 runs (2); most – 1420 (2013). HS 250 v Glamorgan (Worcester) 2013. BB 6-29 (12-96 match) v Lancs (Manchester) 2012. LO HS 158 v Sussex (Horsham) 2011 (CB40). LO BB 4-33 v Notts (Nottingham) 2018 (RLC). T20 HS 121*. T20 BB 5-34.

BARNARD, Edward George (Shrewsbury S), b Shrewsbury, Shrops 20 Nov 1995. Younger brother of M.R.Barnard (Oxford MCCU 2010). 6'1". RHB, RMF. Squad No 30. Debut (Worcestershire) 2015. Shropshire 2012. HS 75 v Durham (Worcester) 2017. BB 6-37 (11-89 match) v Somerset (Taunton) 2018. LO HS 61 v Leics (Leicester) 2019 (RLC). LO BB 3-26 v Yorks (Worcester) 2019 (RLC). T20 HS 42*. T20 BB 3-29.

BROWN, Patrick Rhys (Bourne GS, Lincs), b Peterborough, Cambs 23 Aug 1998. 6'2". RHB, RMF. Squad No 36. Debut (Worcestershire) 2017. Worcestershire 2nd XI debut 2016. Lincolnshire 2016. IT20: 4 (2019-20); HS 4* v NZ (Wellington) 2019-20; BB 1-29 v NZ (Napier) 2019-20. HS 5* v Sussex (Worcester) 2017. BB 2-15 v Leics (Worcester) 2017. LO HS 3 v Somerset (Worcester) 2019 (RLC). LO BB 3-53 v Kent (Worcester) 2018 (RLC). T20 HS 7*. T20 BB 4-21.

COX, Oliver Ben (Bromsgrove S), b Wordsley, Stourbridge 2 Feb 1992. 5'10". RHB, WK. Squad No 10. Debut (Worcestershire) 2009. MCC 2017, 2019. HS 124 v Glos (Cheltenham) 2017. LO HS 122* v Kent (Worcester) 2018 (RLC). T20 HS 59*.

DELL, Joshua Jamie (Cheltenham C), b Tenbury Wells 26 Sep 1997. 6'3". RHB, RMF. Squad No 52. Debut (Worcestershire) 2019. Worcestershire 2nd XI debut 2015. England U19 2016. No 1st XI appearances in 2020. HS 61 v Durham (Worcester) 2019. LO HS 46 v West Indies A (Worcester) 2018.

D'OLIVEIRA, Brett Louis (Worcester SFC), b Worcester 28 Feb 1992. Son of D.B.D'Oliveira (Worcs 1982-95), grandson of B.L.D'Oliveira (Worcs, EP and England 1964-80). 5'9". RHB, LB. Squad No 15. Debut (Worcestershire) 2012. MCC 2018. HS 202* v Glamorgan (Cardiff) 2016. BB 7-92 v Glamorgan (Cardiff) 2019. LO HS 79 North v South (Bridgetown) 2017-18. LO BB 3-35 v Warwks (Worcester) 2013 (Y40). T20 HS 64. T20 BB 4-26.

‡[NQ]**DWARSHUIS, Ben**jamin James, b Kareela, NSW, Australia 23 June 1994. LHB, LFM. New South Wales 2016-17 to date (l-o only). Big Bash: SS 2014-15 to date. Awaiting f-c debut. LO HS 9 NSW v Tas (Sydney, NS) 2018-19. LO BB 2-37 NSW v SA (Adelaide) 2020-21. T20 HS 42*. T20 BB 4-13.

FELL, Thomas Charles (Oakham S; Oxford Brookes U), b Hillingdon, Middx 17 Oct 1993. 6'1". RHB, WK, occ OB. Squad No 29. Oxford MCCU 2013. Worcestershire debut 2013. 1000 runs (1): 1127 (2015). HS 171 v Middx (Worcester) 2015. LO HS 116* v Lancs (Worcester) 2016 (RLC). T20 HS 28.

FINCH, Adam William (Kingswinford S; Oldswinford Hospital SFC), b Wordsley, Stourbridge 28 May 2000. 6'4". RHB, RMF. Squad No 61. Debut (Worcestershire) 2019. Surrey 2020 (on loan). Worcestershire 2nd XI debut 2017. England U19 2018 to 2018-19. HS 18* v Australians (Worcester) 2019. CC HS 17 and Wo BB 2-23 v Glos (Worcester) 2019. BB 4-38 Sy v Essex (Chelmsford) 2020. T20 HS 3*. T20 BB 1-22.

HAYNES, Jack Alexander (Malvern C), b Worcester 30 Jan 2001. Son of G.R.Haynes (Worcestershire 1991-99); younger brother of J.L.Haynes (Worcestershire 2nd XI 2015-16). 6'1". RHB, OB. Squad No 17. Debut (Worcestershire) 2019. Worcestershire 2nd XI debut 2016. England U19 2018. HS 51 v Glos (Bristol) 2020 and 51 v Warwks (Worcester) 2020. LO HS 33 v West Indies A (Worcester) 2018. T20 HS 41.

LEACH, Joseph (Shrewsbury S; Leeds U), b Stafford 30 Oct 1990. Elder brother of S.G.Leach (Oxford MCCU 2014-16). 6'1". RHB, RMF. Squad No 23. Leeds/Bradford MCCU 2012. Worcestershire debut 2012; captain 2017 to date. Staffordshire 2008-09. HS 114 v Glos (Cheltenham) 2013. 50 wkts (3); most – 69 (2017). BB 6-73 v Warwks (Birmingham) 2015. LO HS 63 v Yorks (Leeds) 2016 (RLC). LO BB 4-30 v Northants (Worcester) 2015 (RLC). T20 HS 24. T20 BB 5-33.

LIBBY, Jacob ('Jake') Daniel (Plymouth C; UWIC), b Plymouth, Devon 3 Jan 1993. 5'9". RHB, OB. Squad No 2. Cardiff MCCU 2014. Nottinghamshire 2014-19, scoring 108 v Sussex (Nottingham) on debut. Northamptonshire 2016 (on loan). Worcestershire debut 2020. Cornwall 2011-14. HS 184 and BB2-45 v Glamorgan (Worcester) 2020. LO HS 66 Nt v Leics (Nottingham) 2019 (RLC). T20 HS 75*. T20 BB 1-11.

MILTON, Alexander Geoffrey (Malvern C; Cardiff U), b Redhill, Surrey 19 May 1996. 5'7''. RHB, LB, occ WK. Squad No 12. Cardiff MCCU 2016-18. Worcestershire debut 2018. Worcestershire 2nd XI debut 2012. Glamorgan 2nd XI 2015. Herefordshire 2016. No 1st XI appearances in 2020. HS 104* v Somerset (Worcester) 2018 – on county f-c debut, sharing Wo record 10th wkt partnership of 136 with S.J.Magoffin. LO HS 0.

MITCHELL, Daryl Keith Henry (Prince Henry's HS; University C, Worcester), b Badsey, near Evesham 25 Nov 1983. 5'10''. RHB, RM. Squad No 27. Debut (Worcestershire) 2005; captain 2011-16; benefit 2016. Mountaineers 2011-12. MCC 2015. 1000 runs (5); most – 1334 (2014). HS 298 v Somerset (Taunton) 2009. BB 4-49 v Yorks (Leeds) 2009. LO HS 107 v Sussex (Hove) 2013 (Y40). LO BB 4-19 v Northants (Milton Keynes) 2014 (RLC). T20 HS 68*. T20 BB 5-28.

MORRIS, Charles Andrew John (King's C, Taunton; Oxford Brookes U), b Hereford 6 Jul 1992. 6'0''. RHB, RMF. Squad No 31. Oxford MCCU 2012-14. Worcestershire debut 2013. MCC Univs 2012. Devon 2011-12. HS 53* v Australians (Worcester) 2019. CC HS 29* v Glos (Worcester) 2019. 50 wkts (2); most – 56 (2014). BB 7-45 v Leics (Leicester) 2019. LO HS 16* v Northants (Milton Keynes) 2014 (RLC). LO BB 4-33 v Durham (Gosforth) 2018 (RLC). T20 HS 3. T20 BB 2-30.

PENNINGTON, Dillon Young (Wrekin C), b Shrewsbury, Shrops 26 Feb 1999. 6'2''. RHB, RMF. Squad No 22. Debut (Worcestershire) 2018. Worcestershire 2nd XI debut 2017. Shropshire 2017. HS 37 v Somerset (Worcester) 2018. BB 4-53 v Yorks (Scarborough) 2018. LO HS 4* and LO BB 5-67 v West Indies A (Worcester) 2018. T20 HS 10*. T20 BB 4-9.

‡RODERICK, Gareth Hugh (Maritzburg C), b Durban, South Africa 29 Aug 1991. 6'0''. RHB, WK. Squad No 9. UK passport, qualifying for England in October 2018. KZN 2010-11 to 2011-12. Gloucestershire 2013-20; cap 2013; captain 2016-17. HS 171 Gs v Leics (Bristol) 2014. LO HS 104 Gs v Leics (Leicester) 2015 (RLC). T20 HS 32.

STANLEY, Mitchell Terry (Idsall S, Shifnal; Shrewsbury SFC), b Telford, Shrops 17 Mar 2001. RHB, RFM. Squad No 38. Awaiting 1st XI debut.

TONGUE, Joshua Charles (King's S, Worcester; Worcester SFC), b Redditch 15 Nov 1997. 6'5''. RHB, RM. Squad No 24. Debut (Worcestershire) 2016. Worcestershire 2nd XI debut 2015. HS 41 and BB 6-97 v Glamorgan (Worcester) 2017. LO HS 34 v Warwks (Worcester) 2019 (RLC). LO BB 2-35 v Lancs (Manchester) 2019 (RLC). T20 HS 2*. T20 BB 2-32.

WESSELS, Mattheus Hendrik ('**Riki**') (Woodridge C, Pt Elizabeth; Northampton U), b Marogudoore, Queensland, Australia 12 Nov 1985. Left Australia when 2 months old. Qualified for England after gaining a UK passport in July 2016. Son of K.C.Wessels (OFS, Sussex, WP, NT, Q, EP, GW, Australia and South Africa 1973-74 to 1999-00). 5'11''. RHB, WK. Squad No 99. MCC 2004. Northamptonshire 2005-09. Nondescripts 2007-08. MWR 2009-10 to 2011-12. Nottinghamshire 2011-18; cap 2014. Worcestershire debut 2019. Big Bash: SS 2014-15. 1000 runs (2); most – 1213 (2014). HS 202* Nt v Sussex (Nottingham) 2017. Wo HS 118 v Durham (Worcester) 2019. BB 1-10 MWR v MT (Bulawayo) 2009-10. LO HS 146 Nt v Northants (Nottingham) 2016 (RLC). LO BB 1-0 MWR v MT (Bulawayo) 2009-10. T20 HS 110.

WHITELEY, Ross Andrew (Repton S), b Sheffield, Yorks 13 Sep 1988. 6'2". LHB, LM. Squad No 44. Derbyshire 2008-13. Worcestershire debut 2013. HS 130* De v Kent (Derby) 2011. Wo HS 101 v Yorks (Scarborough) 2015. BB 2-6 De v Hants (Derby) 2012. Wo BB 2-35 v Middx (Worcester) 2019. LO HS 131 v Leics (Leicester) 2019 (RLC). LO BB 4-58 v West Indies A (Worcester) 2018. T20 HS 91*. T20 BB 1-10.

RELEASED/RETIRED

(Having made a County 1st XI appearance in 2020)

PARNELL, W.D. – see NORTHAMPTONSHIRE.

NQRUTHERFORD, Hamish Duncan, b Dunedin, New Zealand 27 Apr 1989. Son of K.R.Rutherford (Gauteng, Otago, Transvaal & New Zealand 1982-83 to 1999-00). Nephew of I.A.Rutherford (C Districts, Otago & Worcestershire 1974-75 to 1983-84). 5'10". LHB, SLA. Otago 2008-09 to date. Essex 2013. Derbyshire 2015-16. Worcestershire 2019. **Tests** (NZ): 16 (2012-13 to 2014-15); HS 171 v E (Dunedin) 2012-13 – on debut. **LOI** (NZ): 4 (2012-13 to 2013-14); HS 11 v E (Napier) 2012-13. **IT20** (NZ): 7 (2012-13 to 2013-14); HS 62 v E (Oval) 2013. F-c Tours (NZ): E 2013, 2014 (NZ A); WI 2014; B 2013-14. 1000 runs (0+1): 1077 (2012-13). HS 239 Otago v Wellington (Dunedin) 2011-12. CC HS 123 v Leics (Leicester) 2019 – on Wo debut. BB – . LO HS 155 Otago v CD (Dunedin) 2019-20. LO BB 1-4 Otago v Wellington (Dunedin) 2017-18. T20 HS 106.

G.L.S.Scrimshaw, B.J.Twohig and O.E.Westbury left the staff without making a County 1st XI appearance in 2020.

WORCESTERSHIRE 2020

RESULTS SUMMARY

	Place	Won	Lost	Drew	NR
Bob Willis Trophy (Central Group)	2nd	2	1	2	
Vitality Blast (Central Group)	6th	2	7		1

BOB WILLIS TROPHY AVERAGES
BATTING AND FIELDING

Cap†		M	I	NO	HS	Runs	Avge	100	50	Ct/St
2020	J.D.Libby	5	9	–	184	498	55.33	1	3	2
2012	B.L.D'Oliveira	5	8	1	174	367	52.42	1	1	2
2013	T.C.Fell	5	9	2	110*	336	48.00	1	1	3
2009	O.B.Cox	5	8	3	45*	225	45.00	–	–	25
2005	D.K.H.Mitchell	5	9	–	110	384	42.66	1	2	7
2019	J.A.Haynes	5	9	–	51	285	40.71	–	2	1
2015	E.G.Barnard	5	6	2	48*	84	21.00	–	–	5
2019	M.H.Wessels	5	8	–	88	157	19.62	–	1	4
2012	J.Leach	5	6	1	17	47	9.40	–	–	1
2018	D.Y.Pennington	3	4	2	11*	15	7.50	–	–	1
2017	J.C.Tongue	4	3	2	1*	1	1.00	–	–	–

Also played: C.A.J.Morris (3 matches – cap 2014) did not bat.

BOWLING

	O	M	R	W	Avge	Best	5wI	10wM
E.G.Barnard	148.5	40	390	18	21.66	4-25	–	–
C.A.J.Morris	99.3	21	315	14	22.50	5-80	1	–
D.Y.Pennington	90.1	22	248	11	22.54	3-30	–	–
J.Leach	169.3	44	490	19	25.78	4-67	–	–
J.C.Tongue	117.1	26	363	14	25.92	3-38	–	–
B.L.D'Oliveira	95	13	312	6	52.00	2-31	–	–

Also bowled: J.D.Libby 14.4-2-46-2; D.K.H.Mitchell 31-7-63-1.

The First-Class Averages (pp 209–221) give the records of Worcestershire players in all first-class county matches.
† Worcestershire revised their capping policy in 2002 and now award players with their County Colours when they make their Championship debut.

WORCESTERSHIRE RECORDS

FIRST-CLASS CRICKET

Highest Total	For	701-6d	v	Surrey	Worcester	2007
	V	701-4d	by	Leics	Worcester	1906
Lowest Total	For	24	v	Yorkshire	Huddersfield	1903
	V	30	by	Hampshire	Worcester	1903
Highest Innings	For	405*	G.A.Hick	v	Somerset	Taunton	1988
	V	331*	J.D.B.Robertson	for	Middlesex	Worcester	1949

Highest Partnership for each Wicket

1st	309	H.K.Foster/F.L.Bowley	v	Derbyshire	Derby	1901
2nd	316	S.C.Moore/V.S.Solanki	v	Glos	Cheltenham	2008
3rd	438*	G.A.Hick/T.M.Moody	v	Hampshire	Southampton[1]	1997
4th	330	B.F.Smith/G.A.Hick	v	Somerset	Taunton	2006
5th	393	E.G.Arnold/W.B.Burns	v	Warwicks	Birmingham	1909
6th	265	G.A.Hick/S.J.Rhodes	v	Somerset	Taunton	1988
7th	256	D.A.Leatherdale/S.J.Rhodes	v	Notts	Nottingham	2002
8th	184	S.J.Rhodes/S.R.Lampitt	v	Derbyshire	Kidderminster	1991
9th	181	J.A.Cuffe/R.D.Burrows	v	Glos	Worcester	1907
10th	136	A.G.Milton/S.J.Magoffin	v	Somerset	Worcester	2018

Best Bowling	For	9- 23	C.F.Root	v	Lancashire	Worcester	1931
(Innings)	V	10- 51	J.Mercer	for	Glamorgan	Worcester	1936
Best Bowling	For	15- 87	A.J.Conway	v	Glos	Moreton-in-M	1914
(Match)	V	17-212	J.C.Clay	for	Glamorgan	Swansea	1937

Most Runs – Season		2654	H.H.I.H.Gibbons	(av 52.03)	1934
Most Runs – Career		34490	D.Kenyon	(av 34.18)	1946-67
Most 100s – Season		10	G.M.Turner		1970
		10	G.A.Hick		1988
Most 100s – Career		106	G.A.Hick		1984-2008
Most Wkts – Season		207	C.F.Root	(av 17.52)	1925
Most Wkts – Career		2143	R.T.D.Perks	(av 23.73)	1930-55
Most Career W-K Dismissals		1095	S.J.Rhodes	(991 ct; 104 st)	1985-2004
Most Career Catches in the Field		528	G.A.Hick		1984-2008

LIMITED-OVERS CRICKET

Highest Total	50ov	404-3		v	Devon	Worcester	1987
	40ov	376-6		v	Surrey	The Oval	2010
	T20	227-6		v	Northants	Kidderminster	2007
Lowest Total	50ov	58		v	Ireland	Worcester	2009
	40ov	86		v	Yorkshire	Leeds	1969
	T20	53		v	Lancashire	Manchester	2016
Highest Innings	50ov	192	C.J.Ferguson	v	Leics	Worcester	2018
	40ov	160	T.M.Moody	v	Kent	Worcester	1991
	T20	127	T.Kohler-Cadmore	v	Durham	Worcester	2016
Best Bowling	50ov	7-19	N.V.Radford	v	Beds	Bedford	1991
	40ov	6-16	Shoaib Akhtar	v	Glos	Worcester	2005
	T20	5-24	A.Hepburn	v	Notts	Worcester	2017

YORKSHIRE

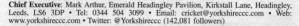

Formation of Present Club: 8 January 1863
Substantial Reorganisation: 10 December 1891
Inaugural First-Class Match: 1864
Colours: Dark Blue, Light Blue and Gold
Badge: White Rose
County Championships (since 1890): (32) 1893, 1896,
1898, 1900, 1901, 1902, 1905, 1908, 1912, 1919, 1922,
1923, 1924, 1925, 1931, 1932, 1933, 1935, 1937, 1938,
1939, 1946, 1959, 1960, 1962, 1963, 1966, 1967, 1968,
2001, 2014, 2015
Joint Champions: (1) 1949
Gillette/C&G Trophy Winners: (3) 1965, 1969, 2002
Benson and Hedges Cup Winners: (1) 1987
Sunday League Winners: (1) 1983
Twenty20 Cup Winners: (0); best – Finalist 2012

Chief Executive: Mark Arthur, Emerald Headingley Pavilion, Kirkstall Lane, Headingley, Leeds, LS6 3DP • Tel: 0344 504 3099 • Email: cricket@yorkshireccc.com • Web: www.yorkshireccc.com • Twitter: @Yorkshireccc (142,081 followers)

Director of Cricket: Martyn Moxon. **1st XI Coach**: Andrew Gale. **Batting Coach**: Paul Grayson. **Bowling Coach**: Richard Pyrah. **Captains**: S.A.Patterson (f-c and 1-o) and D.J.Willey (T20). **Overseas Players**: L.H.Ferguson (T20 only) and D.Olivier. **2021 Testimonial**: A.Lyth. **Head Groundsman**: Andy Fogarty. **Scorer**: John Potter and John Virr. **Vitality Blast Name**: Yorkshire Vikings. ‡ New registration. ^{NQ} Not qualified for England.

BAIRSTOW, Jonathan Marc (St Peter's S, York; Leeds Met U), b Bradford 26 Sep 1989. Son of D.L.Bairstow (Yorkshire, GW and England 1970-90); brother of A.D.Bairstow (Derbyshire 1995). 6'0''. RHB, WK, occ RM. Squad No 21. Debut (Yorkshire) 2009; cap 2011. Inaugural winner of Young Wisden Schools Cricketer of the Year 2008. YC 2011. **ECB L-O Central Contract 2020-21. Tests**: 74 (2012 to 2020-21); 1000 runs (1): 1470 (2016); HS 167* v SL (Lord's) 2016. Took a world record 70 dismissals in 2016, as well as scoring a record number of runs in a calendar year for a keeper. **LOI**: 83 (2011 to 2020); 1000 runs (1): 1025 (2018); HS 141* v WI (Southampton) 2017. **IT20**: 46 (2011 to 2020-21); HS 86* v SA (Cape Town) 2020-21. F-c Tours: A 2013-14, 2017-18; SA 2014-15 (EL), 2015-16, 2019-20; WI 2010-11 (EL), 2018-19; NZ 2017-18; I 2012-13, 2016-17, 2020-21; SL 2013-14 (EL), 2018-19, 2020-21; B 2016-17; UAE 2015-16 (v P). 1000 runs (3); most – 1286 (2016). HS 246 v Hants (Leeds) 2016. LO HS 174 v Durham (Leeds) 2017 (RLC). T20 HS 114.

BALLANCE, Gary Simon (Peterhouse S, Marondera, Zimbabwe; Harrow S; Leeds Met U), b Harare, Zimbabwe 22 Nov 1989. Nephew of G.S.Ballance (Rhodesia B 1978-79) and D.L.Houghton (Rhodesia/Zimbabwe 1978-79 to 1997-98). 6'0''. LHB, LB. Squad No 19. Debut (Yorkshire) 2008; cap 2012; captain 2017 to 2018 (*part*). MWR 2010-11 to 2011-12. No 1st XI appearances in 2020. *Wisden* 2014. **Tests**: 23 (2013-14 to 2017); HS 156 v I (Southampton) 2014; BB – . **LOI**: 16 (2013 to 2014-15); HS 79 v A (Melbourne) 2013-14. F-c Tours: A 2013-14; WI 2014-15; B 2016-17. 1000 runs (4+1); most – 1363 (2013). HS 210 MWR v SR (Masvingo) 2011-12. Y HS 203* v Hants (Southampton) 2017. BB – . LO HS 156 v Leics (Leeds) 2019 (RLC). T20 HS 79.

BESS, Dominic Mark (Blundell's S), b Exeter, Devon 22 Jul 1997. Cousin of Z.G.G.Bess (Devon 2015 to date), J.J.Bess (Devon 2007-18) and L.F.O.Bess (Devon 2017 to date). RHB, OB. Squad No 22. Somerset 2016-19. Yorkshire debut 2019 (on loan). MCC 2018, 2019. Somerset 2nd XI 2013-18. Devon 2015-16. **ECB Incremental Contract 2020-21**. **Tests**: 14 (2018 to 2020-21); HS 57 v P (Lord's) 2018; BB 5-30 v SL (Galle) 2019. F-c Tours: A 2019-20 (EL); SA 2019-20; WI 2017-18 (EL); I 2018-19 (EL), 2020-21; SL 2019-20, 2020-21. HS 107 MCC v Essex (Bridgetown) 2018. CC HS 92 Sm v Hants (Taunton) 2018. Y HS 91* and Y BB 3-45 v Essex (Leeds) 2019. BB 7-117 (10-162 match) Sm v Hants (Taunton) 2017. LO HS 24* South v North (Cave Hill) 2017-18. LO BB 3-35 EL v Pakistan A (Abu Dhabi) 2018-19. T20 HS 5*. T20 BB 2-30.

BIRKHEAD, Benjamin David (Huddersfield New C), b Halifax 28 Oct 1998. 5'9½". RHB, WK. Squad No 30. Yorkshire 2nd XI debut 2016. Awaiting f-c debut. LO HS – . T20 HS – .

BROOK, Harry Cherrington (Sedbergh S), b Keighley 22 Feb 1999. 5'11". RHB, RM. Squad No 88. Debut (Yorkshire) 2016. Yorkshire 2nd XI debut 2015. England U19 2016-17 to 2017. HS 124 v Essex (Chelmsford) 2018. BB 1-54 v Somerset (Scarborough) 2017. LO HS 103 v Leics (Leeds) 2019 (RLC). T20 HS 50*. T20 BB 1-13.

COAD, Benjamin Oliver (Thirsk S & SFC), b Harrogate 10 Jan 1994. 6'2". RHB, RM. Squad No 10. Debut (Yorkshire) 2016; cap 2018. HS 48 v Surrey (Scarborough) 2019. 50 wkts (1): 53 (2017). BB 6-25 v Lancs (Leeds) 2017. LO HS 9 v Hants (Southampton) 2018 (RLC). LO BB 4-63 v Derbys (Leeds) 2017 (RLC). T20 HS 7. T20 BB 3-40.

DUKE, Harry George (QEGS, Wakefield), b Wakefield 6 Sep 2001. 5'8". RHB, WK. Yorkshire 2nd XI debut 2019. Awaiting 1st XI debut.

^{NQ}**FERGUSON, Lachlan** Hammond ('Lockie'), b Auckland, New Zealand 13 Jun 1991. RHB, RF. Auckland 2012-13 to date. Derbyshire 2018. IPL: RPS 2017. KKR 2019 to date. **Tests** (NZ): 1 (2019-20); HS 1* and BB – v A (Perth) 2019-20. **LOI** (NZ): 37 (2016-17 to 2019-20); HS 19 v E (Mt Maunganui) 2017-18; BB 5-45 v P (Dubai, DSC) 2018-19. **IT20** (NZ): 11 (2016-17 to 2020-21); HS 1 v P (Dubai, DSC) 2018-19; BB 5-21 v WI (Auckland) 2020-21. F-c Tour (NZ): A 2019-20; I 2017-18 (NZA). HS 41 Auckland v Canterbury (Rangiora) 2016-17. CC HS 16 De v Kent (Derby) 2018 and 16 De v Middx (Lord's) 2018. BB 7-34 (12-78 match) Auckland v Otago (Auckland) 2017-18. CC BB 4-56 De v Glos (Derby) 2018. LO HS 24 Auckland v Otago (Auckland) 2016-17. LO BB 6-27 Auckland v ND (Auckland) 2016-17. T20 HS 24*. T20 BB 5-21.

FISHER, Matthew David (Easingwold SS), b York 9 Nov 1997. 6'1". RHB, RFM. Squad No 7. Debut (Yorkshire) 2015. MCC 2018. Yorkshire 2nd XI debut 2013, aged 15y 201d. England U19 2014. HS 47* v Kent (Leeds) 2019. BB 5-54 v Warwks (Leeds) 2017. LO HS 36* v Worcs (Worcester) 2017 (RLC). LO BB 3-32 v Leics (Leeds) 2015 (RLC). T20 HS 17*. T20 BB 5-22.

FRAINE, William Alan Richard (Silcoates S; Bromsgrove SFC; Durham U), b Huddersfield, Yorks 13 Jun 1996. 6'2". RHB, RM. Squad No 31. Durham MCCU 2017-18. Nottinghamshire 2018. Yorkshire debut 2019. Worcestershire 2nd XI 2015-16. Nottinghamshire 2nd XI 2017-18. Herefordshire 2016. HS 106 v Surrey (Scarborough) 2019. LO HS 13 Nt v Lancs (Manchester) 2018 (RLC). T20 HS 44*.

HILL, George Christopher Hindley (Sedbergh S), b Keighley 24 Jan 2001. 6'2½". RHB, RMF. Squad No 18. Debut (Yorkshire) 2020. Yorkshire 2nd XI debut 2018. England U19 2018-19. HS 29 and BB 1-27 v Lancs (Leeds) 2020. T20 HS 14. T20 BB 1-9.

KOHLER-CADMORE, Tom (Malvern C), b Chatham, Kent 19 Aug 1994. 6'2". RHB, OB. Squad No 32. Worcestershire 2014-17. Yorkshire debut 2017; cap 2019. 1000 runs (1): 1004 (2019). HS 176 v Leeds/Brad MCCU (Leeds) 2019. CC HS 169 Wo v Glos (Worcester) 2016. LO HS 164 v Durham (Chester-le-St) 2018 (RLC). T20 HS 127 Wo v Durham (Worcester) 2016 – Wo record, winning Walter Lawrence Trophy for fastest 100 (43 balls).

LEECH, Dominic James (Nunthorpe Ac; Q Ethelburga's S, York), b Middlesbrough 10 Jan 2001. 6'2½". RHB, RMF. Squad No 8. Debut (Yorkshire) 2020. Yorkshire 2nd XI debut 2018. HS 1 v Notts (Nottingham) 2020. BB 2-72 v Derbys (Leeds) 2020.

LOTEN, Thomas William (Pocklington S), b York 8 Jan 1999. 6'5". RHB, RMF. Squad No 40. Debut (Yorkshire) 2019. Yorkshire 2nd XI debut 2018. HS 58 v Warwks (Birmingham) 2019. LO HS – .

LYTH, Adam (Caedmon S, Whitby; Whitby Community C), b Whitby 25 Sep 1987. 5'8". LHB, RM. Squad No 9. Debut (Yorkshire) 2007; cap 2010; testimonial 2020-21. MCC 2017. PCA 2014. *Wisden* 2014. **Tests**: 7 (2015); HS 107 v NZ (Leeds) 2015. F-c Tours (EL): SA 2014-15; WI 2010-11. 1000 runs (3); most – 1619 (2014). HS 251 v Lancs (Manchester) 2014, sharing in Y record 6th wicket partnership of 296 with A.U.Rashid. BB 2-9 v Middx (Scarborough) 2016. LO HS 144 v Lancs (Manchester) 2018 (RLC). LO BB 2-27 v Derbys (Leeds) 2019 (RLC). T20 HS 161 v Northants (Leeds) 2017 – Y & UK record; 5th highest score in all T20 cricket. T20 BB 5-31.

MALAN, Dawid Johannes (Paarl HS), b Roehampton, Surrey 3 Sep 1987. Son of D.J.Malan (WP B and Transvaal B 1978-79 to 1981-82), elder brother of C.C.Malan (Loughborough MCCU 2009-10). 6'0". LHB, LB. Squad No 29. Boland 2005-06. Middlesex 2008-19, scoring 132* v Northants (Uxbridge) on debut; cap 2010; T20 captain 2016-19; captain 2018-19. Yorkshire debut/cap 2020. MCC 2010-11, 2013. **ECB Incremental Contract 2020-21**. **Tests**: 15 (2017 to 2018); HS 140 v A (Perth) 2017-18; BB – . **LOI**: 1 (2019); HS 24 v Ire (Dublin) 2019. **IT20**: 19 (2017 to 2020-21); HS 103* v NZ (Napier) 2019-20; BB 1-27 v NZ (Hamilton) 2017-18. F-c Tours: A 2017-18; NZ 2017-18. 1000 runs (3); most – 1137 runs (2014). HS 219 v Derbys (Leeds) 2020. BB 5-61 M v Lancs (Liverpool) 2012. Y BB 2-24 v Notts (Nottingham) 2020. LO HS 185* EL v Sri Lanka A (Northampton) 2016. LO BB 4-25 PDSC v Partex (Savar) 2014-15. T20 HS 117. T20 BB 2-10.

^(NQ)**OLIVIER, Duanne**, b Groblersdal, South Africa 9 May 1992. 6'4". RHB, RFM. Squad No 74. Free State 2010-11 to 2017-18. Knights 2013-14 to 2018-19. Derbyshire 2018. Yorkshire debut 2019; cap 2020. **Tests** (SA): 10 (2016-17 to 2018-19); HS 10* v P (Cape Town) 2018-19; BB 6-37 (11-96 match) v P (Centurion) 2018-19. **LOI** (SA): 2 (2018-19); HS – ; BB 2-73 v P (Port Elizabeth) 2018-19. F-c Tours (SA): E 2017; A 2016 (SAA); I 2018 (SAA); Z 2016 (SAA). HS 72 FS v Namibia (Bloemfontein) 2014-15. CC HS 40* De v Warwks (Birmingham) 2018. Y HS 24 v Kent (Leeds) 2019. 50 wkts (0+3); most – 64 (2016-17). BB 6-37 (*see* Tests). CC BB 5-20 (10-125 match) De v Durham (Chester-le-St) 2018. Y BB 5-96 v Notts (Nottingham) 2019. LO HS 25* and LO BB 4-34 Knights v Lions (Kimberley) 2017-18. T20 HS 15*. T20 BB 4-28.

PATTERSON, Steven Andrew (Malet Lambert CS; St Mary's SFC, Hull; Leeds U), b Beverley 3 Oct 1983. 6'4". RHB, RMF. Squad No 17. Debut (Yorkshire) 2005; cap 2012; testimonial 2017; captain 2018 (*part*) to date. Bradford/Leeds UCCE 2003 (not f-c). HS 63* v Warwks (Birmingham) 2016. 50 wkts (2); most – 53 (2012). BB 6-40 v Essex (Chelmsford) 2018. LO HS 25* v Worcs (Leeds) 2006 (P40). LO BB 6-32 v Derbys (Leeds) 2010. T20 HS 3*. T20 BB 4-30.

NQPILLANS, Mathew William (Pretoria BHS; U of Pretoria), b Durban, South Africa 4 Jul 1991. Qualifies for England in 2023, ancestral visa. 6'6''. RHB, RF. Squad No 13. Northerns 2012-13. KwaZulu-Natal Inland 2013-14 to 2015-16. Dolphins 2013-14 to 2015-16. Surrey 2016-18. Leicestershire 2017 (on loan). Yorkshire debut 2018. HS 56 Le v Northants (Northampton) 2017. Y HS 8 v Notts (Nottingham) 2018. BB 6-67 (10-129 match) Dolphins v Knights (Durban) 2014-15. CC BB 3-63 Le v Sussex (Arundel) 2017. Y BB 2-34 v Leeds/Brad MCCU (Leeds) 2019. LO HS 31 v Worcs (Worcester) 2019 (RLC). LO BB 5-29 v Leics (Leeds) 2019 (RLC). T20 HS 34*. T20 BB 3-15.

POYSDEN, Joshua Edward (Cardinal Newman S, Hove; Anglia RU), b Shoreham-by-Sea, Sussex 8 Aug 1991. 5'9''. LHB, LB. Squad No 14. Cambridge MCCU 2011-13. Warwickshire 2015-18. Yorkshire debut 2018. Unicorns (l-o) 2013. HS 47 CU v Surrey (Cambridge) 2011. CC HS 20* v Lancs (Manchester) 2018. BB 5-29 Wa v Glamorgan (Birmingham) 2018. Y BB 3-128 v Worcs (Scarborough) 2018. LO HS 10* Unicorns v Glos (Wormsley) 2013 (Y40). LO BB 3-33 Unicorns v Middx (Lord's) 2013 (Y40). T20 BB 9*. T20 BB 4-51.

RASHID, Adil Usman (Belle Vue S, Bradford), b Bradford 17 Feb 1988. 5'8''. RHB, LBG. Squad No 3. Debut (Yorkshire) 2006; cap 2008; testimonial 2018. Signed white ball only contract in 2020. MCC 2007-09. Big Bash: AS 2015-16. YC 2007. Match double (114, 48, 8-157 and 2-45) for England U19 v India U19 (Taunton) 2006. **ECB L-O Central Contract 2020-21. Tests**: 19 (2015-16 to 2018-19), taking 5-64 v P (Abu Dhabi) on debut; HS 61 v P (Dubai, DSC) 2015-16; BB 5-49 v SL (Colombo, SSC) 2018-19. **LOI**: 106 (2009 to 2020); HS 69 v NZ (Birmingham) 2015; BB 5-27 v Ire (Bristol) 2017. **IT20**: 52 (2009 to 2020-21); HS 9* v SA (Nottingham) 2009; BB 3-11 v SL (Colombo, RPS) 2018-19. F-c Tours: WI 2010-11 (EL), 2018-19; I 2007-08 (EL), 2016-17; SL 2018-19; B 2006-07 (Eng A), 2016-17; UAE 2015-16 (v P). HS 180 v Somerset (Leeds) 2013. 50 wkts (2); most – 65 (2008). BB 7-107 v Hants (Southampton) 2008. LO HS 71 v Glos (Leeds) 2014 (RLC). LO BB 5-27 (*see LOI*). T20 HS 36*. T20 BB 4-19.

REVIS, Matthew Liam (Ilkley GS), b Steeton 15 Nov 2001. 6'4½''. RHB, RM. Debut (Yorkshire) 2019. Yorkshire 2nd XI debut 2019. HS 9 v Kent (Leeds) 2019. T20 HS 0*.

ROOT, Joseph Edward (King Ecgbert S, Sheffield; Worksop C), b Sheffield 30 Dec 1990. Elder brother of W.T.Root (*see GLAMORGAN*). RHB, OB. Squad No 66. Debut (Yorkshire) 2010; cap 2012. YC 2012. **ECB Test & L-O Central Contract 2020-21. Tests**: 103 (2012-13 to 2020-21, 50 as captain); 1000 runs (2); most – 1477 (2016); HS 254 v P (Manchester) 2016; BB 5-8 v I (Ahmedabad) 2020-21. **LOI**: 149 (2012-13 to 2020); HS 133* v B (Oval) 2017; BB 3-52 v Ire (Lord's) 2017. **IT20**: 32 (2012-13 to 2019); HS 90* v A (Southampton) 2013; BB 2-9 v WI (Kolkata) 2015-16. F-c Tours(C=Captain): A 2013-14, 2017-18C; SA 2015-16, 2019-20C; WI 2014-15, 2018-19C; NZ 2012-13, 2017-18C, 2019-20C; I 2012-13, 2016-17, 2020-21C; B 2016-17. UAE 2015-16 (v P). 1000 runs (3); most – 1228 (2013). HS 254 (*see Tests*). CC HS 236 v Derbys (Leeds) 2013. SL BB 5-8 (*see Tests*). Y BB 4-5 v Lancs (Manchester) 2018. LO HS 133* (*see LOI*). LO BB 3-52 (*see LOI*). T20 HS 92*. T20 BB 2-7.

SHUTT, Jack William (Kirk Balk S; Thomas Rotherham C), b Barnsley 24 Jun 1997. 6'0''. RHB, OB. Squad No 24. Debut (Yorkshire) 2020. Yorkshire 2nd XI debut 2016. HS 7* v Durham (Chester-le-St) 2020. BB 2-14 v Notts (Nottingham) 2020. T20 HS 0*. T20 BB 5-11.

SULLIVAN, Joshua Richard (Temple Moor S), b Leeds 4 Aug 2000. 5'11½''. RHB, LBG. Squad No 4. Yorkshire 2nd XI debut 2018. Awaiting 1st XI debut.

TATTERSALL, Jonathan Andrew (King James S, Knaresborough), b Harrogate 15 Dec 1994. 5'8''. RHB, LB. Squad No 12. Debut (Yorkshire) 2018. HS 135* v Leeds/Brad MCCU (Leeds) 2019. HS 92 v Notts (Scarborough) 2019. LO HS 89 v Hants (Southampton) 2018 (RLC). T20 HS 53*.

THOMPSON, Jordan Aaron (Benton Park S), b Leeds 9 Oct 1996. 5'11". LHB, RM. Squad No 44. Debut (Yorkshire) 2019. Yorkshire 2nd XI debut 2014. HS 98 v Notts (Nottingham) 2020. BB 5-31 Leics (Leeds) 2020. LO BB – . T20 HS 50. T20 BB 3-23.

WAITE, Matthew James (Brigshaw HS), b Leeds 24 Dec 1995. 6'0". RHB, RFM. Squad No 6. Debut (Yorkshire) 2017. No 1st XI appearances in 2020. HS 42 and CC BB 3-91 v Notts (Nottingham) 2018. BB 5-16 v Leeds/Brad MCCU (Leeds) 2019. LO HS 71 v Warwks (Birmingham) 2017 (RLC). LO BB 4-65 v Worcs (Worcester) 2017 (RLC). T20 HS 19*. T20 BB 1-6.

WHARTON, James Henry (Holmfirth HS; Greenhead C), b Huddersfield 1 Feb 2001. 6'4". RHB, OB. Squad No 23. Yorkshire 2nd XI debut 2018. Awaiting f-c debut. T20 HS 8.

WILLEY, David Jonathan (Northampton S), b Northampton 28 Feb 1990. Son of P.Willey (Northants, Leics and England 1966-91). 6'1". LHB, LMF. Squad No 15. Northamptonshire 2009-15; cap 2013. Yorkshire debut/cap 2016; captain 2020 to date (T20 only). Bedfordshire 2008. IPL: CSK 2018. Big Bash: PS 2015-16 to 2018-19. **LOI:** 49 (2015 to 2020); HS 51 v Ire (Southampton) 2020; BB 5-30 v Ire (Southampton) 2020 – separate matches. **IT20:** 28 (2015 to 2019); HS 29* v I (Manchester) 2018; BB 4-7 v WI (Basseterre) 2018-19. HS 104* Nh v Glos (Northampton) 2015. Y HS 46 v Warwks (York) 2019. BB 5-29 (10-75 match) Nh v Glos (Northampton) 2011. Y BB 3-55 v Surrey (Leeds) 2016. LO HS 167 Nh v Warwks (Birmingham) 2013 (Y40). LO BB 5-62 EL v New Zealand A (Bristol) 2014. T20 HS 118. T20 BB 4-7.

WISNIEWSKI, Sam Alex (Yorkshire Foundation Cricket C), b Huddersfield 2 Oct 2001. 5'7½". LHB, SLA. Awaiting f-c debut. T20 BB – .

RELEASED/RETIRED

(Having made a County 1st XI appearance in 2020)

BARNES, E. – see LEICESTERSHIRE.

BRESNAN, T.T. – *see WARWICKSHIRE.*

WARNER, J.D. – see GLOUCESTERSHIRE.

J.E.G.Logan left the staff without making a County 1st XI appearance in 2020.

YORKSHIRE 2020

RESULTS SUMMARY

	Place	Won	Lost	Drew	NR
Bob Willis Trophy (North Group)	1st	3		2	
Vitality Blast (North Group)	5th	3	5		2

BOB WILLIS TROPHY AVERAGES
BATTING AND FIELDING

Cap		M	I	NO	HS	Runs	Avge	100	50	Ct/St
2020	D.J.Malan	3	5	–	219	332	66.40	1	1	2
	J.A.Thompson	5	6	–	98	234	46.80	–	2	2
	J.A.Tattersall	5	7	1	71	265	44.16	–	3	9
	H.C.Brook	5	7	1	66*	258	43.00	–	3	4
2011	J.M.Bairstow	2	3	–	75	102	34.00	–	1	5
2010	A.Lyth	5	8	1	103	220	31.42	1	1	5
2019	T.Kohler-Cadmore	5	8	1	41	127	18.14	–	–	2
2020	D.Olivier	4	4	1	20*	33	11.00	–	–	3
	W.A.R.Fraine	3	4	–	14	32	8.00	–	–	1
	J.W.Shutt	3	4	3	7*	7	7.00	–	–	2
2012	S.A.Patterson	4	4	–	11	23	5.75	–	–	–

Also batted: B.O.Coad (2 matches – cap 2018) 28, 4 (1 ct); M.D.Fisher (2) 1, 1 (2 ct); G.C.H.Hill (2) 4*, 29; D.J.Leech (2) 0*, 1; T.W.Loten (2) 0, 11; J.D.Warner (1) 4.

BOWLING

	O	M	R	W	Avge	Best	5wI	10wM
B.O.Coad	69	28	87	12	7.25	5-18	1	–
J.A.Thompson	104	25	246	15	16.40	5-31	1	–
S.A.Patterson	106.3	37	197	11	17.90	3-27	–	–
M.D.Fisher	67	22	180	10	18.00	4-54	–	–
D.J.Leech	34	5	134	4	33.50	2-72	–	–
D.Olivier	91	18	364	10	36.40	3-29	–	–

Also bowled: H.C.Brook 14.1-1-49-0; G.C.H.Hill 25-8-54-1; A.Lyth 23-3-75-2; D.J.Malan 6-1-24-2; J.W.Shutt 19.2-0-104-2; J.D.Warner 9-0-23-1.

The First-Class Averages (pp 209–221) give the records of Yorkshire players in all first-class county matches.

YORKSHIRE RECORDS
FIRST-CLASS CRICKET

Highest Total	For	887		v	Warwicks	Birmingham	1896
	V	681-7d		by	Leics	Bradford	1996
Lowest Total	For	23		v	Hampshire	Middlesbrough	1965
	V	13		by	Notts	Nottingham	1901
Highest Innings	For	341	G.H.Hirst	v	Leics	Leicester	1905
	V	318*	W.G.Grace	for	Glos	Cheltenham	1876

Highest Partnership for each Wicket

1st	555	P.Holmes/H.Sutcliffe	v	Essex	Leyton	1932
2nd	346	W.Barber/M.Leyland	v	Middlesex	Sheffield	1932
3rd	346	J.J.Sayers/A.McGrath	v	Warwicks	Birmingham	2009
4th	372	J.E.Root/J.M.Bairstow	v	Surrey	Leeds	2016
5th	340	E.Wainwright/G.H.Hirst	v	Surrey	The Oval	1899
6th	296	A.Lyth/A.U.Rashid	v	Lancashire	Manchester	2014
7th	366*	J.M.Bairstow/T.T.Bresnan	v	Durham	Chester-le-St²	2015
8th	292	R.Peel/Lord Hawke	v	Warwicks	Birmingham	1896
9th	246	T.T.Bresnan/J.N.Gillespie	v	Surrey	The Oval	2007
10th	149	G.Boycott/G.B.Stevenson	v	Warwicks	Birmingham	1982

Best Bowling	For	10-10	H.Verity		v	Notts	Leeds	1932
(Innings)	V	10-37	C.V.Grimmett		for	Australians	Sheffield	1930
Best Bowling	For	17-91	H.Verity		v	Essex	Leyton	1933
(Match)	V	17-91	H.Dean		for	Lancashire	Liverpool	1913

Most Runs – Season	2883	H.Sutcliffe	(av 80.08)		1932
Most Runs – Career	38558	H.Sutcliffe	(av 50.20)		1919-45
Most 100s – Season	12	H.Sutcliffe			1932
Most 100s – Career	112	H.Sutcliffe			1919-45
Most Wkts – Season	240	W.Rhodes	(av 12.72)		1900
Most Wkts – Career	3597	W.Rhodes	(av 16.02)		1898-1930
Most Career W-K Dismissals	1186	D.Hunter	(863 ct; 323 st)		1888-1909
Most Career Catches in the Field	665	J.Tunnicliffe			1891-1907

LIMITED-OVERS CRICKET

Highest Total	50ov	411-6		v	Devon	Exmouth	2004
	40ov	352-6		v	Notts	Scarborough	2001
	T20	260-4		v	Northants	Leeds	2017
Lowest Total	50ov	76		v	Surrey	Harrogate	1970
	40ov	54		v	Essex	Leeds	2003
	T20	90-9		v	Durham	Chester-le-St²	2009
Highest Innings	50ov	175	T.M.Head	v	Leics	Leicester	2016
	40ov	191	D.S.Lehmann	v	Notts	Scarborough	2001
	T20	161	A.Lyth	v	Northants	Leeds	2017
Best Bowling	50ov	7-27	D.Gough	v	Ireland	Leeds	1997
	40ov	7-15	R.A.Hutton	v	Worcs	Leeds	1969
	T20	6-19	T.T.Bresnan	v	Lancashire	Leeds	2017

FIRST-CLASS UMPIRES 2021

† New appointment. See page 73 for key to abbreviations.

BAILEY, Robert John (Biddulph HS), b Biddulph, Staffs 28 Oct 1963. 6'3". RHB, OB. Northamptonshire 1982-99; cap 1985; benefit 1993; captain 1996-97. Derbyshire 2000-01; cap 2000. Staffordshire 1980. YC 1984. **Tests:** 4 (1988 to 1989-90); HS 43 v WI (Oval) 1988. **LOI:** 4 (1984-85 to 1989-90); HS 43* v SL (Oval) 1988. F-c Tours: SA 1991-92 (Nh); WI 1989-90; Z 1994-95 (Nh). 1000 runs (13); most – 1987 (1990). HS 224* Nh v Glamorgan (Swansea) 1986. BB 5-54 Nh v Notts (Northampton) 1993. F-c career: 374 matches; 21844 runs @ 40.52, 47 hundreds; 121 wickets @ 42.51; 272 ct. Appointed 2006. Umpired 23 LOI (2011 to 2019). **ICC International Panel 2011-19.**

BAINTON, Neil Laurence, b Romford, Essex 2 October 1970. No f-c appearances. Appointed 2006.

BALDWIN, Paul Kerr, b Epsom, Surrey 18 Jul 1973. No f-c appearances. Umpired 18 LOI (2006 to 2009). Reserve List 2010-14. Appointed 2015.

BLACKWELL, Ian David (Brookfield Community S), b Chesterfield, Derbys 10 Jun 1978. 6'2". LHB, SLA. Derbyshire 1997-99. Somerset 2000-08; cap 2001; captain 2006 (*part*). Durham 2009-12. Warwickshire 2012 (on loan). MCC 2012. **Tests:** 1 (2005-06); HS 4 and BB-v I (Nagpur) 2005-06. **LOI:** 34 (2002-03 to 2005-06); HS 82 v I (Colombo) 2002-03; BB 3-26 v A (Adelaide) 2002-03. F-c Tour: I 2005-06. 1000 runs (3); most – 1256 (2005). HS 247* Sm v Derbys (Taunton) 2003 – off 156 balls and including 204 off 98 balls in reduced post-lunch session. BB 7-52 Du v Australia A (Chester-le-St) 2012. CC BB 7-85 Du v Lancs (Manchester) 2009. F-c career: 210 matches; 11595 runs @ 39.57, 27 hundreds; 398 wickets @ 35.91; 66 ct. Reserve List 2015-17. Appointed 2018.

BURNS, Michael (Walney CS), b Barrow-in-Furness, Lancs 6 Feb 1969. 6'0". RHB, RM, WK. Warwickshire 1992-96. Somerset 1997-2005; cap 1999; captain 2003-04. 1000 runs (2); most – 1133 (2003). HS 221 Sm v Yorks (Bath) 2001. BB 6-54 Sm v Leics (Taunton) 2001. F-c career: 154 matches; 7648 runs @ 32.68, 8 hundreds; 68 wickets @ 42.42; 142 ct, 7 st. Appointed 2016. Umpired 1 LOI (2020). **ICC International Panel 2020 to date.**

COOK, Nicholas Grant Billson (Lutterworth GS), b Leicester 17 Jun 1956. 6'0". RHB, SLA. Leicestershire 1978-85; cap 1982. Northamptonshire 1986-94; cap 1987; benefit 1995. **Tests:** 15 (1983 to 1989); HS 31 v A (Oval) 1989; BB 6-65 (11-83 match) v P (Karachi) 1983-84. **LOI:** 3 (1983-84 to 1989-90); HS – ; BB 2-18 v P (Peshawar) 1987-88. F-c Tours: NZ 1979-80 (DHR), 1983-84; P 1983-84, 1987-88; SL 1985-86 (Eng B); Z 1980-81 (Le), 1984-85 (EC). HS 75 Le v Somerset (Taunton) 1980. 50 wkts (8); most – 90 (1982). BB 7-34 (10-97 match) Nh v Essex (Chelmsford) 1992. F-c career: 356 matches; 3137 runs @ 11.66; 879 wickets @ 29.01; 197 ct. Appointed 2009.

DEBENHAM, Benjamin John, b Chelmsford, Essex 11 Oct 1967. LHB. No f-c appearances. Reserve List 2012-17. Appointed 2018.

GOUGH, Michael Andrew (English Martyrs RCS; Hartlepool SFC), b Hartlepool, Co Durham 18 Dec 1979. Son of M.P.Gough (Durham 1974-77). 6'5". RHB, OB. Durham 1998-2003. F-c Tours (Eng A): NZ 1999-00; B 1999-00. HS 123 Du v CU (Cambridge) 1998. CC HS 103 Du v Essex (Colchester) 2002. BB 5-56 Du v Middx (Chester-le-St) 2001. F-c career: 67 matches; 2952 runs @ 25.44, 2 hundreds; 30 wickets @ 45.00; 57 ct. Reserve List 2006-08. Appointed 2009. Umpired 18 Tests (2016 to 2020) and 63 LOI (2013 to 2020). **ICC Elite Panel 2020 to date.**

GOULD, Ian James (Westgate SS, Slough), b Taplow, Bucks 19 Aug 1957. 5'8". LHB, WK. Middlesex 1975 to 1980-81, 1996; cap 1977. Auckland 1979-80. Sussex 1981-90; cap 1981; captain 1987; benefit 1990. MCC YC. **LOI:** 18 (1982-83 to 1983); HS 42 v A (Sydney) 1982-83. F-c Tours: A 1982-83; P 1980-81 (Int); Z 1980-81 (M). HS 128 M v Worcs (Worcester) 1978. BB 3-10 Sx v Surrey (Oval) 1989. Middlesex coach 1991-2000. Reappeared in one match (v OU) 1996. F-c career: 298 matches; 8756 runs @ 26.05, 4 hundreds; 7 wickets @ 52.14; 603 dismissals (536 ct, 67 st). Appointed 2002. Umpired 74 Tests (2008-09 to 2018-19) and 140 LOI (2006 to 2019). **ICC Elite Panel 2009-19.**

HARTLEY, Peter John (Greenhead GS; Bradford C), b Keighley, Yorks 18 Apr 1960. 6'0". RHB, RMF. Warwickshire 1982. Yorkshire 1985-97; cap 1987; benefit 1996. Hampshire 1998-2000; cap 1998. F-c Tours (Y): SA 1991-92; WI 1986-87; Z 1995-96. HS 127* Y v Lancs (Manchester) 1988. 50 wkts (7); most – 81 (1995). BB 9-41 (inc hat-trick, 4 wkts in 5 balls and 5 in 9; 11-68 match) Y v Derbys (Chesterfield) 1995. Hat-trick 1995. F-c career: 232 matches; 4321 runs @ 19.91, 2 hundreds; 683 wickets @ 30.21; 68 ct. Appointed 2003. Umpired 6 LOI (2007 to 2009). **ICC International Panel 2006-09.**

ILLINGWORTH, Richard Keith (Salts GS), b Bradford, Yorks 23 Aug 1963. 5'11". RHB, SLA. Worcestershire 1982-2000; cap 1986; benefit 1997. Natal 1988-89. Derbyshire 2001. Wiltshire 2005. **Tests:** 9 (1991 to 1995-96); HS 28 v SA (Pt Elizabeth) 1995-96; BB 4-96 v WI (Nottingham) 1995. Took wicket of P.V.Simmons with his first ball in Tests – v WI (Nottingham) 1991. **LOI:** 25 (1991 to 1995-96); HS 14 v P (Melbourne) 1991-92; BB 3-33 v Z (Albury) 1991-92. F-c Tours: SA 1995-96; NZ 1991-92; P 1990-91 (Eng A); SL 1990-91 (Eng A); Z 1989-90 (Eng A), 1990-91 (Wo), 1993-94 (Wo), 1996-97 (Wo). HS 120* Wo v Warwks (Worcester) 1987 – as night-watchman. Scored 106 for England A v Z (Harare) 1989-90 – also as night-watchman. 50 wkts (5); most – 75 (1990). BB 7-50 Wo v OU (Oxford) 1985. F-c career: 376 matches; 7027 runs @ 22.45, 4 hundreds; 831 wickets @ 31.54; 161 ct. Appointed 2006. Umpired 53 Tests (2012-13 to 2020-21) and 69 LOI (2010 to 2020). **ICC Elite Panel 2013 to date.**

KETTLEBOROUGH, Richard Allan (Worksop C), b Sheffield, Yorks 15 Mar 1973. 6'0". LHB, RM. Yorkshire 1994-97. Middlesex 1998-99. F-c Tour (Y): Z 1995-96. HS 108 Y v Essex (Leeds) 1996. BB 2-26 Y v Notts (Scarborough) 1996. F-c career: 33 matches; 1258 runs @ 25.16, 1 hundred; 3 wickets @ 81.00; 20 ct. Appointed 2006. Umpired 68 Tests (2010-11 to 2020) and 90 LOI (2009 to 2020). **ICC Elite Panel 2011 to date.**

LLONG, Nigel James (Ashford North S), b Ashford, Kent 11 Feb 1969. 6'0". LHB, OB. Kent 1990-98; cap 1993. F-c Tour (K): Z 1992-93. HS 130 K v Hants (Canterbury) 1996. BB 5-21 K v Middx (Canterbury) 1996. F-c career: 68 matches; 3024 runs @ 31.17, 6 hundreds; 35 wickets @ 35.97; 59 ct. Appointed 2002. Umpired 62 Tests (2007-08 to 2019-20) and 130 LOI (2006 to 2019-20). **ICC Elite Panel 2012-20.**

LLOYD, Graham David (Hollins County HS), b Accrington, Lancs 1 Jul 1969. Son of D.Lloyd (Lancs and England 1965-83). 5'9". RHB, RM. Lancashire 1988-2002; cap 1992; benefit 2001. **LOI:** 6 (1996 to 1998-99); HS 22 v A (Oval) 1997. F-c Tours: A 1992-93 (Eng A); WI 1995-96 (La). 1000 runs (5); most – 1389 (1992). HS 241 La v Essex (Chelmsford) 1996. BB 1-4. F-c career: 203 matches; 11279 runs @ 38.23, 24 hundreds; 2 wickets @ 220.00; 140 ct. Reserve List 2009-13. Appointed 2014.

MALLENDER, Neil Alan (Beverley GS), b Kirk Sandall, Yorks 13 Aug 1961. 6'0". RHB, RFM. Northamptonshire 1980-86 and 1995-96; cap 1984. Somerset 1987-94; cap 1987; benefit 1994. Otago 1983-84 to 1992-93; captain 1990-91 to 1992-93. **Tests:** 2 (1992); HS 4 v P (Oval) 1992; BB 5-50 v P (Leeds) 1992 – on debut. F-c Tour (Nh): Z 1994-95. HS 100* Otago v CD (Palmerston N) 1991-92. UK HS 87* Sm v Sussex (Hove) 1990. 50 wkts (6); most – 56 (1983). BB 7-27 Otago v Auckland (Auckland) 1984-85. UK BB 7-41 Nh v Derbys (Northampton) 1982. F-c career: 345 matches; 4709 runs @ 17.18, 1 hundred; 937 wickets @ 26.31; 111 ct. Appointed 1999. Umpired 3 Tests (2003-04) and 22 LOI (2001 to 2003-04), including 2002-03 World Cup. **ICC Elite Panel 2004.**

MILLNS, David James (Garibaldi CS; N Notts C; Nottingham Trent U), b Clipstone, Notts 27 Feb 1965. 6'3". LHB, RF. Nottinghamshire 1988-89, 2000-01; cap 2000. Leicestershire 1990-99; cap 1991; benefit 1999. Tasmania 1994-95. Boland 1996-97. F-c Tours: A 1992-93 (Eng A); SA 1996-97 (Le). HS 121 Le v Northants (Northampton) 1997. 50 wkts (4); most – 76 (1994). BB 9-37 (12-91 match) Le v Derbys (Derby) 1991. F-c career: 171 matches; 3082 runs @ 22.01, 3 hundreds; 553 wickets @ 27.35; 76 ct. Reserve List 2007-08. Appointed 2009. Umpired 3 LOI (2020). **ICC International Panel 2020 to date.**

O'SHAUGHNESSY, Steven Joseph (Harper Green SS, Franworth), b Bury, Lancs 9 Sep 1961. 5'10½". RHB, RM. Lancashire 1980-87; cap 1985. Worcestershire 1988-89. Scored 100 in 35 min to equal world record for La v Leics (Manchester) 1983. 1000 runs (1): 1167 (1984). HS 159* La v Somerset (Bath) 1984. BB 4-66 La v Notts (Nottingham) 1982. F-c career: 112 matches; 3720 runs @ 24.31, 5 hundreds; 114 wickets @ 36.03; 57 ct. Reserve List 2009-10. Appointed 2011.

POLLARD, Paul Raymond (Gedling CS), b Carlton, Nottingham 24 Sep 1968. 5'11". LHB, RM. Nottinghamshire 1987-98; cap 1992. Worcestershire 1999-2001. F-c Tour (Nt): SA 1996-97. 1000 runs (3); most – 1463 (1993). HS 180 Nt v Derbys (Nottingham) 1993. BB 2-79 Nt v Glos (Bristol) 1993. F-c career: 192 matches; 9685 runs @ 31.44, 15 hundreds; 4 wkts @ 68.00; 158 ct. Reserve List 2012-17. Appointed 2018.

ROBINSON, Robert Timothy (Dunstable GS; High Pavement SFC; Sheffield U), b Sutton in Ashfield, Notts 21 Nov 1958. 6'0". RHB, RM. Nottinghamshire 1978-99; cap 1983; captain 1988-95; benefit 1992. *Wisden* 1985. **Tests:** 29 (1984-85 to 1989); HS 175 v A (Leeds) 1985. **LOI:** 26 (1984-85 to 1988); HS 83 v P (Sharjah) 1986-87. F-c Tours: A 1987-88; SA 1989-90 (Eng XI), 1996-97 (Nt); NZ 1987-88; WI 1985-86; I/SL 1984-85; P 1987-88. 1000 runs (14) inc 2000 (1): 2032 (1984). HS 220* Nt v Yorks (Nottingham) 1990. BB 1-22. F-c career: 425 matches; 27571 runs @ 42.15, 63 hundreds; 4 wickets @ 72.25; 257 ct. Appointed 2007. Umpired 16 LOI (2013 to 2019). **ICC International Panel 2012-19.**

SAGGERS, Martin John (Springwood HS, King's Lynn; Huddersfield U), b King's Lynn, Norfolk 23 May 1972. 6'2". RHB, RMF. Durham 1996-98. Kent 1999-2009; cap 2001; benefit 2009. MCC 2004. Essex 2007 (on loan). Norfolk 1995-96. **Tests:** 3 (2003-04 to 2004); HS 1 and BB 2-29 v B (Chittagong) 2003-04 – on debut. F-c Tour: B 2003-04. HS 64 K v Worcs (Canterbury) 2004. 50 wkts (4); most – 83 (2002). BB 7-79 K v Durham (Chester-le-St) 2000. F-c career: 119 matches; 1165 runs @ 11.20; 415 wickets @ 25.33; 27 ct. Reserve List 2010-11. Appointed 2012. Umpired 2 LOI (2020). **ICC International Panel 2020 to date.**

TAYLOR, Billy Victor (Bitterne Park S, Southampton), b Southampton 11 Jan 1977. Younger brother of J.L.Taylor (Wiltshire 1998-2002). 6'3". LHB, RMF. Sussex 1999-2003. Hampshire 2004-09; cap 2006; testimonial 2016. Wiltshire 1996-98. HS 40 v Essex (Southampton) 2004. BB 6-32 v Middlesex (Southampton) 2006 (inc hat-trick). F-c career: 54 matches; 431 runs @10.26; 136 wickets @ 33.34; 6 ct. Reserve list 2011-16. Appointed 2017.

WARREN, Russell John (Kingsthorpe Upper S), b Northampton 10 Sep 1971. 6'1". RHB, OB, WK. Northamptonshire 1992-2002; cap 1995. Nottinghamshire 2003-06; cap 2004. 1000 runs (1): 1030 (2001). HS 201* Nh v Glamorgan (Northampton) 2001. F-c career: 146 matches; 7776 runs @ 36.67, 15 hundreds; 128 ct, 5 st. Reserve List: 2015-17. Appointed 2018.

WHARF, Alexander George (Buttershaw Upper S; Thomas Danby C), b Bradford, Yorks 4 Jun 1975. 6'5". RHB, RMF. Yorkshire 1994-97. Nottinghamshire 1998-99. Glamorgan 2000-08, scoring 100* v OU (Oxford) on debut; cap 2000; benefit 2009. **LOI**: 13 (2004 to 2004-05); HS 9 v India (Lord's) 2004; BB 4-24 v Z (Harare) 2004-05. F-c Tour (Eng A): WI 2005-06. HS 128* Gm v Glos (Bristol) 2007. 50 wkts (1): 52 (2003). BB 6-59 Gm v Glos (Bristol) 2005. F-c career: 121 matches; 3570 runs @ 23.03, 6 hundreds; 293 wickets @ 37.34; 63 ct. Reserve List 2011-13. Appointed 2014. Umpired 6 LOI (2018 to 2020). **ICC International Panel 2018 to date.**

RESERVE FIRST-CLASS LIST: Hassan M.S.Adnan, Tom Lungley, James D.Middlebrook, Mark Newell, Neil J.Pratt, Ian N.Ramage, Christopher M.Watts, Robert A.White.

Test Match and LOI statistics to 9 March 2021.

TOURING TEAMS REGISTER 2020

PAKISTAN (A)

Full Names	Birthdate	Birthplace	Team	Type	F-C Debut
ABID ALI	16.10.87	Lahore	Central Punjab	RHB/LB	2007-08
ASAD SHAFIQ	28.01.86	Karachi	Sindh	RHB/OB	2007-08
AZHAR ALI	19.02.85	Lahore	Central Punjab	RHB/LB	2001-02
BABAR AZAM	15.10.94	Lahore	Central Punjab	RHB/OB	2010-11
FAHEEM ASHRAF	16.01.94	Kasur	Central Punjab	RHB/RFM	2013-14
FAKHAR ZAMAN	10.04.90	Mardan	Khyber Pakhtun	LHB/SLA	2012-13
FAWAD ALAM	08.10.85	Karachi	Sindh	LHB/SLA	2003-04
HAIDER ALI	02.10.00	Attock	Northern	RHB/OB	2019-20
IFTIKHAR AHMED	03.09.90	Peshawar	Khyber Pakhtun	RHB/OB	2011-12
IMAM-UL-HAQ	12.12.95	Lahore	Baluchistan	LHB/LB	2012-13
IMRAN KHAN	15.07.87	Lower Dir	Khyber Pakhtun	RHB/RMF	2007-08
KASHIF BHATTI	25.07.86	Nawabshah	Baluchistan	RHB/SLA	2007-08
MOHAMMAD ABBAS	10.03.90	Sialkot	Southern Punjab	RHB/RMF	2008-09
MOHAMMAD RIZWAN	01.06.92	Peshawar	Khyber Pakhtun	RHB/RM	2008-09
NASEEM SHAH	15.02.03		Central Punjab	RHB/RF	2018-19
SARFRAZ AHMED	22.05.87	Karachi	Sindh	RHB/WK	2005-06
SHADAB KHAN	04.10.98	Mianwali	Northern	RHB/LBG	2016-17
SHAHEEN SHAH AFRIDI	06.04.00	Khyber Agency	Northerrn	LHB/LFM	2017-18
SHAN MASOOD	14.10.89	Kuwait	Southern Punjab	LHB/RM	2007-08
SOHAIL KHAN	06.03.84	Malakand	Sindh	RHB/RFM	2007-08
USMAN SHINWARI	01.05.94	Khyber Agency	Khyber Pakhtun	RHB/LMF	2013-14
YASIR SHAH	02.05.86	Swabi	Baluchistan	RHB/LBG	2001-02

WEST INDIES

Full Names	Birthdate	Birthplace	Team	Type	F-C Debut
BLACKWOOD, Jermaine	20.11.91	St Elizabeth	Jamaica	RHB/OB	2011-12
BRATHWAITE, Kraigg Clairmonte	01.12.92	St Michael	Barbados	RHB/OB	2008-09
BROOKS, Sharmarh Shaqad Joshua	01.10.98	St Michael	Barbados	RHB/LB	2006-07
CAMPBELL, John Dillon	21.09.93	St James	Jamaica	LHB/OB	2013-14
CHASE, Roston Lamar	22.03.92	Christ Church	Barbados	RHB/OB	2010-11
CORNWALL, Rahkeem Rashawn Shane	01.02.93	Antigua	Leeward Is	RHB/OB	2014-15
DOWRICH, Shane Omari	30.10.91	St James	Barbados	RHB/WK	2009-10
GABRIEL, Shannon Terry	28.04.88	Trinidad	Trinidad	RHB/RF	2009-10
HOLDER, Jason Omar	05.11.91	St George	Barbados	RHB/RMF	2008-09
HOPE, Shai Diego	10.11.93	Barbados	Barbados	RHB/WK	2012-13
JOSEPH, Alzarri Shaheim	20.11.96	Antigua	Leeward Is	RHB/RFM	2014-15
ROACH, Kemar Andre Jamal	30.06.88	St Lucy	Barbados	RHB/RFM	2007-08

THE 2020 FIRST-CLASS SEASON STATISTICAL HIGHLIGHTS

FIRST TO INDIVIDUAL TARGETS

1000 RUNS	–		Most – 563 A.N.Cook (Essex)
50 WICKETS	–		Most – 38 S.R.Harmer (Essex)

TEAM HIGHLIGHTS († *Team record*)

HIGHEST INNINGS TOTALS

583-8d	England v Pakistan (*3rd Test*)	Southampton
530-1	Kent v Sussex	Canterbury
507-6d	Northamptonshire v Warwickshire	Birmingham

HIGHEST FOURTH INNINGS TOTAL

365-7	Derbyshire (set 365) v Nottinghamshire	Nottingham

LOWEST INNINGS TOTALS

67	Northamptonshire v Somerset	Northampton
70	Gloucestershire v Somerset (*2nd inns*)	Taunton
74	Surrey v Hampshire	Arundel
76	Gloucestershire v Somerset (*1st inns*)	Taunton
97	Nottinghamshire v Yorkshire	Nottingham

HIGHEST MATCH AGGREGATES

1246-31	Worcestershire (455-8 & 276-6d) v Glamorgan (374 & 141-7)	Worcester

LARGE MARGINS OF VICTORY

314 runs	Somerset (237 & 223-1d) beat Gloucestershire (76 & 70)	Taunton
Inns & 52 runs	Hampshire (298) beat Surrey (172 & 74)	Arundel
Inns & 25 runs	Kent (530-1d) beat Sussex (332 & 173)	Canterbury

First instance since 1997 when a side has won a match losing one or fewer wickets in the game.

NARROW MARGINS OF VICTORY

17 runs	Kent (342 & 127) beat Surrey (278 & 174)	The Oval
2 wkts	Essex (298 & 202-8) beat Kent (387 & 112)	Chelmsford

MOST EXTRAS IN AN INNINGS

	B	LB	W	NB		
54	9	7	12	26	Cambridge U (307) v Oxford U	Cambridge
38	5	27	2	4	Yorkshire (260) v Lancashire	Leeds
38	11	9	6	12	Nottinghamshire (355) v Yorkshire	Nottingham

Under ECB regulations, Test matches excluded, two penalty extras were scored for each no-ball.

BATTING HIGHLIGHTS

DOUBLE HUNDREDS

J.M.Cox	238*	Kent v Sussex	Canterbury
Z.Crawley	267	England v Pakistan (*3rd Test*)	Southampton
J.A.Leaning	220*	Kent v Sussex	Canterbury
D.J.Malan	219	Yorkshire v Derbyshire	Leeds
W.M.H.Rhodes	207	Warwickshire v Worcestershire	Worcester

FASTEST HUNDRED AGAINST GENUINE BOWLING

M.de Lange   (113) 62 balls   Glamorgan v Northamptonshire   Northampton

MOST SIXES IN AN INNINGS

9   M.de Lange (113)   Glamorgan v Northamptonshire   Northampton

MOST RUNS FROM BOUNDARIES IN AN INNINGS

Runs	6s	4s			
142	1	34	Z.Crawley	England v Pakistan (*3rd Test*)	Southampton
136	4	28	D.J.Malan	Yorkshire v Derbyshire	Leeds

HUNDRED ON FIRST-CLASS DEBUT

C.Z.Taylor   106   Glamorgan v Northamptonshire   Northampton
    He took just 88 balls to reach his hundred.

HUNDRED ON FIRST-CLASS DEBUT IN BRITAIN

P.D.Daneel   125   Cambridge U v Oxford U   Cambridge

CARRYING BAT THROUGH COMPLETED INNINGS

T.A.Lammonby   107*   Somerset (193) v Worcestershire   Worcester

LONG INNINGS (Qualification 550 mins and/or 350 balls)

Mins	Balls			
541	393	Z.Crawley (267)	England v Pakistan (*3rd Test*)	Southampton
497	399	A.M.Rossington (135*)	Northamptonshire v Warwicks	Birmingham
556	372	D.P.Sibley (120)	England v West Indies (*2nd Test*)	Manchester
487	356	B.A.Stokes (176)	England v West Indies (*2nd Test*)	Manchester

NOTABLE PARTNERSHIPS

Qualifications: 1st-6th wkts: 200 runs; 7th: 175; 8th: 150; 9th: 125; 10th: 100. († Team record)

First Wicket
200   B.T.Slater/H.Hameed   Nottinghamshire v Leics   Leicester
Second Wicket
423†   J.M.Cox/J.A.Leaning   Kent v Sussex   Canterbury
211*   T.A.Lammonby/T.B.Abell   Somerset v Gloucestershire   Taunton
Fourth Wicket
318   J.B.Libby/B.L.D'Oliveira   Worcestershire v Glamorgan   Worcester
260   D.P.Sibley/B.A.Stokes   England v West Indies (*2nd Test*)   Manchester
Fifth wicket
359   Z.Crawley/J.C.Buttler   England v Pakistan (*3rd Test*)   Southampton
200   D.J.Malan/J.A.Tattersall   Yorkshire v Derbyshire   Leeds
Seventh Wicket
200*   A.M.Rossington/L.A.Procter   Northamptonshire v Warwicks   Birmingham
Ninth wicket
180   S.M.Davies/J.Overton   Somerset v Warwickshire   Birmingham
168   D.A.Douthwaite/M.de Lange   Glamorgan v Northamptonshire   Northampton
Tenth Wicket
124   C.Z.Taylor/M.G.Hogan   Glamorgan v Northamptonshire   Northampton
107   S.M.Davies/J.A.Brooks   Somerset v Glamorgan   Taunton

BOWLING HIGHLIGHTS
EIGHT OR MORE WICKETS IN AN INNINGS

S.R.Harmer	8-64	Essex v Surrey	Chelmsford

TEN OR MORE WICKETS IN A MATCH

S.C.J.Broad	10- 67	England v West Indies (*3rd Test*)	Manchester
O.J.Hannon-Dalby	12-110	Warwickshire v Gloucestershire	Bristol
S.R.Harmer	14-131	Essex v Surrey	Chelmsford
R.F.Higgins	11- 96	Gloucestershire v Warwickshire	Bristol
D.T.Moriarty	11-224	Surrey v Sussex	The Oval
J.C.Vitali	10- 92	Cambridge U v Oxford U	Cambridge

HAT-TRICK

J.K.Fuller	Hampshire v Surrey	Arundel

MOST RUNS CONCEDED IN AN INNINGS

Yasir Shah	39-3-173-2	Pakistan v England (*3rd Test*)	Southampton
D.T.Moriarty	37.3-3-154-5	Surrey v Sussex	The Oval

WICKET-KEEPING HIGHLIGHTS
SIX WICKET-KEEPING DISMISSALS IN AN INNINGS

O.G.Robinson	6ct	Kent v Hampshire	Canterbury

NINE OR MORE WICKET-KEEPING DISMISSALS IN A MATCH

C.B.Cooke	7ct,2st	Glamorgan v Worcestershire	Worcester

FIELDING HIGHLIGHTS
FOUR OR MORE CATCHES IN THE FIELD IN AN INNINGS

A.N.Cook	4ct	Essex v Sussex	Hove
S.J.Mullaney	4ct	Nottinghamshire v Yorkshire	Nottingham

SIX OR MORE CATCHES IN THE FIELD IN A MATCH

S.J.Mullaney	7ct	Nottinghamshire v Yorkshire	Nottingham

BOB WILLIS TROPHY 2020
FINAL TABLES

CENTRAL GROUP

		P	W	L	T	D	Bonus Points Bat	Points Bowl	Deduct Points	Total Points
1	Somerset	5	4	–	–	1	10	15	–	97
2	Worcestershire	5	2	1	–	2	14	12	–	74
3	Warwickshire	5	–	1	–	4	7	14	–	53
4	Northamptonshire	5	1	2	–	2	4	13	–	49
5	Gloucestershire	5	1	2	–	2	3	10	–	45
6	Glamorgan	5	–	2	–	3	6	13	–	43

NORTH GROUP

		P	W	L	T	D	Bonus Points Bat	Points Bowl	Deduct Points	Total Points
1	Yorkshire	5	3	–	–	2	11	12	–	87
2	Derbyshire	5	2	1	–	2	13	13	–	74
3	Lancashire	5	2	1	–	2	7	11	–	66
4	Nottinghamshire	5	–	2	–	3	20	15	–	59
5	Leicestershire	5	1	2	–	2	4	13	–	49
6	Durham	5	–	2	–	3	7	10	–	41

SOUTH GROUP

		P	W	L	T	D	Bonus Points Bat	Points Bowl	Deduct Points	Total Points
1	Essex	5	4	–	–	1	6	12	–	90
2	Kent	5	3	1	–	1	12	15	–	82
3	Middlesex	5	2	2	–	1	8	14	–	62
4	Hampshire	5	2	2	–	1	4	13	–	57
5	Surrey	5	1	4	–	–	8	12	–	36
6	Sussex	5	1	4	–	–	9	11	–	12

Kent deducted 1 point each for slow over rate.
Sussex deducted 24 points for ball tampering.

SCORING OF BOB WILLIS TROPHY POINTS 2020

(a) For a win, 16 points, plus any points scored in the first innings.

(b) In a tie, each side to score eight points, plus any points scored in the first innings.

(c) In a drawn match, each side to score eight points, plus any points scored in the first innings (see also paragraph (e) below).

(d) If the scores are equal in a drawn match, the side batting in the fourth innings to score eight points plus any points scored in the first innings, and the opposing side to score three points plus any points scored in the first innings.

(e) **First Innings Points** (awarded only for performances **in the first 110 overs** of each first innings and retained whatever the result of the match; each side to bat for a maximum of 120 overs in the first innings).
   (i) A maximum of five batting points to be available as under:
       200 to 249 runs – 1 point; 250 to 299 runs – 2 points; 300 to 349 runs – 3 points; 350 to 399 runs – 4 points; 400 runs or over – 5 points.
   (ii) A maximum of three bowling points to be available as under:
       3 to 5 wickets taken – 1 point; 6 to 8 wickets taken – 2 points; 9 to 10 wickets taken – 3 points.

(f) If a match is abandoned without a ball being bowled, each side to score five points.

(g) The side which has the highest aggregate of points gained at the end of the season shall be the champion county of their respective group. Should any sides in the table be equal on points, the following tie-breakers will be applied in the order stated: most wins, fewest losses, team achieving most points in contests between teams level on points, most wickets taken, most runs scored. At the end of the season, the two teams with the most points will play off to decide the winner of the trophy.

2020 BOB WILLIS TROPHY FINAL
SOMERSET v ESSEX

At Lord's, London, on 23, 24, 25, 26, 27 September 2020.
Toss: Essex. Result: **MATCH DRAWN** (Essex won on 1st innings).

SOMERSET

B.G.F.Green	b S.J.Cook	24		c A.N.Cook b Beard	41
T.A.Lammonby	lbw b S.J.Cook	0		lbw b Harmer	116
*T.B.Abell	c Wheater b Beard	19		c Brown b Porter	15
E.J.Byrom	lbw b S.J.Cook	117		b Porter	1
G.A.Bartlett	c A.N.Cook b Porter	12		c Westley b Porter	5
†S.M.Davies	c Wheater b S.J.Cook	27		c A.N.Cook b Harmer	19
C.Overton	lbw b Porter	66	(8)	not out	45
L.Gregory	lbw b S.J.Cook	9	(7)	c A.N.Cook b Porter	1
J.H.Davey	not out	17		not out	16
M.J.Leach	lbw b Harmer	3			
J.A.Brooks	b Harmer	0			
Extras	(B 1, LB 4, NB 2)	7		(LB 11, NB 2)	13
Total	**(102 overs)**	**301**		**(7 wkts dec; 76 overs)**	**272**

ESSEX

N.L.J.Browne	c Overton b Gregory	8		c Abell b Gregory	13
Sir A.N.Cook	c Overton b Gregory	172		c Davies b Gregory	31
*T.Westley	c Abell b Lammonby	51		lbw b Overton	0
D.W.Lawrence	c Lammonby b Gregory	6		lbw b Leach	35
P.I.Walter	b Gregory	0		lbw b Leach	21
R.N.ten Doeschate	lbw b Overton	21		c Bartlett b Leach	46
J.A.Porter	b Gregory	13			
†A.J.A.Wheater	not out	26	(7)	not out	14
S.R.Harmer	c Overton b Gregory	0	(8)	not out	0
A.P.Beard	not out	14			
S.J.Cook					
Extras	(B 4, LB 12, NB 10)	26		(B 1, LB 10, NB 8)	19
Total	**(8 wkts; 120 overs)**	**337**		**(6 wkts; 80.3 overs)**	**179**

ESSEX	O	M	R	W		O	M	R	W
Porter	29	9	85	2		23	4	73	4
S.J.Cook	32	10	76	5		16	2	56	0
Beard	11	1	68	1	(5)	4	0	28	1
Harmer	20	6	36	0	(3)	32	9	101	2
Lawrence	1	0	2	0					
Walter	9	1	29	0	(4)	1	0	3	0

SOMERSET	O	M	R	W		O	M	R	W
Overton	29	6	66	1		17	7	37	1
Davey	23	3	70	0		9	3	18	0
Gregory	27	5	72	6		21.3	5	52	2
Brooks	9	3	25	0		8	3	11	0
Abell	2	0	10	0					
Leach	22	4	52	0	(5)	22	10	38	3
Lammonby	8	2	26	1		2	1	8	0
Byrom					(6)	1	0	4	0

FALL OF WICKETS

	Sm	Ex	Sm	Ex
Wkt	1st	1st	2nd	2nd
1st	0	27	105	25
2nd	34	197	155	26
3rd	52	208	167	68
4th	94	208	187	98
5th	139	264	187	131
6th	266	266	188	179
7th	270	303	224	–
8th	279	303	–	–
9th	301		–	–
10th	301		–	–

Umpires: R.J.Bailey and R.J.Warren. Referee: D.A.Cosker.

COUNTY CHAMPIONS

The English County Championship was not officially constituted until December 1889. Prior to that date there was no generally accepted method of awarding the title; although the 'least matches lost' method existed, it was not consistently applied. Rules governing playing qualifications were agreed in 1873 and the first unofficial points system 15 years later.

Research has produced a list of champions dating back to 1826, but at least seven different versions exist for the period from 1864 to 1889 (see *The Wisden Book of Cricket Records*). Only from 1890 can any authorised list of county champions commence.

That first official Championship was contested between eight counties: Gloucestershire, Kent, Lancashire, Middlesex, Nottinghamshire, Surrey, Sussex and Yorkshire. The remaining counties were admitted in the following seasons: 1891 – Somerset, 1895 – Derbyshire, Essex, Hampshire, Leicestershire and Warwickshire, 1899 – Worcestershire, 1905 – Northamptonshire, 1921 – Glamorgan, and 1992 – Durham.

The Championship pennant was introduced by the 1951 champions, Warwickshire, and the Lord's Taverners' Trophy was first presented in 1973. The first sponsors, Schweppes (1977-83), were succeeded by Britannic Assurance (1984-98), PPP Healthcare (1999-2000), CricInfo (2001), Frizzell (2002-05), Liverpool Victoria (2006-15) and Specsavers (from 2016). Based on their previous season's positions, the 18 counties were separated into two divisions in 2000. From 2000 to 2005 the bottom three Division 1 teams were relegated and the top three Division 2 sides promoted. This was reduced to two teams from the end of the 2006 season.

1890	Surrey	1935	Yorkshire	1979	Essex
1891	Surrey	1936	Derbyshire	1980	Middlesex
1892	Surrey	1937	Yorkshire	1981	Nottinghamshire
1893	Yorkshire	1938	Yorkshire	1982	Middlesex
1894	Surrey	1939	Yorkshire	1983	Essex
1895	Surrey	1946	Yorkshire	1984	Essex
1896	Yorkshire	1947	Middlesex	1985	Middlesex
1897	Lancashire	1948	Glamorgan	1986	Essex
1898	Yorkshire	1949	{ Middlesex	1987	Nottinghamshire
1899	Surrey		{ Yorkshire	1988	Worcestershire
1900	Yorkshire	1950	{ Lancashire	1989	Worcestershire
1901	Yorkshire		{ Surrey	1990	Middlesex
1902	Yorkshire	1951	Warwickshire	1991	Essex
1903	Middlesex	1952	Surrey	1992	Essex
1904	Lancashire	1953	Surrey	1993	Middlesex
1905	Yorkshire	1954	Surrey	1994	Warwickshire
1906	Kent	1955	Surrey	1995	Warwickshire
1907	Nottinghamshire	1956	Surrey	1996	Leicestershire
1908	Yorkshire	1957	Surrey	1997	Glamorgan
1909	Kent	1958	Surrey	1998	Leicestershire
1910	Kent	1959	Yorkshire	1999	Surrey
1911	Warwickshire	1960	Yorkshire	2000	Surrey
1912	Yorkshire	1961	Hampshire	2001	Yorkshire
1913	Kent	1962	Yorkshire	2002	Surrey
1914	Surrey	1963	Yorkshire	2003	Sussex
1919	Yorkshire	1964	Worcestershire	2004	Warwickshire
1920	Middlesex	1965	Worcestershire	2005	Nottinghamshire
1921	Middlesex	1966	Yorkshire	2006	Sussex
1922	Yorkshire	1967	Yorkshire	2007	Sussex
1923	Yorkshire	1968	Yorkshire	2008	Durham
1924	Yorkshire	1969	Glamorgan	2009	Durham
1925	Yorkshire	1970	Kent	2010	Nottinghamshire
1926	Lancashire	1971	Surrey	2011	Lancashire
1927	Lancashire	1972	Warwickshire	2012	Warwickshire
1928	Lancashire	1973	Hampshire	2013	Durham
1929	Nottinghamshire	1974	Worcestershire	2014	Yorkshire
1930	Lancashire	1975	Leicestershire	2015	Yorkshire
1931	Yorkshire	1976	Middlesex	2016	Middlesex
1932	Yorkshire	1977	{ Kent	2017	Essex
1933	Yorkshire		{ Middlesex	2018	Surrey
1934	Lancashire	1978	Kent	2019	Essex

COUNTY CHAMPIONSHIP FIXTURES 2021

GROUP 1

	DERBYS	DURHAM	ESSEX	NOTTS	WARKS	WORCS
DERBYS		Derby	C'field	Derby	Derby	Derby
DURHAM	C-le-St		C-le-St	C-le-St	C-le-St	C-le-St
ESSEX	C'ford	C'ford		C'ford	C'ford	C'ford
NOTTS	N'ham	N'ham	N'ham		N'ham	N'ham
WARKS	Birm	Birm	Birm	Birm		Birm
WORCS	Worcs	Worcs	Worcs	Worcs	Worcs	

GROUP 2

	GLOS	HANTS	LEICS	MIDDX	SOM'T	SURREY
GLOS		Chelt	Bristol	Chelt	Bristol	Bristol
HANTS	So'ton		So'ton	So'ton	So'ton	So'ton
LEICS	Leics	Leics		Leics	Leics	Leics
MIDDX	Lord's	Lord's	N'wood		Lord's	Lord's
SOM'T	Taunton	Taunton	Taunton	Taunton		Taunton
SURREY	Oval	Oval	Oval	Oval	Oval	

GROUP 3

	GLAM	KENT	LANCS	N'HANTS	SUSSEX	YORKS
GLAM		Cardiff	Cardiff	Cardiff	Cardiff	Cardiff
KENT	Cant		Cant	Cant	Beck	Cant
LANCS	Man			Man	Man	Man
N'HANTS	No'ton	No'ton	No'ton		No'ton	No'ton
SUSSEX	Hove	Hove	Hove	Hove		Hove
YORKS	Leeds	Leeds	Scar	Leeds	Leeds	

PRINCIPAL LIST A RECORDS 1963-2020

These records cover all the major limited-overs tournaments played by the counties since the inauguration of the Gillette Cup in 1963.

Highest Totals		496-4	Surrey v Glos	The Oval	2007
		445-8	Notts v Northants	Nottingham	2016
Highest Total Batting Second		429	Glamorgan v Surrey	The Oval	2002
Lowest Totals		23	Middlesex v Yorks	Leeds	1974
		36	Leics v Sussex	Leicester	1973
Largest Victory (Runs)			Somerset beat Devon	Torquay	1990
		304	Sussex beat Ireland	Belfast	1996
Highest Scores	268	A.D.Brown	Surrey v Glamorgan	The Oval	2002
	206	A.I.Kallicharran	Warwicks v Oxfords	Birmingham	1984
	203	A.D.Brown	Surrey v Hampshire	Guildford	1997
	201*	R.S.Bopara	Essex v Leics	Leicester	2008
	201	V.J.Wells	Leics v Berkshire	Leicester	1996
Fastest Hundred	36 balls	G.D.Rose	Somerset v Devon	Torquay	1990
	43 balls	R.R.Watson	Scotland v Somerset	Edinburgh	2003
	44 balls	M.A.Ealham	Kent v Derbyshire	Maidstone	1995
	44 balls	T.C.Smith	Lancashire v Worcs	Worcester	2012
	44 balls	D.I.Stevens	Kent v Sussex	Canterbury	2013
Most Sixes (Inns)	15	R.N.ten Doeschate	Essex v Scotland	Chelmsford	2013

Highest Partnership for each Wicket

1st	342	M.J.Lumb/M.H.Wessels	Notts v Northants	Nottingham	2016
2nd	302	M.E.Trescothick/C.Kieswetter	Somerset v Glos	Taunton	2008
3rd	309*	T.S.Curtis/T.M.Moody	Worcs v Surrey	The Oval	1994
4th	234*	D.I.Lloyd/C.H.Lloyd	Lancashire v Glos	Manchester	1978
5th	221*	R.R.Sarwan/M.A.Hardinges	Glos v Lancashire	Manchester	2005
6th	232	D.Wiese/B.C.Brown	Sussex v Hampshire	Southampton	2019
7th	170	D.R.Brown/A.F.Giles	Warwicks v Essex	Birmingham	2003
8th	174	R.W.T.Key/J.C.Tredwell	Kent v Surrey	The Oval	2007
9th	155	C.M.W.Read/A.J.Harris	Notts v Durham	Nottingham	1984
10th	82	G.Chapple/P.J.Martin	Lancashire v Worcs	Manchester	1996
Best Bowling	8-21	M.A.Holding	Derbyshire v Sussex	Hove	1988
	8-26	K.D.Boyce	Essex v Lancashire	Manchester	1971
	8-31	D.L.Underwood	Kent v Scotland	Edinburgh	1987
	8-66	S.R.G.Francis	Somerset v Derbys	Derby	2004
Four Wkts in Four Balls		A.Ward	Derbyshire v Sussex	Derby	1970
		S.M.Pollock	Warwickshire v Leics	Birmingham	1996
		V.C.Drakes	Notts v Derbyshire	Nottingham	1999
		D.A.Payne	Gloucestershire v Essex	Chelmsford	2010
		G.R.Napier	Essex v Surrey	Chelmsford	2013

Most Economical Analyses

8-8-0-0	B.A.Langford	Somerset v Essex	Yeovil	1969
8-7-1-1	D.R.Doshi	Notts v Northants	Northampton	1977
12-9-3-1	J.Simmons	Lancashire v Suffolk	Bury St Eds	1985
8-6-2-3	F.J.Titmus	Middlesex v Northants	Northampton	1972

Most Expensive Analyses

9-0-108-3	S.D.Thomas	Glamorgan v Surrey	The Oval	2002
10-0-107-0	J.W.Dernbach	Surrey v Essex	The Oval	2008
11-0-103-0	G.Welch	Warwicks v Lancs	Birmingham	1995
10-0-101-1	M.J.J.Critchley	Derbyshire v Worcs	Worcester	2016

Century and Five Wickets in an Innings

154*, 5-26	M.J.Procter	Glos v Somerset	Taunton	1972
206, 6-32	A.I.Kallicharran	Warwicks v Oxfords	Birmingham	1984
103, 5-41	C.L.Hooper	Kent v Essex	Maidstone	1993
125, 5-41	I.R.Bell	Warwicks v Essex	Chelmsford	2003

Most Wicket-Keeping Dismissals in an Innings

8 (8 ct)	D.J.S.Taylor	Somerset v British Us	Taunton	1982
8 (8 ct)	D.J.Pipe	Worcs v Herts	Hertford	2001

Most Catches in an Innings by a Fielder

5	J.M.Rice	Hampshire v Warwicks	Southampton	1978
5	D.J.G.Sales	Northants v Essex	Northampton	2007

VITALITY BLAST 2020

In 2020, the Twenty20 competition was again sponsored by Vitality. Between 2003 and 2009, three regional leagues competed to qualify for the knockout stages, but this was reduced to two leagues in 2010, before returning to the three-division format in 2012. In 2014, the competition reverted to two regional leagues. In 2020, due to COVID-19 constraints, it reverted to a three-division format.

CENTRAL GROUP	P	W	L	T	NR	Pts	Net RR
Gloucestershire	10	7	2	–	1	15	+1.01
Northamptonshire	10	5	4	–	1	11	+0.05
Warwickshire	10	5	4	–	1	11	–0.63
Somerset	10	4	5	–	1	9	+0.65
Glamorgan	10	4	5	–	1	9	–0.30
Worcestershire	10	2	7	–	1	5	–0.78

NORTH GROUP	P	W	L	T	NR	Pts	Net RR
Nottinghamshire	10	7	1	–	2	16	+1.31
Lancashire	10	5	3	–	2	12	–0.25
Leicestershire	10	4	3	–	3	11	–0.18
Durham	10	4	5	–	1	9	+0.42
Yorkshire	10	3	5	–	2	8	+0.29
Derbyshire	10	1	7	–	2	4	–1.58

SOUTH GROUP	P	W	L	T	NR	Pts	Net RR
Surrey	10	7	1	1	1	16	+0.65
Sussex	10	6	3	–	1	13	+0.37
Kent	10	5	3	1	1	12	+0.10
Middlesex	10	3	5	1	1	8	–0.29
Essex	10	2	6	1	1	6	0.00
Hampshire	10	2	7	–	1	5	–0.80

QUARTER-FINALS: NOTTINGHAMSHIRE beat Leicestershire on a tie break at Nottingham.
SURREY beat Kent by 56 runs at The Oval.
GLOUCESTERSHIRE beat Northants by seven wickets at Bristol.
LANCASHIRE beat Sussex by 45 runs at Hove.
SEMI-FINALS: SURREY beat Gloucestershire by six wickets at Birmingham.
NOTTINGHAMSHIRE beat Lancashire by five wickets at Birmingham.

LEADING AGGREGATES AND RECORDS 2020

BATTING (400 runs)	M	I	NO	HS	Runs	Avge	100	50	R/100b	Sixes
D.J.Bell-Drummond (Kent)	11	11	1	89	423	42.30	–	3	154.9	12
S.S.Eskinazi (Middx)	10	10	–	84	413	41.30	–	4	148.0	17
L.J.Wright (Sussex)	11	11	–	83	411	37.36	–	2	137.0	7

BOWLING (17 wkts)	O	M	R	W	Avge	BB	4w	R/Over
J.T.Ball (Notts)	34.1	1	259	19	13.63	3-28	–	7.58
D.T.Moriarty (Surrey)	45.0		311	17	18.29	3-25	–	6.91

Highest total	229-8		Somerset v Worcestershire	Birmingham
Highest innings	119	A.J.Hose	Warwickshire v Northants	Birmingham
Highest partnership	171	A.J.Hose/D.R.Mousley	Warwickshire v Northants	Birmingham
Best bowling	6-19	Shaheen Shah Afridi	Hampshire v Middlesex	Southampton
Most economical	4-0-11-3	J.B.Lintott	Warwickshire v Glamorgan	Birmingham
Most expensive	3.4-0-63-2	P.R.Brown	Worcestershire v Glamorgan	Worcester
Most w/k dismissals	12	A.L.Davies (Lancashire)		
Most catches	11	A.D.Hales (Nottinghamshire)		

2020 VITALITY BLAST FINAL
SURREY v NOTTINGHAMSHIRE

At Edgbaston, Birmingham, on 4 October (floodlit).
Result: **NOTTINGHAMSHIRE** won by six wickets.
Toss: Nottinghamshire. Award: D.T.Christian.

SURREY		Runs	Balls	4/6	Fall
J.J.Roy	lbw b Ball	66	47	7/1	5-119
H.M.Amla	c Christian b Patel	3	10	–	1- 18
W.G.Jacks	c Christian b Ball	3	4	–	2- 24
L.J.Evans	c Duckett b Christian	43	23	3/2	3-114
J.Overton	c Moores b Christian	0	1	–	4-115
R.J.Burns	not out	5	5	–	
† B.T.Foakes	c Duckett b Christian	1	3	–	6-122
L.E.Plunkett	c Hales b Christian	4	3	–	7-127
* G.J.Batty					
D.T.Moriarty					
R.J.W.Topley					
Extras	(LB 2)	2			
Total	(7 wkts; 16 overs)	**127**			

NOTTINGHAMSHIRE		Runs	Balls	4/6	Fall
A.D.Hales	c Evans b Topley	0	1	–	1- 0
B.M.Duckett	not out	53	38	8	
J.M.Clarke	c Overton b Jacks	3	6	–	2- 4
S.R.Patel	c Burns b Jacks	7	6	1	3-19
P.D.Trego	lbw b Moriarty	31	21	5/1	4-82
* D.T.Christian	not out	21	1	3	
† T.J.Moores					
S.J.Mullaney					
Imad Wasim					
M.Carter					
J.T.Ball					
Extras	(LB 2, NB 6, W 6)	14			
Total	(4 wkts; 13.2 overs)	**129**			

NOTTINGHAMSHIRE	O	M	R	W	SURREY	O	M	R	W
Patel	4	0	25	1	Topley	3	0	25	1
Ball	3	0	17	2	Jacks	3	0	32	2
Imad Wasim	3	0	28	0	Moriarty	3	0	20	1
Carter	2	0	19	0	Plunkett	1	0	13	0
Mullaney	1	0	13	0	Overton	1	0	16	0
Christian	3	0	23	4	Batty	2.2	0	21	0

Umpires: M.Burns and D.J.Millns

TWENTY20 CUP WINNERS

2003	Surrey	2009	Sussex	2015	Lancashire
2004	Leicestershire	2010	Hampshire	2016	Northamptonshire
2005	Somerset	2011	Leicestershire	2017	Nottinghamshire
2006	Leicestershire	2012	Hampshire	2018	Worcestershire
2007	Kent	2013	Northamptonshire	2019	Essex
2008	Middlesex	2014	Warwickshire	2020	Nottinghamshire

PRINCIPAL TWENTY20 CUP RECORDS 2003-20

Highest Total	260-4		Yorkshire v Northants	Leeds	2017
Highest Total Batting 2nd	231-5		Warwickshire v Northants	Birmingham	2018
Lowest Total	44		Glamorgan v Surrey	The Oval	2019
Largest Victory (Runs)	143		Somerset v Essex	Chelmsford	2011
Largest Victory (Balls)	75		Hampshire v Glos	Bristol	2010
Highest Scores	161	A.Lyth	Yorkshire v Northants	Leeds	2017
	158*	B.B.McCullum	Warwickshire v Derbys	Birmingham	2015
	153*	L.J.Wright	Sussex v Essex	Chelmsford	2014
	152*	G.R.Napier	Essex v Sussex	Chelmsford	2008
	151*	C.H.Gayle	Somerset v Kent	Taunton	2015
Fastest Hundred	34 balls	A.Symonds	Kent v Middlesex	Maidstone	2004
Most Sixes (Innings)	16	G.R.Napier	Essex v Sussex	Chelmsford	2008
Most Runs in Career	4498	L.J.Wright	Sussex		2004-20

Highest Partnership for each Wicket

1st	207	J.L.Denly/D.J.Bell-Drummond	Kent v Essex	Chelmsford	2017
2nd	186	J.L.Langer/C.L.White	Somerset v Glos	Taunton	2006
3rd	171	I.R.Bell/A.J.Hose	Warwickshire v Northants	Birmingham	2018
4th	159*	L.J.Wright/M.W.Machan	Sussex v Essex	Chelmsford	2014
5th	171	A.J.Hose/D.R.Mousley	Warwickshire v Northants	Birmingham	2018
6th	126*	C.S.MacLeod/J.W.Hastings	Durham v Northants	Chester-le-St	2014
7th	80	D.T.Christian/T.S.Roland-Jones	Middlesex v Kent	Canterbury	2014
8th	86*	J.A.Simpson/T.G.Southee	Middlesex v Hampshire	Southampton	2017
9th	69	C.J.Anderson/J.H.Davey	Somerset v Surrey	The Oval	2017
10th	59	H.H.Streak/J.E.Anyon	Warwickshire v Worcs	Birmingham	2005
Best Bowling	7-18	C.N.Ackermann	Leics v Warwicks	Leicester	2019
	6- 5	A.V.Suppiah	Somerset v Glamorgan	Cardiff	2011
	6-16	T.G.Southee	Essex v Glamorgan	Chelmsford	2011
	6-19	T.T.Bresnan	Yorkshire v Lancashire	Leeds	2017
	6-19	Shaheen Shah Afridi	Hampshire v Middlesex	Southampton	2020
	6-21	A.J.Hall	Northants v Worcs	Northampton	2008
	6-24	T.J.Murtagh	Surrey v Middlesex	Lord's	2005
	6-28	J.K.Fuller	Middlesex v Hampshire	Southampton	2018
Most Wkts in Career	172	D.R.Briggs	Hampshire, Sussex		2010-20

Most Economical Innings Analyses (Qualification: 4 overs)

4-2-5-2	A.C.Thomas	Somerset v Hampshire	Southampton	2010
4-0-5-3	D.R.Briggs	Hampshire v Kent	Canterbury	2010

Most Maiden Overs in an Innings

4-2-9-1	M.Morkel	Kent v Surrey	Beckenham	2007
4-2-5-2	A.C.Thomas	Somerset v Hampshire	Southampton	2010
4-2-14-1	S.M.Curran	Surrey v Sussex	Hove	2018

Most Expensive Innings Analyses

4-0-77-0	B.W.Sanderson	Northants v Yorkshire	Leeds	2017
4-0-67-1	R.J.Kirtley	Sussex v Essex	Chelmsford	2008
4-0-67-2	C.P.Wood	Hampshire v Glamorgan	Cardiff	2019

Most Wicket-Keeping Dismissals in Career

114	J.S.Foster	Essex		2003-17

Most Wicket-Keeping Dismissals in an Innings

5 (5 ct)	M.J.Prior	Sussex v Middlesex	Richmond	2006
5 (4 ct, 1 st)	G.L.Brophy	Yorkshire v Durham	Chester-le-St	2008
5 (3 ct, 2 st)	B.J.M.Scott	Worcs v Yorkshire	Worcester	2011
5 (4 ct, 1 st)	G.C.Wilson	Surrey v Hampshire	The Oval	2014
5 (5 ct)	N.J.O'Brien	Leics v Northants	Leicester	2014
5 (3 ct, 2 st)	J.A.Simpson	Middlesex v Surrey	Lord's	2014
5 (4 ct, 1 st)	C.B.Cooke	Glamorgan v Surrey	Cardiff	2016

Most Catches in Career

105	S.J.Croft	Lancashire		2006-20

Most Catches in an Innings by a Fielder

5	M.W.Machan	Sussex v Glamorgan	Hove	2016

THE HUNDRED REGISTER

BIRMINGHAM PHOENIX

Venue: Edgbaston, Birmingham. **Men's Head Coach**: Andrew McDonald. **Women's Head Coach**: Ben Sawyer. **Men's Captain**: Moeen Ali. **Women's Captain**: Sophie Devine.

ABELL, Thomas Benjamin – *see SOMERSET*. £80,000.

ALI, Moeen Munir – *see WORCESTERSHIRE*. £100,000.

BELL-DRUMMOND, Daniel James – *see KENT*. £32,000.

BROOKES, Henry James Hamilton – *see WARWICKSHIRE*. £32,000.

BROWN, Patrick Rhys – *see WORCESTERSHIRE*. £48,000.

COOKE, Christopher Barry – *see GLAMORGAN*. £24,000.

HAMMOND, Miles Arthur Halhead – *see GLOUCESTERSHIRE*. £24,000.

HELM, Thomas George – *see MIDDLESEX*. £60,000.

HOSE, Adam John – *see WARWICKSHIRE*. £40,000.

HOWELL, Benny Alexander Cameron – *see GLOUCESTERSHIRE*. £60,000.

LIVINGSTONE, Liam Stephen – *see LANCASHIRE*. £100,000.

[NO]**SHAHEEN Shah AFRIDI** – *see HAMPSHIRE*. Overseas. £48,000.

SIBLEY, Dominic Peter – *see WARWICKSHIRE*. Central.

[NO]**WILLIAMSON, Kane** Stuart (Tauranga Boys' C), b Tauranga, New Zealand 8 Aug 1990. Cousin of D.Cleaver (C Districts 2010-11 to date). 5'8". RHB, OB. N Districts 2007-08 to date. Gloucestershire 2011-12; cap 2011. Yorkshire 2013-18. IPL: SH 2015-21. Tests (NZ): 83 (2010-11 to 2020-21, 35 as captain); 1000 runs (1): 1172 (2015); HS 251 v WI (Hamilton) 2020-21; scored 131 v I (Ahmedabad) 2010-11 on debut; BB 4-44 v E (Auckland) 2012-13. **LOI** (NZ): 151 (2010 to 2019-20, 77 as captain); 1000 runs (1): 1376 (2015); HS 148 v WI (Manchester) 2019; BB 4-22 v SA (Paarl) 2012-13. **IT20** (NZ): 64 (2011-12 to 2020-21, 46 as captain); HS 95 v I (Hamilton) 2019-20; BB 2-16 v B (Mt Maunganui) 2016-17. F-c Tours (NZ)(C=Captain): E 2013, 2015; A 2011-12, 2015-16, 2019-20C; SA 2012-13, 2016C; WI 2012, 2014; I 2010-11, 2012, 2016-17C; SL 2012-13, 2019C; Z 2011-12, 2016C; B 2013-14; UAE 2014-15 (v P), 2018-19C (v P). HS 284* ND v Wellington (Lincoln) 2011-12. CC HS 189 Y v Sussex (Scarborough) 2014. BB 5-75 ND v Canterbury (Christchurch) 2008-09. CC BB 3-58 Gs v Northants (Northampton) 2012. LO HS 148 (*see LOI*). LO BB 5-51 ND v Auckland (Auckland) 2009-10. T20 HS 101*. T20 BB 3-33. Overseas. £80,000.

WOAKES, Christopher Roger – *see WARWICKSHIRE*. Central.

[NO]**ZAMPA, Adam**, b Shellharbour, NSW, Australia 31 Mar 1992. RHB, LB. New South Wales 2012-13. S Australia 2013-14 to date. Essex 2018-19 (T20 only). IPL: RPS 2016-17. RCB 2020-21. Big Bash: ST 2012-13. AS 2013-14 to 2014-15. MS 2015-16 to date. LOI (A): 61 (2015-16 to 2020-21); HS 22 v SA (Adelaide) 2018-19; BB 4-43 v P (Abu Dhabi) 2018-19. IT20 (A): 41 (2015-16 to 2020-21); HS 13* v NZ (Christchurch) 2020-21; BB 3-14 v SL (Adelaide) 2019-20. HS 74 SA v WA (Adelaide) 2014-15. BB 6-62 (10-119 match) SA v Q (Adelaide) 2016-17. LO HS 66 SA v Q (N Sydney) 2013-14. LO BB 4-18 SA v WA (Brisbane) 2014-15. T20 HS 23. T20 BB 6-19. Overseas. £40,000.

LONDON SPIRIT

Venue: Lord's Cricket Ground, London. **Men's Head Coach**: Shane Warne. **Women's Head Coach**: Trevor Griffin. **Men's Captain**: Eoin Morgan. **Women's Captain**: Heather Knight.

BOPARA, Ravinder Singh – *see SUSSEX*. £60,000.

CRANE, Mason Sydney – *see HAMPSHIRE*. £40,000.

CRAWLEY, Zak – *see KENT*. Central.

DENLY, Joseph Liam – *see KENT*. £48,000.

DERNBACH, Jade Winston – *see SURREY*. £24,000.

LAWRENCE, Daniel William – *see ESSEX*. £48,000.

NQ**MAXWELL, Glenn** James, b Kew, Melbourne, Australia 14 Oct 1988. 5'9". RHB, OB. Victoria 2010-11 to date. Hampshire 2014. Yorkshire 2015. Lancashire 2019. IPL: DD 2012-18. MI 2013. KXIP 2014 to date. Big Bash: MR 2011-12. MS 2012-13 to date. **Tests** (A): 7 (2012-13 to 2017); HS 104 v I (Ranchi) 2016-17; BB 4-127 v I (Hyderabad) 2012-13. **LOI** (A): 116 (2012 to 2020-21); HS 108 v E (Manchester) 2020; BB 4-46 v E (Perth) 2014-15. **IT20** (A): 69 (2012 to 2020-21); HS 145* v SL (Pallekele) 2016; BB 3-10 v E (Hobart) 2017-18. F-c Tours (A): I 2012-13, 2016-17; SA/Z 2013 (Aus A); B 2017; UAE 2014-15 (v P). HS 278 Vic v NSW (Sydney, NO) 2017-18. CC HS 140 Y v Durham (Scarborough) 2015. BB 5-40 La v Middx (Lord's) 2019. LO HS 146 H v Lancs (Manchester) 2014 (RLC). LO BB 4-46 (*see LOI*). T20 HS 145*. T20 BB 3-10. Overseas. £100,000.

NQ**MOHAMMAD AMIR**, b Gujar Khan, Punjab, Pakistan 13 Apr 1992. LHB, LF. Federal Areas 2008-09. National Bank 2008-09 to 2009-10. SSGC 2015-16 to 2018-19. Essex 2017-19. **Tests** (P): 36 (2009 to 2018-19); HS 48 v A (Brisbane) 2016-17; BB 6-44 v WI (Kingston) 2017. **LOI** (P): 61 (2009 to 2019-20); HS 73* v NZ (Abu Dhabi) 2009-10; BB 5-30 v A (Taunton) 2019. **IT20** (P): 50 (2009 to 2020); HS 21* v A (Birmingham) 2010; BB 4-13 v SL (Lahore) 2017-18. F-c Tours (P): E 2010, 2016, 2018; A 2009-10, 2016-17; SA 2018-19; WI 2017; NZ 2009-10, 2016-17; WI 2017; SL 2009; Ire 2018. HS 66 SSGC v Lahore Blues (Lahore) 2015-16. CC HS 28 Ex v Kent (Canterbury) 2019. 50 wkts (0+1): 56 (2008-09). BB 7-61 (10-97 match) NBP v Lahore Shalimar (Lahore) 2008-09. CC BB 5-18 (10-72 match) Ex v Yorks (Scarborough) 2017. LO HS 73* (*see LOI*). LO BB 5-30 (*see LOI*). T20 HS 21*. T20 BB 6-17. Overseas. £80,000.

NQ**MOHAMMAD NABI** – *see NORTHAMPTONSHIRE*. Overseas. £80,000.

MORGAN, Eoin Joseph Gerard – *see MIDDLESEX*. £100,000.

REECE, Luis Michael – *see DERBYSHIRE*. £24,000.

ROSSINGTON, Adam Matthew – *see NORTHAMPTONSHIRE*. £32,000.

VAN DER MERWE, Roelof Erasmus – *see SOMERSET*. £32,000.

WOOD, Christopher Philip – *see HAMPSHIRE*. £40,000.

WOOD, Mark Andrew – *see DURHAM*. £60,000.

MANCHESTER ORIGINALS

Venue: Old Trafford, Manchester. **Men's Head Coach**: Simon Katich. **Women's Head Coach**: Paul Shaw. **Men's Captain**: tba. **Women's Captain**: Kate Cross.

ACKERMANN, Colin Niel – *see LEICESTERSHIRE*. £32,000.

BUTTLER, Joseph Charles – *see LANCASHIRE*. Central.

CLARKE, Joe Michael – *see NOTTINGHAMSHIRE*. £60,000.

FINN, Steven Thomas – *see MIDDLESEX*. £32,000.

GLEESON, Richard James – *see LANCASHIRE*. £24,000.

GURNEY, Harry Frederick – *see NOTTINGHAMSHIRE*. £80,000.

HARTLEY, Tom William – *see LANCASHIRE*. £24,000.

LAMMONBY, Thomas Alexander – *see SOMERSET*. £40,000.

MADSEN, Wayne Lee – *see DERBYSHIRE*. £40,000.

OVERTON, Jamie – *see SURREY*. £48,000.

PARKINSON, Matthew William – *see LANCASHIRE*. £60,000.

NQ**POORAN, Nicolas**, b Trinidad 2 Oct 1995. LHB, WK. Trinidad & Tobago 2014-15. IPL: KXIP 2019 to date. Big Bash: MS 2020-21. Yorkshire 2019 (T20 only). **LOI** (WI): 25 (2018-19 to 2019-20); HS 118 v SL (Chester-le-St) 2019. **IT20** (WI): 24 (2016 to 2020-21); HS 58 v E (Gros Islet) 2018-19. HS 69 WI A v New Zealand A (Nelson) 2020-21. LO HS 118 (*see LOI*). T20 HS 100*. Overseas. £100,000.

NQ**RABADA, Kagiso**, b Johannesburg, South Africa 25 May 1995. 6'3". LHB, RF. Gauteng 2013-14. Lions 2013-14 to 2017-18. Kent 2016. IPL: DD 2017. DC 2019 to date. **Tests** (SA): 45 (2015-16 to 2020-21); HS 34 v NZ (Hamilton) 2016-17; 50 wkts (2); most – 57 (2017); BB 7-112 (13-144 match) v E (Centurion) 2019-16. **LOI** (SA): 75 (2015 to 2019); HS 31* v I (Southampton) 2019; BB 6-16 v B (Dhaka) 2015 – on debut. **IT20** (SA): 26 (2014-15 to 2020-21); HS 22 v A (Johannesburg) 2019-20; BB 3-30 v NZ (Centurion) 2015. F-c Tours (SA): E 2017; A 2014 (SA A), 2016-17; NZ 2016-17; I 2015-16, 2019-20; P 2020-21; SL 2018. HS 48* Lions v Titans (Johannesburg) 2014-15. CC HS 14 and CC BB 4-118 K v Essex (Chelmsford) 2016. BB 9-33 (14-105 match) Lions v Dolphins (Johannesburg) 2014-15. LO HS 31* (*see LOI*). LO BB 6-16 (*see LOI*). T20 HS 44. T20 BB 4-21. Overseas. £100,000.

SALT, Philip Dean – *see SUSSEX*. £80,000.

NQ**SHADAB KHAN**, b Mianwali, Punjab, Pakistan 4 Oct 1998. 5'10". RHB, LBG. Rawalpindi 2016-17. SNGPL 2017-18. Northern 2019-20. Big Bash: BH 2017-18. **Tests** (P): 6 (2017 to 2020); HS 56 v E (Leeds) 2018; BB 3-31 v Ire (Dublin) 2018. **LOI** (P): 43 (2017 to 2019-20); HS 54 v NZ (Wellington) 2017-18; BB 4-28 v Z (Bulawayo) 2018. **IT20** (P): 46 (2016-17 to 2020-21); HS 42 v NZ (Auckland) 2020-21; BB 4-14 v WI (Port of Spain) 2017. F-c Tours (P): E 2016 (PA), 2018, 2020; SA 2018-19; WI 2017; Z 2016-17 (PA); Ire 2018. HS 132 PA v Zimbabwe A (Bulawayo) 2016-17. BB 6-77 (10-157 match) P v Northants (Northampton) 2018. LO HS 56 Rawalpindi v FATA (Islamabad) 2016-17. LO BB 4-28 (*see LOI*). T20 HS 77. T20 BB 4-14. Overseas. £48,000.

NORTHERN SUPERCHARGERS

Venue: Emerald Headingley, Leeds. **Men's Head Coach**: Darren Lehmann. **Women's Head Coach**: Danielle Hazell. **Men's Captain**: Aaron Finch. **Women's Captain**: Lauren Winfield-Hill.

BROOK, Harry Cherrington – *see YORKSHIRE*. £32,000.

CARSE, Brydon Alexander – *see DURHAM*. £40,000.

[NQ]**FINCH, Aaron** James, b Colac, Victoria, Australia 17 Nov 1986. 5'9". RHB, SLA. Victoria 2007-08 to date. Yorkshire 2014-15. Surrey 2016-19; cap 2018. IPL: RR: 2009-10. DD 2011-12. PW 2013. SH 2014. MI 2015. GL 2016-17. KXIP 2018. RCB: 2020-21. Big Bash: MR 2011-12 to date. **Tests** (A): 5 (2018-19); HS 62 v P (Dubai, DSC) 2018-19; BB – . **LOI** (A): 132 (2012-13 to 2020-21, 41 as captain); HS 153* v P (Sharjah) 2018-19; BB 1-2 v I (Pune) 2013-14. **IT20** (A): 68 (2010-11 to 2020-21, 41 as captain); HS 172 v Z (Harare) 2018 – world record IT20 score. F-c Tours (Aus A): SA/Z 2013; Z 2011; UAE 2018-19 (v P)(A). HS 288* Cricket A v New Zealanders (Sydney) 2015-16. CC HS 110 Y v Warwks (Birmingham) 2014 and 110 Sy v Warwks (Guildford) 2016. BB 1-0 Vic v WA (Perth) 2013-14. LO HS 188* Vic v Q (Melbourne) 2019-20. LO BB 2-44 Aus A v EL (Hobart) 2012-13. T20 HS 172. T20 BB 1-9. Overseas. £100,000.

FISHER, Matthew David – *see YORKSHIRE*. £40,000.

KOHLER-CADMORE, Tom – *see YORKSHIRE*. £40,000.

[NQ]**LYNN, Chris**topher Austin, b Herston, Brisbane, Australia 10 Apr 1990. RHB, SLA. Queensland 2009-10 to 2016-17. IPL: DC 2012. KKR 2014-19. Big Bash: BH 2011-12 to date. **LOI** (A): 4 (2016-17 to 2018-19); HS 44 v SA (Adelaide) 2018-19. **IT20** (A): 18 (2013-14 to 2018-19); HS 44 v NZ (Sydney) 2017-18. HS 250 Q v Vic (Brisbane) 2014-15. BB – . LO HS 135 Q v NSW (Sydney, DO) 2018-19. LO BB 1-3 Q v WA (Sydney, BO) 2013-14. T20 HS 113*. T20 BB 2-15. Overseas. £80,000.

LYTH, Adam – *see YORKSHIRE*. £60,000.

[NQ]**MUJEEB ZADRAN** – *see MIDDLESEX*. Overseas. £100,000.

PARKINSON, Callum Francis – *see LEICESTERSHIRE*. £24,000.

POTTS, Matthew James – *see DURHAM*. £48,000.

RASHID, Adil Usman – *see YORKSHIRE*. £80,000.

SIMPSON, John Andrew – *see MIDDLESEX*. £24,000.

STOKES, Benjamin Andrew – *see DURHAM*. Central.

STONE, Oliver Peter – *see WARWICKSHIRE*. £48,000.

WILLEY, David Jonathan – *see YORKSHIRE*. £60,000.

OVAL INVINCIBLES

Venue: The Kia Oval, London. **Men's Head Coach**: Tom Moody. **Women's Head Coach**: Jonathan Batty. **Men's Captain**: tba. **Women's Captain**: Rachael Haynes.

BILLINGS, Samuel William – *see KENT*. £80,000.

BLAKE, Alexander James – *see KENT*. £24,000.

BURNS, Rory Joseph – *see SURREY*. Central.

CLARK, Jordan – *see SURREY*. £32,000.

CURRAN, Samuel Matthew – *see SURREY*. Central.

CURRAN, Thomas Kevin – *see SURREY*. £80,000.

EVANS, Laurie John – *see SURREY*. £40,000.

GLOVER, Brandon Dale – *see NORTHAMPTONSHIRE*. £32,000.

INGRAM, Colin Alexander – *see GLAMORGAN*. £48,000.

JACKS, William George – *see SURREY*. £40,000.

NQ**LAMICHHANE, Sandeep**, b Syangja, Nepal 2 Aug 2000. RHB, LBG. Nepal 2019-20. IPL: DD 2018. DC 2019. Big Bash: MS 2018-19 to 2019-20. HH 2020-21. **LOI** (Nepal): 10 (2018 to 2019-20); HS 28 v Oman (Kirtipur) 2019-20; BB 6-16 v USA (Kirtipur) 2019-20. **IT20** (Nepal): 20 (+ 1 ICC World XI 2018) (2018 to 2019-20); HS 9 v Qatar (Singapore) 2019; BB 4-20 v Neth (Al Amerat) 2019-20. HS 39* and BB 3-84 Nepal v MCC (Kirtipur) 2019-20. LO HS 28 (*see LOI*). LO BB 6-16 (*see LOI*). T20 HS 10*. T20 BB 4-10. Overseas. £60,000.

MAHMOOD, Saqib – *see LANCASHIRE*. £60,000.

NQ**NARINE, Sunil** Philip, b Arima, Trinidad 26 May 1988. LHB, OB. Trinidad & Tobago 2008-09 to 2012-13. IPL: KKR 2012 to date. Big Bash: SS 2012-13. MR 2016-17. **Tests** (WI): 6 (2012 to 2013-14); HS 22* v B (Dhaka) 2012-13; BB 6-91 v NZ (Hamilton) 2013-14. **LOI** (WI): 65 (2011-12 to 2016-17); HS 36 v B (Khulna) 2012-13; BB 6-27 v SA (Providence) 2016. **IT20** (WI): 51 (2011-12 to 2019); HS 30 v P (Dubai, DSC) 2016-17; BB 4-12 v NZ (Lauderhill) 2012. F-c Tours (WI): E 2012; NZ 2013-14; B 2012-13. HS 40* WI A v Bangladesh A (Gros Islet) 2011-12. BB 8-17 (13-39 match) T&T v CC&C (Cave Hill) 2011-12. LO HS 51 T&T v Barbados (Bridgetown) 2017-18. LO BB 6-9 T&T v Guyana (Port of Spain) 2014-15. T20 HS 79. T20 BB 5-19. Overseas. £100,000.

ROY, Jason Jonathan – *see SURREY*. £100,000.

SOWTER, Nathan Adam – *see MIDDLESEX*. £24,000.

TOPLEY, Reece James William – *see SURREY*. £48,000.

SOUTHERN BRAVE

Venue: Ageas Bowl, Southampton. **Men's Head Coach**: Mahela Jayawardena. **Women's Head Coach**: Charlotte Edwards. **Men's Captain**: tba. **Women's Captain**: tba.

ARCHER, Jofra Chioke – *see SUSSEX*. Central.

BRIGGS, Danny Richard – *see WARWICKSHIRE*. £48,000.

DAVIES, Alexander Luke – *see LANCASHIRE*. £40,000.

DAWSON, Liam Andrew – *see HAMPSHIRE*. £60,000.

GARTON, George Henry Simmons – *see SUSSEX*. £32,000.

JORDAN, Christopher James – *see SUSSEX*. £60,000.

MILLS, Tymal Solomon – *see SUSSEX*. £48,000.

OVERTON, Craig – *see SOMERSET*. £24,000.

RAWLINS, Delray Millard Wendell – *see SUSSEX*. £40,000.

[NO]**RUSSELL, Andre** Dwayne, b Jamaica 29 Apr 1988. RHB, RF. Jamaica 2006-07 to 2013-14. IPL: DC 2012-13. KKR 2014 to date. Big Bash: MR 2014-15. ST 2015-16 to 2016-17. Worcestershire 2013 (T20 only). Nottinghamshire 2016 (T20 only). **Tests** (WI): 1 (2010-11); HS 2 and BB 1-73 v SL (Galle). **LOI** (WI): 56 (2010-11 to 2019); HS 92* v I (North Sound) 2011; BB 4-35 v I (Kingston) 2011. **IT20** (WI): 49 (2011 to 2019-20); HS 47 v B (Lauderhill) 2018; BB 2-10 v B (Dhaka) 2013-14. F-c Tours (WI): E 2010 (WI A); SL 2010-11. HS 128 WI A v Bangladesh A (North Sound) 2011-12. BB 5-36 WI A v Bangladesh A (Gros Islet) 2011-12. LO HS 132* (in 56 balls, inc 13 sixes) Sagicor HPC v Bangladesh A (Bridgetown) 2014. LO BB 6-28 Sagicor HPC v Bangladesh A (Lucas Street) 2014. T20 HS 121*. T20 BB 4-11. Overseas. £100,000.

[NO]**STOINIS, Marcus** Peter (Hale S, Wembley Downs, Perth; U of WA), b Perth, W Australia 16 Aug 1989. RHB, RMF. W Australia 2008-09 to date. Victoria 2012-13 to 2016-17. IPL: KXIP 2016-18. RCB 2019. DC 2020-21. Big Bash: PS 2012-13. MS 2013-14 to date. Kent 2018 (T20 only). **LOI** (A): 45 (2015 to 2020-21); HS 146* v NZ (Auckland) 2016-17; BB 3-16 v SA (Perth) 2018-19. **IT20** (A): 25 (2015 to 2020-21); HS 78 v NZ (Dunedin) 2020-21; BB 2-27 v I (Brisbane) 2018-19. F-c Tour (Aus A): I 2015. HS 170 Vic v Tas (Melbourne) 2013-14. BB 4-73 WA v Vic (Perth) 2018-19. LO HS 146* (*see LOI*). LO BB 4-43 Vic v SA (Sydney, BO) 2015-16. T20 HS 147*. T20 BB 4-15. Overseas. £80,000.

VINCE, James Michael – *see HAMPSHIRE*. £80,000.

WALLER, Maximilian Thomas Charles – *see SOMERSET*. £24,000.

[NO]**WARNER, David** Andrew, b Paddington, Sydney, NSW, Australia 27 Oct 1986. 5'7''. LHB, LBG. NSW 2008-09 to date. IPL: DD 2009-13. SH 2014 to date. Big Bash: ST 2011-12 to 2013-14. SS 2012-13. Durham 2009 (T20 only). Middlesex 2010 (T20 and one l-o match). **Tests** (A): 86 (2011-12 to 2020-21); HS 335* v P (Adelaide) 2019-20; BB 2-45 v WI (Bridgetown) 2012. **LOI** (A): 128 (2008-09 to 2020-21); HS 179 v P (Adelaide) 2016-17. **IT20** (A): 81 (2008-09 to 2020); HS 100* v SL (Adelaide) 2019-20. In 2008-09, he became the first man to play for Australia before making f-c debut since 1877. F-c Tours (A): E 2013, 2015, 2019; SA 2013-14, 2017-18; WI 2012, 2015; NZ 2015-16; I 2012-13, 2016-17; SL 2016; B 2017; UAE (v P) 2014-15. HS 335* (*see Tests*). BB 2-45 (*see Tests*). LO HS 197 NSW v Vic (Sydney, NS) 2013-14. LO BB 1-11 NSW v Q (Brisbane) 2009-10. T20 HS 135*. Overseas. £100,000.

WHITELEY, Ross Andrew – *see WORCESTERSHIRE*. £32,000.

TRENT ROCKETS

Venue: Trent Bridge, Nottingham. **Men's Head Coach**: Andy Flower. **Women's Head Coach**: Salliann Briggs. **Men's Captain**: Lewis Gregory. **Women's Captain**: Nat Sciver.

CARTER, Matthew – *see NOTTINGHAMSHIRE*. £40,000.

NQ**COULTER-NILE, Nathan** Mitchell, b Perth, Australia 11 Oct 1987. 6'3''. RHB, RF. W Australia 2009-10 to 2017-18. IPL: MI 2013 to date. DD 2014-16. KKR 2017. Big Bash: PS 2011-12 to 2018-19. MS 2019-20 to date. **LOI** (A): 32 (2013 to 2019); HS 92 v WI (Nottingham) 2019; BB 4-48 v SA (Perth) 2014-15. **IT20** (A): 28 (2012-13 to 2018-19); HS 34 v P (Abu Dhabi) 2018-19; BB 4-31 v E (Hobart) 2013-14. F-c Tours (Aus A): E 2012; SA 2013. HS 64 WA v Tas (Perth) 2014-15. BB 6-84 WA v Q (Brisbane) 2012-13. LO HS 92 (*see LOI*). LO BB 5-26 WA v Vic (Sydney, BO) 2014-15. T20 HS 42*. T20 BB 4-10. Overseas. £60,000.

COX, Oliver **Ben** – *see WORCESTERSHIRE*. £24,000.

GREGORY, Lewis – *see SOMERSET*. £80,000.

HALES, Alexander Daniel – *see NOTTINGHAMSHIRE*. £80,000.

MALAN, Dawid Johannes – *see YORKSHIRE*. £60,000.

MOORES, Thomas James – *see NOTTINGHAMSHIRE*. £40,000.

MULLANEY, Steven John – *see NOTTINGHAMSHIRE*. £48,000.

PATEL, Samit Rohit – *see NOTTINGHAMSHIRE*. £24,000.

NQ**RASHID KHAN** – *see SUSSEX*. Overseas. £100,000.

ROOT, Joseph Edward – *see YORKSHIRE*. Central.

NQ**SHORT, D'Arcy** John Matthew, b Katherine, N Territory, Australia 9 Aug 1990. 5'11''. LHB, SLC. W Australia 2016-17 to date. IPL: RR 2018. Big Bash: HH 2016-17 to date. Durham 2019 (T20 only). **LOI** (A): 8 (2018 to 2019-20); HS 69 v SA (Bloemfontein) 2019-20; BB – . **IT20** (A): 23 (2017-18 to 2020-21); HS 76 v NZ (Auckland) 2017-18 and 76 v P (Harare) 2018; BB 1-13 v P (Abu Dhabi) 2018-19. HS 66 WA v SA (Adelaide, GS) 2017-18. BB 3-78 WA v Vic (Melbourne) 2017-18. LO HS 257 (inc world record 23 sixes) WA v Q (Sydney, HO) 2018-19 – 3rd highest l-o score on record. LO BB 3-53 WA v Vic (Perth) 2017-18. T20 HS 122*. T20 BB 5-21. Overseas. £100,000.

VAN DER GUGTEN, Timm – *see GLAMORGAN*. £48,000.

WOOD, Luke – *see LANCASHIRE*. £32,000.

WRIGHT, Luke James – *see SUSSEX*. £32,000.

WELSH FIRE

Venue: Sophia Gardens, Cardiff. **Men's Head Coach**: Gary Kirsten. **Women's Head Coach**: Matthew Mott. **Men's Captain**: tba. **Women's Captain**: tba.

BAIRSTOW, Jonathan Marc – *see YORKSHIRE*. £100,000.

BALL, Jacob Timothy ('**Jake**') – *see NOTTINGHAMSHIRE*. £60,000.

BANTON, Thomas – *see SOMERSET*. £80,000.

COBB, Joshua James – *see NORTHAMPTONSHIRE*. £40,000.

COCKBAIN, Ian Andrew – *see GLOUCESTERSHIRE*. £48,000.

CRITCHLEY, Matthew James John – *see DERBYSHIRE*. £24,000.

DUCKETT, Ben Matthew – *see NOTTINGHAMSHIRE*. £60,000.

HIGGINS, Ryan Francis – *see GLOUCESTERSHIRE*. £32,000.

LLOYD, David Liam – *see GLAMORGAN*. £24,000.

PAYNE, David Alan – *see GLOUCESTERSHIRE*. £32,000.

PLUNKETT, Liam Edward – *see SURREY*. £40,000.

[NQ]**POLLARD, Kieron** Adrian, b Tacarigua, Trinidad 12 May 1987. RHB, RM. Trinidad & Tobago 2006-07 to 2014-15. IPL: MI 2009-10 to date. Big Bash: AS 2012-13 to 2016-17. MR 2017-18. Somerset 2010-11 (T20 only). **LOI** (WI): 113 (2007 to 2019-20); HS 119 v I (Chennai) 2011-12; BB 3-27 v SA (Rosseau) 2010. **IT20** (WI): 76 (2008 to 2020-21); HS 75* v NZ (Auckland) 2020-21; BB 4-25 v Ire (Basseterre) 2019-20. HS 174 T&T v Barbados (Pointe-a-Pierre) 2008-09. BB 5-36 T&T v Windward Is (Couva) 2014-15. LO HS 119 (*see LOI*). LO BB 5-17 T&T v Barbados (North Sound) 2020-21. T20 HS 104. T20 BB 4-15. Overseas. £100,000.

POPE, Oliver John Douglas – *see SURREY*. Central.

[NQ]**QAIS AHMAD** Kamawal, b Nangarhar, Afghanistan 15 Aug 2000. RHB, LB. Speen Ghar Region 2017-18 to 2018-19. Big Bash: HH 2018-19 to 2019-20. **Tests** (Afg): 1 (2019); HS 14 and BB 1-22 v B (Chittagong) 2019. **IT20** (Afg): 1 (2019-20); HS 0* and BB 3-25 v Ire (Greater Noida) 2019-20. HS 46* Afg A v Bangladesh A (Khulna) 2019. BB 7-41 SGR v Band-e-Amir (Ghazi Amanullah Khan) 2019. **IT20** (A): 11 (2016-17 to 2020-21); HS 11 and BB 2-31 v NZ (Christchurch) 2020-21. HS 71 WA v Tas (Perth) 2017-18. BB 8-47 (11-105 match) WA v NSW (Perth) 2018-19. LO HS 29* WA v Tas (Sydney, HO) 2018-19. T20 HS 33*. T20 BB 4-19. Overseas. £80,000.

[NQ]**RICHARDSON, Jhye** Avon, b Murdoch, W Australia 20 Sep 1996. RHB, RF. W Australia 2015-16 to date. Big Bash: PS 2015-16 to date. **Tests** (A): 2 (2018-19); HS 1 and BB 3-26 v SL (Brisbane) 2018-19. **LOI** (A): 13 (2017-18 to 2019-20); HS 29 v I (Delhi) 2018-19; BB 4-26 v I (Sydney) 2018-19. **IT20** (A): 11 (2016-17 to 2020-21); HS 11 and BB 2-31 v NZ (Christchurch) 2020-21. HS 71 WA v Tas (Perth) 2017-18. BB 8-47 (11-105 match) WA v NSW (Perth) 2018-19. LO HS 29* WA v Tas (Sydney, HO) 2018-19. T20 HS 33*. T20 BB 4-19. Overseas. £80,000.

YOUNG CRICKETER OF THE YEAR

This annual award, made by The Cricket Writers' Club, is currently restricted to players qualified for England, Andrew Symonds meeting that requirement at the time of his award, and under the age of 23 on 1st May. In 1986 their ballot resulted in a dead heat. Up to 8 April 2021 their selections have gained a tally of 2,848 international Test match caps (shown in bracke

1950	R.Tattersall (16)	1974	P.H.Edmonds (51)	1997	B.C.Hollioake (2)
1951	P.B.H.May (66)	1975	A.Kennedy	1998	A.Flintoff (79)
1952	F.S.Trueman (67)	1976	G.Miller (34)	1999	A.J.Tudor (10)
1953	M.C.Cowdrey (114)	1977	I.T.Botham (102)	2000	P.J.Franks
1954	P.J.Loader (13)	1978	D.I.Gower (117)	2001	O.A.Shah (6)
1955	K.F.Barrington (82)	1979	P.W.G.Parker (1)	2002	R.Clarke (2)
1956	B.Taylor	1980	G.R.Dilley (41)	2003	J.M.Anderson (160)
1957	M.J.Stewart (8)	1981	M.W.Gatting (79)	2004	I.R.Bell (118)
1958	A.C.D.Ingleby-Mackenzie	1982	N.G.Cowans (19)	2005	A.N.Cook (161)
1959	G.Pullar (28)	1983	N.A.Foster (29)	2006	S.C.J.Broad (146)
1960	D.A.Allen (39)	1984	R.J.Bailey (4)	2007	A.U.Rashid (19)
1961	P.H.Parfitt (37)	1985	D.V.Lawrence (5)	2008	R.S.Bopara (13)
1962	P.J.Sharpe (12)	1986 {	A.A.Metcalfe	2009	J.W.A.Taylor (7)
1963	G.Boycott (108)		J.J.Whitaker (1)	2010	S.T.Finn (36)
1964	J.M.Brearley (39)	1987	R.J.Blakey (2)	2011	J.M.Bairstow (74)
1965	A.P.E.Knott (95)	1988	M.P.Maynard (4)	2012	J.E.Root (103)
1966	D.L.Underwood (86)	1989	N.Hussain (96)	2013	B.A.Stokes (71)
1967	A.W.Greig (58)	1990	M.A.Atherton (115)	2014	A.Z.Lees
1968	R.M.H.Cottam (4)	1991	M.R.Ramprakash (52)	2015	J.A.Leaning
1969	A.Ward (5)	1992	I.D.K.Salisbury (15)	2016	B.M.Duckett (4)
1970	C.M.Old (46)	1993	M.N.Lathwell (2)	2017	D.W.Lawrence (5)
1971	J.Whitehouse	1994	J.P.Crawley (37)	2018	S.M.Curran (21)
1972	D.R.Owen-Thomas	1995	A.Symonds (26 – Australia)	2019	T.Banton
1973	M.Hendrick (30)	1996	C.E.W.Silverwood (6)	2020	Z.Crawley (12)

THE PROFESSIONAL CRICKETERS' ASSOCIATION

PLAYER OF THE YEAR

Founded in 1967, the Professional Cricketers' Association introduced this award, decided by their membership, in 1970. The award, now known as the Reg Hayter Cup, is presented at the PCA's Annual Awards Dinner in London.

1970 {	M.J.Procter	1987	R.J.Hadlee	2005	A.Flintoff
	J.D.Bond	1988	G.A.Hick	2006	M.R.Ramprakash
1971	L.R.Gibbs	1989	S.J.Cook	2007	O.D.Gibson
1972	A.M.E.Roberts	1990	G.A.Gooch	2008	M.van Jaarsveld
1973	P.G.Lee	1991	Waqar Younis	2009	M.E.Trescothick
1974	B.Stead	1992	C.A.Walsh	2010	N.M.Carter
1975	Zaheer Abbas	1993	S.L.Watkin	2011	M.E.Trescothick
1976	P.G.Lee	1994	B.C.Lara	2012	N.R.D.Compton
1977	M.J.Procter	1995	D.G.Cork	2013	M.M.Ali
1978	J.K.Lever	1996	P.V.Simmons	2014	A.Lyth
1979	J.K.Lever	1997	S.P.James	2015	C.Rushworth
1980	R.D.Jackman	1998	M.B.Loye	2016	B.M.Duckett
1981	R.J.Hadlee	1999	S.G.Law	2017	S.R.Patel
1982	M.D.Marshall	2000	M.E.Trescothick	2018	J.L.Denly
1983	K.S.McEwan	2001	D.P.Fulton	2019	B.A.Stokes
1984	R.J.Hadlee	2002	M.P.Vaughan	2020	C.R.Woakes
1985	N.V.Radford	2003	Mushtaq Ahmed		
1986	C.A.Walsh	2004	A.Flintoff		

2020 FIRST-CLASS AVERAGES

These averages involve the 361 players who appeared in the 54 first-class matches played by 24 teams in England and Wales during the 2020 season.

'Cap' denotes the season in which the player was awarded a 1st XI cap by the county he represented in 2020. If he played for more than one county in 2020, the county(ies) who awarded him his cap is (are) underlined. Durham abolished both their capping and 'awards' system after the 2005 season. Glamorgan's capping system is based on a player's number of appearances. Gloucestershire now cap players on first-class debut. Worcestershire now award county colours when players make their Championship debut.

Team abbreviations: CU – Cambridge University; De – Derbyshire; Du – Durham; E – England; Ex – Essex; Gm – Glamorgan; Gs – Gloucestershire; H – Hampshire; K – Kent; La – Lancashire; Le – Leicestershire; M – Middlesex; Nh – Northamptonshire; Nt – Nottinghamshire; OU – Oxford University; P – Pakistan(is); PW – PCB Whites; Sm – Somerset; Sy – Surrey; Sx – Sussex; Wa – Warwickshire; WI – West Indies; Wo – Worcestershire; Y – Yorkshire.

† Left-handed batsman. Cap: a dash (–) denotes a non-county player. A blank denotes uncapped by his current county.

BATTING AND FIELDING

	Cap	M	I	NO	HS	Runs	Avge	100	50	Ct/St
T.B.Abell (Sm)	2018	6	11	1	119	386	38.60	2	1	5
Abid Ali (P)	–	4	7	–	60	156	22.28	–	1	–
C.N.Ackermann (Le)	2019	5	9	2	94	379	54.14	–	4	6
A.K.Agedah (CU)	–	1	2	–	14	21	10.50	–	–	–
B.W.Aitchison (De)		3	1	–	8	8	8.00	–	–	2
† T.P.Alsop (H)		5	7	–	87	164	23.42	–	1	5
A.R.Amin (CU)	–	1	2	–	23	23	11.50	–	–	2
H.M.Amla (Sy)		1	2	–	26	44	22.00	–	–	1
† J.M.Anderson (E)	–	5	4	1	32	8	8.00	–	–	2
M.K.Andersson (M)		5	9	1	92	227	28.37	–	2	3
J.C.Archer (E)	–	4	4	–	23	42	10.50	–	–	1
Asad Shafiq (P)	–	4	7	1	29	76	12.66	–	–	4
A.A.P.Atkinson (Sy)		2	4	–	15	21	5.25	–	–	–
† M.H.Azad (Le)		5	8	–	58	144	18.00	–	1	3
Azhar Ali (P)	–	4	7	1	141*	244	40.66	1	–	–
Babar Azam (P)	–	4	7	2	69	252	50.40	–	2	1
T.E.Bailey (La)	2018	4	4	1	38*	47	15.66	–	–	–
J.M.Bairstow (Y)	2011	2	3	–	75	102	34.00	–	1	5
† G.P.Balderson (La)		5	7	2	61*	156	31.20	–	1	–
J.T.Ball (Nt)	2016	3	5	1	34	56	14.00	–	–	3
E.R.Bamber (M)		1	1	1	24*	24	–	–	–	–
T.Banton (Sm)		2	3	–	18	33	11.00	–	–	–
T.E.Barber (Nt)		3	3	3	2*	2	–	–	–	–
† K.H.D.Barker (H)		2	4	2	28*	63	31.50	–	–	1
E.G.Barnard (Wo)	2015	6	6	2	48*	84	21.00	–	–	5
E.Barnes (De)		2	1	–	4	4	4.00	–	–	–
G.A.Bartlett (Sm)		4	6	1	100*	160	32.00	1	–	4
† A.P.Beard (Ex)		5	6	2	17	43	10.75	–	–	1
D.G.Bedingham (Du)		5	8	–	96	253	31.62	–	2	3
I.R.Bell (Wa)	2001	5	8	–	90	184	23.00	–	2	5
D.J.Bell-Drummond (K)	2015	5	9	1	45	185	23.12	–	–	3

	Cap	M	I	NO	HS	Runs	Avge	100	50	Ct/St
G.K.Berg (Nh)		2	4	–	45	63	15.75	–	–	3
D.M.Bess (E)	–	6	7	5	31*	111	55.50	–	–	1
S.W.Billings (K)	2015	2	1	–	20	20	20.00	–	–	1
J.Blackwood (WI)	–	3	6	–	95	211	35.16	–	2	1
J.J.Bohannon (La)		5	7	–	94	257	36.71	–	2	4
S.G.Borthwick (Sy)	2018	5	10	–	92	192	19.20	–	2	5
N.Botha (CU)	–	1	2	–	31	38	19.00	–	–	1
† J.R.Bracey (Gs)	2016	1	1	–	4	4	4.00	–	–	–
K.C.Brathwaite (WI)	–	3	6	–	75	176	29.33	–	2	1
T.T.Bresnan (Wa)		4	6	2	105	214	53.50	1	–	5
† S.C.J.Broad (E)	–	5	5	2	62	124	41.33	–	1	1
H.C.Brook (Y)		5	7	1	66*	258	43.00	–	3	4
E.A.Brookes (Wa)		1	2	1	15*	21	21.00	–	–	–
H.J.H.Brookes (Wa)		2	4	–	12	23	5.75	–	–	–
J.A.Brooks (Sm)		5	7	2	72	139	27.80	–	1	1
S.S.J.Brooks (WI)	–	3	6	–	68	195	32.50	–	2	–
B.C.Brown (Sx)	2014	5	10	–	98	270	27.00	–	2	10/1
† N.L.J.Browne (Ex)	2015	4	8	–	61	142	17.75	–	1	4
N.L.Buck (Nh)		2	3	1	32	61	30.50	–	–	–
K.A.Bull (Gm)		4	8	1	23	50	7.14	–	–	1
M.G.K.Burgess (Wa)		5	8	–	39	135	16.87	–	–	15/1
J.T.A.Burnham (Du)		3	5	–	31	72	14.40	–	–	1
† R.J.Burns (E/Sy)	2014	7	11	–	103	409	37.18	1	3	6
G.D.Burrows (La)		2	1	–	1	1	1.00	–	–	–
J.C.Buttler (E)	–	6	9	1	152	416	52.00	1	2	21
† E.J.Byrom (Sm)		6	11	–	117	271	24.63	1	–	3
H.R.C.Came (H)		4	5	–	25	49	9.80	–	–	1
† J.D.Campbell (WI)	–	3	6	1	32	84	16.80	–	–	1
L.J.Carey (Gm)		1	2	–	23	34	17.00	–	–	1
K.S.Carlson (Gm)		4	8	–	79	109	13.62	–	1	2
B.A.Carse (Du)		3	5	–	41	100	20.00	–	–	–
J.J.Carson (Sx)		4	8	–	21	57	7.12	–	–	1
M.Carter (Nt)		3	4	1	22	50	16.66	–	–	3
Z.J.Chappell (Nt)		4	4	1	1	1	0.33	–	–	3
† B.G.Charlesworth (Gs)	2018	4	6	–	51	78	13.00	–	1	–
R.L.Chase (WI)	–	3	6	–	51	157	26.16	–	1	–
V.Chopra (Ex)	2018	2	4	–	41	89	22.25	–	–	4
J.Clark (Sy)		1	2	–	7	8	4.00	–	–	–
† T.G.R.Clark (Sx)		4	8	–	65	110	13.75	–	1	2
J.M.Clarke (Nt)		5	8	1	133	263	37.57	1	1	–
R.Clarke (Sy)	2005	3	6	–	30	91	15.16	–	–	4
† M.E.Claydon (Sx)		4	8	3	24	77	15.40	–	–	–
B.O.Coad (Y)	2018	2	2	–	28	32	16.00	–	–	1
† M.A.R.Cohen (De)		2	3	2	30*	43	43.00	–	–	–
J.M.Coles (Sx)		1	2	–	11	21	10.50	–	–	–
S.Conners (De)		4	4	2	21	45	22.50	–	–	–
† A.N.Cook (Ex)	2005	6	11	1	172	563	56.30	2	1	10
S.J.Cook (Ex)	2020	5	5	1	15*	26	6.50	–	–	–
C.B.Cooke (Gm)	2016	5	10	1	82	294	32.66	–	3	16/2
† J.M.Cooke (Gm)		2	4	–	23	48	12.00	–	–	1

	Cap	M	I	NO	HS	Runs	Avge	100	50	Ct/St
R.R.S.Cornwall (WI)	–	1	2	–	10	12	6.00	–	–	2
P.Coughlin (Du)		4	6	–	90	114	19.00	–	1	2
J.M.Cox (K)		4	6	1	238*	324	64.80	1	–	6
O.B.Cox (Wo)	2009	5	8	3	45*	225	45.00	–	–	25
M.S.Crane (H)		4	5	1	25*	33	8.25	–	–	–
Z.Crawley (E/K)	2019	5	8	–	267	522	65.25	2	3	2
M.J.J.Critchley (De)	2019	5	7	1	63	234	39.00	–	1	4
H.T.Crocombe (Sx)		4	8	4	15	45	11.25	–	–	1
S.J.Croft (La)	2010	4	5	2	63	199	66.33	–	3	6
B.C.Cullen (M)		2	3	–	34	49	16.33	–	–	1
T.N.Cullen (Gm)		3	6	–	26	80	13.33	–	–	6
† M.L.Cummins (M)		3	2	–	25	26	13.00	–	–	–
† B.J.Curran (Nh)		4	8	–	82	238	29.75	–	2	5
† S.M.Curran (E/Sy)	2018	3	3	–	21	52	17.33	–	–	–
S.W.Currie (H)		1	2	–	38	38	19.00	–	–	2
A.K.Dal (De)		4	4	1	78*	108	36.00	–	1	2
A.S.Dale (H)		2	4	1	6	7	2.33	–	–	–
P.D.Daneel (CU)	–	1	2	–	125	147	73.50	1	–	4
J.H.Davey (Sm)		6	9	3	28	113	18.83	–	–	1
A.L.Davies (La)	2017	5	8	1	86	337	48.14	–	4	7
† J.L.B.Davies (M)		1	1	–	13	13	13.00	–	–	–
† S.M.Davies (Sm)	2017	6	10	2	123*	320	40.00	1	1	19
W.S.Davis (Le)		2	2	–	20	28	14.00	–	–	–
L.A.Dawson (H)	2013	1	1	1	43*	43	–	–	–	3
M.de Lange (Gm)	2019	3	5	1	113	131	32.75	1	–	2
D.J.de Silva (OU)	–	1	2	–	1	1	0.50	–	–	–
† H.E.Dearden (Le)		5	9	–	70	234	26.00	–	1	1
J.L.Denly (E/K)	2008	2	3	–	89	136	45.33	–	1	1
† C.D.J.Dent (Gs)	2010	4	7	–	92	170	24.28	–	2	4
J.S.Dhariwal (CU)	–	1	2	–	34	61	30.50	–	–	–
S.R.Dickson (Du)		5	8	–	56	97	12.12	–	1	4
B.L.D'Oliveira (Wo)	2012	5	8	1	174	367	52.42	1	1	2
D.A.Douthwaite (Gm)		5	10	1	86	160	17.77	–	1	3
S.O.Dowrich (WI)	–	3	6	–	61	126	21.00	–	1	7
† J.L.du Plooy (De)		5	7	–	130	296	42.28	1	1	5
† B.M.Duckett (Nt)	2020	5	8	1	150	394	56.28	2	–	3
† M.P.Dunn (Sy)		3	6	1	12	28	5.60	–	–	2
E.J.H.Eckersley (Du)		5	8	2	78*	152	25.33	–	1	3
S.S.Eskinazi (M)	2018	5	10	1	29	151	16.77	–	–	7
† H.A.Evans (Le)		2	3	–	15	16	5.33	–	–	1
L.J.Evans (Sy)		3	6	–	65	172	28.66	–	1	1
S.T.Evans (Le)		3	5	–	85	148	29.60	–	1	3
J.D.M.Evison (Nt)		1	2	–	38	69	34.50	–	–	1
Faheem Ashraf (PW)	–	1	1	–	0	0	0.00	–	–	–
† Fakhar Zaman (PW)	–	1	1	–	22	22	22.00	–	–	–
† Fawad Alam (P/PW)	–	3	4	1	43	64	21.33	–	–	1
T.C.Fell (Wo)	2013	5	9	2	110*	336	48.00	1	1	3
A.W.Finch (Sy)		3	5	1	10	29	7.25	–	–	1
H.Z.Finch (Sx)		5	10	–	69	259	25.90	–	2	6
B.A.J.Fisher (OU)	–	1	2	1	13*	23	23.00	–	–	–

	Cap	M	I	NO	HS	Runs	Avge	100	50	Ct/St
M.D.Fisher (Y)		2	2	–	1	2	1.00	–	–	2
P.J.Flanagan (CU)	–	1	2	–	8	10	5.00	–	–	–
B.T.Foakes (Sy)	2016	2	4	1	118	227	75.66	1	1	4/1
† F.J.H.Foster (OU)	–	1	2	1	50*	51	51.00	–	1	3
W.A.R.Fraine (Y)		3	4	–	14	32	8.00	–	–	1
J.K.Fuller (H)		4	5	1	30	61	15.25	–	–	2
S.T.Gabriel (WI)	–	3	5	3	4	4	2.00	–	–	–
† G.H.S.Garton (Sx)		4	8	1	54*	109	15.57	–	1	4
† E.N.Gay (Nh)		4	6	1	77*	121	24.20	–	1	4
N.N.Gilchrist (K)		1	2	–	25	38	19.00	–	–	–
J.E.Gillespie (CU)	–	1	2	–	16	20	10.00	–	–	–
R.J.Gleeson (La)		1	1	–	6	6	6.00	–	–	–
B.D.Glover (Nh)		1	2	–	0	0	0.00	–	–	–
T.R.W.Gnodde (OU)	–	1	2	–	45	66	33.00	–	–	1
† B.A.Godleman (De)	2015	5	8	–	86	226	28.25	–	3	2
H.O.M.Gouldstone (Nh)		1	–	–	–	–	–	–	–	1
B.G.F.Green (Sm)		3	5	–	54	127	25.40	–	1	–
L.Gregory (Sm)	2015	3	5	–	37	78	15.60	–	–	1
G.T.Griffiths (Le)		3	3	2	11*	23	23.00	–	–	1
T.D.Groenewald (K)		1	–	–	–	–	–	–	–	–
† N.R.T.Gubbins (M)	2016	4	8	–	192	350	43.75	1	1	1
B.D.Guest (De)		1	–	–	–	–	–	–	–	–
Haider Ali (PW)	–	1	1	–	7	7	7.00	–	–	–
S.R.Hain (Wa)	2018	5	8	–	146	146	18.25	–	2	5
† T.J.Haines (Sx)		5	10	1	117	249	27.66	1	–	4
H.Hameed (Nt)	2020	5	7	–	87	272	38.85	–	3	8
Hamidullah Qadri (K)		4	5	2	5	11	3.66	–	–	–
M.A.H.Hammond (Gs)	2013	1	2	–	14	23	11.50	–	–	1
G.T.Hankins (Gs)	2016	5	8	–	69	130	16.25	–	1	7
† O.J.Hannon-Dalby (Wa)	2019	5	7	3	19	43	10.75	–	–	1
G.T.Hargrave (OU)	–	1	2	–	25	35	17.50	–	–	–
S.R.Harmer (Ex)	2018	6	9	1	32	111	13.87	–	–	10
J.A.R.Harris (M)	2015	4	7	2	41	128	25.60	–	–	–
G.J.Harte (Du)		5	8	2	72	250	41.66	–	1	–
† T.W.Hartley (La)		4	4	3	13*	35	35.00	–	–	2
J.A.Haynes (Wo)	2019	5	9	2	51	285	40.71	–	2	1
T.G.Helm (M)	2019	1	2	–	28	29	14.50	–	–	–
C.R.Hemphrey (Gm)		3	6	–	20	62	10.33	–	–	3
R.F.Higgins (Gs)	2018	5	8	1	51	173	24.71	–	1	2
J.C.Hildreth (Sm)	2007	4	6	–	45	124	20.66	–	–	10
G.C.H.Hill (Y)		2	2	1	29	33	33.00	–	–	–
M.G.Hogan (Gm)	2013	4	7	4	33*	78	26.00	–	–	1
† M.D.E.Holden (M)		5	10	–	72	299	29.90	–	1	4
J.O.Holder (WI)	–	3	6	1	46	114	22.80	–	–	5
I.G.Holland (H)		5	7	–	42	115	16.42	–	–	4
S.D.Hope (WI)	–	3	6	–	31	105	17.50	–	–	3
H.R.Hosein (De)		4	6	1	84	167	33.40	–	2	13/1
F.J.Hudson-Prentice (De)		3	5	2	91*	145	48.33	–	1	1
A.L.Hughes (De)	2017	2	2	–	27	40	20.00	–	–	–
L.J.Hurt (La)		2	2	–	2	3	1.50	–	–	–

	Cap	M	I	NO	HS	Runs	Avge	100	50	Ct/St
B.A.Hutton (Nh)		2	1	–	9	9	9.00	–	–	1
E.R.B.Hyde (CU)	–	1	2	–	55	64	32.00	–	1	4
Iftikhar Ahmed (PW)	–	1	1	–	7	7	7.00	–	–	1
† Imam-ul-Haq (PW)	–	1	1	1	41*	41	–	–	–	–
Imran Khan (PW)	–	1	1	–	2	2	2.00	–	–	–
W.G.Jacks (Sy)		5	10	2	84*	248	31.00	–	2	6
L.W.James (Nt)		1	1	1	36*	36	–	–	–	1
K.K.Jennings (La)	2018	5	8	1	81	182	26.00	–	1	8
J.C.A.Job (OU)	–	1	2	–	22	22	11.00	–	–	5
M.A.Jones (Du)		2	3	–	82	84	28.00	–	1	2
R.P.Jones (La)		3	5	–	23	77	15.40	–	–	3
A.S.Joseph (WI)	–	2	3	–	32	59	19.66	–	–	2
Kashif Bhatti (PW)	–	1	1	–	11	11	11.00	–	–	1
R.I.Keogh (Nh)	2019	4	6	–	31	80	13.33	–	–	1
S.C.Kerrigan (Nh)		2	1	–	1	1	1.00	–	–	1
F.I.N.Khushi (Ex)		4	5	–	66	125	25.00	–	1	5
F.J.Klaassen (K)		1	1	1	0*	0	–	–	–	1
D.Klein (Le)		4	5	1	27	53	13.25	–	–	–
T.Kohler-Cadmore (Y)	2019	5	8	1	41	127	18.14	–	–	2
H.G.Kuhn (K)	2018	2	4	1	140	202	67.33	1	–	5
T.C.Lace (Gs)	2020	3	4	–	42	73	18.25	–	–	1
D.J.Lamb (La)		3	4	1	50*	104	34.66	–	1	1
M.J.Lamb (Wa)		3	4	–	65	101	25.25	–	1	1
† T.A.Lammonby (Sm)		6	11	2	116	459	51.00	3	–	4
G.I.D.Lavelle (La)		1	2	–	13	20	10.00	–	–	2
D.W.Lawrence (Ex)	2017	4	6	1	60	144	28.80	–	1	–
J.Leach (Wo)	2012	5	6	1	17	47	9.40	–	–	1
† M.J.Leach (Sm)	2017	2	3	–	21	29	9.66	–	–	1
J.A.Leaning (K)		5	8	1	220*	279	39.85	1	–	9
D.J.Leech (Y)		2	2	1	1	1	1.00	–	–	–
† A.Z.Lees (Du)		5	8	–	106	386	48.25	1	3	4
R.E.Levi (Nh)	2017	1	2	–	11	19	9.50	–	–	1
J.D.Libby (Wo)	2020	5	9	–	184	498	55.33	1	3	2
A.M.Lilley (Le)		1	2	–	13	18	9.00	–	–	1
A.W.Livingstone (OU)	–	1	2	–	3	3	1.50	–	–	–
L.S.Livingstone (La)	2017	2	2	–	23	37	18.50	–	–	1
T.W.Loten (Y)		2	2	–	11	11	5.50	–	–	–
† A.Lyth (Y)	2010	5	8	1	103	220	31.42	1	1	5
M.H.McKiernan (De)		2	4	–	52	103	25.75	–	1	3
L.D.McManus (H)		5	7	–	50	142	20.28	–	1	11/2
W.L.Madsen (De)	2011	5	8	1	103	213	30.42	1	1	10
† D.J.Malan (Y)	2020	3	5	–	219	332	66.40	1	1	2
S.C.Meaker (Sx)		3	6	1	42	106	21.20	–	–	–
D.R.Melton (De)		3	3	1	11	11	5.50	–	–	–
B.W.M.Mike (Le)		4	6	1	51*	99	19.80	–	1	2
C.N.Miles (Wa)		3	5	2	13*	27	9.00	–	–	1
M.E.Milnes (K)		4	6	–	43	96	16.00	–	–	1
D.K.H.Mitchell (Wo)	2005	5	9	–	110	384	42.66	1	2	7
A.J.Moen (CU)	–	1	2	–	41	56	28.00	–	–	–
Mohammad Abbas (P)	–	4	5	1	4	10	2.50	–	–	1

	Cap	M	I	NO	HS	Runs	Avge	100	50	Ct/St
Mohammad Rizwan (P)	–	4	5	–	72	179	35.80	–	2	6/2
T.J.Moores (Nt)		5	7	–	106	207	29.57	1	–	15/1
A.O.Morgan (Gm)		1	2	–	28	28	14.00	–	–	–
† D.T.Moriarty (Sy)		2	3	–	1	1	0.33	–	–	–
† M.Morkel (Sy)	2018	1	2	–	33	33	16.50	–	–	–
† J.P.Morley (La)		1	1	–	3	3	3.00	–	–	–
C.A.J.Morris (Wo)	2014	3	–	–	–	–	–	–	–	–
E.H.T.Moulton (La)		1	2	–	0	0	0.00	–	–	–
† D.R.Mousley (Wa)		2	3	–	71	149	49.66	–	1	1
S.J.Mullaney (Nt)	2013	5	7	–	67	235	33.57	–	2	10
† T.J.Murtagh (M)	2008	4	5	2	11*	26	8.66	–	–	1
B.Muzarabani (Nh)		4	5	2	15	27	9.00	–	–	1
Naseem Shah (P)	–	4	5	1	4	7	1.75	–	–	–
C.D.Nash (Nt)		2	4	–	59	78	19.50	–	1	1
M.A.Naylor (OU)	–	1	2	–	14	14	7.00	–	–	–
S.A.Northeast (H)	2019	5	7	–	81	181	25.85	–	2	–
L.C.Norwell (Wa)		1	2	1	12	19	19.00	–	–	–
D.Olivier (Y)	2020	4	4	1	20*	33	11.00	–	–	3
F.S.Organ (H)		5	7	–	16	60	8.57	–	–	1
M.K.O'Riordan (K)		5	8	3	52*	216	43.20	–	1	1
C.Overton (Sm)	2016	6	10	2	66	248	31.00	–	2	7
J.Overton (Sm/Sy)	2019	5	7	–	120	261	37.28	1	2	9
C.F.Parkinson (Le)		3	3	1	21	42	21.00	–	–	–
R.K.Patel (Le)		1	2	–	19	24	12.00	–	–	–
† R.S.Patel (Sy)		3	6	–	44	78	13.00	–	–	5
S.R.Patel (Nt)	2008	5	7	–	80	210	30.00	–	2	2
S.A.Patterson (Y)	2012	4	4	–	11	23	5.75	–	–	–
D.A.Payne (Gs)	2011	4	5	1	14	24	6.00	–	–	–
D.Y.Pennington (Wo)	2018	3	4	2	11*	15	7.50	–	–	1
T.H.S.Pettman (OU)	–	1	2	–	18	18	9.00	–	–	–
H.W.Podmore (K)	2019	3	3	1	47	79	39.50	–	–	2
O.J.D.Pope (E)	–	6	9	1	91	215	26.87	–	2	2
J.A.Porter (Ex)	2015	6	8	4	13	30	7.50	–	–	3
M.J.Potts (Du)		2	3	–	10	10	3.33	–	–	1
S.W.Poynter (Du)		2	3	–	50	58	19.33	–	1	–
T.J.Price (Gs)	2020	1	2	–	0	0	0.00	–	–	–
† L.A.Procter (Nh)	2020	4	6	2	112*	200	50.00	1	–	1
M.R.Quinn (Ex)		2	2	–	13	13	6.50	–	–	–
† B.A.Raine (Du)		4	7	4	31	124	41.33	–	–	–
† D.M.W.Rawlins (Sx)		5	10	–	65	252	25.20	–	1	–
† L.M.Reece (De)	2019	4	7	1	122	277	46.16	1	2	4
G.H.Rhodes (Le)		4	7	2	22*	83	16.60	–	–	4
† W.M.H.Rhodes (Wa)	2020	5	9	1	207	423	52.87	1	–	2
K.A.J.Roach (WI)	–	3	5	2	5*	15	5.00	–	–	1
O.E.Robinson (Sx)	2019	2	4	–	23	56	14.00	–	–	–
O.G.Robinson (K)		5	6	–	78	138	23.00	–	1	22
S.D.Robson (M)	2013	5	10	1	82*	215	23.88	–	1	8
G.H.Roderick (Gs)	2013	4	7	1	39	101	16.83	–	–	12
J.E.Root (E)	–	5	8	2	68*	224	37.33	–	1	10
† W.T.Root (Gm)		5	10	1	118	286	31.77	1	1	1

	Cap	M	I	NO	HS	Runs	Avge	100	50	Ct/St
A.M.Rossington (Nh)	2019	3	6	1	135*	196	39.20	1	–	8
J.J.Roy (Sy)	2014	1	2	–	14	18	9.00	–	–	1
C.Rushworth (Du)		4	7	2	25	54	10.80	–	–	–
M.E.T.Salisbury (Du)		3	3	–	4	5	1.66	–	–	–
P.D.Salt (Sx)		4	8	–	80	290	36.25	–	3	6
B.W.Sanderson (Nh)	2018	2	3	–	23	23	7.66	–	–	–
Sarfraz Ahmed (PW)	–	1	1	–	26	26	26.00	–	–	2
G.F.B.Scott (Gs)	2020	4	6	2	44*	87	21.75	–	–	–
T.A.R.Scriven (H)		2	3	–	68	84	28.00	–	1	1
C.J.Searle (OU)	–	1	2	–	26	34	17.00	–	–	1
N.J.Selman (Gm)		5	10	–	73	215	21.50	–	2	10
Shadab Khan (P)	–	2	3	–	45	71	23.66	–	–	3
† Shaheen Shah Afridi (P)	–	4	5	1	9*	11	2.75	–	–	–
† Shan Masood (P)	–	4	4	–	156	237	33.85	1	–	1
J.Shaw (Gs)	2016	5	7	–	21	50	7.14	–	–	–
† W.A.Sheffield (Sx)		1	2	–	6	7	3.50	–	–	–
J.W.Shutt (Y)		3	4	3	7*	7	7.00	–	–	2
D.P.Sibley (E)	–	6	9	–	120	324	36.00	1	2	3
R.N.Sidebottom (Wa)		3	2	2	13*	13	–	–	–	–
J.A.Simpson (M)	2011	5	9	2	53	250	35.71	–	1	19/1
B.T.Slater (Le/Nt)		5	7	–	172	425	60.71	2	1	2
J.L.Smith (Sy)		5	10	1	80	274	30.44	–	1	8
R.A.J.Smith (Gm)		1	2	–	23	26	13.00	–	–	–
T.M.J.Smith (Gs)	2013	2	2	1	24*	30	30.00	–	–	1
Sohail Khan (PW)	–	1	1	–	2	2	2.00	–	–	1
N.A.Sowter (M)		2	4	2	20	25	12.50	–	–	5
C.T.Steel (Du)		3	5	–	11	22	4.40	–	–	–
D.I.Stevens (K)	2005	5	6	–	36	77	12.83	–	–	3
R.A.Stevenson (H)		2	1	–	0	0	0.00	–	–	–
G.Stewart (K)		4	6	–	58	129	21.50	–	1	–
† B.A.Stokes (E)		4	7	1	176	372	62.00	1	1	4
O.P.Stone (Wa)	2020	1	1	1	36*	36	–	–	–	–
† M.D.Stoneman (Sy)	2018	4	8	–	45	106	13.25	–	–	1
H.J.Swindells (Le)		5	7	2	52*	188	37.60	–	1	11
J.A.Tattersall (Y)		5	7	1	71	265	44.16	–	3	9
C.Z.Taylor (Gm)		2	4	–	106	153	38.25	1	–	–
J.M.R.Taylor (Gs)	2010	2	4	–	34	71	17.75	–	–	1
J.P.A.Taylor (Sy)		3	5	1	22	34	8.50	–	–	1
M.D.Taylor (Gs)	2013	5	7	2	19*	43	8.60	–	–	1
N.P.Taylor (CU)	–	1	2	–	20	20	10.00	–	–	–
T.A.I.Taylor (Le)		3	3	1	57	78	39.00	–	1	1
R.N.ten Doeschate (Ex)	2006	5	7	–	78	218	31.14	–	1	–
I.A.A.Thomas (K)		2	2	1	3*	3	3.00	–	–	1
A.D.Thomason (Sx)		3	6	–	49	111	18.50	–	–	1
† J.A.Thompson (Y)		5	6	1	98	234	46.80	–	2	2
A.T.Thomson (Wa)		5	8	–	46	146	18.25	–	–	1
C.O.Thurston (Nh)		5	8	–	115	357	44.62	1	2	2
J.C.Tongue (Wo)	2017	4	3	2	1*	1	1.00	–	–	–
P.D.Trego (Nt)		5	8	–	39	116	14.50	–	–	1
Usman Shinwari (PW)	–	1	1	–	0	0	0.00	–	–	–

	Cap	M	I	NO	HS	Runs	Avge	100	50	Ct/St
G.L.van Buuren (Gs)	2016	5	8	–	72	244	30.50	–	2	3
T.van der Gugten (Gm)	2018	4	7	3	30*	98	24.50	–	–	3
R.E.van der Merwe (Sm)		4	6	1	30	57	11.40	–	–	4
† R.S.Vasconcelos (Nh)		5	8	1	58	222	31.71	–	2	13/1
D.J.Vilas (La)	2018	5	7	–	90	247	35.28	–	1	5
G.S.Virdi (Sy)		5	9	4	12	26	5.20	–	–	1
J.C.Vitali (CU)	–	1	2	2	15*	23	–	–	–	–
W.D.N.von Behr (OU)	–	1	1	–	22	36	18.00	–	–	–
G.G.Wagg (Gm)	2013	3	6	1	54	100	20.00	–	1	3
A.G.Wakely (Nh)	2012	1	2	–	9	11	5.50	–	–	1
† T.N.Walallawitta (M)		5	6	2	11	22	5.50	–	–	–
† P.I.Walter (Ex)		5	9	2	46	266	38.00	–	–	1
J.D.Warner (Y)		1	1	–	4	4	4.00	–	–	–
J.J.Weatherley (H)		5	7	1	98	263	43.83	–	2	2
† W.J.Weighell (Le)		1	1	–	23	23	23.00	–	–	1
M.H.Wessels (Wo)	2019	5	8	–	88	157	19.62	–	1	4
T.Westley (Ex)	2013	6	11	1	51	172	17.20	–	1	3
B.T.J.Wheal (H)		3	3	2	14*	24	24.00	–	–	1
A.J.A.Wheater (Ex)	2020	6	9	4	83*	291	58.20	–	2	17/3
† C.White (Nh)		4	4	2	7*	9	4.50	–	–	–
R.G.White (M)		3	5	–	99	176	35.20	–	1	1
D.Wiese (Sx)	2016	1	2	–	57	61	30.50	–	1	1
C.R.Woakes (E)	–	5	5	1	84*	144	36.00	–	1	2
† L.Wood (La)		2	2	–	46	52	26.00	–	–	–
M.A.Wood (E)	–	1	2	–	5	7	3.50	–	–	–
T.A.Wood (De)		1	1	–	26	26	26.00	–	–	–
C.J.C.Wright (Le)		2	2	1	23	33	33.00	–	–	–
Yasir Shah (P)	–	4	5	1	33	71	17.75	–	–	1
† R.M.Yates (Wa)		5	9	1	88	137	17.12	–	1	2
† S.A.Zaib (Nh)		4	5	–	23	36	7.20	–	–	2

BOWLING

See BATTING AND FIELDING section for details of matches and caps

	Cat	O	M	R	W	Avge	Best	5wI	10wM
T.B.Abell (Sm)	RM	16.2	5	50	3	16.66	3- 4	–	–
C.N.Ackermann (Le)	OB	35	12	92	4	23.00	2-24	–	–
B.W.Aitchison (De)	RFM	78	20	211	6	35.16	3-55	–	–
A.R.Amin (CU)	OB	9	0	41	0			–	–
J.M.Anderson (E)	RFM	161	42	408	16	25.50	5-56	1	–
M.K.Andersson (M)	RM	75.5	15	250	14	17.85	4-38	–	–
J.C.Archer (E)	RF	125.4	23	360	8	45.00	3-45	–	–
Asad Shafiq (P)	OB	7	0	24	1	24.00	1-24	–	–
A.A.P.Atkinson (Sy)	RM	35.4	5	128	4	32.00	2-57	–	–
M.H.Azad (Le)	OB	2.1	0	15	1	15.00	1-15	–	–
Azhar Ali (P)	LB	0.1	0	0	0			–	–
T.E.Bailey (La)	RMF	111.4	44	282	13	21.69	3-11	–	–
G.P.Balderson (La)	RM	104	23	296	9	32.88	3-63	–	–
J.T.Ball (Nt)	RFM	112.5	30	336	10	33.60	3-71	–	–
E.R.Bamber (M)	RMF	21	6	79	1	79.00	1-56	–	–

	Cat	O	M	R	W	Avge	Best	5wI	10wM
T.E.Barber (Nt)	LFM	79	9	289	7	41.28	3- 42	–	–
K.H.D.Barker (H)	LMF	66	13	201	7	28.71	2- 44	–	–
E.G.Barnard (Wo)	RMF	148.5	40	390	18	21.66	4- 25	–	–
E.Barnes (De)	RFM	32	6	107	3	35.66	2- 24	–	–
A.P.Beard (Ex)	RFM	78.1	17	265	11	24.09	4- 21	–	–
D.J.Bell-Drummond (K)	RMF	5	0	22	0				
G.K.Berg (Nh)	RMF	47	9	203	6	22.83	4- 64	–	–
D.M.Bess (E)	OB	136.1	25	444	8	55.50	2- 51	–	–
S.G.Borthwick (Sy)	LBG	43	3	161	2	80.50	1- 16	–	–
N.Botha (CU)	OB	44	19	87	5	17.40	4- 43	–	–
K.C.Brathwaite (WI)	OB	6.5	0	18	0				
T.T.Bresnan (Wa)	RFM	116	36	275	10	27.50	4- 99	–	–
S.C.J.Broad (E)	RFM	154.1	48	389	29	13.41	6- 31	1	1
H.C.Brook (Y)	RM	14.1	1	49	0				
E.A.Brookes (Wa)	RMF	3	1	13	0				
H.J.H.Brookes (Wa)	RMF	51	6	203	2	101.50	2- 66	–	–
J.A.Brooks (Sm)	RFM	89.5	23	254	13	19.53	4- 40	–	–
N.L.Buck (Nh)	RMF	64	21	173	9	19.22	3- 42	–	–
K.A.Bull (Gm)	OB	102.3	4	462	9	51.33	3-112	–	–
G.D.Burrows (La)	RFM	40	8	127	4	31.75	2- 20	–	–
E.J.Byrom (Sm)	OB	1	0	4	0				
L.J.Carey (Gm)	RFM	24.5	4	82	3	27.33	3- 54	–	–
K.S.Carlson (Gm)	OB	1	0	2	0				
B.A.Carse (Du)	RF	49	4	245	3	81.66	2-110	–	–
J.J.Carson (Sx)	OB	108.1	17	340	15	22.66	5- 93	1	–
M.Carter (Nt)	OB	149.2	54	263	11	23.90	4- 76	–	–
Z.J.Chappell (Nt)	RFM	131.2	30	431	15	28.73	4- 59	–	–
B.G.Charlesworth (Gs)	RM/OB	27	6	103	1	103.00	1- 40	–	–
R.L.Chase (WI)	OB	94	14	340	10	34.00	5-172	1	–
J.Clark (Sy)	RMF	11	3	30	0				
R.Clarke (Sy)	RMF	88	23	190	13	14.61	5- 20	1	–
M.E.Claydon (Sx)	RMF	102	25	294	11	26.72	3- 23	–	–
B.O.Coad (Y)	RMF	69	28	87	12	7.25	5- 18	1	–
M.A.R.Cohen (De)	LFM	44.2	7	191	7	27.28	3- 47	–	–
J.M.Coles (Sx)	SLA	13	0	35	3	11.66	2- 32	–	–
S.Conners (De)	RM	94.2	23	328	9	36.44	3- 63	–	–
S.J.Cook (Ex)	RFM	140	39	318	17	18.70	5- 76	1	–
R.R.S.Cornwall (WI)	OB	46	7	164	0				
P.Coughlin (Du)	RM	78.4	9	304	3	101.33	3- 46	–	–
M.S.Crane (H)	LB	60.4	8	190	14	13.57	3- 19	–	–
M.J.J.Critchley (De)	LB	128.4	14	457	17	26.88	6- 73	1	–
S.J.Croft (La)	RMF	1	0	6	0				
B.C.Cullen (M)	RMF	30	5	110	3	36.66	2- 51	–	–
M.L.Cummins (M)	RF	92.1	28	269	13	20.69	5- 62	1	–
S.M.Curran (E/Sy)	LMF	85.5	17	268	11	24.36	4- 39	–	–
S.W.Currie (H)	RMF	17	4	58	3	19.33	3- 42	–	–
A.K.Dal (De)	RM	43	10	95	2	47.50	1- 8	–	–
A.S.Dale (H)	RFM	21	4	73	4	18.25	3- 20	–	–
J.H.Davey (Sm)	RMF	150.2	55	331	24	13.79	4- 25	–	–
W.S.Davis (Le)	RFM	30	6	106	3	35.33	2- 75	—	–

	Cat	O	M	R	W	Avge	Best	5wI	10wM
L.A.Dawson (H)	SLA	16.5	5	39	2	19.50	2-39	–	–
M.de Lange (Gm)	RF	81.2	17	218	9	24.22	4-84	–	–
J.L.Denly (E/K)	LB	2	0	12	0				
J.S.Dhariwal (CU)	RMF	1	0	7	0				
B.L.D'Oliveira (Wo)	LB	95	13	312	6	52.00	2-31	–	–
D.A.Douthwaite (Gm)	RMF	121.1	16	473	14	33.78	3-42	–	–
J.L.du Plooy (De)	SLA	9	1	41	2	20.50	1-16	–	–
B.M.Duckett (Nt)	OB	1	0	2	0				
M.P.Dunn (Sy)	RFM	70.4	16	239	5	47.80	3-53	–	–
H.A.Evans (Le)	RFM	35.2	7	140	3	46.66	2-59	–	–
S.T.Evans (Le)	OB	3	0	22	0				
J.D.M.Evison (Nt)	RM	22.5	4	74	4	18.50	3-38	–	–
Faheem Ashraf (PW)	RFM	21	6	33	3	11.00	2-16	–	–
Fawad Alam (P/PW)	SLA	12	0	46	2	23.00	2-46	–	–
A.W.Finch (Sy)	RMF	74.1	9	215	8	26.87	4-38	–	–
B.A.J.Fisher (OU)	RFM	21.2	1	79	5	15.80	3-37	–	–
M.D.Fisher (Y)	RFM	67	22	180	10	18.00	4-54	–	–
P.J.Flanagan (CU)	RMF	31.1	11	83	5	16.60	3-30	–	–
F.J.H.Foster (OU)	SLA	22.2	5	76	2	38.00	2-33	–	–
J.K.Fuller (H)	RFM	70	12	293	9	32.55	4-17	–	–
S.T.Gabriel (WI)	RF	98.1	14	355	11	32.27	5-75	1	–
G.H.S.Garton (Sx)	LF	70.3	13	282	12	23.50	5-26	1	–
N.N.Gilchrist (K)	RFM	9	1	52	0				
R.J.Gleeson (La)	RFM	18	4	52	3	17.33	3-32	–	–
B.D.Glover (Nh)	RFM	24	5	94	4	23.50	2-45	–	–
L.Gregory (Sm)	RMF	102.3	22	318	18	17.66	6-72	1	–
G.T.Griffiths (Le)	RMF	61.5	13	181	5	36.20	3-52	–	–
T.D.Groenewald (K)	RFM	28	5	119	2	59.50	1-53	–	–
N.R.T.Gubbins (M)	LB	1.3	0	2	0				
T.J.Haines (Sx)	RM	25	3	72	2	36.00	1-18	–	–
Hamidullah Qadri (K)	OB	38.4	7	104	1	104.00	1-24	–	–
O.J.Hannon-Dalby (Wa)	RMF	196.3	53	523	25	20.92	6-33	2	1
S.R.Harmer (Ex)	OB	257.1	81	603	38	15.86	8-64	3	1
J.A.R.Harris (Gm)	RFM	89	19	284	9	31.55	2-46	–	–
G.J.Harte (Du)	RM	50.4	5	206	2	103.00	1-41	–	–
T.W.Hartley (La)	SLA	111	28	324	6	54.00	3-79	–	–
T.G.Helm (M)	RMF	24.3	7	66	1	66.00	1-41	–	–
C.R.Hemphrey (Gm)	OB	9	0	37	0				
R.F.Higgins (Gs)	RM	148.4	41	391	17	23.00	7-42	1	1
G.C.H.Hill (Y)	RMF	25	8	54	1	54.00	1-27	–	–
M.G.Hogan (Gm)	RFM	139	32	397	8	49.62	3-59	–	–
J.O.Holder (WI)	RMF	111.5	31	301	10	30.10	6-42	1	–
I.G.Holland (H)	RMF	129	41	297	17	17.47	6-60	1	–
F.J.Hudson-Prentice (De)	RMF	34	8	105	1	105.00	1-44	–	–
A.L.Hughes (De)	RM	21	2	79	1	79.00	1-16	–	–
L.J.Hurt (La)	RMF	48	6	182	7	26.00	4-27	–	–
B.A.Hutton (Nh)	RM	39	8	136	6	22.66	4-77	–	–
Iftikhar Ahmed (PW)	OB	7	3	9	0				
Imran Khan (PW)	RMF	19	1	63	2	31.50	1-28	–	–
W.G.Jacks (Sy)	RM	6	0	17	0				

	Cat	O	M	R	W	Avge	Best	5wI	10wM
L.W.James (Nt)	RMF	16	2	55	1	55.00	1-43	–	–
K.K.Jennings (La)	RM	15	3	28	1	28.00	1-14	–	–
R.P.Jones (La)	LB	3	2	4	0				
A.S.Joseph (WI)	RFM	56.1	11	182	3	60.66	2-45	–	–
Kashif Bhatti (PW)	SLA	7.1	1	13	1	13.00	1- 3	–	–
R.I.Keogh (Nh)	OB	38	10	112	1	112.00	1-96	–	–
S.C.Kerrigan (Nh)	SLA	23.3	4	89	3	29.66	2-54	–	–
F.J.Klaassen (K)	LMF	27	6	80	4	20.00	4-44	–	–
D.Klein (Le)	LMF	95	10	332	9	36.88	3-44	–	–
D.J.Lamb (La)	RM	68.1	13	203	12	16.91	4-55	–	–
T.A.Lammonby (Sm)	LM	12	3	38	2	19.00	1- 4	–	–
D.W.Lawrence (Ex)	LB	2	1	2	0				
J.Leach (Wo)	RMF	169.3	44	490	19	25.78	4-67	–	–
M.J.Leach (Sm)	SLA	52	17	112	3	37.33	3-38	–	–
J.A.Leaning (K)	RMF	2	1	2	0				
D.J.Leech (Y)	RMF	34	5	134	4	33.50	2-72	–	–
A.Z.Lees (Du)	LB	2	0	19	1	19.00	1-12	–	–
J.D.Libby (Wo)	OB	14.4	2	46	2	23.00	2-45	–	–
A.M.Lilley (Le)	OB	6	1	21	3	7.00	3-21	–	–
A.W.Livingstone (OU)	RMF	18	2	81	2	40.50	2-60	–	–
L.S.Livingstone (La)	LB	21.3	2	92	5	18.40	3-79	–	–
A.Lyth (Y)	RM	23	3	75	2	37.50	1-12	–	–
M.H.McKiernan (De)	LB	10.2	2	48	2	24.00	2- 3	–	–
W.L.Madsen (De)	OB	1	0	4	0				
D.J.Malan (Y)	LB	6	1	24	2	12.00	2-24	–	–
S.C.Meaker (Sx)	RFM	46.5	5	225	2	112.50	1-17	–	–
D.R.Melton (De)	RFM	70	13	233	8	29.12	4-22	–	–
B.W.M.Mike (Le)	RM	88.1	13	279	9	31.00	4-39	–	–
C.N.Miles (Wa)	RMF	74	17	265	4	66.25	1-51	–	–
M.E.Milnes (K)	RMF	119.3	29	355	15	23.66	4-46	–	–
D.K.H.Mitchell (Wo)	RM	31	7	63	1	63.00	1- 7	–	–
Mohammad Abbas (P)	RMF	108	34	232	6	38.66	2-28	–	–
A.O.Morgan (Gm)	SLA	11.5	0	43	1	43.00	1-43	–	–
D.T.Moriarty (Sy)	SLA	98.2	15	342	17	20.11	6-70	3	1
M.Morkel (Sy)	RF	14	7	28	0				
J.P.Morley (La)	SLA	40	15	71	5	14.20	4-62	–	–
C.A.J.Morris (Wo)	RMF	99.3	21	315	14	22.50	5-80	1	–
E.H.T.Moulton (La)	RMF	27	4	110	0				
D.R.Mousley (Wa)	OB	9	1	37	0				
S.J.Mullaney (Nt)	RM	80	22	183	4	45.75	1-23	–	–
T.J.Murtagh (M)	RMF	145.5	48	318	25	12.72	5-34	2	–
B.Muzurabani (Nh)	RMF	70.5	17	278	11	25.27	4-29	–	–
Naseem Shah (P)	RF	82	19	260	7	37.14	4-52	–	–
C.D.Nash (Nt)	OB	11.2	1	38	3	12.66	3-20	–	–
L.C.Norwell (Wa)	RMF	44	10	95	4	23.75	4-43	–	–
D.Olivier (Y)	RF	91	18	364	10	36.40	3-29	–	–
F.S.Organ (H)	OB	27	3	90	7	12.85	4-40	–	–
M.K.O'Riordan (K)	OB	62.1	5	255	8	31.87	3-50	–	–
C.Overton (Sm)	RMF	196.2	66	403	30	13.43	5-26	2	–
J.Overton (Sm/Sy)	RFM	89.1	27	256	15	17.06	5-48	1	–

	Cat	O	M	R	W	Avge	Best	5wI	10wM
C.F.Parkinson (Le)	SLA	79.3	22	192	8	24.00	3- 30	–	–
R.S.Patel (Sy)	RMF	14	1	72	0			–	–
S.R.Patel (Nt)	SLA	156.2	36	388	13	29.84	4- 80	–	–
S.A.Patterson (Y)	RMF	106.3	37	197	11	17.90	3- 27	–	–
D.A.Payne (Gs)	LMF	95	29	199	14	14.21	5- 31	1	–
D.Y.Pennington (Wo)	RMF	90.1	22	248	11	22.54	3- 30	–	–
T.H.S.Pettman (OU)	RFM	43	9	121	6	20.16	4- 53	–	–
H.W.Podmore (K)	RMF	117.3	30	307	19	16.15	5- 43	1	–
J.A.Porter (Ex)	RFM	185.5	48	553	27	20.48	5- 60	1	–
M.J.Potts (Du)	RM	36	9	94	2	47.00	1- 19	–	–
S.W.Poynter (Du)	(WK)	4	0	21	0			–	–
T.J.Price (Gs)	RM	18	1	80	1	80.00	1- 69	–	–
L.A.Procter (Nh)	RM	30	5	130	2	65.00	1- 9	–	–
M.R.Quinn (Ex)	RMF	55.3	10	156	3	52.00	1- 19	–	–
B.A.Raine (Du)	RMF	105.1	25	308	9	34.22	3- 53	–	–
D.M.W.Rawlins (Sx)	SLA	69.5	8	261	3	87.00	1- 14	–	–
L.M.Reece (De)	LM	132.3	40	340	13	26.15	3- 51	–	–
W.M.H.Rhodes (Wa)	RMF	79.4	16	245	10	24.50	4- 46	–	–
K.A.J.Roach (WI)	RF	116.4	31	292	8	36.50	4- 72	–	–
O.E.Robinson (Sx)	RMF	73.1	22	175	14	12.50	5- 29	1	–
S.D.Robson (M)	LB	4	3	6	2	3.00	2- 0	–	–
J.E.Root (E)	OB	14.2	2	42	1	42.00	1- 17	–	–
C.Rushworth (Du)	RMF	104	14	358	16	22.37	7-108	1	–
M.E.T.Salisbury (Du)	RMF	53.1	14	148	5	29.60	4- 57	–	–
B.W.Sanderson (Nh)	RMF	55.1	14	166	11	15.09	5- 28	1	–
G.F.B.Scott (Gs)	RM	44	9	129	3	43.00	2- 34	–	–
T.A.R.Scriven (Gs)	RMF	21	3	79	3	26.33	2- 24	–	–
C.J.Searle (OU)	RMF	30	6	97	2	48.50	1- 45	–	–
Shadab Khan (P)	LBG	11.3	0	47	2	23.50	2- 13	–	–
Shaheen Shah Afridi (P)	LMF	96.2	16	305	8	38.12	3- 47	–	–
Shan Masood (P)	RM	9	1	37	1	37.00	1- 12	–	–
J.Shaw (Gs)	RMF	99.5	17	328	8	31.00	3- 13	–	–
W.A.Sheffield (Sx)	LMF	15	0	54	1	54.00	1- 45	–	–
J.W.Shutt (Y)	OB	19.2	0	104	2	52.00	2- 14	–	–
D.P.Sibley (E)	OB	1	0	7	0			–	–
R.N.Sidebottom (Wa)	RMF	88	12	331	8	41.37	3- 37	–	–
R.A.J.Smith (Gm)	RM	14	4	41	3	13.66	3- 41	–	–
T.M.J.Smith (Sy)	SLA	5	0	10	0			–	–
Sohail Khan (PW)	RFM	28	8	66	6	11.00	5- 37	1	–
N.A.Sowter (M)	LB	52.5	16	120	3	40.00	1- 4	–	–
C.T.Steel (Du)	LB	2	0	8	1	8.00	1- 8	–	–
D.I.Stevens (K)	RM	209	64	452	29	15.58	5- 37	3	–
R.A.Stevenson (H)	RMF	32	8	103	5	20.60	4- 70	–	–
G.Stewart (K)	RMF	95.5	19	299	5	59.80	3- 48	–	–
B.A.Stokes (E)	RFM	56	14	158	11	14.36	4- 49	–	–
O.P.Stone (Wa)	RF	17	3	49	4	12.25	4- 39	–	–
C.Z.Taylor (Gm)	OB	26	2	81	2	40.50	1- 20	–	–
J.M.R.Taylor (Gs)	OB	1	0	4	0			–	–
J.P.A.Taylor (Sy)	RM	46	6	171	4	42.75	2- 31	–	–
M.D.Taylor (Gs)	LMF	115	22	330	11	30.00	3- 43	–	–

	Cat	O	M	R	W	Avge	Best	5wI	10wM
T.A.I.Taylor (Le)	RMF	93	25	247	6	41.16	2- 49	–	–
R.N.ten Doeschate (Ex)	RMF	6	0	14	1	14.00	1- 14	–	–
I.A.A.Thomas (K)	RMF	30	3	136	4	34.00	4- 32	–	–
J.A.Thompson (Y)	RM	104	25	246	15	16.40	5- 31	1	–
A.T.Thomson (Wa)	OB	100	14	276	4	69.00	2- 3	–	–
J.C.Tongue (Wo)	RM	117.1	26	363	14	25.92	3- 38	–	–
P.D.Trego (Nt)	RMF	134.3	44	342	12	28.50	3- 33	–	–
Usman Shinwari (PW)	LMF	13	3	48	0				
G.L.van Buuren (Gs)	SLA	21	5	60	1	60.00	1- 7	–	–
T.van der Gugten (Gm)	RFM	119	31	362	12	30.16	3- 45	–	–
R.E.van der Merwe (Sm)	SLA	6	2	8	1	8.00	1- 8	–	–
G.S.Virdi (Sy)	OB	179	26	570	22	25.90	6-101	1	–
J.C.Vitali (CU)	RM	32.5	7	92	10	9.20	6- 34	1	1
W.D.N.von Behr (OU)	OB	39	14	75	3	25.00	2- 38	–	–
G.G.Wagg (Gm)	LM	73	14	272	11	24.72	3- 38	–	–
T.N.Walallawita (M)	SLA	88.2	28	245	6	40.83	3- 28	–	–
P.I.Walter (Ex)	LMF	15	1	53	0				
J.D.Warner (Y)	RFM	9	0	23	1	23.00	1- 23	–	–
W.J.Weighell (Le)	RMF	6	0	29	0				
B.T.J.Wheal (H)	RMF	61	21	203	5	40.60	2- 11	–	–
C.White (Nh)	RFM	88	20	260	13	20.00	4- 35	–	–
D.Wiese (Sx)	RMF	13	3	32	1	32.00	1- 32	–	–
C.R.Woakes (E)	RFM	133	29	348	17	20.47	5- 50	1	–
L.Wood (La)	LFM	44	8	118	3	39.33	2- 31	–	–
M.A.Wood (E)	RF	34	2	110	2	55.00	1- 36	–	–
C.J.C.Wright (Le)	RFM	57	21	141	5	28.20	2- 39	–	–
Yasir Shah (P)	LBG	103	9	375	12	31.25	4- 66	–	–
R.M.Yates (Wa)	OB	22	9	37	0				
S.A.Zaib (Nh)	SLA	28	5	84	4	21.00	2- 11	–	–

FIRST-CLASS CAREER RECORDS

Compiled by Philip Bailey

The following career records are for all players who appeared in first-class and county cricket during the 2020 season, and are complete to the end of that season. Some players who did not appear in 2020 but may do so in 2021 are included, as well as those signed for The Hundred.

BATTING AND FIELDING

'1000' denotes instances of scoring 1000 runs in a season. Where these have been achieved outside the British Isles they are shown after a plus sign.

	M	I	NO	HS	Runs	Avge	100	50	1000	Ct/St
Abbott, K.J.	114	157	30	97*	2427	19.11	–	9	–	18
Abell, T.B.	81	146	14	135	4241	32.12	7	24	–	55
Abid Ali	112	205	16	249*	7485	39.60	20	32	0+1	87/1
Ackermann, C.N.	130	228	27	196*	8243	41.00	17	52	0+1	118
Agedah, A.K.	1	2	–	14	21	10.50	–	–	–	0
Aitchison, B.W.	3	1	–	8	8	8.00	–	–	–	2
Ali, M.M.	194	332	27	250	11202	36.72	20	69	2	111
Allison, B.M.J.	1	1	–	0	0	0.00	–	–	–	0
Alsop, T.P.	49	81	4	150	1999	25.96	2	14	–	65
Amin, A.R.	2	4	–	24	47	11.75	–	–	–	5
Amla, H.M.	238	398	31	311*	17809	48.52	52	88	0+2	186
Anderson, J.M.	253	323	130	81	1858	9.62	–	1	–	148
Andersson, M.K.	13	24	3	92	421	20.04	–	3	–	9
Archer, J.C.	40	58	10	81*	1183	24.64	–	6	–	21
Asad Shafiq	153	255	21	223	9370	40.04	23	49	0+1	145
Atkinson, A.A.P.	2	4	–	15	21	5.25	–	–	–	0
Azad, M.H.	29	46	5	139	1803	43.97	4	11	1	14
Azhar Ali	203	353	29	302*	12685	39.15	40	53	–	143
Babar Azam	65	107	13	266	4057	43.15	8	27	–	42
Bailey, T.E.	60	80	13	68	1175	17.53	–	5	–	14
Bairstow, J.M.	183	302	33	246	11678	43.41	24	63	3	476/24
Balbirnie, A.	30	42	3	205*	1296	33.23	2	8	–	28
Balderson, G.P.	5	7	2	61*	156	31.20	–	1	–	0
Ball, J.T.	66	101	24	49*	1020	13.24	–	–	–	13
Ballance, G.S.	160	262	24	210	11282	47.40	40	51	4+1	119
Bamber, E.R.	14	22	7	27*	160	10.66	–	–	–	2
Bancroft, C.T.	101	185	15	228*	6355	37.38	14	26	–	132/1
Banton, T.	14	24	–	79	603	25.12	–	5	–	7
Barber, T.E.	5	6	4	3	5	2.50	–	–	–	0
Barker, K.H.D.	129	173	31	125	4018	28.29	6	17	–	36
Barnard, E.G.	65	96	16	75	2112	26.40	–	12	–	40
Barnes, E.	2	1	–	4	4	4.00	–	–	–	0
Bartlett, G.A.	29	51	3	137	1338	27.87	4	3	–	8
Batty, G.J.	261	389	68	133	7399	23.04	3	30	–	163
Beard, A.P.	22	24	11	58*	234	18.00	–	1	–	5
Bedingham, D.G.	37	63	6	147	2495	43.77	7	9	–	35
Beer, W.A.T.	27	34	7	97	755	27.96	–	4	–	6
Behardien, F.	114	183	16	150*	6794	41.17	11	44	–	75
Bell, I.R.	312	524	55	262*	20440	43.58	57	105	5	238

222

	M	I	NO	HS	Runs	Avge	100	50	1000	Ct/St
Bell-Drummond, D.J.	117	201	17	206*	5997	32.59	10	30	1	47
Berg, G.K.	133	201	23	130*	5011	28.15	2	27	–	69
Bess, D.M.	47	71	14	107	1379	24.19	1	6	–	22
Billings, S.W.	70	103	11	171	3178	34.54	6	14	–	167/11
Blackwood, J.	104	192	9	248	6080	33.22	5	42	–	107
Blake, A.J.	46	72	6	105*	1511	22.89	1	6	–	25
Blatherwick, J.M.	2	2	2	4*	6	–	–	–	–	0
Bohannon, J.J.	21	28	4	174	984	41.00	1	6	–	10
Bopara, R.S.	221	357	40	229	12821	40.44	31	55	1	118
Borthwick, S.G.	169	285	25	216	9288	35.72	19	50	4	221
Botha, N.	3	4	–	31	65	16.25	–	–	–	2
Bracey, J.R.	39	66	6	156	2096	34.93	5	8	–	49
Brathwaite, C.R.	39	64	9	109	1522	27.67	1	9	–	20
Brathwaite, K.C.	159	285	21	212	10021	37.95	22	53	–	99
Bresnan, T.T.	202	278	43	169*	6813	28.99	7	34	–	107
Briggs, D.R.	108	138	37	120*	1769	17.51	1	1	–	38
Broad, S.C.J.	228	320	53	169	5305	19.86	1	25	–	83
Brook, H.C.	33	54	1	124	1285	24.24	2	6	–	19
Brookes, E.A.	2	3	1	15*	21	10.50	–	–	–	0
Brookes, H.J.H.	19	29	3	84	488	18.76	–	3	–	8
Brooks, J.A.	133	165	58	109*	1827	17.07	1	5	–	32
Brooks, S.S.J.	87	149	13	166	4337	31.88	7	26	–	76
Brown, B.C.	145	229	34	163	7673	39.34	18	42	2	407/18
Brown, P.R.	5	6	4	5*	14	7.00	–	–	–	2
Browne, N.L.J.	95	157	10	255	5673	38.59	15	24	3	73
Buck, N.L.	96	134	37	53	1406	14.49	–	3	–	17
Bull, K.A.	16	28	7	31	202	9.61	–	–	–	5
Burgess, M.G.K.	38	55	4	146	1823	35.74	2	10	–	47/1
Burnham, J.T.A.	42	72	5	135	1688	25.19	1	10	–	14
Burns, R.J.	139	242	14	219*	9618	42.18	19	53	6	120
Burrows, G.D.	2	1	–	1	1	1.00	–	–	–	0
Buttleman, W.E.L.	1	1	–	0	0	0.00	–	–	–	3
Buttler, J.C.	112	181	14	152	5524	33.07	7	32	–	230/2
Byrom, E.J.	27	51	2	152	1379	28.14	3	4	–	15
Came, H.R.C.	5	6	1	25	72	14.40	–	–	–	1
Campbell, J.D.	75	142	6	156	4013	29.50	5	20	–	75
Campbell, J.O.I.	3	4	2	2	2	1.00	–	–	–	0
Carey, L.J.	30	41	6	62*	553	15.80	–	3	–	5
Carlson, K.S.	34	60	2	191	1502	25.89	4	4	–	16
Carse, B.A.	25	32	8	77*	643	26.79	–	2	–	3
Carson, J.J.	4	8	–	21	57	7.12	–	–	–	1
Carter, M.	17	27	2	33	241	9.64	–	–	–	16
Chappell, Z.J.	23	34	6	96	598	21.35	–	2	–	5
Charlesworth, B.G.	15	22	2	77*	417	20.85	–	4	–	5
Chase, R.L.	83	139	19	137*	4518	37.65	9	25	–	40
Chopra, V.	192	317	20	233*	10243	34.48	20	50	3	228
Christian, D.T.	83	141	17	131*	3783	30.50	5	16	–	90
Clark, G.	34	63	1	109	1543	24.88	1	10	–	25
Clark, J.	52	76	8	140	1892	27.82	1	10	–	7
Clark, T.G.R.	5	9	–	65	123	13.66	–	1	–	2
Clarke, J.M.	80	138	10	194	4849	37.88	17	16	1	36
Clarke, R.	256	390	46	214	11195	32.54	17	57	1	378

223

	M	I	NO	HS	Runs	Avge	100	50	1000	Ct/St
Claydon, M.E.	112	145	35	77	1688	15.34	–	4	–	11
Coad, B.O.	38	50	16	48	519	15.26	–	–	–	2
Cobb, J.J.	126	216	22	148*	5155	26.57	4	30	–	53
Cockbain, I.A.	51	86	6	151*	2382	29.77	4	13	–	35
Cohen, M.A.R.	17	20	14	30*	131	21.83	–	–	–	1
Coles, J.M.	1	2	–	11	21	10.50	–	–	–	0
Compton, B.G.	2	3	1	16*	43	21.50	–	–	–	1
Conners, S.	7	6	3	21	65	21.66	–	–	–	0
Cook, A.N.	310	549	42	294	24230	47.79	67	115	9+1	333
Cook, S.J.	34	35	15	37*	140	7.00	–	–	–	3
Cooke, C.B.	89	153	19	171	4772	35.61	4	32	–	157/6
Cooke, J.M.	6	6	–	23	76	12.66	–	–	–	7
Cornwall, R.R.S.	63	110	7	101*	2411	23.40	1	13	–	65
Coughlin, P.	42	66	8	90	1482	25.55	–	8	–	22
Coulter-Nile, N.M.	37	56	3	64	994	18.75	–	3	–	24
Cox, J.M.	7	10	1	238*	395	43.88	1	–	–	7
Cox, O.B.	121	196	27	124	4764	28.18	4	26	–	330/13
Crane, M.S.	42	58	19	29	419	10.74	–	–	–	9
Crawley, Z.	46	77	1	267	2622	34.50	5	14	–	37
Critchley, M.J.J.	53	88	10	137*	2254	28.89	3	10	–	34
Crocombe, H.T.	4	8	4	15	45	11.25	–	–	–	1
Croft, S.J.	180	275	27	156	8462	34.12	13	51	–	182
Cullen, B.C.	2	3	–	34	49	16.33	–	–	–	1
Cullen, T.N.	20	31	3	63	582	20.78	–	4	–	50/1
Cummins, M.L.	82	105	42	29*	434	6.88	–	–	–	31
Curran, B.J.	17	30	3	83*	857	31.74	–	6	–	11
Curran, S.M.	69	107	13	96	2645	28.13	–	18	–	17
Curran, T.K.	59	81	11	60	1241	17.72	–	5	–	20
Currie, S.W.	1	2	–	38	38	19.00	–	–	–	2
Dal, A.K.	19	30	5	92	510	20.40	–	3	–	11
Dale, A.S.	2	4	1	6	7	2.33	–	–	–	0
Daneel, P.D.	3	6	–	125	287	47.83	1	1	–	7
Davey, J.H.	38	61	12	72	838	17.10	–	3	–	13
Davies, A.L.	80	122	6	147	4103	35.37	5	27	1	163/15
Davies, J.L.B.	1	1	–	13	13	13.00	–	–	–	0
Davies, S.M.	231	384	37	200*	13417	38.66	25	62	6	551/33
Davis, W.S.	26	36	12	39*	282	11.75	–	–	–	3
Dawson, L.A.	152	247	27	169	7363	33.46	9	41	1	148
Dearden, H.E.	42	72	2	87	1503	21.47	–	7	–	28
de Lange, M.	85	114	17	113	1581	16.29	1	3	–	36
Delany, G.J.	4	4	–	22	57	14.25	–	–	–	1
Dell, J.J.	7	12	–	61	158	13.16	–	1	–	5
Delport, C.S.	61	106	6	163	3206	32.06	3	19	–	36
Denly, J.L.	212	366	25	227	12474	36.58	29	63	4	88
Dent, C.D.J.	147	263	23	268	9151	38.12	18	53	4	160
Dernbach, J.W.	113	139	47	56*	871	9.46	–	1	–	17
de Silva, D.J.	1	2	–	1	1	0.50	–	–	–	0
Dhariwal, J.S.	1	2	–	34	61	30.50	–	–	–	0
Dickson, S.R.	74	125	9	318	3833	33.04	10	15	–	63
D'Oliveira, B.L.	64	109	4	202*	3160	30.09	8	8	–	30
Donald, A.H.T.	48	86	5	234	2610	32.22	3	15	1	35
Douthwaite, D.A.	14	25	2	100*	603	26.21	1	2	–	4

	M	I	NO	HS	Runs	Avge	100	50	1000	Ct/St
Dowrich, S.O.	109	170	28	131*	4741	33.38	7	28	–	276/25
Duckett, B.M.	95	164	8	282*	6140	39.35	18	26	2	70/3
Dunn, M.P.	42	49	22	31*	174	6.44	–	–	–	9
du Plooy, J.L.	58	91	12	181	3666	46.40	12	19	–	52
Eckersley, E.J.H.	126	223	18	158	6651	32.44	15	24	1	220/3
Eskinazi, S.S.	56	99	5	179	3025	32.18	6	12	–	52
Evans, H.A.	5	8	3	15	32	6.40	–	–	–	1
Evans, L.J.	71	122	6	213*	3474	29.94	6	18	–	56
Evans, S.T.	12	18	1	114	397	23.35	1	1	–	5
Evison, J.D.M.	2	4	–	45	126	31.50	–	–	–	2
Faheem Ashraf	44	63	10	116	1596	30.11	2	7	–	22
Fakhar Zaman	46	75	4	205	2769	39.00	6	16	–	40
Fawad Alam	168	262	44	296*	12286	56.35	34	60	0+3	84
Fell, T.C.	84	143	7	171	4144	30.47	6	17	1	64
Ferguson, L.H.	45	60	23	41	505	13.64	–	–	–	16
Finch, A.J.	88	143	6	288*	4915	35.87	7	33	–	81
Finch, A.W.	11	15	6	18*	90	10.00	–	–	–	1
Finch, H.Z.	53	89	6	135*	2166	26.09	3	13	–	68
Finn, S.T.	157	191	62	56	1266	9.81	–	2	–	49
Fisher, B.A.J.	1	2	1	13*	23	23.00	–	–	–	0
Fisher, M.D.	15	19	3	47*	248	15.50	–	–	–	6
Flanagan, P.J.	1	2	–	8	10	5.00	–	–	–	0
Fletcher, L.J.	117	174	28	92	2029	13.89	–	4	–	28
Foakes, B.T.	111	176	29	141*	5701	38.78	10	31	–	229/24
Foster, F.J.H.	2	3	1	50*	52	26.00	–	1	–	4
Fraine, W.A.R.	16	24	1	106	522	22.69	1	–	–	9
Fuller, J.K.	57	74	10	93	1300	20.31	–	6	–	23
Gabriel, S.T.	106	146	59	20*	474	5.44	–	–	–	25
Garrett, G.A.	3	4	2	24	32	16.00	–	–	–	0
Garton, G.H.S.	17	23	6	59*	322	18.94	–	3	–	10
Gay, E.N.	5	6	1	77*	121	24.20	–	1	–	5
Gilchrist, N.N.	1	2	–	25	38	19.00	–	–	–	0
Gillespie, J.E.	1	2	–	16	20	10.00	–	–	–	0
Gleeson, R.J.	34	39	16	31	259	11.26	–	–	–	8
Glover, B.D.	10	15	6	12*	38	4.22	–	–	–	1
Gnodde, T.R.W.	1	2	–	45	66	33.00	–	–	–	1
Godleman, B.A.	163	293	13	227	9029	32.24	21	41	2	100
Gouldstone, H.O.M.	1	–	–	–	–	–	–	–	–	1
Green, B.G.F.	5	9	–	54	170	18.88	–	1	–	3
Gregory, L.	89	132	13	137	2569	21.58	2	8	–	49
Griffiths, G.T.	26	36	13	40	326	14.17	–	–	–	4
Groenewald, T.D.	139	200	66	78	2375	17.72	–	6	–	45
Gubbins, N.R.T.	77	137	2	201*	4534	33.58	8	27	1	29
Guest, B.D.	3	4	–	17	36	9.00	–	–	–	5
Gurney, H.F.	103	131	63	42*	424	6.23	–	–	–	12
Haggett, C.J.	41	54	13	80	926	22.58	–	2	–	10
Haider Ali	8	14	–	134	652	46.57	2	3	–	4
Hain, S.R.	80	125	12	208	4043	35.77	10	21	–	69
Haines, T.J.	21	35	1	124	832	24.47	2	2	–	6
Hales, A.D.	107	182	6	236	6655	37.81	13	38	3	84
Hameed, H.	68	113	11	122	3179	31.16	5	18	1	43
Hamidullah Qadri	14	25	10	17*	92	6.13	–	–	–	6

	M	I	NO	HS	Runs	Avge	100	50	1000	Ct/St
Hammond, M.A.H.	27	46	3	123*	1014	23.58	2	5	–	23
Handscomb, P.S.P.	111	185	12	215	6500	37.57	14	38	–	177/4
Hankins, G.T.	33	53	2	116	1091	21.39	1	7	–	36
Hankins, H.J.	1	1	–	9	9	9.00	–	–	–	0
Hannon-Dalby, O.J.	75	91	31	40	449	7.48	–	–	–	8
Hargrave, G.T.	2	4	–	146	186	46.50	1	–	–	0
Harmer, S.R.	151	227	44	102*	4401	24.04	2	22	–	150
Harris, J.A.R.	148	216	51	87*	3862	23.40	–	18	–	42
Harris, M.S.	95	172	10	250*	6083	37.54	13	29	0+1	45
Harrison, C.G.	2	3	1	37*	65	32.50	–	–	–	1
Harte, G.J.	25	46	4	114	1201	28.59	3	4	–	6
Hartley, T.W.	4	4	3	13*	35	35.00	–	–	–	2
Haynes, J.A.	10	16	2	51	404	28.85	–	2	–	2
Head, T.M.	105	189	10	192	7025	39.24	12	46	0+1	46
Helm, T.G.	30	41	8	52	559	16.93	–	1	–	9
Hemphrey, C.R.	51	95	6	118	2575	28.93	4	16	–	38
Higgins, R.F.	38	61	9	199	1786	34.34	5	6	–	12
Hildreth, J.C.	267	441	32	303*	17288	42.26	46	77	7	233
Hill, G.C.H.	2	2	1	29	33	33.00	–	–	–	0
Hill, L.J.	41	71	9	126	1459	23.53	1	5	–	96/3
Hogan, M.G.	159	225	89	57	2248	16.52	–	3	–	79
Holden, M.D.E.	43	78	4	153	2031	27.44	3	8	–	15
Holder, J.O.	74	117	12	202*	2727	25.97	3	10	–	61
Holland, I.G.	31	48	6	143	986	23.47	1	5	–	13
Hope, S.D.	62	109	8	215*	3585	35.49	8	13	–	72/1
Hose, A.J.	19	35	1	111	746	21.94	1	4	–	5
Hosein, H.R.	51	86	15	138*	2209	31.11	2	16	–	121/5
Howell, B.A.C.	86	136	13	163	3378	27.46	2	18	–	52
Hudson-Prentice, F.J.	15	25	4	99	571	27.19	–	3	–	2
Hughes, A.L.	73	127	11	142	3317	28.59	6	13	–	53
Hurt, L.J.	3	3	–	38	41	13.66	–	–	–	0
Hutton, B.A.	58	89	12	74	1380	17.92	–	4	–	35
Hyde, E.R.B.	5	9	1	55	144	18.00	–	1	–	13
Iftikhar Ahmed	66	113	10	181	4058	39.39	11	20	–	73
Imad Wasim	77	115	24	207	3702	40.68	6	20	–	35
Imam-ul-Haq	49	87	13	200*	2621	35.14	5	14	–	31
Imran Khan	99	137	44	32	652	7.01	–	–	–	10
Ingram, C.A.	111	195	17	190	6641	37.30	14	30	–	75
Jacks, W.G.	24	39	4	120	996	28.45	1	7	–	28
James, L.W.	2	3	1	36*	50	25.00	–	–	–	1
Jennings, K.K.	138	241	16	221*	7501	33.33	18	28	1	113
Job, J.C.A.	1	2	–	22	22	11.00	–	–	–	5
Jones, M.A.	5	8	–	82	106	13.25	–	1	–	2
Jones, R.P.	30	45	5	122	1175	29.37	2	5	–	27
Jordan, C.J.	114	159	23	166	3443	25.31	3	15	–	137
Joseph, A.S.	36	57	12	89	603	13.40	–	2	–	18
Kashif Bhatti	85	129	15	158	2717	23.83	2	10	–	33
Keogh, R.I.	83	135	8	221	3687	29.03	9	10	–	23/1
Kerrigan, S.C.	106	123	42	62*	1059	13.07	–	3	–	37
Khushi, F.I.N.	4	5	–	66	125	25.00	–	1	–	5
Klaassen, F.J.	3	4	2	14*	37	18.50	–	–	–	3
Klein, D.	68	96	19	94	1443	18.74	–	6	–	19

226

	M	I	NO	HS	Runs	Avge	100	50	1000	Ct/St
Kohler-Cadmore, T.	66	108	8	176	3459	34.59	9	15	1	87
Kuhn, H.G.	175	307	28	244*	11442	41.01	24	58	0+1	374/18
Labuschagne, M.	76	137	9	215	5524	43.15	13	32	1+1	74
Lace, T.C.	19	35	1	143	1157	34.02	3	4	–	13
Lamb, D.J.	8	11	3	50*	210	26.25	–	1	–	2
Lamb, M.J.	19	32	2	173	791	26.36	1	4	–	6
Lamichhane, S.	1	2	1	39*	64	64.00	–	–	–	0
Lammonby, T.A.	6	11	2	116	459	51.00	3	–	–	4
Lavelle, G.I.D.	1	2	–	13	20	10.00	–	–	–	2
Lawrence, D.W.	74	117	13	161	3948	37.96	10	18	1	55
Leach, J.	93	138	17	114	2919	24.12	2	18	–	23
Leach, M.J.	90	124	31	92	1138	12.23	–	3	–	38
Leaning, J.A.	73	116	12	220*	3234	31.09	5	16	–	61
Leech, D.J.	2	2	1	1	1	1.00	–	–	–	0
Lees, A.Z.	115	198	13	275*	6450	34.86	16	30	2	81
Levi, R.E.	106	176	18	168	5722	36.21	10	32	–	89
Libby, J.D.	60	105	6	184	3072	31.03	6	14	–	21
Lilley, A.M.	16	20	5	63	444	29.60	–	2	–	5
Livingstone, A.W.	1	2	–	3	3	1.50	–	–	–	0
Livingstone, L.S.	56	87	14	224	2992	40.98	7	15	–	69
Lloyd, D.L.	69	116	12	119	2939	28.25	4	11	–	34
Loten, T.W.	3	3	–	58	69	23.00	–	1	–	0
Lynn, C.A.	41	71	7	250	2743	43.53	6	12	–	26
Lyth, A.	181	304	15	251	10894	37.69	24	58	3	236
McDermott, B.R.	33	58	6	104	1549	29.78	1	11	–	22
McKerr, C.	14	15	4	29	133	12.09	–	–	–	2
McKiernan, M.H.	3	6	–	52	110	18.33	–	1	–	6
MacLeod, C.S.	28	41	6	84	904	25.82	–	5	–	20
McManus, L.D.	44	63	6	132*	1556	27.29	1	7	–	94/12
Madsen, W.L.	189	337	24	231*	12177	38.90	31	62	5	198
Mahmood, S.	16	18	7	34	154	14.00	–	–	–	1
Malan, D.J.	191	326	21	219	11561	37.90	26	60	3	200
Malan, P.J.	151	251	20	211*	10317	44.66	32	43	0+2	102
Marsh, M.R.	102	176	14	211	5210	32.16	11	21	–	53
Maxwell, G.J.	67	112	10	278	4061	39.81	7	23	–	55
Meaker, S.C.	92	123	25	94	1551	15.82	–	6	–	20
Melton, D.R.	6	7	3	11	12	3.00	–	–	–	1
Mike, B.W.M.	15	24	3	72	392	18.66	–	2	–	4
Miles, C.N.	76	107	17	62*	1447	16.07	–	5	–	19
Mills, T.S.	32	38	15	31*	260	11.30	–	–	–	9
Milnes, M.E.	27	38	11	43	388	14.37	–	–	–	13
Milton, A.G.	14	22	2	104*	358	17.90	1	1	–	12/1
Mitchell, D.K.H.	211	380	39	298	13450	39.44	38	52	6	288
Moen, A.J.	2	4	–	41	62	15.50	–	–	–	0
Mohammad Abbas	110	155	53	40	670	6.56	–	–	–	30
Mohammad Amir	67	102	16	66	1366	15.88	–	2	–	15
Mohammad Nabi	35	57	4	117	1284	24.22	2	5	–	20
Mohammad Rizwan	89	134	22	224	4809	42.93	10	24	–	246/18
Moores, T.J.	39	66	1	106	1372	21.10	2	2	–	92/2
Morgan, A.O.	22	39	4	103*	666	20.18	1	1	–	6
Morgan, E.J.G.	102	169	18	209*	5042	33.39	11	24	1	76/1
Moriarty, D.T.	2	3	–	1	1	0.33	–	–	–	0

227

	M	I	NO	HS	Runs	Avge	100	50	1000	Ct/St
Morkel, M.	153	192	35	82*	2062	13.13	–	4	–	51
Morley, J.P.	1	1	–	3	3	3.00	–	–	–	0
Morris, C.A.J.	63	83	47	53*	454	12.61	–	1	–	12
Moulton, E.H.T.	1	2	–	0	0	0.00	–	–	–	0
Mousley, D.R.	3	5	–	71	152	30.40	–	1	–	1
Mujeeb Zadran	1	2	–	15	18	9.00	–	–	–	0
Mulder, P.W.A.	29	48	10	146	1476	38.84	4	4	–	13
Mullaney, S.J.	143	241	9	179	7727	33.30	15	42	1	142
Munsey, H.G.	4	5	1	100*	224	56.00	1	1	–	1
Murtagh, T.J.	236	313	90	74*	4197	18.82	–	11	–	65
Muzarabani, B.	16	23	7	52*	238	14.87	–	1	–	6
Narine, S.P.	13	18	6	40*	213	17.75	–	–	–	10
Naseem Shah	15	15	5	7	30	3.00	–	–	–	1
Nash, C.D.	208	359	20	184	12552	37.02	24	68	4	123
Naveen-ul-Haq	10	13	1	34	93	7.75	–	–	–	5
Naylor, M.A.	3	5	–	202	235	47.00	1	–	–	0
Neser, M.G.	55	83	11	77	1758	24.41	–	11	–	23
Nijjar, A.S.S.	13	15	5	53	237	23.70	–	1	–	3
Northeast, S.A.	170	288	21	191	10365	38.82	24	53	4	85
Norwell, L.C.	73	94	37	102	842	14.77	1	2	–	16
Olivier, D.	114	146	46	72	1263	12.63	–	3	–	33
Organ, F.S.	12	19	–	100	376	19.78	1	2	–	5
O'Riordan, M.K.	6	10	3	52*	237	33.85	–	1.	–	1
Overton, C.	95	140	18	138	2640	21.63	1	11	–	67
Overton, J.	69	99	21	120	1506	19.30	1	8	–	38
Parkinson, C.F.	28	42	8	75	635	18.67	–	1	–	4
Parkinson, M.W.	20	26	9	14	90	5.29	–	–	–	6
Parnell, W.D.	75	101	11	111*	2502	27.80	2	15	–	23
Parry, S.D.	28	34	2	44	456	14.25	–	–	–	7
Patel, J.S.	293	391	78	120	6695	21.38	3	28	–	155
Patel, R.K.	7	10	–	35	170	17.00	–	–	–	6
Patel, R.S.	26	42	4	100*	926	24.36	1	2	–	14
Patel, S.R.	231	376	20	257*	12692	35.65	26	64	4	140
Paterson, D.	103	128	31	59	1214	12.51	–	1	–	39
Patterson, S.A.	159	190	43	63*	2377	16.17	–	4	–	31
Patterson-White, L.A.	5	8	2	58*	91	15.16	–	1	–	3
Payne, D.A.	99	122	39	67*	1652	19.90	–	6	–	31
Pennington, D.Y.	15	26	5	37	153	7.28	–	–	–	5
Pepper, M.S.	3	6	–	22	61	10.16	–	–	–	6
Pettman, T.H.S.	7	8	1	54*	122	17.42	–	1	–	3
Pillans, M.W.	42	59	5	56	730	13.51	–	1	–	20
Plom, J.H.	1	–	–	–	–	–	–	–	–	0
Plunkett, L.E.	158	216	39	126	4378	24.73	3	22	–	86
Podmore, H.W.	45	65	18	66*	852	18.12	–	3	–	12
Pollard, K.A.	27	44	2	174	1584	37.71	4	7	–	42
Pollock, E.J.	5	7	1	52	184	30.66	–	1	–	1
Pooran, N.	3	6	–	55	143	23.83	–	1	–	2/2
Pope, O.J.D.	43	64	10	251	2972	55.03	9	12	1	50
Porter, J.A.	90	105	38	34	387	5.77	–	–	–	27
Potts, M.J.	11	16	4	53*	176	14.66	–	1	–	2
Poynter, S.W.	41	65	2	170	1437	22.80	2	5	–	117/4
Poysden, J.E.	14	14	4	47	96	9.60	–	–	–	2

228

	M	I	NO	HS	Runs	Avge	100	50	1000	Ct/St
Price, T.J.	1	2	–	0	0	0.00	–	–	–	0
Procter, L.A.	98	155	17	137	4308	31.21	4	22	–	24
Qais Ahmad	12	17	2	46*	226	15.06	–	–	–	7
Qayyum, I.	6	9	4	39	55	11.00	–	–	–	3
Quinn, M.R.	36	46	11	50	360	10.28	–	1	–	7
Rabada, K.	61	83	14	48*	807	11.69	–	–	–	27
Raine, B.A.	83	136	15	82	2589	21.39	–	10	–	16
Rashid, A.U.	175	251	41	180	6822	32.48	10	37	–	79
Rashid Khan	8	11	1	52	231	23.10	–	2	–	0
Rawlins, D.M.W.	19	34	1	100	894	27.09	1	6	–	5
Reece, L.M.	67	120	8	184	3805	33.97	7	22	–	33
Revis, M.L.	1	2	–	9	9	4.50	–	–	–	1
Rhodes, G.H.	28	52	8	61*	956	21.72	–	5	–	14
Rhodes, W.M.H.	55	88	4	207	3097	36.86	6	14	–	33
Richardson, J.A.	17	22	1	71	377	17.95	–	3	–	11
Rimmington, N.J.	53	76	16	102*	1221	20.35	1	4	–	15
Roach, K.A.J.	119	166	33	53	1801	13.54	–	3	–	35
Robinson, O.E.	58	85	16	110	1438	20.84	1	5	–	19
Robinson, O.G.	23	36	2	143	983	28.91	2	4	–	77
Robson, S.D.	162	286	19	231	9965	37.32	23	40	2	152
Roderick, G.H.	100	163	21	171	4902	34.52	6	32	–	277/5
Roland-Jones, T.S.	114	159	30	103*	2824	21.89	1	11	–	33
Root, J.E.	157	273	25	254	11911	48.02	27	66	3	163
Root, W.T.	33	56	3	229	1751	33.03	5	4	–	8
Rossington, A.M.	80	129	13	138*	4099	35.33	7	28	–	175/11
Roy, J.J.	87	144	11	143	4850	36.46	9	23	1	75
Rushworth, C.	131	186	59	57	1514	11.92	–	1	–	28
Russell, A.D.	17	24	1	128	609	26.47	2	–	–	6
Rutherford, H.D.	103	177	3	239	6242	35.87	14	29	0+1	69
Salisbury, M.E.T.	34	56	11	37	379	8.42	–	–	–	4
Salt, P.D.	38	66	2	148	1967	30.73	4	10	–	33
Salter, A.G.	56	87	17	88	1629	23.27	–	8	–	28
Sanderson, B.W.	62	80	30	42	444	8.88	–	–	–	9
Sarfraz Ahmed	157	244	44	213*	7989	39.94	11	56	–	495/53
Scott, G.F.B.	16	24	5	55	344	18.10	–	1	–	5
Scriven, T.A.R.	2	3	–	68	84	28.00	–	1	–	1
Searle, C.J.	4	5	1	26	48	12.00	–	–	–	0
Selman, N.J.	56	103	6	150	2742	28.26	7	13	–	64
Shadab Khan	17	24	2	132	595	27.04	1	3	–	11
Shaheen Shah Afridi	17	22	3	25	101	5.31	–	–	–	1
Shan Masood	127	216	10	199	7212	35.00	14	35	0+1	74
Shaw, J.	39	52	9	42	461	10.72	–	–	–	8
Sheffield, W.A.	1	2	–	6	7	3.50	–	–	–	0
Short, D.J.M.	14	26	1	66	654	26.16	–	4	–	11
Shutt, J.W.	3	4	2	7*	7	7.00	–	–	–	4
Sibley, D.P.	80	134	12	244	5016	41.11	15	22	1	62
Siddle, P.M.	179	239	43	103*	3331	16.99	1	6	–	57
Sidebottom, R.N.	21	30	16	27*	100	7.14	–	–	–	5
Simpson, J.A.	160	254	39	167*	6930	32.23	7	39	–	486/25
Sisodiya, P.	4	5	1	38	83	13.83	–	–	–	2
Slater, B.T.	88	161	7	172	5029	32.65	7	26	1	32
Smith, J.L.	14	25	2	127	739	32.13	1	3	–	13/2

	M	I	NO	HS	Runs	Avge	100	50	1000	Ct/St
Smith, R.A.J.	30	44	6	57*	681	17.92	–	2	–	4
Smith, T.M.J.	50	69	13	84	1346	24.03	–	4	–	15
Snater, S.	3	4	1	50*	73	24.33	–	1	–	1
Sohail Khan	110	143	31	65	1618	14.44	–	4	–	23
Sowter, N.A.	10	17	3	57*	246	17.57	–	2	–	9
Steel, C.T.	40	70	2	224	2007	29.51	3	11	–	18
Steel, S.	2	4	–	39	48	12.00	–	–	–	1
Stevens, D.I.	308	482	30	237	15710	34.75	34	79	3	200
Stevenson, R.A.	7	7	1	51	124	20.66	–	1	–	1
Stewart, G.	21	32	4	103	671	23.96	1	4	–	3
Stirling, P.R.	70	110	5	146	2932	27.92	6	14	–	40
Stoinis, M.P.	61	105	7	170	3255	33.21	4	24	–	22
Stokes, B.A.	143	243	13	258	8221	35.74	18	41	–	117
Stone, O.P.	38	49	11	60	609	16.02	–	1	–	16
Stoneman, M.D.	194	339	8	197	11286	34.09	23	58	5	89
Swindells, H.J.	12	17	2	52*	356	23.73	–	1	–	23/1
Tattersall, J.A.	27	41	4	135*	1273	34.40	1	8	–	64/4
Taylor, B.J.	6	10	3	36	133	19.00	–	–	–	2
Taylor, C.Z.	2	4	–	106	153	38.25	1	–	–	0
Taylor, J.M.R.	79	122	9	156	3300	29.20	7	9	–	40
Taylor, J.P.A.	5	7	3	22	45	11.25	–	–	–	1
Taylor, M.D.	57	74	30	48	557	12.65	–	–	–	7
Taylor, N.P.	3	6	–	59	85	14.16	–	1	–	1
Taylor, T.A.I.	33	49	8	80	821	20.02	–	4	–	8
ten Doeschate, R.N.	193	282	39	259*	10984	45.20	29	50	1	118
Thomas, I.A.A.	35	46	23	13	117	5.08	–	–	–	9
Thomason, A.D.	7	14	–	90	240	17.14	–	1	–	2
Thompson, J.A.	7	9	1	98	270	33.75	–	2	–	2
Thomson, A.T.	14	18	–	46	316	17.55	–	–	–	5
Thurston, C.O.	13	18	–	126	593	32.94	2	2	–	4
Tongue, J.C.	35	46	9	41	393	10.62	–	–	–	4
Topley, R.J.W.	36	43	20	16	100	4.34	–	–	–	8
Trego, P.D.	223	332	38	154*	9644	32.80	15	54	1	90
Trevaskis, L.	11	19	1	64	406	22.55	–	2	–	2
Usman Shinwari	29	31	16	51	291	19.40	–	2	–	8
van Buuren, G.L.	90	140	21	235	4955	41.63	10	30	–	49
van der Gugten, T.	47	69	21	60*	750	15.62	–	3	–	11
van der Merwe, R.E.	71	114	16	205*	3241	33.07	6	19	–	57
van Zyl, S.	175	293	42	228	11132	44.35	27	50	1+1	99
Vasconcelos, R.S.	38	69	6	184	2279	36.17	5	13	–	57/5
Vilas, D.J.	161	246	29	266	9119	42.02	21	42	1	435/20
Vince, J.M.	162	269	20	240	9692	38.92	25	36	2	137
Virdi, G.S.	28	36	18	21*	151	8.38	–	–	–	6
Vitali, J.C.	2	4	3	46*	84	84.00	–	–	–	0
von Behr, W.D.N.	1	2	–	22	36	18.00	–	–	–	0
Wagg, G.G.	164	246	26	200	5904	26.83	5	33	–	54
Waite, M.J.	8	11	1	42	160	16.00	–	–	–	1
Wakely, A.G.	147	235	16	123	6876	31.39	9	37	–	97
Walallawita, T.N.	5	6	2	11	22	5.50	–	–	–	0
Waller, M.T.C.	9	10	1	28	91	10.11	–	–	–	5
Walter, P.I.	15	19	5	68*	506	36.14	–	1	–	2
Warner, D.A.	114	206	10	335*	9630	49.13	32	38	–	83

	M	I	NO	HS	Runs	Avge	100	50	1000	Ct/St
Warner, J.D.	3	3	2	13*	18	18.00	–	–	–	0
Weatherley, J.J.	37	59	4	126*	1421	25.83	1	7	–	16
Weighell, W.J.	16	26	4	84	529	24.04	–	3	–	4
Welch, N.R.	5	7	–	83	179	25.57	–	1	–	1
Wells, L.W.P.	141	237	16	258	7779	35.19	18	33	2	63
Wessels, M.H.	217	359	31	202*	11499	35.05	23	59	2	336/16
Westley, T.	186	310	22	254	10218	35.47	21	48	1	118
Wheal, B.T.J.	28	32	10	25*	181	8.22	–	–	–	11
Wheater, A.J.A.	144	211	28	204*	6664	36.41	12	37	–	252/17
White, C.	4	4	2	7*	9	4.50	–	–	–	0
White, G.G.	39	55	5	65	659	13.18	–	2	–	12
White, R.G.	19	28	1	99	450	16.66	–	2	–	25/2
Whiteley, R.A.	87	142	13	130*	3543	27.46	3	19	–	59
Wiese, D.	124	194	20	208	5814	33.41	11	32	–	70
Willey, D.J.	71	100	12	104*	2350	26.70	2	14	–	17
Williamson, K.S.	148	253	20	284*	11287	48.44	31	59	–	135
Woakes, C.R.	152	224	50	152*	5929	34.07	10	24	–	64
Wood, C.P.	43	62	6	105*	1326	23.67	1	6	–	14
Wood, L.	42	65	14	100	1263	24.76	1	5	–	14
Wood, M.A.	54	89	18	72*	1535	21.61	–	5	–	16
Wood, T.A.	4	6	–	26	73	12.16	–	–	–	3
Worrall, D.J.	45	68	29	50	504	12.92	–	1	–	14
Wright, C.J.C.	164	211	46	77	3031	18.36	–	12	–	29
Wright, L.J.	144	223	23	226*	7622	38.11	17	38	1	58
Yasir Shah	140	195	27	113	2895	17.23	1	7	–	69
Yates, R.M.	17	28	1	141	707	26.18	1	3	–	12
Zaib, S.A.	20	29	3	65*	530	20.38	–	3	–	5
Zampa, A.	38	61	7	74	1177	21.79	–	6	–	9

BOWLING

'50wS' denotes instances of taking 50 or more wickets in a season. Where these have been achieved outside the British Isles they are shown after a plus sign.

	Runs	Wkts	Avge	Best	5wI	10wM	50wS
Abbott, K.J.	9256	442	20.94	9- 40	30	4	3+1
Abell, T.B.	1008	40	25.20	4- 39	–	–	–
Abid Ali	40	2	20.00	1- 2	–	–	–
Ackermann, C.N.	2700	64	42.18	5- 69	1	–	–
Aitchison, B.W.	211	6	35.16	3- 55	–	–	–
Ali, M.M.	13965	368	37.94	6- 29	12	2	–
Allison, B.M.J.	139	4	34.75	3-109	–	–	–
Alsop, T.P.	81	3	27.00	2- 59	–	–	–
Amin, A.R.	123	6	20.50	4- 56	–	–	–
Amla, H.M.	277	1	277.00	1- 10	–	–	–
Anderson, J.M.	24315	975	24.93	7- 42	49	6	4
Andersson, M.K.	489	26	18.80	4- 25	–	–	–
Archer, J.C.	4345	174	24.97	7- 67	8	1	1
Asad Shafiq	650	9	72.22	3- 85	–	–	–
Atkinson, A.A.P.	128	4	32.00	2- 57	–	–	–
Azad, M.H.	17	1	17.00	1- 15	–	–	–
Azhar Ali	2059	47	43.80	4- 34	–	–	–
Babar Azam	423	5	84.60	1- 13	–	–	–

	Runs	Wkts	Avge	Best	5wI	10wM	50wS
Bailey, T.E.	5155	206	25.02	5- 12	9	2	1
Bairstow, J.M.	1	0					
Balbirnie, A.	245	13	18.84	4- 23	–	–	–
Balderson, G.P.	296	9	32.88	3- 63	–	–	–
Ball, J.T.	5770	201	28.70	6- 49	6	–	1
Ballance, G.S.	154	0					
Bamber, E.R.	1233	48	25.68	5- 93	1	–	–
Bancroft, C.T.	77	2	38.50	1- 10	–	–	–
Barber, T.E.	420	7	60.00	3- 42	–	–	–
Barker, K.H.D.	10324	404	25.55	6- 40	15	1	3
Barnard, E.G.	5476	205	26.71	6- 37	5	1	–
Barnes, E.	107	3	35.66	2- 24	–	–	–
Bartlett, G.A.	27	0					
Batty, G.J.	22356	682	32.78	8- 64	27	4	2
Beard, A.P.	1498	49	30.57	4- 21	–	–	–
Bedingham, D.G.	18	0					
Beer, W.A.T.	1480	40	37.00	6- 29	2	1	–
Behardien, F.	1199	32	37.46	3- 48	–	–	–
Bell, I.R.	1615	47	34.36	4- 4	–	–	–
Bell-Drummond, D.J.	263	10	26.30	2- 6	–	–	–
Berg, G.K.	8778	279	31.46	6- 56	5	–	–
Bess, D.M.	3900	129	30.23	7-117	9	1	–
Billings, S.W.	4	0					
Blackwood, J.	698	14	49.85	3- 39	–	–	–
Blake, A.J.	138	3	46.00	2- 9	–	–	–
Blatherwick, J.M.	192	2	96.00	1- 82	–	–	–
Bohannon, J.J.	468	10	46.80	3- 46	–	–	–
Bopara, R.S.	9381	257	36.50	5- 49	3	–	–
Borthwick, S.G.	8101	208	38.94	6- 70	3	–	–
Botha, N.	336	16	21.00	6-108	2	–	–
Bracey, J.R.	35	0					
Brathwaite, C.R.	2098	88	23.84	7- 90	2	–	–
Brathwaite, K.C.	1383	27	51.22	6- 29	1	–	–
Bresnan, T.T.	17367	562	30.90	5- 28	9	–	–
Briggs, D.R.	9390	270	34.77	6- 45	8	–	–
Broad, S.C.J.	21808	808	26.99	8- 15	30	4	–
Brook, H.C.	181	1	181.00	1- 54	–	–	–
Brookes, E.A.	54	0					
Brookes, H.J.H.	2066	55	37.56	4- 54	–	–	–
Brooks, J.A.	12885	475	27.12	6- 65	20	–	4
Brooks, S.S.J.	548	7	78.28	2- 68	–	–	–
Brown, B.C.	109	1	109.00	1- 48	–	–	–
Brown, P.R.	266	7	38.00	2- 15	–	–	–
Browne, N.L.J.	175	0					
Buck, N.L.	8699	259	33.58	6- 34	8	–	–
Bull, K.A.	1323	31	42.67	4- 62	–	–	–
Burgess, M.G.K.	14	0					
Burnham, J.T.A.	17	0					
Burns, R.J.	127	2	63.50	1- 18	–	–	–
Burrows, G.D.	127	4	31.75	2- 20	–	–	–
Buttler, J.C.	11	0					
Byrom, E.J.	43	0					

	Runs	Wkts	Avge	Best	5wI	10wM	50wS
Campbell, J.D.	1805	57	31.66	7- 73	2	–	–
Campbell, J.O.I.	261	1	261.00	1- 43	–	–	–
Carey, L.J.	2830	83	34.09	4- 54	–	–	–
Carlson, K.S.	295	6	49.16	5- 28	1	–	–
Carse, B.A.	2090	61	34.26	6- 26	3	–	–
Carson, J.J.	340	15	22.66	5- 93	1	–	–
Carter, M.	1989	50	39.78	7- 56	2	1	–
Chappell, Z.J.	1800	53	33.96	6- 44	1	–	–
Charlesworth, B.G.	234	8	29.25	3- 25	–	–	–
Chase, R.L.	4671	144	32.43	8- 60	7	1	–
Chopra, V.	128	0					
Christian, D.T.	5679	163	34.84	5- 24	3	–	–
Clark, G.	58	2	29.00	1- 10	–	–	–
Clark, J.	3394	99	34.28	5- 58	2	–	–
Clarke, J.M.	22	0					
Clarke, R.	15714	518	30.33	7- 55	8	–	–
Claydon, M.E.	9889	310	31.90	6-104	9	–	2
Coad, B.O.	3130	157	19.93	6- 25	9	2	1
Cobb, J.J.	1607	18	89.27	2- 11	–	–	–
Cockbain, I.A.	44	1	44.00	1- 23	–	–	–
Cohen, M.A.R.	1497	57	26.26	5- 40	2	–	–
Coles, J.M.	35	3	11.66	2- 32	–	–	–
Conners, S.	441	14	31.50	3- 63	–	–	–
Cook, A.N.	211	7	30.14	3- 13	–	–	–
Cook, S.J.	2461	104	23.66	7- 23	7	1	–
Cooke, J.M.	308	3	102.66	1- 26	–	–	–
Cornwall, R.R.S.	7306	303	24.11	8- 51	19	4	0+2
Coughlin, P.	3130	89	35.16	5- 49	2	1	–
Coulter-Nile, N.M.	3557	124	28.68	6- 84	2	–	–
Crane, M.S.	4334	96	45.14	5- 35	2	–	–
Crawley, Z.	33	0					
Critchley, M.J.J.	3678	82	44.85	6- 73	2	1	–
Crocombe, H.T.	245	3	81.66	2- 36	–	–	–
Croft, S.J.	2980	72	41.38	6- 41	1	–	–
Cullen, B.C.	110	3	36.66	2- 51	–	–	–
Cummins, M.L.	5941	231	25.71	7- 45	10	1	–
Curran, S.M.	5649	194	29.11	7- 58	7	1	–
Curran, T.K.	5613	195	28.78	7- 20	7	1	1
Currie, S.W.	58	3	19.33	3- 42	–	–	–
Dal, A.K.	276	11	25.09	3- 11	–	–	–
Dale, A.S.	73	4	18.25	3- 20	–	–	–
Davey, J.H.	2309	105	21.99	5- 21	2	–	–
Davies, A.L.	6	0					
Davis, W.S.	2323	72	32.26	7-146	1	–	–
Dawson, L.A.	7220	205	35.21	7- 51	3	–	–
Dearden, H.E.	108	2	54.00	1- 0	–	–	–
de Lange, M.	9386	314	29.89	7- 23	11	2	–
Delany, G.J.	144	4	36.00	3- 48	–	–	–
Delport, C.S.	723	14	51.64	2- 10	–	–	–
Denly, J.L.	2710	68	39.85	4- 36	–	–	–
Dent, C.D.J.	813	9	90.33	2- 21	–	–	–
Dernbach, J.W.	10139	311	32.60	6- 47	10	–	1

233

	Runs	Wkts	Avge	Best	5wI	10wM	50wS
Dhariwal, J.S.	7	0					
Dickson, S.R.	53	2	26.50	1-15	–	–	–
D'Oliveira, B.L.	2849	57	49.98	7-92	2	–	–
Douthwaite, D.A.	1375	35	39.28	4-48	–	–	–
Duckett, B.M.	67	1	67.00	1-21	–	–	–
Dunn, M.P.	4092	117	34.97	5-43	4	–	–
du Plooy, J.L.	1218	25	48.72	3-76	–	–	–
Eckersley, E.J.H.	67	2	33.50	2-29	–	–	–
Eskinazi, S.S.	4	0					
Evans, H.A.	369	10	36.90	3-49	–	–	–
Evans, L.J.	270	2	135.00	1-29	–	–	–
Evans, S.T.	46	0					
Evison, J.D.M.	107	4	26.75	3-38	–	–	–
Faheem Ashraf	3442	128	26.89	6-65	6	–	–
Fakhar Zaman	189	8	23.62	2- 2	–	–	–
Fawad Alam	2166	52	41.65	4-27	–	–	–
Fell, T.C.	17	0					
Ferguson, L.H.	3975	161	24.68	7-34	11	1	–
Finch, A.J.	318	5	63.60	1- 0	–	–	–
Finch, A.W.	897	20	44.85	4-38	–	–	–
Finch, H.Z.	118	2	59.00	1- 9	–	–	–
Finn, S.T.	15981	551	29.00	9-37	14	1	2
Fisher, B.A.J.	79	5	15.80	3-37	–	–	–
Fisher, M.D.	1257	41	30.65	5-54	1	–	–
Flanagan, P.J.	83	5	16.60	3-30	–	–	–
Fletcher, L.J.	9654	343	28.14	5-27	6	–	–
Foakes, B.T.	6	0					
Foster, F.J.H.	156	5	31.20	2-33	–	–	–
Fuller, J.K.	5257	159	33.06	6-24	5	1	–
Gabriel, S.T.	8930	300	29.76	8-62	9	1	–
Garrett, G.A.	302	8	37.75	2-53	–	–	–
Garton, G.H.S.	1331	40	33.27	5-26	1	–	–
Gilchrist, N.N.	52	0					
Gleeson, R.J.	3053	143	21.34	6-43	10	1	–
Glover, B.D.	827	24	34.45	4-83	–	–	–
Godleman, B.A.	35	0					
Green, B.G.F.	17	1	17.00	1- 8	–	–	–
Gregory, L.	7100	282	25.17	6-32	14	2	1
Griffiths, G.T.	1936	60	32.26	6-49	1	1	–
Groenewald, T.D.	11904	403	29.53	6-50	16	–	–
Gubbins, N.R.T.	54	0					
Gurney, H.F.	9472	310	30.55	6-25	8	–	–
Haggett, C.J.	3008	89	33.79	4-15	–	–	–
Haider Ali	19	0					
Hain, S.R.	31	0					
Haines, T.J.	366	9	40.66	1- 9	–	–	–
Hales, A.D.	173	3	57.66	2-63	–	–	–
Hameed, H.	21	0					
Hamidullah Qadri	930	24	38.75	5-60	1	–	–
Hammond, M.A.H.	368	2	184.00	1-29	–	–	–
Handscomb, P.S.P.	79	0					
Hankins, G.T.	13	0					

	Runs	Wkts	Avge	Best	5wI	10wM	50wS
Hankins, H.J.	101	0					
Hannon-Dalby, O.J.	6107	200	30.53	6-33	7	1	–
Harmer, S.R.	17506	646	27.09	9-95	37	7	3+1
Harris, J.A.R.	14194	494	28.73	9-34	15	2	3
Harris, M.S.	64	0					
Harrison, C.G.	113	3	37.66	1-30	–	–	–
Harte, G.J.	635	15	42.33	4-15	–	–	–
Hartley, T.W.	324	6	54.00	3-79	–	–	–
Head, T.M.	2975	43	69.18	3-42	–	–	–
Helm, T.G.	2359	79	29.86	5-36	3	–	–
Hemphrey, C.R.	640	8	80.00	2-56	–	–	–
Higgins, R.F.	2746	127	21.62	7-42	5	1	1
Hildreth, J.C.	492	6	82.00	2-39	–	–	–
Hill, G.C.H.	54	1	54.00	1-27	–	–	–
Hill, L.J.	6	0					
Hogan, M.G.	14749	602	24.50	7-92	23	2	3
Holden, M.D.E.	452	5	90.40	2-59	–	–	–
Holder, J.O.	4877	196	24.88	6-42	10	1	–
Holland, I.G.	1493	57	26.19	6-60	1	–	–
Hope, S.D.	5	0					
Howell, B.A.C.	3222	96	33.56	5-57	1	–	–
Hudson-Prentice, F.J.	621	21	29.57	3-27	–	–	–
Hughes, A.L.	1814	36	50.38	4-46	–	–	–
Hurt, L.J.	248	7	35.42	4-27	–	–	–
Hutton, B.A.	5181	193	26.84	8-57	9	2	–
Iftikhar Ahmed	1790	62	28.87	6-39	1	–	–
Imad Wasim	4392	141	31.14	8-81	3	1	–
Imam-ul-Haq	58	1	58.00	1- 4	–	–	–
Imran Khan	8571	351	24.41	9-69	20	3	0+3
Ingram, C.A.	2133	50	42.66	4-16	–	–	–
Jacks, W.G.	104	0					
James, L.W.	123	4	30.75	3-54	–	–	–
Jennings, K.K.	988	30	32.93	3-37	–	–	–
Jones, R.P.	42	1	42.00	1-18	–	–	–
Jordan, C.J.	10730	335	32.02	7-43	10	–	1
Joseph, A.S.	2906	114	25.49	7-46	6	–	–
Kashif Bhatti	7620	332	22.95	8-50	19	3	–
Keogh, R.I.	3871	89	43.49	9-52	1	1	–
Kerrigan, S.C.	9933	325	30.56	9-51	13	3	2
Klaassen, F.J.	250	6	41.66	4-44	–	–	–
Klein, J.	6372	221	28.83	8-72	10	1	–
Kuhn, H.G.	12	0					
Labuschagne, M.	2480	58	42.75	3-45	–	–	–
Lamb, D.J.	438	18	24.33	4-55	–	–	–
Lamb, M.J.	254	6	42.33	1-15	–	–	–
Lamichhane, S.	134	3	44.66	3-84	–	–	–
Lammonby, T.A.	38	2	19.00	1- 4	–	–	–
Lawrence, D.W.	379	9	42.11	2-63	–	–	–
Leach, J.	8615	330	26.10	6-73	13	1	3
Leach, M.J.	7544	293	25.74	8-85	20	3	3
Leaning, J.A.	457	8	57.12	2-20	–	–	–
Leech, D.J.	134	4	33.50	2-72	–	–	–

	Runs	Wkts	Avge	Best	5wI	10wM	50wS
Lees, A.Z.	96	3	32.00	2-51	–	–	–
Libby, J.D.	342	6	57.00	2-45	–	–	–
Lilley, A.M.	1428	43	33.20	5-23	2	–	–
Livingstone, A.W.	81	2	40.50	2-60	–	–	–
Livingstone, L.S.	1304	39	33.43	6-52	1	–	–
Lloyd, D.L.	2812	61	46.09	3-36	–	–	–
Lynn, C.A.	64	0					
Lyth, A.	1699	36	47.19	2- 9	–	–	–
McDermott, B.R.	75	0					
McKerr, C.	1054	38	27.73	5-54	2	1	–
McKiernan, M.H.	48	2	24.00	2- 3	–	–	–
MacLeod, C.S.	444	16	27.75	4-66	–	–	–
Madsen, W.L.	1712	33	51.87	3-45	–	–	–
Mahmood, S.	1214	42	28.90	4-48	–	–	–
Malan, D.J.	2455	61	40.24	5-61	1	–	–
Malan, P.J.	467	20	23.35	5-35	1	–	–
Marsh, M.R.	4838	158	30.62	6-84	2	–	–
Maxwell, G.J.	3174	77	41.22	5-40	1	–	–
Meaker, S.C.	8926	281	31.76	8-52	11	2	1
Melton, D.R.	382	10	38.20	4-22	–	–	–
Mike, B.W.M.	1313	40	32.82	5-37	1	–	–
Miles, C.N.	7612	276	27.57	6-63	14	1	3
Mills, T.S.	2008	55	36.50	4-25	–	–	–
Milnes, M.E.	2468	87	28.36	5-68	2	–	1
Mitchell, D.K.H.	1358	29	46.82	4-49	–	–	–
Moen, A.J.	16	0					
Mohammad Amir	5850	260	22.50	7-61	13	2	0+1
Mohammad Abbas	9782	462	21.17	8-46	34	10	1+2
Mohammad Nabi	2178	94	23.17	6-33	3	–	–
Mohammad Rizwan	122	3	40.66	2-10	–	–	–
Morgan, A.O.	1046	16	65.37	2-37	–	–	–
Morgan, E.J.G.	94	2	47.00	2-24	–	–	–
Moriarty, D.T.	342	17	20.11	6-70	3	1	–
Morkel, M.	14416	567	25.42	6-23	20	2	1
Morley, J.P.	71	5	14.20	4-62	–	–	–
Morris, C.A.J.	5779	197	29.33	7-45	6	. –	2
Moulton, E.H.T.	110	0					
Mousley, D.R.	37	0					
Mujeeb Zadran	75	1	75.00	1-75	–	–	–
Mulder, P.W.A.	1967	84	23.41	7-25	1	–	–
Mullaney, S.J.	4084	113	36.14	5-32	1	–	–
Murtagh, T.J.	20836	841	24.77	7-82	37	4	8
Muzarabani, B.	1004	42	23.90	5-32	1	–	–
Narine, S.P.	1398	65	21.50	8-17	8	3	–
Naseem Shah	1059	47	22.53	6-59	3	–	–
Nash, C.D.	3309	81	40.85	4-12	–	–	–
Naveen-ul-Haq	782	31	25.22	8-35	1	–	–
Neser, M.G.	4680	181	25.85	6-57	3	–	–
Nijjar, A.S.S.	785	19	41.31	2-28	–	–	–
Northeast, S.A.	147	1	147.00	1-60	–	–	–
Norwell, L.C.	7145	266	26.86	8-43	11	3	2
Olivier, D.	10544	456	23.12	6-37	24	4	0+3

	Runs	Wkts	Avge	Best	5wI	10wM	50wS
Organ, F.S.	215	15	14.33	5- 25	1	–	–
O'Riordan, M.K.	288	8	36.00	3- 50	–	–	–
Overton, C.	7862	322	24.41	6- 24	9	–	–
Overton, J.	5319	179	29.71	6- 95	4	–	–
Parkinson, C.F.	2340	54	43.33	8-148	1	1	–
Parkinson, M.W.	1564	62	25.22	6- 23	3	1	–
Parnell, W.D.	6542	220	29.73	7- 51	7	1	–
Parry, S.D.	1926	58	33.20	5- 23	2	–	–
Patel, J.S.	29239	892	32.77	8- 36	38	7	7
Patel, R.S.	773	15	51.53	6- 5	1	–	–
Patel, S.R.	13650	357	38.23	7- 68	5	1	–
Paterson, D.	8579	355	24.16	7- 20	13	1	0+2
Patterson, S.A.	11651	420	27.74	6- 40	8	–	2
Patterson-White, L.A.	420	20	21.00	5- 73	1	–	–
Payne, D.A.	8413	277	30.37	6- 26	4	–	–
Pennington, D.Y.	1327	41	32.36	4- 53	–	–	–
Pettman, T.H.S.	698	33	21.15	5- 19	2	–	–
Pillans, M.W.	3710	131	28.32	6- 67	3	1	0+1
Plunkett, L.E.	14433	453	31.86	6- 33	11	1	3
Podmore, H.W.	3756	149	25.20	6- 36	4	–	1
Pollard, K.A.	436	14	31.14	5- 36	1	–	–
Porter, J.A.	8554	356	24.02	7- 41	13	2	5
Potts, M.J.	809	19	42.57	3- 48	–	–	–
Poynter, S.W.	21	0					
Poysden, J.E.	1084	33	32.84	5- 29	2	–	–
Price, T.J.	80	1	80.00	1- 69	–	–	–
Procter, L.A.	3949	108	36.56	7- 71	3	–	–
Qais Ahmad	1395	68	20.51	7- 41	5	3	–
Qayyum, I.	524	12	43.66	3-158	–	–	–
Quinn, M.R.	3715	123	30.20	7- 76	1	1	–
Rabada, K.	6260	264	23.71	9- 33	11	5	0+1
Raine, B.A.	7279	276	26.37	6- 27	8	–	3
Rashid, A.U.	17949	512	35.05	7-107	20	1	2
Rashid Khan	1012	58	17.44	8- 74	7	2	–
Rawlins, D.M.W.	818	14	58.42	3- 19	–	–	–
Reece, L.M.	2612	101	25.86	7- 20	4	–	1
Rhodes, G.H.	631	6	105.16	2- 83	–	–	–
Rhodes, W.M.H.	1753	53	33.07	5- 111	1	–	–
Richardson, J.A.	1591	67	23.74	8- 47	2	1	–
Rimmington, N.J.	4235	134	31.60	5- 27	3	–	–
Roach, K.A.J.	9920	380	26.10	7- 23	15	1	–
Robinson, O.E.	5445	250	21.78	8- 34	14	4	2
Robson, S.D.	205	6	34.16	2- 0	–	–	–
Roland-Jones, T.S.	10387	403	25.77	7- 52	19	4	2
Root, J.E.	2461	49	50.22	4- 5	–	–	–
Root, W.T.	176	8	22.00	3- 29	–	–	–
Rossington, A.M.	86	0					
Roy, J.J.	495	14	35.35	3- 9	–	–	–
Rushworth, C.	11634	510	22.81	9- 52	26	4	5
Russell, A.D.	1104	54	20.44	5- 36	3	–	–
Rutherford, H.D.	81	0					
Salisbury, M.E.T.	2952	95	31.07	6- 37	1	–	–

	Runs	Wkts	Avge	Best	5wI	10wM	50wS
Salt, P.D.	32	1	32.00	1- 32	–	–	–
Salter, A.G.	4130	86	48.02	4- 80	–	–	–
Sanderson, B.W.	4842	244	19.84	8- 73	13	2	3
Sarfraz Ahmed	8	0					
Scott, G.F.B.	396	8	49.50	2- 34	–	–	–
Scriven, T.A.R.	79	3	26.33	2- 24	–	–	–
Searle, C.J.	399	8	49.87	2- 31	–	–	–
Selman, N.J.	36	1	36.00	1- 22	–	–	–
Shadab Khan	1753	68	25.77	6- 77	2	1	–
Shaheen Shah Afridi	1647	61	27.00	8- 39	2	–	–
Shan Masood	584	8	73.00	2- 52	–	–	–
Shaw, J.	3485	97	35.92	5- 79	2	–	–
Sheffield, W.A.	54	1	54.00	1- 45	–	–	–
Short, D.J.M.	682	20	34.10	3- 78	–	–	–
Shutt, J.W.	104	2	52.00	2- 14	–	–	–
Sibley, D.P.	271	4	67.75	2-103	–	–	–
Siddle, P.M.	16573	617	26.86	8- 54	24	–	0+1
Sidebottom, R.N.	1697	59	28.76	6- 35	1	1	–
Simpson, J.A.	23	0					
Sisodiya, P.	369	15	24.60	4- 79	–	–	–
Slater, B.T.	113	0					
Smith, R.A.J.	2329	68	34.25	5- 87	1	–	–
Smith, T.M.J.	3868	78	49.58	4- 35	–	–	–
Snater, S.	324	12	27.00	5- 88	2	–	–
Sohail Khan	11801	477	24.74	9-109	36	7	0+4
Sowter, N.A.	795	18	44.16	3- 42	–	–	–
Steel, C.T.	638	21	30.38	2- 7	–	–	–
Steel, S.	16	0					
Stevens, D.I.	13472	546	24.67	8- 75	29	2	4
Stevenson, R.A.	460	9	51.11	4- 70	–	–	–
Stewart, G.	1407	44	31.97	6- 22	1	–	–
Stirling, P.R.	1118	27	41.40	2- 21	–	–	–
Stoinis, M.P.	2686	66	40.69	4- 73	–	–	–
Stokes, B.A.	9711	330	29.42	7- 67	7	1	–
Stone, O.P.	3157	130	24.28	8- 80	6	1	–
Stoneman, M.D.	165	0					
Taylor, B.J.	544	13	41.84	4- 64	–	–	–
Taylor, C.Z.	81	2	40.50	1- 20	–	–	–
Taylor, J.M.R.	3345	75	44.60	4- 16	–	–	–
Taylor, J.P.A.	322	11	29.27	3- 26	–	–	–
Taylor, M.D.	5064	153	33.09	5- 15	5	–	1
Taylor, T.A.I.	3084	96	32.12	6- 47	3	1	–
ten Doeschate, R.N.	7207	213	33.83	6- 20	7	–	–
Thomas, I.A.A.	2260	74	30.54	5- 91	1	–	–
Thomason, A.D.	358	4	89.50	2-107	–	–	–
Thompson, J.A.	351	20	17.55	5- 31	1	–	–
Thomson, A.T.	771	20	38.55	6-138	1	–	–
Thurston, C.O.	16	0					
Tongue, J.C.	3037	124	24.49	6- 97	5	–	–
Topley, R.J.W.	3482	133	26.18	6- 29	7	2	–
Trego, P.D.	14359	395	36.35	7- 84	5	1	1
Trevaskis, L.	536	7	76.57	2- 96	–	–	–

	Runs	Wkts	Avge	Best	5wI	10wM	50wS
Usman Shinwari	2311	91	25.39	6- 66	2	–	–
van Buuren, G.L.	2872	88	32.63	4- 12	–	–	–
van der Gugten, T.	4466	165	27.06	7- 42	10	1	1
van der Merwe, R.E.	4527	134	33.78	4- 22	–	–	–
van Zyl, S.	2535	68	37.27	5- 32	1	–	–
Vasconcelos, R.S.	9	0					
Vilas, D.J.	3	0					
Vince, J.M.	1031	22	46.86	5- 41	1	–	–
Virdi, G.S.	2556	91	28.08	8- 61	4	1	–
Vitali, J.C.	150	12	12.50	6- 34	1	1	–
von Behr, W.D.N.	75	3	25.00	2- 38	–	–	–
Wagg, G.G.	16034	465	34.48	6- 29	12	1	2
Waite, M.J.	583	23	25.34	5- 16	1	–	–
Wakely, A.G.	426	6	71.00	2- 62	–	–	–
Walallawita, T.N.	245	6	40.83	3- 28	–	–	–
Waller, M.T.C.	493	10	49.30	3- 33	–	–	–
Walter, P.I.	593	13	45.61	3- 44	–	–	–
Warner, D.A.	455	6	75.83	2- 45	–	–	–
Warner, J.D.	164	5	32.80	3- 35	–	–	–
Weatherley, J.J.	228	4	57.00	1- 2	–	–	–
Weighell, W.J.	1501	52	28.86	7- 32	2	–	–
Wells, L.W.P.	3172	69	45.97	5- 63	1	–	–
Wessels, M.H.	130	3	43.33	1- 10	–	–	–
Westley, T.	2693	59	45.64	4- 55	–	–	–
Wheal, B.T.J.	2283	61	37.42	6- 51	1	–	–
Wheater, A.J.A.	86	1	86.00	1- 86	–	–	–
White, C.	260	13	20.00	4- 35	–	–	–
White, G.G.	2730	65	42.00	6- 44	1	–	–
Whiteley, R.A.	2064	40	51.60	2- 6	–	–	–
Wiese, D.	9638	344	28.01	6- 58	10	1	–
Willey, D.J.	5416	178	30.42	5- 29	5	1	–
Williamson, K.S.	3692	85	43.43	5- 75	1	–	–
Woakes, C.R.	13092	514	25.47	9- 36	21	4	3
Wood, C.P.	3174	105	30.22	5- 39	3	–	–
Wood, L.	3326	99	33.59	5- 40	3	–	–
Wood, M.A.	4708	176	26.75	6- 46	10	–	–
Worrall, D.J.	4903	183	26.79	7- 64	7	1	–
Wright, C.J.C.	15294	464	32.96	6- 22	13	–	2
Wright, L.J.	4862	120	40.51	5- 65	3	–	–
Yasir Shah	16671	578	28.84	8- 41	32	4	–
Yates, R.M.	37	0					
Zaib, S.A.	497	17	29.23	6-115	2	–	–
Zampa, A.	5068	105	48.26	6- 62	2	1	–

LIMITED-OVERS CAREER RECORDS

Compiled by Philip Bailey

The following career records, to the end of the 2020 season, include all players currently registered with first-class counties or teams in The Hundred. These records are restricted to performances in limited-overs matches of 'List A' status as defined by the Association of Cricket Statisticians and Historians now incorporated by ICC into their Classification of Cricket. The following matches qualify for List A status and are included in the figures that follow: Limited-Overs Internationals; Other International matches (e.g. Commonwealth Games, 'A' team internationals); Premier domestic limited-overs tournaments in Test status countries; Official tourist matches against the main first-class teams.

The following matches do NOT qualify for inclusion: World Cup warm-up games; Tourist matches against first-class teams outside the major domestic competitions (e.g. Universities, Minor Counties etc.); Festival, pre-season friendly games and Twenty20 Cup matches.

	M	Runs	Avge	HS	100	50	Wkts	Avge	Best	Econ
Abbott, K.J.	104	485	15.64	56	–	1	141	29.06	4-21	5.22
Abell, T.B.	25	636	31.80	106	1	1	2	13.00	2-19	4.33
Ackermann, C.N.	83	2260	36.45	152*	2	15	42	39.59	4-48	4.83
Ali, M.M.	223	5085	28.09	158	11	20	160	44.92	4-33	5.36
Alsop, T.P.	48	1465	32.55	130*	4	6	–	–	–	33/5
Amla, H.M.	243	9972	45.12	159	30	52	0	–	–	10.50
Anderson, J.M.	261	378	9.00	28	–	–	358	28.57	5-23	4.82
Archer, J.C.	31	219	18.25	45	–	–	51	26.76	5-42	4.98
Bailey, T.E.	15	81	16.20	33	–	–	20	33.00	3-31	5.83
Bairstow, J.M.	151	5129	41.36	174	13	23	–	–	–	90/8
Ball, J.T.	95	198	8.60	28	–	–	118	33.51	5-51	5.87
Ballance, G.S.	110	4360	49.54	156	8	26	–	–	–	–
Bancroft, C.T.	56	1882	41.82	176	3	12	–	–	–	48/1
Banton, T.	24	658	29.90	112	2	4	–	–	–	16/1
Barber, T.E.	7	1	0.16	1	–	–	9	35.77	3-62	6.44
Barker, K.H.D.	62	560	20.00	56	–	1	69	32.79	4-33	5.79
Barnard, E.G.	44	554	29.15	61	–	3	53	35.22	3-26	5.87
Bartlett, G.A.	9	207	34.50	57*	–	1	–	–	–	–
Batty, G.J.	271	2374	15.21	83*	–	5	255	32.48	5-35	4.63
Beard, A.P.	2	24	24.00	22*	–	–	3	32.33	3-51	5.10
Bedingham, D.G.	20	504	29.64	104*	2	2	0	–	–	3.84
Beer, W.A.T.	60	444	15.85	75	–	1	54	41.59	3-27	5.18
Bell-Drummond, D.J.	89	3381	42.26	171*	6	22	5	24.20	2-22	4.68
Berg, G.K.	103	1474	23.03	75	–	7	97	32.82	5-26	5.25
Billings, S.W.	96	3009	42.98	175	7	20	–	–	–	85/8
Birkhead, B.D.	1	–	–	–	–	–	–	–	–	1/0
Blake, A.J.	106	2125	30.35	116	1	12	4	55.75	2-13	6.55
Blatherwick, J.M.	3	6	6.00	3*	–	–	1	72.00	1-55	9.00
Bohannon, J.J.	15	210	26.25	55*	–	1	1	208.00	1-33	8.32
Bopara, R.S.	323	9845	40.18	201*	15	60	248	29.02	5-63	5.33
Borthwick, S.G.	99	1350	22.13	87	–	7	69	40.18	5-38	6.05
Bracey, J.R.	9	487	60.87	113*	1	4	1	23.00	1-23	7.66
Brathwaite, C.R.	92	1350	20.14	113	2	4	103	28.77	5-27	5.16
Bresnan, T.T.	279	3221	21.61	95*	–	10	315	34.26	5-48	5.24

	M	Runs	Avge	HS	100	50	Wkts	Avge	Best	Econ
Briggs, D.R.	107	402	12.56	37*	–	–	112	37.39	4-32	5.11
Broad, S.C.J.	151	620	11.92	45*	–	–	216	30.51	5-23	5.27
Brook, H.C.	15	343	31.18	103	1	1	0	–	–	6.33
Brookes, H.J.H.	12	13	4.33	12*	–	–	17	35.35	3-50	6.54
Brooks, J.A.	36	49	4.90	10	–	–	37	34.48	3-30	4.83
Brown, B.C.	74	1102	24.48	73*	–	8	–	–	–	67/12
Brown, P.R.	10	3	3.00	3	–	–	12	36.50	3-53	6.28
Browne, N.L.J.	21	557	30.94	99	–	3	–	–	–	–
Buck, N.L.	61	141	7.83	21	–	–	69	38.14	4-39	6.24
Burgess, M.G.K.	19	363	21.35	58	–	2	–	–	–	10/1
Burnham, J.T.A.	13	139	23.16	45	–	–	–	–	–	–
Burns, R.J.	57	1722	35.14	95	–	12	–	–	–	–
Buttler, J.C.	215	6020	44.26	150	11	36	–	–	–	227/37
Carey, L.J.	18	124	24.80	39	–	–	12	62.91	2-57	5.56
Carlson, K.S.	17	341	22.73	63	–	2	1	47.00	1-30	6.71
Carse, B.A.	7	2	2.00	2	–	–	10	22.30	3-52	5.46
Carter, M.	16	65	7.22	21*	–	–	23	27.17	4-40	5.34
Chappell, Z.J.	17	141	17.62	59*	–	1	17	45.00	3-45	6.27
Charlesworth, B.G.	1	14	14.00	14	–	–	–	–	–	–
Chopra, V.	114	4789	46.04	160	12	28	0	–	–	6.00
Christian, D.T.	119	2844	32.68	117	2	14	107	33.50	6-48	5.52
Clark, G.	32	665	21.45	114	1	2	3	6.00	3-18	4.50
Clark, J.	51	954	30.77	79*	–	5	34	45.17	4-34	6.34
Clarke, J.M.	62	1846	34.18	139	4	9	–	–	–	22/2
Clarke, R.	232	4087	25.22	98*	–	21	154	37.66	5-26	5.42
Claydon, M.E.	110	276	8.36	19	–	–	138	32.61	5-31	5.62
Coad, B.O.	17	15	15.00	9	–	–	20	37.40	4-63	5.87
Cobb, J.J.	99	3330	38.27	146*	7	21	35	48.91	3-34	5.84
Cockbain, I.A.	68	1633	34.02	108*	2	10	–	–	–	–
Cohen, M.A.R.	4	16	16.00	16	–	–	3	53.33	1-17	5.00
Conners, S.	3	4	4.00	4	–	–	2	75.00	1-45	6.52
Cook, A.N.	168	6055	39.06	137	12	35	0	–	–	3.33
Cook, S.J.	12	9	4.50	6	–	–	11	41.54	3-37	4.71
Cooke, C.B.	88	2607	36.20	161	3	14	–	–	–	54/5
Coulter-Nile, N.M.	80	703	17.57	92	–	3	146	24.98	5-26	5.07
Cox, J.M.	1	21	21.00	21	–	–	–	–	–	1/0
Cox, O.B.	74	1371	27.97	122*	1	5	–	–	–	80/9
Crane, M.S.	39	112	28.00	28*	–	–	67	29.98	4-30	6.08
Crawley, Z.	23	743	35.38	120	1	4	0	–	–	8.50
Critchley, M.J.J.	43	685	27.40	64*	–	2	31	54.00	4-48	6.56
Croft, S.J.	157	4252	36.65	127	3	31	62	41.30	4-24	5.51
Cummins, M.L.	35	62	10.33	20	–	–	48	26.16	4-27	4.77
Curran, B.J.	3	102	34.00	69	–	1	–	–	–	–
Curran, S.M.	54	605	19.51	57	–	1	71	31.09	4-32	5.54
Curran, T.K.	82	728	21.41	47*	–	–	120	28.40	5-16	5.57
Dal, A.K.	5	72	36.00	52	–	1	–	–	–	–
Davey, J.H.	86	1210	23.26	91	–	5	105	26.77	6-28	5.33
Davies, A.L.	49	1380	32.09	147	1	7	–	–	–	48/11

	M	Runs	Avge	HS	100	50	Wkts	Avge	Best	Econ
Davies, S.M.	184	5645	35.50	127*	9	35	–	–	–	147/42
Davis, W.S.	4	17	17.00	15*	–	–	2	89.00	1-60	7.91
Dawson, L.A.	159	3499	33.00	113*	3	18	161	30.04	6-47	4.72
Dearden, H.E.	10	341	34.10	91	–	3	–	–	–	–
de Lange, M.	95	750	15.62	58*	–	2	169	25.28	5-49	5.47
Dell, J.J.	1	46	46.00	46	–	–	–	–	–	–
Delport, C.S.	107	2765	30.38	169*	3	15	38	42.00	4-42	6.09
Denly, J.L.	159	4902	36.58	150*	8	26	47	25.51	4-35	5.11
Dent, C.D.J.	70	1946	32.43	151*	3	6	12	34.33	4-43	5.64
Dernbach, J.W.	144	242	7.56	31	–	–	228	27.10	6-35	5.90
Dickson, S.R.	42	992	27.55	99	–	8	0	–	–	10.00
D'Oliveira, B.L.	66	1032	22.93	79	–	6	50	43.32	3-35	5.27
Donald, A.H.T.	30	424	16.30	57	–	2	–	–	–	–
Douthwaite, D.A.	4	99	49.50	52*	–	1	5	25.20	3-43	5.47
Duckett, B.M.	73	2341	38.37	220*	3	16	–	–	–	38/3
Dunn, M.P.	1	–	–	–	–	–	2	16.00	2-32	5.33
du Plooy, J.L.	45	1865	58.28	155	5	10	11	35.36	3-19	5.84
Eckersley, E.J.H.	44	1041	28.91	108	1	5	–	–	–	27/1
Eskinazi, S.S.	17	496	35.42	107*	1	1	–	–	–	–
Evans, L.J.	63	1735	37.71	134*	3	5	1	82.00	1-29	9.11
Evans, S.T.	1	20	20.00	20	–	–	–	–	–	–
Fell, T.C.	45	1369	35.10	116*	1	11	–	–	–	–
Ferguson, L.H.	69	177	7.69	24	–	–	126	25.50	6-27	5.38
Finch, A.J.	214	8281	41.19	188*	22	47	9	48.77	2-44	5.49
Finn, S.T.	143	411	12.08	42*	–	–	199	29.27	5-33	5.14
Fisher, M.D.	34	228	28.50	36*	–	–	32	42.68	3-32	5.92
Fletcher, L.J.	75	495	20.62	53*	–	1	81	36.24	5-56	5.66
Foakes, B.T.	73	1941	37.32	92	–	18	–	–	–	86/11
Fraine, W.A.R.	4	27	13.50	13	–	–	–	–	–	–
Fuller, J.K.	62	759	23.00	55*	–	1	75	32.29	6-35	5.93
Garton, G.H.S.	24	103	11.44	38	–	–	29	34.24	4-43	6.32
Gleeson, R.J.	21	53	6.62	13	–	–	28	29.14	5-47	5.82
Glover, B.D.	6	55	18.33	27	–	–	4	49.50	2-60	5.03
Godleman, B.A.	69	2559	43.37	137	6	12	–	–	–	–
Green, B.G.F.	3	35	35.00	26*	–	–	1	70.00	1-52	6.36
Gregory, L.	76	1206	23.64	105*	1	7	106	27.79	4-23	5.98
Griffiths, G.T.	22	29	14.50	15*	–	–	29	33.72	4-30	6.01
Groenewald, T.D.	109	793	19.82	57	–	2	123	32.93	4-22	5.62
Gubbins, N.R.T.	56	2067	39.00	141	5	12	–	–	–	–
Guest, B.D.	2	41	20.50	36	–	–	–	–	–	0/1
Gurney, H.F.	93	61	5.54	13*	–	–	114	33.94	5-24	5.90
Hain, S.R.	58	2810	59.78	161*	10	15	–	–	–	–
Hales, A.D.	175	6260	38.40	187*	17	32	0	–	–	15.00
Hameed, H.	19	556	34.75	88	–	4	–	–	–	–
Hamidullah Qadri	3	4	4.00	4	–	–	1	61.00	1-31	6.00
Hammond, M.A.H.	8	185	30.83	95	–	1	5	19.40	2-18	5.10
Handscomb, P.S.P.	108	3165	37.67	140	3	20	–	–	–	99/5
Hankins, G.T.	15	535	38.21	92	–	5	–	–	–	–

242

	M	Runs	Avge	HS	100	50	Wkts	Avge	Best	Econ
Hannon-Dalby, O.J.	43	91	15.16	21*	–	–	65	31.92	5-27	6.29
Harmer, S.R.	83	1002	20.44	44*	–	–	78	42.29	4-42	5.13
Harris, J.A.R.	64	417	14.37	117	1	–	88	30.10	4-38	5.82
Harris, M.S.	44	1184	28.87	84	–	7	–	–	–	–
Haynes, J.A.	1	33	33.00	33	–	–	–	–	–	–
Head, T.M.	94	3202	37.23	202	7	17	21	60.38	2- 9	5.89
Helm, T.G.	40	206	12.87	30	–	–	56	31.10	5-33	5.75
Hemphrey, C.R.	22	430	21.50	87	–	2	2	75.50	1-18	5.80
Higgins, R.F.	33	680	28.33	81*	–	3	24	35.20	4-50	5.54
Hildreth, J.C.	212	5781	35.46	159	7	27	6	30.83	2-26	7.40
Hill, L.J.	41	846	24.17	118	1	3	–	–	–	24/2
Hogan, M.G.	69	171	17.10	27	–	–	102	29.57	5-44	5.09
Holden, M.D.E.	11	412	45.77	166	1	2	1	93.00	1-29	4.65
Holland, I.G.	21	400	25.00	75	–	3	17	41.35	3-11	5.78
Hose, A.J.	29	761	33.08	101*	1	4	–	–	–	–
Hosein, H.R.	13	139	23.16	41*	–	–	–	–	–	8/3
Howell, B.A.C.	86	2050	35.34	122	1	13	76	34.73	3-37	5.20
Hudson-Prentice, F.J.	3	67	33.50	48	–	–	0	–	–	8.00
Hughes, A.L.	65	852	23.66	96*	–	3	43	44.13	4-44	5.61
Hurt, L.J.	5	34	34.00	15*	–	–	7	27.57	2-24	5.84
Hutton, B.A.	15	173	28.83	34*	–	–	16	48.50	3-72	6.39
Ingram, C.A.	186	7584	47.40	142	18	48	40	33.62	4-39	5.44
Jacks, W.G.	22	506	24.09	121	1	2	11	38.45	2-32	5.26
James, L.W.	1	0	0.00	0	–	–	–	–	–	–
Jennings, K.K.	68	2271	41.29	139	4	17	11	55.81	2-19	6.20
Jones, M.A.	8	281	35.12	87	–	3	–	–	–	–
Jones, R.P.	13	205	25.62	65	–	1	2	61.00	1- 3	6.00
Jordan, C.J.	84	634	15.46	55	–	1	121	30.02	5-28	5.73
Keogh, R.I.	46	1272	32.61	134	2	11	8	115.62	2-26	5.53
Kerrigan, S.C.	35	30	3.33	10	–	–	28	46.50	3-21	5.36
Klaassen, F.J.	19	59	9.83	13	–	–	28	26.53	3-30	4.93
Klein, D.	33	206	13.73	46	–	–	49	27.91	5-35	5.20
Kohler-Cadmore, T.	56	1808	34.11	164	3	10	–	–	–	–
Kuhn, H.G.	174	4859	34.46	141*	13	22	–	–	–	179/22
Labuschagne, M.	43	1567	39.17	135	2	13	8	62.12	3-46	6.29
Lace, T.C.	9	115	16.42	48	–	–	2	10.00	2-20	10.00
Lamb, D.J.	2	5	–	4*	–	–	4	27.00	2-51	5.40
Lamb, M.J.	3	61	20.33	47	–	–	0	–	–	9.00
Lamichhane, S.	34	117	9.00	28	–	–	70	17.55	6-16	4.05
Lawrence, D.W.	28	670	26.80	115	1	4	11	54.27	3-35	6.25
Leach, J.	38	539	26.95	63	–	1	43	39.97	4-30	6.04
Leach, M.J.	16	22	7.33	18	–	–	21	30.52	3- 7	4.66
Leaning, J.A.	50	1061	29.47	131*	2	5	9	31.77	5-22	5.66
Lees, A.Z.	54	1533	34.84	115	2	12	–	–	–	–
Levi, R.E.	140	4614	36.61	166	8	29	–	–	–	–
Libby, J.D.	7	117	23.40	66	–	1	–	–	–	–
Lilley, A.M.	19	100	10.00	25	–	–	15	35.33	4-30	5.57
Livingstone, L.S.	55	1552	36.09	129	1	10	23	49.30	3-51	5.21

243

	M	Runs	Avge	HS	100	50	Wkts	Avge	Best	Econ
Lloyd, D.L.	46	942	24.78	92	–	5	17	43.58	5-53	5.96
Loten, T.W.	1	–	–	–	–	–	–	–	–	–
Lynn, C.A.	50	1597	36.29	135	2	12	1	45.00	1- 3	3.91
Lyth, A.	122	3765	35.18	144	5	18	6	62.16	2-27	6.21
McDermott, B.R.	21	936	49.26	117	3	5	–	–	–	20/0
McKerr, C.	6	56	14.00	26*	–	–	8	41.75	3-56	6.44
McManus, L.D.	32	430	21.50	47	–	–	–	–	–	24/8
Madsen, W.L.	105	3323	41.53	138	6	19	16	35.81	3-27	5.14
Mahmood, S.	31	129	18.42	45	–	–	55	25.85	6-37	5.69
Malan, D.J.	149	5135	41.41	185*	10	25	40	32.75	4-25	5.83
Malan, P.J.	109	4270	44.94	169*	12	19	0	–	–	6.88
Marsh, M.R.	116	3232	37.14	124	3	22	94	32.06	5-33	5.42
Maxwell, G.J.	185	4948	33.43	146	5	30	94	44.82	4-46	5.47
Meaker, S.C.	73	198	9.90	50	–	1	80	35.52	4-37	6.17
Mike, B.W.M.	4	80	20.00	41	–	–	1	145.00	1-47	9.66
Miles, C.N.	37	115	9.58	31	–	–	44	37.09	4-29	6.30
Mills, T.S.	23	7	1.75	3*	–	–	22	35.77	3-23	5.97
Milnes, M.E.	8	77	15.40	26	–	–	16	30.87	5-79	6.87
Milton, A.G.	1	0	0.00	0	–	–	–	–	–	0/0
Mitchell, D.K.H.	135	3466	33.65	107	4	22	81	36.11	4-19	5.51
Mohammad Amir	84	413	18.77	73*	–	2	123	26.65	5-30	4.63
Mohammad Abbas	52	136	8.00	15*	–	–	67	30.19	4-31	4.81
Mohammad Nabi	159	3786	29.12	146	3	18	178	30.75	5-12	4.25
Moores, T.J.	21	566	35.37	76	–	5	–	–	–	18/5
Morgan, A.O.	3	32	16.00	29	–	–	2	40.50	2-49	5.78
Morgan, E.J.G.	372	11456	38.83	161	22	66	0	–	–	7.00
Morris, C.A.J.	34	58	9.66	16*	–	–	40	34.47	4-33	5.89
Mujeeb Zadran	47	73	6.63	15	–	–	71	23.39	5-50	3.92
Mulder, P.W.A.	35	491	22.31	66	–	1	35	32.00	3-32	5.37
Mullaney, S.J.	123	2611	35.28	124	2	19	100	34.58	4-29	5.21
Murtagh, T.J.	211	820	10.00	35*	–	–	275	29.57	5-21	4.99
Narine, S.P.	96	606	11.88	51	–	1	160	20.33	6- 9	3.72
Naveen-ul-Haq	16	77	11.00	30	–	–	24	37.45	5-40	6.24
Neser, M.G.	54	631	22.53	122	1	1	61	36.34	4-41	5.28
Nijjar, A.S.S.	3	21	21.00	21	–	–	1	107.00	1-39	5.09
Northeast, S.A.	106	2986	33.93	132	4	17	–	–	–	–
Norwell, L.C.	17	47	5.87	16	–	–	23	31.13	6-52	5.50
Olivier, D.	49	201	13.40	25*	–	–	63	28.20	4-34	5.29
Organ, F.S.	4	0	0.00	0	–	–	2	16.50	1- 6	3.14
Overton, C.	69	756	22.23	66*	–	2	90	31.33	5-18	5.32
Overton, J.	42	798	17.34	40*	–	–	114	30.54	4-42	6.28
Parkinson, C.F.	13	222	27.75	52*	–	1	4	147.25	1-34	6.40
Parkinson, M.W.	27	43	14.33	15*	–	–	42	28.04	5-51	5.17
Parnell, W.D.	165	2088	25.15	129	2	6	233	28.96	6-51	5.45
Patel, R.K.	3	65	21.66	35	–	–	–	–	–	–
Patel, R.S.	3	57	28.50	41*	–	–	2	41.00	2-65	6.83
Patel, S.R.	245	6270	35.22	136*	8	33	225	33.29	6-13	5.40
Paterson, D.	83	283	11.32	29	–	–	115	30.71	5-19	5.12

244

	M	Runs	Avge	HS	100	50	Wkts	Avge	Best	Econ
Patterson, S.A.	96	249	13.10	25*	–	–	122	28.88	6-32	5.13
Payne, D.A.	66	171	17.10	36*	–	–	110	24.96	7-29	5.74
Pennington, D.Y.	3	7	7.00	4*	–	–	8	22.25	5-67	6.84
Pillans, M.W.	19	133	16.62	31	–	–	32	21.50	5-29	5.62
Plunkett, L.E.	214	1675	20.42	72	–	3	282	30.29	5-52	5.54
Podmore, H.W.	18	111	18.50	40	–	–	18	50.55	4-57	6.30
Pollard, K.A.	151	3341	26.72	119	3	16	88	29.65	4-32	5.55
Pollock, E.J.	17	362	24.13	57	–	2	–	–	–	–
Pooran, N.	43	1424	43.15	118	1	10	–	–	–	19/1
Porter, J.A.	31	35	8.75	7*	–	–	33	36.15	4-29	5.19
Potts, M.J.	9	53	17.66	30	–	–	13	24.53	4-62	5.90
Poynter, S.W.	47	581	18.74	109	1	–	–	–	–	42/3
Poysden, J.E.	32	35	3.50	10*	–	–	30	41.60	3-33	5.84
Price, T.J.	1	0	0.00	0	–	–	0	–	–	8.66
Procter, L.A.	45	710	30.86	97	–	5	23	45.30	3-29	5.73
Qais Ahmad	10	107	26.75	66	–	1	13	35.46	3-53	5.17
Qayyum, I.	29	99	7.61	26*	–	–	29	40.62	4-33	5.16
Quinn, M.R.	34	128	16.00	36	–	–	46	36.56	4-71	5.88
Rabada, K.	93	308	13.39	31*	–	–	138	29.31	6-16	5.11
Raine, B.A.	28	392	21.77	83	–	1	27	43.00	3-31	5.68
Rashid, A.U.	223	1761	19.14	71	–	2	300	31.15	5-27	5.43
Rashid Khan	73	926	19.29	60*	–	4	137	18.64	7-18	4.18
Rawlins, D.M.W.	11	285	25.90	53	–	2	3	89.66	1-27	5.38
Reece, L.M.	40	908	29.29	128	1	5	19	50.73	4-35	6.16
Rhodes, G.H.	10	228	38.00	106	1	1	5	50.40	2-34	6.30
Rhodes, W.M.H.	32	569	21.88	69	–	2	13	47.07	2-22	5.83
Richardson, J.A.	37	224	17.23	29*	–	–	60	29.86	4-26	5.47
Roach, K.A.J.	116	400	13.79	34	–	–	155	29.10	6-27	4.99
Robinson, O.E.	14	122	17.42	30	–	–	14	40.57	3-31	5.91
Robinson, O.G.	8	132	26.40	49	–	–	–	–	–	4/0
Robson, S.D.	20	603	33.50	106	1	3	1	43.00	1-27	7.16
Roderick, G.H.	51	1184	33.82	104	2	8	–	–	–	50/4
Roland-Jones, T.S.	79	684	21.37	65	–	1	126	25.24	4-10	5.19
Root, J.E.	187	7175	47.83	133*	17	41	39	50.46	3-52	5.58
Root, W.T.	24	773	48.31	113*	2	3	6	51.66	2-36	6.36
Rossington, A.M.	49	1381	37.32	97	–	11	–	–	–	34/5
Roy, J.J.	188	6464	37.80	180	16	33	0	–	–	12.00
Rushworth, C.	72	188	12.53	38*	–	–	111	24.90	5-31	5.28
Russell, A.D.	93	1953	32.55	132*	2	8	131	26.09	6-28	5.42
Salisbury, M.E.T.	13	8	8.00	5*	–	–	14	35.14	4-55	5.78
Salt, P.D.	16	494	32.93	137*	1	2	–	–	–	–
Salter, A.G.	36	371	20.61	51	–	1	17	67.94	2-41	5.38
Sanderson, B.W.	33	99	11.00	31	–	–	37	35.29	3-36	5.94
Scott, G.F.B.	11	194	27.71	63	–	1	1	239.00	1-65	6.63
Selman, N.J.	9	242	26.88	92	–	1	–	–	–	–
Shadab Khan	56	549	26.14	56	–	–	80	29.16	4-28	5.21
Shaheen Shah Afridi	24	45	15.00	19*	–	–	45	24.62	6-35	5.59
Shaw, J.	1	–	–	–	–	–	0	–	–	7.42

245

	M	Runs	Avge	HS	100	50	Wkts	Avge	Best	Econ
Short, D.J.M.	42	1291	36.88	257	3	4	19	46.52	3-53	5.98
Sibley, D.P.	22	416	23.11	115	1	–	1	62.00	1-20	6.88
Siddle, P.M.	63	251	11.40	62	–	1	74	34.05	4-27	4.75
Simpson, J.A.	93	1587	26.01	82*	–	8	–	–	–	81/19
Slater, B.T.	36	3222	55.55	148*	10	18	–	–	–	–
Smith, J.L.	5	110	22.00	40	–	–	–	–	–	2/0
Smith, R.A.J.	18	71	8.87	14	–	–	18	32.83	4- 7	6.19
Smith, T.M.J.	83	513	22.30	65	–	1	68	40.67	4-26	5.40
Snater, S.	16	68	8.50	23*	–	–	14	40.07	5-60	5.36
Sowter, N.A.	19	134	14.88	31	–	–	36	25.77	6-62	5.52
Steel, C.T.	11	181	20.11	77	–	1	0	–	–	9.40
Steel, S.	8	227	32.42	68	–	2	1	53.00	1-38	5.88
Stevens, D.I.	314	7612	29.50	147	7	46	160	31.97	6-25	4.80
Stevenson, R.A.	3	0	0.00	0	–	–	2	71.00	1-28	7.10
Stewart, G.	5	69	23.00	44	–	–	8	19.00	3-17	3.76
Stoinis, M.P.	94	2478	32.60	146*	4	14	71	36.78	4-43	5.67
Stokes, B.A.	165	4522	37.68	164	7	26	133	32.93	5-61	5.74
Stone, O.P.	30	122	24.40	24*	–	–	24	42.62	4-71	5.45
Stoneman, M.D.	82	2763	37.84	144*	6	17	1	8.00	1- 8	12.00
Swindells, H.J.	4	43	21.50	28	–	–	–	–	–	2/0
Tattersall, J.A.	15	375	41.66	89	–	4	–	–	–	16/3
Taylor, B.J.	18	355	35.50	69	–	3	15	44.06	4-26	4.65
Taylor, J.M.R.	51	1100	33.33	75	–	9	29	35.41	4-38	5.20
Taylor, J.P.A.	1	6	–	6*	–	–	2	33.00	2-66	9.42
Taylor, M.D.	28	41	13.66	16	–	–	20	58.70	3-39	5.63
Taylor, T.A.I.	12	484	48.40	98*	–	4	26	46.30	3-48	6.00
ten Doeschate, R.N.	225	6053	45.17	180	11	31	174	30.21	5-50	5.76
Thomason, A.D.	17	176	25.14	28	–	–	14	32.85	4-45	7.11
Thompson, J.A.	1	–	–	–	–	–	0	–	–	8.60
Thomson, A.T.	9	258	43.00	68*	–	2	13	29.15	3-27	5.05
Thurston, C.O.	4	128	32.00	53	–	1	–	–	–	–
Tongue, J.C.	13	76	19.00	34	–	–	14	42.85	2-35	6.80
Topley, R.J.W.	56	54	9.00	19	–	–	94	25.50	4-16	5.50
Trego, P.D.	198	4962	32.86	147	10	26	171	32.56	5-40	5.56
Trevaskis, L.	8	16	5.33	16	–	–	7	26.71	2-37	4.45
van Buuren, G.L.	70	1454	29.08	119*	1	7	52	33.75	5-35	4.76
van der Gugten, T.	58	350	16.66	36	–	–	68	35.01	5-24	5.56
van der Merwe, R.E.	187	2901	26.86	165*	1	11	250	26.62	5-26	4.87
van Zyl, S.	120	3400	34.69	114*	5	18	20	46.35	4-24	5.26
Vasconcelos, R.S.	26	713	29.70	112	1	4	–	–	–	19/2
Vilas, D.J.	172	4888	37.03	166	9	24	–	–	–	172/29
Vince, J.M.	139	4905	39.87	190	9	23	3	54.00	1-18	5.58
Waite, M.J.	13	278	34.75	71	–	1	16	32.62	4-65	6.44
Wakely, A.G.	90	2532	32.88	109*	2	18	5	26.20	2-14	5.77
Walker, R.I.	1	7	–	7*	–	–	0	–	–	5.25
Waller, M.T.C.	58	109	15.57	25*	–	–	45	37.68	3-37	5.65
Walter, P.I.	10	96	19.20	25	–	–	13	28.84	4-37	6.85
Warner, D.A.	172	7058	43.56	197	23	26	4	39.50	1-11	6.58

	M	Runs	Avge	HS	100	50	Wkts	Avge	Best	Econ
Warner, J.D.	1	–	–	–	–	–	0	–	–	6.40
Weatherley, J.J.	20	509	31.81	105*	1	3	8	27.62	4-25	4.05
Welch, N.R.	5	102	20.40	52	–	1	–	–	–	–
Wells, L.W.P.	26	232	11.60	62	–	1	10	38.40	3-19	5.27
Wessels, M.H.	179	4764	30.93	146	5	26	1	48.00	1- 0	5.87
Westley, T.	88	2853	36.57	134	5	22	21	41.00	4-60	4.98
Wheal, B.T.J.	28	63	7.00	18*	–	–	44	26.22	4-38	5.24
Wheater, A.J.A.	80	1713	28.55	135	2	9	–	–	–	–
White, G.G.	85	543	15.08	41*	–	–	92	29.44	6-37	5.05
White, R.G.	9	99	19.80	21*	–	–	–	–	–	15/2
Whiteley, R.A.	81	1660	27.66	131	1	10	14	40.21	4-58	6.66
Wiese, D.	148	3580	36.53	171	2	21	133	37.12	5-25	5.37
Willey, D.J.	132	1859	25.46	167	3	7	148	31.61	5-30	5.68
Williamson, K.S.	212	8294	46.33	148	17	51	67	35.56	5-51	5.18
Woakes, C.R.	186	2056	23.36	95*	–	6	227	33.02	6-45	5.50
Wood, C.P.	79	400	12.90	41	–	–	106	27.96	5-22	5.38
Wood, L.	4	73	73.00	52	–	1	5	25.00	2-36	5.95
Wood, M.A.	87	118	6.55	24	–	–	110	32.90	4-33	5.32
Wood, T.A.	2	44	44.00	44	–	–	–	–	–	–
Worrall, D.J.	30	59	14.75	16	–	–	37	36.43	5-62	5.23
Wright, C.J.C.	103	263	11.43	42	–	–	102	36.92	4-20	5.61
Wright, L.J.	211	5126	33.07	166	11	19	111	38.11	4-12	5.34
Yates, R.M.	1	66	66.00	66	–	1	–	–	–	–
Zaib, S.A.	10	73	10.42	17	–	–	3	67.33	2-22	6.96
Zampa, A.	99	633	14.72	66	–	3	147	32.82	4-18	5.39

TWENTY20 CAREER RECORDS

Compiled by Philip Bailey

The following career records, to the end of the 2020 season, include all players currently registered with first-class counties or teams in The Hundred.

	M	Runs	Avge	HS	100	50	Wkts	Avge	Best	Econ
Abbott, K.J.	153	320	13.33	30	–	–	155	28.36	5-14	8.24
Abbott, S.A.	88	430	10.23	39	–	–	107	21.38	5-16	8.42
Abell, T.B.	46	974	30.43	101*	1	4	2	50.00	1-11	10.00
Ackermann, C.N.	116	2700	28.72	79*	–	15	55	26.38	7-18	6.93
Ali, M.M.	164	3501	25.18	121*	2	19	109	26.82	5-34	7.67
Allison, B.M.J.	1	1	–	1*	–	–	1	32.00	1-32	10.66
Alsop, T.P.	39	772	23.39	85	–	3	–	–	–	15/3
Amla, H.M.	163	4563	31.04	104*	2	30	0	–	–	15.00
Anderson, J.M.	44	23	5.75	16	–	–	41	32.14	3-23	8.47
Andersson, M.K.	11	95	9.50	24	–	–	0	–	–	13.75
Archer, J.C.	98	419	16.76	36	–	–	124	22.70	4-18	7.83
Atkinson, A.A.P.	9	30	30.00	14	–	–	7	28.57	2-18	9.52
Bailey, T.E.	19	18	6.00	10	–	–	21	22.00	5-17	8.88
Bairstow, J.M.	122	2541	27.92	114	2	11	–	–	–	75/12
Ball, J.T.	74	31	6.20	8*	–	–	87	24.16	3-27	8.63
Ballance, G.S.	91	1648	23.21	79	–	6	–	–	–	–
Bancroft, C.T.	50	1090	32.05	87*	–	8	–	–	–	19/5
Banton, T.	40	1093	29.54	100	1	8	–	–	–	20/3
Barber, T.E.	10	2	0.50	2	–	–	11	32.90	4-28	11.74
Barker, K.H.D.	65	383	13.67	46	–	–	69	23.01	4-19	7.90
Barnard, E.G.	75	463	16.53	42*	–	–	48	37.41	3-29	8.92
Barnes, E.	4	0	–	0	–	–	4	40.50	2-27	11.57
Bartlett, G.A.	3	41	13.66	24	–	–	–	–	–	–
Batty, G.J.	181	623	10.38	87	–	1	147	26.74	4-13	7.30
Beard, A.P.	10	26	13.00	13	–	–	10	28.80	3-41	10.66
Bedingham, D.G.	32	597	22.11	73	–	3	–	–	–	9/1
Beer, W.A.T.	118	350	9.45	37	–	–	97	26.67	3-14	7.45
Bell-Drummond, D.J.	100	2887	31.38	112*	1	22	5	35.80	2-19	10.22
Berg, G.K.	94	1083	21.66	90	–	3	74	29.22	4-20	8.00
Billings, S.W.	175	3262	23.46	95*	–	19	–	–	–	99/14
Birkhead, B.D.	1	0	–	0	–	–	–	–	–	1/0
Blake, A.J.	128	1772	21.09	71*	–	9	1	89.00	1-17	7.41
Bohannon, J.J.	21	77	9.62	23	–	–	–	–	–	–
Bopara, R.S.	368	7235	27.61	105*	1	35	234	25.50	6-16	7.51
Borthwick, S.G.	94	561	17.53	62	–	1	67	23.37	4-18	8.10
Bracey, J.R.	24	370	19.47	64	–	1	–	–	–	8/8
Brathwaite, C.R.	173	1604	15.72	64*	–	2	154	27.44	4-15	8.13
Bresnan, T.T.	182	1639	20.48	51	–	1	180	25.85	6-19	8.14
Briggs, D.R.	169	100	9.09	13	–	–	186	21.99	5-19	7.21
Broad, S.C.J.	85	152	7.60	18*	–	–	100	21.44	4-24	7.19
Brook, H.C.	25	556	27.80	50*	–	1	1	26.00	1-13	13.00
Brookes, H.J.H.	24	94	10.44	31*	–	–	31	25.09	3-26	8.87

	M	Runs	Avge	HS	100	50	Wkts	Avge	Best	Econ
Brooks, J.A.	56	59	14.75	33*	–	–	47	27.27	5-21	7.47
Brown, B.C.	82	840	15.00	68	–	1	–	–	–	41/7
Brown, P.R.	48	22	7.33	7*	–	–	60	23.71	4-21	8.80
Browne, N.L.J.	14	165	16.50	38	–	–	–	–	–	–
Buck, N.L.	63	70	8.75	16*	–	–	71	25.46	4-26	8.76
Burgess, M.G.K.	38	384	16.00	56	–	1	–	–	–	17/6
Burnham, J.T.A.	24	189	11.11	53*	–	1	0	–	–	0.00
Burns, R.J.	54	640	17.29	56*	–	2	–	–	–	21/2
Buttler, J.C.	254	5903	30.90	95*	–	41	–	–	–	140/27
Byrom, E.J.	14	226	18.83	54*	–	1	–	–	–	–
Carey, L.J.	9	7	7.00	5	–	–	4	52.25	1-15	9.08
Carlson, K.S.	22	339	18.83	58	–	1	0	–	–	6.00
Carse, B.A.	23	219	16.84	35	–	–	12	47.33	1-11	8.62
Carter, M.	22	34	11.33	16*	–	–	23	22.56	3-14	7.41
Chappell, Z.J.	16	67	8.37	16	–	–	13	35.53	3-23	9.72
Chopra, V.	115	2896	29.25	116	2	20	–	–	–	–
Christian, D.T.	326	4844	23.28	129	2	13	240	28.60	5-14	8.38
Clark, G.	58	1322	24.94	91*	–	9	0	–	–	12.42
Clark, J.	87	916	22.34	60	–	1	53	28.41	4-22	8.85
Clarke, J.M.	66	1653	28.01	124*	2	9	–	–	–	16/0
Clarke, R.	169	2285	21.35	79*	–	6	113	24.76	4-16	7.54
Claydon, M.E.	149	191	9.55	19	–	–	162	26.85	5-26	8.46
Coad, B.O.	12	14	4.66	7	–	–	13	24.84	3-40	8.93
Cobb, J.J.	157	3321	24.78	103	1	19	59	32.79	4-22	7.84
Cockbain, I.A.	122	3064	32.94	123	1	16	–	–	–	–
Cohen, M.A.R.	9	15	15.00	7*	–	–	7	33.42	2-17	8.45
Conners, S.	6	2	–	2*	–	–	3	40.00	2-38	10.00
Cook, A.N.	32	892	31.85	100*	1	5	–	–	–	–
Cook, S.J.	12	0	0.00	0*	–	–	8	40.37	2-25	9.50
Cooke, C.B.	113	1880	24.41	72	–	6	–	–	–	69/9
Coughlin, P.	43	511	25.55	53	–	1	47	20.82	5-42	9.58
Coulter-Nile, N.M.	120	625	14.88	42*	–	–	140	23.38	4-20	7.76
Cox, J.M.	15	133	16.62	39*	–	–	–	–	–	6/2
Cox, O.B.	120	1785	27.46	59*	–	4	–	–	–	53/27
Cracknell, J.B.	4	123	30.75	50	–	1	–	–	–	0/0
Crane, M.S.	37	43	21.50	12*	–	–	42	21.26	3-15	7.08
Crawley, Z.	24	652	31.04	108*	1	3	–	–	–	–
Critchley, M.J.J.	60	678	17.84	72*	–	1	43	26.30	4-36	7.80
Croft, S.J.	195	4148	29.84	94*	–	24	73	28.06	3- 6	7.43
Cummins, M.L.	14	14	14.00	10	–	–	7	43.28	3-19	8.95
Curran, B.J.	5	54	10.80	29	–	–	–	–	–	–
Curran, S.M.	69	838	19.04	55*	–	4	63	30.28	4-11	8.65
Curran, T.K.	126	889	18.52	62	–	2	152	24.04	4-22	8.66
Currie, S.W.	4	2	2.00	2	–	–	1	58.00	1-28	9.66
Dal, A.K.	21	159	15.90	35	–	–	0	–	–	8.00
Das, R.J.	1	7	7.00	7	–	–	–	–	–	–
Davey, J.H.	49	210	17.50	24	–	–	52	21.84	4-34	8.69
Davies, A.L.	64	1439	28.78	94*	–	11	–	–	–	36/10

249

	M	Runs	Avge	HS	100	50	Wkts	Avge	Best	Econ
Davies, J.L.B.	4	48	12.00	23	–	–	–	–	–	0/0
Davies, S.M.	151	2826	21.08	99*	–	16	–	–	–	69/24
Davis, W.S.	19	6	3.00	4*	–	–	16	25.56	3-24	8.55
Dawson, L.A.	168	1894	20.14	82	–	5	119	27.35	5-17	7.28
Dearden, H.E.	22	348	19.33	61	–	1	–	–	–	–
de Lange, M.	101	263	11.43	28*	–	–	111	25.65	4-23	8.63
Delport, C.S.	246	5779	25.79	129	5	29	68	28.45	4-17	8.03
Denly, J.L.	213	5238	27.86	127	4	30	34	23.85	4-19	7.93
Dent, C.D.J.	60	1096	23.31	87	–	7	5	33.60	1- 4	8.40
Dernbach, J.W.	160	178	7.41	24*	–	–	173	26.64	4-22	8.53
Dickson, S.R.	21	250	22.72	53	–	1	1	9.00	1- 9	9.00
D'Oliveira, B.L.	92	1098	23.36	64	–	5	45	36.17	4-26	7.82
Donald, A.H.T.	54	927	20.15	76	–	5	–	–	–	–
Douthwaite, D.A.	16	139	13.90	24	–	–	5	48.40	1- 7	9.30
Duckett, B.M.	108	2442	29.78	96	–	14	–	–	–	45/2
Dunn, M.P.	20	3	1.50	2	–	–	26	21.15	3- 8	8.80
du Plooy, J.L.	49	918	30.60	70	–	5	13	15.61	4-15	7.42
Eckersley, E.J.H.	66	702	15.60	43	–	–	–	–	–	20/7
Eskinazi, S.S.	39	1125	34.09	84	–	9	–	–	–	–
Evans, L.J.	156	3624	33.55	104*	1	25	1	35.00	1- 5	9.54
Fell, T.C.	7	62	12.40	28	–	–	–	–	–	–
Ferguson, L.H.	51	23	5.75	8*	–	–	47	28.31	4-26	7.69
Finch, A.J.	287	9039	36.15	172	8	60	7	51.28	1- 9	9.24
Finch, A.W.	5	6	–	3*	–	–	8	36.75	1-22	9.18
Finch, H.Z.	24	230	15.33	35*	–	–	–	–	–	–
Finn, S.T.	112	59	9.83	8*	–	–	137	22.20	5-16	7.89
Fisher, M.D.	27	33	8.25	17*	–	–	31	25.19	5-22	9.20
Fletcher, L.J.	76	113	7.06	27	–	–	87	24.33	5-43	8.17
Foakes, B.T.	77	856	21.40	75*	–	4	–	–	–	38/10
Fraine, W.A.R.	19	242	17.28	44*	–	–	–	–	–	–
Fuller, J.K.	99	844	21.10	53*	–	2	97	24.97	6-28	8.89
Garrett, G.A.	2	0	–	0	–	–	1	39.00	1-19	9.75
Garton, G.H.S.	23	103	25.75	34*	–	–	25	20.12	4-16	8.24
Gleeson, R.J.	50	24	4.80	7*	–	–	50	25.76	3-12	7.85
Glover, B.D.	25	2	2.00	1*	–	–	35	17.22	4-12	7.35
Godleman, B.A.	88	1820	24.26	92	–	12	–	–	–	–
Goldsworthy, L.P.	3	38	–	38*	–	–	5	17.20	2-21	7.81
Green, B.G.F.	4	36	18.00	14	–	–	4	22.25	4-26	9.88
Gregory, L.	113	1468	21.91	76*	–	5	109	26.18	4-15	8.83
Griffiths, G.T.	47	41	41.00	11	–	–	39	26.94	4-35	8.29
Groenewald, T.D.	114	401	14.32	41	–	–	99	28.57	4-21	8.21
Gubbins, N.R.T.	36	491	14.87	53	–	1	0	–	–	8.00
Guest, B.D.	4	36	–	22*	–	–	–	–	–	3/0
Gurney, H.F.	156	27	3.85	6	–	–	190	22.58	5-30	7.84
Hain, S.R.	66	1976	36.59	95	–	13	–	–	–	–
Hales, A.D.	269	7351	29.76	116*	3	48	0	–	–	14.00
Hamidullah Qadri	1	0	–	0	–	–	0	–	–	12.00
Hammond, M.A.H.	39	845	24.14	63	–	3	0	–	–	8.50

250

	M	Runs	Avge	HS	100	50	Wkts	Avge	Best	Econ
Handscomb, P.S.P.	84	1318	24.40	103*	1	5	–	–	–	43/13
Hankins, G.T.	8	24	6.00	14	–	–	–	–	–	–
Hannon-Dalby, O.J.	60	53	10.60	14*	–	–	75	24.38	4-20	8.76
Harmer, S.R.	107	739	18.47	43	–	–	82	30.52	4-19	7.62
Harris, J.A.R.	58	164	10.93	18	–	–	48	33.20	4-23	9.28
Harris, M.S.	48	970	21.08	85	–	4	–	–	–	–
Hartley, T.W.	11	4	4.00	4	–	–	6	42.66	2-21	7.11
Haynes, J.A.	7	149	21.28	41	–	–	–	–	–	–
Head, T.M.	80	2036	31.32	101*	1	9	21	25.95	3-16	8.62
Helm, T.G.	43	93	13.28	28*	–	–	54	22.94	5-11	8.60
Higgins, R.F.	75	1221	24.91	77*	–	4	47	25.38	5-13	8.85
Hildreth, J.C.	196	3694	24.46	107*	1	16	10	24.70	3-24	8.76
Hill, G.C.H.	4	21	7.00	14	–	–	1	50.00	1- 9	7.69
Hill, L.J.	51	585	18.28	58	–	1	–	–	–	18/2
Hogan, M.G.	97	78	9.75	17*	–	–	105	24.42	5-17	7.82
Holden, M.D.E.	16	419	29.92	102*	1	1	0	–	–	12.00
Holland, I.G.	14	173	34.60	65	–	1	4	53.00	1-25	7.52
Hollman, L.B.K.	7	139	34.75	46	–	–	9	18.11	3-18	6.79
Hose, A.J.	54	1457	30.35	119	1	9	–	–	–	–
Hosein, H.R.	10	11	–	10*	–	–	–	–	–	8/0
Howell, B.A.C.	121	1605	22.92	57	–	4	132	19.28	5-18	6.95
Hudson-Prentice, F.J.	15	110	18.33	31*	–	–	12	31.00	2- 2	9.07
Hughes, A.L.	87	803	16.38	43*	–	–	53	34.58	4-42	8.01
Hurt, L.J.	4	0	0.00	0	–	–	2	55.00	2-29	11.00
Hutton, B.A.	9	50	16.66	18*	–	–	5	51.00	2-28	8.89
Ingram, C.A.	265	6658	30.12	127*	4	40	38	32.81	4-32	7.88
Jacks, W.G.	36	681	25.22	65	–	5	13	19.15	4-15	7.04
Jennings, K.K.	62	954	35.33	108	1	3	22	28.54	4-37	7.38
Jones, R.P.	12	77	25.66	38*	–	–	–	–	–	–
Jordan, C.J.	200	1020	14.16	45*	–	–	213	26.27	4- 6	8.48
Kelley, V.V.	1	5	5.00	5	–	–	–	–	–	0/2
Keogh, R.I.	59	574	22.07	59*	–	1	16	24.81	3-30	7.94
Khushi, F.I.N.	1	0	0.00	0	–	–	–	–	–	–
Klaassen, F.J.	47	41	5.85	13	–	–	47	30.10	3-31	8.78
Klein, D.	33	128	11.63	31*	–	–	26	28.61	3-27	7.85
Kohler-Cadmore, T.	81	2197	29.68	127	1	16	–	–	–	–
Kuhn, H.G.	133	2425	25.79	83*	1	13	–	–	–	80/6
Labuschagne, M.	10	97	12.12	28	–	–	1	81.00	1-25	11.57
Lamb, D.J.	22	123	30.75	29*	–	–	17	25.64	3-30	8.07
Lamb, M.J.	5	102	34.00	35	–	–	–	–	–	–
Lamichhane, S.	88	63	4.84	10*	–	–	117	18.15	4-10	6.71
Lammonby, T.A.	18	209	23.22	43*	–	–	9	29.22	2-32	10.52
Lavelle, G.I.D.	2	18	9.00	12	–	–	–	–	–	0/0
Lawrence, D.W.	60	1276	27.14	86	–	6	21	20.80	3-21	7.40
Leach, J.	54	261	10.44	24	–	–	52	26.05	5-33	9.57
Leaning, J.A.	63	1153	28.82	64	–	3	1	88.00	1-15	8.80
Lees, A.Z.	55	1350	29.34	77*	–	8	–	–	–	–
Levi, R.E.	215	5422	28.09	117*	3	34	–	–	–	–

	M	Runs	Avge	HS	100	50	Wkts	Avge	Best	Econ
Libby, J.D.	29	687	36.15	75*	–	3	1	54.00	1-11	7.71
Lilley, A.M.	94	1064	19.00	69	–	2	43	31.76	3-31	7.41
Lintott, J.B.	13	36	7.20	12	–	–	14	21.14	3-11	6.60
Livingstone, L.S.	114	2707	27.07	100	1	15	42	18.19	4-17	7.87
Lloyd, D.L.	53	1099	24.42	97*	–	6	5	16.20	2-13	9.00
Lynn, C.A.	193	5237	31.93	113*	2	34	3	31.00	2-15	7.15
Lyth, A.	122	2934	26.67	161	1	17	21	22.23	5-31	7.18
McDermott, B.R.	61	1258	29.95	114	1	4	–	–	–	26/2
McKiernan, M.H.	9	72	12.00	25	–	–	2	79.00	2-22	7.18
McManus, L.D.	48	475	15.83	59	–	1	–	–	–	15/9
Madsen, W.L.	124	3006	29.76	86*	–	20	19	33.94	2-20	7.86
Mahmood, S.	28	17	8.50	6	–	–	27	25.25	4-14	8.38
Malan, D.J.	209	5672	33.16	117	5	32	23	31.39	2-10	7.64
Malan, P.J.	36	1091	41.96	140*	1	5	2	15.00	2-30	7.50
Marsh, M.R.	92	1952	30.98	93*	–	9	49	28.12	4- 6	8.51
Maxwell, G.J.	271	6016	27.34	145*	3	33	97	30.81	3-10	7.67
Meaker, S.C.	32	46	9.20	17	–	–	26	29.76	4-30	8.94
Melton, D.R.	4	0	–	0	–	–	4	31.00	2-37	9.53
Mike, B.W.M.	14	140	17.50	37	–	–	8	29.75	3-38	9.98
Miles, C.N.	13	13	4.33	8	–	–	15	23.40	3-25	7.94
Mills, T.S.	123	65	5.00	10	–	–	131	25.42	4-22	7.84
Milnes, M.E.	11	6	6.00	3	–	–	7	51.85	3-19	9.30
Mitchell, D.K.H.	170	2260	23.06	68*	–	7	98	29.51	5-28	7.66
Mohammad Abbas	24	32	10.66	15*	–	–	20	34.25	3-22	8.35
Mohammad Amir	166	215	6.71	21*	–	–	199	21.12	6-17	6.94
Mohammad Nabi	270	4107	22.56	89	–	11	267	23.26	5-15	6.90
Moores, T.J.	63	1114	27.17	80*	–	6	–	–	–	33/7
Morgan, A.O.	9	59	9.83	24	–	–	0	–	–	7.60
Morgan, E.J.G.	290	6423	26.98	91	–	36	–	–	–	–
Moriarty, D.T.	13	0	–	0	–	–	17	18.29	3-25	6.91
Morris, C.A.J.	13	6	6.00	3	–	–	11	35.63	2-30	9.48
Mousley, D.R.	3	101	50.50	58*	–	1	1	22.00	1- 9	11.00
Mujeeb Zadran	122	139	9.92	27	–	–	131	23.24	4-12	6.60
Mulder, P.W.A.	35	400	22.22	63	–	4	22	30.22	2-13	8.40
Mullaney, S.J.	137	1203	17.43	55	–	2	101	28.98	4-19	7.90
Munsey, H.G.	47	1114	27.17	127*	1	5	–	–	–	–
Murtagh, T.J.	107	227	9.08	40*	–	–	113	25.18	6-24	8.16
Narine, S.P.	341	2385	15.28	79	–	8	385	20.28	5-19	6.00
Nash, C.D.	167	3679	26.85	112*	1	23	49	24.93	4- 7	7.17
Naveen-ul-Haq	45	99	12.37	20*	–	–	47	23.57	4-14	7.11
Neser, M.G.	71	417	14.37	40*	–	–	71	27.52	3-24	8.48
Nijjar, A.S.S.	12	9	4.50	5	–	–	12	28.16	3-22	7.86
Northeast, S.A.	125	2960	28.73	114	1	20	–	–	–	–
Norwell, L.C.	25	5	–	2*	–	–	13	54.30	3-27	9.49
Olivier, D.	47	81	13.50	15*	–	–	56	23.26	4-28	8.36
Organ, F.S.	3	21	7.00	9	–	–	3	18.00	2-21	6.75
O'Riordan, M.K.	1	0	–	0	–	–	0	–	–	6.50
Overton, C.	49	267	16.68	35*	–	–	42	33.95	3-17	9.44

	M	Runs	Avge	HS	100	50	Wkts	Avge	Best	Econ
Overton, J.	58	542	16.93	40*	–	–	110	30.16	5-47	9.63
Parkinson, C.F.	52	192	14.76	27*	–	–	52	24.19	4-20	7.57
Parkinson, M.W.	49	17	4.25	7*	–	–	80	16.08	4-23	7.31
Parnell, W.D.	206	1460	19.72	99	–	4	209	25.27	4-13	7.81
Patel, R.S.	7	7	3.50	5*	–	–	0	–	–	10.28
Patel, S.R.	290	4965	26.26	90*	–	29	237	27.00	4- 5	7.28
Paterson, D.	88	147	9.18	24*	–	–	91	25.27	4-24	7.70
Patterson, S.A.	63	9	1.80	3*	–	–	61	29.68	4-30	8.42
Payne, D.A.	93	49	5.44	10	–	–	115	22.18	5-24	8.33
Pennington, D.Y.	22	27	9.00	10*	–	–	21	28.28	4- 9	9.13
Pepper, M.S.	9	102	20.40	34*	–	–	–	–	–	4/0
Pillans, M.W.	43	184	16.72	34*	–	–	40	28.75	3-15	8.82
Plom, J.H.	5	7	3.50	5	–	–	7	18.42	3-32	7.74
Plunkett, L.E.	158	825	14.47	41	–	–	146	27.52	5-31	8.05
Podmore, H.W.	21	32	6.40	9	–	–	18	31.77	3-13	9.35
Pollard, K.A.	512	10208	31.12	104	1	50	287	24.21	4-15	8.18
Pollock, E.J.	34	724	21.29	77	–	4	–	–	–	–
Pooran, N.	138	2626	24.77	100*	1	13	–	–	–	76/12
Porter, J.A.	19	5	5.00	1*	–	–	17	28.00	4-20	8.78
Potts, M.J.	22	28	7.00	12	–	–	30	18.90	3- 8	7.89
Poynter, S.W.	67	725	23.38	61*	–	1	–	–	–	36/10
Poysden, J.E.	32	13	6.50	9*	–	–	26	28.88	4-51	7.58
Procter, L.A.	37	240	14.11	25*	–	–	14	31.28	3-22	8.87
Qais Ahmad	51	202	11.88	33	–	–	59	21.22	5-18	7.27
Qayyum, I.	45	51	17.00	21*	–	–	45	25.73	5-21	8.07
Quinn, M.R.	65	28	14.00	8*	–	–	70	26.84	4-20	8.83
Rabada, K.	81	163	8.15	44	–	–	107	21.39	4-21	7.76
Raine, B.A.	67	876	21.36	113	1	3	55	28.38	3- 7	9.10
Rashid, A.U.	176	691	12.56	36*	–	–	199	22.45	4-19	7.46
Rashid Khan	221	939	12.03	56*	–	1	307	17.42	5- 3	6.32
Rawlins, D.M.W.	43	827	22.97	69	–	3	15	27.86	3-21	7.33
Reece, L.M.	51	1066	24.79	97*	–	8	24	29.04	3-33	8.20
Revis, M.L.	2	0	–	0*	–	–	–	–	–	–
Rhodes, G.H.	20	103	11.44	30*	–	–	10	16.40	4-13	8.63
Rhodes, W.M.H.	42	401	12.53	46	–	–	22	26.22	3-27	8.99
Richardson, J.A.	45	145	20.71	33*	–	–	49	26.73	4-19	7.93
Roach, K.A.J.	46	59	7.37	12	–	–	28	43.89	3-18	8.08
Robinson, O.E.	44	61	5.08	18*	–	–	40	28.85	4-15	8.80
Robinson, O.G.	14	140	14.00	53	–	1	–	–	–	8/2
Robson, S.D.	4	53	26.50	28*	–	–	–	–	–	–
Roderick, G.H.	41	213	13.31	32	–	–	–	–	–	20/1
Roland-Jones, T.S.	54	317	16.68	40	–	–	64	24.20	5-21	8.72
Root, J.E.	77	1897	33.28	92*	–	13	17	31.00	2- 7	8.63
Root, W.T.	32	372	20.66	40	–	–	0	–	–	12.33
Rossington, A.M.	84	1548	21.20	85	–	9	–	–	–	38/14
Roy, J.J.	215	5556	27.78	122*	4	38	1	39.00	1-23	13.00
Rushworth, C.	85	20	3.33	5	–	–	78	27.19	3-14	7.84
Russell, A.D.	330	5587	27.38	121*	2	21	294	25.99	4-11	8.28

	M	Runs	Avge	HS	100	50	Wkts	Avge	Best	Econ
Sale, O.R.T.	10	20	10.00	14*	–	–	13	26.23	3-32	10.43
Salisbury, M.E.T.	8	2	–	1*	–	–	10	25.60	2-19	8.93
Salt, P.D.	74	1709	26.29	78*	–	13	–	–	–	–
Salter, A.G.	77	337	15.31	39*	–	–	53	28.64	4-12	8.11
Sanderson, B.W.	45	36	9.00	12*	–	–	51	24.31	4-21	8.75
Scott, G.F.B.	31	341	22.73	38*	–	–	3	39.66	1-14	9.91
Scriven, T.A.R.	2	2	2.00	2	–	–	0	–	–	8.00
Selman, N.J.	18	396	28.28	78	–	2	–	–	–	–
Shadab Khan	126	844	15.62	77	–	4	149	21.37	4-14	6.98
Shaheen Shah Afridi	52	25	2.50	9*	–	–	64	22.73	6-19	7.68
Shaw, J.	9	1	1.00	1	–	–	4	53.25	2-39	9.68
Short, D.J.M.	82	2954	39.91	122*	2	23	38	30.89	5-21	8.34
Shutt, J.W.	11	0	0.00	0*	–	–	12	22.58	5-11	7.52
Sibley, D.P.	35	859	29.62	74*	–	7	5	67.60	2-33	8.89
Siddle, P.M.	60	48	6.00	11	–	–	59	25.25	4-29	7.29
Simpson, J.A.	118	2047	24.36	84*	–	7	–	–	–	56/21
Sisodiya, P.	11	4	–	4*	–	–	11	27.45	3-26	6.86
Slater, B.T.	11	472	21.45	57	–	2	–	–	–	–
Smeed, W.C.F.	5	94	18.80	82	–	1	–	–	–	–
Smith, J.L.	12	96	24.00	38*	–	–	–	–	–	6/0
Smith, R.A.J.	25	89	14.83	22*	–	–	20	29.75	4- 6	8.32
Smith, T.M.J.	138	294	19.60	36*	–	–	137	23.11	5-16	7.31
Snater, S.	25	49	8.16	16*	–	–	22	30.18	3-42	10.08
Sole, T.B.	19	160	20.00	41*	–	–	6	33.00	2-15	6.82
Sowter, N.A.	63	84	7.00	13*	–	–	56	28.91	4-23	8.06
Steel, C.T.	6	93	15.50	37	–	–	2	44.00	2-60	11.00
Steel, S.	21	409	24.05	70	–	2	11	24.90	3-20	6.85
Stevens, D.I.	212	4001	26.49	90	–	17	114	26.03	4-14	7.92
Stevenson, R.A.	21	54	9.00	17	–	–	14	41.85	2-28	9.52
Stewart, G.	15	86	12.28	21*	–	–	9	46.66	2-23	8.93
Stirling, P.R.	227	5731	26.65	109	1	40	72	25.93	4-10	7.32
Stoinis, M.P.	117	2514	33.07	147*	1	13	62	27.66	4-15	8.73
Stokes, B.A.	123	2330	24.78	103*	1	8	68	31.70	4-16	8.41
Stone, O.P.	51	66	9.42	22*	–	–	48	29.27	3-22	8.89
Stoneman, M.D.	73	1285	20.39	89*	–	7	–	–	–	–
Swindells, H.J.	18	281	18.73	63	–	3	–	–	–	6/0
Tattersall, J.A.	31	364	26.00	53*	–	1	–	–	–	22/6
Taylor, B.J.	8	23	7.66	9*	–	–	4	32.00	2-20	7.38
Taylor, C.Z.	11	99	14.14	23	–	–	3	17.33	2- 9	7.42
Taylor, J.M.R.	91	1061	20.80	80	–	2	26	33.15	4-16	8.15
Taylor, J.P.A.	2	3	3.00	3	–	–	1	34.00	1- 6	17.00
Taylor, M.D.	38	28	7.00	9*	–	–	34	29.73	3-16	8.80
Taylor, T.A.I.	7	240	20.00	50*	–	2	8	34.25	2-38	8.56
ten Doeschate, R.N.	369	7524	29.97	121*	2	34	114	25.63	4-24	8.16
Thomason, A.D.	32	309	18.17	47	–	–	24	27.91	3-33	10.80
Thompson, J.A.	26	202	16.83	50	–	1	20	32.00	3-23	9.01
Thomson, A.T.	11	39	13.00	14	–	–	10	27.70	4-35	8.14
Thurston, C.O.	8	98	14.00	41	–	–	–	–	–	–

	M	Runs	Avge	HS	100	50	Wkts	Avge	Best	Econ
Tongue, J.C.	5	3	–	2*	–	–	3	40.66	2-32	8.71
Topley, R.J.W.	84	22	4.40	5*	–	–	115	20.82	4-20	8.18
Trego, P.D.	202	4001	24.24	94*	–	21	78	31.42	4-27	8.51
Trevaskis, L.	31	144	10.28	31*	–	–	27	22.40	4-16	7.18
van Buuren, G.L.	67	698	22.51	64	–	4	45	24.42	5- 8	6.86
van der Gugten, T.	96	267	12.13	40*	–	–	114	20.08	5-21	7.79
van der Merwe, R.E.	241	2570	22.34	89*	–	10	226	24.84	5-32	7.10
van Zyl, S.	73	1509	25.57	86*	–	9	7	27.28	2-14	8.68
Vasconcelos, R.S.	13	193	21.44	45*	–	–	–	–	–	7/0
Vilas, D.J.	166	3012	28.68	75*	–	12	–	–	–	93/28
Vince, J.M.	224	5833	29.91	107*	1	36	3	29.00	1- 5	6.69
Waite, M.J.	6	34	–	19*	–	–	2	40.50	1- 6	8.10
Wakely, A.G.	133	2597	26.23	64	–	14	0	–	–	14.50
Walallawita, T.N.	1	0	0.00	0	–	–	3	6.33	3-19	4.75
Walker, R.I.	3	1	1.00	1	–	–	5	23.80	3-39	10.05
Waller, M.T.C.	133	96	7.38	17	–	–	132	23.80	4-16	7.28
Walter, P.I.	48	461	20.95	76	–	1	28	30.00	3-24	9.13
Warner, D.A.	282	9276	37.86	135*	8	76	0	–	–	13.00
Weatherley, J.J.	20	302	16.77	68	–	1	0	–	–	9.00
Welch, N.R.	5	101	20.20	43	–	–	–	–	–	–
Wells, L.W.P.	5	18	3.60	11	–	–	0	–	–	24.00
Wessels, M.H.	226	5384	28.94	110	1	25	–	–	–	89/15
Westley, T.	86	2143	30.18	109*	2	7	7	42.28	2-27	7.58
Wharton, J.H.	2	12	6.00	8	–	–	–	–	–	–
Wheal, B.T.J.	12	22	11.00	16	–	–	11	28.81	3-20	8.49
Wheater, A.J.A.	119	1527	19.08	78	–	4	–	–	–	45/23
White, G.G.	116	380	15.83	37*	–	–	92	26.68	5-22	8.00
White, R.G.	3	11	11.00	11*	–	–	–	–	–	1/0
Whiteley, R.A.	130	2215	25.17	91*	–	5	4	45.25	1-10	10.64
Wiese, D.	237	2546	23.79	79*	–	6	176	27.35	5-19	8.45
Willey, D.J.	187	2722	23.66	118	2	11	180	22.88	4- 7	7.85
Williamson, K.S.	181	4593	30.21	101*	1	31	30	29.50	3-33	7.00
Wisniewski, S.A.	2	0	0.00	0	–	–	0	–	–	8.00
Woakes, C.R.	111	803	24.33	57*	–	2	121	25.12	4-21	8.38
Wood, C.P.	131	325	10.83	27	–	–	137	26.79	5-32	8.28
Wood, L.	38	41	5.12	11	–	–	31	26.83	3-16	8.14
Wood, M.A.	32	106	17.66	27*	–	–	38	23.86	4-25	8.28
Wood, T.A.	4	100	33.33	67	–	1	–	–	–	–
Worrall, D.J.	32	55	11.00	16	–	–	26	33.26	4-23	8.27
Wright, C.J.C.	62	30	4.28	6*	–	–	53	34.60	4-24	9.00
Wright, L.J.	325	7999	29.08	153*	7	42	79	32.44	3-17	8.54
Yates, R.M.	4	89	22.25	37	–	–	–	–	–	–
Young, W.A.	65	1406	25.10	96	–	7	–	–	–	–
Zaib, S.A.	13	123	15.37	30	–	–	2	65.00	1-20	8.12
Zampa, A.	150	168	6.22	17*	–	–	172	21.83	6-19	7.29

FIRST-CLASS CRICKET RECORDS

To the end of the 2020 season

TEAM RECORDS
HIGHEST INNINGS TOTALS

1107	Victoria v New South Wales	Melbourne	1926-27
1059	Victoria v Tasmania	Melbourne	1922-23
952-6d	Sri Lanka v India	Colombo	1997-98
951-7d	Sind v Baluchistan	Karachi	1973-74
944-6d	Hyderabad v Andhra	Secunderabad	1993-94
918	New South Wales v South Australia	Sydney	1900-01
912-8d	Holkar v Mysore	Indore	1945-46
910-6d	Railways v Dera Ismail Khan	Lahore	1964-65
903-7d	England v Australia	The Oval	1938
900-6d	Queensland v Victoria	Brisbane	2005-06
887	Yorkshire v Warwickshire	Birmingham	1896
863	Lancashire v Surrey	The Oval	1990
860-6d	Tamil Nadu v Goa	Panjim	1988-89
850-7d	Somerset v Middlesex	Taunton	2007

Excluding penalty runs in India, there have been 36 innings totals of 800 runs or more in first-class cricket. Tamil Nadu's total of 860-6d was boosted to 912 by 52 penalty runs.

HIGHEST SECOND INNINGS TOTAL

770	New South Wales v South Australia	Adelaide	1920-21

HIGHEST FOURTH INNINGS TOTAL

654-5	England (set 696 to win) v South Africa	Durban	1938-39

HIGHEST MATCH AGGREGATE

2376-37	Maharashtra v Bombay	Poona	1948-49

RECORD MARGIN OF VICTORY

Innings and 851 runs: Railways v Dera Ismail Khan	Lahore	1964-65

MOST RUNS IN A DAY

721	Australians v Essex	Southend	1948

MOST HUNDREDS IN AN INNINGS

6	Holkar v Mysore	Indore	1945-46

LOWEST INNINGS TOTALS

12	†Oxford University v MCC and Ground	Oxford	1877
12	Northamptonshire v Gloucestershire	Gloucester	1907
13	Auckland v Canterbury	Auckland	1877-78
13	Nottinghamshire v Yorkshire	Nottingham	1901
14	Surrey v Essex	Chelmsford	1983
15	MCC v Surrey	Lord's	1839
15	†Victoria v MCC	Melbourne	1903-04
15	†Northamptonshire v Yorkshire	Northampton	1908
15	Hampshire v Warwickshire	Birmingham	1922

† Batted one man short

There have been 28 instances of a team being dismissed for under 20.

LOWEST MATCH AGGREGATE BY ONE TEAM

34 (16 and 18)	Border v Natal	East London	1959-60

LOWEST COMPLETED MATCH AGGREGATE BY BOTH TEAMS

105	MCC v Australians	Lord's	1878

FEWEST RUNS IN AN UNINTERRUPTED DAY'S PLAY

95	Australia (80) v Pakistan (15-2)	Karachi	1956-57

TIED MATCHES

Before 1949 a match was considered to be tied if the scores were level after the fourth innings, even if the side batting last had wickets in hand when play ended. Law 22 was amended in 1948 and since then a match has been tied only when the scores are level after the fourth innings have been completed. There have been 61 tied first-class matches, five of which would not have qualified under the current law. The most recent is:
Lancashire (99 & 170) v Somerset (192 & 77)   Taunton   2018

BATTING RECORDS
35,000 RUNS IN A CAREER

	Career	I	NO	HS	Runs	Avge	100
J.B.Hobbs	1905-34	1315	106	316*	**61237**	50.65	197
F.E.Woolley	1906-38	1532	85	305*	**58969**	40.75	145
E.H.Hendren	1907-38	1300	166	301*	**57611**	50.80	170
C.P.Mead	1905-36	1340	185	280*	**55061**	47.67	153
W.G.Grace	1865-1908	1493	105	344	**54896**	39.55	126
W.R.Hammond	1920-51	1005	104	336*	**50551**	56.10	167
H.Sutcliffe	1919-45	1088	123	313	**50138**	51.95	149
G.Boycott	1962-86	1014	162	261*	**48426**	56.83	151
T.W.Graveney	1948-71/72	1223	159	258	**47793**	44.91	122
G.A.Gooch	1973-2000	990	75	333	**44846**	49.01	128
T.W.Hayward	1893-1914	1138	96	315*	**43551**	41.79	104
D.L.Amiss	1960-87	1139	126	262*	**43423**	42.86	102
M.C.Cowdrey	1950-76	1130	134	307	**42719**	42.89	107
A.Sandham	1911-37/38	1000	79	325	**41284**	44.82	107
G.A.Hick	1983/84-2008	871	84	405*	**41112**	52.23	136
L.Hutton	1934-60	814	91	364	**40140**	55.51	129
M.J.K.Smith	1951-75	1091	139	204	**39832**	41.84	69
W.Rhodes	1898-1930	1528	237	267*	**39802**	30.83	58
J.H.Edrich	1956-78	979	104	310*	**39790**	45.47	103
R.E.S.Wyatt	1923-57	1141	157	232	**39405**	40.04	85
D.C.S.Compton	1936-64	839	88	300	**38942**	51.85	123
G.E.Tyldesley	1909-36	961	106	256*	**38874**	45.46	102
J.T.Tyldesley	1895-1923	994	62	295*	**37897**	40.60	86
K.W.R.Fletcher	1962-88	1167	170	228*	**37665**	37.77	63
C.G.Greenidge	1970-92	889	75	273*	**37354**	45.88	92
J.W.Hearne	1909-36	1025	116	285*	**37252**	40.98	96
L.E.G.Ames	1926-51	951	95	295	**37248**	43.51	102
D.Kenyon	1946-67	1159	59	259	**37002**	33.63	74
W.J.Edrich	1934-58	964	92	267*	**36965**	42.39	86
J.M.Parks	1949-76	1227	172	205*	**36673**	34.76	51
M.W.Gatting	1975-98	861	123	258	**36549**	49.52	94
D.Denton	1894-1920	1163	70	221	**36479**	33.37	69
G.H.Hirst	1891-1929	1215	151	341	**36323**	34.13	60
I.V.A.Richards	1971/72-93	796	63	322	**36212**	49.40	114
A.Jones	1957-83	1168	72	204*	**36049**	32.89	56
W.G.Quaife	1894-1928	1203	185	255*	**36012**	35.37	72
R.E.Marshall	1945/46-72	1053	59	228*	**35725**	35.94	68
M.R.Ramprakash	1987-2012	764	93	301*	**35659**	53.14	114
G.Gunn	1902-32	1061	82	220	**35208**	35.96	62

HIGHEST INDIVIDUAL INNINGS

501*	B.C.Lara	Warwickshire v Durham	Birmingham	1994
499	Hanif Mohammed	Karachi v Bahawalpur	Karachi	1958-59
452*	D.G.Bradman	New South Wales v Queensland	Sydney	1929-30
443*	B.B.Nimbalkar	Maharashtra v Kathiawar	Poona	1948-49
437	W.H.Ponsford	Victoria v Queensland	Melbourne	1927-28

429		W.H.Ponsford	Victoria v Tasmania	Melbourne	1922-23
428		Aftab Baloch	Sind v Baluchistan	Karachi	1973-74
424		A.C.MacLaren	Lancashire v Somerset	Taunton	1895
405*		G.A.Hick	Worcestershire v Somerset	Taunton	1988
400*		B.C.Lara	West Indies v England	St John's	2003-04
394		Naved Latif	Sargodha v Gujranwala	Gujranwala	2000-01
390		S.C.Cook	Lions v Warriors	East London	2009-10
385		B.Sutcliffe	Otago v Canterbury	Christchurch	1952-53
383		C.W.Gregory	New South Wales v Queensland	Brisbane	1906-07
380		M.L.Hayden	Australia v Zimbabwe	Perth	2003-04
377		S.V.Manjrekar	Bombay v Hyderabad	Bombay	1990-91
375		B.C.Lara	West Indies v England	St John's	1993-94
374		D.P.M.D.Jayawardena	Sri Lanka v South Africa	Colombo	2006
369		D.G.Bradman	South Australia v Tasmania	Adelaide	1935-36
366		N.H.Fairbrother	Lancashire v Surrey	The Oval	1990
366		M.V.Sridhar	Hyderabad v Andhra	Secunderabad	1993-94
365*		C.Hill	South Australia v NSW	Adelaide	1900-01
365*		G.St A.Sobers	West Indies v Pakistan	Kingston	1957-58
364		L.Hutton	England v Australia	The Oval	1938
359*		V.M.Merchant	Bombay v Maharashtra	Bombay	1943-44
359*		S.B.Gohel	Gujarat v Orissa	Jaipur	2016-17
359		R.B.Simpson	New South Wales v Queensland	Brisbane	1963-64
357*		R.Abel	Surrey v Somerset	The Oval	1899
357		D.G.Bradman	South Australia v Victoria	Melbourne	1935-36
356		B.A.Richards	South Australia v W Australia	Perth	1970-71
355*		G.R.Marsh	W Australia v S Australia	Perth	1989-90
355*		K.P.Pietersen	Surrey v Leicestershire	The Oval	2015
355		B.Sutcliffe	Otago v Auckland	Dunedin	1949-50
354*		L.D.Chandimal	Sri Lanka Army v Saracens	Katunayake	2020
353		V.V.S.Laxman	Hyderabad v Karnataka	Bangalore	1999-00
352		W.H.Ponsford	Victoria v New South Wales	Melbourne	1926-27
352		C.A.Pujara	Saurashtra v Karnataka	Rajkot	2012-13
351*		S.M.Gugale	Maharashtra v Delhi	Mumbai	2016-17
351		K.D.K.Vithanage	Tamil Union v SL Air	Katunayake	2014-15
350		Rashid Israr	Habib Bank v National Bank	Lahore	1976-77

There have been 230 triple hundreds in first-class cricket, W.V.Raman (313) and Arjan Kripal Singh (302*) for Tamil Nadu v Goa at Panjim in 1988-89 providing the only instance of two batsmen scoring 300 in the same innings.

MOST HUNDREDS IN SUCCESSIVE INNINGS

6	C.B.Fry	Sussex and Rest of England		1901
6	D.G.Bradman	South Australia and D.G.Bradman's XI		1938-39
6	M.J.Procter	Rhodesia		1970-71

TWO DOUBLE HUNDREDS IN A MATCH

244	202*	A.E.Fagg	Kent v Essex	Colchester	1938
201	231	A.K.Perera	Nondescripts v Sinhalese	Colombo (PSO)	2018-19

TRIPLE HUNDRED AND HUNDRED IN A MATCH

333	123	G.A.Gooch	England v India	Lord's	1990
319	105	K.C.Sangakkara	Sri Lanka v Bangladesh	Chittagong	2013-14

DOUBLE HUNDRED AND HUNDRED IN A MATCH MOST TIMES

4	Zaheer Abbas	Gloucestershire	1976-81

TWO HUNDREDS IN A MATCH MOST TIMES

8	Zaheer Abbas	Gloucestershire and PIA	1976-82
8	R.T.Ponting	Tasmania, Australia and Australians	1992-2006

MOST HUNDREDS IN A SEASON

18	D.C.S.Compton	1947	16	J.B.Hobbs	1925

100 HUNDREDS IN A CAREER

	Total		100th Hundred	
	Hundreds	*Inns*	*Season*	*Inns*
J.B.Hobbs	197	1315	1923	821
E.H.Hendren	170	1300	1928-29	740
W.R.Hammond	167	1005	1935	679
C.P.Mead	153	1340	1927	892
G.Boycott	151	1014	1977	645
H.Sutcliffe	149	1088	1932	700
F.E.Woolley	145	1532	1929	1031
G.A.Hick	136	871	1998	574
L.Hutton	129	814	1951	619
G.A.Gooch	128	990	1992-93	820
W.G.Grace	126	1493	1895	1113
D.C.S.Compton	123	839	1952	552
T.W.Graveney	122	1223	1964	940
D.G.Bradman	117	338	1947-48	295
I.V.A.Richards	114	796	1988-89	658
M.R.Ramprakash	114	764	2008	676
Zaheer Abbas	108	768	1982-83	658
A.Sandham	107	1000	1935	871
M.C.Cowdrey	107	1130	1973	1035
T.W.Hayward	104	1138	1913	1076
G.M.Turner	103	792	1982	779
J.H.Edrich	103	979	1977	945
L.E.G.Ames	102	951	1950	915
G.E.Tyldesley	102	961	1934	919
D.L.Amiss	102	1139	1986	1081

MOST 400s: 2 – B.C.Lara, W.H.Ponsford

MOST 300s or more: 6 – D.G.Bradman; 4 – W.R.Hammond, W.H.Ponsford

MOST 200s or more: 37 – D.G.Bradman; 36 – W.R.Hammond; 22 – E.H.Hendren

MOST RUNS IN A MONTH

1294 (avge 92.42)	L.Hutton	Yorkshire	June 1949

MOST RUNS IN A SEASON

Runs			*I*	*NO*	*HS*	*Avge*	*100*	*Season*
3816	D.C.S.Compton	Middlesex	50	8	246	90.85	18	1947
3539	W.J.Edrich	Middlesex	52	8	267*	80.43	12	1947
3518	T.W.Hayward	Surrey	61	8	219	66.37	13	1906

The feat of scoring 3000 runs in a season has been achieved 28 times, the most recent instance being by W.E.Alley (3019) in 1961. The highest aggregate in a season since 1969 is 2755 by S.J.Cook in 1991.

1000 RUNS IN A SEASON MOST TIMES

28   W.G.Grace (Gloucestershire), F.E.Woolley (Kent)

HIGHEST BATTING AVERAGE IN A SEASON

(Qualification: 12 innings)

Avge			*I*	*NO*	*HS*	*Runs*	*100*	*Season*
115.66	D.G.Bradman	Australians	26	5	278	2429	13	1938
106.50	K.C.Sangakkara	Surrey	16	2	200	1491	8	2017
104.66	D.R.Martyn	Australians	14	5	176*	942	5	2001
103.54	M.R.Ramprakash	Surrey	24	2	301*	2278	8	2006
102.53	G.Boycott	Yorkshire	20	5	175*	1538	6	1979
102.00	W.A.Johnston	Australians	17	16	28*	102	–	1953
101.70	G.A.Gooch	Essex	30	3	333	2746	12	1990
101.30	M.R.Ramprakash	Surrey	25	5	266*	2026	10	2007
100.12	G.Boycott	Yorkshire	30	5	233	2503	13	1971

FASTEST HUNDRED AGAINST AUTHENTIC BOWLING

35 min	P.G.H.Fender	Surrey v Northamptonshire	Northampton	1920

FASTEST DOUBLE HUNDRED

103 min	Shafiqullah Shinwari	Kabul v Boost	Asadabad	2017-18

FASTEST TRIPLE HUNDRED

181 min	D.C.S.Compton	MCC v NE Transvaal	Benoni	1948-49

MOST SIXES IN AN INNINGS

23	C.Munro	Central Districts v Auckland	Napier	2014-15

MOST SIXES IN A MATCH

24	Shafiqullah Shinwari	Kabul v Boost	Asadabad	2017-18

MOST SIXES IN A SEASON

80	I.T.Botham	Somerset and England		1985

MOST BOUNDARIES IN AN INNINGS

72	B.C.Lara	Warwickshire v Durham	Birmingham	1994

MOST RUNS OFF ONE OVER

36	G.St A.Sobers	Nottinghamshire v Glamorgan	Swansea	1968
36	R.J.Shastri	Bombay v Baroda	Bombay	1984-85

Both batsmen hit for six all six balls of overs bowled by M.A.Nash and Tilak Raj respectively.

MOST RUNS IN A DAY

390*	B.C.Lara	Warwickshire v Durham	Birmingham	1994

There have been 19 instances of a batsman scoring 300 or more runs in a day.

LONGEST INNINGS

1015 min	R.Nayyar (271)	Himachal Pradesh v Jammu & Kashmir	Chamba	1999-00

HIGHEST PARTNERSHIPS FOR EACH WICKET

First Wicket

561	Waheed Mirza/Mansoor Akhtar	Karachi W v Quetta	Karachi	1976-77
555	P.Holmes/H.Sutcliffe	Yorkshire v Essex	Leyton	1932
554	J.T.Brown/J.Tunnicliffe	Yorkshire v Derbys	Chesterfield	1898

Second Wicket

580	Rafatullah Mohmand/Aamer Sajjad	WAPDA v SSGC	Sheikhupura	2009-10
576	S.T.Jayasuriya/R.S.Mahanama	Sri Lanka v India	Colombo	1997-98
480	D.Elgar/R.R.Rossouw	Eagles v Titans	Centurion	2009-10
475	Zahir Alam/L.S.Rajput	Assam v Tripura	Gauhati	1991-92
465*	J.A.Jameson/R.B.Kanhai	Warwickshire v Glos	Birmingham	1974

Third Wicket

624	K.C.Sangakkara/D.P.M.D.Jayawardena	Sri Lanka v South Africa	Colombo	2006
594*	S.M.Gugale/A.R.Bawne	Maharashtra v Delhi	Mumbai	2016-17
539	S.D.Jogiyani/R.A.Jadeja	Saurashtra v Gujarat	Surat	2012-13
523	M.A.Carberry/N.D.McKenzie	Hampshire v Yorkshire	Southampton	2011

Fourth Wicket

577	V.S.Hazare/Gul Mahomed	Baroda v Holkar	Baroda	1946-47
574*	C.L.Walcott/F.M.M.Worrell	Barbados v Trinidad	Port-of-Spain	1945-46
502*	F.M.M.Worrell/J.D.C.Goddard	Barbados v Trinidad	Bridgetown	1943-44
470	A.I.Kallicharran/G.W.Humpage	Warwickshire v Lancs	Southport	1982

Fifth Wicket

520*	C.A.Pujara/R.A.Jadeja	Saurashtra v Orissa	Rajkot	2008-09
494	Marchall Ayub/Mehrab Hossain Jr	Central Zone v East Zone	Bogra	2012-13
479	Misbah-ul-Haq/Usman Arshad	Sui NGP v Lahore Shalimar	Lahore	2009-10
464*	M.E.Waugh/S.R.Waugh	NSW v W Australia	Perth	1990-91
428*	B.C.Williams/M.Marais	Border v Eastern Province	East London	2017-18
423	Mosaddek Hossain/Al-Amin	Barisal v Rangpur	Savar	2014-15
420	Mohd. Ashraful/Marshall Ayub	Dhaka v Chittagong	Chittagong	2006-07

410*	A.S.Chopra/S.Badrinath	India A v South Africa A	Delhi	2007-08
405	S.G.Barnes/D.G.Bradman	Australia v England	Sydney	1946-47
401	M.B.Loye/D.Ripley	Northants v Glamorgan	Northampton	1998

Sixth Wicket

487*	G.A.Headley/C.C.Passailaigue	Jamaica v Tennyson's	Kingston	1931-32
428	W.W.Armstrong/M.A.Noble	Australians v Sussex	Hove	1902
417	W.P.Saha/L.R.Shukla	Bengal v Assam	Kolkata	2010-11
411	R.M.Poore/E.G.Wynyard	Hampshire v Somerset	Taunton	1899

Seventh Wicket

460	Bhupinder Singh jr/P.Dharmani	Punjab v Delhi	Delhi	1994-95
399	A.N.Khare/A.J.Mandal	Chhattisgarh v Uttarakhand	Naya Raipur	2019-20
371	M.R.Marsh/S.M.Whiteman	Australia A v India A	Brisbane	2014
366*	J.M.Bairstow/T.T.Bresnan	Yorkshire v Durham	Chester-le-Street	2015

Eighth Wicket

433	V.T.Trumper/A.Sims	Australians v C'bury	Christchurch	1913-14
392	A.Mishra/J.Yadav	Haryana v Karnataka	Hubli	2012-13
332	I.J.L.Trott/S.C.J.Broad	England v Pakistan	Lord's	2010

Ninth Wicket

283	J.Chapman/A.Warren	Derbys v Warwicks	Blackwell	1910
268	J.B.Commins/N.Boje	SA 'A' v Mashonaland	Harare	1994-95
261	W.L.Madsen/T.Poynton	Derbys v Northants	Northampton	2012
251	J.W.H.T.Douglas/S.N.Hare	Essex v Derbyshire	Leyton	1921

Tenth Wicket

307	A.F.Kippax/J.E.H.Hooker	NSW v Victoria	Melbourne	1928-29
249	C.T.Sarwate/S.N.Banerjee	Indians v Surrey	The Oval	1946
239	Aqil Arshad/Ali Raza	Lahore Whites v Hyderabad	Lahore	2004-05

BOWLING RECORDS
2000 WICKETS IN A CAREER

	Career	Runs	Wkts	Avge	100w
W.Rhodes	1898-1930	69993	**4187**	16.71	23
A.P.Freeman	1914-36	69577	**3776**	18.42	17
C.W.L.Parker	1903-35	63817	**3278**	19.46	16
J.T.Hearne	1888-1923	54352	**3061**	17.75	15
T.W.J.Goddard	1922-52	59116	**2979**	19.84	16
W.G.Grace	1865-1908	51545	**2876**	17.92	10
A.S.Kennedy	1907-36	61034	**2874**	21.23	15
D.Shackleton	1948-69	53303	**2857**	18.65	20
G.A.R.Lock	1946-70/71	54709	**2844**	19.23	14
F.J.Titmus	1949-82	63313	**2830**	22.37	16
M.W.Tate	1912-37	50571	**2784**	18.16	13+1
G.H.Hirst	1891-1929	51282	**2739**	18.72	15
C.Blythe	1899-1914	42136	**2506**	16.81	14
D.L.Underwood	1963-87	49993	**2465**	20.28	10
W.E.Astill	1906-39	57783	**2431**	23.76	9
J.C.White	1909-37	43759	**2356**	18.57	14
W.E.Hollies	1932-57	48656	**2323**	20.94	14
F.S.Trueman	1949-69	42154	**2304**	18.29	12
J.B.Statham	1950-68	36999	**2260**	16.37	13
R.T.D.Perks	1930-55	53771	**2233**	24.07	16
J.Briggs	1879-1900	35431	**2221**	15.95	12
D.J.Shepherd	1950-72	47302	**2218**	21.32	12
E.G.Dennett	1903-26	42571	**2147**	19.82	12
T.Richardson	1892-1905	38794	**2104**	18.43	10
T.E.Bailey	1945-67	48170	**2082**	23.13	9
R.Illingworth	1951-83	42023	**2072**	20.28	10
F.E.Woolley	1906-38	41066	**2068**	19.85	8

	Career	Runs	Wkts	Avge	100w
N.Gifford	1960-88	48731	**2068**	23.56	4
G.Geary	1912-38	41339	**2063**	20.03	11
D.V.P.Wright	1932-57	49307	**2056**	23.98	10
J.A.Newman	1906-30	51111	**2032**	25.15	9
A.Shaw	1864-97	24580	**2026**+1	12.12	9
S.Haigh	1895-1913	32091	**2012**	15.94	11

ALL TEN WICKETS IN AN INNINGS

This feat has been achieved 82 times in first-class matches (excluding 12-a-side fixtures).

Three Times: A.P.Freeman (1929, 1930, 1931)

Twice: V.E.Walker (1859, 1865); H.Verity (1931, 1932); J.C.Laker (1956)

Instances since 1945:

W.E.Hollies	Warwickshire v Notts	Birmingham	1946
J.M.Sims	East v West	Kingston on Thames	1948
J.K.R.Graveney	Gloucestershire v Derbyshire	Chesterfield	1949
T.E.Bailey	Essex v Lancashire	Clacton	1949
R.Berry	Lancashire v Worcestershire	Blackpool	1953
S.P.Gupte	President's XI v Combined XI	Bombay	1954-55
J.C.Laker	Surrey v Australians	The Oval	1956
K.Smales	Nottinghamshire v Glos	Stroud	1956
G.A.R.Lock	Surrey v Kent	Blackheath	1956
J.C.Laker	England v Australia	Manchester	1956
P.M.Chatterjee	Bengal v Assam	Jorhat	1956-57
J.D.Bannister	Warwicks v Combined Services	Birmingham (M & B)	1959
A.J.G.Pearson	Cambridge U v Leicestershire	Loughborough	1961
N.I.Thomson	Sussex v Warwickshire	Worthing	1964
P.J.Allan	Queensland v Victoria	Melbourne	1965-66
I.J.Brayshaw	Western Australia v Victoria	Perth	1967-68
Shahid Mahmood	Karachi Whites v Khairpur	Karachi	1969-70
E.E.Hemmings	International XI v W Indians	Kingston	1982-83
P.Sunderam	Rajasthan v Vidarbha	Jodhpur	1985-86
S.T.Jefferies	Western Province v OFS	Cape Town	1987-88
Imran Adil	Bahawalpur v Faisalabad	Faisalabad	1989-90
G.P.Wickremasinghe	Sinhalese v Kalutara	Colombo	1991-92
R.L.Johnson	Middlesex v Derbyshire	Derby	1994
Naeem Akhtar	Rawalpindi B v Peshawar	Peshawar	1995-96
A.Kumble	India v Pakistan	Delhi	1998-99
D.S.Mohanty	East Zone v South Zone	Agartala	2000-01
O.D.Gibson	Durham v Hampshire	Chester-le-Street	2007
M.W.Olivier	Warriors v Eagles	Bloemfontein	2007-08
Zulfiqar Babar	Multan v Islamabad	Multan	2009-10
P.M.Pushpakumara	Colombo v Saracens	Moratuwa	2018-19

MOST WICKETS IN A MATCH

19	J.C.Laker	England v Australia	Manchester	1956

MOST WICKETS IN A SEASON

Wkts		Season	Matches	Overs	Mdns	Runs	Avge
304	A.P.Freeman	1928	37	1976.1	423	5489	18.05
298	A.P.Freeman	1933	33	2039	651	4549	15.26

The feat of taking 250 wickets in a season has been achieved on 12 occasions, the last instance being by A.P.Freeman in 1933. 200 or more wickets in a season have been taken on 59 occasions, the last being by G.A.R.Lock (212 wickets, average 12.02) in 1957.

The highest aggregates of wickets taken in a season since the reduction of County Championship matches in 1969 are as follows:

Wkts		Season	Matches	Overs	Mdns	Runs	Avge
134	M.D.Marshall	1982	22	822	225	2108	15.73
131	L.R.Gibbs	1971	23	1024.1	295	2475	18.89
125	F.D.Stephenson	1988	22	819.1	196	2289	18.31
121	R.D.Jackman	1980	23	746.2	220	1864	15.40

Since 1969 there have been 50 instances of bowlers taking 100 wickets in a season.

MOST HAT-TRICKS IN A CAREER

7	D.V.P.Wright
6	T.W.J.Goddard, C.W.L.Parker
5	S.Haigh, V.W.C.Jupp, A.E.G.Rhodes, F.A.Tarrant

ALL-ROUND RECORDS
THE 'DOUBLE'

3000 runs and 100 wickets: J.H.Parks (1937)

2000 runs and 200 wickets: G.H.Hirst (1906)

2000 runs and 100 wickets: F.E.Woolley (4), J.W.Hearne (3), W.G.Grace (2), G.H.Hirst (2), W.Rhodes (2), T.E.Bailey, D.E.Davies, G.L.Jessop, V.W.C.Jupp, J.Langridge, F.A.Tarrant, C.L.Townsend, L.F.Townsend

1000 runs and 200 wickets: M.W.Tate (3), A.E.Trott (2), A.S.Kennedy

Most Doubles: 16 – W.Rhodes; 14 – G.H.Hirst; 10 – V.W.C.Jupp

Double in Debut Season: D.B.Close (1949) – aged 18, the youngest to achieve this feat.

The feat of scoring 1000 runs and taking 100 wickets in a season has been achieved on 305 occasions, R.J.Hadlee (1984) and F.D.Stephenson (1988) being the only players to complete the 'double' since the reduction of County Championship matches in 1969.

WICKET-KEEPING RECORDS
1000 DISMISSALS IN A CAREER

	Career	Dismissals	Ct	St
R.W.Taylor	1960-88	**1649**	1473	176
J.T.Murray	1952-75	**1527**	1270	257
H.Strudwick	1902-27	**1497**	1242	255
A.P.E.Knott	1964-85	**1344**	1211	133
R.C.Russell	1981-2004	**1320**	1192	128
F.H.Huish	1895-1914	**1310**	933	377
B.Taylor	1949-73	**1294**	1083	211
S.J.Rhodes	1981-2004	**1263**	1139	124
D.Hunter	1889-1909	**1253**	906	347
H.R.Butt	1890-1912	**1228**	953	275
J.H.Board	1891-1914/15	**1207**	852	355
H.Elliott	1920-47	**1206**	904	302
J.M.Parks	1949-76	**1181**	1088	93
R.Booth	1951-70	**1126**	948	178
L.E.G.Ames	1926-51	**1121**	703	418
C.M.W.Read	1997-2017	**1104**	1051	53
D.L.Bairstow	1970-90	**1099**	961	138
G.Duckworth	1923-47	**1096**	753	343
H.W.Stephenson	1948-64	**1082**	748	334
J.G.Binks	1955-75	**1071**	895	176
T.G.Evans	1939-69	**1066**	816	250
A.Long	1960-80	**1046**	922	124
G.O.Dawkes	1937-61	**1043**	895	148
R.W.Tolchard	1965-83	**1037**	912	125
W.L.Cornford	1921-47	**1017**	675	342

MOST DISMISSALS IN AN INNINGS

9	(8ct, 1st)	Tahir Rashid	Habib Bank v PACO	Gujranwala	1992-93
9	(7ct, 2st)	W.R.James	Matabeleland v Mashonaland CD	Bulawayo	1995-96
8	(8ct)	A.T.W.Grout	Queensland v W Australia	Brisbane	1959-60
8	(8ct)	D.E.East	Essex v Somerset	Taunton	1985
8	(8ct)	S.A.Marsh	Kent v Middlesex	Lord's	1991
8	(6ct, 2st)	T.J.Zoehrer	Australians v Surrey	The Oval	1993
8	(7ct, 1st)	D.S.Berry	Victoria v South Australia	Melbourne	1996-97
8	(7ct, 1st)	Y.S.S.Mendis	Bloomfield v Kurunegala Youth	Colombo	2000-01
8	(7ct, 1st)	S.Nath	Assam v Tripura (on debut)	Gauhati	2001-02
8	(8ct)	J.N.Batty	Surrey v Kent	The Oval	2004
8	(8ct)	Golam Mabud	Sylhet v Dhaka	Dhaka	2005-06
8	(8ct)	D.C.de Boorder	Otago v Wellington	Wellington	2009-10
8	(8ct)	R.S.Second	Free State v North West	Bloemfontein	2011-12
8	(8ct)	T.L.Tsolekile	South Africa A v Sri Lanka A	Durban	2012
8	(7ct, 1st)	M.A.R.S.Fernando	Chilaw Marians v Colts	Columbo (SSC)	2017-18

MOST DISMISSALS IN A MATCH

14	(11ct, 3st)	I.Khaleel	Hyderabad v Assam	Guwahati	2011-12
13	(11ct, 2st)	W.R.James	Matabeleland v Mashonaland CD	Bulawayo	1995-96
12	(8ct, 4st)	E.Pooley	Surrey v Sussex	The Oval	1868
12	(9ct, 3st)	D.Tallon	Queensland v NSW	Sydney	1938-39
12	(9ct, 3st)	H.B.Taber	NSW v South Australia	Adelaide	1968-69
12	(12ct)	P.D.McGlashan	Northern Districts v Central Districts	Whangarei	2009-10
12	(11ct, 1st)	T.L.Tsolekile	Lions v Dolphins	Johannesburg	2010-11
12	(12ct)	Kashif Mahmood	Lahore Shalimar v Abbottabad	Abbottabad	2010-11
12	(12ct)	R.S.Second	Free State v North West	Bloemfontein	2011-12

MOST DISMISSALS IN A SEASON

128	(79ct, 49st)	L.E.G.Ames			1929

FIELDING RECORDS
750 CATCHES IN A CAREER

1018	F.E.Woolley	1906-38	784	J.G.Langridge	1928-55
887	W.G.Grace	1865-1908	764	W.Rhodes	1898-1930
830	G.A.R.Lock	1946-70/71	758	C.A.Milton	1948-74
819	W.R.Hammond	1920-51	754	E.H.Hendren	1907-38
813	D.B.Close	1949-86			

MOST CATCHES IN AN INNINGS

7	M.J.Stewart	Surrey v Northamptonshire	Northampton	1957
7	A.S.Brown	Gloucestershire v Nottinghamshire	Nottingham	1966
7	R.Clarke	Warwickshire v Lancashire	Liverpool	2011

MOST CATCHES IN A MATCH

10	W.R.Hammond	Gloucestershire v Surrey	Cheltenham	1928
9	R.Clarke	Warwickshire v Lancashire	Liverpool	2011

MOST CATCHES IN A SEASON

78	W.R.Hammond	1928	77	M.J.Stewart	1957

ENGLAND LIMITED-OVERS INTERNATIONALS 2020

SOUTH AFRICA v ENGLAND

LIMITED-OVERS INTERNATIONALS

Newlands, Cape Town, 4 February. Toss: South Africa. **SOUTH AFRICA** won by seven wickets. England 258-8 (50; J.L.Denly 87, T.Shamsi 3-38). South Africa 259-3 (47.4; Q.de Kock 107, T.Bavuma 98). Award: Q.de Kock. England debuts: T.Banton, M.W.Parkinson.

Kingsmead, Durban, 7 February. Toss: England. **NO RESULT**. South Africa 71-2 (11.2).

Wanderers, Johannesburg, 9 February. Toss: England. **ENGLAND** won by two wickets. South Africa 256-7 (50; D.A.Miller 69*, Q.de Kock 69, A.U.Rashid 3-51). England 257-8 (43.2; J.L.Denly 66, B.E.Hendricks 3-59, L.T.Ngidi 3-63). Award: A.U.Rashid. Series award: Q.de Kock. England debut: S.Mahmood.

TWENTY20 INTERNATIONALS

Buffalo Park, East London, 12 February. Toss: England. **SOUTH AFRICA** won by 1 run. South Africa 177-8 (20; T.Bavuma 43). England 176-9 (20; J.J.Roy 70, E.J.G.Morgan 52, L.T.Ngidi 3-30). Award: L.T.Ngidi.

Kingsmead, Durban, 14 February. Toss: South Africa. **ENGLAND** won by 2 runs. England 204-7 (20; B.A.Stokes 47*, J.J.Roy 40, L.T.Ngidi 3-48). South Africa 202-7 (20; Q.de Kock 65, H.E.van der Dussen 43*). Award: M.M.Ali (39 in 11 balls).

Q.de Kock reached 50 in 17 balls (1 four, 7 sixes), a record for South Africa.

SuperSport Park, Centurion, 16 February. Toss: South Africa. **ENGLAND** won by five wickets. South Africa 222-6 (20; H.Klaasen 66, T.Bavuma 49). England 226-5 (19.1; J.M.Bairstow 64, E.J.G.Morgan 57*, J.C.Buttler 57). Award: E.J.G.Morgan. Series award: E.J.G.Morgan.

E.J.G.Morgan reached 50 in 21 balls (7 sixes), equalling the record for England.

ENGLAND v IRELAND

LIMITED-OVERS INTERNATIONALS

Rose Bowl, Southampton, 30 July. Toss: England. **ENGLAND** won by six wickets. Ireland 172 (44.4; C.Campher 59*, D.J.Willey 5-30). England 174-4 (27.5; S.W.Billings 67*). Award: D.J.Willey.

Rose Bowl, Southampton, 1 August. Toss: Ireland. **ENGLAND** won by four wickets. Ireland 212-9 (50; C.Campher 68, A.U.Rashid 3-34). England 216-6 (32.3; J.M.Bairstow 82, J.B.Little 3-60). Award: J.M.Bairstow.

Rose Bowl, Southampton, 4 August. Toss: Ireland. **IRELAND** won by seven wickets. England 328 (49.5; E.J.G.Morgan 106, T.Banton 58, D.J.Willey 51, C.A.Young 3-53). Ireland 329-3 (49.5; P.R.Stirling 142, A.Balbirnie 113). Award: P.R.Stirling. Series award: D.J.Willey.

TWENTY20 INTERNATIONALS

Old Trafford, Manchester, 28 August. Toss: Pakistan. **NO RESULT**. England 131-6 (16.1; T.Banton 71).

Old Trafford, Manchester, 30 August. Toss: England. **ENGLAND** won by five wickets. Pakistan 195-4 (20; Mohammad Hafeez 69, Babar Azam 56). England 199-5 (19.1; E.J.G.Morgan 66, D.J.Malan 54*, J.M.Bairstow 44, Shadab Khan 3-34). Award: E.J.G.Morgan.

Old Trafford, Manchester, 1 September. Toss: England. **PAKISTAN** won by 5 runs. Pakistan 190-4 (20; Mohammad Hafeez 86*, Haider Ali 54). England 185-8 (20; M.M.Ali 61, T.Banton 46). Award: Mohammad Hafeez. Series award: Mohammad Hafeez.

ENGLAND v AUSTRALIA

TWENTY20 INTERNATIONALS

Rose Bowl, Southampton, 4 September. Toss: Australia. **ENGLAND** won by 2 runs. England 162-7 (20; D.J.Malan 66, J.C.Buttler 44). Australia 160-6 (20; D.A.Warner 58, A.J.Finch 46). Award: D.J.Malan.

Rose Bowl, Southampton, 6 September. Toss: Australia. **ENGLAND** won by six wickets. Australia 157-7 (20; A.J.Finch 40). England 158-4 (18.5; J.C.Buttler 77*, D.J.Malan 42). Award: J.C.Buttler.

Rose Bowl, Southampton, 8 September. Toss: Australia. **AUSTRALIA** won by five wickets. England 145-6 (20; J.M.Bairstow 55). Australia 146-5 (19.3; A.U.Rashid 3-21). Award: M.R.Marsh (39*). Series award: J.C.Buttler.

LIMITED-OVERS INTERNATIONALS

Old Trafford, Manchester, 11 September. Toss: England. **AUSTRALIA** won by 19 runs. Australia 294-9 (50; G.J.Maxwell 77, M.R.Marsh 73, M.A.Wood 3-54, J.C.Archer 3-57). England 275-9 (50; S.W.Billings 118, J.M.Bairstow 84, A.Zampa 4-55, J.R.Hazlewood 3-26). Award: J.R.Hazlewood.

Old Trafford, Manchester, 13 September. Toss: England. **ENGLAND** won by 24 runs. England 231-9 (50; A.Zampa 3-36). Australia 207 (48.4; A.J.Finch 73, C.R.Woakes 3-32, J.C.Archer 3-34, S.M.Curran 3-35). Award: J.C.Archer.

Old Trafford, Manchester, 16 September. Toss: England. **AUSTRALIA** won by three wickets. England 302-7 (50; J.M.Bairstow 112, S.W.Billings 57, C.R.Woakes 53*, A.Zampa 3-51, M.A.Starc 3-74). Australia 305-7 (49.4; G.J.Maxwell 108, A.T.Carey 106). Award: G.J.Maxwell. Series award: G.J.Maxwell.

SOUTH AFRICA v ENGLAND

TWENTY20 INTERNATIONALS

Newlands, Cape Town, 27 November. Toss: England. **ENGLAND** won by five wickets. South Africa 179-6 (20; F.du Plessis 58, S.M.Curran 3-28). England 183-5 (19.2; J.M.Bairstow 86*). Award: J.M.Bairstow.

Boland Park, Paarl, 29 November. Toss: England. **ENGLAND** won by four wickets. South Africa 146-6 (20). England 147-6 (19.5; D.J.Malan 55, T.Shamsi 3-19). Award: D.J.Malan.

Newlands, Cape Town, 1 December. Toss: South Africa. **ENGLAND** won by nine wickets. South Africa 191-3 (20; H.E.van der Dussen 74*, F.du Plessis 52*). England 192-1 (17.4; D.J.Malan 99*, J.C.Buttler 67*). Award: D.J.Malan. Series award: D.J.Malan.

A planned limited-over series was abandoned after an outbreak of Coronavirus in the touring party.

ENGLAND RESULTS IN 2020

	P	W	L	T	NR
Limited Overs	9	4	4	–	1
Twenty20	12	8	3	–	1
Overall	21	12	7	–	2

250 RUNS IN LIMITED-OVERS INTERNATIONALS IN 2020

	P	I	NO	HS	Runs	Ave	100	50	S/Rate
J.M.Bairstow	9	8	–	112	346	43.25	1	2	100.87
S.W.Billings	6	6	2	118	315	78.75	1	2	95.74
E.J.G.Morgan	9	8	1	106	250	35.71	1	–	97.65

10 WICKETS IN LIMITED-OVERS INTERNATIONALS IN 2020

	P	O	M	Runs	W	Ave	Best	4wI	Econ
A.U.Rashid	7	67.2	4	362	12	30.16	3-34	–	5.37

250 RUNS IN TWENTY20 INTERNATIONALS IN 2020

	P	I	NO	HS	Runs	Ave	100	50	S/Rate
D.J.Malan	10	10	2	99*	397	49.62	–	4	142.29
J.M.Bairstow	12	11	1	86*	329	32.90	–	3	150.91
J.C.Buttler	8	8	2	77*	291	48.50	–	3	150.77
E.J.G.Morgan	11	10	2	66	276	34.50	–	3	168.29

12 WICKETS IN TWENTY20 INTERNATIONALS IN 2020

	P	O	M	Runs	W	Ave	Best	4wI	Econ
A.U.Rashid	12	42.0	–	316	12	26.33	3-21	–	7.52
C.J.Jordan	12	40.3	–	371	12	30.91	2-28	–	9.16

LIMITED-OVERS INTERNATIONALS CAREER RECORDS

These records, complete to 9 March 2021, include all players registered for county cricket and The Hundred for the 2021 season at the time of going to press, plus those who have appeared in LOI matches for ICC full member countries since 26 September 2019. Some players who may return to LOI action have also been listed, even if their most recent game was earlier than this date.

ENGLAND – BATTING AND FIELDING

	M	I	NO	HS	Runs	Avge	100	50	Ct/St
M.M.Ali	106	86	14	128	1790	24.86	3	5	32
J.M.Anderson	194	79	43	28	273	7.58	–	–	53
J.C.Archer	17	9	5	8*	27	6.75	–	–	5
J.M.Bairstow	83	76	8	141*	3207	47.16	10	13	39/2
J.T.Ball	18	6	2	28	38	9.50	–	–	5
G.S.Ballance	16	15	1	79	279	21.21	–	2	8
T.Banton	6	5	–	58	134	26.80	–	1	2
G.J.Batty	10	8	2	17	30	5.00	–	–	4
S.W.Billings	21	18	–	118	586	36.62	1	4	16
R.S.Bopara	120	109	21	101*	2695	30.62	1	14	35
S.G.Borthwick	2	2	–	15	18	9.00	–	–	–
T.T.Bresnan	85	64	20	80	871	19.79	–	1	20
D.R.Briggs	1								–
S.C.J.Broad	121	68	25	45*	529	12.30	–	–	27
J.C.Buttler	145	120	23	150	3855	39.74	9	20	177/32
R.Clarke	20	13	–	39	144	11.07	–	–	11
A.N.Cook	92	92	4	137	3204	36.40	5	19	36
S.M.Curran	5	4	–	15	25	6.25	–	–	–
T.K.Curran	24	16	9	47*	292	41.71	–	–	5
S.M.Davies	8	8	–	87	244	30.50	–	1	8
L.A.Dawson	3	2	–	10	14	7.00	–	–	–
J.L.Denly	16	13	–	87	446	34.30	–	4	7
J.W.Dernbach	24	8	1	5	19	2.71	–	–	5
B.M.Duckett	3	3	–	63	123	41.00	–	2	–
S.T.Finn	69	30	13	35	136	8.00	–	–	15
B.T.Foakes	1	1	1	61*	61	–	–	–	2/1
H.F.Gurney	10	6	4	6*	15	7.50	–	–	1
A.D.Hales	70	67	3	171	2419	37.79	6	14	27
C.J.Jordan	34	23	9	38*	170	12.14	–	–	19
S.Mahmood	4	1	–	12	12	12.00	–	–	1
D.J.Malan	1	1	–	24	24	24.00	–	–	–
S.C.Meaker	2	2	–	1	2	1.00	–	–	–
E.J.G.Morgan †	219	202	31	148	6854	40.08	13	41	77
C.Overton	1								2
M.W.Parkinson	2								–
S.R.Patel	36	22	7	70*	482	32.13	–	1	7
L.E.Plunkett	89	50	19	56	646	20.83	–	1	26
A.U.Rashid	106	48	14	69	644	18.94	–	1	31
T.S.Roland-Jones	1	1	1	37*	37	–	–	–	–
J.E.Root	149	140	21	133*	5962	50.10	16	33	74
J.J.Roy	93	89	2	180	3483	40.03	9	18	32
B.A.Stokes	95	81	15	102*	2682	40.63	3	20	45
O.P.Stone	4	1	1	9*	9	–	–	–	–
R.J.W.Topley	11	5	4	6	7	7.00	–	–	3
J.M.Vince	16	14	–	51	322	23.00	–	1	5

	M	I	NO	HS	Runs	Avge	100	50	Ct/St
D.J.Willey	49	29	13	51	377	23.56	–	2	22
C.R.Woakes	104	72	21	95*	1315	25.78	–	5	45
M.A.Wood	53	17	10	13	56	8.00	–	–	12
L.J.Wright	50	39	4	52	707	20.20	–	2	18

ENGLAND – BOWLING

	O	M	R	W	Avge	Best	4wI	R/Over
M.M.Ali	820.4	10	4305	85	50.64	4-46	1	5.24
J.M.Anderson	1597.2	125	7861	269	29.22	5-23	13	4.92
J.C.Archer	151.5	12	720	30	24.00	3-27	–	4.74
J.T.Ball	157.5	5	980	21	46.66	5-51	1	6.20
G.J.Batty	73.2	1	366	5	73.20	2-40	–	4.99
R.S.Bopara	310	11	1523	40	38.07	4-38	1	4.91
S.G.Borthwick	9	0	72	0	–	–	–	8.00
T.T.Bresnan	703.3	35	3813	109	34.98	5-48	4	5.42
D.R.Briggs	10	0	39	2	19.50	2-39	–	3.90
S.C.J.Broad	1018.1	56	5364	178	30.13	5-23	10	5.26
R.Clarke	78.1	3	415	11	37.72	2-28	–	5.30
S.M.Curran	28	0	169	5	33.80	3-35	–	6.03
T.K.Curran	178	8	1066	28	38.07	5-35	2	5.98
L.A.Dawson	14	0	96	3	32.00	2-70	–	6.85
J.L.Denly	17	0	101	1	101.00	1-24	–	5.94
J.W.Dernbach	205.4	6	1308	31	42.19	4-45	1	6.35
S.T.Finn	591.4	38	2996	102	29.37	5-33	6	5.06
H.F.Gurney	75.5	4	432	11	39.27	4-55	1	5.69
C.J.Jordan	269.4	5	1611	45	35.80	5-29	1	5.97
S.Mahmood	32.5	2	156	5	31.20	2-36	–	4.75
S.C.Meaker	19	1	110	2	55.00	1-45	–	5.78
C.Overton	7	0	55	0	–	–	–	7.85
M.W.Parkinson	10.4	0	63	0	–	–	–	5.90
S.R.Patel	197.5	4	1091	24	45.45	5-41	1	5.51
L.E.Plunkett	689.3	14	4010	135	29.70	5-52	7	5.81
A.U.Rashid	875.5	10	4909	155	31.67	5-27	9	5.60
T.S.Roland-Jones	7	2	34	1	34.00	1-34	–	4.85
J.E.Root	258.4	2	1491	26	57.34	3-52	–	5.76
B.A.Stokes	485.2	7	2920	70	41.71	5-61	2	6.01
O.P.Stone	16	0	97	1	97.00	1-23	–	6.06
R.J.W.Topley	86.1	7	441	17	25.94	4-50	1	5.11
J.M.Vince	7	0	38	1	38.00	1-18	–	5.42
D.J.Willey	357.1	21	2037	60	33.95	5-30	3	5.70
C.R.Woakes	816	41	4521	149	30.34	6-45	12	5.54
M.A.Wood	449.5	14	2479	64	38.73	4-33	–	5.51
L.J.Wright	173	2	884	15	58.93	2-34	–	5.10

† E.J.G.Morgan has also made 23 appearances for Ireland (see below).

AUSTRALIA – BATTING AND FIELDING

	M	I	NO	HS	Runs	Avge	100	50	Ct/St
S.A.Abbott	2	2	–	4	7	3.50	–	–	–
A.C.Agar	14	12	2	46	217	21.70	–	–	7
A.T.Carey	42	37	7	106	1091	36.36	1	4	49/5
D.T.Christian	19	18	5	39	273	21.00	–	–	10
N.M.Coulter-Nile	32	21	6	92	252	16.80	–	1	7
P.J.Cummins	69	44	15	36	285	9.82	–	–	16

AUSTRALIA – BATTING AND FIELDING (continued)

	M	I	NO	HS	Runs	Avge	100	50	Ct/St
A.J.Finch	132	128	3	153*	5232	41.85	17	29	63
C.Green	1	1	–	21	21	21.00	–	–	–
P.S.P.Handscomb	22	20	1	117	632	33.26	1	4	14
J.R.Hazlewood	54	18	15	11*	53	17.66	–	–	16
T.M.Head	42	39	2	128	1273	34.40	1	10	12
M.C.Henriques	13	12	2	22	105	10.50	–	–	5
M.Labuschagne	13	12	–	108	473	39.41	1	3	4
C.A.Lynn	4	4	–	44	75	18.75	–	–	3
M.R.Marsh	60	56	9	102*	1615	33.36	1	12	28
G.J.Maxwell	116	106	12	108	3230	34.36	2	22	72
M.G.Neser	2	2	–	.6	8	4.00	–	–	–
J.A.Richardson	13	8	3	29	92	18.40	–	–	4
K.W.Richardson	25	12	7	24*	75	15.00	–	–	7
D.J.M.Short	8	8	1	69	211	30.14	–	1	2
P.M.Siddle	20	6	3	10*	31	10.33	–	–	1
S.P.D.Smith	128	113	12	164	4378	43.34	11	25	70
B.Stanlake	7	5	2	2	4	1.33	–	–	1
M.A.Starc	96	54	21	52*	401	12.15	–	1	32
M.P.Stoinis	45	42	7	146*	1106	31.60	1	6	12
A.J.Turner	6	5	1	84*	142	35.50	–	1	2
D.A.Warner	128	126	6	179	5710	45.45	18	23	56
D.J.Worrall	3	1	1	6*	6	–	–	–	1
A.Zampa	61	27	7	22	128	6.40	–	–	11

AUSTRALIA – BOWLING

	O	M	R	W	Avge	Best	4wI	R/Over
S.A.Abbott	15	0	109	2	54.50	1-25	–	7.26
A.C.Agar	119	3	663	12	55.25	2-44	–	5.57
D.T.Christian	121.1	4	595	20	29.75	5-31	1	4.91
N.M.Coulter-Nile	279.4	10	1555	52	29.90	4-48	1	5.56
P.J.Cummins	608.3	38	3195	111	28.78	5-70	6	5.25
A.J.Finch	47.2	0	259	4	64.75	1- 2	–	5.47
C.Green	4	0	27	0	–	–	–	6.75
J.R.Hazlewood	480.5	33	2304	88	26.18	6-52	4	4.79
T.M.Head	127.3	0	737	12	61.41	2-22	–	5.78
M.C.Henriques	67	1	347	8	43.37	3-32	–	5.17
M.Labuschagne	4	0	36	0	–	–	–	9.00
M.R.Marsh	324.5	8	1803	49	36.79	5-33	2	5.55
G.J.Maxwell	473.2	9	2683	51	52.60	4-46	2	5.66
M.G.Neser	16.4	0	120	2	60.00	2-46	–	7.20
J.A.Richardson	118	11	690	24	28.75	4-26	1	5.84
K.W.Richardson	218.4	11	1240	39	31.79	5-68	1	5.67
D.J.M.Short	15	0	114	0	–	–	–	7.60
P.M.Siddle	150.1	10	743	17	43.70	3-55	–	4.94
S.P.D.Smith	179.2	1	971	28	34.67	3-16	–	5.41
B.Stanlake	59	3	324	7	46.28	3-35	–	5.49
M.A.Starc	822.4	40	4262	184	23.16	6-28	18	5.18
M.P.Stoinis	246	2	1506	33	45.63	3-16	–	6.12
D.A.Warner	1	0	8	0	–	–	–	8.00
D.J.Worrall	26.2	0	171	1	171.00	1-43	–	6.49
A.Zampa	541.2	5	3004	92	32.65	4-43	3	5.54

SOUTH AFRICA – BATTING AND FIELDING

	M	I	NO	HS	Runs	Avge	100	50	Ct/St
K.J.Abbott	28	13	4	23	76	8.44	–	–	7
H.M.Amla	181	178	14	159	8113	49.46	27	39	87
T.Bavuma	6	6	–	113	335	55.83	1	1	4
Q.de Kock	121	121	6	178	5135	44.65	15	25	164/9
M.de Lange	4	–	–	–	–	–	–	–	–
F.du Plessis	143	136	20	185	5507	47.47	12	35	81
J.P.Duminy	199	179	40	150*	5117	36.81	4	27	82
D.M.Dupavillon	1	–	–	–	–	–	–	–	–
B.C.Fortuin	1	–	–	–	–	–	–	–	–
B.E.Hendricks	7	2	1	3	5	5.00	–	–	2
R.R.Hendricks	21	21	2	102	507	26.68	1	2	13
Imran Tahir	107	36	16	29	157	7.85	–	–	25
C.A.Ingram	31	29	3	124	843	32.42	3	3	12
H.Klaasen	17	16	4	123*	493	41.08	1	3	17/3
K.A.Maharaj	7	3	–	17	27	9.00	–	–	1
J.N.Malan	3	3	1	129*	152	76.00	1	–	3
A.K.Markram	26	24	1	67*	643	27.95	–	2	12
D.A.Miller	132	114	34	139	3231	40.38	5	14	61
C.H.Morris	42	27	4	62	467	20.30	–	1	9
P.W.A.Mulder	10	8	3	19*	74	14.80	–	–	4
L.T.Ngidi	26	9	6	19*	47	15.66	–	–	8
A.A.Nortje	7	2	1	8	9	9.00	–	–	2
D.Olivier	2	–	–	–	–	–	–	–	–
W.D.Parnell	65	38	14	56	508	21.16	–	1	12
D.Paterson	4	–	–	–	–	–	–	–	2
A.L.Phehlukwayo	58	34	15	69*	563	29.63	–	1	13
D.Pretorius	22	10	1	50	135	15.00	–	1	6
K.Rabada	75	28	12	31*	259	16.18	–	–	22
T.Shamsi	22	3	2	0*	0	0.00	–	–	5
L.L.Sipamla	4	1	1	10*	10	–	–	–	1
J.T.Smuts	5	4	1	84	163	54.33	–	1	2
H.E.van der Dussen	21	16	6	95	707	70.70	–	7	9
R.E.van der Merwe †	13	7	3	12	39	9.75	–	–	3
D.Wiese	6	6	1	41*	102	20.40	–	–	–
K.Verreynne	3	3	–	50	101	33.66	–	1	3

SOUTH AFRICA – BOWLING

	O	M	R	W	Avge	Best	4wI	R/Over
K.J.Abbott	217.1	13	1051	34	30.91	4-21	1	4.83
M.de Lange	34.5	2	198	10	19.80	4-46	1	5.68
F.du Plessis	32	0	189	2	94.50	1- 8	–	5.90
J.P.Duminy	585.3	9	3143	69	45.55	4-16	1	5.36
D.M.Dupavillon	6	0	21	1	21.00	1-21	–	3.50
B.E.Hendricks	39	1	211	5	42.20	3-59	–	5.41
R.R.Hendricks	7	0	47	1	47.00	1-13	–	6.71
Imran Tahir	923.3	38	4297	173	24.83	7-45	10	4.65
C.A.Ingram	1	0	17	0	–	–	–	17.00
H.Klaasen	3	0	19	0	–	–	–	6.33
K.A.Maharaj	61.1	0	312	7	44.57	3-25	–	5.10
A.K.Markram	20	0	132	3	44.00	2-18	–	6.60
C.H.Morris	315.4	10	1756	48	36.58	4-31	2	5.56
P.W.A.Mulder	53	0	308	8	38.50	2-59	–	5.81
L.T.Ngidi	205	15	1140	53	21.50	6-58	3	5.56
A.A.Nortje	55.4	1	283	14	20.21	3-57	–	5.08
D.Olivier	19	0	124	3	41.33	2-73	–	6.52

SOUTH AFRICA – BOWLING (continued)

	O	M	R	W	Avge	Best	4wI	R/Over
W.D.Parnell	485.1	20	2738	94	29.12	5-48	5	5.64
D.Paterson	34.5	1	217	4	54.25	3-44	–	6.22
A.L.Phehlukwayo	383.1	15	2151	69	31.17	4-22	3	5.61
D.Pretorius	170.2	9	813	29	28.03	3- 5	–	4.77
K.Rabada	640.2	42	3199	117	27.34	6-16	7	4.99
T.Shamsi	186.3	4	993	26	38.19	4-33	1	5.32
L.L.Sipamla	24.2	1	122	2	61.00	1-40	–	5.01
J.T.Smuts	22	1	97	3	32.33	2-42	–	4.40
R.E.van der Merwe	117.3	2	561	17	33.00	3-27	–	4.77
D.Wiese	49	0	316	9	35.11	3-50	–	6.44

† R.E.van der Merwe has also made 2 appearances for Netherlands (see below).

WEST INDIES – BATTING AND FIELDING

	M	I	NO	HS	Runs	Avge	100	50	Ct/St
F.A.Allen	14	12	3	51	143	15.88	–	1	6
S.W.Ambris	16	15	2	148	473	36.38	1	2	2
N.E.Bonner	3	3	–	31	51	17.00	–	–	–
C.R.Brathwaite	44	37	3	101	559	16.44	1	1	11
D.M.Bravo	113	108	13	124	2902	30.54	3	18	34
R.L.Chase	30	23	3	94	520	26.00	–	2	11
S.S.Cottrell	35	17	10	17	84	12.00	–	–	19
M.L.Cummins	11	3	1	5	10	5.00	–	–	1
J.Da Silva	2	2	–	9	14	7.00	–	–	1/1
S.O.Dowrich	1	1	–	6	6	6.00	–	–	–
J.N.Hamilton	1	1	–	5	5	5.00	–	–	–
K.J.Harding	1	1	1	1*	1	–	–	–	–
S.O.Hetmyer	45	42	3	139	1430	36.66	5	4	18
C.K.Holder	1	1	–	0*	0	–	–	–	–
J.O.Holder	115	92	19	99*	1821	24.94	–	9	50
S.D.Hope	78	73	10	170	3289	52.20	9	17	83/10
A.J.Hosein	3	3	1	12*	13	6.50	–	–	1
A.S.Joseph	31	16	7	29*	153	17.00	–	–	10
B.A.King	4	4	–	39	97	24.25	–	–	3
E.Lewis	51	48	3	176*	1610	35.77	3	8	17
A.M.McCarthy	2	2	–	12	15	7.50	–	–	–
K.R.Mayers	3	3	–	40	51	17.00	–	–	–
J.N.Mohammed	31	27	1	91*	596	22.92	–	4	4
S.P.Narine	65	45	12	36	363	11.00	–	–	14
K.Y.Ottley	2	2	–	24	25	12.50	–	–	1
K.M.A.Paul	19	13	4	46	214	23.77	–	–	10
K.Pierre	3	2	–	21	39	19.50	–	–	–
K.A.Pollard	113	104	8	119	2496	26.00	3	10	61
N.Pooran	25	23	4	118	932	49.05	1	7	8/1
R.Powell	37	34	3	101	786	25.35	1	2	14
R.A.Reifer	5	4	–	27	36	9.00	–	–	–
K.A.J.Roach	92	57	34	34	308	13.39	–	–	21
A.D.Russell	56	47	9	92*	1034	27.21	–	4	11
R.Shepherd	5	3	–	8	15	5.00	–	–	2
O.R.Thomas	20	10	5	6*	13	2.60	–	–	–
H.R.Walsh †	9	4	2	46*	72	36.00	–	–	2

WEST INDIES – BOWLING

	O	M	R	W	Avge	Best	4wI	R/Over
F.A.Allen	66	0	397	4	99.25	2-40	–	6.01
N.E.Bonner	2.5	0	15	0	–	–	–	5.29
C.R.Brathwaite	304.1	11	1766	43	41.06	5-27	3	5.80
R.L.Chase	148.5	3	719	15	47.93	3-30	–	4.83
S.S.Cottrell	268	10	1577	49	32.18	5-46	3	5.88
M.L.Cummins	75	3	474	9	52.66	3-82	–	6.32
K.J.Harding	10	0	88	0	–	–	–	8.80
C.K.Holder	3	0	26	0	–	–	–	8.66
J.O.Holder	891.1	48	4948	136	36.38	5-27	6	5.55
A.J.Hosein	29.2	1	117	4	29.25	3-26	–	3.98
A.S.Joseph	260.1	11	1479	50	29.58	5-56	5	5.68
A.M.McCarthy	2	0	10	0	–	–	–	5.00
K.R.Mayers	9	0	49	1	49.00	1-34	–	5.44
J.N.Mohammed	42.2	1	195	2	97.50	1-19	–	4.60
S.P.Narine	590	35	2435	92	26.46	6-27	6	4.12
K.M.A.Paul	145.4	0	881	23	38.30	3-44	–	6.04
K.Pierre	26	0	158	1	158.00	1-50	–	6.07
K.A.Pollard	364.4	0	2105	53	39.71	3-27	–	5.77
R.Powell	40.5	0	243	3	81.00	1- 7	–	5.95
R.A.Reifer	23.5	0	133	5	26.60	2-23	–	5.58
K.A.J.Roach	743.1	53	3763	124	30.34	6-27	6	5.06
A.D.Russell	381.4	0	2229	70	31.84	4-35	5	5.84
R.Shepherd	38.2	3	174	4	43.50	2-32	–	4.53
O.R.Thomas	128.3	1	866	27	32.07	5-21	2	6.73
H.R.Walsh	61.4	0	322	12	26.83	4-36	1	5.22

† *H.R.Walsh has also made 1 appearance for the USA v PNG.*

NEW ZEALAND – BATTING AND FIELDING

	M	I	NO	HS	Runs	Avge	100	50	Ct/St
H.K.Bennett	19	7	5	4*	10	5.00	–	–	3
T.A.Blundell	2	2	–	22	31	15.50	–	–	1
T.A.Boult	90	40	23	21*	159	9.35	–	–	31
M.S.Chapman	6	6	1	124*	161	32.20	1	–	1
C.de Grandhomme	42	33	7	74*	722	27.76	–	4	14
L.H.Ferguson	37	16	7	19	63	7.00	–	–	10
M.J.Guptill	183	180	19	237*	6843	42.50	16	37	91
M.J.Henry	52	21	7	48*	211	15.07	–	–	17
K.A.Jamieson	2	1	1	25*	25	–	–	–	2
T.W.M.Latham	99	92	10	137	2696	32.87	4	16	82/7
C.Munro	57	53	2	87	1271	24.92	–	8	22
J.D.S.Neesham	63	54	10	97*	1286	29.22	–	6	23
H.M.Nicholls	49	47	10	124*	1329	35.91	1	11	18
M.J.Santner	72	56	22	67	924	27.17	–	2	27
I.S.Sodhi	33	14	3	24	81	7.36	–	–	8
T.G.Southee	143	86	32	55	679	12.57	–	1	39
L.R.P.L.Taylor	232	216	39	181*	8574	48.44	21	51	139
K.S.Williamson	151	144	14	148	6173	47.48	13	39	60

NEW ZEALAND – BOWLING

	O	M	R	W	Avge	Best	4wI	R/Over
H.K.Bennett	148.4	5	820	33	24.84	4-16	3	5.51
T.A.Boult	824	58	4148	164	25.29	7-34	12	5.03
C.de Grandhomme	243	9	1180	27	43.70	3-26	–	4.85
L.H.Ferguson	326	6	1779	69	25.78	5-45	3	5.45

NEW ZEALAND – BOWLING (continued)

	O	M	R	W	Avge	Best	4wI	R/Over
M.J.Guptill	18.1	0	98	4	24.50	2- 6	–	5.39
M.J.Henry	450.3	27	2437	92	26.48	5-30	9	5.40
K.A.Jamieson	20	1	95	3	31.66	2-42	–	4.75
C.Munro	92	1	481	7	68.71	2-10	–	5.22
J.D.S.Neesham	327.5	4	2012	61	32.98	5-31	3	6.13
M.J.Santner	543.1	12	2661	71	37.47	5-50	1	4.89
I.S.Sodhi	270	9	1508	43	35.06	4-58	1	5.58
T.G.Southee	1199.1	74	6558	190	34.51	7-33	7	5.46
L.R.P.L.Taylor	7	0	35	0	–	–	–	5.00
K.S.Williamson	244.3	2	1310	37	35.40	4-22	1	5.35

INDIA – BATTING AND FIELDING

	M	I	NO	HS	Runs	Avge	100	50	Ct/St
M.A.Agarwal	5	5	–	32	86	17.20	–	–	2
J.J.Bumrah	67	17	11	10*	19	3.16	–	–	17
Y.S.Chahal	54	10	4	18*	53	8.83	–	–	15
D.L.Chahar	3	2	1	12	18	18.00	–	–	–
S.Dhawan	139	136	7	143	5808	45.02	17	30	65
S.Dube	1	1	–	9	9	9.00	–	–	–
S.S.Iyer	21	19	1	103	807	44.83	1	8	8
R.A.Jadeja	168	113	39	87	2411	32.58	–	13	60
K.M.Jadhav	73	52	19	120	1389	42.09	2	6	33
K.D.Karthik	94	79	21	79	1752	30.20	–	9	64/7
V.Kohli	251	242	39	183	12040	59.31	43	60	129
Kuldeep Yadav	61	21	12	19	118	13.11	–	–	8
B.Kumar	114	52	15	53*	526	14.21	–	1	27
Mohammed Shami	79	38	17	25	161	7.66	–	–	28
T.Natarajan	1	–	–	–	–	–	–	–	–
M.K.Pandey	26	21	7	104*	492	35.14	1	2	7
H.H.Pandya	57	41	7	92*	1167	34.32	–	6	22
R.R.Pant	16	14	–	71	374	26.71	–	1	8/1
K.L.Rahul	35	34	5	112	1332	45.93	4	8	18/2
N.A.Saini	7	4	3	45	92	92.00	–	–	3
R.G.Sharma	224	217	32	264	9115	49.27	29	43	77
P.P.Shaw	3	3	–	40	84	28.00	–	–	–
Shubman Gill	3	3	–	33	49	16.33	–	–	–
S.N.Thakur	12	6	2	22*	77	19.25	–	–	3

INDIA – BOWLING

	O	M	R	W	Avge	Best	4wI	R/Over
M.A.Agarwal	1	0	10	0	–	–	–	10.00
J.J.Bumrah	587.1	39	2736	108	25.33	5-27	6	4.65
Y.S.Chahal	482.1	13	2511	92	27.29	6-42	4	5.20
D.L.Chahar	21	0	129	2	64.50	1-37	–	6.14
S.Dube	7.5	0	68	0	–	–	–	8.68
S.S.Iyer	2	0	15	0	–	–	–	7.50
R.A.Jadeja	1426.1	50	7024	188	37.36	5-36	8	4.92
K.M.Jadhav	197.5	1	1020	27	37.77	3-23	–	5.15
V.Kohli	106.5	1	665	4	166.25	1-15	–	6.22
Kuldeep Yadav	542	12	2778	105	26.45	6-25	5	5.12
B.Kumar	908.3	68	4568	132	34.60	5-42	5	5.02
Mohammed Shami	674	39	3793	148	25.62	5-69	10	5.62
T.Natarajan	10	1	70	2	35.00	2-70	–	7.00
H.H.Pandya	398.4	5	2219	55	40.34	3-31	–	5.56

INDIA – BOWLING (continued)

	O	M	R	W	Avge	Best	4wI	R/Over
N.A.Saini	65	0	454	6	75.66	2-58	–	6.98
R.G.Sharma	98.5	2	515	8	64.37	2-27	–	5.21
S.N.Thakur	97	2	660	15	44.00	4-52	1	6.80

PAKISTAN – BATTING AND FIELDING

	M	I	NO	HS	Runs	Avge	100	50	Ct/St
Abid Ali	6	6	1	112	234	39.00	1	1	3
Babar Azam	77	75	11	125*	3580	55.93	12	16	36
Faheem Ashraf	25	16	2	28	185	13.21	–	–	5
Fakhar Zaman	47	47	4	210*	1960	45.58	4	13	21
Haider Ali	2	2	–	29	42	21.00	–	–	1
Haris Rauf	2	–	–	–	–	–	–	–	1
Haris Sohail	42	41	5	130	1685	46.80	2	14	17
Hasan Ali	53	29	9	59	280	14.00	–	2	12
Iftikhar Ahmed	7	7	3	32*	114	28.50	–	–	5
Imad Wasim	55	40	17	63*	986	42.86	–	5	12
Imam-ul-Haq	40	40	5	151	1831	52.40	7	7	8
Khushdil Shah	1	1	–	33	33	33.00	–	–	1
Mohammad Abbas	3	–	–	–	–	–	–	–	–
Mohammad Amir	61	30	10	73*	363	18.15	–	2	8
Mohammad Hasnain	6	3	1	28	31	15.50	–	–	2
Mohammad Nawaz	15	12	3	53	199	22.11	–	–	5
Mohammad Rizwan	35	31	7	115	730	30.41	2	3	32/1
Musa Khan	2	1	1	9*	9	–	–	–	–
Sarfraz Ahmed	116	90	22	105	2302	33.85	2	11	116/24
Shadab Khan	43	22	9	54	337	25.92	–	3	8
Shaheen Shah Afridi	22	10	7	19*	52	17.33	–	–	3
Usman Khan	17	4	1	6	6	2.00	–	–	3
Wahab Riaz	91	66	15	54*	740	14.50	–	3	29

PAKISTAN – BOWLING

	O	M	R	W	Avge	Best	4wI	R/Over
Faheem Ashraf	167.2	8	831	21	39.57	5-22	1	4.96
Fakhar Zaman	22.3	0	111	1	111.00	1-19	–	4.93
Haris Rauf	17	1	88	1	88.00	1-31	–	5.17
Haris Sohail	107	0	613	11	55.72	3-45	–	5.72
Hasan Ali	424.4	14	2381	82	29.03	5-34	4	5.60
Iftikhar Ahmed	43	0	201	6	33.50	5-40	1	4.67
Imad Wasim	400.3	8	1957	44	44.47	5-14	1	4.88
Mohammad Abbas	27	0	153	1	153.00	1-44	–	5.66
Mohammad Amir	502.1	34	2400	81	29.62	5-30	2	4.77
Mohammad Hasnain	51	0	329	10	32.90	5-26	1	6.45
Mohammad Nawaz	116.3	2	607	17	35.70	4-42	1	5.21
Musa Khan	16.1	0	101	2	50.50	2-21	–	6.24
Sarfraz Ahmed	2	0	15	0	–	–	–	7.50
Shadab Khan	348	7	1750	59	29.66	4-28	3	5.02
Shaheen Shah Afridi	184	9	974	45	21.64	6-35	6	5.29
Usman Khan	128	8	633	34	18.61	5-34	5	4.94
Wahab Riaz	721.1	20	4117	120	34.30	5-46	6	5.70

SRI LANKA – BATTING AND FIELDING

	M	I	NO	HS	Runs	Avge	100	50	Ct/St
D.M.de Silva	45	42	7	84	895	25.57	–	5	20
P.W.H.de Silva	15	13	3	42*	190	19.00	–	–	5
A.N.P.R.Fernando	45	23	16	7	29	4.14	–	–	6
B.O.P.Fernando	6	6	–	49	128	21.33	–	–	1
W.I.A.Fernando	18	18	–	127	653	36.27	2	3	6
M.D.Gunathilleke	38	37	1	133	1249	34.69	2	8	12
G.S.N.F.G.Jayasuriya	12	10	1	96	195	21.66	–	1	1
F.D.M.Karunaratne	31	27	2	97	683	27.32	–	5	10
C.B.R.L.S.Kumara	13	6	3	7*	17	5.66	–	–	3
R.A.S.Lakmal	85	48	22	26	244	9.38	–	–	19
A.D.Mathews	217	187	48	139*	5830	41.94	3	40	53
B.K.G.Mendis	76	74	3	119	2167	30.52	2	17	39
A.K.Perera	6	4	–	31	52	13.00	–	–	1
M.D.K.J.Perera	101	96	5	135	2825	31.04	5	14	43/3
M.K.P.A.D.Perera	36	27	5	50*	283	12.86	–	1	14
N.L.T.C.Perera	164	131	16	140	2316	20.13	1	10	62
C.A.K.Rajitha	9	3	2	0*	0	0.00	–	–	1
M.B.Ranasinghe	1	1	–	36	36	36.00	–	–	–
W.S.R.Samarawickrama	7	7	–	54	138	19.71	–	1	1
P.A.D.L.R.Sandakan	24	14	4	6	34	3.40	–	–	8
M.D.Shanaka	22	19	1	68	468	26.00	–	3	3
H.D.R.L.Thirimanne	127	106	14	139*	3194	34.71	4	21	38
I.Udana	18	15	3	78	190	15.83	–	1	5

SRI LANKA – BOWLING

	O	M	R	W	Avge	Best	4wI	R/Over
D.M.de Silva	179.2	1	928	22	42.18	3-32	–	5.17
P.W.H.de Silva	97.1	3	547	17	32.17	3-15	–	5.62
A.N.P.R.Fernando	353.1	18	2099	57	36.82	4-31	2	5.94
B.O.P.Fernando	2	0	16	0	–	–	–	8.00
M.D.Gunathilleke	51	1	296	6	49.33	3-48	–	5.80
G.S.N.F.G.Jayasuriya	52	1	277	3	92.33	1-15	–	5.32
F.D.M.Karunaratne	2.4	0	18	0	–	–	–	6.75
C.B.R.L.S.Kumara	90.4	0	623	13	47.92	2-26	–	6.87
R.A.S.Lakmal	637.2	35	3478	107	32.50	4-13	3	5.45
A.D.Mathews	865.1	54	4003	120	33.35	6-20	3	4.62
B.K.G.Mendis	3.2	0	28	0	–	–	–	8.40
A.K.Perera	6	0	33	0	–	–	–	5.50
M.K.P.A.D.Perera	295.3	5	1506	51	29.52	6-29	4	5.09
N.L.T.C.Perera	971.2	28	5668	172	32.95	6-44	9	5.83
C.A.K.Rajitha	58.5	0	379	9	42.11	2-17	–	6.44
P.A.D.L.R.Sandakan	179.2	0	1161	20	58.05	4-52	1	6.47
M.D.Shanaka	47	0	274	10	27.40	5-43	1	5.82
H.D.R.L.Thirimanne	17.2	0	94	3	31.33	2-36	–	5.42
I.Udana	130.3	1	810	16	50.62	3-82	–	6.20

A.N.P.R.Fernando is also known as N.Pradeep; D.S.M.Kumara is also known as D.S.K.Madushanka; M.K.P.A.D.Perera is also known as A.Dananjaya; M.B.Ranasinghe is also known as M.Bhanuka.

ZIMBABWE – BATTING AND FIELDING

	M	I	NO	HS	Runs	Avge	100	50	Ct/St
R.P.Burl	18	15	3	53	243	20.25	–	1	8
R.W.Chakabva	41	38	2	78*	646	17.94	–	1	29/4
B.B.Chari	14	14	–	39	186	13.28	–	–	3/1

	M	I	NO	HS	Runs	Avge	100	50	Ct/St
T.L.Chatara	70	45	20	23	165	6.60	–	–	6
C.J.Chibhabha	107	107	2	99	2418	23.02	–	16	33
T.S.Chisoro	21	17	6	42*	146	13.27	–	–	6
C.R.Ervine	96	93	11	130*	2616	31.90	3	15	44
T.S.Kamunhukamwe	6	6	–	51	93	15.50	–	1	1
W.N.Madhevere	6	6	–	55	227	37.83	–	2	1
P.J.Moor	49	45	5	58*	827	20.67	–	4	22/1
C.B.Mpofu	84	41	21	9*	57	2.85	–	–	11
C.T.Mumba	7	7	3	13	32	8.00	–	–	1
C.T.Mutombodzi	14	13	1	34	177	14.75	–	–	7
R.Mutumbami	36	34	2	74	618	19.31	–	3	24/5
B.Muzarabani	21	17	7	17	38	3.80	–	–	7
R.Ngarava	12	8	3	10	15	3.00	–	–	1
Sikandar Raza	103	99	15	141	2856	34.00	3	16	41
B.R.M.Taylor	199	198	15	145*	6530	35.68	11	39	131/29
D.T.Tiripano	35	26	8	55*	344	19.11	–	1	4
C.K.Tshuma	2	1	–	0	0	0.00	–	–	–
S.C.Williams	136	132	19	129*	3958	35.02	4	32	51

ZIMBABWE – BOWLING

	O	M	R	W	Avge	Best	4wI	R/Over
R.P.Burl	35	1	207	7	29.57	4-32	1	5.91
T.L.Chatara	571.5	45	2905	95	30.57	4-33	1	5.08
C.J.Chibhabha	279.5	12	1631	35	46.60	4-25	1	5.82
T.S.Chisoro	150	7	684	24	28.50	3-16	–	4.56
W.N.Madhevere	29.2	0	160	2	80.00	1-38	–	5.45
C.B.Mpofu	660	41	3581	93	38.50	6-52	3	5.42
C.T.Mumba	45.2	0	326	7	46.57	3-69	–	7.19
C.T.Mutombodzi	61.5	0	359	7	51.28	2-33	–	5.80
B.Muzarabani	158	5	869	25	34.76	5-49	2	5.50
R.Ngarava	85.5	2	545	10	54.50	2-37	–	6.34
Sikandar Raza	525.2	21	2558	61	41.93	3-21	–	4.86
B.R.M.Taylor	66	0	406	9	45.11	3-54	–	6.15
D.T.Tiripano	233.2	12	1337	33	40.51	5-63	1	5.73
C.K.Tshuma	11	1	83	1	83.00	1-35	–	7.54
S.C.Williams	708	31	3449	72	47.90	4-43	1	4.87

BANGLADESH – BATTING AND FIELDING

	M	I	NO	HS	Runs	Avge	100	50	Ct/St
Afif Hossain	1	1	–	7	7	7.00	–	–	–
Al-Amin Hossain	15	7	5	2*	4	2.00	–	–	1
Anumul Haque	38	35	–	120	1052	30.05	3	3	10
Hasan Mahmud	2	–	–	–	–	–	–	–	–
Liton Das	39	39	3	176	1115	30.97	3	3	28/3
Mahmudullah	191	165	44	128*	4143	34.23	3	22	64
Mashrafe Mortaza †	218	156	28	51*	1773	13.85	–	1	61
Mehedi Hasan	44	26	4	51	393	17.86	–	1	14
Mithun Ali	27	23	3	63	575	28.75	–	5	7
Mohammad Naim	1	–	–	–	–	–	–	–	2
Mohammad Saifuddin	23	14	5	51*	295	32.77	–	2	3
Mosaddek Hossain	35	30	10	52*	549	27.45	–	2	13
Mushfiqur Rahim	221	207	36	144	6266	36.64	7	39	186/46
Mustafizur Rahman	61	27	17	18*	78	7.80	–	–	12
Nazmul Hossain	8	8	–	29	93	11.62	–	–	2

	M	I	NO	HS	Runs	Avge	100	50	Ct/St
Rubel Hossain	103	52	24	17	140	5.00	–	–	20
Sabbir Rahman	66	59	7	102	1333	25.63	1	6	37
Shafiul Islam	60	34	12	24*	134	6.09	–	–	8
Shakib Al Hasan	209	197	28	134*	6436	38.08	9	48	50
Soumya Sarkar	58	55	3	127*	1735	33.36	2	11	33
Taijul Islam	9	5	1	39*	63	15.75	–	–	1
Tamim Iqbal	210	208	9	158	7360	36.98	13	49	55
Taskin Ahmed	33	16	6	14	41	4.10	–	–	8

BANGLADESH – BOWLING

	O	M	R	W	Avge	Best	4wI	R/Over
Afif Hossain	2	0	12	1	12.00	1-12	–	6.00
Al-Amin Hossain	110.3	7	608	22	27.63	4-51	2	5.50
Hasan Mahmud	15	1	82	4	20.50	3-28	–	5.46
Mahmudullah	690.4	14	3572	76	47.00	3- 4	–	5.17
Mashrafe Mortaza	1804.3	122	8785	269	32.65	6-26	8	4.86
Mehedi Hasan	375.5	13	1697	47	36.10	4-25	2	4.51
Mohammad Saifuddin	174.3	7	1023	34	30.08	4-41	1	5.86
Mosaddek Hossain	150.2	1	787	14	56.21	3-13	–	5.23
Mustafizur Rahman	500.5	25	2571	115	22.35	6-43	8	5.13
Nazmul Hossain	1	0	4	0	–	–	–	4.00
Rubel Hossain	769.4	28	4357	126	34.57	6-26	8	5.66
Sabbir Rahman	51	0	345	3	115.00	1-12	–	6.76
Shafiul Islam	423.2	26	2529	70	36.12	4-21	4	5.97
Shakib Al Hasan	1775	85	7907	266	29.72	5-29	11	4.45
Soumya Sarkar	57.1	0	340	10	34.00	3-56	–	5.94
Taijul Islam	85	7	337	12	28.08	4-11	1	3.96
Tamim Iqbal	1	0	13	0	–	–	–	13.00
Taskin Ahmed	243.5	7	1433	46	31.15	5-28	3	5.87

† *Mashrafe Mortaza also made 2 appearances for an Asia XI.*

IRELAND – BATTING AND FIELDING

	M	I	NO	HS	Runs	Avge	100	50	Ct/St
M.R.Adair	15	12	2	32	164	16.40	–	–	5
A.Balbirnie	75	72	4	145*	2122	31.20	6	10	24
C.Campher	8	7	1	68	305	50.83	–	3	1
G.J.Delany	9	9	3	22	120	20.00	–	–	2
S.C.Getkate	3	2	1	16*	23	23.00	–	–	1
J.B.Little	7	3	1	9	9	4.50	–	–	–
A.R.McBrine	53	33	10	79	378	16.43	–	1	20
B.J.McCarthy	35	24	6	18	156	8.66	–	–	11
J.A.McCollum	10	10	–	73	188	18.80	–	2	2
E.J.G.Morgan †	23	23	2	115	744	35.42	1	5	9
T.J.Murtagh	58	36	12	23*	188	7.83	–	–	16
K.J.O'Brien	152	140	18	142	3619	29.66	2	18	67
W.T.S.Porterfield	139	136	3	139	4091	30.75	11	17	64
S.W.Poynter	21	19	5	36	185	13.21	–	–	22/1
W.B.Rankin ‡	68	32	20	18*	95	7.91	–	–	17
Simi Singh	24	23	2	54*	377	17.95	–	1	13
P.R.Stirling	125	122	3	177	4697	39.47	12	24	47
H.T.Tector	8	8	1	33	172	24.57	–	–	3
L.J.Tucker	16	15	1	83	331	23.64	–	2	23/1
C.A.Young	22	12	5	12*	54	7.71	–	–	6

LOI   IRELAND – BOWLING

	O	M	R	W	Avge	Best	4wI	R/Over
M.R.Adair	114.3	3	743	17	43.70	4-19	2	6.48
A.Balbirnie	10	0	68	2	34.00	1-26	–	6.80
C.Campher	42.3	3	245	8	30.62	2-31	–	5.76
G.J.Delany	22	0	148	3	49.33	1-10	–	6.72
S.C.Getkate	27	2	120	6	20.00	2-30	–	4.44
J.B.Little	61.5	4	411	11	37.36	4-45	1	6.64
A.R.McBride	432.5	22	1924	55	34.98	5-29	1	4.44
B.J.McCarthy	287	10	1700	59	28.81	5-46	3	5.92
T.J.Murtagh	503.2	45	2290	74	30.94	5-21	5	4.54
K.J.O'Brien	716	309	3726	114	32.68	4-13	5	5.20
W.B.Rankin	617	42	2955	106	27.87	4-15	4	4.78
Simi Singh	169.1	11	661	28	23.60	5-10	1	3.90
P.R.Stirling	402.5	8	1926	43	44.79	6-55	2	4.78
H.T.Tector	8	0	52	1	52.00	1-52	–	6.50
C.A.Young	182.3	8	1026	37	27.72	5-46	1	5.62‡

† *E.J.G.Morgan has also made 219 appearances for England (see above).‡ W.B.Rankin also made 7 appearances for England.*

AFGHANISTAN – BATTING AND FIELDING

	M	I	NO	HS	Runs	Avge	100	50	Ct/St
Asghar Stanikzai	114	108	10	101	2424	24.73	1	12	24
Azmatullah Omarzai	1	1	–	2	2	2.00	–	–	1
Dawlat Zadran	82	56	27	47*	513	17.68	–	–	16
Gulbadin Naib	68	58	8	82*	1079	21.58	–	5	16
Hamid Hassan	38	22	6	17	107	6.68	–	–	5
Hashmatullah Shahidi	41	41	6	97*	1154	32.97	–	10	11
Hazratullah Zazai	16	16	–	67	361	22.56	–	2	3
Ibrahim Zadran	1	1	–	2	2	2.00	–	–	1
Ikram Ali Khil	12	12	3	86	234	26.00	–	2	3/3
Javed Ahmadi	47	44	–	81	1049	23.84	–	7	11
Mohammad Nabi	127	114	12	116	2817	27.61	1	15	56
Mohammad Shahzad	84	84	3	131*	2727	33.66	6	14	64/25
Mujeeb Zadran	43	23	12	18*	88	8.00	–	–	6
Najibullah Zadran	70	64	9	104*	1615	29.36	1	11	37
Naveen-ul-Haq	7	5	4	10*	21	21.00	–	–	2
Noor Ali Zadran	51	50	1	114	1216	24.81	1	7	15
Rahmanullah Gurbaz	3	3	–	127	180	60.00	1	–	2/2
Rahmat Shah	76	72	2	114	2467	35.75	5	16	19
Rashid Khan	74	58	9	60*	1008	20.57	–	5	52
Samiullah Shinwari	84	74	12	96	1811	29.20	–	11	21
Sharafuddin Ashraf	17	10	3	21	66	9.42	–	–	5
Yamin Ahmadzai	4	2	1	3*	3	3.00	–	–	2

AFGHANISTAN – BOWLING

	O	M	R	W	Avge	Best	4wI	R/Over
Asghar Stanikzai	23.1	1	91	3	30.33	1- 1	–	3.92
Azmatullah Omarzai	4	0	24	0	–	–	–	6.00
Dawlat Zadran	628.1	42	3423	115	29.76	4-22	3	5.44
Gulbadin Naib	384.4	11	2091	61	34.27	6-43	3	5.43
Hamid Hassan	289	24	1330	59	22.54	5-45	3	4.60
Hashmatullah Shahidi	3	0	25	0	–	–	–	8.33
Javed Ahmadi	75.2	0	363	9	40.33	4-37	1	4.81
Mohammad Nabi	1016.3	39	4372	132	33.12	4-30	3	4.30
Mujeeb Zadran	388.5	29	1543	70	22.04	5-50	3	3.96

AFGHANISTAN – BOWLING (continued)

	O	M	R	W	Avge	Best	4wI	R/Over
Najibullah Zadran	5	0	30	0	–	–	–	6.00
Naveen-ul-Haq	61.3	0	356	14	25.42	4-42	1	5.78
Rahmat Shah	87.2	2	504	14	36.00	5-32	1	5.77
Rashid Khan	622	27	2601	140	18.57	7-18	9	4.18
Samiullah Shinwari	351.5	10	1729	46	37.58	4-31	1	4.91
Sharafuddin Ashraf	127.2	3	559	13	43.00	3-29	–	4.39
Yamin Ahmadzai	26.4	3	139	2	69.50	1-23	–	5.21

ASSOCIATES – BATTING AND FIELDING

	M	I	NO	HS	Runs	Avge	100	50	Ct/St
J.H.Davey (Scot)	31	28	6	64	497	22.59	–	2	10
B.D.Glover (Neth)	1	–	–	–	–	–	–	–	1
I.G.Holland (USA)	8	8	–	75	244	30.50	–	2	3
M.A.Jones (Scot)	8	8	–	87	281	35.12	–	3	3
F.J.Klaassen (Neth)	4	3	1	13	30	15.00	–	–	2
S.Lamichhane (Nepal)	10	8	2	28	78	13.00	–	–	2
R.A.J.Smith (Scot)	2	1	–	10	10	10.00	–	–	–
S.Snater (Neth)	2	2	–	12	12	6.00	–	–	3
R.N.ten Doeschate (Neth)	33	32	9	119	1541	67.00	5	9	13
T.van der Gugten (Neth)	4	2	–	2	4	2.00	–	–	–
R.E.van der Merwe (Neth)	2	1	–	57	57	57.00	–	1	1
B.T.J.Wheal (Scot)	13	7	3	14	16	4.00	–	–	3

ASSOCIATES – BOWLING

	O	M	R	W	Avge	Best	4wI	R/Over
J.H.Davey	216.5	18	1082	49	22.08	6-28	3	4.99
B.D.Glover	10	0	37	1	37.00	1-37	–	3.70
I.G.Holland	45.5	2	209	7	29.85	3-11	–	4.56
F.J.Klaassen	40	3	150	10	15.00	3-30	–	3.75
S.Lamichhane	89.1	8	375	23	16.30	6-16	3	4.20
R.A.J.Smith	15	0	97	1	97.00	1-34	–	6.46
S.Snater	11.5	1	63	1	63.00	1-41	–	5.32
R.N.ten Doeschate	263.2	18	1327	55	24.12	4-31	3	5.03
T.van der Gugten	21	3	85	8	10.62	5-24	1	4.04
R.E.van der Merwe	14	0	97	1	97.00	1-57	–	6.92
B.T.J.Wheal	114.3	9	508	23	22.08	3-34	–	4.43

LIMITED-OVERS INTERNATIONALS RESULTS

1970-71 to 9 March 2021

This chart excludes all matches involving multinational teams.

	Opponents	Matches	Won														Tied	NR
			E	A	SA	WI	NZ	I	P	SL	Z	B	Ire	Afg	Ass		
England	Australia	152	63	84	–	–	–	–	–	–	–	–	–	–	–	2	3
	South Africa	63	28	–	30	–	–	–	–	–	–	–	–	–	–	1	4
	West Indies	102	52	–	–	44	–	–	–	–	–	–	–	–	–	–	6
	New Zealand	91	41	–	–	–	43	–	–	–	–	–	–	–	–	3	4
	India	100	42	–	–	–	–	53	–	–	–	–	–	–	–	2	3
	Pakistan	88	53	–	–	–	–	–	32	–	–	–	–	–	–	–	3
	Sri Lanka	75	36	–	–	–	–	–	–	36	–	–	–	–	–	1	2
	Zimbabwe	30	21	–	–	–	–	–	–	–	8	–	–	–	–	–	1
	Bangladesh	21	17	–	–	–	–	–	–	–	–	4	–	–	–	–	–
	Ireland	13	10	–	–	–	–	–	–	–	–	–	2	–	–	–	1
	Afghanistan	2	2	–	–	–	–	–	–	–	–	–	–	–	–	–	–
	Associates	15	13	–	–	–	–	–	–	–	–	–	–	–	0	–	1
Australia	South Africa	103	–	48	51	–	–	–	–	–	–	–	–	–	–	3	1
	West Indies	140	–	74	–	60	–	–	–	–	–	–	–	–	–	3	3
	New Zealand	138	–	92	–	–	39	–	–	–	–	–	–	–	–	–	7
	India	143	–	80	–	–	–	53	–	–	–	–	–	–	–	–	10
	Pakistan	104	–	68	–	–	–	–	32	–	–	–	–	–	–	1	3
	Sri Lanka	97	–	61	–	–	–	–	–	32	–	–	–	–	–	–	4
	Zimbabwe	30	–	27	–	–	–	–	–	–	2	–	–	–	–	–	1
	Bangladesh	21	–	19	–	–	–	–	–	–	–	1	–	–	–	–	1
	Ireland	5	–	4	–	–	–	–	–	–	–	–	0	–	–	–	1
	Afghanistan	3	–	3	–	–	–	–	–	–	–	–	–	0	–	–	–
	Associates	16	–	16	–	–	–	–	–	–	–	–	–	–	0	–	–
S Africa	West Indies	62	–	–	44	15	–	–	–	–	–	–	–	–	–	1	2
	New Zealand	71	–	–	41	–	25	–	–	–	–	–	–	–	–	–	5
	India	84	–	–	46	–	–	35	–	–	–	–	–	–	–	–	3
	Pakistan	79	–	–	50	–	–	–	28	–	–	–	–	–	–	–	1
	Sri Lanka	77	–	–	44	–	–	–	–	31	–	–	–	–	–	1	1
	Zimbabwe	41	–	–	38	–	–	–	–	–	2	–	–	–	–	–	1
	Bangladesh	21	–	–	17	–	–	–	–	–	–	4	–	–	–	–	–
	Ireland	5	–	–	5	–	–	–	–	–	–	–	0	–	–	–	–
	Afghanistan	1	–	–	1	–	–	–	–	–	–	–	–	0	–	–	–
	Associates	18	–	–	18	–	–	–	–	–	–	–	–	–	0	–	–
W Indies	New Zealand	65	–	–	–	30	28	–	–	–	–	–	–	–	–	–	7
	India	133	–	–	–	63	–	64	–	–	–	–	–	–	–	2	4
	Pakistan	134	–	–	–	71	–	–	60	–	–	–	–	–	–	3	–
	Sri Lanka	60	–	–	–	28	–	–	–	29	–	–	–	–	–	–	3
	Zimbabwe	48	–	–	–	36	–	–	–	–	10	–	–	–	–	1	1
	Bangladesh	41	–	–	–	21	–	–	–	–	–	18	–	–	–	–	2
	Ireland	12	–	–	–	10	–	–	–	–	–	–	1	–	–	–	1
	Afghanistan	9	–	–	–	5	–	–	–	–	–	–	–	3	–	–	1
	Associates	19	–	–	–	18	–	–	–	–	–	–	–	–	1	–	–
N Zealand	India	110	–	–	–	–	49	55	–	–	–	–	–	–	–	1	5
	Pakistan	107	–	–	–	–	48	–	55	–	–	–	–	–	–	1	3
	Sri Lanka	99	–	–	–	–	49	–	–	41	–	–	–	–	–	1	8
	Zimbabwe	38	–	–	–	–	27	–	–	–	9	–	–	–	–	1	1
	Bangladesh	35	–	–	–	–	25	–	–	–	–	10	–	–	–	–	–
	Ireland	4	–	–	–	–	4	–	–	–	–	–	0	–	–	–	–
	Afghanistan	2	–	–	–	–	2	–	–	–	–	–	–	0	–	–	–
	Associates	12	–	–	–	–	12	–	–	–	–	–	–	–	0	–	–
India	Pakistan	132	–	–	–	–	–	55	73	–	–	–	–	–	–	–	4
	Sri Lanka	159	–	–	–	–	–	91	–	56	–	–	–	–	–	1	11
	Zimbabwe	63	–	–	–	–	–	51	–	–	10	–	–	–	–	2	–
	Bangladesh	36	–	–	–	–	–	30	–	–	–	5	–	–	–	–	1
	Ireland	3	–	–	–	–	–	3	–	–	–	–	0	–	–	–	–
	Afghanistan	3	–	–	–	–	–	2	–	–	–	–	–	0	–	1	–
	Associates	24	–	–	–	–	–	22	–	–	–	–	–	–	2	–	–
Pakistan	Sri Lanka	155	–	–	–	–	–	–	92	58	–	–	–	–	–	1	4
	Zimbabwe	62	–	–	–	–	–	–	54	–	4	–	–	–	–	2	2

Team	Opponents	Matches	E	A	SA	WI	NZ	I	P	SL	Z	B	Ire	Afg	Ass	Tied	NR
	Bangladesh	37	–	–	–	–	–	–	32	–	–	5	–	–	–	–	–
	Ireland	7	–	–	–	–	–	–	5	–	–	–	1	–	–	1	–
	Afghanistan	4	–	–	–	–	–	–	4	–	–	–	–	0	–	–	–
	Associates	21	–	–	–	–	–	–	21	–	–	–	–	–	0	–	–
Sri Lanka	Zimbabwe	57	–	–	–	–	–	–	–	44	11	–	–	–	–	–	2
	Bangladesh	48	–	–	–	–	–	–	–	39	–	7	–	–	–	–	2
	Ireland	4	–	–	–	–	–	–	–	4	–	–	0	–	–	–	2
	Afghanistan	4	–	–	–	–	–	–	–	3	–	–	–	1	–	–	–
	Associates	17	–	–	–	–	–	–	–	16	–	–	–	–	1	–	–
Zimbabwe	Bangladesh	75	–	–	–	–	–	–	–	–	28	47	–	–	–	–	–
	Ireland	13	–	–	–	–	–	–	–	–	6	–	6	–	–	1	–
	Afghanistan	25	–	–	–	–	–	–	–	–	10	–	–	15	–	–	–
	Associates	50	–	–	–	–	–	–	–	–	38	–	–	–	9	1	2
Bangladesh	Ireland	10	–	–	–	–	–	–	–	–	–	7	2	–	–	–	1
	Afghanistan	8	–	–	–	–	–	–	–	–	–	5	–	3	–	–	–
	Associates	26	–	–	–	–	–	–	–	–	–	18	–	–	8	–	–
Ireland	Afghanistan	30	–	–	–	–	–	–	–	–	–	–	13	16	–	–	1
	Associates	58	–	–	–	–	–	–	–	–	–	–	44	–	10	2	2
Afghanistan	Associates	38	–	–	–	–	–	–	–	–	–	–	–	24	13	–	1
Associates	Associates	157	–	–	–	–	–	–	–	–	–	–	–	–	152	–	5
		4265	378	576	385	401	351	514	488	389	138	131	69	62	197	39	148

MERIT TABLE OF ALL L-O INTERNATIONALS

	Matches	Won	Lost	Tied	No Result	% Won (exc NR)
South Africa	625	385	216	6	18	63.42
Australia	952	576	333	9	34	62.74
India	990	514	426	9	41	54.16
Pakistan	930	488	413	9	20	53.62
England	752	378	337	9	28	52.20
West Indies	825	401	384	10	30	50.44
Afghanistan	129	62	63	1	3	49.20
New Zealand	772	351	374	7	40	48.01
Sri Lanka	852	389	421	5	37	47.73
Ireland	164	69	84	3	8	44.23
Bangladesh	379	131	241	–	7	35.21
Zimbabwe	532	138	375	8	11	26.48
Associate Members (v Full*)	314	45	260	3	6	14.61

* Results of games between two Associate Members and those involving multi-national sides are excluded from this list; Associate Members have participated in 471 LOIs, 157 LOIs being between Associate Members.

TEAM RECORDS

HIGHEST TOTALS

† Batting Second

481-6	(50 overs)	England v Australia	Nottingham	2018
444-3	(50 overs)	England v Pakistan	Nottingham	2016
443-9	(50 overs)	Sri Lanka v Netherlands	Amstelveen	2006
439-2	(50 overs)	South Africa v West Indies	Johannesburg	2014-15
438-9†	(49.5 overs)	South Africa v Australia	Johannesburg	2005-06
438-4	(50 overs)	South Africa v India	Mumbai	2015-16
434-4	(50 overs)	Australia v South Africa	Johannesburg	2005-06
418-5	(50 overs)	South Africa v Zimbabwe	Potchefstroom	2006-07
418-5	(50 overs)	India v West Indies	Indore	2011-12
418-6	(50 overs)	England v West Indies	St George's	2018-19

417-6	(50 overs)	Australia v Afghanistan	Perth	2014-15
414-7	(50 overs)	India v Sri Lanka	Rajkot	2009-10
413-5	(50 overs)	India v Bermuda	Port of Spain	2006-07
411-8†	(50 overs)	Sri Lanka v India	Rajkot	2009-10
411-4	(50 overs)	South Africa v Ireland	Canberra	2014-15
408-5	(50 overs)	South Africa v West Indies	Sydney	2014-15
408-9	(50 overs)	England v New Zealand	Birmingham	2015
404-5	(50 overs)	India v Sri Lanka	Kolkata	2014-15
402-2	(50 overs)	New Zealand v Ireland	Aberdeen	2008
401-3	(50 overs)	India v South Africa	Gwalior	2009-10
399-6	(50 overs)	South Africa v Zimbabwe	Benoni	2010-11
399-9	(50 overs)	England v South Africa	Bloemfontein	2015-16
399-1	(50 overs)	Pakistan v Zimbabwe	Bulawayo	2018
398-5	(50 overs)	Sri Lanka v Kenya	Kandy	1995-96
398-5	(50 overs)	New Zealand v England	The Oval	2015
397-5	(44 overs)	New Zealand v Zimbabwe	Bulawayo	2005
397-6	(50 overs)	England v Afghanistan	Manchester	2019
393-6	(50 overs)	New Zealand v West Indies	Wellington	2014-15
392-6	(50 overs)	South Africa v Pakistan	Pretoria	2006-07
392-4	(50 overs)	India v New Zealand	Christchurch	2008-09
392-4	(50 overs)	India v Sri Lanka	Mohali	2017-18
391-4	(50 overs)	England v Bangladesh	Nottingham	2005
389	(48 overs)	West Indies v England	St George's	2018-19
389-4	(50 overs)	Australia v India	Sydney	2020-21
387-5	(50 overs)	India v England	Rajkot	2008-09
387-5	(50 overs)	India v West Indies	Visakhapatnam	2019-20
386-6	(50 overs)	England v Bangladesh	Cardiff	2019
385-7	(50 overs)	Pakistan v Bangladesh	Dambulla	2010
384-6	(50 overs)	South Africa v Sri Lanka	Centurion	2016-17
383-6	(50 overs)	India v Australia	Bangalore	2013-14
381-6	(50 overs)	India v England	Cuttack	2016-17
381-3	(50 overs)	West Indies v Ireland	Dublin	2019
381-5	(50 overs)	Australia v Bangladesh	Nottingham	2019
378-5	(50 overs)	Australia v New Zealand	Canberra	2016-17
377-6	(50 overs)	Australia v South Africa	Basseterre	2006-07
377-8	(50 overs)	Sri Lanka v Ireland	Dublin	2016
377-5	(50 overs)	India v West Indies	Mumbai (BS)	2018-19
376-2	(50 overs)	India v New Zealand	Hyderabad, India	1999-00
376-9	(50 overs)	Australia v Sri Lanka	Sydney	2014-15
375-3	(50 overs)	Pakistan v Zimbabwe	Lahore	2015
375-5	(50 overs)	India v Sri Lanka	Colombo (RPS)	2017

The highest score for Zimbabwe is 351-7 (v Kenya, Mombasa, 2008-09), for Afghanistan is 338 (v Ire, Greater Noida, 2016-17), for Bangladesh is 333 (v A, Nottingham, 2019) and for Ireland is 331-8 (v Z, Hobart, 2014-15) and 331-6 (v Scotland, Dubai, 2017-18).

HIGHEST MATCH AGGREGATES

872-13	(99.5 overs)	South Africa v Australia	Johannesburg	2005-06
825-15	(100 overs)	India v Sri Lanka	Rajkot	2009-10
807-16	(98 overs)	West Indies v England	St George's	2018-19

LARGEST RUNS MARGINS OF VICTORY

290 runs	New Zealand beat Ireland	Aberdeen	2008
275 runs	Australia beat Afghanistan	Perth	2014-15
272 runs	South Africa beat Zimbabwe	Benoni	2010-11
258 runs	South Africa beat Sri Lanka	Paarl	2011-12
257 runs	India beat Bermuda	Port of Spain	2006-07
257 runs	South Africa beat West Indies	Sydney	2014-15
256 runs	Australia beat Namibia	Potchefstroom	2002-03
256 runs	India beat Hong Kong	Karachi	2008
255 runs	Pakistan beat Ireland	Dublin	2016
245 runs	Sri Lanka beat India	Sharjah	2000-01

244 runs	Pakistan beat Zimbabwe	Bulawayo	2018
243 runs	Sri Lanka beat Bermuda	Port of Spain	2006-07
242 runs	England beat Australia	Nottingham	2018
234 runs	Sri Lanka beat Pakistan	Lahore	2008-09
233 runs	Pakistan beat Bangladesh	Dhaka	1999-00
232 runs	Australia beat Sri Lanka	Adelaide	1984-85
231 runs	South Africa beat Netherlands	Mohali	2010-11
229 runs	Australia beat Netherlands	Basseterre	2006-07
226 runs	Ireland beat UAE	Harare	2017-18
224 runs	Australia beat Pakistan	Nairobi	2002
224 runs	India beat West Indies	Mumbai (BS)	2018-19
221 runs	South Africa beat Netherlands	Basseterre	2006-07

LOWEST TOTALS (Excluding reduced innings)

35	(18.0 overs)	Zimbabwe v Sri Lanka	Harare	2003-04
35	(12.0 overs)	USA v Nepal	Kirtipur	2019-20
36	(18.4 overs)	Canada v Sri Lanka	Paarl	2002-03
38	(15.4 overs)	Zimbabwe v Sri Lanka	Colombo (SSC)	2001-02
43	(19.5 overs)	Pakistan v West Indies	Cape Town	1992-93
43	(20.1 overs)	Sri Lanka v South Africa	Paarl	2011-12
44	(24.5 overs)	Zimbabwe v Bangladesh	Chittagong	2009-10
45	(40.3 overs)	Canada v England	Manchester	1979
45	(14.0 overs)	Namibia v Australia	Potchefstroom	2002-03
54	(26.3 overs)	India v Sri Lanka	Sharjah	2000-01
54	(23.2 overs)	West Indies v South Africa	Cape Town	2003-04
54	(13.5 overs)	Zimbabwe v Afghanistan	Harare	2016-17
55	(28.3 overs)	Sri Lanka v West Indies	Sharjah	1986-87
58	(18.5 overs)	Bangladesh v West Indies	Dhaka	2010-11
58	(17.4 overs)	Bangladesh v India	Dhaka	2014
58	(16.1 overs)	Afghanistan v Zimbabwe	Sharjah	2015-16
61	(22.0 overs)	West Indies v Bangladesh	Chittagong	2011-12
63	(25.5 overs)	India v Australia	Sydney	1980-81
63	(18.3 overs)	Afghanistan v Scotland	Abu Dhabi	2014-15
64	(35.5 overs)	New Zealand v Pakistan	Sharjah	1985-86
65	(24.0 overs)	USA v Australia	Southampton	2004
65	(24.3 overs)	Zimbabwe v India	Harare	2005
67	(31.0 overs)	Zimbabwe v Sri Lanka	Harare	2008-09
67	(24.4 overs)	Canada v Netherlands	King City	2013
67	(24.0 overs)	Sri Lanka v England	Manchester	2014
67	(25.1 overs)	Zimbabwe v Pakistan	Bulawayo	2018
68	(31.3 overs)	Scotland v West Indies	Leicester	1999
69	(28.0 overs)	South Africa v Australia	Sydney	1993-94
69	(22.5 overs)	Zimbabwe v Kenya	Harare	2005-06
69	(23.5 overs)	Kenya v New Zealand	Chennai	2010-11
70	(25.2 overs)	Australia v England	Birmingham	1977
70	(26.3 overs)	Australia v New Zealand	Adelaide	1985-86
70	(23.5 overs)	West Indies v Australia	Perth	2012-13
70	(24.4 overs)	Bangladesh v West Indies	St George's	2014

The lowest for England is 86 (v A, Manchester, 2001) and for Ireland is 77 (v SL, St George's, 2007).

LOWEST MATCH AGGREGATES

71-12	(17.2 overs)	USA (35) v Nepal (36-2)	Kirtipur	2019-20
73-11	(23.2 overs)	Canada (36) v Sri Lanka (37-1)	Paarl	2002-03
75-11	(27.2 overs)	Zimbabwe (35) v Sri Lanka (40-1)	Harare	2003-04
78-11	(20.0 overs)	Zimbabwe (38) v Sri Lanka (40-1)	Colombo (SSC)	2001-02

284

		LOI	I	NO	HS	Runs	Avge	100	50
S.R.Tendulkar	I	463	452	41	200*	18426	44.83	49	96
K.C.Sangakkara	SL/Asia/ICC	404	380	41	169	14234	41.98	25	93
R.T.Ponting	A/ICC	375	365	39	164	13704	42.03	30	82
S.T.Jayasuriya	SL/Asia	445	433	18	189	13430	32.36	28	68
D.P.M.D.Jayawardena	SL/Asia	448	418	39	144	12650	33.37	19	77
V.Kohli	I	251	242	39	183	12040	59.31	43	60
Inzamam-ul-Haq	P/Asia	378	350	53	137*	11739	39.52	10	83
J.H.Kallis	SA/Afr/ICC	328	314	53	139	11579	44.36	17	86
S.C.Ganguly	I/Asia	311	300	23	183	11363	41.02	22	72
R.S.Dravid	I/Asia/ICC	344	318	40	153	10889	39.16	12	83
M.S.Dhoni	I/Asia	350	297	84	183*	10773	50.57	10	73
C.H.Gayle	WI/ICC	301	294	17	215	10480	37.83	25	54
B.C.Lara	WI/ICC	299	289	32	169	10405	40.48	19	63
T.M.Dilshan	SL	330	303	41	161*	10290	39.27	22	47
Mohammad Yousuf	P/Asia	288	272	40	141*	9720	41.71	15	64
A.C.Gilchrist	A/ICC	287	279	11	172	9619	35.89	16	55
A.B.de Villiers	SA/Afr	228	218	39	176	9577	53.50	25	53
M.Azharuddin	I	334	308	54	153*	9378	36.92	7	58
P.A.de Silva	SL	308	296	30	145	9284	34.90	11	64
R.G.Sharma	I	224	217	32	264	9115	49.27	29	43
Saeed Anwar	P	247	244	19	194	8824	39.21	20	43
S.Chanderpaul	WI	268	251	40	150	8778	41.60	11	59
Yuvraj Singh	I/Asia	304	278	40	150	8701	36.55	14	52
D.L.Haynes	WI	238	237	28	152*	8648	41.37	17	57
L.R.P.L.Taylor	NZ	232	216	39	181*	8574	48.44	21	51
M.S.Atapattu	SL	268	259	32	132*	8529	37.57	11	59
M.E.Waugh	A	244	236	20	173	8500	39.35	18	50
V.Sehwag	I/Asia/ICC	251	245	9	219	8273	35.05	15	38
H.M.Amla	SA	181	178	14	159	8113	49.46	27	39
H.H.Gibbs	SA	248	240	16	175	8094	36.13	21	37
Shahid Afridi	P/Asia/ICC	398	369	27	124	8064	23.57	6	39
S.P.Fleming	NZ/ICC	280	269	21	134*	8037	32.40	8	49
M.J.Clarke	A	245	223	44	130	7981	44.58	8	58
E.J.G.Morgan	E/Ire	242	225	33	148	7598	39.57	14	46
S.R.Waugh	A	325	288	58	120*	7569	32.90	3	45
Shoaib Malik	P	287	258	40	143	7534	34.55	9	44
A.Ranatunga	SL	269	255	47	131*	7456	35.84	4	49
Javed Miandad	P	233	218	41	119*	7381	41.70	8	50
Tamim Iqbal	B	210	208	9	158	7360	36.98	13	49
Younus Khan	P	265	255	23	144	7249	31.24	7	48
Salim Malik	P	283	256	38	102	7170	32.88	5	47
N.J.Astle	NZ	223	217	14	145*	7090	34.92	16	41
G.C.Smith	SA/Afr	197	194	10	141	6989	37.98	10	47
W.U.Tharanga	SL/Asia	235	223	17	174*	6951	33.74	15	37
M.G.Bevan	A	232	196	67	108*	6912	53.58	6	46
M.J.Guptill	NZ	183	180	19	237*	6843	42.50	16	37
G.Kirsten	SA	185	185	19	188*	6798	40.95	13	45
A.Flower	Z	213	208	16	145	6786	35.34	4	55
I.V.A.Richards	WI	187	167	24	189*	6721	47.00	11	45
Mohammad Hafeez	P	218	216	15	140*	6614	32.90	11	38
G.W.Flower	Z	221	214	18	142*	6571	33.52	6	40
B.R.M.Taylor	Z	199	198	15	145*	6530	35.68	11	39
A.R.Border	A	273	252	39	127*	6524	30.62	3	39
Shakib Al Hasan	B	209	197	28	134*	6436	38.08	9	48
Mushfiqur Rahim	B	221	207	36	144	6266	36.64	7	39
R.B.Richardson	WI	224	217	30	122	6248	33.41	5	44
K.S.Williamson	NZ	151	144	14	148	6173	47.48	13	39
M.L.Hayden	A/ICC	161	155	15	181*	6133	43.80	10	36

		LOI	I	NO	HS	**Runs**	Avge	100	50
B.B.McCullum	NZ	260	228	28	166	**6083**	30.41	5	32
D.M.Jones	A	164	161	25	145	**6068**	44.61	7	46

The most runs for Ireland is 4697 by P.R.Stirling (122 innings) and for Afghanistan 2817 by Mohammad Nabi (114 innings).

HIGHEST INDIVIDUAL INNINGS

264	R.G.Sharma	India v Sri Lanka	Kolkata	2014-15
237*	M.J.Guptill	New Zealand v West Indies	Wellington	2014-15
219	V.Sehwag	India v West Indies	Indore	2011-12
215	C.H.Gayle	West Indies v Zimbabwe	Canberra	2014-15
210*	Fakhar Zaman	Pakistan v Zimbabwe	Bulawayo	2018
209	R.G.Sharma	India v Australia	Bangalore	2013-14
208*	R.G.Sharma	India v Sri Lanka	Mohali	2017-18
200*	S.R.Tendulkar	India v South Africa	Gwalior	2009-10
194*	C.K.Coventry	Zimbabwe v Bangladesh	Bulawayo	2009
194	Saeed Anwar	Pakistan v India	Madras	1996-97
189*	I.V.A.Richards	West Indies v England	Manchester	1984
189*	M.J.Guptill	New Zealand v England	Southampton	2013
189	S.T.Jayasuriya	Sri Lanka v India	Sharjah	2000-01
188*	G.Kirsten	South Africa v UAE	Rawalpindi	1995-96
186*	S.R.Tendulkar	India v New Zealand	Hyderabad	1999-00
185*	S.R.Watson	Australia v Bangladesh	Dhaka	2010-11
185	F.du Plessis	South Africa v Sri Lanka	Cape Town	2016-17
183*	M.S.Dhoni	India v Sri Lanka	Jaipur	2005-06
183	S.C.Ganguly	India v Sri Lanka	Taunton	1999
183	V.Kohli	India v Pakistan	Dhaka	2011-12
181*	M.L.Hayden	Australia v New Zealand	Hamilton	2006-07
181*	L.R.P.L.Taylor	New Zealand v England	Dunedin	2017-18
181	I.V.A.Richards	West Indies v Sri Lanka	Karachi	1987-88
180*	M.J.Guptill	New Zealand v South Africa	Hamilton	2016-17
180	J.J.Roy	England v Australia	Melbourne	2017-18
179	D.A.Warner	Australia v Pakistan	Adelaide	2016-17
179	J.D.Campbell	West Indies v Ireland	Dublin	2019
178*	H.Masakadza	Zimbabwe v Kenya	Harare	2009-10
178	D.A.Warner	Australia v Afghanistan	Perth	2014-15
178	Q.de Kock	South Africa v Australia	Centurion	2016-17
177	P.R.Stirling	Ireland v Canada	Toronto	2010
176*	E.Lewis	West Indies v England	The Oval	2017
176	A.B.de Villiers	South Africa v Bangladesh	Paarl	2017-18
176	Liton Das	Bangladesh v Zimbabwe	Sylhet	2019-20
175*	Kapil Dev	India v Zimbabwe	Tunbridge Wells	1983
175	H.H.Gibbs	South Africa v Australia	Johannesburg	2005-06
175	S.R.Tendulkar	India v Australia	Hyderabad, India	2009-10
175	V.Sehwag	India v Bangladesh	Dhaka	2010-11
175	C.S.MacLeod	Scotland v Canada	Christchurch	2013-14
174*	W.U.Tharanga	Sri Lanka v India	Kingston	2013
173	M.E.Waugh	Australia v West Indies	Melbourne	2000-01
173	D.A.Warner	Australia v South Africa	Cape Town	2016-17
172*	C.B.Wishart	Zimbabwe v Namibia	Harare	2002-03
172	A.C.Gilchrist	Australia v Zimbabwe	Hobart	2003-04
172	L.Vincent	New Zealand v Zimbabwe	Bulawayo	2005
171*	G.M.Turner	New Zealand v East Africa	Birmingham	1975
171*	R.G.Sharma	India v Australia	Perth	2015-16
171	A.D.Hales	England v Pakistan	Nottingham	2016
170*	L.Ronchi	New Zealand v Sri Lanka	Dunedin	2014-15
170	S.D.Hope	West Indies v Ireland	Dublin	2019

The highest for Afghanistan is 131* by Mohammad Shahzad (v Z, Sharjah, 2015-16).

HUNDRED ON DEBUT

D.L.Amiss	103	England v Australia	Manchester	1972
D.L.Haynes	148	West Indies v Australia	St John's	1977-78
A.Flower	115*	Zimbabwe v Sri Lanka	New Plymouth	1991-92
Salim Elahi	102*	Pakistan v Sri Lanka	Gujranwala	1995-96
M.J.Guptill	122*	New Zealand v West Indies	Auckland	2008-09
C.A.Ingram	124	South Africa v Zimbabwe	Bloemfontein	2010-11
R.J.Nicol	108*	New Zealand v Zimbabwe	Harare	2011-12
P.J.Hughes	112	Australia v Sri Lanka	Melbourne	2012-13
M.J.Lumb	106	England v West Indies	North Sound	2013-14
M.S.Chapman	124*	Hong Kong v UAE	Dubai	2015-16
K.L.Rahul	100*	India v Zimbabwe	Harare	2016
T.Bavuma	113	South Africa v Ireland	Benoni	2016-17
Imam-ul-Haq	100	Pakistan v Sri Lanka	Abu Dhabi	2017-18
R.R.Hendricks	102	South Africa v Sri Lanka	Pallekele	2018
Abid Ali	112	Pakistan v Australia	Dubai, DSC	2018-19
Rahmanullah Gurbaz	127	Afghanistan v Ireland	Abu Dhabi	2020-21

Shahid Afridi scored 102 for P v SL, Nairobi, 1996-97, in his second match having not batted in his first.

Fastest 100	31 balls	A.B.de Villiers (149)	SA v WI	Johannesburg	2014-15
Fastest 50	16 balls	A.B.de Villiers (149)	SA v WI	Johannesburg	2014-15

16 HUNDREDS

		Inns	100	E	A	SA	WI	NZ	I	P	SL	Z	B	Ire	Afg	Ass
S.R.Tendulkar	I	452	49	2	9	5	4	5	–	5	8	5	1	–	–	5
V.Kohli	I	242	43	3	8	4	9	5	–	2	8	1	3	–	–	–
R.T.Ponting	A	365	30*	5	–	2	2	6	6	1	4	1	1	–	–	1
R.G.Sharma	I	217	29	2	8	3	3	1	–	2	6	1	3	–	–	–
S.T.Jayasuriya	SL	433	28	4	2	–	1	5	7	3	–	1	4	–	–	1
H.M.Amla	SA	178	27	2	1	–	5	2	2	3	5	3	2	1	–	1
A.B.de Villiers	SA	218	25	2	1	–	5	1	6	3	2	3	1	–	–	1
C.H.Gayle	WI	294	25	4	–	3	–	2	4	3	1	3	1	–	–	4
K.C.Sangakkara	SL	380	25	4	2	2	–	2	6	2	–	–	5	–	–	2
S.C.Ganguly	I	300	22	1	1	3	–	3	–	2	4	3	1	–	–	4
T.M.Dilshan	SL	303	22	2	1	2	–	3	4	2	–	2	4	–	–	2
L.R.P.L.Taylor	NZ	216	21	5	2	1	1	–	3	3	2	2	2	–	–	–
H.H.Gibbs	SA	240	21	2	3	–	5	2	2	2	1	1	2	1	–	1
Saeed Anwar	P	244	20	–	1	–	2	4	4	–	7	2	–	–	–	–
B.C.Lara	WI	289	19	1	3	3	–	2	–	5	2	1	1	–	–	1
D.P.M.D.Jayawardena	SL	418	19*	5	–	1	3	4	2	–	1	1	1	–	1	1
D.A.Warner	A	126	18	1	–	4	–	2	3	3	3	–	1	–	1	–
M.E.Waugh	A	236	18	1	–	2	3	3	3	1	1	3	–	–	–	1
A.J.Finch	A	128	17	7	–	2	–	–	4	2	1	–	–	–	–	1
S.Dhawan	I	136	17	–	4	3	2	–	–	1	4	1	–	1	–	1
D.L.Haynes	WI	237	17	2	6	–	–	2	2	4	1	–	–	–	–	–
J.H.Kallis	SA	314	17	1	1	–	4	3	2	1	3	1	–	–	–	1
J.E.Root	E	140	16	–	–	2	4	3	3	1	2	1	–	–	–	–
M.J.Guptill	NZ	180	16	2	1	2	2	–	1	1	2	2	3	–	–	–
N.J.Astle	NZ	217	16	2	1	1	1	–	5	2	–	3	–	–	–	1
A.C.Gilchrist	A	279	16*	2	–	2	–	2	1	1	6	1	–	–	–	1

* = Includes hundred scored against multi-national side.

The most for Zimbabwe is 11 by B.R.M.Taylor (198 innings), for Bangladesh 13 by Tamim Iqbal (208), for Ireland 12 by P.R.Stirling (122), and for Afghanistan 6 by Mohammad Shahzad (84).

HIGHEST PARTNERSHIP FOR EACH WICKET

1st	365	J.D.Campbell/S.D.Hope	West Indies v Ireland	Dublin	2019
2nd	372	C.H.Gayle/M.N.Samuels	West Indies v Zimbabwe	Canberra	2014-15
3rd	258	D.M.Bravo/D.Ramdin	West Indies v Bangladesh	Basseterre	2014
4th	275*	M.Azharuddin/A.Jadeja	India v Zimbabwe	Cuttack	1997-98

5th	256*	D.A.Miller/J.P.Duminy			South Africa v Zimbabwe	Hamilton		2014-15
6th	267*	G.D.Elliott/L.Ronchi			New Zealand v Sri Lanka	Dunedin		2014-15
7th	177	J.C.Buttler/A.U.Rashid			England v New Zealand	Birmingham		2015
8th	138*	J.M.Kemp/A.J.Hall			South Africa v India	Cape Town		2006-07
9th	132	A.D.Mathews/S.L.Malinga			Sri Lanka v Australia	Melbourne		2010-11
10th	106*	I.V.A.Richards/M.A.Holding			West Indies v England	Manchester		1984

BOWLING RECORDS

200 WICKETS IN A CAREER

		LOI	Balls	R	W	Avge	Best	5w	R/Over
M.Muralitharan	SL/Asia/ICC	350	18811	12326	**534**	23.08	7-30	10	3.93
Wasim Akram	P	356	18186	11812	**502**	23.52	5-15	6	3.89
Waqar Younis	P	262	12698	9919	**416**	23.84	7-36	13	4.68
W.P.J.U.C.Vaas	SL/Asia	322	15775	11014	**400**	27.53	8-19	4	4.18
Shahid Afridi	P/Asia/ICC	398	17620	13632	**395**	34.51	7-12	9	4.62
S.M.Pollock	SA/Afr/ICC	303	15712	9631	**393**	24.50	6-35	5	3.67
G.D.McGrath	A/ICC	250	12970	8391	**381**	22.02	7-15	7	3.88
B.Lee	A	221	11185	8877	**380**	23.36	5-22	9	4.76
S.L.Malinga	SL	226	10936	9760	**338**	28.87	6-38	8	5.35
A.Kumble	I/Asia	271	14496	10412	**337**	30.89	6-12	2	4.30
S.T.Jayasuriya	SL	445	14874	11871	**323**	36.75	6-29	4	4.78
J.Srinath	I	229	11935	8847	**315**	28.08	5-23	3	4.44
D.L.Vettori	NZ/ICC	295	14060	9674	**305**	31.71	5- 7	2	4.12
S.K.Warne	A/ICC	194	10642	7541	**293**	25.73	5-33	1	4.25
Saqlain Mushtaq	P	169	8770	6275	**288**	21.78	5-20	6	4.29
A.B.Agarkar	I	191	9484	8021	**288**	27.85	6-42	2	5.07
Z.Khan	I/Asia	200	10097	8301	**282**	29.43	5-42	1	4.93
J.H.Kallis	SA/Afr/ICC	328	10750	8680	**273**	31.79	5-30	2	4.84
A.A.Donald	SA	164	8561	5926	**272**	21.78	6-23	2	4.15
Mashrafe Mortaza	B/Asia	220	10922	8893	**270**	32.93	6-26	1	4.88
J.M.Anderson	E	194	9584	7861	**269**	29.22	5-23	2	4.92
Abdul Razzaq	P/Asia	265	10941	8564	**269**	31.83	6-35	3	4.69
Harbhajan Singh	I/Asia	236	12479	8973	**269**	33.35	5-31	3	4.31
M.Ntini	SA/ICC	173	8687	6559	**266**	24.65	6-22	4	4.53
Shakib Al Hasan	B	209	10650	7907	**266**	29.72	5-29	2	4.45
Kapil Dev	I	225	11202	6945	**253**	27.45	5-43	1	3.72
Shoaib Akhtar	P/Asia/ICC	163	7764	6169	**247**	24.97	6-16	4	4.76
K.D.Mills	NZ	170	8230	6485	**240**	27.02	5-25	1	4.72
M.G.Johnson	A	153	7489	6038	**239**	25.26	6-31	3	4.83
H.H.Streak	Z/Afr	189	9468	7129	**239**	29.82	5-32	1	4.51
D.Gough	E/ICC	159	8470	6209	**235**	26.42	5-44	2	4.39
C.A.Walsh	WI	205	10822	6918	**227**	30.47	5- 1	1	3.83
C.E.L.Ambrose	WI	176	9353	5429	**225**	24.12	5-17	4	3.48
Abdur Razzak	B	153	7965	6065	**207**	29.29	5-29	4	4.56
C.J.McDermott	A	138	7460	5018	**203**	24.71	5-44	1	4.03
C.Z.Harris	NZ	250	10667	7613	**203**	37.50	5-42	1	4.28
C.L.Cairns	NZ/ICC	215	8168	6594	**201**	32.80	5-42	1	4.84

The most wickets for Ireland is 114 by K.J.O'Brien (152 matches) and for Afghanistan 140 by Rashid Khan (74).

BEST FIGURES IN AN INNINGS

8-19	W.P.J.U.C.Vaas	Sri Lanka v Zimbabwe	Colombo (SSC)	2001-02
7-12	Shahid Afridi	Pakistan v West Indies	Providence	2013
7-15	G.D.McGrath	Australia v Namibia	Potchefstroom	2002-03
7-18	Rashid Khan	Afghanistan v West Indies	Gros Islet	2017
7-20	A.J.Bichel	Australia v England	Port Elizabeth	2002-03
7-30	M.Muralitharan	Sri Lanka v India	Sharjah	2000-01
7-33	T.G.Southee	New Zealand v England	Wellington	2014-15
7-34	T.A.Boult	New Zealand v West Indies	Christchurch	2017-18
7-36	Waqar Younis	Pakistan v England	Leeds	2001
7-37	Aqib Javed	Pakistan v India	Sharjah	1991-92
7-45	Imran Tahir	South Africa v West Indies	Basseterre	2016
7-51	W.W.Davis	West Indies v Australia	Leeds	1983

6- 4	S.T.R.Binny	India v Bangladesh	Dhaka	2014
6-12	A.Kumble	India v West Indies	Calcutta	1993-94
6-13	B.A.W.Mendis	Sri Lanka v India	Karachi	2008
6-14	G.J.Gilmour	Australia v England	Leeds	1975
6-14	Imran Khan	Pakistan v India	Sharjah	1984-85
6-14	M.F.Maharoof	Sri Lanka v West Indies	Mumbai	2006-07
6-15	C.E.H.Croft	West Indies v England	Kingstown	1980-81
6-16	Shoaib Akhtar	Pakistan v New Zealand	Karachi	2001-02
6-16	K.Rabada	South Africa v Bangladesh	Dhaka	2015
6-16	S.Lamichhane	Nepal v USA	Kirtipur	2019-20
6-18	Azhar Mahmood	Pakistan v West Indies	Sharjah	1999-00
6-19	H.K.Olonga	Zimbabwe v England	Cape Town	1999-00
6-19	S.E.Bond	New Zealand v Zimbabwe	Harare	2005
6-20	B.C.Strang	Zimbabwe v Bangladesh	Nairobi	1997-98
6-20	A.D.Mathews	Sri Lanka v India	Colombo (RPS)	2009-10
6-22	F.H.Edwards	West Indies v Zimbabwe	Harare	2003-04
6-22	M.Ntini	South Africa v Australia	Cape Town	2005-06
6-23	A.A.Donald	South Africa v Kenya	Nairobi	1996-97
6-23	A.Nehra	India v England	Durban	2002-03
6-23	S.E.Bond	New Zealand v Australia	Port Elizabeth	2002-03
6-24	Imran Tahir	South Africa v Zimbabwe	Bloemfontein	2018-19
6-25	S.B.Styris	New Zealand v West Indies	Port of Spain	2002
6-25	W.P.J.U.C.Vaas	Sri Lanka v Bangladesh	Pietermaritzburg	2002-03
6-25	Kuldeep Yadav	India v England	Nottingham	2018
6-26	Waqar Younis	Pakistan v Sri Lanka	Sharjah	1989-90
6-26	Mashrafe Mortaza	Bangladesh v Kenya	Nairobi	2006
6-26	Rubel Hossain	Bangladesh v New Zealand	Dhaka	2013-14
6-26	Yasir Shah	Pakistan v Zimbabwe	Harare	2015-16
6-27	Naved-ul-Hasan	Pakistan v India	Jamshedpur	2004-05
6-27	C.R.D.Fernando	Sri Lanka v England	Colombo (RPS)	2007-08
6-27	M.Kartik	India v Australia	Mumbai	2007-08
6-27	K.A.J.Roach	West Indies v Netherlands	Delhi	2010-11
6-27	S.P.Narine	West Indies v South Africa	Providence	2016
6-28	H.K.Olonga	Zimbabwe v Kenya	Bulawayo	2002-03
6-28	J.H.Davey	Scotland v Afghanistan	Abu Dhabi	2014-15
6-28	M.A.Starc	Australia v New Zealand	Auckland	2014-15
6-29	B.P.Patterson	West Indies v India	Nagpur	1987-88
6-29	S.T.Jayasuriya	Sri Lanka v England	Moratuwa	1992-93
6-29	B.A.W.Mendis	Sri Lanka v Zimbabwe	Harare	2008-09
6-29	M.K.P.A.D.Perera	Sri Lanka v South Africa	Colombo (RPS)	2018
6-30	Waqar Younis	Pakistan v New Zealand	Auckland	1993-94
6-31	P.D.Collingwood	England v Bangladesh	Nottingham	2005
6-31	M.G.Johnson	Australia v Sri Lanka	Pallekele	2011
6-33	T.A.Boult	New Zealand v India	Hamilton	2016-17
6-34	Zahoor Khan	UAE v Ireland	Dubai (ICCA)	2016-17
6-35	S.M.Pollock	South Africa v West Indies	East London	1998-99
6-35	Abdul Razzaq	Pakistan v Bangladesh	Dhaka	2001-02
6-35	Shaheen Shah Afridi	Pakistan v Bangladesh	Lord's	2019

The best figures for Ireland are 6-55 by P.R.Stirling (v Afg, Greater Noida, 2016-17).

HAT-TRICKS

Jalaluddin	Pakistan v Australia	Hyderabad	1982-83
B.A.Reid	Australia v New Zealand	Sydney	1985-86
C.Sharma	India v New Zealand	Nagpur	1987-88
Wasim Akram	Pakistan v West Indies	Sharjah	1989-90
Wasim Akram	Pakistan v Australia	Sharjah	1989-90
Kapil Dev	India v Sri Lanka	Calcutta	1990-91
Aqib Javed	Pakistan v India	Sharjah	1991-92
D.K.Morrison	New Zealand v India	Napier	1993-94
Waqar Younis	Pakistan v New Zealand	East London	1994-95
Saqlain Mushtaq	Pakistan v Zimbabwe	Peshawar	1996-97
E.A.Brandes	Zimbabwe v England	Harare	1996-97
A.M.Stuart	Australia v Pakistan	Melbourne	1996-97
Saqlain Mushtaq	Pakistan v Zimbabwe	The Oval	1999

W.P.J.U.C.Vaas	Sri Lanka v Zimbabwe	Colombo (SSC)	2001-02
Mohammad Sami	Pakistan v West Indies	Sharjah	2001-02
W.P.J.U.C.Vaas[1]	Sri Lanka v Bangladesh	Pietermaritzburg	2002-03
B.Lee	Australia v Kenya	Durban	2002-03
J.M.Anderson	England v Pakistan	The Oval	2003
S.J.Harmison	England v India	Nottingham	2004
C.K.Langeveldt	South Africa v West Indies	Bridgetown	2004-05
Shahadat Hossain	Bangladesh v Zimbabwe	Harare	2006
J.E.Taylor	West Indies v Australia	Mumbai	2006-07
S.E.Bond	New Zealand v Australia	Hobart	2006-07
S.L.Malinga[2]	Sri Lanka v South Africa	Providence	2006-07
A.Flintoff	England v West Indies	St Lucia	2008-09
M.F.Maharoof	Sri Lanka v India	Dambulla	2010
Abdur Razzak	Bangladesh v Zimbabwe	Dhaka	2010-11
K.A.J.Roach	West Indies v Netherlands	Delhi	2010-11
S.L.Malinga	Sri Lanka v Kenya	Colombo (RPS)	2010-11
S.L.Malinga	Sri Lanka v Australia	Colombo (RPS)	2011
D.T.Christian	Australia v Sri Lanka	Melbourne	2011-12
N.L.T.C.Perera	Sri Lanka v Pakistan	Colombo (RPS)	2012
C.J.McKay	Australia v England	Cardiff	2013
Rubel Hossain	Bangladesh v New Zealand	Dhaka	2013-14
P.Utseya	Zimbabwe v South Africa	Harare	2014
Taijul Islam	Bangladesh v Zimbabwe	Dhaka	2014-15
S.T.Finn	England v Australia	Melbourne	2014-15
J.P.Duminy	South Africa v Sri Lanka	Sydney	2014-15
K.Rabada	South Africa v Bangladesh	Mirpur	2015
J.P.Faulkner	Australia v Sri Lanka	Colombo (RPS)	2016
Taskin Ahmed	Bangladesh v Sri Lanka	Dambulla	2016-17
P.W.H.de Silva	Sri Lanka v Zimbabwe	Galle	2017
Kuldeep Yadav	India v Australia	Kolkata	2017-18
D.S.K.Madushanka	Sri Lanka v Bangladesh	Dhaka	2017-18
Imran Tahir	South Africa v Zimbabwe	Bloemfontein	2018-19
T.A.Boult	New Zealand v Pakistan	Abu Dhabi	2018-19
Mohammed Shami	India v Afghanistan	Southampton	2019
T.A.Boult	New Zealand v Australia	Lord's	2019
Kuldeep Yadav	India v West Indies	Visakhapatnam	2019-20

[1] The first three balls of the match. Took four wickets in opening over (W W W 4 wide W 0).
[2] Four wickets in four balls.

WICKET-KEEPING RECORDS

150 DISMISSALS IN A CAREER

Total			LOI	Ct	St
482‡‡	K.C.Sangakkara	Sri Lanka/Asia/ICC	360	384	98
472‡	A.C.Gilchrist	Australia/ICC	287	417	55
444	M.S.Dhoni	India/Asia	350	321	123
424	M.V.Boucher	South Africa/Africa	295	402	22
287‡	Moin Khan	Pakistan	219	214	73
242‡‡	B.B.McCullum	New Zealand	185	227	15
233	I.A.Healy	Australia	168	194	39
230	Mushfiqur Rahim	Bangladesh	221	184	46
220‡	Rashid Latif	Pakistan	166	182	38
209	J.C.Buttler	England	145	177	32
206‡	R.S.Kaluwitharana	Sri Lanka	187	131	75
204‡	P.J.L.Dujon	West Indies	169	183	21
189	R.D.Jacobs	West Indies	147	160	29
188	D.Ramdin	West Indies	139	181	7
187	Kamran Akmal	Pakistan	154	156	31
181	B.J.Haddin	Australia	126	170	11
173	Q.de Kock	South Africa	121	164	9
165	D.J.Richardson	South Africa	122	148	17

290

Total				*LOI*	*Ct*	*St*
165†‡	A.Flower	Zimbabwe		213	133	32
163†‡	A.J.Stewart	England		170	148	15
154‡	N.R.Mongia	India		140	110	44

† Excluding catches taken in the field. ‡ Excluding matches when not wicket-keeper.

The most for Ireland is 96 by N.J.O'Brien (103 matches) and for Afghanistan 88 by Mohammad Shahzad (84).

SIX DISMISSALS IN AN INNINGS

6	(6ct)	A.C.Gilchrist	Australia v South Africa	Cape Town	1999-00
6	(6ct)	A.J.Stewart	England v Zimbabwe	Manchester	2000
6	(5ct/1st)	R.D.Jacobs	West Indies v Sri Lanka	Colombo (RPS)	2001-02
6	(6ct)	A.C.Gilchrist	Australia v England	Sydney	2002-03
6	(6ct)	A.C.Gilchrist	Australia v Namibia	Potchefstroom	2002-03
6	(6ct)	A.C.Gilchrist	Australia v Sri Lanka	Colombo (RPS)	2003-04
6	(6ct)	M.V.Boucher	South Africa v Pakistan	Cape Town	2006-07
6	(5ct/1st)	M.S.Dhoni	India v England	Leeds	2007
6	(6ct)	A.C.Gilchrist	Australia v India	Baroda	2007-08
6	(5ct/1st)	A.C.Gilchrist	Australia v India	Sydney	2007-08
6	(6ct)	M.J.Prior	England v South Africa	Nottingham	2008
6	(6ct)	J.C.Buttler	England v South Africa	The Oval	2013
6	(6ct)	M.H.Cross	Scotland v Canada	Christchurch	2013-14
6	(5ct/1st)	Q.de Kock	South Africa v New Zealand	Mt Maunganui	2014-15
6	(6ct)	Sarfraz Ahmed	Pakistan v South Africa	Auckland	2014-15

FIELDING RECORDS
100 CATCHES IN A CAREER

Total			*LOI*	*Total*			*LOI*
218	D.P.M.D.Jayawardena	Sri Lanka/Asia	448	120	B.C.Lara	West Indies/ICC	299
160	R.T.Ponting	Australia/ICC	375	118	T.M.Dilshan	Sri Lanka	330
156	M.Azharuddin	India	334	113	Inzamam-ul-Haq	Pakistan/Asia	378
140	S.R.Tendulkar	India	463	111	S.R.Waugh	Australia	325
139	L.R.P.L.Taylor	New Zealand	232	109	R.S.Mahanama	Sri Lanka	213
133	S.P.Fleming	New Zealand/ICC	280	108	P.D.Collingwood	England	197
131	J.H.Kallis	South Africa/Africa/ICC	328	108	M.E.Waugh	Australia	244
130	Younus Khan	Pakistan	265	108	H.H.Gibbs	South Africa	248
130	M.Muralitharan	Sri Lanka/Asia/ICC	350	108	S.M.Pollock	South Africa/Africa/ICC	303
129	V.Kohli	India	251	106	M.J.Clarke	Australia	245
127	A.R.Border	Australia	273	105	M.E.K.Hussey	Australia	185
127	Shahid Afridi	Pakistan/Asia/ICC	398	105	G.C.Smith	South Africa/Africa	197
124	C.H.Gayle	West Indies/ICC	301	105	J.N.Rhodes	South Africa	245
124	R.S.Dravid	India/Asia/ICC	344	102	S.K.Raina	India	226
123	S.T.Jayasuriya	Sri Lanka/Asia	445	101	I.V.A.Richards	West Indies	187
120	C.L.Hooper	West Indies	227	100	S.C.Ganguly	India/Asia	311

The most for Zimbabwe is 86 by G.W.Flower (221), for Bangladesh 64 by Mahmudullah (191), for Ireland 67 by K.J.O'Brien (152), and for Afghanistan 56 by Mohammad Nabi (127).

FIVE CATCHES IN AN INNINGS

5	J.N.Rhodes	South Africa v West Indies	Bombay (BS)	1993-94

APPEARANCE RECORDS – 250 MATCHES

463	S.R.Tendulkar	India		295	M.V.Boucher	South Africa/Africa
448	D.P.M.D.Jayawardena	Sri Lanka/Asia		295	D.L.Vettori	New Zealand/ICC
445	S.T.Jayasuriya	Sri Lanka/Asia		288	Mohammad Yousuf	Pakistan/Asia
404	K.C.Sangakkara	Sri Lanka/Asia/ICC		287	A.C.Gilchrist	Australia/ICC
398	Shahid Afridi	Pakistan/Asia/ICC		287	Shoaib Malik	Pakistan
378	Inzamam-ul-Haq	Pakistan/Asia		283	Salim Malik	Pakistan
375	R.T.Ponting	Australia/ICC		280	S.P.Fleming	New Zealand/ICC
356	Wasim Akram	Pakistan		273	A.R.Border	Australia
350	M.S.Dhoni	India/Asia		271	A.Kumble	India/Asia
350	M.Muralitharan	Sri Lanka/Asia/ICC		269	A.Ranatunga	Sri Lanka
344	R.S.Dravid	India/Asia/ICC		268	M.S.Atapattu	Sri Lanka
334	M.Azharuddin	India		268	S.Chanderpaul	West Indies
330	T.M.Dilshan	Sri Lanka		267	Abdul Razzaq	Pakistan/Asia
328	J.H.Kallis	South Africa/Africa/ICC		265	Younus Khan	Pakistan
325	S.R.Waugh	Australia		262	Waqar Younis	Pakistan
322	W.P.J.U.C.Vaas	Sri Lanka/Asia		260	B.B.McCullum	New Zealand
311	S.C.Ganguly	India/Asia		251	V.Kohli	India
308	P.A.de Silva	Sri Lanka		251	V.Sehwag	India/Asia/ICC
304	Yuvraj Singh	India/Asia		250	C.Z.Harris	New Zealand
303	S.M.Pollock	South Africa/Africa/ICC		250	Ijaz Ahmed	Pakistan
301	C.H.Gayle	West Indies/ICC		250	G.D.McGrath	Australia/ICC
299	B.C.Lara	West Indies/ICC				

The most for England is 219 by E.J.G.Morgan, for Zimbabwe 221 by G.W.Flower, for Bangladesh 221 by Mushfiqur Rahim, for Ireland 152 by K.J.O'Brien, and for Afghanistan 127 by Mohammad Nabi.

The most consecutive appearances is 185 by S.R.Tendulkar for India (Apr 1990-Apr 1998).

100 MATCHES AS CAPTAIN

LOI			W	L	T	NR	% Won (exc NR)
230	R.T.Ponting	Australia/ICC	165	51	2	12	75.68
218	S.P.Fleming	New Zealand	98	106	1	13	47.80
200	M.S.Dhoni	India	110	74	5	11	58.20
193	A.Ranatunga	Sri Lanka	89	95	1	8	48.10
178	A.R.Border	Australia	107	67	1	3	61.14
174	M.Azharuddin	India	90	76	2	6	53.57
150	G.C.Smith	South Africa/Africa	92	51	1	6	63.88
147	S.C.Ganguly	India/Asia	76	66	–	5	53.52
139	Imran Khan	Pakistan	75	59	1	4	55.55
138	W.J.Cronje	South Africa	99	35	1	3	73.33
129	D.P.M.D.Jayawardena	Sri Lanka	71	49	1	8	58.67
125	B.C.Lara	West Indies	59	59	–	7	50.42
120	E.J.G.Morgan	England	72	39	2	7	63.71
118	S.T.Jayasuriya	Sri Lanka	66	47	2	3	57.39
113	W.T.S.Porterfield	Ireland	50	55	2	6	46.72
109	Wasim Akram	Pakistan	66	41	2	–	60.55
106	A.D.Mathews	Sri Lanka	49	51	1	5	48.51
106	S.R.Waugh	Australia	67	35	3	1	63.80
105	I.V.A.Richards	West Indies	67	36	–	2	65.04
103	A.B.de Villers	South Africa	59	39	1	4	59.59

The most for Zimbabwe is 86 by A.D.R.Campbell, for Bangladesh 88 by Mashrafe Mortaza, and for Afghanistan 59 by Asghar Afghan.

150 LOI UMPIRING APPEARANCES

211	Alim Dar	Pakistan	16.02.2000	to	03.11.2020
209	R.E.Koertzen	South Africa	09.12.1992	to	09.06.2010
200	B.F.Bowden	New Zealand	23.03.1995	to	06.02.2016
181	S.A.Bucknor	West Indies	18.03.1989	to	29.03.2009
174	D.J.Harper	Australia	14.01.1994	to	19.03.2011
174	S.J.A.Taufel	Australia	13.01.1999	to	02.09.2012
172	D.R.Shepherd	England	09.06.1983	to	12.07.2005
154	R.B.Tiffin	Zimbabwe	25.10.1992	to	22.07.2018

ENGLAND TWENTY20 INTERNATIONALS
CAREER RECORDS

These records, complete to 11 March 2021, include all players registered for county cricket for the 2021 season at the time of going to press.

BATTING AND FIELDING

	M	I	NO	HS	Runs	Avge	100	50	Ct/St
M.M.Ali	34	31	8	72*	392	17.04	–	2	8
J.M.Anderson	19	4	3	1*	1	1.00	–	–	3
J.C.Archer	7	–	–	–	–	–	–	–	–
J.M.Bairstow	46	40	7	86*	932	28.24	–	6	33
J.T.Ball	2	–	–	–	–	–	–	–	1
T.Banton	9	9	–	71	205	22.77	–	1	6
G.J.Batty	1	1	–	4	4	4.00	–	–	–
S.W.Billings†	29	26	4	87	387	17.59	–	2	16/1
R.S.Bopara	38	35	10	65*	711	28.44	–	3	7
S.G.Borthwick	1	1	–	14	14	14.00	–	–	1
T.T.Bresnan	34	22	9	47*	216	16.61	–	–	10
D.R.Briggs	7	1	1	0*	0	–	–	–	1
S.C.J.Broad	56	26	10	18*	118	7.37	–	–	21
P.R.Brown	4	1	1	4*	4	–	–	–	2
J.C.Buttler	74	66	13	77*	1551	29.26	–	10	31/5
A.N.Cook	4	4	–	26	61	15.25	–	–	1
M.S.Crane	2	–	–	–	–	–	–	–	–
S.M.Curran	8	5	1	24	43	10.75	–	–	–
T.K.Curran	27	11	7	14*	54	13.50	–	–	8
S.M.Davies	5	5	–	33	102	20.40	–	–	2/1
L.A.Dawson	6	2	1	10	17	17.00	–	–	2
J.L.Denly	13	12	2	30	125	12.50	–	–	4
J.W.Dernbach	34	7	2	12	24	4.80	–	–	8
B.M.Duckett	1	1	–	9	9	9.00	–	–	1
S.T.Finn	21	3	3	8*	14	–	–	–	6
B.T.Foakes	1	–	–	–	–	–	–	–	1
L.Gregory	8	6	1	15	35	7.00	–	–	–
H.F.Gurney	2	–	–	–	–	–	–	–	–
A.D.Hales	60	60	7	116*	1664	31.01	1	8	32
C.J.Jordan	55	32	15	36	247	14.52	–	–	29
L.S.Livingstone	2	2	–	16	16	8.00	–	–	–
S.Mahmood	6	2	1	4	7	7.00	–	–	1
D.J.Malan	19	19	3	103*	855	53.43	1	9	4
S.C.Meaker	2	–	–	–	–	–	–	–	1
T.S.Mills†	4	1	–	0	0	0.00	–	–	1
E.J.G.Morgan	97	94	19	91	2278	30.37	–	14	41
M.W.Parkinson	2	–	–	–	–	–	–	–	–
S.D.Parry	5	1	–	1	1	1.00	–	–	2
S.R.Patel	18	14	2	67	189	15.75	–	1	3
L.E.Plunkett	22	11	4	18	42	6.00	–	–	7
A.U.Rashid	52	18	10	9*	56	7.00	–	–	12
J.E.Root	32	30	5	90*	893	35.72	–	5	18
J.J.Roy	38	38	–	78	890	23.42	–	5	5
B.A.Stokes	29	25	6	47*	358	18.84	–	–	14
J.M.Vince	12	12	–	59	340	28.33	–	1	5
D.J.Willey	28	19	7	29*	166	13.83	–	–	12
C.R.Woakes	8	7	4	37	93	30.33	–	–	1
M.A.Wood	11	2	2	51*	10	–	–	–	–
L.J.Wright	51	45	5	99*	759	18.97	–	4	14

BOWLING

	O	M	R	W	Avge	Best	4wI	R/Over
M.M.Ali	73.2	0	630	17	37.05	2-21	–	8.59
J.M.Anderson	70.2	1	552	18	30.66	3-23	–	7.84
J.C.Archer	27	0	216	7	30.85	2-29	–	8.00
J.T.Ball	7	0	83	2	41.50	1-39	–	11.85
G.J.Batty	3	0	17	0	–	–	–	5.66
R.S.Bopara	53.4	1	387	16	24.18	4-10	1	7.21
S.G.Borthwick	4	0	15	1	15.00	1-15	–	3.75
T.T.Bresnan	110.3	1	887	24	36.95	3-10	–	8.02
D.R.Briggs	18	0	199	5	39.80	2-25	–	11.05
S.C.J.Broad	195.3	2	1491	65	22.93	4-24	1	7.62
P.R.Brown	13	0	128	3	42.66	1-29	–	9.84
M.S.Crane	8	0	62	1	62.00	1-38	–	7.75
S.M.Curran	27	0	240	9	26.66	3-28	–	8.88
T.K.Curran	88	1	812	26	31.23	4-36	1	9.22
L.A.Dawson	20	0	152	5	30.40	3-27	–	7.60
J.L.Denly	12	0	93	7	13.28	4-19	1	7.75
J.W.Dernbach	117	1	1020	39	26.15	4-22	1	8.71
S.T.Finn	80	0	583	27	21.59	3-16	–	7.28
L.Gregory	11	0	92	1	92.00	1-10	–	8.36
H.F.Gurney	8	0	55	3	18.33	2-26	–	6.87
C.J.Jordan	192	0	1671	66	25.31	4- 6	2	8.70
S.Mahmood	18	0	190	3	63.33	1-20	–	10.55
D.J.Malan	2	0	27	1	27.00	1-27	–	13.50
S.C.Meaker	7.5	0	70	2	35.00	1-28	–	8.93
T.S.Mills	16	0	116	3	38.66	1-27	–	7.25
M.W.Parkinson	6	0	61	5	12.20	4-47	1	10.16
S.D.Parry	16	0	138	3	46.00	2-33	–	8.62
S.R.Patel	42	0	321	7	45.85	2- 6	–	7.64
L.E.Plunkett	79.2	1	627	25	25.08	3-21	–	7.90
A.U.Rashid	175	1	1316	51	25.80	3-11	–	7.52
J.E.Root	14	0	139	6	23.16	2- 9	–	9.92
B.A.Stokes	69.4	1	611	16	38.18	3-26	–	8.77
D.J.Willey	92.5	0	761	34	22.38	4- 7	1	8.19
C.R.Woakes	27	0	253	7	36.14	2-40	–	9.37
M.A.Wood	39.3	0	360	18	20.00	3- 9	–	9.11
L.J.Wright	55	0	465	18	25.83	2-24	–	8.45

† S.W.Billings and T.S.Mills also played one game for an ICC World XI v West Indies at Lord's in 2018.

From 1 January 2019, the ICC granted official IT20 status to all 20-over matches between its 105 members. As a result, there has been a vast increase in the number of games played, many featuring very minor nations. In the records that follow, except for the first-ranked record, only those IT20s featuring a nation that has also played a full LOI are listed.

MATCH RESULTS

2004-05 to 11 March 2021

	Opponents	Matches	Won E	A	SA	WI	NZ	I	P	SL	Z	B	Ire	Afg	Ass	Tied	NR
England	Australia	19	8	10	–	–	–	–	–	–	–	–	–	–	–	–	1
	South Africa	21	11	–	9	–	–	–	–	–	–	–	–	–	–	–	1
	West Indies	18	7	–	–	11	–	–	–	–	–	–	–	–	–	–	–
	New Zealand	21	12	–	–	–	7	–	–	–	–	–	–	–	–	1	1
	India	14	7	–	–	–	–	7	–	–	–	–	–	–	–	–	–
	Pakistan	18	11	–	–	–	–	–	5	–	–	–	–	–	–	1	1
	Sri Lanka	9	5	–	–	–	–	–	–	4	–	–	–	–	–	–	–
	Zimbabwe	1	1	–	–	–	–	–	–	–	0	–	–	–	–	–	–
	Bangladesh	0	–	–	–	–	–	–	–	–	–	0	–	–	–	–	–
	Ireland	1	0	–	–	–	–	–	–	–	–	–	0	–	–	–	1
	Afghanistan	2	2	–	–	–	–	–	–	–	–	–	–	0	–	–	–
	Associates	2	0	–	–	–	–	–	–	–	–	–	–	–	2	–	–
Australia	South Africa	21	–	13	8	–	–	–	–	–	–	–	–	–	–	–	–
	West Indies	11	–	5	–	6	–	–	–	–	–	–	–	–	–	–	–
	New Zealand	14	–	9	–	–	4	–	–	–	–	–	–	–	–	1	–
	India	23	–	9	–	–	–	13	–	–	–	–	–	–	–	–	1
	Pakistan	23	–	9	–	–	–	–	12	–	–	–	–	–	–	1	1
	Sri Lanka	16	–	8	–	–	–	–	–	8	–	–	–	–	–	–	–
	Zimbabwe	3	–	2	–	–	–	–	–	–	1	–	–	–	–	–	–
	Bangladesh	4	–	4	–	–	–	–	–	–	–	0	–	–	–	–	–
	Ireland	1	–	1	–	–	–	–	–	–	–	–	0	–	–	–	–
	Afghanistan	0	–	0	–	–	–	–	–	–	–	–	–	0	–	–	–
	Associates	1	–	1	–	–	–	–	–	–	–	–	–	–	0	–	–
S Africa	West Indies	10	–	–	6	4	–	–	–	–	–	–	–	–	–	–	–
	New Zealand	15	–	–	11	–	4	–	–	–	–	–	–	–	–	–	–
	India	15	–	–	6	–	–	9	–	–	–	–	–	–	–	–	–
	Pakistan	17	–	–	9	–	–	–	8	–	–	–	–	–	–	–	–
	Sri Lanka	13	–	–	7	–	–	–	–	5	–	–	–	–	–	1	–
	Zimbabwe	5	–	–	5	–	–	–	–	–	0	–	–	–	–	–	–
	Bangladesh	6	–	–	6	–	–	–	–	–	–	0	–	–	–	–	–
	Ireland	0	–	–	0	–	–	–	–	–	–	–	0	–	–	–	–
	Afghanistan	2	–	–	2	–	–	–	–	–	–	–	–	0	–	–	–
	Associates	2	–	–	2	–	–	–	–	–	–	–	–	–	0	–	–
W Indies	New Zealand	16	–	–	–	3	8	–	–	–	–	–	–	–	–	3	2
	India	17	–	–	–	6	–	10	–	–	–	–	–	–	–	–	1
	Pakistan	14	–	–	–	3	–	–	11	–	–	–	–	–	–	–	–
	Sri Lanka	14	–	–	–	7	–	–	–	7	–	–	–	–	–	–	–
	Zimbabwe	3	–	–	–	2	–	–	–	–	1	–	–	–	–	–	–
	Bangladesh	12	–	–	–	6	–	–	–	–	–	5	–	–	–	–	1
	Ireland	7	–	–	–	3	–	–	–	–	–	–	2	–	–	–	2
	Afghanistan	7	–	–	–	4	–	–	–	–	–	–	–	3	–	–	–
	Associates	0	–	–	–	–	–	–	–	–	–	–	–	–	0	–	–
N Zealand	India	16	–	–	–	–	8	6	–	–	–	–	–	–	–	2	–
	Pakistan	24	–	–	–	–	10	–	14	–	–	–	–	–	–	–	–
	Sri Lanka	19	–	–	–	–	10	–	–	7	–	–	–	–	–	1	1
	Zimbabwe	6	–	–	–	–	6	–	–	–	0	–	–	–	–	–	–
	Bangladesh	7	–	–	–	–	7	–	–	–	–	0	–	–	–	–	–
	Ireland	1	–	–	–	–	1	–	–	–	–	–	0	–	–	–	–
	Afghanistan	0	–	–	–	–	–	–	–	–	–	–	–	0	–	–	–
	Associates	3	–	–	–	–	3	–	–	–	–	–	–	–	0	–	–
India	Pakistan	8	–	–	–	–	–	6	1	–	–	–	–	–	–	1	–
	Sri Lanka	19	–	–	–	–	–	13	–	5	–	–	–	–	–	–	1

	Opponents	Matches	E	A	SA	WI	NZ	I	P	SL	Z	B	Ire	Afg	Ass	Tied	NR
	Zimbabwe	7	–	–	–	–	–	5	–	–	2	–	–	–	–	–	–
	Bangladesh	11	–	–	–	–	–	10	–	–	–	1	–	–	–	–	–
	Ireland	3	–	–	–	–	–	3	–	–	–	–	0	–	–	–	–
	Afghanistan	2	–	–	–	–	–	2	–	–	–	–	–	0	–	–	–
	Associates	2	–	–	–	–	–	1	–	–	–	–	–	–	0	–	1
Pakistan	Sri Lanka	21	–	–	–	–	–	–	13	8	–	–	–	–	–	–	–
	Zimbabwe	14	–	–	–	–	–	–	14	–	0	–	–	–	–	–	–
	Bangladesh	12	–	–	–	–	–	–	10	–	–	2	–	–	–	–	–
	Ireland	1	–	–	–	–	–	–	1	–	–	–	0	–	–	–	–
	Afghanistan	1	–	–	–	–	–	–	1	–	–	–	–	0	–	–	–
	Associates	7	–	–	–	–	–	–	7	–	–	–	–	–	0	–	–
Sri Lanka	Zimbabwe	3	–	–	–	–	–	–	–	3	0	–	–	–	–	–	–
	Bangladesh	11	–	–	–	–	–	–	–	7	–	4	–	–	–	–	–
	Ireland	1	–	–	–	–	–	–	–	1	–	–	0	–	–	–	–
	Afghanistan	1	–	–	–	–	–	–	–	1	–	–	–	0	–	–	–
	Associates	4	–	–	–	–	–	–	–	4	–	–	–	–	0	–	–
Zimbabwe	Bangladesh	13	–	–	–	–	–	–	–	–	4	9	–	–	–	–	–
	Ireland	3	–	–	–	–	–	–	–	–	1	–	2	–	–	–	–
	Afghanistan	9	–	–	–	–	–	–	–	–	1	–	–	8	–	–	–
	Associates	12	–	–	–	–	–	–	–	–	8	–	–	–	2	2	–
Bangladesh	Ireland	5	–	–	–	–	–	–	–	–	–	3	1	–	–	–	1
	Afghanistan	6	–	–	–	–	–	–	–	–	–	2	–	4	–	–	–
	Associates	9	–	–	–	–	–	–	–	–	–	6	–	–	3	–	–
Ireland	Afghanistan	18	–	–	–	–	–	–	–	–	–	–	3	14	–	–	1
	Associates	57	–	–	–	–	–	–	–	–	–	–	33	–	20	1	3
Afghanistan	Associates	33	–	–	–	–	–	–	–	–	–	–	–	26	7	–	–
Associates	Associates	339	–	–	–	–	–	–	–	–	–	–	–	–	326	3	10
		1126	64	71	71	55	68	85	97	60	18	32	41	55	360	19	30

MATCH RESULTS SUMMARY

	Matches	Won	Lost	Tied	NR	% Won (ex NR)
Afghanistan	81	55	25	1	0	67.90
India	137	85	45	3	4	63.90
Pakistan	160	97	58	3	2	61.39
South Africa	127	71	54	1	1	56.34
Australia	136	71	60	2	3	53.38
England	126	64	55	2	5	52.89
New Zealand	142	68	62	8	4	49.27
Sri Lanka	131	60	67	2	2	46.51
Ireland	98	41	48	2	7	45.05
West Indies	129	55	65	3	6	44.71
Bangladesh	96	32	62	0	2	34.04
Associates (v Full)	132	34	91	3	4	26.56
Zimbabwe	79	18	59	2	0	22.78

Results of games between two Associate Members and Pakistan's three IT20s v a World XI in 2017 (W2, L1) and West Indies' IT20 v an ICC World XI in 2018 (W1) are excluded from these figures.

INTERNATIONAL TWENTY20 RECORDS
(To 11 March 2021)

TEAM RECORDS
HIGHEST INNINGS TOTALS † Batting Second

278-3	Afghanistan v Ireland	Dehradun	2018-19
263-3	Australia v Sri Lanka	Pallekele	2016
260-6	Sri Lanka v Kenya	Johannesburg	2007-08
260-5	India v Sri Lanka	Indore	2017-18
252-3	Scotland v Netherlands	Dublin	2019
248-6	Australia v England	Southampton	2013

245-6	West Indies v India	Lauderhill	2016
245-5†	Australia v New Zealand	Auckland	2017-18
244-4†	India v West Indies	Lauderhill	2016
243-5	New Zealand v West Indies	Mt Maunganui	2017-18
243-6	New Zealand v Australia	Auckland	2017-18
241-6	South Africa v England	Centurion	2009-10
241-3	England v New Zealand	Napier	2019-20
240-3	Namibia v Botswana	Windhoek	2019
240-3	India v West Indies	Mumbai	2019-20
238-3	New Zealand v West Indies	Mt Maunganui	2020-21
236-6†	West Indies v South Africa	Johannesburg	2014-15
236-3	Nepal v Bhutan	Kirtipur	2019-20
233-8	Afghanistan v Ireland	Greater Noida	2016-17
233-2	Australia v Sri Lanka	Adelaide	2019-20
231-7	South Africa v West Indies	Johannesburg	2014-15
230-8†	England v South Africa	Mumbai	2015-16
229-4	South Africa v England	Mumbai	2015-16
229-2	Australia v Zimbabwe	Harare	2018
226-5†	England v South Africa	Centurion	2019-20
225-7	Ireland v Afghanistan	Abu Dhabi	2013-14

The highest total for Pakistan is 205-3 (v West Indies, Karachi, 2017-18), for Zimbabwe 200-2 (v New Zealand, Hamilton, 2011-12) and for Bangladesh is 215-5 (v Sri Lanka, Colombo (RPS), 2017-18).

LOWEST COMPLETED INNINGS TOTALS † Batting Second

21† (8.3)	Turkey v Czech Republic	Ilfov County	2019
39 (10.3)	Netherlands v Sri Lanka	Chittagong	2013-14
45† (11.5)	West Indies v England	Basseterre	2018-19
46 (12.1)	Botswana v Namibia	Kampala	2019
53 (14.3)	Nepal v Ireland	Belfast	2015
56† (18.4)	Kenya v Afghanistan	Sharjah	2013-14
60† (15.3)	New Zealand v Sri Lanka	Chittagong	2013-14
60† (13.4)	West Indies v Pakistan	Karachi	2017-18
61-8	Iran v UAE	Al Amerat	2019-20
64 (11.0)	Nepal v Oman	Al Amerat	2019-20
66-9	Cayman Islands v USA	Sandys Parish	2019
66-9	Nigeria v Ireland	Abu Dhabi	2019-20
66	Thailand v Nepal	Bangkok	2019-20
67 (17.2)	Kenya v Ireland	Belfast	2008
68† (16.4)	Ireland v West Indies	Providence	2009-10
68-8	Cayman Islands v USA	Hamilton, Ber	2019
68	Ireland v West Indies	Providence	2020
69† (17.0)	Hong Kong v Nepal	Chittagong	2013-14
69† (17.4)	Nepal v Netherlands	Amstelveen	2015
70	Bermuda v Canada	Belfast	2008
70† (15.4)	Bangladesh v New Zealand	Kolkata	2015-16
70† (12.3)	Ireland v India	Dublin	2018

The lowest total for England is 80 (v India, Colombo (RPS), 2012-13).

LARGEST RUNS MARGIN OF VICTORY

257 runs	Czech Republic beat Turkey	Ilfov County	2019
172 runs	Sri Lanka beat Kenya	Johannesburg	2007
143 runs	Pakistan beat West Indies	Karachi	2017-18
143 runs	India beat Ireland	Dublin	2018
141 runs	Nepal beat Bhutan	Kirtipur	2019-20
137 runs	England beat West Indies	Basseterre	2018-19

There have been 22 victories by ten wickets, with Austria beating Turkey by a record margin of 104 balls remaining (Ilfov County, 2019).

BATTING RECORDS
1600 RUNS IN A CAREER

Runs			M	I	NO	HS	Avge	50	R/100B
2928	V.Kohli	I	85	79	21	94*	50.48	25	138.4
2839	M.J.Guptill	NZ	99	95	7	105	32.26	19	136.2
2773	R.G.Sharma	I	108	100	15	118	32.62	25	138.7
2346	A.J.Finch	A	71	71	10	172	38.45	16	152.1
2335	Shoaib Malik	P/ICC	116	106	31	75	31.13	8	124.2
2323	Mohammad Hafeez	P	99	94	11	99*	27.98	14	121.3
2278	E.J.G.Morgan	E	97	94	19	91	30.37	14	138.9
2265	D.A.Warner	A	81	81	9	100*	31.45	19	139.7
2140	B.B.McCullum	NZ	71	70	10	123	35.66	15	136.2
2124	P.R.Stirling	Ire	78	77	6	95	29.91	18	139.2
1936	Mohammad Shahzad	Afg	65	65	3	118*	31.22	13	134.8
1934	J.P.Duminy	SA	81	75	25	96*	38.68	11	126.2
1909	L.R.P.L.Taylor	NZ	102	94	20	63	26.15	7	122.3
1889	T.M.Dilshan	SL	80	79	12	104*	28.19	14	120.5
1805	K.S.Williamson	NZ	67	65	8	95	31.66	13	125.0
1780	G.J.Maxwell	A	72	65	9	145*	31.78	12	158.9
1758	Tamim Iqbal	B/Wd	78	78	5	103*	24.08	8	116.9
1730	Babar Azam	P	47	45	9	97*	48.05	16	130.2
1724	C.Munro	NZ	65	62	7	109*	31.34	14	156.4
1690	Umar Akmal	P	84	79	14	94	26.00	8	122.7
1672	A.B.de Villiers	SA	78	75	11	79*	26.12	10	135.1
1672	K.J.O'Brien	Ire	96	89	10	124	21.16	4	135.9
1669	S.Dhawan	I	64	62	3	92	28.28	11	128.2
1662	H.Masakadza	Z	66	66	2	93*	25.96	11	117.2
1656	C.H.Gayle	WI	61	57	4	117	31.24	15	140.8
1644	A.D.Hales	E	60	60	7	116*	31.01	9	136.6
1617	M.S.Dhoni	I	98	85	42	56	37.60	2	126.1
1611	M.N.Samuels	WI	67	65	10	89*	29.29	10	116.2
1605	S.K.Raina	I	78	66	11	101	29.18	6	134.8

HIGHEST INDIVIDUAL INNINGS

Score	Balls				
172	76	A.J.Finch	A v Z	Harare	2018
162*	62	Hazratullah Zazai	Afg v Ire	Dehradun	2018-19
156	63	A.J.Finch	A v E	Southampton	2013
145*	65	G.J.Maxwell	A v SL	Pallekele	2016
127*	56	H.G.Munsey	Scot v Neth	Dublin	2019
125*	62	E.Lewis	WI v I	Kingston	2017
124*	71	S.R.Watson	A v I	Sydney	2015-16
124	62	K.J.O'Brien	Ire v HK	Al Amerat	2019-20
123	58	B.B.McCullum	NZ v B	Pallekele	2012-13
122	60	Babar Hayat	HK v Oman	Fatullah	2015-16
119	56	F.du Plessis	SA v WI	Johannesburg	2014-15
118*	67	Mohammad Shahzad	Afg v Z	Sharjah	2015-16
118	43	R.G.Sharma	I v SL	Indore	2017-18
117*	51	R.E.Levi	SA v NZ	Hamilton	2011-12
117*	68	Shaiman Anwar	UAE v PNG	Abu Dhabi	2017
117	57	C.H.Gayle	WI v SA	Johannesburg	2007-08
116*	56	B.B.McCullum	NZ v A	Christchurch	2009-10
116*	64	A.D.Hales	E v SL	Chittagong	2013-14
114*	70	M.N.van Wyk	SA v WI	Durban	2014-15
113*	55	G.J.Maxwell	A v I	Bengaluru	2018-19
111*	62	Ahmed Shehzad	P v B	Dhaka	2013-14

111*	61	R.G.Sharma	I v WI	Lucknow	2018-19
110*	51	K.L.Rahul	I v WI	Lauderhill	2016
109*	58	C.Munro	NZ v I	Rajkot	2017-18
108	51	G.D.Phillips	NZ v WI	Mt Maunganui	2020-21
107*	60	T.P.Ura	PNG v Phil	Port Moresby	2018-19
107	55	G.Malla	Nep v Bhut	Kirtipur	2019-20
106*	52	P.Khadka	Nep v Sing	Singapore	2019-20
106	66	R.G.Sharma	I v SA	Dharamsala	2015-16
105	54	M.J.Guptill	NZ v A	Auckland	2017-18
104*	57	T.M.Dilshan	SL v A	Pallekele	2011
104*	64	Mohammad Rizwan	P v SA	Lahore	2020-21
104	53	C.Munro	NZ v WI	Mt Maunganui	2017-18
103*	63	Tamim Iqbal	B v Oman	Dharamsala	2015-16
103*	58	G.J.Maxwell	A v E	Hobart	2017-18
103*	51	D.J.Malan	E v NZ	Napier	2019-20

The highest score for Zimbabwe is 94 by S.F.Mire (v P, Harare, 2018).

MOST SIXES IN AN INNINGS

16	Hazratullah Zazai (162*)	Afg v Ire	Dehradun	2018-19
14	A.J.Finch (156)	A v E	Southampton	2013
14	H.G.Munsey (127*)	Scot v Neth	Dublin	2019
13	R.E.Levi (117*)	SA v NZ	Hamilton	2011-12
12	E.Lewis (125*)	WI v I	Kingston	2017

HIGHEST PARTNERSHIP FOR EACH WICKET

1st	236	Hazratullah Zazai/Usman Ghani	Afg v Ire	Dehradun	2018-19
2nd	167	J.C.Buttler/D.J.Malan	E v SA	Cape Town	2020-21
3rd	184	D.P.Conway/G.D.Phillips	NZ v WI	Mt Maunganui	2020-21
4th	161	D.A.Warner/G.J.Maxwell	A v SA	Johannesburg	2015-16
5th	119*	Shoaib Malik/Misbah-ul-Haq	P v A	Johannesburg	2007-08
6th	101*	C.L.White/M.E.K.Hussey	A v SL	Bridgetown	2009-10
7th	92	M.P.Stoinis/D.R.Sams	A v NZ	Dunedin	2020-21
8th	80	P.L.Mommsen/S.M.Sharif	Scot v Neth	Edinburgh	2015
9th	66	D.J.Bravo/J.E.Taylor	WI v P	Dubai	2016-17
10th	38	Mohammad Adnan/Usman Ali	Saud v Qat	Al Amerat	2018-19

BOWLING RECORDS

55 WICKETS IN A CAREER

Wkts			Matches	Overs	Mdns	Runs	Avge	Best	R/Over
107	S.L.Malinga	SL	84	299.5	1	2225	20.79	5- 6	7.42
98	Shahid Afridi	P/Wd	99	361.2	4	2396	24.44	4-11	6.63
93	T.G.Southee	NZ	80	287.0	2	2422	26.04	5-18	8.43
92	Shakib Al Hasan	B	76	277.5	2	1894	20.58	5-20	6.81
89	Rashid Khan	Afg/IC	48	183.0	1	1124	12.62	5- 3	6.14
85	Umar Gul	P	60	200.3	2	1443	16.97	5- 6	7.19
85	Saeed Ajmal	P	64	238.2	2	1516	17.83	4-19	6.36
76	G.H.Dockrell	Ire	77	228.2	1	1624	21.36	4-20	7.11
69	I.S.Sodhi	NZ	55	189.3	–	1524	22.08	4-28	8.04
69	Mohammad Nabi	Afg	78	260.4	5	1871	27.11	4-10	7.17
66	B.A.W.Mendis	SL	39	147.3	5	952	14.42	6- 8	6.45
66	K.M.D.N.Kulasekara	SL	58	205.1	6	1530	23.18	4-31	7.45
66	C.J.Jordan	E	55	192.0	1	1671	25.31	4- 6	8.70
65	S.C.J.Broad	E	56	195.3	2	1491	22.93	4-24	7.62
64	D.W.Steyn	SA	47	169.1	3	1175	18.35	4- 9	6.94
63	Imran Tahir	SA/Wd	38	140.5	–	948	15.04	5-23	6.73
62	D.J.Bravo	WI	74	203.5	–	1682	27.12	4-28	8.25

Wkts			Matches	Overs	Mdns	Runs	Avge	Best	R/Over
60	M.J.Santner	NZ	52	174.2	1	1287	21.45	4-11	7.38
59	J.J.Bumrah	I	50	179.1	7	1195	20.25	3-11	6.66
59	Mohammad Amir	P	50	179.5	5	1263	21.40	4-13	7.02
59	Y.S.Chahal	I	45	175.3	1	1456	24.67	6-25	8.29
58	K.J.O'Brien	Ire	96	150.3	–	1134	19.55	4-45	7.53
58	Mustafizur Rahman	B	41	150.1	3	1191	20.53	5-22	7.93
58	N.L.McCullum	NZ	63	187.1	–	1278	22.03	4-16	6.82
56	S.Badree	WI/Wd	52	191.0	4	1180	21.07	4-15	6.17
55	W.B.Rankin	E/Ire	50	178.0	2	1219	22.16	3-16	6.84

The most wickets for Australia is 48 by S.R.Watson (58 matches) and for Zimbabwe 35 by A.G.Cremer (29 matches).

BEST FIGURES IN AN INNINGS

6- 7	D.L.Chahar	I v B	Nagpur	2019-20
6- 8	B.A.W.Mendis	SL v Z	Hambantota	2012-13
6-16	B.A.W.Mendis	SL v A	Pallekele	2011
6-25	Y.S.Chahal	I v E	Bangalore	2016-17
6-30	A.C.Agar	A v NZ	Wellington	2020-21
5- 3	H.M.R.K.B.Herath	SL v NZ	Chittagong	2013-14
5- 3	Rashid Khan	Afg v Ire	Greater Noida	2016-17
5- 4	Khizar Hayat	Malay v HK	Kuala Lumpur	2019-20
5- 6	Umar Gul	P v NZ	The Oval	2009
5- 6	Umar Gul	P v SA	Centurion	2012-13
5- 6	S.L.Malinga	SL v NZ	Pallekele	2019
5- 9	C.Viljoen	Nam v Bots	Kampala	2019
5-11	Karim Janat	Afg v WI	Lucknow	2019-20
5-13	Elias Sunny	B v Ire	Belfast	2012
5-13	Samiullah Shenwari	Afg v Ken	Sharjah	2013-14
5-14	Imad Wasim	P v WI	Dubai	2016-17
5-15	K.M.A.Paul	WI v B	Dhaka	2018-19
5-15	D.Ravu	PNG v Vanu	Apia	2019
5-15	Aamir Kaleem	Oman v Nep	Al Amerat	2019-20
5-16	Haroon Arshad	HK v Nep	Bangkok	2019-20
5-17	N.Vanua	PNG v Vanu	Apia	2019
5-17	D.Pretorius	SA v P	Lahore	2020-21
5-18	T.G.Southee	NZ v P	Auckland	2010-11
5-18	A.C.Douglas	Ber v Cay Is	Sandys Parish	2019
5-19	R.McLaren	SA v WI	North Sound	2009-10
5-19	Ahsan Malik	Neth v SA	Chittagong	2013-14
5-19	N.Nipiko	Vanu v PNG	Apia	2019
5-20	N.Odhiambo	Ken v Sc	Nairobi (Gym)	2009-10
5-20	Shakib Al Hasan	B v WI	Dhaka	2018-19

The best figures for England are 4-6 by C.J.Jordan (v WI, Basseterre, 2018-19), for Zimbabwe 4-28 by W.P.Masakadza (v Sc, Nagpur, 2015-16), and for Ireland 4-11 by A.R.Cusack (v WI, Kingston, 2013-14).

HAT-TRICKS

B.Lee	Australia v Bangladesh	Melbourne	2007-08
J.D.P.Oram	New Zealand v Sri Lanka	Colombo (RPS)	2009
T.G.Southee	New Zealand v Pakistan	Auckland	2010-11
N.L.T.C.Perera	Sri Lanka v India	Ranchi	2015-16
S.L.Malinga	Sri Lanka v Bangladesh	Colombo (RPS)	2016-17
Faheem Ashraf	Pakistan v Sri Lanka	Abu Dhabi	2017-18
Rashid Khan†	Afghanistan v Ireland	Dehradun	2018-19
S.L.Malinga†	Sri Lanka v New Zealand	Pallekele	2019

Mohammad Hasnain	Pakistan v Sri Lanka	Lahore		2019-20
Khawar Ali	Oman v Netherlands	Al Amerat		2019-20
N.Vanua	PNG v Bermuda	Dubai		2019-20
D.L.Chahar	India v Bangladesh	Nagpur		2019-20
A.C.Agar	Australia v South Africa	Johannesburg		2019-20
M.K.P.A.D.Perera	Sri Lanka v West Indies	Antigua		2020-21

† *Four wickets in four balls.*

WICKET-KEEPING RECORDS – 34 DISMISSALS IN A CAREER

Dis			Matches	Ct	St
91	M.S.Dhoni	India	98	57	34
63	D.Ramdin	West Indies	71	43	20
61	Mushfiqur Rahim	Bangladesh	86	32	29
60	Kamran Akmal	Pakistan	58	28	32
54	Mohammad Shahzad	Afghanistan	65	26	28
52	Q.de Kock	South Africa	47	41	11
45	K.C.Sangakkara	Sri Lanka	56	25	20
45	Sarfraz Ahmed	Pakistan	59	35	10
36†	G.C.Wilson	Ireland	81	29	7
34	J.C.Buttler	England	74	29	5

† *Excluding catches taken in the field.*

MOST DISMISSALS IN AN INNINGS

5 (3 ct, 2 st)	Mohammad Shahzad	Afghanistan v Oman	Abu Dhabi	2015-16
5 (5 ct)	M.S.Dhoni	India v England	Bristol	2018
5 (2 ct, 3 st)	I.A.Karim	Kenya v Ghana	Kampala	2019
5 (5 ct)	K.Doriga	PNG v Vanuatu	Apia	2019

FIELDING RECORDS – 40 CATCHES IN A CAREER

Total			Matches	Total			Matches
57	D.A.Miller	South Africa	81	42	S.K.Raina	India	78
56	M.J.Guptill	New Zealand	99	42	V.Kohli	India	85
50	Shoaib Malik	Pakistan/ICC	116	41	T.G.Southee	New Zealand	80
46	L.R.P.L.Taylor	New Zealand	102	41	E.J.G.Morgan	England	97
44†	A.B.de Villiers	South Africa	78	40	G.H.Dockrell	Ireland	77
44	Mohammad Nabi	Afghanistan	78	40	R.G.Sharma	India	108
44	D.A.Warner	Australia	81				

† *Excluding catches taken as a wicket-keeper.*

MOST CATCHES IN AN INNINGS

4	D.J.G.Sammy	West Indies v Ireland	Providence	2009-10
4	P.W.Borren	Netherlands v Bangladesh	The Hague	2012
4	C.J.Anderson	New Zealand v South Africa	Port Elizabeth	2012-13
4	L.D.Chandimal	Sri Lanka v Bangladesh	Chittagong	2013-14
4	A.M.Rahane	India v England	Birmingham	2014
4	Babar Hayat	Hong Kong v Afghanistan	Dhaka	2015-16
4	D.A.Miller	South Africa v Pakistan	Cape Town	2018-19
4	L.Siaka	PNG v Vanuatu	Apia	2019
4	C.S.MacLeod	Scotland v Ireland	Dublin	2019
4	T.H.David	Singapore v Scotland	Dubai	2019-20
4	C.de Grandhomme	New Zealand v England	Wellington	2019-20
4	P.Sarraf	Nepal v Malaysia	Bangkok	2019-20

APPEARANCE RECORDS – 80 APPEARANCES

116	Shoaib Malik	Pakistan/ICC	85	V.Kohli	India
108	R.G.Sharma	India	84	S.L.Malinga	Sri Lanka
102	L.R.P.L.Taylor	New Zealand	84	N.L.T.C.Perera	Sri Lanka/ICC/World
99	M.J.Guptill	New Zealand	84	Umar Akmal	Pakistan
99	Mohammad Hafeez	Pakistan	81	J.P.Duminy	South Africa
99	Shahid Afridi	Pakistan/ICC	81	D.A.Miller	South Africa/World
98	M.S.Dhoni	India	81	D.A.Warner	Australia
97	E.J.G.Morgan	England	81	G.C.Wilson	Ireland
96	K.J.O'Brien	Ireland	80	T.M.Dilshan	Sri Lanka
87	Mahmudullah	Bangladesh	80	T.G.Southee	New Zealand
86	Mushfiqur Rahim	Bangladesh			

The most appearances for West Indies 79 by K.A.Pollard, for Zimbabwe 66 by H.Masakadza, and for Afghanistan 78 by Mohammad Nabi.

40 MATCHES AS CAPTAIN

			W	L	T	NR	%age wins
72	M.S.Dhoni	India	41	28	1	2	58.57
56	W.T.S.Porterfield	Ireland	26	26	–	4	50.00
54	E.J.G.Morgan	England	31	20	2	1	58.49
49	Asghar Stanikzai	Afghanistan	39	9	1	–	79.59
49	K.S.Williamson	New Zealand	23	24	1	1	47.91
47	D.J.G.Sammy	West Indies	27	17	1	2	60.00
44	A.J.Finch	Australia	22	20	–	2	52.38
44	Shahid Afridi	ICC/Pakistan	19	24	1	–	43.18
40	F.du Plessis	South Africa	24	15	1	–	60.00
40	V.Kohli	India	24	12	2	2	63.15

UNIVERSITY MATCH RESULTS

Played: 175. Wins: Cambridge 61; Oxford 58. Drawn: 56. Abandoned: 1

In 2001, for the very first time, Cambridge hosted the University Match, cricket's oldest surviving first-class fixture, after the ECB's re-organisation of university cricket around six centres of excellence had removed it from Lord's. Dating from 1827 it has, wartime interruptions apart, been played annually since 1838. With the exception of five matches played in the area of Oxford (1829, 1843, 1846, 1848 and 1850), all the previous fixtures had been staged at Lord's. Since 2001 it has been played over four days rather than three.

1827	Drawn	1880	Cambridge	1929	Drawn	1980	Drawn
1829	Oxford	1881	Oxford	1930	Cambridge	1981	Drawn
1836	Oxford	1882	Cambridge	1931	Oxford	1982	Cambridge
1838	Oxford	1883	Cambridge	1932	Drawn	1983	Drawn
1839	Cambridge	1884	Oxford	1933	Drawn	1984	Oxford
1840	Cambridge	1885	Cambridge	1934	Drawn	1985	Drawn
1841	Cambridge	1886	Oxford	1935	Cambridge	1986	Cambridge
1842	Cambridge	1887	Oxford	1936	Cambridge	1987	Drawn
1843	Cambridge	1888	Drawn	1937	Oxford	1988	Abandoned
1844	Drawn	1889	Cambridge	1938	Drawn	1989	Drawn
1845	Cambridge	1890	Cambridge	1939	Oxford	1990	Drawn
1846	Oxford	1891	Cambridge	1946	Oxford	1991	Drawn
1847	Cambridge	1892	Oxford	1947	Drawn	1992	Cambridge
1848	Oxford	1893	Cambridge	1948	Oxford	1993	Oxford
1849	Cambridge	1894	Oxford	1949	Cambridge	1994	Drawn
1850	Oxford	1895	Cambridge	1950	Drawn	1995	Oxford
1851	Cambridge	1896	Oxford	1951	Oxford	1996	Drawn
1852	Oxford	1897	Cambridge	1952	Drawn	1997	Drawn
1853	Oxford	1898	Oxford	1953	Cambridge	1998	Cambridge
1854	Oxford	1899	Drawn	1954	Drawn	1999	Drawn
1855	Oxford	1900	Drawn	1955	Drawn	2000	Drawn
1856	Cambridge	1901	Drawn	1956	Drawn	2001	Oxford
1857	Oxford	1902	Cambridge	1957	Cambridge	2002	Drawn
1858	Oxford	1903	Oxford	1958	Cambridge	2003	Oxford
1859	Cambridge	1904	Drawn	1959	Oxford	2004	Oxford
1860	Cambridge	1905	Cambridge	1960	Drawn	2005	Oxford
1861	Cambridge	1906	Cambridge	1961	Drawn	2006	Oxford
1862	Cambridge	1907	Cambridge	1962	Drawn	2007	Drawn
1863	Oxford	1908	Oxford	1963	Drawn	2008	Drawn
1864	Oxford	1909	Drawn	1964	Drawn	2009	Cambridge
1865	Oxford	1910	Oxford	1965	Drawn	2010	Oxford
1866	Oxford	1911	Oxford	1966	Drawn	2011	Cambridge
1867	Cambridge	1912	Cambridge	1967	Drawn	2012	Drawn
1868	Cambridge	1913	Cambridge	1968	Drawn	2013	Oxford
1869	Cambridge	1914	Oxford	1969	Drawn	2014	Drawn
1870	Cambridge	1919	Oxford	1970	Drawn	2015	Cambridge
1871	Oxford	1920	Drawn	1971	Drawn	2016	Drawn
1872	Cambridge	1921	Cambridge	1972	Cambridge	2017	Cambridge
1873	Oxford	1922	Cambridge	1973	Drawn	2018	Oxford
1874	Oxford	1923	Oxford	1974	Drawn	2019	Oxford
1875	Oxford	1924	Cambridge	1975	Drawn	2020	Cambridge
1876	Cambridge	1925	Drawn	1976	Oxford		
1877	Oxford	1926	Cambridge	1977	Drawn		
1878	Cambridge	1927	Cambridge	1978	Drawn		
1879	Cambridge	1928	Drawn	1979	Cambridge		

CAMBRIDGE UNIVERSITY RECORDS
ALL FIRST-CLASS MATCHES

Highest Total	For 703-9d		v	Sussex	Hove	1890
	V 730-3		by	W Indians	Cambridge	1950
Lowest Total	For 30		v	Yorkshire	Cambridge	1928
	V 32		by	Oxford U	Lord's	1878
Highest Innings	For 254*	K.S.Duleepsinhji	v	Middlesex	Cambridge	1927
	V 313*	S.S.Agarwal	for	Oxford U	Cambridge	2013
Highest Partnership						
(2nd wicket)	429*	J.G.Dewes/G.H.G.Doggart	v	Essex	Cambridge	1949
Best Innings Bowling	10-69	S.M.J.Woods	v	Thornton's XI	Cambridge	1890
Best Match Bowling	15-88	S.M.J.Woods	v	Thornton's XI	Cambridge	1890
Most Runs – Season	1581		D.S.Sheppard	(av 79.05)		1952
Most Runs – Career	4310		J.M.Brearley	(av 38.48)		1961-68
Most 100s – Season	7		D.S.Sheppard			1952
Most 100s – Career	14		D.S.Sheppard			1950-52
Most Wkts – Season	80		O.S.Wheatley	(av 17.63)		1958
Most Wkts – Career	208		G.Goonesena	(av 21.82)		1954-57

UNIVERSITY MATCH RECORDS

Highest Total	604		Oxford	2002
Lowest Total	39		Lord's	1858
Highest Innings	211	G.Goonesena	Lord's	1957
Best Innings Bowling	8-44	G.E.Jeffery	Lord's	1873
Best Match Bowling	13-73	A.G.Steel	Lord's	1878

Hat-Tricks: F.C.Cobden (1870), A.G.Steel (1879), P.H.Morton (1880), J.F.Ireland (1911), R.G.H.Lowe (1926)

OXFORD UNIVERSITY RECORDS
ALL FIRST-CLASS MATCHES

Highest Total	For 651		v	Sussex	Hove	1895
	V 679-7d		by	Australians	Oxford	1938
Lowest Total	For 12		v	MCC	Oxford	1877
	V 24		by	MCC	Oxford	1846
Highest Innings	For 313*	S.S.Agarwal	v	Cambridge U	Cambridge	2013
	V 338	W.W.Read	for	Surrey	The Oval	1888
Highest Partnership						
(3rd wicket)	408	S.Oberoi/D.R.Fox	v	Cambridge U	Cambridge	2005
Best Innings Bowling	10-38	S.E.Butler	v	Cambridge U	Lord's	1871
Best Match Bowling	15-65	B.J.T.Bosanquet	v	Sussex	Oxford	1900
Most Runs – Season	1307		Nawab of Pataudi sr	(av 93.35)		1931
Most Runs – Career	3319		N.S.Mitchell-Innes	(av 47.41)		1934-37
Most 100s – Season	6		Nawab of Pataudi sr			1931
	6		M.P.Donnelly			1946
Most 100s – Career	9		A.M.Crawley			1927-30
	9		Nawab of Pataudi sr			1928-31
	9		N.S.Mitchell-Innes			1934-37
	9		M.P.Donnelly			1946-47
Most Wkts – Season	70		I.A.R.Peebles	(av 18.15)		1930
Most Wkts – Career	182		R.H.B.Bettington	(av 19.38)		1920-23

UNIVERSITY MATCH RECORDS

Highest Total	611-5d		Oxford	2010
Lowest Total	32		Lord's	1878
Highest Innings	313*	S.S.Agarwal	Cambridge	2013
Best Innings Bowling	10-38	S.E.Butler	Lord's	1871
Best Match Bowling	15-95	S.E.Butler	Lord's	1871

Match Doubles: P.R.le Couteur (160 and 11-66 in 1910); G.J.Toogood (149 and 10-93 in 1985)

INDIAN PREMIER LEAGUE 2020

The 13th IPL tournament was held in the UAE between 19 September and 10 November.

Team	P	W	L	T	NR	Pts	Net RR
1 Mumbai Indians (1)	14	9	5	–	–	18	+1.10
2 Delhi Capitals (3)	14	8	6	–	–	16	–0.10
3 Sunrisers Hyderabad (4)	14	7	7	–	–	14	+0.60
4 Royal Challengers Bangalore (8)	14	7	7	–	–	14	–0.17
5 Kolkata Knight Riders (5)	14	7	7	–	–	14	–0.21
6 Kings XI Punjab (6)	14	6	8	–	–	12	–0.16
7 Chennai Super Kings (2)	14	6	8	–	–	12	–0.45
8 Rajasthan Royals (7)	14	6	8	–	–	12	–0.56

1st Qualifying Match: At Dubai International Cricket Stadium, 5 November (floodlit). Toss: Delhi Capitals. **MUMBAI INDIANS** won by 57 runs. Mumbai Indians 200-5 (20; I.P.K.P.Kishan 55*, S.A.Yadav 51, Q.de Kock 40, R.Ashwin 3-29). Delhi Capitals 143-8 (20; M.P.Stoinis 65, A.R.Patel 42, J.J.Bumrah 4-14). Award: J.J.Bumrah.

Eliminator: At Sheikh Zayed Stadium, Abu Dhabi, 6 November (floodlit). Toss: Sunrisers Hyderabad. **SUNRISERS HYDERABAD** won by six wickets. Royal Challengers Bangalore 131-7 (20; A.B.de Villiers 56, J.O.Holder 3-25). Sunrisers Hyderabad 132-4 (19.4; K.S.Williamson 50*). Award: K.S.Williamson.

2nd Qualifying Match: At Sheikh Zayed Stadium, Abu Dhabi, 8 November (floodlit). Toss: Delhi Capitals. **DELHI CAPITALS** won by 17 runs. Delhi Capitals 189-3 (20; S.Dhawan 78, S.O.Hetmyer 42*). Sunrisers Hyderabad 172-8 (20; K.S.Williamson 67, K.Rabada 4-29, M.P.Stoinis 3-26). Award: M.P.Stoinis.

FINAL: At Dubai International Cricket Stadium, 10 November (floodlit). Toss: Delhi Capitals. **MUMBAI INDIANS** won by five wickets. Delhi Capitals 156-7 (20; S.S.Iyer 65*, R.R.Pant 56, T.A.Boult 3-30). Mumbai Indians 157-5 (18.4; R.G.Sharma 68). Award: T.A.Boult. Series award: J.C.Archer (RR).

IPL winners:	2008	Rajasthan Royals	2009	Deccan Chargers
	2010	Chennai Super Kings	2011	Chennai Super Kings
	2012	Kolkata Knight Riders	2013	Mumbai Indians
	2014	Kolkata Knight Riders	2015	Mumbai Indians
	2016	Sunrisers Hyderabad	2017	Mumbai Indians
	2018	Chennai Super Kings	2019	Mumbai Indians

TEAM RECORDS
HIGHEST TOTALS

263-5 (20)	Bangalore v Pune	Bangalore	2013
248-3 (20)	Bangalore v Gujarat	Bangalore	2016

LOWEST TOTALS

49 (9.4)	Bangalore v Kolkata	Kolkata	2017
58 (15.1)	Rajasthan v Bangalore	Cape Town	2009

LARGEST MARGINS OF VICTORY

146 runs	Mumbai (212-3) beat Delhi (66)	Delhi	2017
87 balls	Mumbai (68-2) beat Kolkata (67)	Mumbai	2008

There have been 14 victories in IPL history by ten wickets.

BATTING RECORDS
MOST RUNS IN IPL

5878	V.Kohli	Bangalore	2008-20
5368	S.K.Raina	Chennai, Gujarat	2008-19

800 RUNS IN A SEASON

Runs			Year	M	I	NO	HS	Ave	100	50	6s	4s	R/100B
973	V.Kohli	Bangalore	2016	16	16	4	113	81.08	4	7	38	83	152.0
848	D.A.Warner	Hyderabad	2016	17	17	3	93*	60.57	–	9	31	88	151.4

305

HIGHEST SCORES

Score	Balls				
175*	66	C.H.Gayle	Bangalore v Pune	Bangalore	2013
158*	73	B.B.McCullum	Kolkata v Bangalore	Bangalore	2008
133*	59	A.B.de Villiers	Bangalore v Mumbai	Mumbai	2015
129*	52	A.B.de Villiers	Bangalore v Mumbai	Bangalore	2016
128*	62	C.H.Gayle	Bangalore v Delhi	Delhi	2012
128*	63	R.R.Pant	Delhi v Hyderabad	Delhi	2018

K.P.Pietersen 103* (Delhi v Deccan at Delhi, 2012), B.A.Stokes 103* (Pune v Gujarat at Pune, 2017) and 107* (Rajasthan v Mumbai at Abu Dhabi, 2020) and J.M.Bairstow 114 (Hyderabad v Bangalore at Hyderabad, 2019) are the only England-qualified centurions in the IPL.

FASTEST HUNDRED

30 balls	C.H.Gayle (175*)	Bangalore v Pune	Bangalore	2013

MOST SIXES IN AN INNINGS

17	C.H.Gayle	Bangalore v Pune	Bangalore	2013

HIGHEST STRIKE RATE IN A SEASON (Qualification: 100 runs or more)

R/100B	Runs	Balls			
204.81	510	249	A.D.Russell	Kolkata	2019

HIGHEST STRIKE RATE IN AN INNINGS (Qualification: 30 runs, 350+ strike rate)

R/100B	Runs	Balls			
422.2	38*	9	C.H.Morris	Delhi v Pune	Pune	2017
387.5	31	8	A.B.de Villiers	Bangalore v Pune	Bangalore	2013
372.7	41	11	A.B.de Villiers	Bangalore v Mumbai	Bangalore	2015
369.2	48*	13	A.D.Russell	Kolkata v Bangalore	Bangalore	2019
350.0	35	10	C.H.Gayle	Bangalore v Hyderabad	Hyderabad	2015
350.0	35*	10	S.N.Khan	Bangalore v Hyderabad	Bangalore	2016

BOWLING RECORDS
MOST WICKETS IN IPL

170	S.L.Malinga	Mumbai		2009-19
160	A.Mishra	Deccan, Delhi, Hyderabad		2008-20

27 WICKETS IN A SEASON

Wkts			Year	P	O	M	Runs	Avge	Best	4w	R/Over
32	D.J.Bravo	Chennai	2013	18	62.3	–	497	15.53	4-42	1	7.95
30	K.Rabada	Delhi	2020	17	65.4	1	548	18.26	4-24	2	8.34
28	S.L.Malinga	Mumbai	2011	16	63.0	2	375	13.39	5-13	1	5.95
28	J.P.Faulkner	Rajasthan	2013	16	63.1	2	427	15.25	5-16	2	6.75
27	J.J.Bumrah	Mumbai	2020	15	60.0	2	404	14.96	4-14	2	6.73

BEST BOWLING FIGURES IN AN INNINGS

6-12	A.S.Joseph	Mumbai v Hyderabad	Hyderabad	2109
6-14	Sohail Tanvir	Rajasthan v Chennai	Jaipur	2008
6-19	A.Zampa	Pune v Hyderabad	Visakhapatnam	2016
5- 5	A.Kumble	Bangalore v Rajasthan	Cape Town	2009

A.D.Mascarenhas 5-25 (Punjab v Pune at Mohali, 2012) is the only England-qualified bowler to take five wickets in an innings in the IPL.

MOST ECONOMICAL BOWLING ANALYSIS

O	M	R	W				
4	1	6	0	F.H.Edwards	Deccan v Kolkata	Cape Town	2009
4	1	6	1	A.Nehra	Delhi v Punjab	Bloemfontein	2009
4	1	6	1	Y.S.Chahal	Bangalore v Chennai	Chennai	2019

MOST EXPENSIVE BOWLING ANALYSIS

O	M	R	W				
4	0	70	0	Basil Thampi	Hyderabad v Bangalore	Bangalore	2018
4	0	66	0	I.Sharma	Hyderabad v Chennai	Hyderabad	2013
4	0	66	0	Mujeeb Zadran	Punjab v Hyerabad	Hyderabad	2019

BIG BASH 2020-21

The tenth Big Bash tournament was held in Australia between 10 December and 6 February.

	Team	P	W	L	T	NR	Pts	Net RR
1	Sydney Sixers (2)	14	9	5	–	–	18	+0.25
2	Perth Scorchers (6)	14	8	5	–	1	17	+0.85
3	Sydney Thunder (5)	14	8	6	–	–	16	+0.94
4	Brisbane Heat (7)	14	7	7	–	–	14	–0.28
5	Adelaide Strikers (3)	14	7	7	–	–	14	+0.10
6	Hobart Hurricanes (4)	14	7	7	–	–	14	–0.18
7	Melbourne Stars (1)	14	5	8	–	1	11	+0.14
8	Melbourne Renegades (8)	14	4	10	–	–	8	–1.72

Knockout: At Canberra Oval, 31 January (floodlit). Toss: Brisbane Heat. **BRISBANE HEAT** won by seven wickets. Sydney Thunder 158-8 (20). Brisbane Heat 162-3 (19.1; S.D.Heazlett 74*). Award: S.D.Heazlett.

Challenger: At Canberra Oval, 4 February. Toss: Brisbane Heat. **PERTH SCORCHERS** won by 49 runs (D/L method). Perth Scorchers 189-1 (18.1; L.S.Livingstone 77, C.T.Bancroft 58*). Brisbane Heat 150-9 (18; A.M.Hardie 3-46). Award: L.S.Livingstone.

FINAL: At Sydney Cricket Ground, 6 February. Toss: Perth Scorchers. **SYDNEY SIXERS** won by 27 runs. Sydney Sixers 188-6 (20; J.M.Vince 95). Perth Scorchers 161-9 (20; B.J.Dwarshuis 3-37). Award: J.M.Vince. Series award: J.R.Philippe (Sydney Sixers).

Big Bash winners:

2011-12 Sydney Sixers	2012-13 Brisbane Heat
2013-14 Perth Scorchers	2014-15 Perth Scorchers
2015-16 Sydney Thunder	2016-17 Perth Scorchers
2017-18 Adelaide Strikers	2018-19 Melbourne Renegades
2019-20 Sydney Sixers	

TEAM RECORDS
HIGHEST TOTALS

232-5 (20)	Thunder v Sixers	Adelaide	2020-21
223-8 (20)	Hurricanes v Renegades	Melbourne (Dock)	2016-17

LOWEST TOTALS

57 (12.4)	Renegades v Stars	Melbourne (Dock)	2014-15
60 (10.4)	Renegades v Sixers	Hobart	2020-21

LARGEST MARGINS OF VICTORY

145 runs	Renegades (60) v Sixers (205-4)	Hobart	2020-21
10 wickets	Scorchers (171-0) v Renegades (170-4)	Melbourne (Dock)	2015-16
10 wickets	Strikers (154-5) v Hurricanes (158-0)	Adelaide	2018-19
10 wickets	Stars (156-8) v Heat (158-0)	Brisbane	2018-19
10 wickets	Heat (100) v Strikers (104-0)	Adelaide	2019-20

BATTING RECORDS
MOST RUNS IN BIG BASH

2790 (av 37.20)	C.A.Lynn	Heat	2011-21
2431 (av 34.23)	A.J.Finch	Renegades	2011-21

MOST RUNS IN A SEASON

Runs		Year	M	I	NO	HS	Ave	100	50	6s	4s	R/100B
705	M.P.Stoinis	Stars	2019-20	17	17	4	147*	54.23	1	6	28	62	136.6

HIGHEST SCORES

Score	Balls				
147*	79	M.P.Stoinis	Stars v Sixers	Melbourne	2019-20
130*	61	M.S.Wade	Hurricanes v Strikers	Adelaide	2019-20
122*	69	D.J.M.Short	Hurricanes v Heat	Brisbane	2017-18

FASTEST HUNDRED

39 balls	C.J.Simmons (102)	Scorchers v Strikers	Perth	2013-14

MOST SIXES IN AN INNINGS

11	C.H.Gayle (100*)	Thunder v Strikers	Sydney (SA)	2011-12
11	C.J.Simmons (112)	Scorchers v Sixers	Sydney	2013-14
11	C.A.Lynn (98*)	Heat v Scorchers	Perth	2016-17
11	C.A.Lynn (94)	Heat v Sixers	Sydney	2019-20

HIGHEST STRIKE RATE IN AN INNINGS (Qualification: 25 runs, 325+ strike rate)

R/100B	Score	Balls				
377.7	34	9	D.T.Christian	Heat v Hurricanes	Hobart	2014-15
329.4	56	17	C.H.Gayle	Renegades v Strikers	Melbourne (Dk)	2015-16
327.2	36*	11	B.J.Rohrer	Renegades v Heat	Melbourne (Dk)	2013-14

HIGHEST PARTNERSHIPS

207	M.P.Stoinis/H.W.R.Cartwright	Stars v Sixers	Melbourne	2019-20
203	M.S.Wade/D.J.M.Short	Hurricanes v Strikers	Adelaide	2019-20

BOWLING RECORDS
MOST WICKETS IN BIG BASH

111	B.Laughlin	Strikers, Heat, Hurricanes	2011-21
106	S.A.Abbott	Sixers, Thunder	2011-21

MOST WICKETS IN A SEASON

Wkts			Year	P	O	M	Runs	Avge	Best	4w	R/Over
30	D.R.Sams	Thunder	2019-20	17	58.5	2	461	15.36	4-34	1	7.83

BEST BOWLING FIGURES IN AN INNINGS

6- 7	S.L.Malinga	Stars v Scorchers	Perth	2012-13
6-11	I.S.Sodhi	Strikers v Thunder	Sydney (Show)	2016-17
5-14	D.T.Christian	Hurricanes v Strikers	Hobart	2016-17

MOST ECONOMICAL BOWLING ANALYSIS

O	M	R	W				
4	2	3	3	M.G.Johnson	Scorchers v Stars	Perth	2016-17
4	0	6	1	A.F.Milne	Thunder v Strikers	Adelaide	2020-21

MOST EXPENSIVE BOWLING ANALYSIS

O	M	R	W				
4	0	61	0	B.J.Dwarshuis	Sixers v Stars	Melbourne	2019-20
4	0	60	0	D.J.Worrall	Stars v Hurricanes	Melbourne	2014-15
4	0	60	1	B.Laughlin	Heat v Scorchers	Perth	2019-20

WICKET-KEEPING RECORDS
MOST DISMISSALS IN BIG BASH

51	A.T.Carey	Strikers	2017-21

MOST DISMISSALS IN A SERIES

16	J.R.Philippe	Sixers	2020-21

MOST DISMISSALS IN AN INNINGS

5 (5ct)	T.I.F.Triffitt	Scorchers v Renegades	Perth	2012-13
5 (4ct, 1st)	J.J.Peirson	Heat v Strikers	Brisbane	2019-20

IRELAND INTERNATIONALS

The following players have played for Ireland in any format of international cricket since 1 October 2019. Details correct to 18 March 2021.

ADAIR, Mark Richard (Sullivan Upper S, Holywood), b Belfast 27 Mar 1996. 6'2". RHB, RFM. Warwickshire 2015-16. Northern debut 2018. Ireland Wolves 2018-19 to 2020-21. **Tests**: 1 (2019); HS 8 and BB 3-32 v E (Lord's) 2019. **LOI**: 15 (2019 to 2020-21); HS 32 v E (Dublin) 2019; BB 4-19 v Afg (Belfast) 2019. **IT20**: 18 (2019 to 2020-21); HS 38 v Z (Bready) 2019; BB 4-40 v Z (Bready) 2019 – on debut, different matches. HS 91 Northern v Leinster (Dublin, Sandymount) 2018. BB 3-32 (*see Tests*). LO HS 44 Northern v NW (La Manga) 2019. LO BB 4-19 (*see LOI*). T20 HS 38. T20 BB 4-14.

BALBIRNIE, Andrew (St Andrew's C, Dublin; UWIC), b Dublin 28 Dec 1990. 6'2". RHB, OB. Cardiff MCCU 2012-13. Ireland debut 2012. Middlesex 2012-15. Leinster debut 2017. Ireland Wolves 2017-18. Glamorgan 2020 (T20 only). **Tests**: 3 (2018 to 2019); HS 82 v Afg (Dehradun) 2018-19. **LOI**: 75 (2010 to 2020-21, 11 as captain); HS 145* v Afg (Dehradun) 2018-19; BB 1-26 v Afg (Dubai, DSC) 2014-15. **IT20**: 43 (2015 to 2019-20, 6 as captain); HS 83 v Neth (Al Amerat) 2018-19. HS 205* Ire v Neth (Dublin) 2017. BB 4-23 Lein v NW (Bready) 2017. LO HS 160* Ire W v Bangladesh A (Dublin, CA) 2018. LO BB 1-26 (*see LOI*). T20 HS 99*.

CAMPHER, Curtis (St Stithians C), b Johannesburg, South Africa 20 Apr 1999. RHB, RM. Ireland Wolves debut 2020-21. Leinster 2020 (not f-c). **LOI**: 8 (2020 to 2020-21); HS 68 v E (Southampton); BB 2-31 v UAE (Abu Dhabi) 2020-21. HS 39 v Bangladesh Emerging (Chittagong) 2020-21. LO HS 68 (*see LOI*). LO BB 4-46 Lein v NW (Bready) 2020. T20 HS 62*. T20 BB 1-20.

DELANY, David Colin Alex, b Dublin 28 Dec 1997. Cousin of G.J.Delany. LHB, RMF. Leinster 2017-18. Northern debut 2019. **IT20**: 8 (2019 to 2019-20); HS 7 v Scot (Dublin) 2019; BB 2-12 v Jersey (Abu Dhabi, TO) 2019-20. HS 17 Northern v Leinster (Dublin) 2019. BB 4-31 Leinster v Northern (Dublin, CA) 2017. LO HS 18 and LO BB 2-62 Northern v Leinster (Dublin) 2020. T20 HS 25. T20 BB 2-12.

DELANY, Gareth James, b Dublin 28 Apr 1997. Cousin of D.C.A.Delany. RHB, LBG. Leinster debut 2017. Ireland Wolves 2018-19 to 2020-21. Leicestershire 2020 (T20 only). **LOI**: 9 (2019-20 to 2020-21); HS 22 v E (Southampton) 2020; BB 1-10 v UAE (Abu Dhabi) 2020-21. **IT20**: 23 (2019 to 2019-20); HS 89* v Oman (Abu Dhabi, TO) 2019-20; BB 2-21 v Afg (Greater Noida) 2019-20. HS 22 Ire W v Sri Lanka A (Colombo, SSC) 2018-19. BB 3-48 Leinster v Northern (Bready) 2017. LO HS 67 Leinster v NW (Dublin, OL) 2018. LO BB 3-47 Leinster v NW (Bready) 2018. T20 HS 89*. T20 BB 3-8.

DOCKRELL, George Henry (Gonzaga C, Dublin), b Dublin 22 Jul 1992. 6'3". RHB, SLA. Ireland 2010 to date. Somerset 2011-14. Sussex 2015. Leinster debut 2017. Ireland Wolves 2017-18. **Tests**: 1 (2018-19); HS 39 and BB 2-63 v Afg (Dehradun) 2018-19. **LOI**: 87 (2009-10 to 2019); HS 62* v Afg (Sharjah) 2017-18; BB 4-24 v Scot (Belfast) 2013. **IT20**: 77 (2009-10 to 2019-20); HS 34* v Afg (Dehradun) 2018-19; BB 4-20 v Neth (Dubai) 2009-10. HS 92 Leinster v NW (Bready) 2018. BB 6-27 Sm v Middx (Taunton) 2012. LO HS 98* and LO BB 5-21 Leinster v Northern (Dublin, V) 2018. T20 HS 40*. T20 BB 4-20.

GETKATE, Shane Charles, b Durban, South Africa 2 Oct 1991. Grandson of R.S.Getkate (Natal 1936-37). RHB, RMF. Northern debut 2017. Ireland Wolves 2018-19. Warwickshire 2nd XI 2011. MCC YC 2013-14. Northamptonshire 2nd XI 2014. **LOI**: 3 (2019); HS 16* v Z (Bready) 2019; BB 2-30 v Z (Belfast) 2019. **IT20**: 15 (2018-19 to 2019-20); HS 24 v Afg (Dehradun) 2018-19; BB 2-15 v Scotland (Al Amerat) 2018-19. HS 70 Northern v Leinster (Comber) 2018. BB 4-62 Northern v Leinster (Dublin, CA) 2017. LO HS 86 Ire W v Sri Lanka A (Colombo, SSC) 2018-19. LO BB 5-44 Northern v Leinster (Downpatrick) 2017. T20 HS 49. T20 BB 5-8.

LITTLE, Joshua Brian, b Dublin 1 Nov 1999. RHB, LFM. Leinster debut 2018. Ireland Wolves 2018-19. **LOI**: 7 (2019 to 2020-21); HS 9 and BB 4-45 v E (Dublin) 2019. **IT20**: 17 (2016 to 2019-20); HS 7 v Neth (Al Amerat) 2018-19; BB 3-29 v WI (St George's) 2019-20. HS 27 Leinster v NW (Bready) 2018. BB 3-95 Leinster v Northern (Dublin) 2018. LO HS 9 (*see LOI*). LO BB 4-45 (*see LOI*). T20 HS 7. T20 BB 3-17.

McBRINE, Andrew Robert, b Londonderry 30 Apr 1993. Son of A.McBrine (Ireland 1985-92), nephew of J.McBrine (Ireland 1986). LHB, OB. Ireland debut 2013. North-West debut 2017. Ireland Wolves 2017-18. **Tests**: 2 (2018 to 2019); HS 11 v E (Lord's) 2019; BB 2-77 v Afg (Dehradun) 2018-19. **LOI**: 53 (2014 to 2020-21); HS 79 v SL (Dublin) 2016; BB 5-29 v Afg (Abu Dhabi) 2020-21. **IT20**: 19 (2013-14 to 2016-17); HS 14* v UAE (Dubai, DSC) 2016-17; BB 2-7 v PNG (Townsville) 2015-16. HS 77 NW v Northern (Comber) 2018. BB 4-35 NW v Northern (Bready) 2018. LO HS 89 Ire W v Bangladesh A (Dublin, CA) 2018. LO BB 5-29 (*see LOI*). T20 HS 52*. T20 BB 3-19.

McCARTHY, Barry John (St Michael's C, Dublin; University C, Dublin), b Dublin 13 Sep 1992. 5'11". RHB, RMF. Durham 2015-18. Leinster debut 2019. **LOI**: 35 (2016 to 2020-21); HS 18 v Afg (Belfast) 2019; BB 5-46 v Afg (Sharjah) 2017-18. **IT20**: 10 (2016-17 to 2019-20); HS 18* v WI (Basseterre) 2019-20; BB 4-33 v Afg (Greater Noida) 2016-17. HS 51* Du v Hants (Chester-le-St) 2016. BB 6-63 Du v Kent (Canterbury) 2017. LO HS 43 Du v Leics (Leicester) 2018 (RLC). LO BB 5-46 (*see LOI*). T20 HS 18*. T20 BB 4-31.

McCOLLUM, James Alexander (Methodist C, Belfast; Durham U), b Craigavon 1 Aug 1995. RHB, RM. Durham MCCU 2017. Northern debut 2017. Ireland Wolves 2018-19 to 2020-21. **Tests**: 2 (2018-19 to 2019); HS 39 v Afg (Dehradun) 2018-19. **LOI**: 10 (2018-19 to 2020-21); HS 73 v Z (Belfast) 2019. HS 119* Northern v Leinster (Belfast) 2017. BB 5-32 Northern v NW (Bready) 2018. LO HS 102 Ire W v Sri Lanka A (Colombo, RPS) 2018-19. LO BB 1-14 Northern v NW (Eglinton) 2018. T20 HS 79*.

O'BRIEN, Kevin Joseph (Marian C, Dublin; Tallaght I of Tech), b Dublin 4 Mar 1984. RHB, RM. Son of B.A.O'Brien (Ireland 1966-81) and younger brother of N.J.O'Brien (Kent, Northamptonshire, Leicestershire, North-West and Ireland 2004-18). Ireland debut 2006-07. Nottinghamshire 2009. Surrey 2014. Leicestershire 2015-16 (l-o and T20 only). Leinster debut 2017. Gloucestershire 2011 (T20 only). Somerset 2012 (T20 only). **Tests**: 3 (2018 to 2019); HS 118 v P (Dublin) 2018 – on debut and Ire record; BB – . **LOI**: 152 (2006 to 2020-21, 4 as captain); HS 142 v Kenya (Nairobi) 2006-07; BB 4-13 v Neth (Amstelveen) 2013. **IT20**: 96 (2008 to 2019-20, 4 as captain); HS 124 v Hong Kong (Al Amerat) 2019-20 – Ire record; BB 4-45 v Afg (Greater Noida) 2016-17. HS 171* Ire v Kenya (Nairobi) 2008-09. BB 5-39 Ire v Canada (Toronto) 2010. LO HS 142 (*see LOI*). LO BB 4-13 (*see LOI*). T20 HS 124. T20 BB 4-22.

PORTERFIELD, William Thomas Stuart (Strabane GS; Leeds Met U), b Londonderry 6 Sep 1984. 5'11". LHB, OB. Ireland 2006-07 to date. Gloucestershire 2008-10; cap 2008. Warwickshire 2011-17; cap 2011. North West debut 2018. MCC 2017. **Tests**: 3 (2018 to 2019, 3 as captain); HS 32 v P (Dublin) 2018. **LOI**: 139 (2006 to 2019-20, 113 as captain); HS 139 v UAE (Dubai, ICCA) 2017-18. **IT20**: 61 (2008 to 2018, 56 as captain); HS 72 v UAE (Abu Dhabi) 2015-16. HS 207 NW v Leinster (Bready) 2018. BB 1-29 Ire v Jamaica (Spanish Town) 2009-10. LO HS 139 (*see LOI*). T20 HS 127*.

RANKIN, William Boyd (Strabane GS; Harper Adams UC), b Londonderry, Co Derry 5 Jul 1984. Brother of R.J.Rankin (Ireland U19 2003-04). 6'8". LHB, RFM. Ireland 2006-07 to date. Derbyshire 2007. Warwickshire 2008-17; cap 2013. Became available for England in 2012, before rejoining Ireland in 2015-16. North West debut 2018. **Tests** (E/Ire): 3 (1 for E 2013-14, 2 for Ire 2018 to 2019); HS 17 Ire v P (Dublin) 2018; BB 2-5 Ire v E (Lord's) 2019. **LOI** (E/Ire): 75 (68 for Ire 2006-07 to 2019-20, 7 for E 2013 to 2013-14); HS 18* Ire v SL (Dublin) 2016; BB 4-15 Ire v UAE (Harare) 2017-18). **IT20** (E/Ire): 50 (48 for Ire 2009 to 2019-20, 2 for E 2013); HS 16* Ire v UAE (Abu Dhabi) 2015-16; BB 3-16 Ire v UAE (Dubai, DSC) 2016-17. F-c Tour (E): A 2013-14. HS 56* Wa v Worcs (Birmingham) 2015. 50 wkts (1): 55 (2011). BB 6-55 Wa v Yorks (Leeds) 2015. LO HS 18* Wa v Northants (Northampton) 2013 (Y40) and *see LOI*. LO BB 4-15 (*see LOI*). T20 HS 16*. T20 BB 4-9.

SINGH, Simranjit ('Simi'), b Bathlana, Punjab, India 4 Feb 1987. RHB, OB. Leinster debut 2017. Ireland debut 2017. Ireland Wolves 2017-18. **LOI:** 24 (2017 to 2020-21); HS 54* and BB 5-10 v UAE (Abu Dhabi) 2020-21. **IT20:** 24 (2018 to 2019-20); HS 57* v Neth (Rotterdam) 2018; BB 3-15 v Oman (Al Amerat) 2018-19. HS 121 Ire W v Bangladesh A (Sylhet) 2017-18. BB 5-38 Leinster v Northern (Dublin) 2019. LO HS 121* Leinster v Northern (Dublin, V) 2018. LO BB 5-10 (*see LOI*). T20 HS 109. T20 BB 3-11.

STIRLING, Paul Robert (Belfast HS), b Belfast, N Ireland 3 Sep 1990. Father Brian Stirling was an international rugby referee. 5'10". RHB, OB. Middlesex 2007-08 to date. Middlesex 2013-19; cap 2016. Northamptonshire 2020 (T20 only). **Tests:** 3 (2018 to 2019); HS 36 v E (Lord's) 2019; BB – . **LOI:** 125 (2008 to 2020-21); HS 177 v Canada (Toronto) 2010 – Ire record; BB 6-55 v Afg (Greater Noida) 2016-17 – Ire record. **IT20:** 78 (2009 to 2019-20); HS 95 v WI (St George's) 2019-20; BB 3-21 v B (Belfast) 2012. HS 146 Ire v UAE (Dublin) 2015. CC HS 138 and BB 2-21 M v Glamorgan (Radlett) 2019. LO HS 177 (*see LOI*). LO BB 6-55 (*see LOI*). T20 HS 109. T20 BB 4-10.

TECTOR, Harry Tom, b Dublin 6 Nov 1999. Younger brother of J.B.Tector (Leinster 2017 to date). RHB, OB. Northern debut 2018. Ireland Wolves 2018-19 to 2020-21. **LOI:** 8 (2020 to 2020-21); HS 33 v UAE (Abu Dhabi) 2020-21; BB 1-52 v Afg (Abu Dhabi) 2020-21. **IT20:** 20 (2019 to 2020-21); HS 60 v Neth (Dublin) 2019. HS 146 Northern v Leinster (Dublin) 2019. BB 4-70 Northern v NW (Bready) 2018. LO HS 103 Ire W v Sri Lanka A (Colombo, SSC) 2018-19. LO BB 5-36 Northern v NW (La Manga) 2019. T20 HS 91. T20 BB 4-21.

THOMPSON, Stuart Robert (Limavady GS; U of Northumbria), b Eglinton, Londonderry 15 Aug 1991. LHB, RM. Ireland debut 2012. North-West debut 2017. Ireland Wolves 2017-18. Played county 2nd XI cricket for four counties 2012-15. **Tests:** 3 (2018 to 2019); HS 53 v P (Dublin) 2018; BB 3-28 v Afg (Dehradun) 2018-19. **LOI:** 39 v Scot (Dublin) 2014; BB 2-17 v WI (Kingston) 2013-14. **IT20:** 41 (2013-14 to 2019-20); HS 56 v Afg (Greater Noida) 2016-17; BB 4-18 v Neth (Al Amerat) 2018-19. HS 148 NW v Leinster (Dublin, SP) 2018. BB 3-28 (*see Tests*). LO HS 68 Ire W v Bangladesh A (Oak Hill) 2018. LO BB 4-55 NW v Northern (La Manga) 2019. T20 HS 56. T20 BB 4-18.

TUCKER, Lorcan John, b Dublin 10 Sep 1996. RHB, WK. Leinster debut 2017. Ireland Wolves 2018-19 to 2020-21. **LOI:** 16 (2019 to 2020-21); HS 83 v Afg (Abu Dhabi) 2020-21. **IT20:** 17 (2016 to 2019-20); HS 22* v Oman (Al Amerat) 2018-19. HS 80 Ire W v Sri Lanka A (Hambantota) 2018-19. LO HS 109 Ire W v Sri Lanka A (Hambantota) 2018-19. T20 HS 51.

WILSON, Gary Craig (Methodist C, Belfast; Manchester Met U), b Dundonald 5 Feb 1986. 5'10". RHB, WK. Ireland 2005 to date. Surrey 2010-16; cap 2014. Derbyshire 2017-18; T20 captain 2018. **Tests:** 2 (2018 to 2019); HS 33* v P (Dublin) 2018. **LOI:** 105 (2007 to 2019); HS 113 v Neth (Dublin) 2010. **IT20:** 81 (2008 to 2019-20, 26 as captain); HS 65* v Scot (Dubai, DSC) 2016-17. HS 160* Sy v Leics (Oval) 2014. BB – . LO HS 113 (*see LOI*). T20 HS 80.

YOUNG, Craig Alexander (Strabane HS; North West IHE, Belfast), b Londonderry 4 Apr 1990. RHB, RM. Ireland debut 2013. North-West debut 2017. Ireland Wolves 2018-19. Sussex 2nd XI 2010-13. Hampshire 2nd XI 2016. **LOI:** 22 (2014 to 2020-21); HS 12* v Afg (Abu Dhabi) 2020-21; BB 5-46 v Scot (Dublin) 2014. **IT20:** 32 (2015 to 2019-20); HS 8 v WI (Basseterre) 2019-20; BB 4-13 v Nigeria (Abu Dhabi) 2019-20. HS 23 and BB 5-37 NW v Northern (Eglinton) 2017. LO HS 27 NW v Northern (La Manga) 2019. LO BB 5-46 (*see LOI*). T20 HS 8*. T20 BB 5-15.

ENGLAND WOMEN INTERNATIONALS

The following players have played for England since 1 July 2019 and are still available for selection. Details correct to 8 April 2021.

BEAUMONT, Tamsin ('**Tammy**') Tilley, b Dover, Kent 11 Mar 1991. RHB, WK. MBE 2018. Kent 2007 to date. Diamonds 2007-12. Sapphires 2008. Emeralds 2011-13. Surrey Stars 2016-17. Adelaide Strikers 2016-17 to 2017-18. Southern Vipers 2018-19. Melbourne Renegades 2019-20. Sydney Thunder 2020-21. *Wisden* 2018. **Tests**: 4 (2013 to 2019); HS 70 v A (Sydney) 2017-18. **LOI**: 74 (2009-10 to 2020-21); HS 168* v P (Taunton) 2016. **IT20**: 91 (2009-10 to 2020-21); HS 116 v SA (Taunton) 2018.

BRUNT, Katherine Helen, b Barnsley, Yorks 2 Jul 1985. RHB, RMF. Yorkshire 2004 to date. Sapphires 2006-08. Diamonds 2011-12. Perth Scorchers 2015-16 to 2017-18. Yorkshire Diamonds 2016-18. Northern Diamonds 2020. Melbourne Stars 2020-21. **Tests**: 12 (2004 to 2019); HS 52 v A (Worcester) 2005; BB 6-69 v A (Worcester) 2009. **LOI**: 125 (2004-05 to 2020-21); HS 72* v SA (Worcester) 2018; BB 5-18 v A (Wormsley) 2011. **IT20**: 89 (2005 to 2020-21); HS 42* v SA (Taunton) 2018; BB 3-6 v NZ (Lord's) 2009.

CROSS, Kathryn ('**Kate**') Laura, b Manchester, Lancs 3 Oct 1991. RHB, RMF. Lancashire 2005 to date. Sapphires 2007-08. Emeralds 2012. W Australia 2017-18 to 2018-19. Brisbane Heat 2015-16. Lancashire Thunder 2016-19. Perth Scorchers 2018-19. Thunder 2020. **Tests**: 3 (2013-14 to 2015); HS 4* v A (Canterbury) 2015; BB 3-29 v I (Wormsley) 2014. **LOI**: 28 (2013-14 to 2020-21); HS 8* v A (Canterbury) 2019; BB 5-24 v NZ (Lincoln) 2014-15. **IT20**: 13 (2013-14 to 2019-20); HS 0*; BB 2-18 v I (Guwahati) 2018-19.

DAVIES, Freya Ruth, b Chichester, Sussex 27 Oct 1995. RHB, RMF. Sussex 2012 to date. Western Storm 2016-19. South East Stars 2020. **LOI**: 3 (2019-20 to 2020-21); HS 2 v NZ (Dunedin) 2020-21; BB 1-30 v NZ (Christchurch) 2020-21. **IT20**: 11 (2018-19 to 2020-21); HS 1* v NZ (Wellington) 2020-21; BB 4-23 v NZ (Wellington) 2020-21 – separate matches.

DUNKLEY, Sophia Ivy Rose, b Lambeth, Surrey 16 Jul 1998. RHB, LB. Middlesex 2013 to date. Surrey Stars 2016-18. Lancashire Thunder 2019. South East Stars 2020. **IT20**: 15 (2018-19 to 2020-21); HS 35 v WI (Gros Islet) 2018-19; BB 1-6 v SL (Colombo, PSS) 2018-19.

ECCLESTONE, Sophie (Helsby HS), b Chester 6 May 1999. 5'11". RHB, SLA. Cheshire 2013-14. Lancashire 2015 to date. Lancashire Thunder 2016-19. Thunder 2020. **Tests**: 2 (2017-18 to 2019); HS 9* v A (Taunton) 2019; BB 3-107 v A (Sydney) 2017-18. **LOI**: 27 (2016-17 to 2020-21); HS 27 v A (Leicester) 2019; BB 4-14 v I (Nagpur) 2017-18. **IT20**: 42 (2016 to 2020-21); HS 17* v A (Hove) 2019; BB 4-18 v NZ (Taunton) 2018.

ELWISS, Georgia Amanda, b Wolverhampton, Staffs 31 May 1991. RHB, RMF. Staffordshire 2004-10. Sapphires 2006-12. Diamonds 2008. Australia CT 2009-10 to 2010-11. Emeralds 2011. Sussex 2011 to date. Rubies 2013. Loughborough Lightning 2016-19. Melbourne Stars 2017-18 to 2018-19. **Tests**: 3 (2015 to 2019); HS 46 v A (Canterbury) 2015; BB 1-40 v A (Sydney) 2017-18. **LOI**: 36 (2011-12 to 2018-19); HS 77 v P (Taunton) 2016; BB 3-17 v I (Wormsley) 2012. **IT20**: 14 (2011-12 to 2019); HS 18 v SA (Paarl) 2015-16; BB 2-9 v P (Chennai) 2015-16.

FARRANT, Natasha ('**Tash**') Eleni (Sevenoaks S), b Athens, Greece 29 May 1996. LHB, LMF. Kent 2012 to date. Sapphires 2013. W Australia 2016-17. Southern Vipers 2018-19. South East Stars 2020. **LOI**: 3 (2013-14 to 2020-21); HS 1* v WI (Port of Spain) 2013-14; BB 2-31 v NZ (Christchurch) 2020-21. **IT20**: 15 (2013 to 2020-21); HS 3* v A (Mumbai, BS) 2017-18; BB 2-15 v P (Loughborough) 2013.

GLENN, Sarah, b Derby 27 Feb 1999. RHB, LB. Derbyshire 2013-18. Worcestershire 2019. Loughborough Lightning 2017-19. Central Sparks 2020. Perth Scorchers 2020-21. **LOI**: 6 (2019-20 to 2020-21); HS 11 v NZ (Dunedin) 2020-21; BB 4-18 v P (Kuala Lumpur) 2019-20. **IT20**: 18 (2019-20 to 2020-21); HS 26 v WI (Derby) 2020; BB 3-15 v P (Canberra) 2019-20.

GORDON, Kirstie Louise, b Huntly, Aberdeenshire 20 Oct 1997. RHB, SLA. Nottinghamshire 2016 to date. Loughborough Lightning 2018-19. Lightning 2020. **Tests**: 1 (2019); HS – ; BB 2-50 v A (Taunton) 2019. **IT20**: 5 (2018-19); HS 1* v A (North Sound) 2018-19; BB 3-16 v B (Gros Islet) 2018-19.

JONES, Amy Ellen, b Solihull, Warwicks 13 Jun 1993. RHB, WK. Warwickshire 2008 to date. Diamonds 2011. Emeralds 2012. Rubies 2013. W Australia 2017-18. Loughborough Lightning 2016-19. Sydney Sixers 2016-17 to 2017-18. Perth Scorchers 2018-19 to date. Central Sparks 2020. **Tests**: 1 (2019); HS 64 v A (Taunton) 2019. **LOI**: 47 (2012-13 to 2020-21); HS 94 v I (Nagpur) 2017-18. **IT20**: 57 (2013 to 2020-21); HS 89 v P (Kuala Lumpur) 2019-20.

KNIGHT, Heather Clare, b Rochdale, Lancs 26 Dec 1990. RHB, OB. OBE 2018. Devon 2008-09. Emeralds 2008-13. Berkshire 2010 to date. Sapphires 2011-12. Tasmania 2014-15 to 2015-16. Hobart Hurricanes 2015-16 to 2019-20. Western Storm 2016 to date. Sydney Thunder 2020-21. *Wisden* 2017. **Tests**: 7 (2010-11 to 2019, 2 as captain); HS 157 v A (Wormsley) 2013; BB 2-25 v A (Taunton) 2019. **LOI**: 104 (2009-10 to 2020-21, 49 as captain); HS 106 v P (Leicester) 2017; BB 5-26 v P (Leicester) 2016. **IT20**: 814 (2010-11 to 2020-21, 48 as captain); HS 108* v Thai (Canberra) 2019-20; BB 3-9 v I (North Sound) 2018-19.

SCIVER, Natalie Ruth (Epsom C), b Tokyo, Japan 20 Aug 1992. RHB, RM. Surrey 2010 to date. Rubies 2011. Emeralds 2012-13. Melbourne Stars 2015-16 to date. Surrey Stars 2016-19. Perth Scorchers 2017-18 to 2019-20. Northern Diamonds 2020. *Wisden* 2017. **Tests**: 5 (2013-14 to 2019); HS 88 v A (Taunton) 2019; BB 1-30 v A (Perth) 2013-14. **LOI**: 70 (2013 to 2020-21); HS 137 v P (Leicester) 2017; BB 3-3 v WI (Bristol) 2017. **IT20**: 83 (2013 to 2020-21, 1 as captain); HS 82 v WI (Derby) 2020. BB 4-15 v A (Cardiff) 2015.

SHRUBSOLE, Anya, b Bath, Somerset 7 Dec 1991. RHB, RMF. MBE 2018. Somerset 2004-18. Rubies 2006-12. Emeralds 2006-13. Berkshire 2019. Western Storm 2016 to date. Perth Scorchers 2016-17. *Wisden* 2017. **Tests**: 6 (2013 to 2019); HS 20 v A (Sydney) 2017-18; BB 4-51 v A (Perth) 2013-14. **LOI**: 70 (2008 to 2019-20, 1 as captain); HS 32* v WI (Worcester) 2019; BB 6-46 v I (Lord's) 2017, in World Cup final. **IT20**: 79 (2008 to 2020); HS 29 v WI (Gros Islet) 2018-19; BB 5-11 v NZ (Wellington) 2011-12.

VILLIERS, Mady Kate, b Havering, Essex 26 Aug 1998. RHB, OB. Essex 2013 to date. Surrey Stars 2018-19. Sunrisers 2020. **IT20**: 12 (2019 to 2020-21); HS 1* v WI (Derby) 2020; BB 3-10 v NZ (Wellington) 2020-21.

WILSON, Frances Claire, b Aldershot, Hants 7 Nov 1991. RHB, OB. Somerset 2006-14. Diamonds 2011. Emeralds 2012. Rubies 2013. Middlesex 2015-18. Wellington 2016-17 to 2017-18. Kent 2019. Western Storm 2016-19. Sydney Thunder 2017-18. Hobart Hurricanes 2019-20. Sunrisers 2020. **Tests**: 1 (2017-18); HS 13 v A (Sydney) 2017-18. **LOI**: 33 (2010-11 to 2020-21); HS 85* v P (Kuala Lumpur) 2019-20. **IT20**: 30 (2010-11 to 2020-21); HS 43* v P (Southampton) 2016.

WINFIELD-HILL, Lauren, b York 16 Aug 1990. RHB, WK. Yorkshire 2007 to date. Diamonds 2011. Sapphires 2012. Rubies 2013. Brisbane Heat 2015-16 to 2016-17. Yorkshire Diamonds 2016-19. Hobart Hurricanes 2017-18. Adelaide Strikers 2019-20. Northern Diamonds 2020. **Tests**: 3 (2014 to 2017-18); HS 35 v I (Wormsley) 2014. **LOI**: 43 (2013 to 2020-21); HS 123 v P (Worcester) 2016. **IT20**: 40 (2013 to 2019-20); HS 74 v SA (Birmingham) 2014 and 74 v P (Bristol) 2016.

WYATT, Danielle ('Danni') Nicole, b Stoke-on-Trent, Staffs 22 Apr 1991. RHB, OB/RM. Staffordshire 2005-12. Emeralds 2011-13. Victoria 2011-12 to 2015-16. Nottinghamshire 2013-15. Sussex 2016 to date. Melbourne Renegades 2015-16 to 2019-20. Lancashire Thunder 2016. Southern Vipers 2017 to date. **LOI**: 77 (2009-10 to 2020-21); HS 110 v P (Kuala Lumpur) 2019-20; BB 3-7 v SA (Cuttack) 2012-13. **IT20**: 116 (2009-10 to 2020-21); HS 124 v I (Mumbai, BS) 2017-18; BB 4-11 v SA (Basseterre) 2010.

WOMEN'S TEST CRICKET RECORDS

1934-35 to 2 April 2021

RESULTS SUMMARY

	Opponents	Tests	E	A	NZ	SA	WI	I	P	SL	Ire	H	Drawn
England	Australia	50	9	12	–	–	–	–	–	–	–	–	29
	New Zealand	23	6	–	0	–	–	–	–	–	–	–	17
	South Africa	6	2	–	–	0	–	–	–	–	–	–	4
	West Indies	3	2	–	–	–	0	–	–	–	–	–	1
	India	13	1	–	–	–	–	2	–	–	–	–	10
Australia	New Zealand	13	–	4	1	–	–	–	–	–	–	–	8
	West Indies	2	–	0	–	–	0	–	–	–	–	–	2
	India	9	–	4	–	–	–	0	–	–	–	–	5
New Zealand	South Africa	3	–	–	1	0	–	–	–	–	–	–	2
	India	6	–	–	0	–	–	0	–	–	–	–	6
South Africa	India	2	–	–	–	0	–	2	–	–	–	–	–
	Netherlands	1	–	–	–	1	–	–	–	–	–	0	–
West Indies	India	6	–	–	–	–	1	1	–	–	–	–	4
	Pakistan	1	–	–	–	–	0	–	0	–	–	–	1
Pakistan	Sri Lanka	1	–	–	–	–	–	–	0	1	–	–	–
	Ireland	1	–	–	–	–	–	–	0	–	1	–	–
		140	20	20	2	1	1	5	0	1	1	0	89

	Tests	Won	Lost	Drawn	Toss Won
England	95	20	14	61	55
Australia	74	20	10	44	26
New Zealand	45	2	10	33	21
South Africa	12	1	5	6	6
West Indies	12	1	3	8	6†
India	36	5	6	25	18†
Pakistan	3	–	2	1	1
Sri Lanka	1	1	–	–	1
Ireland	1	1	–	–	1
Netherlands	1	–	1	–	1

† Results of tosses in five of the six India v West Indies Tests in 1976-77 are not known

TEAM RECORDS
HIGHEST INNINGS TOTALS

569-6d	Australia v England	Guildford	1998
525	Australia v India	Ahmedabad	1983-84
517-8	New Zealand v England	Scarborough	1996
503-5d	England v New Zealand	Christchurch	1934-35
497	England v South Africa	Shenley	2003
467	India v England	Taunton	2002
455	England v South Africa	Taunton	2003
448-9d	Australia v England	Sydney	2017-18
440	West Indies v Pakistan	Karachi	2003-04
427-4d	Australia v England	Worcester	1998
426-7d	Pakistan v West Indies	Karachi	2003-04
426-9d	India v England	Blackpool	1986
420-8d	Australia v England	Taunton	2019
414	England v New Zealand	Scarborough	1996
414	England v Australia	Guildford	1998
404-9d	India v South Africa	Paarl	2001-02

| 403-8d | New Zealand v India | Nelson | 1994-95 |
| 400-6d | India v South Africa | Mysore | 2014-15 |

The highest totals for countries not included above are:

316	South Africa v England	Shenley	2003
193-3d	Ireland v Pakistan	Dublin	2000
108	Netherlands v South Africa	Rotterdam	2007

LOWEST INNINGS TOTALS

35	England v Australia	Melbourne	1957-58
38	Australia v England	Melbourne	1957-58
44	New Zealand v England	Christchurch	1934-35
47	Australia v England	Brisbane	1934-35
50	Netherlands v South Africa	Rotterdam	2007
53	Pakistan v Ireland	Dublin	2000

The lowest innings totals for countries not included above are:

65	India v West Indies	Jammu	1976-77
67	West Indies v England	Canterbury	1979
89	South Africa v New Zealand	Durban	1971-72

BATTING RECORDS
1000 RUNS IN TESTS

		Career	M	I	NO	HS	Avge	100	50
1935	J.A.Brittin (E)	1979-98	27	44	5	167	49.61	5	11
1645	C.M.Edwards (E)	1996-2014	22	41	5	117	45.69	4	9
1594	R.Heyhoe-Flint (E)	1960-79	22	38	3	179	45.54	3	10
1301	D.A.Hockley (NZ)	1979-96	19	29	4	126*	52.04	4	7
1164	C.A.Hodges (E)	1984-92	18	31	2	158*	40.13	2	6
1110	S.Agarwal (I)	1984-95	13	23	1	190	50.45	4	4
1078	E.Bakewell (E)	1968-79	12	22	4	124	59.88	4	7
1030	S.C.Taylor (E)	1999-2009	15	27	2	177	41.20	4	2
1007	M.E.Maclagan (E)	1934-51	14	25	1	119	41.95	2	6
1002	K.L.Rolton (A)	1995-2009	14	22	4	209*	55.66	2	5

HIGHEST INDIVIDUAL INNINGS

242	Kiran Baluch	P v WI	Karachi	2003-04
214	M.Raj	I v E	Taunton	2002
213*	E.A.Perry	A v E	Sydney	2017-18
209*	K.L.Rolton	A v E	Leeds	2001
204	K.E.Flavell	NZ v E	Scarborough	1996
204‡	M.A.J.Goszko	A v E	Shenley	2001
200	J.Broadbent	A v E	Guildford	1998
193	D.A.Annetts	A v E	Collingham	1987
192	M.D.T.Kamini	I v SA	Mysore	2014-15
190	S.Agarwal	I v E	Worcester	1986
189	E.A.Snowball	E v NZ	Christchurch	1934-35
179	R.Heyhoe-Flint	E v A	The Oval	1976
177	S.C.Taylor	E v SA	Shenley	2003
176*	K.L.Rolton	A v E	Worcester	1998
167	J.A.Brittin	E v A	Harrogate	1998
161*	E.C.Drumm	E v A	Christchurch	1994-95
160	B.A.Daniels	E v NZ	Scarborough	1996
158*	C.A.Hodges	E v NZ	Canterbury	1984
157	H.C.Knight	E v A	Wormsley	2013
155*	P.F.McKelvey	NZ v E	Wellington	1968-69

‡ *On debut*

FIVE HUNDREDS

		Opponents								
		M	I	E	NZ	SA	WI	IND	P	SL	IRE
5	J.A.Brittin (E)	27	44	–	3	1	–	1	–		

HIGHEST PARTNERSHIP FOR EACH WICKET

1st	241	Kiran Baluch/Sajjida Shah	P v WI	Karachi	2003-04
2nd	275	M.D.T.Kamini/P.G.Raut	I v SA	Mysore	2014-15
3rd	309	L.A.Reeler/D.A.Annetts	A v E	Collingham	1987
4th	253	K.L.Rolton/L.C.Broadfoot	A v E	Leeds	2001
5th	138	J.Logtenberg/C.van der Westhuizen	SA v E	Shenley	2003
6th	229	J.M.Fields/R.L.Haynes	A v E	Worcester	2009
7th	157	M.Raj/J.Goswami	I v E	Taunton	2002
8th	181	S.J.Griffiths/D.L.Wilson	A v NZ	Auckland	1989-90
9th	107	B.Botha/M.Payne	SA v NZ	Cape Town	1971-72
10th	119	S.Nitschke/C.R.Smith	A v E	Hove	2005

BOWLING RECORDS
50 WICKETS IN TESTS

Wkts		Career	M	Balls	Runs	Avge	Best	5wI	10wM
77	M.B.Duggan (E)	1949-63	17	3734	1039	13.49	7- 6	5	–
68	E.R.Wilson (A)	1948-58	11	2885	803	11.80	7- 7	4	2
63	D.F.Edulji (I)	1976-91	20	5098†	1624	25.77	6- 64	1	–
60	M.E.Maclagan (E)	1934-51	14	3432	935	15.58	7- 10	3	–
60	C.L.Fitzpatrick (A)	1991-2006	13	3603	1147	19.11	5- 29	2	–
60	S.Kulkarni (I)	1976-91	19	3320†	1647	27.45	6- 99	5	–
57	R.H.Thompson (A)	1972-85	16	4304	1040	18.24	5- 33	1	–
55	J.Lord (NZ)	1966-79	15	3108	1049	19.07	6-119	4	1
50	E.Bakewell (E)	1968-79	12	2697	831	16.62	7- 61	3	1

† Excludes balls bowled in Sixth Test v West Indies 1976-77

TEN WICKETS IN A TEST

13-226	Shaiza Khan	P v WI	Karachi	2003-04
11- 16	E.R.Wilson	A v E	Melbourne	1957-58
11- 63	J.M.Greenwood	E v WI	Canterbury	1979
11-107	L.C.Pearson	E v A	Sydney	2002-03
10- 65	E.R.Wilson	A v NZ	Wellington	1947-48
10- 75	E.Bakewell	E v WI	Birmingham	1979
10- 78	J.Goswami	I v E	Taunton	2006
10-107	K.Price	A v I	Lucknow	1983-84
10-118	D.A.Gordon	A v E	Melbourne	1968-69
10-137	J.Lord	NZ v A	Melbourne	1978-79

SEVEN WICKETS IN AN INNINGS

8-53	N.David	I v E	Jamshedpur	1995-96
7- 6	M.B.Duggan	E v A	Melbourne	1957-58
7- 7	E.R.Wilson	A v E	Melbourne	1957-58
7-10	M.E.Maclagan	E v A	Brisbane	1934-35
7-18	A.Palmer	A v E	Brisbane	1934-35
7-24	L.Johnston	A v NZ	Melbourne	1971-72
7-34	G.E.McConway	E v I	Worcester	1986
7-41	J.A.Burley	NZ v E	The Oval	1966
7-51	L.C.Pearson	E v A	Sydney	2002-03
7-59	Shaiza Khan	P v WI	Karachi	2003-04
7-61	E.Bakewell	E v WI	Birmingham	1979

HAT-TRICKS

E.R.Wilson	Australia v England	Melbourne	1957-58
Shaiza Khan	Pakistan v West Indies	Karachi	2003-04
R.M.Farrell	Australia v England	Sydney	2010-11

WICKET-KEEPING AND FIELDING RECORDS

25 DISMISSALS IN TESTS

Total			Tests	Ct	St	
58	C.Matthews	Australia	20	46	12	1984-95
43	J.Smit	England	21	39	4	1992-2006
36	S.A.Hodges	England	11	19	17	1969-79
28	B.A.Brentnall	New Zealand	10	16	12	1966-72

EIGHT DISMISSALS IN A TEST

9 (8ct, 1st)	C.Matthews	A v I	Adelaide	1990-91
8 (6ct, 2st)	L.Nye	E v NZ	New Plymouth	1991-92

SIX DISMISSALS IN AN INNINGS

8 (6ct, 2st)	L.Nye	E v NZ	New Plymouth	1991-92
6 (2ct, 4st)	B.A.Brentnall	NZ v SA	Johannesburg	1971-72

20 CATCHES IN THE FIELD IN TESTS

Total			Tests	
25	C.A.Hodges	England	18	1984-92
21	S.Shah	India	20	1976-91
20	L.A.Fullston	Australia	12	1984-87

APPEARANCE RECORDS

25 TEST MATCH APPEARANCES

27	J.A.Brittin	England	1979-98

12 MATCHES AS CAPTAIN

			Won	Lost	Drawn	
14	P.F.McKelvey	New Zealand	2	3	9	1966-79
12	R.Heyhoe-Flint	England	2	–	10	1966-76
12	S.Rangaswamy	India	1	2	9	1976-84

WOMEN'S LIMITED-OVERS RECORDS

1973 to 6 March 2021
RESULTS SUMMARY

	Matches	Won	Lost	Tied	No Result	% Won (exc NR)
Australia	332	261	63	2	6	80.06
England	351	206	132	2	11	60.58
India	272	151	116	1	4	56.34
South Africa	199	100	88	3	8	52.35
New Zealand	344	171	165	2	6	50.59
West Indies	177	80	91	1	5	46.51
Sri Lanka	167	56	106	–	5	34.56
Trinidad & Tobago	6	2	4	–	–	33.33
Pakistan	168	48	116	1	3	29.09
Ireland	148	39	103	–	6	27.64
Bangladesh	38	9	27	–	2	25.00
Jamaica	5	1	4	–	–	20.00
Netherlands	101	19	81	–	1	19.00
Denmark	33	6	27	–	–	18.18
International XI	18	3	14	–	1	17.64
Young England	6	1	5	–	–	16.66
Scotland	8	1	7	–	–	12.50
Japan	5	–	5	–	–	0.00

TEAM RECORDS – HIGHEST INNINGS TOTALS

491-4 (50 overs)	New Zealand v Ireland	Dublin	2018
455-5 (50 overs)	New Zealand v Pakistan	Christchurch	1996-97
440-3 (50 overs)	New Zealand v Ireland	Dublin	2018
418 (49.5 overs)	New Zealand v Ireland	Dublin	2018
412-3 (50 overs)	Australia v Denmark	Mumbai	1997-98
397-4 (50 overs)	Australia v Pakistan	Melbourne	1996-97
378-5 (50 overs)	England v Pakistan	Worcester	2016

LARGEST RUNS MARGIN OF VICTORY

408 runs	New Zealand beat Pakistan	Christchurch	1996-97
374 runs	Australia beat Pakistan	Melbourne	1996-97

LOWEST INNINGS TOTALS

22 (23.4 overs)	Netherlands v West Indies	Deventer	2008
23 (24.1 overs)	Pakistan v Australia	Melbourne	1996-97
24 (21.3 overs)	Scotland v England	Reading	2001

BATTING RECORDS – 2700 RUNS IN A CAREER

Runs		Career	M	I	NO	HS	Avge	100	50
6888	M.Raj (I)	1999-2019	209	189	53	125*	50.64	7	53
5992	C.M.Edwards (E)	1997-2016	191	180	23	173*	38.16	9	46
4844	B.J.Clark (A)	1991-2005	118	114	12	229*	47.49	5	30
4814	K.L.Rolton (A)	1995-2009	141	132	32	154*	48.14	8	33
4754	S.R.Taylor (WI)	2008-2019	126	123	15	171	44.01	5	36
4548	S.W.Bates (NZ)	2006-2020	125	119	12	168	42.50	10	27
4101	S.C.Taylor (E)	1998-2011	126	120	18	156*	40.20	8	23
4067	A.E.Satterthwaite (NZ)	2007-2021	125	119	16	147	39.48	7	22
4064	D.A.Hockley (NZ)	1982-2000	118	115	18	117	41.89	4	34
4056	S.J.Taylor (E)	2006-2019	126	119	13	147	38.26	7	20
3856	M.M.Lanning (A)	2011-2020	82	82	12	152*	55.08	14	15
3492	A.J.Blackwell (A)	2003-2017	144	124	27	114	36.00	3	25
3277	M.du Preez (SA)	2007-2021	132	123	22	116*	32.44	2	14
3022	E.A.Perry (A)	2007-2019	112	89	31	112*	52.10	2	27
2935	H.C.Knight (E)	2010-2021	104	99	23	106	38.61	1	21
2919	H.M.Tiffen (NZ)	1999-2009	117	111	16	100	30.72	1	18
2856	A.Chopra (I)	1995-2012	127	112	21	100	31.38	1	18
2844	E.C.Drumm (NZ)	1992-2006	101	94	13	116	35.11	2	19

Runs		Career	M	I	NO	HS	Avge	100	50
2833	D.J.S.Dottin (WI)	2008-2019	117	111	11	104*	28.33	1	19
2744	Javeria Khan (P)	2008-2021	106	103	12	133*	30.15	2	15
2728	L.C.Sthalekar (A)	2001-2013	125	111	22	104*	30.65	2	16

HIGHEST INDIVIDUAL INNINGS

232*	A.C.Kerr	New Zealand v Ireland	Dublin	2018
229*	B.J.Clark	Australia v Denmark	Mumbai	1997-98
188	D.B.Sharma	India v Ireland	Potchefstroom	2017
178*	A.C.Jayangani	Sri Lanka v Australia	Bristol	2017
173*	C.M.Edwards	England v Ireland	Pune	1997-98
171*	H.Kaur	India v Australia	Derby	2017
171	S.R.Taylor	West Indies v Sri Lanka	Mumbai	2012-13
168*	T.T.Beaumont	England v Pakistan	Taunton	2016
168	S.W.Bates	New Zealand v Pakistan	Sydney	2008-09
157	R.H.Priest	New Zealand v Sri Lanka	Lincoln	2015-16
156*	L.M.Keightley	Australia v Pakistan	Melbourne	1996-97
156*	S.C.Taylor	England v India	Lord's	2006
154*	K.L.Rolton	Australia v Sri Lanka	Christchurch	2000-01
153*	J.Logtenberg	South Africa v Netherlands	Deventer	2007
152*	M.M.Lanning	Australia v Sri Lanka	Bristol	2017
151	K.L.Rolton	Australia v Ireland	Dublin	2005
151	S.W.Bates	New Zealand v Ireland	Dublin	2018

HIGHEST PARTNERSHIP FOR EACH WICKET

1st	320	D.B.Sharma/P.G.Raut	India v Ireland	Potchefstroom	2017
2nd	295	A.C.Kerr/L.M.Kasperek	New Zealand v Ireland	Dublin	2018
3rd	244	K.L.Rolton/L.C.Sthalekar	Australia v Ireland	Dublin	2005
4th	224*	J.Logtenberg/M.du Preez	South Africa v Netherlands	Deventer	2007
5th	188*	S.C.Taylor/J.Cassar	England v Sri Lanka	Lincoln	2000-01
6th	142	S.Luus/C.L.Tryon	South Africa v Ireland	Dublin	2016
7th	104*	S.J.Tsukigawa/N.J.Browne	New Zealand v England	Chennai	2006-07
8th	88	N.N.De Silva/O.U.Ranasinghe	Sri Lanka v England	Hambantota	2018-19
9th	73	L.R.F.Askew/I.T.Guha	England v New Zealand	Chennai	2006-07
10th	76	A.J.Blackwell/K.M.Beams	Australia v India	Derby	2017

BOWLING RECORDS – 100 WICKETS IN A CAREER

	LOI	Balls	Runs	W	Avge	Best	4w	R/Over
J.Goswami (I) 2002-2019	182	8835	4835	225	21.48	6-31	8	3.28
C.L.Fitzpatrick (A) 1993-2007	109	6017	3023	180	16.79	5-14	11	3.01
K.H.Brunt (E) 2005-2021	125	6077	3540	153	23.13	5-18	7	3.49
E.A.Perry (A) 2007-2019	112	5110	3693	152	24.29	7-22	4	4.33
A.Mohammed (WI) 2003-2019	122	5368	3098	151	20.51	7-14	12	3.46
Sana Mir (P) 2005-2019	120	5942	3665	151	24.27	5-32	8	3.70
L.C.Sthalekar (A) 2001-2013	125	5964	3646	146	24.97	5-35	2	3.66
S.Ismail (SA) 2007-2021	101	4910	2962	143	20.71	6-10	5	3.61
S.R.Taylor (WI) 2008-2019	126	5309	3032	142	21.35	4-17	5	3.42
N.David (I) 1995-2008	97	4892	2305	141	16.34	5-20	6	2.82
J.L.Gunn (E) 2004-2019	144	5906	3822	136	28.10	5-22	6	3.88
D.van Niekerk (SA) 2009-2020	102	4344	2549	130	19.60	5-17	8	3.52
L.A.Marsh (E) 2006-2019	103	5328	3463	129	26.84	5-15	4	3.89
M.Kapp (SA) 2009-2021	110	4809	2961	126	23.50	4-14	4	3.69
H.A.S.D.Siriwardene (SL) 2003-2019	118	5449	3577	124	28.84	4-11	6	3.93
J.L.Jonassen (A) 2012-2020	71	3294	2180	109	20.00	5-27	8	3.97
C.E.Taylor (E) 1988-2005	105	5140	2443	102	23.95	4-13	2	2.85
I.T.Guha (E) 2001-2011	83	3767	2345	101	23.21	5-14	4	3.73
S.Luus (SA) 2012-2021	82	2661	1990	100	19.90	6-36	8	4.48
N.Al Khadeer (I) 2002-2012	78	4036	2402	100	24.02	5-14	5	3.57

SIX OR MORE WICKETS IN AN INNINGS

7- 4	Saijida Shah	Pakistan v Japan	Amsterdam	2003
7- 8	J.M.Chamberlain	England v Denmark	Haarlem	1991

7-14	A.Mohammed	West Indies v Pakistan	Dhaka	2011-12
7-22	E.A.Perry	Australia v England	Canterbury	2019
7-24	S.Nitschke	Australia v England	Kidderminster	2005
6-10	J.Lord	New Zealand v India	Auckland	1981-82
6-10	M.Maben	India v Sri Lanka	Kandy	2003-04
6-10	S.Ismail	South Africa v Netherlands	Savar	2011-12
6-20	G.L.Page	New Zealand v Trinidad & T	St Albans	1973
6-20	D.B.Sharma	India v Sri Lanka	Ranchi	2015-16
6-20	Khadija Tul Kubra	Bangladesh v Pakistan	Cox's Bazar	2018-19
6-31	J.Goswami	India v New Zealand	Southgate	2011
6-32	B.H.McNeill	New Zealand v England	Lincoln, NZ	2007-08
6-36	S.Luus	South Africa v Ireland	Dublin	2016
6-45	S.Luus	South Africa v New Zealand	Hamilton	2019-20
6-46	A.Shrubsole	England v India	Lord's	2017

WICKET-KEEPING AND FIELDING RECORDS – 100 DISMISSALS IN A CAREER

Total			LOI	Ct	St
160	T.Chetty	South Africa	114	112	48
136	S.J.Taylor	England	126	85	51
133	R.J.Rolls	New Zealand	104	89	44
114	J.Smit	England	109	69	45
102	M.R.Aguillera	West Indies	112	76	26

SIX DISMISSALS IN AN INNINGS

6 (4ct, 2st)	S.L.Illingworth	New Zealand v Australia	Beckenham	1993
6 (1ct, 5st)	V.Kalpana	India v Denmark	Slough	1993
6 (2ct, 4st)	Batool Fatima	Pakistan v West Indies	Karachi	2003-04
6 (4ct, 2st)	Batool Fatima	Pakistan v Sri Lanka	Colombo (PSS)	2011

50 CATCHES IN THE FIELD IN A CAREER

Total			LOI	Career
67	S.W.Bates	New Zealand	125	2006-2020
64	J.Goswami	India	182	2002-2019
58	S.R.Taylor	West Indies	126	2008-2019
55	A.J.Blackwell	Australia	144	2003-2017
53	M.Raj	India	209	1999-2019
52	D.van Niekerk	South Africa	102	2009-2020
52	L.S.Greenway	England	126	2003-2016
52	C.M.Edwards	England	191	1997-2016

FOUR CATCHES IN THE FIELD IN AN INNINGS

4	Z.J.Goss	Australia v New Zealand	Adelaide	1995-96
4	J.L.Gunn	England v New Zealand	Lincoln, NZ	2014-15
4	Nahida Khan	Pakistan v Sri Lanka	Dambulla	2017-18

APPEARANCE RECORDS – 130 APPEARANCES

209	M.Raj	India	1999-2019
191	C.M.Edwards	England	1997-2016
182	J.Goswami	India	2002-2019
144	A.J.Blackwell	Australia	2003-2017
144	J.L.Gunn	England	2004-2019
141	K.L.Rolton	Australia	1995-2009
134	S.J.McGlashan	New Zealand	2002-2016
132	M.du Preez	South Africa	2007-2021

100 CONSECUTIVE APPEARANCES

109	M.Raj	India	17.04.2004 to 07.02.2013
101	M.du Preez	South Africa	08.03.2009 to 05.02.2018

100 MATCHES AS CAPTAIN

			Won	Lost	No Result	
132	M.Raj	India	82	47	3	2004-2019
117	C.M.Edwards	England	72	38	7	2005-2016
101	B.J.Clark	Australia	83	17	1	1994-2005

WOMEN'S INTERNATIONAL TWENTY20 RECORDS

2004 to 27 March 2021

As for the men's IT20 records, in the section that follows, except for the first-ranked record and the highest partnerships, only those games featuring a nation that has also played a full LOI are listed.

MATCH RESULTS SUMMARY

	Matches	Won	Lost	Tied	NR	Win %
Zimbabwe	14	14	–	–	–	100.0
England	149	107	38	3	1	72.29
Australia	141	93	45	3	–	65.95
New Zealand	130	75	52	2	1	58.13
India	123	67	54	–	2	55.37
West Indies	135	70	58	5	2	52.63
South Africa	114	51	61	–	2	45.53
Pakistan	120	48	67	3	2	40.67
Bangladesh	75	27	48	–	–	36.00
Ireland	71	20	50	–	1	28.57
Sri Lanka	100	24	72	–	4	25.00

WOMEN'S INTERNATIONAL TWENTY20 RECORDS
TEAM RECORDS – HIGHEST INNINGS TOTALS † Batting Second

314-2	Uganda v Mali	Rwanda	2019
255-2	Bangladesh v Maldives	Pokhara	2019-20
250-3	England v South Africa	Taunton	2018
226-3	Australia v England	Chelmsford	2019
226-2	Australia v Sri Lanka	Sydney (NS)	2019-20
217-4	Australia v Sri Lanka	Sydney (NS)	2019-20
216-1	New Zealand v South Africa	Taunton	2018
213-4	Ireland v Netherlands	Deventer	2019
209-4	Australia v England	Mumbai (BS)	2017-18
205-1	South Africa v Netherlands	Potchefstroom	2010-11
204-2	England v Sri Lanka	Colombo (PSS)	2018-19
199-3†	England v India	Mumbai (BS)	2017-18

LOWEST COMPLETED INNINGS TOTALS † Batting Second

6† (12.1)	Maldives v Bangladesh	Pokhara	2019-20
6 (9.0)	Mali v Rwanda	Rwanda	2019
27† (13.4)	Malaysia v India	Kuala Lumpur	2018
30† (18.4)	Malaysia v Pakistan	Kuala Lumpur	2018
30† (12.5)	Bangladesh v Pakistan	Cox's Bazar	2018-19
35† (19.2)	Mozambique v Zimbabwe	Harare	2019
35 (12.1)	Nigeria v Zimbabwe	Harare	2019

The lowest score for England is 87 (v Australia, Hove, 2015).

BATTING RECORDS – 2000 RUNS IN A CAREER

Runs			M	I	NO	HS	Avge	50	R/100B
3301	S.W.Bates	NZ	122	119	9	124*	30.00	22	110.6
3062	S.R.Taylor	WI	108	106	21	90	36.02	21	101.3†
2859	M.M.Lanning	A	107	101	22	133*	36.18	15	115.9
2605	C.M.Edwards	E	95	93	14	92*	32.97	12	106.9
2565	D.J.S.Dottin	WI	118	116	19	112*	26.44	14	123.5†
2457	S.F.M.Devine	NZ	97	94	12	105	29.96	15	124.7
2364	M.Raj	I	89	84	21	97*	37.52	17	96.3†
2225	Bismah Maroof	P	108	102	21	70*	27.46	11	92.8

Runs			M	I	NO	HS	Avge	50	R/100B
2186	H.Kaur	I	114	102	21	103	26.98	7	102.0†
2177	S.J.Taylor	E	90	87	12	77	29.02	16	110.6
2107	A.J.Healy	A	115	100	16	148*	25.08	13	131.6

† No information on balls faced for games at Roseau on 22 and 23 February 2012.

HIGHEST INDIVIDUAL INNINGS

Score	Balls				
148*	61	A.J.Healy	A v SL	Sydney (NS)	2019-20
133*	63	M.M.Lanning	A v E	Chelmsford	2019
126	65	M.M.Lanning	A v Ire	Sylhet	2013-14
124*	66	S.W.Bates	NZ v SA	Taunton	2018
124	64	D.N.Wyatt	E v I	Mumbai (BS)	2017-18
117*	70	B.L.Mooney	A v E	Canberra	2017-18
116*	71	S.A.Fritz	SA v Neth	Potchefstroom	2010-11
116	52	T.T.Beaumont	E v SA	Taunton	2018

HIGHEST PARTNERSHIP FOR EACH WICKET

1st	182	S.W.Bates/S.F.M.Devine	NZ v SA	Taunton	2018
2nd	162*	H.K.Matthews/C.N.Nation	WI v Ire	Dublin	2019
3rd	236*	Nigar Sultana/Fargana Hoque	B v Mald	Pokhara	2019-20
4th	147*	K.L.Rolton/K.A.Blackwell	A v E	Taunton	2005
5th	119*	M.M.Lanning/R.L.Haynes	A v NZ	Sydney	2018-19
6th	84	M.A.A.Sanjeewani/N.N.D.de Silva	SL v P	Colombo (SSC)	2017-18
7th	60	Bismah Maroof/Sidra Nawaz	P v E	Kuala Lumpur	2019-20
8th	39	L.E.Kaushalya/K.A.D.A.Kanchana	SL v I	Ranchi	2015-16
9th	33*	D.Hazell/H.L.Colvin	E v WI	Bridgetown	2013-14
10th	33	M.L.Green/R.A.Mair	NZ v E	Wellington	2020-21

BOWLING RECORDS – 85 WICKETS IN A CAREER

Wkts			Matches	Overs	Mdns	Runs	Avge	Best	R/Over
120	A.Mohammed	WI	111	373.3	6	2077	17.30	5-10	5.56
114	E.A.Perry	A	120	376.5	6	2209	19.37	4-12	5.86
106	S.Ismail	SA	95	333.5	14	1908	18.00	5-12	5.71
102	A.Shrubsole	E	79	266.2	10	1587	15.55	5-11	5.95
99	Nida Dar	P	105	336.1	6	1817	18.35	5-21	5.40
95	Poonam Yadav	I	67	242.0	5	1367	14.38	4-9	5.64
94	S.R.Taylor	WI	108	280.5	4	1587	16.88	4-12	5.65
94	S.F.M.Devine	NZ	97	255.0	6	1609	17.11	4-22	6.30
93	M.Schutt	A	70	235.3	6	1424	15.31	4-18	6.04
93	K.H.Brunt	E	89	321.5	15	1758	18.90	3- 6	5.46
89	Sana Mir	P	106	378.2	9	2085	23.42	4-13	5.51
85	D.Hazell	E	85	317.3	6	1764	20.75	4-12	5.55

BEST FIGURES IN AN INNINGS

6- 0	Anjali Chand	Nep v Mald	Pokhara	2019-20
6-17	A.E.Satterthwaite	NZ v E	Taunton	2007
5- 5	D.J.S.Dottin	WI v B	Providence	2018-19
5- 8	S.Luus	SA v Ire	Chennai	2015-16
5-10	A.Mohammed	WI v SA	Cape Town	2009-10
5-10	M.Strano	A v NZ	Geelong	2016-17
5-11	A.Shrubsole	E v NZ	Wellington	2011-12
5-11	J.Goswami	I v A	Visakhapatnam	2011-12
5-12	A.Mohammed	WI v NZ	Bridgetown	2013-14
5-12	W.Liengprasert	Thai v SL	Kuala Lumpur	2018
5-12	J.L.Jonassen	A v I	Melbourne (JO)	2019-20
5-12	S.Ismail	SA v P	Durban	2020-21

HAT-TRICKS

Asmavia Iqbal	Pakistan v England	Loughborough	2012
Ekta Bisht	Sri Lanka v India	Colombo (NCC)	2012-13
M.Kapp	South Africa v Bangladesh	Potchefstroom	2013-14
N.R.Sciver	England v New Zealand	Bridgetown	2013-14
Sana Mir	Pakistan v Sri Lanka	Sharjah	2014-15
A.M.Peterson	New Zealand v Australia	Geelong	2016-17
M.Schutt	Australia v India	Mumbai (BS)	2017-18
Fahima Khatun	Bangladesh v UAE	Utrecht	2018
A.Mohammed	West Indies v South Africa	Tarouba	2018-19
A.Shrubsole	England v South Africa	Gros Islet	2018-19
O.Kamchomphu	Thailand v Ireland	Deventer	2019

WICKET-KEEPING RECORDS – 50 DISMISSALS IN A CAREER

Dis			Matches	Ct	St
93	A.J.Healy	Australia	115	42	51
74	S.J.Taylor	England	90	23	51
72	R.H.Priest	New Zealand	75	41	31
70	M.R.Aguilleira	West Indies	95	36	34
67	T.Bhatia	India	50	23	44
64	T.Chetty	South Africa	76	37	27
50	Batool Fatima	Pakistan	45	11	39

FIVE DISMISSALS IN AN INNINGS

5 (1ct, 4st)	Kycia A.Knight	West Indies v Sri Lanka	Colombo (RPS)	2012-13
5 (1ct, 4st)	Batool Fatima	Pakistan v Ireland	Dublin	2013
5 (1ct, 4st)	Batool Fatima	Pakistan v Ireland	Dublin	2013
5 (3ct, 2st)	B.Bezuidenhout	New Zealand v Ireland	Dublin	2018
5 (1ct, 4st)	S.J.Bryce	Scotland v Netherlands	Arbroath	2019

FIELDING RECORDS – 35 CATCHES IN A CAREER

Total			Matches	Total			Matches
64	S.W.Bates	New Zealand	122	38	V.Krishnamurthy	India	76
58	J.L.Gunn	England	104	38	M.M.Lanning	Australia	107
54	L.S.Greenway	England	85	36	E.A.Perry	Australia	120
43	H.Kaur	India	114	35	A.E.Satterthwaite	New Zealand	105
40	N.R.Sciver	England	83				

FOUR CATCHES IN AN INNINGS

4	L.S.Greenway	England v New Zealand	Chelmsford	2010
4	V.Krishnamurthy	India v Australia	Providence	2018-19

APPEARANCE RECORDS – 108 APPEARANCES

122	S.W.Bates	New Zealand		114	H.Kaur	India
120	E.A.Perry	Australia		111	A.Mohammed	West Indies
118	D.J.S.Dottin	West Indies		108	Bismah Maroof	Pakistan
116	D.N.Wyatt	England		108	S.R.Taylor	West Indies
115	A.J.Healy	Australia				

60 MATCHES AS CAPTAIN

			W	L	T	NR	%age wins
93	C.M.Edwards	England	68	23	1	1	73.91
75	M.M.Lanning	Australia	57	17	1	–	76.00
73	M.R.Aguilleira	West Indies	39	29	3	2	54.92
65	Sana Mir	Pakistan	26	36	2	1	40.62
65	Salma Khatun	Bangladesh	27	38	–	–	41.53
64	S.W.Bates	New Zealand	39	24	1	–	60.93

RACHAEL HEYHOE FLINT TROPHY 2020

The 50-over tournament was held between 29 August and 27 September.

NORTH GROUP

		P	W	L	T	NR	Pts	Net RR
1	Northern Diamonds	6	5	1	–	–	23	+1.00
2	Central Sparks	6	3	3	–	–	13	–0.28
3	Thunder	6	2	4	–	–	9	–0.51
4	Lightning	6	2	5	–	–	8	–0.11

SOUTH GROUP

		P	W	L	T	NR	Pts	Net RR
1	Southern Vipers	6	6	–	–	–	27	+1.01
2	Western Storm	6	4	2	–	–	18	+0.51
3	South East Stars	6	2	4	–	–	10	–0.19
4	Sunrisers	6	–	6	–	–	0	–1.36

4 points for a win, with a bonus point if the winning side has a run rate 1.25 times greater than the opposition. 2 points for no result/tie.

FINAL: At Edgbaston, Birmingham, 27 September. Toss: Northern Diamonds. **SOUTHERN VIPERS** won by 38 runs. Southern Vipers 231 (49.5; G.L.Adams 80, K.A.Levick 3-49). Northern Diamonds 193 (42.2; S.L.Kalis 55, C.M.Taylor 6-34). Award: C.M.Taylor.

TEAM RECORDS – HIGHEST TOTALS

303-5 (50)	Lightning v Central Sparks	Leicester
289-8 (50)	South East Stars v Sunrisers	Beckenham
288-1 (50)	Southern Vipers v Western Storm	Southampton
288-6 (50)	Western Storm v Sunrisers	Bristol

LOWEST TOTAL

98 (36.5)	South East Stars v Southern Vipers	Hove

LARGEST MARGINS OF VICTORY

111 runs	Southern Vipers (209) beat South East Stars (98)	Hove
9 wickets	Northern Diamonds (145-1) beat Central Sparks (144)	Birmingham

BATTING RECORDS – MOST RUNS

500 (ave 83.33)	G.L.Adams	Southern Vipers
395 (ave 79.00)	S.J.Bryce	Lightning

HIGHEST SCORES

Score	Balls			
154*	155	G.L.Adams	Southern Vipers v Storm	Southampton
136*	133	S.J.Bryce	Lightning v Central Sparks	Leicester

HIGHEST STRIKE RATE IN AN INNINGS (Qualification: 30 runs, 150+ strike rate)

R/100B	Score	Balls			
157.8	30	19	G.J.Gibbs	SE Stars v Southern Vipers	The Oval

BOWLING RECORDS – MOST WICKETS

		P	O	M	Runs	Avge	Best	4w	R/Over
15	C.M.Taylor	Southern Vipers	5	44.0	2	152	10.13	6-34	2	3.45
14	K.E.Bryce	Lightning	6	55.4	4	216	15.42	5-29	2	3.88

BEST BOWLING FIGURES IN AN INNINGS

6-34	C.M.Taylor	Southern Vipers v Northern Diamonds	Birmingham
5-20	K.H.Brunt	Northern Diamonds v Central Sparks	Birmingham
5-26	F.M.K.Morris	Western Storm v Sunrisers	Chelmsford
5-29	K.E.Bryce	Lightning v Northern Diamonds	Chester-le-St

PRINCIPAL WOMEN'S FIXTURES 2021

| F | Floodlit match | | RHF | Rachael Heyhoe Flint Trophy (50 overs) |
| 100 | The Hundred | | T20 | Women's Regional T20 competition |

Sat 29 May
RHF	Leeds	Diamonds v Central Sparks
RHF	Southampton	Southern Vipers v Lightning
RHF	Derby	Sunrisers v SE Stars
RHF	Bristol	Western Storm v Thunder

Mon 31 May
RHF	Birmingham	Central Sparks v Western Storm
RHF	tbc	Lightning v Diamonds
RHF	Beckenham	SE Stars v Southern Vipers
RHF	tbc	Thunder v Sunrisers

Sat 5 June
RHF	The Oval	SE Stars v Western Storm
RHF	Hove	Southern Vipers v Central Sparks
RHF	tbc	Sunrisers v Diamonds
RHF	tbc	Thunder v Lightning

Sat 12 June
RHF	Worcester	Central Sparks v Thunder
RHF	tbc	Lightning v Sunrisers
RHF	Leeds	Diamonds v SE Stars
RHF	tbc	Western Storm v Southern Vipers

Sat 26 June
T20F	Birmingham	Central Sparks v Southern Vipers
T20	Nottingham	Lightning v SE Stars
T20	Leeds	Diamonds v Thunder
T20	Taunton	Western Storm v Sunrisers

Fri 2 July
| T20F | Chelmsford | Sunrisers v Diamonds |

Sat 3 July
T20	Canterbury	SE Stars v Central Sparks
T20	tbc	Southern Vipers v Lightning
T20	tbc	Thunder v Western Storm

Fri 9 July
| T20 | Manchester | Thunder v Sunrisers |

Sat 10 July
T20	tbc	Lightning v Central Sparks
T20	Beckenham	SE Stars v Southern Vipers
T20	Taunton	Western Storm v Diamonds

Wed 21 July
| 100 | The Oval | Invincibles v Originals |

Fri 23 July
| 100 | Birmingham | Phoenix v London Spirit |

Sat 24 July
| 100 | Leeds | Superchargers v Welsh Fire |
| 100 | Nottingham | Trent Rockets v Southern Brave |

Sun 25 July
| 100 | Lord's | London Spirit v Invincibles |
| 100 | Manchester | Originals v Phoenix |

Mon 26 July
| 100 | Nottingham | Trent Rockets v Superchargers |

Tue 27 July
| 100 | Cardiff | Welsh Fire v Southern Brave |

Wed 28 July
| 100 | Manchester | Originals v Superchargers |

Thu 29 July
| 100 | Lord's | London Spirit v Trent Rockets |

Fri 30 July
| 100 | Southampton | Southern Brave v Phoenix |

Sat 31 July
| 100 | Leeds | Superchargers v Invincibles |
| 100 | Cardiff | Welsh Fire v Originals |

Sun 1 August
| 100 | Birmingham | Phoenix v Trent Rockets |
| 100 | Lord's | London Spirit v Southern Brave |

Mon 2 August
| 100 | The Oval | Invincibles v Welsh Fire |

Tue 3 August
| 100 | Lord's | London Spirit v Superchargers |

Wed 4 August
| 100 | Birmingham | Phoenix v Invincibles |

Thu 5 August
| 100 | Manchester | Originals v Southern Brave |

Fri 6 August
| 100 | Cardiff | Welsh Fire v Trent Rockets |

Sat 7 August
| 100 | Southampton | Southern Brave v Superchargers |

Sun 8 August
| 100 | The Oval | Invincibles v Trent Rockets |

Mon 9 August
| 100 | Birmingham | Phoenix v Welsh Fire |

Tue 10 August
| 100 | Manchester | Originals v London Spirit |

Wed 11 August
100 Southampton Southern Brave v Welsh Fire

Thu 12 August
100 Leeds Superchargers v Originals

Fri 13 August
100 Nottingham Trent Rockets v Phoenix

Sat 14 August
100 The Oval Invincibles v London Spirit

Sun 15 August
100 Nottingham Trent Rockets v Originals

Mon 16 August
100 Southampton Southern Brave v Invincibles

Tue 17 August
100 Leeds Superchargers v Phoenix

Wed 18 August
100 Cardiff Welsh Fire v London Spirit

Fri 20 August
100 The Oval Eliminator

Sat 21 August
100 Lord's FINAL

Wed 25 August
T20 tbc Diamonds v Sunrisers
T20 Guildford SE Stars v Lightning
T20 Hove Southern Vipers v Central Sparks
T20 Cardiff Western Storm v Thunder

Sat 28 August
T20 Worcester Central Sparks v Lightning
T20 Chester-le-St Diamonds v Western Storm

Details of any international fixtures for the summer had not been confirmed at the time of going to press.

T20 tbc Southern Vipers v SE Stars
T20 Northampton Sunrisers v Thunder

Mon 30 August
T20 Worcester Central Sparks v SE Stars
T20 Derby Lightning v Southern Vipers
T20 tbc Sunrisers v Western Storm
T20 tbc Thunder v Diamonds

Sun 5 September
T20 tbc Semi-final and FINAL

Fri 10 September
RHF Chester-le-St Diamonds v Western Storm
RHF Beckenham SE Stars v Lightning
RHF tbc Sunrisers v Central Sparks
RHF tbc Thunder v Southern Vipers

Sun 12 September
RHF Worcester Central Sparks v SE Stars
RHF Chester-le-St Diamonds v Thunder
RHF tbc unrisers v Southern Vipers
RHF Bristol Western Storm v Lightning

Sat 18 September
RHF tbc Lightning v Central Sparks
RHF Beckenham SE Stars v Thunder
RHF Southampton Southern Vipers v Diamonds
RHF Bristol Western Storm v Sunrisers

Wed 22 September
RHF tbc Play-off

Sat 25 September
RHF tbc FINAL

THE HUNDRED FIXTURES 2021

Thu 22 July
The Oval   Invincibles v Originals

Fri 23 July
Birmingham   Phoenix v London Spirit

Sat 24 July
Leeds   Superchargers v Welsh Fire
Nottingham   Trent Rockets v Southern Brave

Sun 25 July
Manchester   Originals v Phoenix
Lord's   London Spirit v Invincibles

Mon 26 July
Nottingham   Trent Rockets v Superchargers

Tue 27 July
Cardiff   Welsh Fire v Southern Brave

Wed 28 July
Manchester   Originals v Superchargers

Thu 29 July
Lord's   London Spirit v Trent Rockets

Fri 30 July
Southampton   Southern Brave v Phoenix

Sat 31 July
Leeds   Superchargers v Invincibles
Cardiff   Welsh Fire v Originals

Sun 1 August
Birmingham   Phoenix v Trent Rockets
Lord's   London Spirit v Southern Brave

Mon 2 August
The Oval   Invincibles v Welsh Fire

Tue 3 August
Lord's   London Spirit v Superchargers

Wed 4 August
Birmingham   Phoenix v Invincibles

Thu 5 August
Manchester   Originals v Southern Brave

Fri 6 August
Cardiff   Welsh Fire v Trent Rockets

Sat 7 August
Southampton   Southern Brave v Superchargers

Sun 8 August
The Oval   Invincibles v Trent Rockets

Mon 9 August
Birmingham   Phoenix v Welsh Fire

Tue 10 August
Manchester   Originals v London Spirit

Wed 11 August
Southampton   Southern Brave v Welsh Fire

Thu 12 August
Leeds   Superchargers v Originals

Fri 13 August
Nottingham   Trent Rockets v Phoenix

Sat 14 August
The Oval   Invincibles v London Spirit

Sun 15 August
Nottingham   Trent Rockets v Originals

Mon 16 August
Southampton   Southern Brave v Invincibles

Tue 17 August
Leeds   Superchargers v Phoenix

Wed 18 August
Cardiff   Welsh Fire v London Spirit

Fri 20 August
The Oval   Eliminator

Sat 21 August
Lord's   FINAL

SECOND XI CHAMPIONSHIP FIXTURES 2021

FOUR-DAY MATCHES

APRIL

Tue 6	Taunton Vale	Somerset v Glamorgan
Mon 12	Billericay	Essex v Durham
	Northwood	Middlesex v Kent/Sussex
	Birm EFSG	Warwicks v Somerset
	Kidderminster	Worcs v Glos
Tue 13	Northampton	Northants v Derbyshire
	Notts SC	Notts v Lancashire
Mon 19	tbc	Durham v Derbyshire
	Billericay	Essex v Surrey
	Bristol	Glos v Yorkshire
	Polo Farm, Cant	Kent/Sussex v Hampshire
	Crosby	Lancashire v Glamorgan
	Notts SC	Notts v Leics
	Taunton Vale	Somerset v Worcs
Mon 26	Kibworth	Leics v Derbyshire
	Guildford	Surrey v Yorkshire
	Birm EFSG	Warwicks v Notts
	Kidderminster	Worcs v Lancashire
Tue 27	Southampton	Hampshire v Middlesex

MAY

Mon 3	Derby	Derbyshire v Warwicks
	Darlington	Durham v Notts
	Billericay	Essex v Yorkshire
	Canterbury	Kent v Northants
	Crosby	Lancashire v Leics
	Taunton Vale	Somerset v Glos
	Hove	Sussex v Surrey
Tue 4	Worcester	Worcs v Glamorgan
Mon 10	Derby	Derbyshire v Notts
	Newport	Glamorgan v Glos
	Southampton	Hampshire v Sussex
	Radlett	Middlesex v Somerset
	Scarborough	Yorkshire v Lancashire
Mon 17	Manchester	Lancashire v Middlesex
	Kibworth	Leics v Durham
	New Malden	Surrey v Hampshire
	Birm EFSG	Warwicks v Northants
	York	Yorkshire v Notts
Tues 18	Blackstone	Sussex v Essex
Mon 24	Belper Mead	Derbyshire v Lancashire
	Newport	Glamorgan v Warwicks
	Milton Keynes	Northants v Worcs
	Leeds Wwood	Yorkshire v Durham

JUNE

Mon 28	Billericay	Essex v Middlesex

	Newport	Glamorgan v Leics
	Rockhampton	Glos v Northants
	Southport	Lancashire v Notts
	Taunton Vale	Somerset v Surrey
	Blackstone	Sussex v Kent
	Leeds Wwood	Yorkshire v Warwicks

JULY

Mon 5	tbc	Durham v Kent
	Newport	Glamorgan v Northants
	Rockhampton	Glos v Hampshire
	Kibworth	Leics v Yorkshire
	Notts SC	Notts v Worcs
	New Malden	Surrey v Middlesex
	Birm EFSG	Warwicks v Lancashire

AUGUST

Mon 16	Billericay	Essex v Hampshire
	Rockhampton	Glos v Sussex
	Desborough	Northants v Leics
	Notts SC	Notts v Durham
	Leeds Wwood	Yorkshire v Derbyshire
Mon 23	tbc	Durham v Lancashire
	Rockhampton	Glos v Glamorgan
	Folkestone	Kent v Hampshire
	Notts SC	Notts v Derbyshire
	Taunton Vale	Somerset v Essex
	Worcester	Worcs v Warwicks
Tue 24	Radlett	Middlesex v Sussex
Mon 30	Polo Farm, Cant	Kent v Surrey
	Notts SC	Notts v Northants
Tue 31	Belper Mead	Derbyshire v Glamorgan
	Chester BH	Lancashire v Yorkshire

SEPTEMBER

Mon 6	tbc	Derbyshire v Middlesex
	Newport	Glamorgan v Yorkshire
	Rockhampton	Glos v Surrey
	tbc	Kent v Essex
	Kibworth	Leics v Notts
	Milton Keynes	Northants v Somerset
	Blackstone	Sussex v Durham
Tue 7	Southampton	Hampshire v Warwicks
Mon 13	Rockhampton	Glos v Warwicks
	Northwood	Middlesex v Essex
	Scarborough	Yorkshire v Worcs
Tue 14	Southampton	Hampshire v Somerset
	Southport	Lancashire v Durham

SECOND XI TWENTY20 CUP FIXTURES 2021

MAY				tbc	Northants v Warwicks
Thu 27	Southend	Essex v Kent		tbc	Notts v Derbyshire
Mon 31	Derby	Derbyshire v Leics		Taunton Vale	Somerset v Glamorgan
	Southend	Essex v Sussex		Kidderminster	Worcs v Glos
	Southampton	Hampshire v Surrey	Wed 9	tbc	Durham v Notts (x 2)
	Birm EFSG	Warwicks v Glamorgan		New Malden	Surrey v Hampshire
	Barnt Green	Worcs v Somerset		Birm EFSG	Warwicks v Glos
JUNE			Thu 10	tbc	Durham v Leics (x 2)
Tue 1	Derby	Derbyshire v Lancashire		Polo Farm, Cant	Kent v Essex
	Newport	Glamorgan v Somerset		Liverpool	Lancashire v Yorkshire
	Bristol	Glos v Northants (x 2)		Taunton Vale	Somerset v Worcs
	tbc	Notts v Yorkshire (x 2)		New Malden	Surrey v Middlesex
	New Malden	Surrey v Sussex	Fri 11	Liverpool	Lancashire v Derbyshire
Wed 2	Newport	Glamorgan v Northants		Northwood	Middlesex v Sussex
	Rockhampton	Glos v Worcs		tbc	Northants v Glamorgan
	Southampton	Hampshire v Kent (x 2)	Sun 13	New Malden	Surrey v Kent
	Kibworth	Leics v Derbyshire	Mon 14	tbc	Durham v Lancashire (x 2)
	New Malden	Surrey v Essex		tbc	Essex v Middlesex
Thu 3	Rockhampton	Glos v Somerset		Newport	Glamorgan v Glos
	Manchester	Lancashire v Notts (x 2)		Polo Farm, Cant	Kent v Sussex
	Hove	Sussex v Kent		Kibworth	Leics v Notts
	Hove	Sussex v Middlesex		Barnt Green	Worcs v Northants
	Barnt Green	Worcs v Warwicks (x 2)		Doncaster	Yorkshire v Derbyshire
	Leeds Wwood	Yorkshire v Durham (x 2)	Tue 15	Rockhampton	Glos v Glamorgan
Fri 4	tbc	Durham v Derbyshire (x 2)		Northwood	Middlesex v Surrey
	Northwood	Middlesex v Hampshire		Hove	Sussex v Hampshire (x 2)
	Northampton	Northants v Worcs		Moseley	Warwicks v Somerset
	Taunton Vale	Somerset v Warwicks		Doncaster	Yorkshire v Leics
	Hove	Sussex v Essex	Wed 16	tbc	Derbyshire v Notts
Mon 7	Derby	Derbyshire v Yorkshire		tbc	Essex v Surrey
	tbc	Essex v Hampshire (x 2)		Beckenham	Kent v Middlesex
	Newport	Glamorgan v Worcs		Manchester	Lancashire v Leics (x 2)
	Northwood	Middlesex v Kent		tbc	Northants v Somerset
	tbc	Notts v Leics	Thu 17	Rockhampton	Glos v Warwicks
	Taunton Vale	Somerset v Glos		Stourbridge	Worcs v Glamorgan
	Blackstone	Sussex v Surrey		Leeds Wwood	Yorkshire v Lancashire
	Birm EFSG	Warwicks v Northants	Fri 18	Newport	Glamorgan v Warwicks
Tue 8	Polo Farm, Cant	Kent v Surrey		Newclose IoW	Hampshire v Middlesex
	Kibworth	Leics v Yorkshire		Taunton Vale	Somerset v Northants
	Northwood	Middlesex v Essex	Thu 24	Arundel	Semi-finals and FINAL

329

PRINCIPAL FIXTURES 2021

CC1   LV= Insurance County Championship Group 1
CC2   LV= Insurance County Championship Group 2
CC3   LV= Insurance County Championship Group 3 — Floodlit
FCF   First-Class Friendly
LOI   Royal London Limited-Overs International

50L   Royal London One-Day Cup
T20   Vitality Blast
IT20   Vitality Twenty20 International
TM   Test Match
UCCE   University Centre of Cricketing Excellence
Uni   University match

Wed 24 – Fri 26 March

Uni	Nottingham	Notts v Oxford UCCE
Uni	Kidderminster	Worcs v Durham UCCE

Mon 29 – Wed 31 March

Uni	Cardiff	Glamorgan v Cardiff UCCE
Uni	Leicester	Leics v Loughboro UCCE
Uni	Leeds	Yorkshire v Leeds/Brad UCCE

Sat 3 – Mon 5 April

Uni	Derby	Derbyshire v Cardiff UCCE
Uni	Leeds W'wood	Leeds/Brad UCCE v Warwicks
Uni	Leeds	Yorkshire v Durham UCCE

Thu 8 – Sun 11 April

CC1	Chelmsford	Essex v Worcs
CC1	Nottingham	Notts v Durham
CC1	Birmingham	Warwicks v Derbyshire
CC2	Bristol	Glos v Surrey
CC2	Leicester	Leics v Hampshire
CC2	Lord's	Middlesex v Somerset
CC3	Northampton	Northants v Kent
CC3	Hove	Sussex v Lancashire
CC3	Leeds	Yorkshire v Glamorgan

Thu 15 – Sun 18 April

CC1	Derby	Derbyshire v Worcs
CC1	Chelmsford	Essex v Durham
CC1	Nottingham	Notts v Warwicks
CC2	Southampton	Hampshire v Middlesex
CC2	Taunton	Somerset v Glos
CC2	The Oval	Surrey v Leics
CC3	Cardiff	Glamorgan v Sussex
CC3	Canterbury	Kent v Yorkshire
CC3	Manchester	Lancashire v Northants

Thu 22 – Sun 25 April

CC1	Chester-le-St	Durham v Derbyshire
CC1	Birmingham	Warwicks v Essex
CC1	Worcester	Worcs v Notts
CC2	Southampton	Hampshire v Glos
CC2	Lord's	Middlesex v Surrey
CC2	Leicester	Leics v Somerset
CC3	Canterbury	Kent v Lancashire
CC3	Northampton	Northants v Glamorgan
CC3	Hove	Sussex v Yorkshire

Thu 29 Apr – Sun 2 May

CC1	Derby	Derbyshire v Notts
CC1	Chester-le-St	Durham v Warwicks
CC1	Worcester	Worcs v Essex
CC2	Bristol	Glos v Leics
CC2	Taunton	Somerset v Middlesex
CC2	The Oval	Surrey v Hampshire
CC3	Cardiff	Glamorgan v Kent
CC3	Manchester	Lancashire v Sussex
CC3	Leeds	Yorkshire v Northants

Thu 6 – Sun 9 May

CC1	Nottingham	Notts v Essex
CC1	Birmingham	Warwicks v Worcs
CC2	Southampton	Hampshire v Somerset
CC2	Leicester	Leics v Surrey
CC2	Lord's	Middlesex v Glos
CC3	Manchester	Lancashire v Glamorgan
CC3	Northampton	Northants v Sussex
CC3	Leeds	Yorkshire v Kent

Thu 13 – Sun 16 May

CC1	Chester-le-St	Durham v Worcs
CC1	Chelmsford	Essex v Derbyshire
CC2	Lord's	Middlesex v Hampshire
CC2	Taunton	Somerset v Surrey
CC3	Cardiff	Glamorgan v Yorkshire
CC3	Hove	Sussex v Kent

Thu 20 – Sun 23 May

CC1	Derby	Derbyshire v Durham
CC1	Chelmsford	Essex v Warwicks
CC1	Nottingham	Notts v Worcs
CC2	Bristol	Glos v Somerset
CC2	Southampton	Hampshire v Leics
CC2	The Oval	Surrey v Middlesex
CC3	Canterbury	Kent v Glamorgan
CC3	Northampton	Northants v Lancashire

Tue 25 – Fri 28 May

FCF	Taunton	Somerset v New Zealanders

Thu 27-Sun 30 May

CC1	Chester-le-St	Durham v Essex
CC1	Birmingham	Warwicks v Notts
CC1	Worcester	Worcs v Derbyshire
CC2	Leicester	Leics v Middlesex

CC2	The Oval	Surrey v Glos
CC3	Manchester	Lancashire v Yorkshire
CC3	Hove	Sussex v Northants

Wed 2 – Sun 6 June

TM1	Lord's	**ENGLAND v NEW ZEALAND**

Thu 3 – Sun 6 June

CC1	Derby	Derbyshire v Warwicks
CC1	Chelmsford	Essex v Notts
CC1	Worcester	Worcs v Durham
CC2	Leicester	Leics v Glos
CC2	Taunton	Somerset v Hampshire
CC3	Cardiff	Glamorgan v Lancashire
CC3	Canterbury	Kent v Northants
CC3	Leeds	Yorkshire v Sussex

Wed 9 June

T20^F	Canterbury	Kent v Hampshire
T20	Manchester	Lancashire v Derbyshire
T20^F	Taunton	Somerset v Essex
T20	Worcester	Worcs v Notts

Thu 10 – Mon 14 June

TM2	Birmingham	**ENGLAND v NEW ZEALAND**

Thu 10 June

T20^F	Cardiff	Glamorgan v Glos
T20^F	Manchester	Lancashire v Leics
T20^F	Lord's	Middlesex v Surrey
T20^F	Leeds	Yorkshire v Warwicks

Fri 11 June

T20^F	Chester-le-St	Durham v Yorkshire
T20^F	Chelmsford	Essex v Hampshire
T20^F	Bristol	Glos v Sussex
T20^F	Canterbury	Kent v Middlesex
T20^F	Leicester	Leics v Derbyshire
T20^F	Northampton	Northants v Worcs
T20^F	Nottingham	Notts v Warwicks
T20^F	Taunton	Somerset v Surrey

Sat 12 June

T20^F	Hove	Sussex v Hampshire

Sun 13 June

T20	Derby	Derbyshire v Warwicks
T20	Cardiff	Glamorgan v Essex
T20	Canterbury	Kent v Glos
T20	Leicester	Leics v Durham
T20	Northampton	Northants v Notts
T20	Worcester	Worcs v Lancashire

Mon 14 June

T20^F	The Oval	Surrey v Glamorgan

Tue 15 June

T20^F	Derby	Derbyshire v Lancashire
T20^F	Chester-le-St	Durham v Notts

T20^F	Chelmsford	Essex v Sussex
T20	Radlett	Middlesex v Hampshire
T20^F	Northampton	Northants v Warwicks
T20^F	Taunton	Somerset v Kent
T20^F	Leeds	Yorkshire v Leics

Wed 16 June

T20^F	Cardiff	Glamorgan v Kent
T20^F	Leicester	Leics v Warwicks
T20	Worcester	Worcs v Yorkshire

Thu 17 June

T20^F	Derby	Derbyshire v Northants
T20	Chester-le-St	Durham v Lancashire
T20	Radlett	Middlesex v Glos
T20^F	The Oval	Surrey v Sussex

Fri 18 – Tue 22 June

TM	Southampton	**INDIA v NEW ZEALAND**

Fri 18 June

50o^F	Canterbury	Kent v Sri Lankans
T20^F	Chelmsford	Essex v Glos
T20^F	Cardiff	Glamorgan v Middlesex
T20^F	Nottingham	Notts v Derbyshire
T20^F	The Oval	Surrey v Hampshire
T20^F	Hove	Sussex v Somerset
T20^F	Birmingham	Warwicks v Lancashire
T20	Worcester	Worcs v Northants
T20^F	Leeds	Yorkshire v Durham

Sat 19 June

T20^F	Taunton	Somerset v Glamorgan

Sun 20 June

T20	Chester-le-St	Durham v Warwicks
T20	Bristol	Glos v Hampshire
T20	Canterbury	Kent v Essex
T20	Manchester	Lancashire v Notts
T20	Northampton	Northants v Leics
T20	Leeds	Yorkshire v Derbyshire
20o	Hove	Sussex v Sri Lankans

Mon 21 June

T20^F	The Oval	Surrey v Essex

Tue 22 June

T20^F	Derby	Derbyshire v Leics
T20^F	Bristol	Glos v Kent
T20^F	Nottingham	Notts v Worcs
T20^F	Hove	Sussex v Glamorgan

Wed 23 June

IT20^F	Cardiff	**England v Sri Lanka**
T20^F	Chester-le-St	Durham v Northants
T20^F	The Oval	Surrey v Somerset
T20^F	Leeds	Yorkshire v Worcs

Thu 24 June
IT20^F	Cardiff	England v Sri Lanka
T20^F	Bristol	Glos v Glamorgan
T20^F	Lord's	Middlesex v Essex
T20^F	Birmingham	Warwicks v Derbyshire

Fri 25 June
T20^F	Derby	Derbyshire v Notts
T20^F	Chelmsford	Essex v Kent
T20^F	Leicester	Leics v Yorkshire
T20^F	Northampton	Northants v Lancashire
T20^F	Taunton	Somerset v Hampshire
T20^F	The Oval	Surrey v Middlesex
T20^F	Hove	Sussex v Glos
T20	Worcester	Worcs v Durham

Sat 26 June
IT20	Southampton	England v Sri Lanka
T20	Nottingham	Notts v Lancashire
T20	Birmingham	Warwicks v Durham
T20	Leeds	Yorkshire v Northants

Sun 27 – Wed 30 June
| FCF | Derby | Derbyshire v India A |

Sun 27 June
T20	Radlett	Middlesex v Glamorgan
T20	Hove	Sussex v Surrey
T20	Worcester	Worcs v Leics

Mon 28 June
| T20^F | Southampton | Hampshire v Middlesex |
| T20^F | Canterbury | Kent v Somerset |

Tue 29 June
LOI	Chester-le-St	England v Sri Lanka
T20^F	Chelmsford	Essex v Somerset
T20^F	Cardiff	Glamorgan v Surrey
T20^F	Leicester	Leics v Northants
T20^F	Hove	Sussex v Kent

Wed 30 June
T20^F	Southampton	Hampshire v Surrey
T20^F	Northampton	Northants v Durham
T20^F	Birmingham	Warwicks v Yorkshire

Thu 1 July
LOI^F	The Oval	England v Sri Lanka
T20^F	Chelmsford	Essex v Glamorgan
T20^F	Bristol	Glos v Somerset
T20^F	Manchester	Lancashire v Worcs
T20^F	Lord's	Middlesex v Sussex
T20^F	Nottingham	Notts v Leics

Fri 2 July
T20^F	Derby	Derbyshire v Worcs
T20^F	Chester-le-St	Durham v Leics
T20^F	Cardiff	Glamorgan v Sussex
T20^F	Southampton	Hampshire v Glos

T20^F	Canterbury	Kent v Surrey
T20^F	Taunton	Somerset v Middlesex
T20^F	Birmingham	Warwicks v Notts
T20^F	Leeds	Yorkshire v Lancashire

Sun 4 – Wed 7 July
CC1	Nottingham	Notts v Derbyshire
CC1	Birmingham	Warwicks v Durham
CC2	Southampton	Hampshire v Surrey
CC2	Taunton	Somerset v Leics
CC3	Manchester	Lancashire v Kent
CC3	Northampton	Northants v Yorkshire
CC3	Hove	Sussex v Glamorgan
FCF	Chelmsford	Essex v India A

Sun 4 July
| LOI | Bristol | England v Sri Lanka |

Mon 5 – Thu 8 July
| CC2 | Cheltenham | Glos v Middlesex |

Thu 8 July
| LOI^F | Cardiff | England v Pakistan |

Fri 9 July
T20^F	Chester-le-St	Durham v Derbyshire
T20	Cheltenham	Glos v Middlesex
T20^F	Southampton	Hampshire v Somerset
T20^F	Manchester	Lancashire v Northants
T20^F	Nottingham	Notts v Yorkshire
T20^F	The Oval	Surrey v Kent
T20^F	Hove	Sussex v Essex
T20	Worcester	Worcs v Warwicks

Sat 10 July
| LOI | Lord's | England v Pakistan |

Sun 11 – Wed 14 July
CC1	Chesterfield	Derbyshire v Essex
CC1	Chester-le-St	Durham v Notts
CC1	Worcester	Worcs v Warwicks
CC2	Cheltenham	Glos v Hampshire
CC2	Northwood	Middlesex v Leics
CC2	The Oval	Surrey v Somerset
CC3	Cardiff	Glamorgan v Northants
CC3	Beckenham	Kent v Sussex
CC3	Scarborough	Yorkshire v Lancashire

Mon 12 – Thu 15 July
| FCF | Leicester | FCC XI v India A |

Tue 13 July
| LOI^F | Birmingham | England v Pakistan |

Fri 16 July
IT20^F	Nottingham	England v Pakistan
T20^F	Cardiff	Glamorgan v Somerset
T20	Cheltenham	Glos v Surrey
T20	Southampton	Hampshire v Essex

T20[F]	Southampton	Hampshire v Sussex
T20[F]	Manchester	Lancashire v Durham
T20[F]	Leicester	Leics v Notts
T20[F]	Lord's	Middlesex v Kent
T20[F]	Northampton	Northants v Derbyshire
T20[F]	Birmingham	Warwicks v Worcs

Sat 17 July

T20	Manchester	Lancashire v Yorkshire

Sun 18 July

IT20	**Leeds**	**England v Pakistan**
T20	Chesterfield	Derbyshire v Yorkshire
T20[F]	Chelmsford	Essex v Middlesex
T20[F]	Southampton	Hampshire v Glamorgan
T20[F]	Canterbury	Kent v Sussex
T20[F]	Leicester	Leics v Worcs
T20[F]	Nottingham	Notts v Durham
T20[F]	Taunton	Somerset v Glos
T20[F]	Birmingham	Warwicks v Northants

Tue 20 July

IT20[F]	**Manchester**	**England v Pakistan**

Wed 21 – Sat 24 July

FCF	Northampton	Indians v India A

Thu 22 July

50L	Cardiff	Glamorgan v Warwicks
50L	Southampton	Hampshire v Essex
50L	tbc	Kent v Durham
50L	Leicester	Leics v Derbyshire
50L	Scarborough	Yorkshire v Surrey

Fri 23 July

50L	tbc	Lancashire v Sussex

Sun 25 July

50L	Chelmsford	Essex v Middlesex
50L	Bristol	Glos v Lancashire
50L	Leicester	Leics v Yorkshire
50L	Northampton	Northants v Glamorgan
50L[F]	Taunton	Somerset v Derbyshire
50L	Hove	Sussex v Durham
50L	Birmingham	Warwicks v Notts
50L	Worcester	Worcs v Kent

Tue 27 July

50L	Derby	Derbyshire v Warwicks
50L	Bristol	Glos v Worcs
50L	Southampton	Hampshire v Sussex
50L	Radlett	Middlesex v Durham
50L	Guildford	Surrey v Notts

Wed 28 – Sat 31 July

FCF	Leicester	Indians v India A

Wed 28 July

50L	tbc	Kent v Lancashire

50L	Taunton	Somerset v Glamorgan
50L	Scarborough	Yorkshire v Northants

Thu 29 July

50L	Scarborough	Durham v Glos
50L	Chelmsford	Essex v Worcs
50L	Birmingham	Warwicks v Leics

Fri 30 July

50L	Derby	Derbyshire v Glamorgan
50L	Radlett	Middlesex v Hampshire
50L	Welbeck	Notts v Somerset
50L	The Oval	Surrey v Northants
50L	Hove	Sussex v Kent

Sun 1 August

50L	Chelmsford	Essex v Kent
50L	Southampton	Hampshire v Lancashire
50L	Northampton	Northants v Derbyshire
50L	Welbeck	Notts v Leics
50L	Taunton	Somerset v Yorkshire
50L	Hove	Sussex v Glos
50L	Worcester	Worcs v Middlesex

Tue 3 August

50L	Cardiff	Glamorgan v Surrey
50L	Bristol	Glos v Essex
50L	Manchester	Lancashire v Middlesex
50L	York	Yorkshire v Warwicks

Wed 4 – Sun 8 August

TM1	Nottingham	**ENGLAND v INDIA**

Wed 4 August

50L	Southampton	Hampshire v Worcs
50L	Derby	Notts v Derbyshire

Thu 5 August

50L	Gosforth	Durham v Lancashire
50L	Leicester	Leics v Glamorgan
50L	The Oval	Surrey v Somerset

Fri 6 August

50L	Bristol	Glos v Hampshire
50L	Radlett	Middlesex v Kent
50L	Birmingham	Warwicks v Northants
50L	Worcester	Worcs v Sussex
50L	York	Yorkshire v Notts

Sat 7 August

50L	Leicester	Leics v Surrey

Sun 8 August

50L	Chesterfield	Derbyshire v Yorkshire
50L	Chester-le-St	Durham v Essex
50L	Cardiff	Glamorgan v Notts
50L	tbc	Kent v Hampshire
50L	Blackpool	Lancashire v Worcs

50L	Radlett	Middlesex v Glos
50L	Northampton	Northants v Somerset

Tue 10 August

50L	Chelmsford	Essex v Sussex
50L	Grantham	Notts v Northants
50L	Taunton	Somerset v Leics
50L	The Oval	Surrey v Warwicks
50L	Worcester	Worcs v Durham

Thu 12 – Mon 16 August

TM2	Lord's	ENGLAND v INDIA

Thu 12 August

50L	Derby	Derbyshire v Surrey
50L	Chester-le-St	Durham v Hampshire
50L	Cardiff	Glamorgan v Yorkshire
50L	tbc	Kent v Glos
50L	Manchester	Lancashire v Essex
50L	Northampton	Northants v Leics
50L	Hove	Sussex v Middlesex
50L	Birmingham	Warwicks v Somerset

Sat 14 August

50L	tbc	Quarter-finals 1 & 2

Tue 17 August

50L	tbc	Semi-finals 1 & 2

Thu 19 August

50L	Nottingham	FINAL

Tue 24 August

T20	tbc	Quarter-final 1

Wed 25 – Sun 29 August

TM3	Leeds	ENGLAND v INDIA

Wed 25 August

T20	tbc	Quarter-final 2

Thu 26 August

T20	tbc	Quarter-final 3

Fri 27 August

T20	tbc	Quarter-final 4

Mon 30 Aug – Thu 2 September

CC	tbc	Division Stage, Round 1

Thu 2 – Mon 6 September

TM4	The Oval	ENGLAND v INDIA

Sun 5 – Wed 8 September

CC	tbc	Division Stage, round 2

Fri 10 – Tue 14 September

TM5	Manchester	ENGLAND v INDIA

Sun 12 – Wed 15 September

CC	tbc	Division Stage, Round 3

Sat 18 September

T20^F	Birmingham	Semi-finals and FINAL

Tue 21 – Fri 24 September

CC	tbc	Division Stage, Round 4

Mon 27 September – Fri 1 October

CC	Lord's	Bob Willis Trophy Final

FIELDING CHART

(For a right-handed batsman)

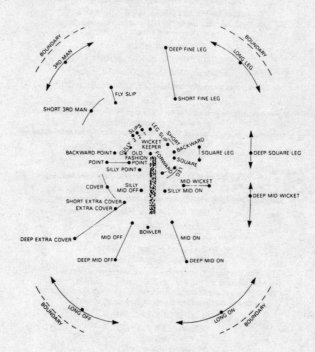

First published in 2021

by HEADLINE PUBLISHING GROUP

Front cover photograph Zak Crawley (Kent and England)

Back cover photograph Joe Root (Yorkshire and England)

2

Cataloguing in Publication Data is available from the British Library

ISBN: 978 1 4722 6754 2

Typeset in Times by
Letterpart Limited, Caterham on the Hill, Surrey

Printed and bound in Great Britain by
Clays Ltd, Elcograf S.p.A.

HEADLINE PUBLISHING GROUP

An Hachette UK Company
Carmelite House
50 Victoria Embankment
London EC4Y 0DZ

www.headline.co.uk
www.hachette.co.uk